Reproducing Women

Reproducing Women

Medicine, Metaphor, and Childbirth
in Late Imperial China

Yi-Li Wu

UNIVERSITY OF CALIFORNIA PRESS
Berkeley · Los Angeles · London

University of California Press, one of the most
distinguished university presses in the United States,
enriches lives around the world by advancing scholarship in the humanities, social sciences, and natural
sciences. Its activities are supported by the UC Press
Foundation and by philanthropic contributions from
individuals and institutions. For more information,
visit www.ucpress.edu.

University of California Press
Berkeley and Los Angeles, California

University of California Press, Ltd.
London, England

Library of Congress Cataloging-in-Publication Data

Wu, Yi-Li, 1965–
    Reproducing women : medicine, metaphor, and
childbirth in late imperial China / Yi-Li Wu.
        p. cm.
    Includes bibliographical references and index.
    ISBN 978-0-520-26068-9 (cloth : alk. paper)
    1. Childbirth—China—History. 2. Women—
Medical care—History. 3. China—Social life and
customs—1644–1912. I. Title.
    [DNLM: 1. Reproductive Medicine—history—
China. 2. Gynecology—history—China.
3. History, Modern 1601—China. 4. Metaphor—
China. WQ 11 JC6 W959r 2010]
    RG518.C6W8 2010
    362.198'400951—dc22   2010001036

Manufactured in the United States of America

19 18 17 16 15 14 13 12 11 10
10 9 8 7 6 5 4 3 2 1

This book is printed on Cascades Enviro 100, a
100% post consumer waste, recycled, de-inked fiber.
FSC recycled certified and processed chlorine free. It
is acid free, Ecologo certified, and manufactured by
BioGas energy.

To Michael, Rachel, and Emily

Contents

List of Illustrations   ix

Acknowledgments   xi

Introduction   1

1. Late Imperial *Fuke* and the Literate Medical Tradition   15

2. Amateur as Arbiter: Popular *Fuke* Manuals in the Qing   54

3. Function and Structure in the Female Body   84

4. An Uncertain Harvest: Pregnancy and Miscarriage   120

5. "Born Like a Lamb": The Discourse of Cosmologically Resonant Childbirth   147

6. To Generate and Transform: Strategies for Postpartum Health   188

Epilogue: Body, Gender, and Medical Legitimacy   224

Notes   237

Glossary   311

Bibliography   319

Index   343

Illustrations

TABLE

1. Members of the Chen family (1127–ca. 1900)   32

FIGURES

1. A page from *Transmitted Secrets of Women's Medicine from the Bamboo Grove (Zhulin fuke michuan)*, 1890 edition   61
2. Woman giving birth after praying to the Bodhisattva Guanyin, *Lotus Sutra (Saddharmapundarikasutra)*, Dunhuang, ca. tenth century   66
3. Title page, *Treatise on Easy Childbirth (Dasheng bian)*, ca. 1850   80
4. Diagram of internal organs from Li Chan, *An Introduction to Medicine (Yixue rumen)*, 1666 edition   102
5. Diagram of internal organs from Zhang Jiebin, *Illustrated Supplement to "The* Inner Classic *Explicated by Topic" (Leijing tuyi)*, 1624 edition   103
6. Instructions for safe childbirth, expanded edition of *Treatise on Easy Childbirth (Zengguang Dasheng pian)*, 1888   149
7. Charles Bell's engraving of a soldier with tetanus from *The Anatomy and Philosophy of Expression as Connected with the Fine Arts*, 1847 edition   195
8. Woman suffering from abscesses during the postpartum period, *Imperially Compiled Golden Mirror of Medical Learning (Yuzuan yizong jinjian)*, 1742   198

Acknowledgments

Books, like babies, develop at their own pace, and this one has taken longer than others. It is thus an immense pleasure to finally thank the many people who have helped me in so many different ways over the years. My first debt is to my teachers at Yale University, where I learned to be a historian. This book began as a seminar project for a course taught by Beatrice Bartlett and eventually turned into a dissertation directed by Jonathan Spence, Valerie Hansen, and John Warner. I thank them, as well as Emily Honig, for making Yale such a nurturing place to be a graduate student, and I will always be grateful for the care and effort they invested in me. My work would also not have been possible without the pioneering scholarship of Charlotte Furth, who originally sparked my interest in the history of gender and medicine in China. For close to two decades, she has continually inspired me with her personal and intellectual generosity, and I also thank her for many insightful suggestions on earlier iterations of this book. For just as long, Nathan Sivin has been a role model of scholarly rigor who showed me how to think harder and more clearly about Chinese science and medicine. Likewise, Marta Hanson has supported me in too many ways to list, sending me contacts, data, critiques, and encouragement, and generally energizing me with her enthusiasm and creativity. As this project made the transition from dissertation to book, I was also blessed with the incisive comments of Ruth Rogaski and Dorothy Ko, who helped me find the right analytical and narrative voice. The expert guidance of Reed Malcolm at the University of California Press made it possible for this project to finally come to fruition, and Kalicia Pivorotto and Jacqueline Volin helped me navigate the myriad details of the production process. I also thank Bruce Tindall and Bonita Hurd for their meticulous copyediting.

The professors and students of the Institute for the History of Medicine and Medical Literature at the China Academy of Traditional Chinese Medicine (now the China Academy of Chinese Medical Sciences) hosted me as a doctoral student and facilitated my research in numerous ways. I also received crucial assistance from Fu Weikang, Gao Yuqiu, and Xu Binchao of the Shanghai University of Traditional Chinese Medicine and Pharmacology; Ma Boying of the Shanghai Medical University; Wang Shuiyuan and Zhu Jianping of the Zhejiang Research Institute of Traditional Chinese Medicine; Shan Shouchang of the Xiaoshan Bureau of Health; Xu Shuming of the Tongxiang County Gazetteer Office; and Lu Xiaodong of the Shaoxing County Number Two Hospital. My research in Xiaoshan would have been impossible without the help of Shi Jianong of the Xiaoshan Cultural Relics Management Committee and Wang Yifeng. The staff of the Peking Union Medical Library and the library of the Chinese Academy of Sciences made my time there fruitful and smooth. I am also profoundly grateful to the doctors who spoke with me about their families' medical traditions and provided me with valuable documents: Cai Xiaomin, He Shixi, and Zhu Nansun in Shanghai; Chen Shouchun in Xiaoshan; Qian Chuanyao in Shaoxing; Song Lili in Jiaxing; and Song Shixian in Ningbo.

I am also grateful to the libraries and research institutions that I have revisited over the years, and I would especially like to acknowledge the kind assistance of Qiu Jian, Yan Kangwei, Cheng Ying, Liu Junhui, and Jiang Yan of the library of the China Academy of Chinese Medical Sciences. Many thanks also to John Moffett, Sue Bennett, and Chris Cullen of the Needham Research Institute for their warm hospitality, which has turned Cambridge into my home away from home. The staff of the National Library of China and the Shanghai Library graciously expedited my research requests. Raymond Lum and Ma Xiao-He of the Harvard-Yenching Library, Rachael Cross of the Wellcome Library, and Xia Lei of the Shanghai Library generously helped me obtain images from their collections and the permissions to reproduce them here. I also thank the Johns Hopkins Press for permission to reuse, in chapter 2, portions of my article previously published as "The Bamboo Grove Monastery and Popular Gynecology in Qing China," *Late Imperial China* 21:1 (June 2000): 41–76 © Johns Hopkins University Press, and I thank Koninklijke

Brill NV for permission to reuse, in chapter 4, portions of my article published as "Ghost Fetuses, False Pregnancies, and the Parameters of Medical Uncertainty in Classical Chinese Gynecology," *Nan Nü: Men, Women, and Gender in Early and Imperial China* 4:2 (2002): 170–206.

A fellowship from the Committee on Scholarly Communication with China made my doctoral research possible, and a dissertation fellowship from the Yale University Council on East Asian Studies allowed me to concentrate on my writing. A fellowship from the National Endowment for the Humanities in 2002–3 gave me the time to research new book chapters, and a resident fellowship at the University of Michigan's Eisenberg Institute for Historical Studies in 2005–6 provided me with a stimulating environment in which to restructure the project. Over the past decade, several grants from the Hewlett-Mellon Fund for Faculty Development at Albion College have enabled me to take supplemental research trips and acquire additional materials. I am deeply grateful to these institutions for their support of my work.

Long-term projects require ongoing inputs of intellectual stimulation and moral support. In addition to help from those already mentioned, I benefited from valuable discussions with Bridie Andrews, Miranda Brown, James L. Carter, Yüan-ling Chao, Chang Che-chia, Chang Chia-feng, Ronald Cyr, Ryan Dunch, Aileen Gatten, Asaf Goldschmidt, TJ Hinrichs, Timothy R. Johnson, Paul Katz, James Z. Lee, Lee Jen-der, Li Jianmin, Vivienne Lo, Ma Dazheng, Molly Mullin, Dian Murray, Cynthia J. Paces, Katharine Park, Volker Scheid, Sarah Schneewind, Hugh Shapiro, Kim Taylor, Daniel Todes, and Sabine Wilms. Deborah Kanter, Marcy Sacks, and Rudolfo Zúñiga provided logistical assistance at key junctures. Tobie Meyer-Fong and Janet Theiss ensured I always maintained a proper sense of perspective.

This book is dedicated to my family, whose good humor and love make my work possible and my life meaningful. Rachel fixed breakfast for her little sister when I needed to squeeze in an extra hour of revisions on a Saturday morning. Emily always made sure to steal onto my lap as quietly as possible, so as not to interrupt my train of thought. They were my constant emotional link to the Chinese parents of long ago who likewise delighted in their children, and a window into the sorrow of those who remained childless despite their best efforts. But my deepest debt of all is to Michael. Perhaps the only thing harder than writing a book yourself is watching your spouse do it, and I have been amazed and humbled by his infinite patience, steadfast support, and unflagging faith in me. Thank you, for everything.

Introduction

To die in childbirth is tragedy enough without also dying from an apparent medical error. But so it was in the winter of 1713, when Ms. Shen began to suffer fits of raving and hallucinations shortly after delivering her child.[1] Her husband, Yan Chunxi, was a hardworking scholar, trying to make his way through the tiered examinations for government posts that spelled success for Chinese men. Some years later, he would so impress educational officials from his native place of Xuanhua Prefecture, Zhili Province, that they would sponsor his direct entrance into the National University and thence to an official government position.[2] Alongside his professional accomplishments, however, Yan weathered personal disappointment, for Ms. Shen suffered repeated miscarriages. Now, having carried a child to term, she fell ill soon after giving birth.

By this time, Yan Chunxi had been studying medicine for over a decade. Like many of his literati contemporaries, he considered knowledge of the healing arts to be a desirable and natural outgrowth of the scholar's classical formation, a tangible expression of the virtuous gentleman's concern for humanity. Influenced by his wife's miscarriages, he also gave special attention to the subdiscipline known as *fuke,* or "medicine for women." But in 1713, he was not at home when his wife fell ill. Local officials were rushing to deliver a shipment of military grain rations to the storehouses by year's end, and Yan was assigned to assist with the project. In his absence, the doctor diagnosed Ms. Shen as afflicted by upsurging internal fire, invasion of wind, and stagnation of phlegm. Accordingly, he treated her with drugs to purge, subdue, and dissipate these pathological manifestations. But when these remedies provoked convulsions, the household dispatched a servant to ask Yan Chunxi for instructions. A glance at the prescription convinced Yan that the doctor had misdiagnosed Ms. Shen's illness, giving her drugs that were not only ineffective but would positively "hasten death." Alarmed, flustered, and unable to examine his wife in person, Yan could only send back emphatic instructions to administer large doses of ginseng, a powerful replenisher. To Yan Chunxi, it was obvious that his wife's illness was rooted in depletion, not in excess or invasion. But the doctor rejected the orders, and when a messenger reported that Ms. Shen had again been treated with purgatives, Yan rushed home in the deepest dread.

By then it was evening. Upon arrival Yan found his wife barely breathing and already moved to an outlying building in anticipation of her imminent death. Seizing the household's entire supply of ginseng, he decocted it into a broth, dissolved some additional drugs into it, and forced it down her throat.[3] By midnight her condition had improved noticeably and she was able to sit up and speak. Yan therefore judged that they could wait for the morning markets to open before buying more ginseng to continue the treatment. But the ginseng's effects wore off just as the night was ending. Ms. Shen again began to rave and hallucinate, and this time she could not be saved. "Some said," Yan recalled, "that this was predestined by fate." But he was not so easily mollified. Fate notwithstanding, he charged that his wife's death had been caused by the doctor's incorrect use of drugs.

Eighteenth-century Chinese law recognized "incompetent physicians killing and harming people" (yongyi shashang ren) as a crime, but history does not reveal whether Yan Chunxi ever made any formal complaint against the doctor.[4] What we do know, however, is that Yan included this story as a cautionary tale in his own text on women's medicine, Essential Teachings on Childbearing (Taichan xinfa), completed around 1725. That same year, Yan Chunxi was appointed circuit intendant in Guangxi. He was successful enough that he could now afford to publish his work, but apparently he was too busy to do so before 1730. When he did, he used Ms. Shen's case to argue that one should not administer purgatives and dispelling drugs to postpartum women. Over the next century and a half, Yan's text was reprinted dozens of times, joining a burgeoning corpus of Chinese writings on female reproductive health.[5] In this context, the story of Ms. Shen engaged with broader long-standing debates in the medical literature: How should one classify, diagnose, and treat the potentially fatal complications of childbirth? More broadly put, what constituted the proper approach to managing female fertility and reproductive health? Disagreements over the relative preponderance of stagnation or depletion in childbearing women were never simply doctrinal or academic matters, for the illnesses of women like Ms. Shen were inescapable material facts that demanded explanation and remediation.

This book examines how Yan Chunxi and other medical thinkers of late imperial China approached a set of universal concerns that have occupied all societies: promoting fertility, sustaining pregnancy, ensuring the safe delivery of healthy babies, and facilitating women's postpartum recovery. In the lingo of the medical historian, my aim is to understand how people during this time "framed" women's reproductive bodies.[6] What meanings did they assign to the observable bodily phenomena connected to conception, gestation, and labor? What epistemological, institutional, cultural, or material factors shaped the criteria that they used to define health and pathology, and how did they decide what interventions were necessary and appropriate? In particular, how was medicine for women shaped by different gender norms, and how did medical ideas in turn shape the range of ways that people thought about the similarities between male and female bodies? Finally, how were the answers that people gave to these questions distinctive to the late imperial period?

APPROACHING THE FEMALE BODY

Open the leaves of a typical *fuke* text from late imperial China, and you enter into a realm of bodily flows, aches, swellings, and injuries, all connected somehow to women's childbearing functions. Some of these disorders have obvious analogues in biomedicine: infertility, morning sickness, eclampsia (what the Chinese called "pregnancy convulsions"), postpartum hemorrhage, and internal infections. Others elude modern understanding, such as accounts of two-year-long pregnancies or unborn children crying within the womb. Yet all were a part of the late imperial Chinese conceptual universe and served as points of reference against which people defined the healthy and pathological states of women's bodies. Abdominal pains during menstruation, foul smelling discharges, "joining bones" of the pelvis that failed to open during labor *(jiaogu bu kai)*, genital lacerations, prolapsed wombs that fell down between the thighs, breast sores during lactation—these underscored the physicality of the female body that literate medicine sought to address. But as the rich scholarship on the history and anthropology of the body has shown, people in different times and contexts have understood their bodies in vastly diverse ways. Skin and sinew, blood and breath, penis and vagina—all "expressed" different meanings to different observers, whose investigation of such phenomena was inevitably mediated by broader systems of beliefs: how men and women were different from or similar to one another, how emotional and physical health were connected, whether supernatural or superhuman beings influenced disease and healing, and what constituted the nature and sources of valid medical knowledge.[7] Such perspectives are especially valuable for histories of childbirth, reminding us of the many different ways that societies have "medicalized" the female body, defining certain aspects as pathological and in need of medical oversight and therapeutic remediation.

By analyzing the female ailments that Chinese medical experts recognized and tried to treat, I seek to map the repertoire of ideas that they used to understand women's ailments, ideas that both drew on and revised the beliefs of their predecessors. What I find is that the intellectual vanguard of late imperial *fuke* was distinguished by a markedly optimistic view of female bodies, epitomized by the idea that "women's ailments are fundamentally the same as men's," and by the teaching that childbirth was an inherently safe process that replicated the spontaneous ease of cosmogenesis. We can best appreciate the distinctiveness of such perspectives by comparing them to medical teachings of earlier periods, which emphasized the uniqueness of female bodily function and the inherent danger of childbearing, as well as to popular practices and religious teachings that emphasized the polluting and debilitating effects of parturition. To be sure, the very existence of *fuke* literature bespoke a continued belief that women had special medical needs that required special care, and the perception that childbirth was dangerous continued to be a salient point of reference for all. But by Yan Chunxi's lifetime, the center of gravity in the male-authored tradition of literate medicine had shifted to diminish earlier emphases on female bodily difference.

My exploration of these changing ideas will highlight the ways in which late imperial *fuke* was shaped by its particular historical, material, and social setting as well as how it drew on different philosophical and epistemological traditions. Men might well write authoritative works on "women's diseases," yet childbirth took place at home, under the direction of midwives and female relatives. A central issue in the history of *fuke* is thus how educated medical men sought to assert their authority over the reproductive female body, wielding their knowledge of medical cosmology in an attempt to discredit midwives and lesser male practitioners. Furthermore, if the medical beliefs discussed here sometimes seem elusive to modern readers, it is not simply because they are unfamiliar with the concepts of yin-yang or the five phases. It is also because we are discussing illnesses that people in developed countries now rarely see. The advent of vaccines, antibiotics, in vitro fertilization, ultrasound fetal imaging, routine cesarean sections, and hospital-based childbirth are but some of the more salient developments of the last century that have transformed the way that women and their household members experience childbearing and the gestational body. Those of us who live in the world's prosperous nations have only the faintest cultural memory of what it means to be crippled by polio or killed by measles, nor do we remember what it means to confront illness with no other diagnostic tool than the powers of unassisted human perception. Here I hasten to add that I have no intention of disparaging older systems of healing as less "advanced" or of idealizing the achievements of biomedicine. Instead, my purpose is to emphasize that we must analyze late imperial medicine on its own terms, and in its own historical setting, in order to appreciate how thoughtful, intelligent women and men of that time negotiated the potential challenges associated with childbearing.

MEDICINE IN LATE IMPERIAL CHINA

My chronological focus will be the seventeenth through early nineteenth centuries, a period roughly corresponding to the last decades of the Ming dynasty (1386–1644) and the first two-thirds of the Qing dynasty (1644–1911). The well-known political, social, and economic developments of this late imperial era make it a particularly useful and important period for studying Chinese views of the female reproductive body, and the ways in which these ideas themselves were reproduced and disseminated throughout the empire. Founded by the Manchus of Northeast Asia, who seized power after an internal rebellion crippled the ruling Ming house, the Qing in its heyday presided over a territorially vast, multiethnic empire characterized by rapid population growth, economic expansion, intellectual vibrancy, and a flourishing print culture that permeated all levels of society. To a large extent, these developments were a continuation of trends that had begun in the mid-sixteenth century and reemerged with greater strength after the disruption of the Manchu conquest had dissipated. To strengthen their political legitimacy and gain the support of the scholar-official elite, the Qing rulers also portrayed themselves as champions of traditional Chinese values, sponsoring a Neo-Confucian

revival that included an intensified emphasis on gender segregation and
female chastity. Chinese scholars, for their part, took advantage of Qing-
sponsored publishing projects and the growth of private libraries and
academies to promote new norms of evidential research, grounded in rigorous philological inquiry into ancient canonical works.[8] Medicine, too,
was shaped by these broader forces. As we shall see, educated doctors
actively reinterpreted and systematized the medical canon, affirming the
inherent veracity of older teachings while using them to articulate new
and competing doctrines. Besides seeking ever more effective cures, they
also strove to elevate the status of medicine from a technical art to a noble offshoot of classical learning. The proliferation of medical literature
during this time also owed much to the burgeoning number of educated
but unemployed men who took up medicine as an alternate career and
needed instructional texts. As medical literature proliferated, so did specialized works on the different subfields of medicine, including "medicine for women."

THE LITERATURE OF CHILDBIRTH

In late imperial China, as in other societies throughout history, childbirth
was not simply a personal issue, a women's issue, or a medical issue but
a matter of broad social consequence. Chinese philosophy articulated this
belief with special eloquence, endowing procreation with cosmological
and political significance. The relationship between parent and child was
the foundation for human society, and a well-regulated human society
was the precondition for a smoothly functioning universe.[9] Particularly
crucial was the birth of sons, who were responsible for ensuring their
parents' welfare and for leading the ancestral rites to honor the dead
and harmonize the ongoing relationship between family members past
and present. Childbearing, in other words, was the warp on which the
fabric of society was woven. When the thirteenth-century physician Chen
Ziming wrote his seminal compendium on the special ailments of
women, it was entirely natural that he should cite Mencius's famous
dictum that failure to produce heirs was a supreme violation of duty:
"It is when there are husbands and wives that there can be fathers and
sons. After one marries, it is imperative to seek heirs. Therefore the sages
said, 'Of the three violations of filial piety, the most serious is the failure to produce descendants.' "[10]

The seventeenth-century physician Xiao Xun was among the many
later writers who described protecting female reproductive health as both

a medical and a moral imperative. In the preface to his 1684 compilation of famous teachings on women's illnesses, Xiao Xun reminded his readers that the ancient classics at the core of Chinese elite culture had all depicted marriage as being of primary importance. That was because the coupling of male and female allowed children to be born and society to continue:

> The sages handed down the teachings of the Six Classics to the myriad generations. The *Classic of Changes* opens with *qian* and *kun* [the male and female cosmic principles]. The first poem in the *Classic of Odes* is [the love poem] "Call of the Osprey." The *Classic of Documents* transmits the story of the Emperor Yao sending his daughters down to marry Shun. The *Classic of Rites* writes of the "Inner Principles" [on the duties of a wife]. The *Spring and Autumn Annals* chronicles [the marriage alliance of] the King of Zhou's daughter.
>
> Thus did they consider the husband-wife relationship to be the beginning of the Way of humans, and women are the root of the transformation of the primordial whereby offspring are engendered. Therefore those who deploy the skills of regulating and harmonizing [i.e., doctors] cannot fail to regard the treatment of women's diseases as singularly important.[11]

Historically, this pronatalist impulse focused attention on the female body, whence life issued forth. Whether or not a woman bore children, how many, and of what sex, determined the very survival and prosperity of family and lineage. By the time Yan Chunxi recorded his late wife's story, centuries of concern for ensuring fertility and fecundity had produced a huge corpus of medical writings devoted to the special medical needs of women. The earliest extant manuscript dedicated to pregnancy and childbirth was compiled around the early second century B.C.E., and the medical classics of the former and latter Han dynasties (second century B.C.E. to second century C.E.) pointed out that women suffered from special illnesses.[12] During the Sui (581–617) and Tang (617–907) dynasties, imperial physicians and other prominent healers began to produce systematic treatises on women's reproductive ailments. During the Song dynasty (960–1279), "childbirth medicine" *(chanke)* was established as an independent department of the imperial medical service, and physicians like Chen Ziming subsumed "remedies for women" in an expanded system of medical cosmology, knitting women's diseases firmly into the sphere of male, literate, medical practice. In subsequent centuries, writings on women's special illnesses continued to proliferate. These appear throughout the traditional medical literature, in general medical works—collections of cases and comprehensive textbooks—as well as in treatises on diagnosis, etiology, and pharmacology. In addition, Chinese medical experts and laypeople alike produced texts that focused exclusively on the treatment of women's reproductive disorders. These include works bearing the designation of "medicine for married women" *(fuke)*, "medicine for females" *(nüke)*, "childbirth medicine" *(chanke)*, or "producing children" or "childbearing" *(taichan)*, terms that by late imperial times were often used interchangeably. They also included more narrowly defined works labeled as treatises on "proliferation of descendants" *(guangsi)* and "planting sons" *(zhongzi)*. The sheer numbers of extant pre-twentieth-century medical works on female reproductive health testifies to the continual production and circulation of this literature in the late imperial era. A standard bibliographic reference, the *Union Catalog of Chinese Medicine Works in Chinese Libraries (Quanguo zhongyi tushu lianhe mulu)*, lists some three hundred extant works on *fuke, chanke,* and *guangsi* compiled between the ninth century and the end of the nineteenth century. Many other works have now been lost, but their titles are recorded in the bibliographic sections of local gazetteers, which list altogether hundreds of specialized works on women's diseases compiled by local worthies in China's counties, prefectures, and provinces.[13]

To understand the parameters of late imperial *fuke,* I will broadly sample this pool of knowledge. Readers unfamiliar with the literature may be disconcerted when I cite a seventh-century text in the same paragraph as an eighteenth-century one; readers sensitive to the geographical variations of Chinese practice may wonder how I can discuss a writer from Sichuan together with an author from Suzhou. I do not wish to elide the important temporal and spatial variations that characterized medicine in China; indeed a major theme of this book is the multiplicity of coexisting medical opinions and strategies. But to understand the medical ideas of this time requires us to consider the many texts that people continued to read, study, and quote during the late imperial period. Whether reproduced in their entirety or anthologized in new medical collections, earlier works served as constant points of reference for late imperial readers. Like present-day constitutional lawyers seeking case precedents, Qing medical thinkers justified their views by invoking the practices of their predecessors, even as they bent old ways to new purposes. In addition, the wide production and circulation of printed medical literature in late imperial times meant that these medical texts formed part of a common culture that was potentially familiar to all Chinese with some degree of literacy. Furthermore, the proliferation of medical publishing during the Qing, and the rapidity with which texts produced in one place subsequently appeared in another, meant that text producers and readers were in virtual conversation with others across the empire.[14] Thus, even while individual medical works could embody distinctive regional perspectives, they nevertheless formed part of a shared empirewide discourse on the nature of healing and illness. From high-quality editions aimed at bibliophiles to cheap and crudely printed treatises intended for free distribution, a multitude of works on women's reproductive ailments circulated throughout the empire. While elite gender norms during the Qing may have emphasized feminine modesty and the spiritual and physical confinement of women to the household, the details of their reproductive ailments—vaginal discharges, genital injuries, blocked wombs, pregnancy-induced constipation—were accessible to anyone with the ability to buy or borrow a book.

To be sure, the works I discuss here were authored by literate men who comprised but a fraction of the Chinese population. Almost all are printed works, and thus my sources do not account for medical manuscripts, which can include different visual and textual conventions.[15] My texts also favor a drug-based approach to treatment over other therapeutic modalities such as religious or ritual healing and manual techniques such as acupuncture, moxibustion, or massage. Similarly, the activities of nonliterate practitioners and lower-class healers, including midwives, are heard only through the voices of male writers. What we are looking at, therefore, is a particular subsection of the wider repertoire of Chinese healing beliefs. But even if printed medical sources cannot encompass all forms of healing in China, text-based medicine still constituted an important benchmark for thinking about bodies, health, and disease in China, and it is one that remains to be fully understood. Of particular interest is the heterogeneous nature of the textual record itself, in which scholarly doctrines and folk remedies freely intermingled.

PLURALITY AND SYNTHESIS

My investigations are indebted to earlier scholarship on *fuke*, which has explored how cultural and institutional constructions of gender intersected with patterns of medical thought and practice.[16] More than just a discursive arena, *fuke* was also a repertoire of technical strategies that women could deploy to influence their own fertility and thus their status in the patrilineal family.[17] But while the broad conceptual parameters of Qing *fuke* are well known, we still need an account of the varied and sometimes discordant ways in which people deployed these ideas. A principal aim of this book, therefore, is to chart the points of disagreement and consensus that appear in Ming-Qing writings on women's reproductive diseases, namely, to examine what Volker Scheid has termed "plurality and synthesis" in Chinese healing practices.[18] As Scheid points out in his study of twentieth-century "traditional Chinese medicine" (TCM), all medical systems are inherently pluralistic, with the dimensions of this plurality shaped by the shifting intersections between the "infrastructures" present in a society. Scheid thus examines factors such as the historical degree and nature of government intervention, career patterns and aspirations of doctors, educational institutions, and the particular mix of healing systems coexisting at any given point in time, analyzing how these have fostered the multiplicity of practices and practitioners that are presently grouped under the rubric of TCM. But even as these infrastructures promote diversity in TCM, Scheid shows that they also serve as vehicles for creating shared professional identities organized around a perceived common medical heritage.

In the case of late imperial "medicine for women," the texts I use were unified by the assumption that the management of women's reproductive functions constituted a distinct subfield of healing that people could be more or less skilled at understanding and managing. The men who wrote these texts, furthermore, shared a broad understanding that literate gentlemen were specially qualified to assess an illness and prescribe its treatments. But exactly what kind of medical training did the gentleman need to make informed judgments? What therapeutic strategies were most effective and reliable? In the pages that follow, we will see how Yan Chunxi and others negotiated the existing intellectual, material, and social infrastructures of late imperial medicine to arrive at different answers to the questions posed by female reproductive functions. Debates over the postpartum use of purgatives or restoratives, for example, were not simply disagreements over drugs. They were also inseparable from disagreements about the nature of women's bodies, their difference from or similarity to men's, and the significance that one should assign to a woman's gestative state during diagnosis or therapy. In practical terms, too, the appeal of a specific strategy might very well depend on the perceived qualifications of the practitioner who recommended it. Assessments of medical efficacy, in other words, were inseparable from judgments about medical legitimacy. Furthermore, the diversity of social and cultural resources that could confer medical legitimacy meant that such judgments were always contingent and shifting.

Placing the themes of "plurality and synthesis" at the center of a history of Chinese *fuke* also directs us to a subtler consideration of the gender implications of this corpus. Earlier analyses have tended to depict literate medicine as embodying the heavy hand of Chinese patriarchy. It was assumed that *fuke* texts were one of many ideological tools that men used to discipline and control women, and that they thus embodied a set of authoritative ideas that women might "resist" or subvert. But we must not overstate the presumed social or epistemological power of these literate physicians, who operated in a pluralistic medical environment where they enjoyed no special institutional or social status. One might even argue that it was educated male doctors who were on the defensive, trying with varying levels of success to claim a privileged place for themselves in the face of multiple challenges from competing practitioners, medical amateurs of various skill levels, and the preconceptions of their own clients. Likewise, we should beware of portraying male medical exhortations and attempts to regulate the behavior of gestating women as inherently misogynistic. Indeed, as we will see, learned medicine of the Qing promoted a view of female reproductive function that was relatively benign when compared to religious views of childbirth as polluting or folk views of the parturient woman as sickly.

More broadly, we find significant diversity in how medical knowledge about women's bodies was created, interpreted, and legitimated. To be sure, the textual corpus took its broad outlines from physicians who wrote works promoting their favored doctrines or model curricula. But the ranks of men who compiled and authored medical texts at large comprised a diverse range of individuals, ranging from lifelong practitioners to those who dabbled in healing as a hobby or charitable pursuit. Some of them were even motivated by their suspicion of or disillusionment with doctors. At the same time, the textual record was shaped by the tastes of men and women who had no particular commitment to medicine as a body of knowledge or practice, but who printed and distributed medical texts because of religious and philanthropic motives. Thus, new ideas turned into accepted practice not just because doctors saw fit to promote them but also because they resonated with popular beliefs about what constituted useful and legitimate medical knowledge. While the extant literature on women's diseases was certainly dominated by male voices, these never spoke as one, and writers routinely disagreed on the best ways to diagnose and treat women's reproductive illnesses.

OUTLINE OF THE BOOK

Late imperial *fuke* was a historically negotiated body of knowledge and techniques, shaped by a specific set of material concerns and the perceptions of a diverse assemblage of actors. Pluralism in the late imperial medical marketplace was thus inseparable from pluralism within literate medicine itself. The substantive chapters of this book develop these themes along three lines. The first section of the book foregrounds the historical and cultural context in which text-based knowledge about women's bodies was created and legitimated. What actors and institutions shaped the creation of the written record, and why? Chapter 1 surveys the history of *fuke* as a distinct subfield of a male-directed medical sphere and examines how male doctors sought to legitimate themselves as healers of women's diseases. We will see that they continually negotiated between two approaches to treating women's ailments: as a specialized subfield of medicine, and as an extension of general medicine. We will also see how these approaches could overlap with two important sources of medical legitimacy: medicine as an outgrowth of scholarly formation, and medicine as proprietary knowledge handed down through a medical lineage. The expansion of scholarly medicine was accompanied by a more universalistic approach to female gestative illnesses, epitomized by the emergence of the teaching that "the diseases of women are fundamentally no different from those of men."[19]

Chapter 2 examines the role of popular print culture in shaping *fuke* literature, focusing particularly on the resonances between religious beliefs and amateur medical publishing. Here we will examine two groups of texts that became a staple of popular medical literature beginning in the late seventeenth and early eighteenth centuries: the gynecological handbooks attributed to the Bamboo Grove Monastery (Zhulinsi) of Xiaoshan, and the many editions of Lay Buddhist Jizhai's *Treatise on Easy Childbirth (Dasheng bian)* of 1715. Upper-class sponsors of the monks' texts promoted a group of healers and a style of healing that elite doctors disdained. The pseudonymous scholar who wrote *Easy Childbirth* benefited from the belief that gentlemanly amateurs made more reliable healers than those who practiced for pay. In both cases, the texts' wide circulation was driven by people who sought to obtain karmic rewards through the charitable dissemination of medical knowledge.

Following this discussion of how *fuke* texts were created and evaluated, the book highlights the repertoire of models and metaphors that appeared in the medical literature and framed how late imperial medical writers envisioned women's reproductive health and illness. Chapter 3 examines the body of *fuke* and provides a revisionist reading of a key issue in the historiography of Chinese medicine: how doctors perceived the relationship between the structures and functions of the human body. Although the womb never constituted a focus for constructions of gender difference, medical writers throughout history nevertheless recognized the womb as a key node in the distinctly female pattern of Blood flow that enabled conception and gestation. The health of Blood (capitalized here to distinguish it from biomedical "blood") and the health of the womb were thus inextricably linked. Consequently the acknowledged physicality of the womb continued to color medical discourse throughout the Qing, even as writers continually expanded a model of female reproductive health that showcased the behavior of Blood. Chapter 4 examines the metaphorical frameworks that guided understandings of conception and gestation and, in particular, the related problems of abnormal pregnancy and pregnancy loss. Here we will explore the resonances and contradictions between two possible ways of envisioning gestation: cosmological frameworks that explained women's bodies in terms of a bodily economy of yin and yang forces, and a set of agricultural metaphors that portrayed the child as a ripening fruit whose development could be terminated or impeded at any moment by perturbations in the maternal environment. Although these explanatory models could point to very different pharmacological strategies, both also assumed that pregnancy loss was always rooted in identifiable human error or negligence. The pregnant woman was thus simultaneously liable and powerful, held responsible for miscarriage yet ultimately endowed with full power to ensure the healthy development of her unborn child.

The last two chapters present case studies of medical change and innovation in Qing *fuke*, examining how social, medical, and technical considerations converged to legitimate new approaches to potentially life-threatening issues. Chapter 5 analyzes what I call the doctrine of cosmologically resonant childbirth, the idea that human birth was meant to reiterate the spontaneous ease of cosmogenesis. This view became salient beginning in the eighteenth century, epitomized in the huge success of Jizhai's *Treatise on Easy Childbirth* of 1715. The idealization of "easy birth" became widespread among male physicians, who by the Qing had definitively distanced themselves from hands-on obstetrics. Rather than seeking better ways of extracting the baby from the birth canal, the male physician sought a better understanding of cosmological principles that would allow one to best preserve the innate ease of childbirth. In a similar vein,

Chapter 6 examines the rise of Generating and Transforming Decoction *(shenghua tang)* from an obscure recipe in the seventeenth century to a well-known postpartum remedy by the nineteenth. Using the history of this formula as a focal point, I examine the changing ways in which late imperial doctors tried to address the alarming and sometimes fatal complications of the postpartum period. The popularity of Generating and Transforming Decoction owed much to changes both within and outside medicine: learned doctors promoted Generating and Transforming Decoction as a better alternative to older remedies championed by the Song dynasty medical bureau, while popular medical works touted Generating and Transforming Decoction as a divinely revealed secret formula and postpartum panacea. In sum, the overall portrait that emerges of late imperial *fuke* is that of a pluralistic, contested body of knowledge and practice whose most innovative thinkers promoted the de-exoticization of female difference and an increasingly benign view of female reproductive bodies.

CHAPTER I

Late Imperial *Fuke* and the Literate Medical Tradition

Shi Jiefan's wife unexpectedly became pregnant for the first time in her thirties, and to compound the surprise, she gave birth to twins.[1] The family was surely relieved to see how hale she was following delivery. Over the next several days, however, she developed an intensifying fever with abdominal distension, and her family called on the doctor Wei Zhixiu (1722–72). Originally of humble social origins and orphaned as a child, Wei ultimately rose through his own diligence to become a successful healer and accomplished poet, sufficiently talented to attract the support of eminent literati from his home county of Hangzhou.[2] Examining Mrs. Shi's pulse signs, and noting that her lochia (bloody postpartum discharges) had stopped flowing, Wei Zhixiu diagnosed her as afflicted by stagnant Blood and prescribed drugs to break up the stagnation. But the family feared that such drugs were too harsh for a woman who had just given birth and refused to use them.[3] Instead, they summoned an "expert in the discipline" *(zhuanke),* namely, a male practitioner known for his special skill in a medical subfield, in this case the subject of "medicine for women" *(fuke).* The expert claimed that, because Mrs. Shi had given birth for the first time at a relatively advanced age, her vitalities had become injured. She was suffering not from stagnation, as Wei had said, but rather from a pathological depletion, and she needed warming and Blood-replenishing drugs. After Mrs. Shi took the expert's medicine, however, her fever intensified and she began raving and babbling. The family then called upon a second "expert," whose recommendations were the same as the first, and whose medicines caused Mrs. Shi's condition to deteriorate even further. Unable to sleep, Mrs. Shi became "delirious, deranged, and insensible to her surroundings, and at times she would suddenly start singing in a loud voice."

It was then that the family went back to Wei Zhixiu, who was in no mood to be polite. Mrs. Shi's lochia had stopped flowing, he pointedly reminded them, and the significance of this symptom was obvious. "Even if you just grabbed someone off the street and told him about this," Wei said, "he would certainly also know that it was a case of stagnant and obstructed Blood. If you want her to live, you can just quickly administer my earlier remedy." Left without any alternative, the family followed his instructions. Soon after she took Wei's prescription, Mrs. Shi's lochia started to flow again, and within hours she expelled what was identified as a blackened placenta. In retrospect, Wei surmised, the attending midwife must have failed to detect the presence of this second placenta, mistakenly thinking that "the two children had shared a single placenta." The cause of illness now eliminated, Mrs. Shi recovered.

Some time later, Wei incorporated Mrs. Shi's story into *A Continuation of the* Cases from Famous Doctors, Arranged by Category (*Xu mingyi lei'an,* ca. 1770), a collection of more than fifty-two hundred medical cases representing the experiences of more than three hundred practitioners—including Wei himself—culled from published medical texts, local historical chronicles, and literary collections.[4] Although some readers criticized Wei's collection for being carelessly edited, late-eighteenth-century government compilers regarded it highly enough to include it in the imperially commissioned *Complete Library of the Four Treasuries (Siku quanshu).*[5] The title of Wei Zhixiu's work announced his intent to supplement a famous earlier collection of cases compiled in 1549 by the Anhui physician Jiang Guan. Beginning in the sixteenth century, the medical case collection had become an important textual genre, serving to showcase the erudition of individual physicians as well as provide training and reference for practicing and aspiring doctors.[6] Massive in size and catholic in its orientations, Wei Zhixiu's *Continuation of the* Cases from Famous Doctors was well positioned to become a standard reference in the field. His account of Mrs. Shi's illness employed a common rhetorical device in the literature, asserting his medical authority through the superior subtlety of his own medical insights while simultaneously portraying his adversaries as unimaginative, narrow-minded, and mired in convention. As a historical artifact, Wei's narrative also directs us to consider a central question in the history of *fuke:* whence did literate male medical practi-

tioners and writers derive their authority as interpreters of female bodies and arbiters of women's reproductive health?

In the story of Mrs. Shi, Wei Zhixiu's competitors were the two male
"experts," with the midwife being generally irrelevant to the medical con-
test. Unlike their contemporaries in western Europe, male physicians in
late imperial China never sought to take over the delivery of babies themselves, viewing the midwife's role as inevitable. Indeed, it was not uncommon for male-authored texts on *fuke* to give advice on how to select a capable midwife.[7] Instead, Chinese male doctors focused their
energies on articulating pharmacological remedies and behavioral regimens to ensure female health in all other areas related to reproduction:
menstruation, conception, pregnancy, postpartum. To be sure, their efforts always assumed that the male doctor's knowledge was inherently
superior to that of midwives. Furthermore, as we shall see in chapter 5,
physicians taught that easy labor would naturally follow if the woman's
bodily and emotional states were properly managed prior to delivery, a
belief that depicted the midwife's presence as largely superfluous. But
in the writings of men like Wei Zhixiu, the most significant interpractitioner struggles for medical authority were not between male and female
healers but rather among male doctors who all drew on the same body
of textual knowledge yet promoted very different ideas of how to apply
it. This is particularly important for understanding Ming and Qing medicine, which was characterized by the proliferation of competing "currents
of learning" *(xuepai)* that drew their identity from a shifting combination of different factors: doctrinal orientations, therapeutic preferences,
master-disciple networks, and family and regional allegiances.[8] To understand the history of *fuke*, therefore, we must consider how male practitioners negotiated a special sphere of therapeutic expertise that was separate from—even if implicitly superior to—that of female healers.

The specific medical debates that animated late imperial *fuke* are detailed in later chapters. Meanwhile, an examination of the historical, social, intellectual factors that allowed men to claim expertise in treating
women's diseases will provide the background for such discussions. The
development of *fuke* as a subfield of the male-authored, classical medical tradition owed much to the institutionalization of medical specialties in the government medical service and the concomitant integration
of childbirth medicine into a learned medical paradigm informed by Neo-
Confucian cosmological inquiry. From its inception as a distinct field of
study, therefore, medicine for women was integrated into the masculine
outer sphere of public service and moral stewardship. The idea that male

practitioners could possess privileged insights into women's illnesses was also nurtured by the tradition of hereditary medical lineages, many of which claimed to possess proprietary techniques for treating certain classes of illness such as *fuke*. Although women did participate in lineage medicine, medical knowledge and authority ultimately came from the strength and longevity of the medical patriline. Finally, starting in the seventeenth century, male doctors' efforts to weld medicine more closely to Neo-Confucian cosmology produced a subtle but significant shift in thinking about women's illnesses, one that now became the mark of the insightful physician. In contrast to supposedly lesser healers, who assumed that women's reproductive functions made them fundamentally different from men, learned physicians now promoted the idea that women's illnesses were essentially no different from men's, with a few exceptions related to childbearing.

FUKE AS A MALE-AUTHORED TRADITION

Wei Zhixiu's contemporaries recognized numerous causes of human illness: attacks by ghosts, demons, or offended ancestors; fate or karmic retribution for sins committed in a past life; climatic extremes or insalubrious terrains; gluttony and lasciviousness; physical and mental strain; excessive emotion; and general carelessness in the activities of everyday life. To promote health and treat illness, people employed a diverse repertoire of techniques to regulate body and psyche and harmonize the relationship between the human and nonhuman realms: religious rituals and prophylactic charms; dietetic regimens; calisthenic or meditative exercises; external cauterization or needling; poultices and suppositories; and internally ingested decoctions and pills made of various animal, mineral, and vegetable substances.[9] People regularly treated themselves on the basis of folk practices, household lore, or healing texts of varying complexity, supplementing these with advice from outside experts, including physicians, herbalists, priests, and geomancers. With the exception of government physicians, who underwent regular examinations and evaluations, those who performed healing activities were unbounded by any institutional, legal, or educational regulations. In effect, the only essential qualification to become a healer was the ability to attract clients.

From shamanesses *(nüwu)* to midwives, from smallpox-inoculating "grannies" to medicine sellers, female healers of all kinds were also a standard part of the Chinese medical landscape. Although they provided services to patients of all ages and both sexes, female practitioners were particularly indispensable in caring for women and children, so much so that Ming-Qing male writers continually fretted about the influence of these medical "grannies" over their womenfolk.[10] The historical breadth of female healing is especially well documented in the activities of the Lodge of Ritual and Ceremony, which recruited, evaluated, and supervised female practitioners for service in the imperial household during the Ming dynasty (1368–1644). These included midwives and wet nurses, but also "female physicians" *(yipo)* trained in pulse-taking and prescription. A Ming literatus who interviewed one such doctor, a girl of fifteen or sixteen, judged that her knowledge of medicine "could not have been surpassed by the great specialists in prescription and sphygmology."[11] Since the Lodge itself did not train healers, these female practitioners would have obtained their knowledge elsewhere, indicating a widespread tradition of women learning medicine. Some of these were certainly the wives and daughters of medical families. Besides those women who made their living as healers, educated women from the upper classes also took an interest in healing, reading medical texts and giving medical advice to friends and family. Their ranks included Wu Bai (d. ca. 1660) of Hangzhou, who assumed the life of a cloistered, virtuous widow after her fiancé died, maintaining her connections with the outside world through study and correspondence. According to Dorothy Ko, Wu Bai was "an avid reader [who] delved not only into geography but also into poetry and herbal medicine."[12] Tang Yaoqing (1763–1831), one of the "talented women of the Zhang family" studied by Susan Mann, spent her time as a magistrate's wife tending to the poor and infirm and had sufficient knowledge of medicine to compound a formula that she used to expel a baby from its mother's body after the woman died in labor.[13] Similarly, Zeng Jifen (1852–1942), the daughter of the Hunanese statesman and general Zeng Guofan, scoured the printed literature for useful medical formulas, also collecting prescriptions from relatives, acquaintances, and medicine shops. Besides using these to treat family members and friends, she distributed medicine as a form of charity.[14]

    With a few notable exceptions, however, such women left no formal records of their healing knowledge. For example, a standard catalog of extant Chinese medical works in Chinese libraries lists some twelve thousand titles, of which only three are known to have been authored by women. Charlotte Furth has extensively discussed the earliest of these, Tan Yunxian (1461–1554), who authored a collection of her own medical cases. Tan was the daughter of a *jinshi* degree holder and grand-

daughter of a physician, and her family background helped her gain respect and recognition as a healer.[15] We also have a collection of cases by
Gu Dehua, who was active as a doctor during the Daoguang and Tongzhi
reigns (1821–74).[16] Gu came from a Suzhou gentry family that enjoyed
a modest record of office holding and literary activity, and she herself
produced a volume of poetry.[17] Tan's and Gu's clients were all female,
but they treated them for a wide range of illnesses. A third female author is Zeng Yi (b. ca. 1852), born into a prominent gentry family whose
men distinguished themselves in the civil service and whose women earned
public recognition for their personal virtue and literary and artistic skill.[18]
Zeng Yi began studying medicine as a child, leafing through the medical
texts in her family's library.[19] By her late teens or early twenties she was
skilled enough to offer her services as a healer during a local epidemic,
and she continued to treat the sick for most of her life.[20] In her fifties,
Zeng Yi wrote a comprehensive, eight-chapter *(juan)* medical work discussing medical diagnosis, seasonal epidemics, medicine for women, pediatrics, external ailments, and other "unclassified" illnesses *(zabing)*.[21]

Why are there so few extant medical works by women? One could
posit that Chinese female healers were mostly from the lower classes and
thus illiterate, but this does not explain why the many writings left by
China's literate women include so few medical works. A partial answer
is that the historical survival of any medical works—regardless of the
author's sex—depended on the existence of people with the interest and
financial means to preserve or reproduce the work. If the author was unable to do this him- or herself, the task would fall to disciples, descendants, or even philanthropically minded amateurs seeking to disseminate
useful information (this latter dynamic is discussed further in chapter 2).
The lack of such networks may explain the loss of a three-*juan* work titled *Compiled Essentials of Medicine for Women (Nüke zuanyao)*, authored by the female healer Wang Hengqi. Hengqi was the eldest daughter of the scholar-doctor Wang Zhu of Jiading County, Jiangsu Province.
Both father and daughter wrote medical works, their titles listed in the
Gazetteer of Jiading County of 1881, but none of these works appears
to have survived. In his old age, we are told, Wang Zhu lost his eyesight
and depended on his daughter to read aloud to him, a situation that suggests a relatively low level of familial and economic resources.[22]

The small number of extant medical works by women may also suggest that relatively few were ever produced. As the voluminous scholarship on Chinese female poets shows, the dominant cultural values served
to valorize certain kinds of female literary production while positively

discouraging others. For centuries, poetry had been the literary vehicle par excellence that both men and women used to demonstrate their wit, erudition, and moral cultivation. Distinctly female poetic genres developed, and women could also identify their efforts with worthy predecessors such as the poetesses represented in the *Classic of Odes,* one of the canonical works at the core of the male scholar's education. Thus "poetry conjoined, as no other genre did, the requisites for opening up a women's tradition: a well-marked social function, a group of stylistic and personal models . . . and contexts in which the display of talent was permissible and might eventually become truly public."[23] Some men even suggested that women's poetry was superior to men's because women were undistracted by the pursuit of official position and so their emotions were purer and more sincere. Beginning in the sixteenth century, these factors helped spur the publication of women's poetry anthologies, which eventually numbered in the thousands.[24] By contrast, there were no women among the many authors who were then also producing novels for a growing commercial reading audience. Fiction writing was considered lower class, and it was not until the end of the nineteenth century that women became significant as novelists.[25]

Writing medical texts seems to have been similarly incompatible with the sanctioned scope of female literary activity. The vast majority of catalogued extant medical works are printed texts that were produced as a public act. Whether intended for government use, teaching purposes, or promotion of new doctrines, the authorship of such texts was a natural extension of male norms of public service and intellectual life. Women's intellectual activities, by contrast, inspired ambivalence.[26] A woman's poetic ability was a sign of good breeding if kept within proper limits, but poetesses like Luo Qilan (1755–1813?) drew criticism when they sought public recognition for their abilities.[27] Hence the common trope of the woman who burned her poetry lest it tempt her away from her domestic duties.[28] In this context it is worth noting that the medical texts by Tan Yunxian and Zeng Yi were both published by sons who wished to commemorate their mothers. The dictates of filial piety thus allowed the celebration of a mother's medical activities, especially when they could also be described as an expression of her benevolent concern for humanity.[29] Such themes were especially salient in the case of Zeng Yi, whose medical treatise was published in 1907 together with a cookbook and a treatise on "female education" *(nüxue).* Both of these latter works were meant to teach turn-of-the-century Chinese women how to be productive citizens of a modernizing nation and to integrate new ideas such as love-based marriage between equals, "home economics" *(jiating jingji xue)*, and "hygiene" *(weisheng)* into the performance of their domestic duties.[30] As for Gu Dehua, her casebook was published in 1936 by male medical reformers at a time when Chinese elites were trying both to modernize medicine and to elevate the social status of women.[31] Interest in the writings of Zeng and Gu was thus enhanced by the growth of feminist and reformist thought in late Qing and early Republican China. In short, women's medical writings—to the extent that they existed—were most likely to survive only if there was a serendipitous convergence between women's own record keeping and the interests of male family members and associates. By contrast, as we shall see later, there were numerous positive incentives for upper-class men to compile and publish works about the illnesses of women.

Finally, it appears that female knowledge of women's bodies was simply not a useful source of epistemological authority in the world of literate *fuke*. It is notable, for example, that there is no Chinese analogy to the medieval European *Trotula*, where the name of a female healer was attached to a text on gynecology as a way of imparting greater authority to it.[32] Instead, the text-based tradition of medicine for women historically derived its organizational models and legitimacy from male institutions: intellectual lineages founded on classical texts, government service, the patriline, and Neo-Confucian norms of moral cultivation and empirical inquiry.

FUKE AND CLASSICAL MEDICINE

The *fuke* that we are investigating was a subfield of *yi*, the standard modern Chinese word for "medicine." We must note, however, that the "medicine" of Wei Zhixiu's time was qualitatively different from what is now known as "traditional Chinese medicine" (TCM). As Kim Taylor has documented, TCM is a twentieth-century formulation, selectively fashioned from older text-based practices and institutionalized in its present form by Chinese state-run medical schools. TCM was intended from the outset to make Chinese practices more compatible with modern science and thus easier to use in conjunction with Western medicine.[33] By contrast, while late imperial Chinese doctors certainly argued over whose teachings were most important and correct, there was never any institutionalized attempt to impose uniformity or orthodoxy on medical knowledge and practice.[34]

In this unregulated and diverse marketplace, the "medicine" that Wei practiced was distinguished by its self-identification with a set of ancient, canonical texts, customarily known by the collective title *Yellow Emperor's Inner Classic (Huangdi neijing)*. This collection of teachings dating from around the second and first centuries B.C.E. had gradually coalesced into a set of more or less cohesive texts over the course of the Han dynasty. Written in the form of a dialogue between the mythical Yellow Emperor and his ministers, most famously Qi Bo, the *Inner Classic* served as the epistemological source of authority for doctors in subsequent centuries. Indeed, the phrase "to be skilled in the arts of Qi Bo and the Yellow Emperor" *(jing Qi-Huang)* was a standard phrase used to describe someone as a medical expert. The received version of the *Yellow Emperor's Inner Classic, Basic Questions (Suwen)* originated in the Tang dynasty (618–907), when it became required reading in government medical schools; in the latter part of the eleventh century, the Song dynasty's Imperial Editorial Office directed the compilation of what would become the standard edition.[35] Beginning in the mid-twelfth century, furthermore, doctors could also refer to an authoritative recension of the second component text of the *Inner Classic*, the *Divine Pivot (Lingshu)*.[36] The goal of literate physicians like Wei Zhixiu was to improve their discernment of the universal insights set forth in these esoteric works, adapting and applying them to diseases old and new.

To be an expert in the Yellow Emperor's art was to engage in a form of healing that located the primary dynamics of illness and cure within the body itself. As Paul Unschuld explains, this view developed in contradistinction to older, coexisting frameworks that attributed illness to demonic possession and vengeance of dead ancestors.[37] The *Inner Classic* saw the human body as a literal microcosmos whose material form and dynamic functioning reiterated that of the universe. Like all things in the cosmos, the body was constituted of and animated by qi, a concept that simultaneously encompassed all material existence and all transformative potential in the cosmos. Modern scholars have explained it with phrases such as "psychophysical energy," "vital force," or the "stuff" that constituted all discernable "substance, activity, and vitality."[38] The central question driving philosophical and empirical inquiry in China was how to properly discern and characterize the principles *(li)* that governed the transformations and manifestations of qi as well as the dynamic patterns by which these transformations influenced each other. To describe these, Chinese thinkers drew on two metaphorical frameworks. The most fundamental was that of yin and yang, which envisioned the universe as an infinite series of paired opposites, joined in a mutually dependent relationship where one existed only in reference to the other: dark and light, night and day, down and up, inner and outer, Earth and Heaven, female and male, stillness and movement. Everything had a yin and yang aspect, and each could again be divided into yin and yang: while women were yin, for example, a robust young woman would be yang compared to an old frail woman. The second conceptual system was that of the five phases *(wu xing)*, which employed the metaphors of water, fire, wood, metal, and earth to explain the nature of phenomena and the interactions between them. These interactions could follow a cycle of production and nurturing or a cycle of destruction and hampering: water engendered wood, for example, but it checked fire. Yin-yang and five phase doctrine provided the scaffolding for a complex and elaborate system of correlative thinking or "system of correspondences" that explained the cause, form, and unfolding of all phenomena. Late imperial doctors took it for granted that these correspondences could explain and predict the onset and course of disease as well as the expected effect of drugs and other therapeutic interventions.

A literate male doctor like Wei Zhixiu would explain that the primordial qi bestowed at conception was supplemented after birth with qi derived from the transformation of food, water, and air by the organs of the body. The key organs were collectively known as the "five depots and six palaces" *(wu zang liu fu)*, organs differentiated by whether they were primarily responsible for storing qi or for disseminating qi throughout the body. The spleen, heart, kidney, lungs, and liver were the depot organs, defined as yin, and seen as most internal and most vital to life. The palace organs, which constituted their yang counterparts, were the stomach, large intestine, small intestines, bladder, gall bladder, and the "triple burner" *(sanjiao)*. Together, the organs ensured the adequate production of qi and its smooth and regular movement throughout a network of circulation channels. Doctors recognized many different manifestations of qi in the body, and they drew distinctions between them based on their functions and their yin or yang attributes.[39] The most basic distinction was between the yang aspect of general bodily qi, also called qi, and the yin aspect, called Blood *(xue)*. This distinction was present in the phrase "qi and Blood" *(qi xue)*, which was the standard way of referring to the ensemble of vital forces that animated and nurtured the body. When used in this manner, the term *Blood* encompassed not only the red liquid that flowed from the body but also bodily fluids in general. For example, excessive perspiration could deplete Blood, and Blood constituted the basis of menses and breast milk in women.

Illness arose from imbalances in the various yin and yang forms of bodily qi, broadly described in terms of deficiency and vacuity *(xu)*, excess and plethora *(shi)*, blockage, stagnation, or contrary flow. Curing illness required one to correctly identify the nature, location, and root cause of qi perturbations and then employ treatments to eliminate pathology and restore smooth functioning. To diagnose illness, doctors employed the "four examinations"—namely, "looking" *(wang)* at the patient's appearance and movements, including the color and form of the tongue; "listening [to] and smelling" *(wen)* signs such as the patient's breathing and bodily odors; "asking" *(wen)* about the nature and history of the patient's malaise; and "palpation" *(qie)* of the pulse at the patient's wrists to read the state of qi flow through the body. Although acupuncture was the dominant therapy in the original *Inner Classic* texts, the Northern Song dynasty (960–1127) ushered in a vast expansion of materia medica at the expense of other therapies.[40] During late imperial times, the therapeutic hallmark of an educated physician like Wei Zhixiu was the use of drugs, administered singly or in combination, taken orally in the form of powders, pills, or boiled decoctions.[41]

While the principles of qi transformation were universal, their manifestations in a specific body varied according to time, place, and individual. In addition to considering a patient's diet, habits, personality, social class, age, profession, and gender, doctors also had to factor in the prevailing forces of geography, season, and day.[42] The heart of classical diagnostic and therapy was to discern the general principles at work in any specific instance of illness.[43] A well-trained doctor with superior insights into yin, yang, and the five phases could in theory treat any illness that he encountered, and one did not need specific expertise in women's diseases to cure women successfully. At the same time, however, the myriad possible variations of the human condition meant that specialization was seen as a useful mechanism for ensuring deep mastery in identifiable classes of ailments. And when Wei Zhixiu's contemporaries thought about the treatment of women's ailments, they took it for granted that *fuke* constituted a distinct body of knowledge that people could deploy with greater or lesser skill.

THE "CURRICULUM" OF WOMEN'S ILLNESSES

The Yellow Emperor served as the intellectual progenitor for all who claimed mastery in medicine. To evoke the antiquity of specialization in women's illnesses, writers also referred to the legendary physician Bian

Que of the Warring States period (403–221 B.C.E.).[44] Reputedly endowed with the power to see through the human body, Bian Que was later canonized as a "god of medicine" and the patron deity of doctors and medicine sellers.[45] He was also the apocryphal author of the *Classic of Difficult Issues (Nanjing,* ca. first century C.E.), a foundational work that Paul Unschuld describes as "marking the apex of the application of the concepts of yin-yang and the Five Phases to medicine in Chinese antiquity."[46] A biography of Bian Que famously appears in *Records of the Historian (Shiji)* compiled by Sima Qian (ca. 145–90 B.C.E.), who recounted how the master physician was equally skilled at healing numerous types of ailments, tailoring his therapeutic focus according to the demands of people in different regions. These included women's diseases, denoted in this early text by the term of illnesses "below the girdle" *(daixia):*[47] "When [Bian Que] was passing through Handan, he heard that the people there esteemed their women, so he became a doctor of 'below the girdle' ailments. When he passed through Luoyang, he heard that the Zhou people loved their old people, so he became a doctor of vision and hearing disorders. When he entered Xianyang, he heard that the Qin people loved children, so he became a doctor of children's diseases. Thus he altered to accord with local customs."[48]

During the thirteenth century, the doctor Qi Zhongfu questioned whether Bian Que's activities indeed constituted "the dawn of the specialized curriculum *[zhuanke]* of medicine for women." Qi pointed out that Bian Que had not left any texts, and he situated the origins of *fuke* in his own age—the Song dynasty—when he and other male writers began to compile systematic treatises on women's special illnesses.[49] Nevertheless, references to Bian Que as the mythic ancestor of *fuke* continued to surface in late imperial texts, and the phrase "passing through Handan" *(guo Handan)* was understood as a synonym for "treating women's ailments."[50]

Qi Zhongfu's skepticism about Bian Que's historical significance echoes a question that occupies medical historians today: where should we locate the origins of "gynecology" in China? Whereas Qi Zhongfu used text compilation as the yardstick, modern scholars have looked for a systematic body of medical knowledge constructed around explicit statements of female gender difference. The archeological and historical record attests to continual awareness, concern, and fascination with female procreative functions, and special medical recipes for women were written down as early as the first century C.E. on the basis of earlier folk and oral practices.[51] But at what point do such discussions of women's special bodily functions and illnesses constitute a true discourse of gender difference and at what point does this gender difference become medically relevant? While scholars disagree on the exact periodization, it is clear that a recognizable literate subfield of medicine for women emerged over the course of the fifth to thirteenth centuries.[52] During the first part of this period, dominated by the Sui (581–618) and Tang (618–907) dynasties, male practitioners identified women's diseases as an area that they should be concerned with, and they undertook the systematization of earlier practices. Especially influential was Sun Simiao's *Essential Prescriptions Worth a Thousand Golds for Managing Urgent Situations* (*Beiji qianjin yaofang*, 651), which opened its discussion of disease and therapy with three chapters on the treatment of women's illnesses. Here Sun also set forth what historians consider to be the earliest explicit statement on gender difference, explaining that women needed special prescriptions because their reproductive functions made them more sickly than men.[53] Tang doctors also addressed the rituals used for mitigating the pollution of childbirth, and one innovation was the creation of birthing charts that synthesized earlier diagrams on orienting the birthing room and burying the placenta.[54]

During the second half of this period, roughly corresponding to the Song dynasty (960–1279), state medical activism and the fusion of classical medicine with Neo-Confucian metaphysical inquiry nurtured the growth of a sophisticated, doctrinally self-aware "curriculum" *(ke)* of medicine for women.[55] Emperors and government officials alike saw medical activism as a vehicle for demonstrating benevolent rule and enhancing the state's legitimacy. To project its cultural hegemony over the marginally assimilated southern frontiers of the empire, the state notably promoted classical medicine as an alternative to spirit-healing. A wave of epidemics in the mid-eleventh century also intensified this existing interest in medical affairs. The court sponsored important medical publishing projects, including the compilation of an authoritative version of the *Basic Questions*, and actively sought to entice educated men to join the government medical service.

In 1060, the Song imperial government launched a reform of the state medical bureaucracy, raising the requirements for entry into the imperial medical college, revising its curriculum, and overhauling the system of medical examinations. At this time as well, it established *chanke*, that is, "medicine for childbearing," as one of nine departments in the Imperial Medical Service *(taiyi ju)*.[56] This subfield of medicine eventually became known as *fuke*, literally the "curriculum of medicine for married women" but broadly understood as meaning "medicine for women." Indeed, a common synonym for this term was *nüke*, or "the curriculum of medicine for females."[57] When the Song rulers divided their government medical service into different areas of specialization, they significantly expanded a pattern developed by the preceding Tang dynasty (618– 907).[58] The Tang Imperial Medical Office *(taiyi shu)* had trained and deployed its doctors according to four departments, each wielding a different therapeutic technique: acupuncture, massage, exorcism, and "medicine" *(yi)*, that is, the use of drugs. The Song medical service diminished the relative importance of ritual and manual therapies by giving pride of place to drug-based medicine, which it further subdivided into a number of distinct fields. The number of specialized divisions was eventually increased to thirteen, and the phrase "the thirteen curricula" *(shisan ke)* even became used as a synonym for "medicine" in general. Within this institutional setting, the training, assessment, and job assignments of central-government doctors were all structured around distinct medical subdisciplines. Compiling texts on women's medicine was a logical accompaniment to these developments. It was on this basis that Qi Zhongfu located the origin of medical specialization in the Song, an era when the various medical subfields were supported by institutional frameworks: "Not only do they have officials but also [special] areas of study; not only do they have areas of study but also [distinct] departments."[59]

The elaboration of *fuke* during the Song was also nurtured by the expansion of medical cosmological frameworks, both in terms of their intellectual sophistication and their range of applications. It was during the Northern Song that the medico-cosmological doctrine of the "five circulatory phases and six seasonal influences" *(wu yun liu qi)* assumed its mature form, "gradually pervad[ing] every field of medicine: prognosis, diagnosis, prevention, pharmacotherapy, and acupuncture."[60] So too, doctors began to apply medical cosmology to earlier teachings about how to care for reproductive women. During the Tang dynasty, medical writings on women's diseases framed them in terms of "girdle discharges" *(daixia)*, a rubric that evoked concerns with female pollution. Song dynasty doctors, by comparison, articulated a nosology of women's ailments defined in terms of yin and yang. The *Yellow Emperor's Inner Classic* had pointed out that "men are ruled by qi, and women by Blood," thus pointing out the special affinities between the yang of humankind (man) with the yang aspect of bodily vitalities (qi), and the yin of humankind (woman) with the yin of the body (Blood). This formulation simultaneously acknowledged distinctions between the sexes while subordinating these differences to a universalistic cosmological body.[61] Thus when Song dynasty *fuke* texts taught that "in women, Blood is the main principle," they aimed both to explain the origins of women's special medical needs and to affirm that male scholar-philosophers had something important to say about them. By 1237, when Chen Ziming wrote his seminal *Comprehensive Compendium of Good Formulas for Women* (*Furen daquan liangfang*), physicians had identified a wide range of female ailments rooted in female Blood, including but not limited to those directly related to reproduction.[62] Song dynasty teachings served as an important reference point for later writers, whose revisions of the Song tradition are discussed throughout the later parts of this book.

The development of *fuke* as a distinct subfield was thus nurtured by the growing scholarly interest in medicine as well as the administrative demands of the state. The practice of dividing medicine into different curricula continued to be the basic pattern in the medical services of dynasties after the Song as well. While the precise departmental divisions and labels varied over time, they included functional departments distinguished by nosological categories (cold damage, pox, internal or external ailments), the part of body afflicted (eye diseases, throat diseases), techniques used ("prescriptions and pulse taking," acumoxa, bone setting), and special ailments of certain populations (women and children). During the Qing, government regulations followed a long precedent in specifying that, "in practicing their métier, the medical officials, medical doctors, and medical students will be directed to develop special expertise in a medical subdiscipline."[63] The examinations that the palace medical staff took every six years also specifically tested them on their areas of therapeutic expertise.[64]

Outside the government medical service, specialization also shaped the reputation and practice of doctors, although the degree to which it did so was much more variable. The medical biography sections of county, prefectural, and provincial gazetteers show that, while the majority of publicly recognized healers were known for being generally "good at medicine," numerous others built their reputations through treating certain classes of illness.[65] These, then, were the kinds of people that Wei Zhixiu referred to when he spoke of "experts in the discipline." Their ranks included Hu Jishi, a native of Tongxiang County, who "achieved renown in his time as a doctor of wounds [*yangyi*]."[66] Similarly, Qian Qingshi and Qian Biyi, both county licentiates, "made medicine for women their area of expertise" *(zhuan nüke).*[67] Tan Jinzhang, an "expert in children's medicine" *(erke zhuanjia),* was furthermore noted for his particular skill in treating "pox and variola," a subcategory of pediatrics.[68] Others were also described as "practicing" *(xi)* or "making a profession of" *(ye)* one area of medicine. While such practitioners may not necessarily have treated one type of disease to the exclusion of others, their social identities were shaped by their perceived specializations. Indeed, the name of the medical subfield was commonly used as synonym for the practitioner. Wei Zhixiu's case anthology, for example, described how one doctor had "made inquiries among the *chanke*" (literally, the "medicine for childbearing") to see whether any of these practitioners had ever encountered a case of bodily swelling during pregnancy accompanied by watery blisters in the vagina.[69]

HEREDITARY PHYSICIANS AND *FUKE*

Prominent among the many "experts in the discipline" who plied their craft were practitioners claiming to be descended from families with a tradition of producing doctors, the so-called hereditary physicians *(shiyi).* The transmission of therapeutic secrets from father to son or from master to disciple was the oldest form of medical education. Within families, furthermore, possession of proprietary medical knowledge constituted a form of socioeconomic capital to be handed down for the benefit of successive generations. These de facto practices had loose institutional referents during the Yuan (1279–1368) and Ming (1368–1644) dynasties, when the government designated certain occupations as hereditary status groups in order to guarantee a supply of skilled labor to the state. These groups included the "medical households" *(yihu),* selected from among existing medical lineages, and their responsibilities included staffing local government medical schools and dispensaries.[70] These hereditary occupational designations were permeable, however, and individuals from medical families pursued alternative occupations, while other medical lineages thrived even without special legal status.[71] After the mid-seventeenth century, furthermore, the Qing rulers eliminated these hereditary occupations. For the late imperial period, therefore, the *shiyi* label is best understood as referring to a particular family background and to the values that it evoked: access to proprietary methods and the accumulated wisdom of successive generations of forebears.

While many medical lineages claimed an expertise in medicine generally, numerous others constructed their reputation around expertise in a

specific medical subfield such as *fuke*.[72] Three particularly well-documented and long-lived *fuke* families were the Chens of Jiaxing, the Guos
of Hangzhou, and the Songs of Ningbo. All hailed from northern Zhejiang Province, located in the Jiangnan region of southeastern China. Since
the Song dynasty, Jiangnan had been the most economically and culturally advanced region of China, its native children dominating the ranks
of China's scholar-officials, women poets, and medical worthies. All three
families claimed a transmitted *fuke* practice that dated from the Tang or
Song dynasty and endured into the Qing. So successful were the Chens
and Songs, in fact, that their descendants were still practicing medicine
in China at the end of the twentieth century. Their histories illustrate the
diverse strategies that men from medical lineages could use to assert their
expertise as healers of women.

The Chen Family: Imperial Physician as Progenitor

The Chen family history exemplifies a common dynamic in Chinese medicine: a practitioner who became famous for treating certain classes of
illness could use this knowledge to establish a family medical tradition.
The Chens traced their origins to a Tang dynasty imperial physician, Chen
Shiliang, but the family's fame as gynecological practitioners was established by the twelfth-century doctor Chen Yi. It was not uncommon for
the court to put out a general appeal to skilled doctors of the land when
government doctors were unable to treat a particularly difficult case.[73]
This was likely how Chen Yi came to prominence, for local histories re-
late that he was made an imperial physician after he cured one of the
Southern Song imperial concubines of a "dangerous disease" *(wei ji)*. As
a further token of favor, Chen Yi received a palace fan that served as a
kind of passport, granting him access to the imperial family's quarters
whenever he was summoned to treat his patients. This also earned him
the sobriquet "Chen of the wooden fan" (Chen Mushan). Subsequently,
his biography tells us, Chen Yi's descendants "continued his occupation
in each generation by practicing medicine for women."[74] Historical and
medical records name twenty-eight members of the Chen family who lived
from approximately 1127 to 1900, of whom twenty-one are described
as having engaged in some medical activity, including eleven described as
active in *fuke* (table 1). One of these was the Ming dynasty figure Chen
Wenzhao, who edited the only extant copy of a *fuke* text attributed to Chen
Yi.[75] Chen Yi's descendants also employed his fan as a symbol of their
practice, using it to remind potential clients of their illustrious ancestor

TABLE 1. MEMBERS OF THE CHEN FAMILY (1127–CA. 1900)

Dynasty	Name	Government Office/Degree	Medical Activities?
Song	Yi	Imperial Medical Service	Yes, *fuke*, wrote medical book
	Jingfu		—
	Qingyin		—
Yuan	Zhongchang		Yes, *fuke*
	Yishan		Yes, *fuke*
Ming	Weikang		Yes, *fuke*
	Chun		Yes, *fuke*
	Lin	Imperial Academy of Medicine	Yes
	Gao		
	Mo	Prefectural physician	Yes
	Jian		Yes, *fuke*, wrote medical book
	Jin		Yes
	Zhuan		Yes
	Ding	Imperial Academy of Medicine	Yes
	Zi	Imperial Academy of Medicine	Yes
	Yinquan		Yes
	Yinchuan		Yes, wrote medical book
	Xiebiao		Yes, *fuke*
	Wenzhao		Yes, wrote medical book
Qing	Hongdian	County licentiate	Yes, *fuke*, wrote medical book
	Mengxiong	County licentiate	Yes, *fuke*
	Dejie		—
	Shannan		Yes, *fuke*, wrote medical book
	Yi'nan		—
	Wenfu		—
	Weimei		Yes, *fuke*
	Sishu		—
	Hongxing		Yes

SOURCES: Chen Qiong et al., comp., *Mingguo Hangzhou fuzhi*, 149:9b–10a, 27a–b; Geng Weihu, ed., *Shimen xianzhi*, 16:33a–b; *LDYJ*; Li Yang, "Chenshi fuke shijia"; Wei Yuan, ed., *Kangxi Qiantang xianzhi*, 26:16b–17a; Yan Chen et al., comp., *Tongxiang xianzhi*, 15:4b; *Zhonghua quanguo zhongyi xuehui Zhejiang fenhui and Zhejiang zhongyiyao yanjiusuo*, ed., *Yilin huicui*; Zhu Xuzeng, *Kaiyouyi zhai*, 4:9b–10a.

as well as the generations of experience that the Chen family doctors had in curing women's illnesses. This strategy notably appears in an early-nineteenth-century account by the official Zhu Xuzeng, who described a visit to the Chen family home in Jiaxing: "In front of their gate they display a wooden fan and on it are written eight characters: 'A palace fan bestowed by the Song; hereditary doctors who followed the court south" *(Song si gongshan, nan du shiyi)*. They are still practicing women's medicine as a hereditary occupation."[76]

The idealized view of hereditary practice was that medical knowledge was personally handed down from father to son in an unbroken line of transmission. In reality, however, this ideal of continuous transmission was not necessarily achieved. As table 1 shows, medical practice frequently skipped one or more generations and the level of medical activity might consist of no more than editing or publishing a medical book. And although the Chens claimed a hereditary transmission in women's medicine, not all their members were necessarily known as experts in *fuke*. But even if history does not completely substantiate the claim that a particular doctor was descended from several hundred years' worth of practitioners, the success of the Chen family shows that these validating legends were powerful sources of medical legitimacy.

The Guo Family: Divinely Imparted Secrets

Hereditary medicine also drew power from the assumption that such doctors possessed secret, proprietary remedies. This assumption owed much to medicine's historical status as a technical art, whose skilled practitioners would be expected to develop closely held trade secrets that would be passed on only to worthy successors. Li Jianmin has shown that the secret transmission of proprietary techniques in fact typified medical education during the Han dynasty, when the classical medical tradition was coalescing.[77] The mystique of secret techniques was further bolstered by historical overlaps between medicine, religious healing, and the occult arts. As described by the eighteenth-century physician Xu Dachun (1693–1771), common wisdom held that "the medicines used in secret prescriptions are inevitably prepared with extraordinary methods and combined in ingenious ways. . . . They usurp the power of yin and yang, and spy into the mechanisms of creation."[78] The wondrous efficacy of these secret methods was also explained in terms of their divine origins, for many of these were believed to be transmitted by "extraordinary persons, scholarly recluses, divine immortals, bodhisattvas, demons, or spirits," who would reveal their secrets only to deserving mortals.[79] Indeed, Bian Que himself had been but a hostel keeper until he received secret medical methods from Chang Sangjun, a divinity disguised as a traveler. Such beliefs were found at all levels of society, discussed in fictional and factual accounts alike, and they were integral to the founding legend of the Guo family, a prominent family of "childbirth doctors" from Haining County, Hangzhou Prefecture.[80]

According to Hangzhou local histories, the Guo lineage traced its origins back to the Prince of Fenyang.[81] The first Guo ancestor identified by name was Guo Yuan, whom the Song Jianlong emperor (r. 960–62) honored with the title of "faithful and virtuous" *(jiegan)*. It was Guo Yuan's grandson Guo Zhaoqian who reportedly began the family's medical practice. At the beginning of the Song Xiangfu reign (1008–17), Zhaoqian left his native place of Henan and went to Hangzhou, where he "performed many unpublicized good deeds" *(duo yinde)*.[82] One of Zhaoqian's good deeds included giving shelter to an "unusual person" *(yiren)*, who rewarded him with three peony blossoms. On the petals of the flowers were written thirteen formulas for treating women's ailments.[83] With these formulas, Zhaoqian became a successful doctor of medicine for women, transmitting the practice to his son and grandson. During the Jianyan reign (1127–30) of the Southern Song dynasty, Zhaoqian's great-grandson Shiyi and Shiyi's mother, Ms. Feng, used these very formulas to cure the Empress Dowager Meng. A grateful emperor subsequently rewarded them with various imperial titles and the fief of Haichang. County, prefectural, and provincial gazetteers compiled during the Qing Kangxi reign (1662–1722) identify sixteen members of the Guo family who were active as healers around this time, including two women.[84] The Guos appeared to have declined in prominence by the end of the Qing dynasty, however, for later gazetteers do not name any additional Guo family doctors.

Surviving textual fragments suggest that the Guo family's "peony formulas" were nothing unusual, relying on standard drugs for regulating female Blood.[85] But the legend of the peony blossoms was cited in local historical accounts, as well as in the title of the Guo family's ancestral medical text. It thereby served to underscore the founding Guo physician's benevolence and morality, while also providing a ready explanation for how and why this man decided to specialize in *fuke*. In this context, the spectacular cure of a royal client served primarily to affirm the inherent power of the divinely imparted formulas.

The Song Family: Wife as Medical Founder

Many of the woman healers whose names have survived were members of medical families, be it as daughters, wives, or daughters-in-law of medical men.[86] As we saw earlier, for example, Ms. Feng helped establish the Guo lineage's fortune by curing the Empress Dowager Meng. During the seventeenth century, Guo Shaoqu's wife, Ms. Wu, practiced medicine, as did his daughter-in-law Ms. Mao.[87] All of these women are named in local histories, suggesting that their activities were a source of pride for the Guo family. But the case of the Song family of Ningbo shows that women's medical contributions might also be viewed with ambivalence. The lineage ancestor was the eminent Tang dynasty official Song Jing, enfeoffed as the Duke of Guangping in 717.[88] According to family legend, however, it was Song Jing's wife, Ms. Yu, who established medicine for women as the lineage's hereditary métier. The earliest account of her activities dates from 1612, written by the lineage member and physician Song Lin'gao in a preface to his own text on *fuke:* "[Jing's] wife, Ms. Yu, secretly obtained *[qie]* his methods and circulated them in the world. Even among the wives of the commoners, there were none who did not receive her beneficence. And so her transmission was exclusively in this subject of women's medicine."[89]

The basic meaning of *qie* is "to steal" and, by extension, "to usurp" or "to spy out"—in other words, to obtain property or knowledge that one is not supposed to have. By using this word, Song Lin'gao's account implies that Song Jing may have had some proprietary techniques that he did not wish to share, and that his wife initially learned them without his knowledge or consent. If there were any other female practitioners in long history of the Song family, their names have been forgotten, and it is not until the mid-twentieth century that we again find Song family women named as doctors.[90]

But even if women like Ms. Yu made significant contributions to a medical lineage's social capital, the legitimacy of the lineage's practice ultimately depended on the transmission of knowledge between its male members. In the absence of sons, it was not uncommon for medical families to seek uxorilocal sons-in-law to continue the lineage's occupation.[91] In one branch of the Guo medical family of Haining, for example, a fifteenth-century son-in-law took the Guo surname, learned the Guo medical tradition, and passed it on to his descendants. Another Ming dynasty doctor, Shu Gui, likewise had no sons and so transmitted his secret book of medicine to a son-in-law, Yuan Xiang. Yuan Xiang himself also lacked a male heir and in turn transmitted the family learning to his own son-in-law, Qian E.[92] Carefully husbanded, a lineage's medical expertise could endure for generations, depending on the talents and inclinations of its male descendants. The fact that a man's sons or grandsons followed him into medicine showed that his methods were effective and worth transmitting. Conversely, the fact that a doctor's ancestors had practiced medicine immediately endowed him with the authority of accumulated generations of wisdom. Song Lin'gao evoked these ideas in a poem describing his family's medical skills, in which he emphasized both the antiquity of their transmission and their diagnostic acumen:

> Their skills have passed through numerous generations and their origins are ancient;
> In the Tang, Song, Yuan, and Ming dynasties, their benefit to the world has been profound.
> They see straight to the heart of obscure dynamics, like an arrow striking a target;
> Never are they led astray by the pursuit of false knowledge.[93]

In sum, while Ms. Yu's healing activities might have directed the Song family's medical energies toward *fuke*, the perceived efficacy of their remedies had little to do with any privileged knowledge their womenfolk might have had about women's bodies. Instead, the perceived worth of the family's therapeutic methods was proven by their ability to provide a livelihood for successive generations of male practitioners.

SCHOLARLY MEDICINE IN LATE IMPERIAL CHINA

In his account of Mrs. Shi's postpartum ailments, Wei Zhixiu implied that his medical knowledge was superior to that of the "experts in the discipline." To properly contextualize this rhetoric, we must realize that medical specialization in late imperial China evoked a set of cultural associations that differed significantly from those in the well-studied histories of European and American medicine. In the West, competition for institutional and legal control over the medical profession invested the issue of specialization with symbolic importance.[94] Prior to the twentieth century, elite physicians argued that the truly capable healer was one who could treat all diseases with equal skill. Specializing in a single field was an admission that one's medical knowledge was limited, and tantamount to quackery. Beginning in the twentieth century, however, specialization became associated with a class of medical elites, who were certified as specialists only after mastering knowledge beyond that of the general practitioner. In late imperial China, by comparison, medical specialization had no such symbolic meaning and carried no intrinsic stigma or superiority. The idea that medical education and practice would be organized by subfields was entirely normal, institutionalized as it was in the government medical service. Similarly, acquiring knowledge in a special medical subfield could provide sufficient social capital to found a medical lineage. Given this context, it is clear that Wei Zhixiu is not concerned about the intrinsic value of generalization or specialization as a mode of organizing medicine. Instead, his concern is with the need to be flexible and insightful in one's approach to illness. And whereas access to proprietary knowledge constituted the hereditary practitioner's supposed claim to fame, this sort of mental perspicacity was the avowed hallmark of the scholar-physician *(ruyi)*.[95] As I will show later, the expansion of scholarly ideals of medicine also fostered changes in medical definitions of women's bodies beginning in the seventeenth century. It will thus be helpful first to examine the history of these norms in some detail.

The Scholarly Medical Ideal

The term *scholar-physician* and the values it came to embody had its roots in the Song dynasty, nurtured simultaneously by new central government policies and by changes in the makeup and cultural outlook of the elite class. We saw earlier that Song emperors and statesmen promoted classical medicine as part of state-building and sought to improve the quality of government doctors by persuading educated men to take up medicine. In was in this context that Fan Zhongyan (989–1052), a leading proponent of medical reform, made his famous statement "If you cannot be a good minister, then become a good doctor."[96] Asaf Goldschmidt has analyzed how these efforts intensified under the reign of Emperor Huizong (1101–25), who elevated the bureaucratic status of the government medical school and created more prestigious titles for medical officials that mirrored those of regular civil servants. In an imperial edict of 1113, the court also began using the term *scholar-physician* to refer to the kind of doctors it aimed to recruit and cultivate.[97]

At the same time, educated men themselves were also taking a greater interest in medicine. Whereas Tang government and society were dominated by aristocratic clans, these gave way in the Song to an elite class that derived its status and self-identity from success in the civil service examinations and the scholarly formation that underlay it. Thanks to government-sponsored medical compilations and the expansion of printing at this time, educated men also had greater access than ever before to the medical writings of their contemporaries and predecessors. While the remunerative practice of medicine may still have been beneath a gentleman's dignity, the study of medical texts now became a laudable pursuit for scholars, who depicted it as a humane art and proper vehicle for expressing the gentleman's benevolent concern for the suffering of the world. In subsequent centuries, references to scholar-physicians referred both to gentlemanly connoisseurs of medicine and to practitioners who embodied literati values.

Following its conquest of the Southern Song in 1279, the Mongol Yuan dynasty enacted policies that made medicine an increasingly attractive occupation for upper-class men.[98] To curb the influence of the Han Chinese majority, the court suspended the civil service examinations, leaving scholars in need of alternative career paths. At the same time, the Yuan rulers highly esteemed the technical arts, including medicine, and established an extensive empirewide system of medical schools and bureaus. Although a government doctor's official rank was relatively low, he still enjoyed the status and advantages of serving in the civil service, and ambitious physicians were also able to cultivate useful ties to highly placed patrons. This general trend of educated men becoming doctors continued in subsequent centuries, and preliminary evidence suggests that scholars-turned-doctors had achieved a kind of critical mass by the end of the Ming (1368–1644), becoming a significant subgroup within the ranks of those who practiced medicine as a remunerative trade. Such developments are notably suggested by changes in the personal backgrounds of the men listed in the medical biography sections of local gazetteers. These were individuals who attained public recognition on the basis of their healing activities. Taking the northern Zhejiang prefectures of Hangzhou, Jiaxing, Shaoxing, and Ningbo as a case study, I have shown elsewhere that there was a dramatic increase from the Ming to the Qing in the number of doctors with civil service examination degrees. Only 6 percent of doctors identified as Ming dynasty figures had a degree (12 of 204 individuals), compared to 30 percent for the Qing (83 of 278 individuals). Notably, three-fourths of the Qing degree holders were county licentiates—the lowest level of certification—suggesting that medicine had become a routine alternative for men who could not advance in the examinations.[99] Whether this pattern held true throughout China will require further study. However, it is also supported by other circumstantial evidence. For example, late imperial observers commented that failed examination candidates were flocking to medicine (and also complained that far too many of these had but a cursory knowledge of medical books and medical principles).[100] Such developments were consistent with a well-documented phenomenon: the expansion in the absolute numbers of educated men who took the examinations but were unable to pass. When Ming Taizu (r. 1368–98) added a lower tier of examinations at the county level, it made the civil service more accessible and attractive than ever to an increasing number of men. At the same time, the Chinese population was rapidly expanding, either doubling or tripling between 1500 and 1800.[101] But the number of available government posts remained relatively stable, resulting in ever-smaller pass rates that could be as low as 1.5 percent at any given tier of examinations.[102] For those who failed, medicine could serve as a substitute for officialdom or as way to maintain a living while continuing one's studies and hoping to pass the exams. The hapless Tutor Chen of the popular play *The Peony Pavilion* (1589), who supplemented his teaching income with bumbling attempts to treat the sick, represented the comic aspects of what had become a well-known figure.

Scholarly versus Hereditary Medicine

When the sixteenth-century physician Li Chan sat down to classify the famous doctors of history into different categories, he depicted the scholar-physicians as men "who are thoroughly knowledgeable in the classics and widely versed in the histories, who cultivate their personal morality and are judicious in their behavior, who have achieved recognition as accomplished scholars, and who concurrently have a mastery of medicine."[103] Just as *hereditary physician* denoted a particular kind of family background, the label *scholar-physician* indicated above all a certain kind of personal formation and moral character. At the most basic level, the scholar *(ru)* was a man who had mastered a canon of books comprising the teachings of Confucius, major commentaries on the same, and books that the Sage had deemed essential for the proper nurturing of worthy men: odes and poetry, histories, rituals and government regulations from model states, and yin-yang cosmology. This curriculum provided the core content of the civil service examinations used to select men for government service. More broadly, however, the aim of this classical study was to provide the foundation and framework for a life of erudition, virtue, and continuous self-cultivation. As described by Volker Scheid, the ideal scholar-physician therefore represented "a perfected human being inspired by a deeply felt desire to help others and guided by a profound understanding of cosmic process. . . . Such perfection did not arise by itself but had to be developed through strategies of self-cultivation shared by all educated men."[104] Intellectual acumen and exemplary morality were thus preconditions for medical efficacy.

Such scholarliness was by no means incompatible with other personal attributes, and the history of Chinese medicine is peopled by practitioners who could simultaneously claim to be scholars and members of medical families. As Ch'iu Chung-lin has found, many Ming dynasty medical lineages even owed their medical tradition to an ancestor who started as a scholar and then became a doctor.[105] This included men who took posts in the government medical service, whether as imperial doctor or local medical official. At the same time, medical lineages with sufficient means would train their men for the examinations. Thus the ranks of scholars-turned-doctors included many sons of medical families who initially aimed for examination success but later returned to their ancestral profession. These notably included members of the Chen and Guo lineages of *fuke* doctors.[106] During the late imperial period, then, the distinctions between hereditary and scholarly doctors were largely heuristic and rhetorical.

Nevertheless, as more men of scholarly background became doctors, they also intensified their efforts to assert the superiority of classically trained practitioners over other healers. This is exemplified by the late imperial debate over a famous saying from the *Book of Rites (Liji),* which said, "If a doctor does not have three generations of medicine, do not take his drugs" *(Yi bu san shi, bu fu qi yao).* The prevailing interpretation was that this referred to a man descended from a medical lineage, someone whose father and grandfather had also practiced medicine. As Yüan-ling Chao has shown, however, beginning in the fourteenth century, and with increasing vigor during the Ming and Qing, literate doctors argued that the *Book of Rites* in fact referred to a scholarly physician who had mastered three ancient medical classics. By emphasizing classical formation, Chao finds, these doctors sought "to counter a trend perceived by many in which hereditary physicians relied too much on the use of secret formulae passed down within the family."[107] Simultaneously, Ming-Qing medical scholars sought to raise the status of medicine by identifying an intellectual lineage of medical sages emulating that of the great Confucian thinkers.[108]

The norms of scholarly medicine thus claimed that a doctor who lacked the requisite intellectual training and moral judgment was but a technician relying on precedent and tricks of the trade. Nor was it enough merely to have some scholarly formation, and elite doctors were as critical of the Tutor Chens of the world as they were of their nonscholarly competitors. These concerns to elevate the intellectual quality and social status of medicine motivated doctors to compile medical primers that laid out model curricula for the medical and moral training of would-be physicians. As Angela Leung shows, furthermore, these primers routinely emulated the rhetoric and form of the Confucian primers with which scholars began their studies.[109] When authors described the kind of mental acuity that medicine required, they repeatedly referred to the need to understand *li*, the principles that governed the cosmos. Such statements portrayed medical study as part of the Neo-Confucian project that joined enlightened self-cultivation to cosmological mastery.[110] As articulated by eleventh-century philosophers and famously synthesized by Zhu Xi (1130–1200), Neo-Confucianism was centrally concerned with discerning the nature of and relationship between *li* and qi. Qi, as we saw earlier, was the basis of all material existence and transformative change, while *li* referred to the principles or patterns governing the manifestations of qi. Zhu Xi gave primacy to *li*, and he called for "investigating things to extend knowledge to the fullest" *(gewu zhizhi)*, seeking the principles inherent in each thing that would reveal the unitary cosmic principle whence it came and of which it formed an integral part. This search for cosmic principle encompassed "both natural and moral orders," for the scholar's study of "the myriad things" would also allow him to discern the proper patterns to which individuals and societies should harmonize themselves.[111] Health and illness, as manifestations of qi transformation, were also governed by principle, and only well-educated doctors would be able to correctly discern the underlying patterns at work in any given case. Zhu Zhenheng had famously depicted medicine as an integral part of Neo-Confucian empirical investigation in the title and preface to his fourteenth-century medical treatise, *Additional Discourses on Extending Knowledge through the Investigation of Things (Gezhi yulun)*. The editors of the *Imperially Compiled Golden Mirror of Medical Learning (Yuzuan yizong jinjian*, 1742) had the same connections in mind when they wrote this prefatory comment to their work, intended as a statement of correct medical practice: "If doctors are not intimately familiar with books, they will not understand principle *[li]*. If they do not understand principle, they will not be able to recognize the situation clearly. Then when they go to treat illness, they will vacillate and be indecisive, their medicines will not accord with the sickness, and it will be difficult to obtain an efficacious result."[112]

These ideals of scholarly discernment also permeated *fuke,* eventually constituting the central ideal around which the educated male practitioner articulated his superiority over midwives and other competitors. As educated men sought better solutions to women's reproductive illnesses, they increasingly subordinated observed bodily differences to the universalistic cosmic principles governing all bodies, male and female. By the early seventeenth century, medical thinkers had significantly reduced the perceived scope of female difference, ultimately permitting a more benign view of the female body.

DE-EXOTICIZATION OF FEMALE DIFFERENCE

The existence of *fuke* as a specialized medical subfield arose from the a priori assumption that women had unique illnesses requiring unique therapeutic strategies. The question, however, was how much importance to assign to these differences. A long-standing and prevalent view— grounded in ancient texts—was that women were inherently more sickly and harder to treat than men. The late imperial period, however, presented a new, alternative view: that male and female illnesses were fundamentally the same. To appreciate the dimensions of this change, it is helpful to contrast Sun Simiao's seventh-century description of female illnesses with a corresponding passage in the *Golden Mirror* of 1742.

When Sun Simiao wrote his *Essential Prescriptions Worth a Thousand Golds for Managing Urgent Situations (Beiji qianjin yaofang,* 651), he opened his discussion of women's diseases with a description of female sickliness that all late imperial doctors would have known. To appreciate his rhetoric—and how later writers modified it—it is worth quoting it at length:

> The reason that there are separate prescriptions for women is that they differ in experiencing pregnancy, childbirth, and injury from [Blood] collapse. Therefore the illnesses of women are ten times harder to treat than those of men. The *Classic* says, women are gathering places for yin influences, and they routinely dwell in dampness. From the age of fourteen on, their yin qi wells up and overflows. Myriad thoughts run through their minds, damaging their organs within and injuring their complexions without. The discharge and retention of their menses is now early, now late. Obstructed Blood stagnates and congeals, so that their central pathways are cut off. The injuries that result from this cannot be fully enumerated. Their organs are cold or hot, vacuity and repletion alternate chaotically, corrupted Blood seeps internally, and the vessels of qi are injured and exhausted. Some are immoderate in their diet, causing numerous injuries.

Some have sexual intercourse before their [vaginal] sores are healed. Some relieve themselves on an elevated privy, and wind enters them from below, further leading to the twelve kinds of internal solidifications. Therefore, separate prescriptions have been established for women.

If the illness is one caused by the qi of the four seasons, or if it is an affliction of depletion, repletion, cold, or heat, then these are the same as their husbands' [illnesses]. It is just that those who fall ill during pregnancy should avoid toxic medicines. The unclassified illnesses *[zabing]* are the same as their husbands' and are distributed throughout the other chapters of this book where one can learn about them.

Nevertheless, women's cravings and desires exceed their husbands' and they contract illnesses at twice the rate of men. On top of this, when women experience affection and longing, love and hatred, envy and jealousy, and worry and rancor, their attachment to their desires is stubborn, and they are unable to control their emotions by themselves. Therefore the roots of their disorders are deep and it is difficult to cure them.[113]

Here Sun articulates female difference in terms of two main issues. The first is that women need separate prescriptions because they have special reproductive functions, and these functions make them ill. We see, for example, that once a girl reaches fourteen, the canonical age of sexual maturity for females, the welling up of yin qi that makes her fertile also provokes mental upheaval and a cascade of illnesses that damage her both internally and externally. Second, women have distinctive constitutional attributes, being gathering places for yin and inherently prone to excessive emotionality. Although Sun did mention that nonreproductive ailments of women were to be treated the same as men's, this point is bracketed and subsumed by his emphasis on the unique difficulty posed by women's ailments. Even if women's "unclassified illnesses" are in principle like men's, their special physical and emotional predispositions still make women fundamentally more difficult to treat.

The overall effect of Sun's essay was to emphasize the innate nature of female difference and to depict the illnesses associated with childbearing as the fundamental determinant of female health. In other words, women's illnesses were *different* from men's, except those *unrelated* to childbirth. The *Golden Mirror,* however, presents the converse view: women's illnesses were the *same* as men's, except those *related* to childbirth. In contrast to Sun Simiao, who introduced his section on women's prescriptions by emphasizing female difference, the *Golden Mirror* opened its discussion of *fuke* with the affirmation that female and male illnesses were more alike than not. This idea was summed up in a set of easy-to-learn mnemonic verses, followed by a lengthier commentary:

[Verses] Male and female diseases are treated in the same way.
The points where they differ are in regulating menses, Blood collapse,
   girdle discharges, internal accumulations,
Nourishing descendants, pregnancy, and postpartum.
Genital and breast diseases are dissimilar.

[Commentary] The diseases of women are fundamentally no different from
those of men *[furen zhubing ben yu nanzi wu yi]*. Therefore they are treated
the same. Where they differ from men is only in the illnesses of irregular
menses, stopped up menses, turbid girdle discharges, collapse and leaking,
verifiable and illusory internal accumulations *[zhengjia]*, producing descendants, pregnancy, and postpartum. Also, the illness manifestations of the
breast and the genitals are dissimilar. Therefore the curriculum of women's
ailments was established as a separate category to detail the methods of
treating these. Those who would make this discipline their occupation must
first read all the books on the essentials of prescriptions and pulse before
reading this [section on women's medicine]. Then they will naturally experience the marvelous effect of everything suddenly becoming clear.[114]

The distinction between the perspective of Sun Simiao and that of the
Golden Mirror is both as subtle and significant as whether one sees a
glass as half empty or half full. No one denied that the maladies associated with childbearing were unique to women. Where they differed, however, was in the extent to which they used these illnesses to define female
bodies as qualitatively different from men's. The "same as men" perspective, in effect, allowed a de-exoticization of female bodies, portraying gestative illnesses as an exception to the rule that women and men were the
same, rather than as a master narrative of female difference.

It is especially significant that such a view should appear in the *Golden
Mirror*. As Marta Hanson has shown, the imperial physicians who directed the compilation of the *Golden Mirror* intended it to be a guiding
statement of correct medical doctrine, and it was one shaped by the leading intellectual currents of the day. The *Golden Mirror*'s compilers, as
well as the source authors whom they favored, hailed from Jiangnan, the
leading center of literati culture—including medical scholarship—in
China. Furthermore, all were proponents of the "evidential scholarship"
(kaozheng) movement, which sought to recover the true form of the ancient Han dynasty classics through rigorous philological research.[115] From
the time of its compilation to the end of the dynasty, the *Golden Mirror*
served as a benchmark of correct practice for the doctors responsible for
maintaining the health of the imperial family.[116] It was also one of the
perennial bestsellers of the late imperial book market.[117] Although the

extent to which the *Golden Mirror* influenced practice outside the court remains to be determined, it was clearly a prominent version of mainstream medical practice, embodying the best judgments of highly educated physicians.

Beyond the special status of the *Golden Mirror* in late imperial medicine, its viewpoints are historically significant because they represented the full articulation of an epistemological shift that had its roots in the Song and came to full flower around the seventeenth century. This shift can be discerned in the way that Sun Simiao's statement on female sickliness was reworked in three important texts of the thirteenth to seventeenth centuries: Chen Ziming's *Comprehensive Compendium* of 1237, Xue Ji's later redaction of Chen Ziming in 1547, and Zhang Jiebin's essays on *fuke,* written sometime between 1624 and 1640.[118] The changes from one to another suggest that medical thinkers over time were assigning greater importance to social factors as a cause of female disease, thereby muting the idea that women's bodies were inherently sickly. In all three cases, furthermore, these changes in gender rhetoric occurred within texts authored by men who sought to apply universal principles more thoroughly to the conceptualization of women's ailments.

Social Customs

When Chen Ziming compiled his thirteenth-century synthesis of *fuke* knowledge, he reprinted Sun Simiao's full essay on the need for women's remedies and also repeated the familiar tropes of female sickliness.[119] But Chen Ziming also included a long essay from the government official and pharmacologist Kou Zongshi (twelfth century) that offered an alternative to the image of innate female sickliness. While Sun Simiao highlighted the debilitating effects of childbirth, Kou attributed the difficulty of curing women to social customs, namely, the gender segregation that hindered male doctors' ability to assess their female patients: "In today's high-ranking families [the women] dwell within obscure rooms, placed amid curtains and screens, and furthermore they cover her arm with a cotton handkerchief. Thereupon one cannot carry out the marvelous method of inspecting the complexion, nor can one fully employ the ingenious method of taking the pulse. Out of four [diagnostic methods], two are omitted."[120] Unable to examine the patient's "form and qi, luster and color," the doctor had no choice but to ask as many questions as possible to determine the true nature of the illness. "But when patients

see how many questions there are," Kou sighed, "they come to the conclusion that the medical profession lacks excellence. So it frequently happens that you give them medicine but they refuse to take it."[121]

The medical case literature suggests that concerns about propriety did
not actually prevent male doctors from diagnosing and treating female
patients on a regular basis.[122] But although Kou still assumed that women
were harder to cure, his emphasis was on the effects of social habits rather
than any innate characteristics of women's bodies. In 1547, when Xue
Ji revised Chen Ziming's compendium, he gave even further emphasis to
contextual factors. As Charlotte Furth has discussed, Xue incorporated
new doctrines that led him to reorganize and rework Chen's text in important ways.[123] Chen Ziming's original focused on female Blood as a
locus of pathology, vulnerable to being afflicted by pathological influences
of cold and wind. By contrast, Xue emphasized that Blood disorders had
their roots in nongendered bodily organs: spleen, stomach, heart, and
liver. His innovations built on the teachings of Li Gao and Zhu Zhenheng, two of the prominent Jin-Yuan era physicians who sought to identify universalistic dynamics that underlay all forms of illness. Li Gao
argued that, because the spleen and stomach were responsible for transforming food and water into qi, regulation of these two organs was the
key to ensuring the healthy state of qi and thus of Blood. Zhu Zhenheng,
by contrast, posited that the body had an innate preponderance toward
an excess of fire (generated in the heart), and therefore of yang. Zhu's
famous teaching that "yang is usually in excess, yin is usually deficient"
(yang chang you yu, yin chang bu zu) thus envisioned pathologies of Blood
in terms of a more dispersed bodily imbalance of yin and yang, rather
than as a malfunction of specifically female reproductive essences.

Alongside these etiological reorientations, Xue Ji notably condensed,
modified, and even omitted passages from Chen Ziming's original that
assumed an innate female sickliness. An illustrative example is Xue's
redaction of Chen Ziming's chapter on the "myriad illnesses" *(zhong ji)*,
a term referring to the multitude of ailments that could arise from menstrual irregularity. Chen Ziming originally began this chapter with an excerpt from Chen Yan's famous etiological treatise of 1174, an excerpt affirming that the illnesses of women were indeed ten times harder to treat
than men's. Xue Ji, however, deleted this entire passage.[124] He performed
similar surgery on the section in which Chen Ziming cited Sun Simiao's
essay explaining why women need separate prescriptions. While Chen
Ziming had originally reproduced the entire essay, Xue Ji's version of *Comprehensive Compendium* excised five-sixths of Sun's discussion, reword-

ing it into this brief account: "The Treatise says: 'The fact that women reside in seclusion means that they frequently experience loss of regulation in Blood and qi. They differ in pregnancy, childbirth, and injurious flooding, and when compared to men are ten times harder to treat. If their seven emotions are not properly regulated, or they are intemperate in eating or drinking, or they engage in intercourse before birthing sores are healed, or cold wind enters the mouth of their genitals when they ascend the privy, then this easily causes deep-rooted disease.' "[125]

The belief that pregnancy, childbirth, and uncontrolled menses make women harder to treat is still evident in Xue's discussion. Overall, however, his summary of Sun Simiao foregrounds different factors. Notably missing from Xue's edition is Sun's earlier concern about the maladies brought by sexual maturation, his description of the female body as "gathering place for yin," and the statement that women are more emotional than men. Instead, the emphasis is placed on women's loss of regulation, now blamed on the social practice of female seclusion or on women's own careless habits. And whereas Sun's original explained that women's illnesses were "deeply rooted" because of excessive emotion compared to men, Xue attributed women's "deep-rooted disease" to lack of self-discipline, sexual carelessness, and exposure to wind. In sum, Xue's discussion of the roots of female sickliness shifts attention away from bodily disposition and toward behavior and social environment.

During the seventeenth century, literate male doctors also began to foreground the similarity between female and male diseases. The *jinshi* scholar Wu Zhiwang, author of *A Comprehensive Guide to Benefiting Yin (Jiyin gangmu)* of 1620, notably opened his preface by pointing out that "the unclassified illnesses of women are generally the same as men's, and it is only the ailments of menses and childbirth that would constitute a separate category."[126] To be sure, Wu continued by saying that women's special diseases could take innumerable forms that would confound unskilled doctors, a statement that echoed earlier rhetoric about sickly women. Nevertheless, his initial emphasis on the similarities between male and female disease is noteworthy because Wu's text also significantly narrowed the nosological scope of female illnesses. As Charlotte Furth shows, Wu and his later editors deleted many of the female ailments previously discussed under the rubric of women's "unclassified disorders" *(zazheng)*, namely, those not specifically associated with childbirth. The resulting text presented "a more limited range of disorders 'unique to women alone.' "[127] A little over a decade later, Zhang Jiebin presented the baldest affirmation to date of the inherent sameness of male and female ailments. For Zhang, mastery of medicine and mastery of cosmic principle were a single enterprise, a belief summed up in his teaching that "medicine and the *Classic of Changes* are one." In chapter 3, I examine Zhang's ideas in greater detail, showing how his search for bodily universals led him to affirm that both men and women had wombs. Here we will focus on Zhang's claim that male and female illnesses were basically alike, a claim that opened his discussion of women's diseases:

> The nine illnesses of women: The diseases of women are fundamentally no different from those of men, and where there is any difference [it] lies only in matters pertaining to menstruation and childbearing. Accordingly, this section will address only nine types of illnesses, namely, those related to menses, pregnancy, childbirth, postpartum, girdle discharges and noxious flows, breast ailments, promoting fecundity, solid and shifting accumulations, and genital disorders. These nine are the most crucial ailments, and one cannot dispense with a separate section that details the relevant remedies and teachings. As for the other ailments that fall outside these categories, they are the same as men's, and the treatment for each will be discussed under its own heading.[128]

In addition to affirming that male and female illnesses were similar, Zhang's statement is noteworthy because it rhetorically reduced the quantitative scope of female disorders to "only nine types of illnesses." Since at least the second century, doctors had used the phrase "the thirty-six diseases of women" *(furen sanshiliu bing)* to refer to an ensemble of gynecological disorders associated with impaired menstrual flow.[129] Primarily centered on the urogenital and lower abdominal region, these notably included various types of noxious discharges, pains, pathological coldness, injured orifices, and internal accumulations. When discussed together with the other classes of illness associated with pregnancy and postpartum, the trope of "women's thirty-six diseases" reinforced the perception that women's reproductive capacities made them both different from and more sickly than men.[130] Such rhetoric appears, for example, in Wei Yilin's 1337 compendium, *Efficacious Prescriptions from a Hereditary Medical Family (Shiyi dexiao fang)*. Wei's section on *fuke* opens with these lines: "Now of the ways that can benefit the world, none takes precedence over medicine. And in discussing the difficulty of medicine, benefiting yin is especially urgent. Why is that? Now women's illnesses are ten times harder to treat than men's. Some speak of the seven verifiable accumulations, the eight illusory accumulations, the nine pains, and the twelve girdle discharges, being thirty-six illnesses in all."[131]

At one level, Zhang Jiebin's claim that women only had nine diseases simply collapsed formerly distinct rubrics into larger umbrella categories. So for example, whereas some earlier texts counted the "seven verifiable accumulations" *(zheng)* and "eight illusory accumulations" *(jia)* as fifteen distinct illnesses, Zhang spoke of them as one single category of "verifiable and illusory accumulations" *(zhengjia).* More than simple re-labeling, however, Zhang's new nosology rhetorically reduced the qualitative magnitude of female difference. By subsuming the entirety of female disease into just nine categories, he reinforced his contention that "the illnesses of women are fundamentally the same as men's."

Alongside this quantitative reconfiguration, Zhang explicitly rejected the idea that women were fundamentally harder to treat than men. Those who held to this belief, he pointed out, had failed to understand that male and female illnesses were actually alike.[132] The difference between men and women, Zhang explained, was merely in the nature of their *qing,* or "emotions." And as Zhang explained the distinctive aspects of female emotion, he emphasized that it arose from their social environment:

> The adage says, "I would rather treat ten men than one woman." What this means is that the illnesses of women are not easy to treat. Why is that? People do not know that the illnesses of women are fundamentally the same as men's, but their emotions *[qing]* are different from men's. In general it is because women live in seclusion with frequent pent-up feelings that they cannot express. It is the nature of yin to be recalcitrant, and things can never be resolved. On top of this, they experience affection and longing, love and hatred, envy and jealousy, and worry and rancor. They do not know the way of propriety *[wang zhi yi ming]* and are always full of re-sentment. Some harbor feelings that they cannot freely act upon, some have illnesses that they cannot tell others about. Some have confidence in religious masters and shamans, while some are awed by [the supposed therapeutic properties of] drugs and foods. Thus their attachment to their desires is stubborn, the roots and stems [of their illness] are deep and firm, and treating them is not easy. These are things brought about by their emotions.[133]

Expanding on Kou Zongshi and Xue Ji, Zhang Jiebin foregrounded the social causes of women's illnesses, placing particular emphasis on female seclusion and women's inability to express or act on their feelings. This also made it difficult, Zhang suggested, for women to obtain the broader perspectives, moral discipline, and intellectual detachment needed to transcend petty disagreements. By the seventeenth century, therefore, the belief that female sickliness was a function of social circumstance had helped to foster the conviction that the illnesses of men and women were fundamentally the same. It was this more benign view of female difference that the compilers of the *Golden Mirror* used to introduce their chapters on the treatment of women. Echoing Zhang Jiebin, they asserted that women's and men's illnesses were essentially treated the same, and that there were only nine kinds of distinctly female ailments that required a separate discussion. In so doing, the *Golden Mirror* firmly integrated the "same as men" perspective into the realm of best practices as defined by an elite group of scholarly physicians, physicians committed to recovering the original meaning of classical texts and applying these teachings to medical problems.

In sum, while the "same as men" rhetoric departed from older medical teachings about female difference, its appearance in the *Golden Mirror* also implied that it was the recovery of a forgotten medical truth, one based on a new and superior understanding of yin and yang as set out in the ancient canons. Another influential work that made this connection was Xu Dachun's *Treatise on the Origins of Medical Learning* (*Yixue yuanliu lun,* 1757). Xu Dachun was a scholar-doctor and devotee of Han learning *(hanxue)* who sought to cleanse the medical classics of later Song dynasty accretions.[134] So while he saw himself as a reformer of contemporary medicine, the nature of that reform was to return medicine back to its uncorrupted roots. Like the editors of the *Golden Mirror,* Xu emphasized the essential similarity between men and women, and he further limited the scope of female difference to the two rubrics of menstruation and childbearing and the Blood associated with these functions: "There is no difference between the illnesses of women and those of men. The only place where they are not alike *(bu tong)* is in illnesses related to menstruation and producing children. Moreover, women are frequently afflicted by verifiable and illusory internal accumulations *(zheng-jia).*[135] The reason that they are prone to these accumulations is also that the Blood of menses and childbearing easily congeals and stagnates. Therefore women have these accumulations more than men."[136]

The prominence and wide circulation of the *Golden Mirror* and Xu Dachun's *Treatise* meant that the "same as men" viewpoint also became a salient medical reference point for contemporary and later doctors.[137] A notable example of its continued influence is Wang Shixiong's well-received 1853 redaction of Wei Zhixiu's *A Continuation of the* Cases from Famous Doctors, Arranged by Category. When he revised Wei's work, Wang Shixiong added a new introductory essay to the section on women's diseases, one that began by quoting Xu Dachun's statement that there was no difference between male and female diseases.[138] The influence of these heuristic works in late imperial times also explains how the optimistic view of female difference found its way into amateur compilations of the nineteenth century. For example, the government secretary and medical enthusiast Zhou Jichang produced a *fuke* handbook in 1823 in which he declared that "the difference between women's illnesses and those of men consists only of menstruation and childbearing."[139] The Suzhou scholar-official Pan Wei, who produced a *fuke* text in 1877, similarly believed that "the illnesses of women are all the same as men's. Only in the case of [ailments] before and after menstruation, and before and after childbirth, are there differences in treatment."[140]

CONCLUSION

If measured on a strictly numerical basis, proponents of the view that "women's illnesses are fundamentally no different from men's" were, admittedly, in the minority. As works on women's illnesses proliferated in late imperial times, their authors and preface writers repeatedly evoked old tropes about women's illnesses being dangerous and difficult to treat.[141] But the emergence of a more benign view of female difference reveals an important reorientation within the elite echelons of scholarly medicine. Heuristic works such as the *Golden Mirror* aimed to promote model standards of medical excellence in which medical ability was inseparable from inspired mastery of cosmological patterns. In this context, the learned doctor's awareness that male and female bodies were governed by the same dynamics of illness and health became a sign of his superiority over lesser healers who persisted in seeing women as governed by a separate logic. These notably included female healers, who owed their reason for existence to social norms of gender segregation that assumed a fundamental distinction between discrete male and female spheres. Inferior male practitioners, including those who made women's diseases their "special area of expertise," might also be overly reliant on the tricks of the trade or cling to conventional wisdom even when it was inappropriate to the situation at hand. The superior physician, by contrast, understood the eternal transformations of yin and yang and adroitly addressed himself to a universal body, where male and female were but situational variants of a master pattern.

This increasing emphasis on the contextual causes of female emotionality also resonated deeply with broader social and medical trends of the late imperial period. While Chinese doctors had long recognized unhealthy behavior and unregulated emotion as a major cause of illness, there is evidence that such concerns had become especially acute over the course of the sixteenth century. The well-studied economic expansion of the mid-Ming, driven by urbanization, commercialization, and monetization, nurtured the growth of a wealthy merchant class and increased opportunities for conspicuous overconsumption. But this pursuit of pleasure was also a potential threat to one's emotional and physical equilibrium, and physicians such as Wang Ji (1463–1539) fretted about the poor health of men who overindulged in alcohol, rich food, and sexual activity. Concern over the social and behavioral causes of illness is also illustrated by the expanded literature on "nourishing life" *(yangsheng),* which extolled the benefits for men of sexual continence and nurturing seminal essence.[142] Beginning in the late sixteenth century, concerns about uncontrolled emotion were also reinforced by the cult of *qing,* which Dorothy Ko has called the "hallmark of the seventeenth-century Jiangnan urban culture."[143] Fueled by the proliferation of literary and theatrical works such as *The Peony Pavilion,* the cult of *qing* glorified the place of love in human relations, particularly the kind of love that could transcend death. Both men and women were now recognized as emotional creatures, but women were especially so. Thus while anxieties about overconsumption focused on the bodies of men, the cult of *qing* highlighted the dangers of female emotionality.[144] The proliferation of female-authored poetry anthologies beginning in the sixteenth century, with their poems allegedly "saved from burning," also drew attention to the tension between a woman's personal aspirations and the duties of a proper Confucian lady. It was in this social context that Xue Ji and Zhang Jiebin emphasized the contextual causes of illnesses in women rooted in social customs that doomed them to thwarted desires. One imagines that such tensions grew more acute under the Qing rulers, when a government-sponsored Neo-Confucian revival intensified norms of female chastity even while economic growth and increased social mobility offered new possibilities for female agency.

The increased rhetorical emphasis on the social causes of female sickliness that we see in medical texts thus resonated with well-known historical changes. While more studies are needed to fully flesh out lines of influence and causation, it is worth noting that there were other changes in Ming-Qing medicine that similarly reflected the increasingly benign view of female reproductive function that underlay the "same as men" perspective. A telling touchstone is the late Ming transformation of the concept of "fetal poison" *(taidu),* a term that Song dynasty writers used to explain childhood skin eruptions, including smallpox. Once thought to be a kind of maternally generated poison linked to birthing pollution, during the late sixteenth and early seventeenth centuries fetal poison was increasingly defined as a pathology rooted in the body of the baby rather than the mother.[145] Similarly, the growth of a textual tradition of "female alchemy" *(nüdan)* beginning in the last quarter of the seventeenth century offered an alternative way of envisioning female Blood. Rather than a source of pollution or illness, Blood now served as the female equivalent of male semen, a bodily vitality that could be retained, recirculated, and refined within the body to endow the practitioner with immortality. Elena Valussi has suggested that the maturation of *nüdan* in the nineteenth century owed much to moralists who aimed to control female religious behavior, channeling it into text-based practices so that women would not associate with male teachers or unsavory female adepts.[146] Even if this was the case, the view of Blood in female alchemy was consistent with medical narratives that diminished the scope of female difference and redefined the distinctive attributes of women's bodies in more universalistic terms.

And yet, the objective fact of childbirth and its continued social association with the female sphere meant that this universalizing impulse could only be partial and situational. As we will see, the choices made by literate doctors continually alternated between these gendered and universalistic inflections of the female body, and medical debates about how to treat women revolved around this very problem of how much importance to assign to unique female functions. Should a woman's gestational state be the primary factor guiding therapy, or was it to be just one factor among others? Whether the glass of gender difference was half empty or half full was always more than a rhetorical issue, for the way one answered this question could mean the difference between life and death. When people sought reliable answers to childbearing-related problems, they frequently concluded that such matters were too important to be left to doctors. The growth of scholarly medicine in late imperial China also allowed fuller voice to a host of medical amateurs who promised to help householders successfully negotiate those ailments specific to women.

CHAPTER 2

Amateur as Arbiter

Popular Fuke *Manuals in the Qing*

Wu Yu's sister-in-law suffered miscarriage after miscarriage, until finally his brother went to consult the monks of the Bamboo Grove Monastery. Located in Xiaoshan, across the Qiantang River from Wu Yu's home prefecture of Hangzhou in Zhejiang Province, the Bamboo Grove monks were known throughout the region for their success in curing women's diseases. They sent Wu's brother home with wrapped packages of medicine. After taking several doses, Wu Yu's sister-in-law successfully carried her next pregnancy to term, ultimately giving birth to a son. In the years following his nephew's birth, Wu Yu recalled, his interest was further piqued as he heard more stories of the monks' successes. Because the monks jealously guarded their secret recipes, however, he had not been able to learn what methods they used. One day, Wu Yu was visiting Fan Yuanpu, his wife's sister's husband, when Fan brought out a book that purported to reveal the monks' proprietary formulas. Knowing that Wu had made a study of medicine, Fan suggested that he review and edit the text. Delighted, Wu Yu took the text home, where he also made a copy for himself, finishing his work some time in 1793.[1]

Although Wu Yu did not know it, a printed text attributed to the monks had already appeared several years earlier, and many more versions would follow. By the time one Cao Binggang found and published Wu Yu's manuscript in 1886, dozens of texts attributed to the Bamboo Grove monks had been produced in all corners of the Chinese empire.[2] The wide circulation of these works owed much to the interests and tastes of literate men like Wu, people with various levels of medical interest and knowledge who did not, however, see themselves as doctors. To the contrary, the majority of men who compiled and edited the Bamboo Grove Monastery texts depicted themselves as laypeople or medical hobbyists who were making valuable knowledge widely available so that people did not have to rely on doctors at all. Suspicious of physicians' claims to superior knowledge, and confident in their own ability to judge what constituted effective treatment, these literate amateurs exerted a formative influence on the late imperial *fuke* repertoire. These dynamics are particularly salient in the history of the Bamboo Grove texts and that of the *Treatise on Easy Childbirth (Dasheng bian)* of 1715.[3] Both groups of texts circulated widely in the eighteenth and nineteenth centuries and are among the best-known works of the Qing period. In the case of the Bamboo Grove Monastery texts, laypeople took a leading role in disseminating the knowledge of a locally prominent lineage of monastic healers. In the case of *Easy Childbirth*, a brief, plainspoken work by an anonymous literatus became one of the most widely circulating childbirth texts of its time. When Cao Binggang printed Wu Yu's Bamboo Grove text in 1886, he even suggested that the monks' work be read in conjunction with *Easy Childbirth*. We will examine these works together, exploring what they reveal about amateur participation in creating and disseminating knowledge about women's reproductive functions. Three factors merit particular attention: the growth of medical publishing in late imperial China, religious motivations for distributing medical texts, and the particular forms of medical legitimacy that amateurship conferred.

AMATEURS AND MEDICAL PUBLISHING

In Qing China, as in other societies during the same time, self-diagnosis and self-dosing were important patterns of medical care, and there was a repertoire of popular knowledge about what foods, drugs, and exercises could be used to maintain health and cure illness. Depending on talent and interest, individuals could also possess various levels of formal medical ability. While some claimed no expertise beyond the ability to look up remedies in a book, others were sufficiently skilled to provide medical advice and treatment to others. At this higher level of expertise, there was a functional overlap between the learned amateur and the physician who made his living from medicine. But despite the fluidity of these spheres of knowledge and practice, late imperial observers clearly considered certain people to be "doctors" and others not.[4] This distinction is particularly important for understanding medicine in the late imperial period. Although Chinese doctors never defined themselves in terms of occupational institutions or guilds, learned physicians of the time actively articulated normative standards for medical practice, standards that provided the basis for a group identity by defining who was or was not a competent and qualified medical practitioner.[5] These cultural norms thus make it possible to discuss distinctions between medical men and laypeople. When I use the term *amateur*, therefore, I refer to people who did not consider themselves to be doctors and who were not identified as such by other people, regardless of their actual level of medical ability.

The relationship between doctors and amateurs could be a fraught one. In a 1757 essay, the physician Xu Dachun criticized the literate men who imagined that browsing through medical works qualified them to treat illness.[6] There were three kinds of people, Xu wrote, whose medical mistakes could bring about a person's death: doctors, the patients themselves, and "bystanders who have made a superficial study of medical texts" *(she-lie yishu)*. This last group included the scholars who erroneously believed that their classical training qualified them to interpret and apply medical works. "They occasionally pore through some medical texts," Xu said, "and believe themselves to have already acquired a thorough mastery of the subject." Sick people trusted such men, Xu noted, because of their learning and status. Furthermore, because these learned amateurs were often better educated than many ordinary doctors—such as those who came from the ranks of failed examination candidates—they could often prevail in arguments about medical treatment. Buoyed by the confidence that "although so-and-so is a famous doctor, I am better than he," these browsers of medicine then blithely went about treating the illnesses of others, taking credit for cures and avoiding blame for failures. Some of these scholars, Xu observed, also wrote medical texts expounding their own pet theories, thereby disseminating erroneous doctrines that could only harm later generations. People of this ilk, he lamented, were innumerable.

For their part, medical consumers and amateur text compilers alike also had numerous complaints against doctors.[7] Typical was this comment by Wang Dejun, who held an unidentified position in a Beijing military unit: "Today there is no shortage of doctors who make women's diseases their area of special expertise *[zhuanmen fuke zhi yi]*. But it is not possible to distinguish between the good doctors and the charlatans. When engaging [these doctors], moreover, one cannot have confidence in them, for how can one be sure that their therapies will have the intended effect?"[8] Such perceptions were fed in large part by the intense competition among doctors seeking to build up a clientele in a fluid marketplace. As Xu Dachun observed, doctors' desire to impress their clients and stand out from their competitors often led to harmful practices and even fraudulent claims:

> Some invent unusual remedies in order to distinguish themselves. Some use uncommon drugs to delude the masses. Some use heat-replenishing drugs like ginseng and deer antler to flatter the rich and noble. Some falsely claim to have remedies transmitted by immortals and Buddhas and use them to cheat the ignorant. Some establish lofty discourses and strange doctrines to astound the world and illegitimately make a name for themselves. Some fabricate fake classics and false teachings to deceive people and amaze the common folk. Some see clearly that the [patient's] illness is easy to manage, but they falsely call it something else in order to demonstrate their unusual abilities.[9]

Even having a reputation as a "famous doctor" *(mingyi)* was no guarantee against a client's skepticism, and people were quick to blame practitioners when things went wrong. For example, in the Zhang family of Changzhou studied by Susan Mann, Zhang Qi (1765–1833) betrothed his son Zhang Juesun to a daughter of the Fa family, a famous lineage of physicians. But when a Fa family physician failed to save Juesun from dying of a fever, Zhang Qi charged that they were "mediocre doctors" and completely lost faith in them.[10] Such attitudes were commonplace and provided a role for amateurs, who portrayed themselves as a necessary corrective to the shortcomings of medical practitioners. Their stated goal was to uncover and disseminate practically useful therapies, making medical knowledge widely available so that people would not be at the mercy of doctors. In practical terms, this meant publishing, editing, and even compiling medical works. And whatever their purported level of medical expertise, such amateurs claimed the authority to judge what constituted legitimate medical knowledge, in some cases promoting modes of healing that conflicted with the values of learned physicians. Just as they challenged physicians' medical authority in face-to-face encounters, these amateurs also challenged it within the context of the medical literature.

POPULAR MEDICAL PUBLISHING

The Song and the Ming dynasties both witnessed a significant expansion in printing and publishing that also profoundly shaped the medical corpus. Literate medical amateurship first became significant during the Song, when studying medical works became a respectable pursuit for educated men and the growth of printing made medical information more accessible than ever. In the name of Confucian benevolence, many scholars also published their own works on medicine to make useful knowledge widely available. No less celebrated a figure than Su Shi (courtesy name Dongpo) compiled a book of prescriptions, in which he promoted a favorite medicine for treating epidemic diseases. As described by TJ Hinrichs, Su claimed to have received Sagely Powder *(shengsanzi)* from a mysterious individual, and he "extolled it precisely because it did not require adjustment according to the particular patterns of the disorder in the individual patient or over the course of the illness, and because it was inexpensive and easy to prepare."[11] For their part, learned physicians criticized Su Shi's collection for its allegedly uncritical approach to diagnosis and therapy. But amateur compilation of medical texts continued to be important in the late imperial period, nurtured by a second era of expanding print culture that began in the sixteenth century. There has been much scholarly debate about how to assess the relative significance and magnitude of the Ming expansion in printing compared to that of the earlier period. Nevertheless, it is clear that late imperial publishing was marked by a quantitative and qualitative expansion in the range of actors, works, and geographic scope of publishing activities. One notable change was the emergence of what Joseph McDermott terms "*shengyuan* book culture."[12] High-ranking scholar-officials had historically played a leading role as writers, editors, and compilers, but now lower-level literati (holders of the bottom-tier *shengyuan* degree) joined them, playing a formative role in the "creation, consumption, and preservation of literati culture." Many of the *shengyuan* writers, in fact, turned to authorship to make a living when they failed to advance in the examinations. As a result, McDermott explains, "for the first time in Chinese history, a significant portion of the literati and major private book collectors were neither themselves high officials or high-degree holders nor from families of high officials or high-degree holders." In chapter 1 we saw that many of these lower-level literati turned to making their living as doctors. In a similar vein, many now also compiled and disseminated medical works as part of a wider range of literary and philanthropic activities.

The particular dynamics of the Qing also reinforced these trends. The Manchu conquest devastated the historically dominant publishing centers of Jiangnan, in southeastern China, and thereby brought about a geographic decentralization of publishing activities. Many new regional and subregional publishing centers sprang up, including some in relatively remote mountainous regions. Medical works were a staple of these publishing houses' booklists, bespeaking a wide commercial demand for medical literature produced at a range of price points.[13] These findings from historians of the Chinese book coincide with medical historians' observations that there was a real expansion in the kind and number of medical works published after the sixteenth century. These included collections of medical cases designed to showcase the teachings of a single practitioner, as well as medical primers and study guides aimed at would-be physicians.[14] The overall effect was that, during the late imperial period, a wide variety of simplified medical texts and collections of mnemonic verses circulated as part of a flourishing print culture, aimed at the burgeoning audience of scholars-turned-doctors but also available to a broader readership.[15] This increased accessibility of medical literature facilitated amateur compilation by expanding the pool of available raw material from which any literate person could compile his own work. In turn, each additional amateur work that was produced further swelled the pool of existing resources. The result was a proliferation of medical literature that could draw on classically informed sources even as its broader aim was to challenge doctors' claims to privileged knowledge. Among the notable works that embodied these impulses were the texts attributed to the Bamboo Grove Monastery and the *Treatise on Easy Childbirth*.

THE BAMBOO GROVE MONASTERY

The Monastery of Benevolent Aid (Huijisi), which locals referred to as the "Bamboo Grove Monastery" (Zhulinsi), was located on the northern outskirts of Xiaoshan City, in Shaoxing Prefecture, Zhejiang Province.[16] The legend explaining the origins of the monks' medical practice repeats a familiar narrative of secret medical knowledge imparted by a deity or immortal in disguise. According to monastery records, the tenth-century monk Gaotan encountered a mysterious "wandering man of the Way" *(daoren)*, whom he invited to stay at the monastery. This stranger's sprightly and agile appearance showed that he was "no ordinary person," and Gaotan treated him with great reverence. One day the visitor mysteriously disappeared. To repay Gaotan's kindness, however, he left behind a medical treatise discussing women's reproductive illnesses and providing wondrously effective remedies for curing them. Gaotan studied this book assiduously and became a successful healer. Henceforth medicine also became an important activity for the monastery. During the Shaoding reign (1228–33) of the Song dynasty, the monastery's reputation was burnished after the monk Jingxian cured an imperial consort. A grateful Song Lizong bestowed several tokens of appreciation on

the monks, including the honorific title of "Kings of Medicine" on Jingxian, his four immediate predecessors, and five generations of successors.
By the end of the nineteenth century, the monks claimed a medical tradition that had been passed down from the Song to the Qing dynasties
through 106 successive generations of monks.[17]

Qing sources show that the monks enjoyed a thriving medical practice, and that medicine was an important source of income for the
monastery. In the Kangxi reign, for example, the head monk Jikong used
money earned entirely from medical practice to finance the wholesale reconstruction of the monastery, which had been devastated by the battles
of the Qing conquest.[18] One eighteenth-century writer also observed that,
"in the three prefectures of Hangzhou, Jiaxing, and Huzhou, the gentry
families admire them as if they were immortals, all heavily bestowing them
with money and silks. . . . I heard that the monks had amassed tens of
thousands of pieces of cash."[19] Beginning in the late eighteenth century,
woodblock texts that claimed to reveal the monks' medical methods began to circulate throughout China. Bearing titles such as *Secret Formulas
of Women's Medicine from the Bamboo Grove Monastery (Zhulinsi nüke
mifang)*, most of these works took the form of a dosing manual that listed
a number of "syndromes" *(zheng)*, described their observable symptoms,
and provided appropriate remedies for each ailment.[20] The men who wrote
the prefaces for these works described them as easy-to-use handbooks that
people with no medical knowledge could use to treat women's illnesses
at home. The monks themselves apparently had nothing to do with the
publication of these works, however. Some of the men who wrote prefaces to these texts recount how they (or a friend) ingratiated themselves
with the monks, insinuated themselves into the monastery, and then copied
down medical formulas behind the monks' backs. Another story suggests
that despite the monks' reputed penchant for secrecy, they did take some
outside disciples, who then transmitted their texts to the outside world.
Workers who helped manufacture the monastery's ready-made medicines
may also have disseminated the monks' methods.[21] Whatever the mechanism of transmission, the monks' proprietary formulas were circulating
widely in print by the mid-Qing. The earliest known Bamboo Grove text
was compiled in the late eighteenth century, and the first printed edition
appeared in 1786.[22] During the nineteenth century, these books were published throughout the empire, produced in the frontier regions of Yunnan,
Sichuan, Guangdong, Fujian, and Taiwan, as well as in the heartland provinces of Zhejiang, Jiangsu, Anhui, Henan, and Zhili. Some eighty distinct
Qing-dynasty editions are still extant today.[23]

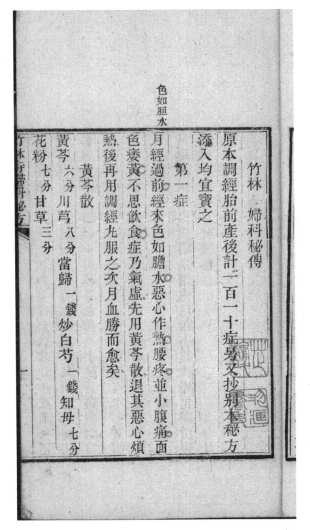

色如膽水

竹林　婦科秘傳

原本調經胎前產後計二百一十症另文抄別本秘方
添入均宜寶之

第一症

月經過前經來色如膽水惡心作熱腰疼並小腹痛面
色痿黃不思飲食症乃氣虛先用黃芩散退其惡心煩
熱後再用調經先服之次月血勝而愈矣

黃芩散

黃芩六分川芎八分當歸一錢炒白芍一錢知母七分
花粉七分甘草三分

竹林寺婦科必方

Figure 1. This edition of *Transmitted Secrets of Women's Medicine from the Bamboo Grove* lists 110 different ailments of menstruation, pregnancy, and the postpartum period. It comes from a batch of copies that Pan Yantong, the provincial educational commissioner of Zhejiang, distributed to examination candidates in 1890. The man who obtained this copy added a handwritten table of contents to it. The punctuation marks he made in the text show that he read it carefully. (Zhulinsi seng, *Zhulin fuke michuan* [Hangzhou: Gu Haizhou woodblock edition, 1890, with handwritten material added in 1892], ST no. 482812), in the collection of the Shanghai Library. Courtesy of the Shanghai Library.

Elite Patronage

Upper-class Chinese not only patronized the Bamboo Grove monks, they also legitimated the monks' medical knowledge by circulating and endorsing their texts. These endorsements notably appeared in the prefaces and afterwords to these texts. Of thirty-seven different individuals who wrote prefaces for the Bamboo Grove Monastery works, five were provincial-level officials, and altogether about a third of the preface writers worked in the Chinese bureaucracy, holding positions ranging from district jailer to provincial governor.[24] Others were lower-level literati working as personal secretaries or legal consultants to local officials, and some wrote on behalf of officials who had paid for the text's printing. Still others mentioned that they were close relatives of government officials. In sum, one-half to two-thirds of the prefaces contained direct or indirect endorsements by men from China's examination-taking and office-holding elite class. Equally significant, scholar-officials actively contributed to the geographic dispersal of Bamboo Grove Monastery texts, disseminating them as they traveled around the country on official business. From 1860 to 1888, for example, three provincial-level officials and a county magistrate passed a single edition of *Secret Formulas of Women's Medicine* from hand to hand, carrying it from Guangxi to Zhili provinces, and reprinting it on three separate occasions.[25] A similar network of personal and official connections shaped the publication of an edition of *Treatments for Women's Illnesses from the Bamboo Grove Monastery (Zhulinsi nüke zhengzhi)* first printed in 1895.[26] This particular text had been obtained by Bian Shiying, employed on the staff of Shanghai Circuit Administrator Pan Jingru, scion of a prominent Suzhou family of scholar-officials. Pan Jingru took the text with him on a visit to his elder brother, Pan Wei, then serving as governor of Guizhou.[27] Pan Wei himself was known for his medical acumen and had compiled a number of his own medical texts, including one on *fuke*. In 1886, when his brother asked him to write a preface for Bian's text, Pan Wei dashed off an enthusiastic endorsement of the Bamboo Grove Monastery work.[28] Another admirer was the eminent Guangzhou scholar-official Pan Yantong (1841–99). In 1890, while he was serving as educational commissioner of Zhejiang, Pan distributed free copies of a Bamboo Grove Monastery text to candidates taking the provincial examinations.[29]

This upper-class support for the monks requires some explanation, for by the elite standards of the day, the monks were neither particularly good monks nor particularly good doctors. The lecherous, hypocritical monk was a stock stereotype in Chinese literature and popular culture from early times, and monks who made their living treating female illnesses played to the worst of these prejudices.[30] Qing-era descriptions of the monks' diagnostic and therapeutic measures also portray them as unlettered and crude. Most telling, such criticisms appear in several prefaces written for the Bamboo Grove Monastery texts themselves. A 1795 preface, for example, reported that the county magistrate once closed down the Bamboo Grove Monastery because he "thought it strange that they would treat women's diseases, and [thereby] contradict Buddhist teachings."[31] Almost a century later, similar criticisms appeared in a 1888 preface by Song Chun, then serving as the administration commissioner of Zhili Province, who wrote that the monks violated Buddhist teachings by exposing themselves to "female pollution" (ban).[32] And whereas the learned physician was a master of pulse and prescription, the monks allegedly diagnosed the patient's illness solely based on her description of the symptoms, and they prescribed drugs by rote.[33] In a 1876 preface, for example, one Yu Zan depicted the monks as unlettered and cavalier. "The monks do not discuss the pulse, nor do they consider the properties of medicines," he charged, "and none of them are clear about whether a word is written correctly or incorrectly. They rely exclusively on asking about the illness and copying out medical formulas."[34] Wu Yu, in fact, had noted that the monks simply gave their clients a "wrapped package of medicine" so that no one would know what was in their cures.[35] These suspicions of sexual impropriety and medical ignorance were accompanied by charges that the monks were base profiteers. Whereas the good doctor should be motivated by a desire to help others, Yu Zan noted, the monks were interested only in "seeking profit so as to satiate themselves on worldly pleasures."[36] Song Chun similarly charged that that the monks' claim to have obtained medical secrets from a divinity was nothing but a ploy to cheat people of their money.[37]

The prefaces by Yu Zan and Song Chun are particularly noteworthy, for they simultaneously condemn and endorse the monks, thus revealing an important tension: the monks and their medicine could affront upper-class sensibilities, yet literate Chinese believed that the monks' formulas truly worked. As Yu Zan explained, "I admire the wondrous efficacy of the monks' medical formulas, but I despise the baseness and stinginess of these vulgar monks." Yu recounted that he had personally tested the Bamboo Grove Monastery formulas on women whom he knew. His success in curing their ailments convinced him that "these are indeed good remedies." Although he himself did not have the means to fund the book's publication, Yu hoped that others would undertake the task. Song Chun echoed these sentiments. In light of the monks' bad character, Song argued, their texts should not be allowed to circulate. Yet the monks' medicine must be truly effective, he reasoned, else their texts would not be so popular. Ultimately, Song was forced to conclude that "one can record [the monks'] skills without necessarily discussing their persons." In sum, the perceived utility of the monks' remedies outweighed any distaste that upper-class men like Song Chun and Yu Zan may have felt toward the monks themselves.

Medical Legitimacy and Medical Efficacy

The modern-day reader will want to know whether Song Chun's and Yu Zan's faith in the monks' remedies was justified. Did the Bamboo Grove Monastery medicines actually work? As medical anthropologists have shown, judgments about efficacy are culturally dependent and must be understood as part of a broader system of beliefs.[38] In general, we can state that people would have believed the monks' remedies to be effective if they perceived a significant, positive change in the patient's condition following treatment, and if they were predisposed to credit these changes to the monks' medicine, rather than to coincidence or other causes.[39] As concerns the first factor, the Bamboo Grove Monastery texts show that the monks' remedies consisted almost exclusively of herbal therapies, many of which were similar to those found in learned texts. Present-day medical researchers have demonstrated that many ingredients in such formulas do produce measurable physiological effects consistent with the traditional Chinese usage, and modern clinicians report that they have successfully used formulas selected from the Bamboo Grove Monastery books to cure women's illnesses.[40] While it is beyond the scope of this chapter to give a detailed accounting of which parts of which formulas might be validated by modern science, we can assume that the monks' remedies did produce noticeable physiological changes often enough for people to believe in their curative effects. As for the second factor, the monks certainly possessed many legitimating resources that would have gained the confidence of their clients. In addition to their founding legend of divinely bestowed formulas and their claimed centuries of experience, the historically close association between medical and religious healing also served to legitimate the monks' healing activities.

For Chinese people of all social classes, religious rituals and institutions were an integral part of the healing repertoire. The Buddha himself was called "the King of Medicine," and Chinese Buddhist monks had a long history of providing charitable medical services.[41] Indeed, the boundaries between religious practice and pharmaceutical therapies were often blurred. Temple-goers requested herbal remedies from the gods by throwing joss sticks, for example, and local deities might also impart special formulas during spirit-writing sessions *(luan bi)*.[42] And, as we have seen, one authoritative source of medical formulas was the immortal in disguise, who bestowed "secret formulas" *(mifang)* on worthy individuals. Medicoreligious healing was especially important for women. Popular religion included a vast pantheon of popular deities who specialized in preventing or curing illness, and these included those with the power to promote conception, grant smooth childbirth, and ensure the survival of newborns.[43] Prominent among such divinities was Bixia yuanjun, goddess of Mount Tai. Popular Buddhist texts also portrayed the "white-robed Guanyin" as a fertility goddess, and devotees sought the bodhisattva's favor by chanting specified sutras and also by printing and distributing the scriptures that bore her name.[44] Besides worshipping a given deity, people could also donate money to monasteries in the hope of obtaining a male heir. A story about the "Phoenix Grove Monastery" of Nanjing, for example, related how a rich Buddhist layman promised to make contributions to the monastery if the monks could help him father a son.[45] Such practices were certainly a key source of the Bamboo Grove monks' substantial income. In short, the Bamboo Grove Monastery's medicine for women was a natural extension of the long association between religious rituals and female fertility.

More broadly, Qing observers imbued the monks' medical practice with religious meaning, and their identities as monks reinforced assumptions about their ability to heal. In a stele commemorating the reconstruction of the monastery, Xiaoshan native Wang Honglie, a *juren* (provincial graduate) degree holder of 1642, depicted Buddhist figures and holy places as the source of the monks' medical knowledge and efficacy. "They consider the ancient Buddha to be their medical master," he explained, "and consider the Mount of Sacred Eagles [Grdhrakuta] to be their 'upper spring.'"[46] This latter analogy compared the monks to the legendary Bian Que, who acquired superhuman powers of diagnosis after ingesting magical herbs with "water from the upper spring" *(shangchi shui)*, namely, rainwater or dew that had not yet touched the ground. Just as upper-spring water allowed Bian Que to see through the human

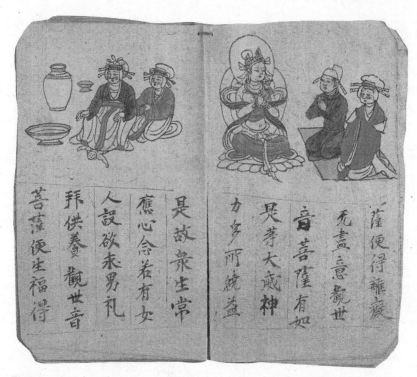

菩薩便生福得　拜供養觀世音　人設欲求男兒　應心念若有女　是故眾生常　　力多所饒益　是菩薩大威神　童菩薩有如　无盡意觀世　薩便得離疲

Figure 2. People in late imperial China routinely prayed to deities for assistance in conceiving and delivering children, and these practices had long historical roots. One of the most popular deities was the Bodhisattva Guanyin (Avalokiteśvara), shown in this set of images from an edition of the *Lotus Sutra (Saddharmapundarikasutra)* produced around the tenth century near Dunhuang. Reading from right to left, we see a couple praying to Guanyin, followed by the woman giving birth. The accompanying text explains that people who make obeisance to the deity will obtain sons and daughters endowed with many virtues. (Or. 8210/S.6983, ff.9V-10R).

body, so too did the Buddhist sacred mountain endow the monks with medical abilities. Furthermore, Wang continued, the monks viewed the Buddhist sutras in the same way that learned physicians viewed the *Yellow Emperor's Inner Classic, Basic Questions*—as the source of their medical knowledge—and they revered the Buddha's ten disciples as their medical models, just as scholarly doctors revered the famous physicians Bian Que and Zhang Ji. So even though the monks' known therapies did not include ritual practices, their reputation as healers was clearly enhanced by the close association between religion and medicine in Chinese culture.

THE *TREATISE ON EASY CHILDBIRTH*

In the case of the Bamboo Grove Monastery texts, upper-class men disseminated what they believed to be a worthy collection of effective medical remedies from a long-lived lineage of religious healers. The history of the *Treatise on Easy Childbirth* reveals a different side of amateur publishing: the creation of *fuke* knowledge by literate amateurs. *Easy Childbirth* was a brief, two-chapter text written by an anonymous lower-level literatus, who simply signed his preface with the sobriquet "Lay Buddhist Jizhai" (Jizhai jushi). In this book, Jizhai proposed a set of strategies that he claimed would forever banish the misfortune of difficult labor. As I will discuss further in chapter 5, Jizhai argued that childbirth was an innately trouble free process that became difficult only when people tried to manage or hasten it. He thus called for nonintervention in labor, and he criticized any one—doctor, midwife, family members—who would try to expedite birth through drugs, rituals, or manipulations. Jizhai stated that he had verified the efficacy of his methods through personal trials undertaken during his "spare time" from work. Beyond this, he made no claim to medical expertise other than having read through works by "the ancients." He made no mention of any family background in medicine or to discipleship with famous masters, and he only fleetingly mentioned a couple of medical works that he consulted when compiling his text. By the author's own admission, furthermore, the text was written in plain language that educated men would surely scoff at.

Despite its humble origins, this modest book by an obscure author became one of the most famous works on childbirth of late imperial China. The *Union Catalog of Chinese Medicine Texts in Chinese Libraries* records 182 distinct Qing editions held in Chinese libraries today, representing texts published in different years by different individuals in print shops throughout the empire.[47] As late imperial observers themselves noted, *Easy Childbirth* was being continually reprinted and disseminated by their countrymen.[48] Besides circulating as an independent text, *Easy Childbirth* was also reproduced in part or in full in numerous other works on women's diseases. These included the frequently reprinted *Essentials of Fecundity (Dasheng yaozhi),* compiled in 1762 by Tang Qianqing, a scholar-turned-physician from Shanghai.[49] *Easy Childbirth* was so well known, in fact, that Qing medical authors used it as rhetorical point of reference: a writer who wanted to praise a particular text might claim that it was superior even to *Easy Childbirth*.[50] The text was also known to foreigners in China, who by 1825 had translated the book into English, Russian, German, and Polish.[51] *Easy Childbirth* continued to be reprinted well into the twentieth century, most notably in thirty different editions of *The Medical Books of Chen Xiuyuan (Chen Xiuyuan yishu)* produced between 1902 and 1955. These were encyclopedic collections of medical books that had been authored or collected by the famous physician Chen Nianzu (1766–1833, courtesy name Xiuyuan).[52] Chen himself had praised *Easy Childbirth* in his own *fuke* compilation, affirming that "every word is a pearl."[53] Being included in Chen's anthologies effectively made *Easy Childbirth* a must-read book for medical students and amateur medical enthusiasts of the early twentieth century. In fact, by this time *Easy Childbirth* had become synonymous with "basic knowledge about childbirth." A Beijing literatus writing in 1909, for example, criticized ignorant midwives who "haven't even read the *Treatise on Easy Childbirth*."[54] The text also served as a reference point for later medical reformers such as the Western-trained physician Yu Songyun. When Yu wrote a textbook on Western obstetrics in 1933, he titled it *A Scientific* Treatise on Easy Childbirth *(Kexue de Dasheng bian)*, an allusion that he clearly assumed his readers would recognize.[55] A few years later, Dr. Marion Yang (Yang Chongrui), the leading figure in the Nationalist government's midwifery reform efforts, lamented the fact that prenatal and obstetrical care in China consisted of little more than women memorizing passages from *Easy Childbirth*, a state of affairs that she blamed for high rates of maternal mortality.[56] In recognition of its obvious popularity and influence, modern textbooks of TCM gynecology identify the *Treatise on Easy Childbirth* as one of the six most important works of traditional *fuke*.[57]

The Authorship of the Treatise on Easy Childbirth

Although the author of the *Treatise on Easy Childbirth* identified himself only as "Lay Buddhist Jizhai" he signaled to his readers that he was a member of the educated classes, someone who had studied for the civil service examinations. In his preface, for example, he averred that promoting safe childbirth was a matter that "we Confucian scholars" *(wu ru)*, concerned for the well-being of all creation, should take seriously.[58] The signature line of his preface also noted that he had written it in the "Nanchang Prefectural Office," thus showing that he was engaged in some form of government service. While Jizhai's real name would have remained a mystery to late imperial readers of *Easy Childbirth*, the historian can reliably identify him as one Ye Feng, courtesy name Weifeng, a literatus from Huoshan County in the southeastern province of Anhui.[59] The Ye family was one of the many families who occupied the lower rungs of the scholar-elite class, never attaining official position yet successful enough to enjoy a certain moral and social standing in their community.[60] Ye Feng's great-grandfather Ye Wanpu had once been a prosperous merchant of salt and foodstuffs in Shanghai, but the family business declined soon after the early death of his son Ye Mengyu. Mengyu's widow, Ms. Wang, only about nineteen years old at the time, was left to raise their four-month-old son, Ye Sheng (b. ca. 1615). Ms. Wang would eventually be memorialized among the exemplary women listed in the *Huoshan County Gazetteer (Huoshan xianzhi),* praised for her steadfast commitment to remain a chaste widow, her filial devotion to her parents-in law, and the moral rectitude she instilled in her son, Ye Sheng. While Ye Sheng was "unable to attain the profession of the *Odes* and *Classics,*" he successfully negotiated the turmoil of the Manchu conquest and was sufficiently well off in 1648 to make significant monetary contributions toward suppressing a local bandit rebellion, one of the many that followed in the wake of the Ming dynasty's collapse. By this time, the family had relocated to Huoshan, where Ye Feng was born.

In many ways, Ye Feng exemplified the lower-level literatus who maintained the mien of the gentleman-scholar even as he scraped together a living to the best of his ability. The *Huoshan County Gazetteer* paints him as a man of uncompromising virtue and intellectual rigor, a diligent philologist who "intensely studied ancient poems and writings, always exerting himself to trace their origins back to the Tang and Song and earlier." In middle age, he served as a staff advisor *(muyou)* in the Nanchang prefectural yamen in Jiangxi Province. It was then that he composed the *Treatise on Easy Childbirth* under his sobriquet, Jizhai. Eventually, he quit his post because he "detested being entangled in sordid matters," namely, the influence-peddling, infighting, and other common but insalubrious concomitants of government life.[61] Like numerous world-weary scholars before him, he took up the life of a recluse, devoting himself to medical studies. The county gazetteer described how Ye Feng erected several thatched huts, planted around with dozens of banana plants, where he spent his days "lying in their midst on his back, communing with the ancients until his lapels and sleeves were all green." Here Ye Feng enjoyed the later years of a life in which medicine partnered with literature as a vehicle for expressing his scholarly aspirations and compassion for humanity. Besides the *Treatise on Easy Childbirth,* Ye Feng wrote several other works on medicine as well as collections of poems and essays, although he was too impecunious to print more than a handful of historical writings. He also maintained a foothold in the local gentry: his son once served as the director of the local medical school, and his grandson attained the status of government scholar *(shengyuan)*, the first rung on the examination ladder. Well regarded in his time, Ye Feng was also later recognized by having one of his poems and one of his essays reprinted in the "literary selections" portion of the official county gazetteer of 1776.[62]

The Literate Amateur as Medical Compiler

The Huoshan County chroniclers noted that "those who delight in works of goodness have already printed and circulated dozens of copies [of *Easy Childbirth*], all of which refer to him as Jizhai, without knowing that it came from Ye Feng's hand."[63] But even if Qing readers did not know the details of Ye Feng's life, they would have mentally grouped "Jizhai" among the many educated men who were actively disseminating medical knowledge in print. There was a range of ways that these literate amateurs participated in the creation and circulation of medical knowledge, depending on finances, interest, and level of medical expertise. The simplest was to reprint an existing work such as the Bamboo Grove Monastery texts. A wealthier individual could himself pay for woodblocks to be carved, but once the woodblocks were made, others could ask the print shop to run off additional copies at a more accessible price. At a deeper level of involvement, people could add new material to existing works during the reprinting process, incorporating medical information that they themselves had found useful. This was the case with Gong Chunpu, a vice commandant in Haiyan County.[64] In his spare time, Gong would discuss medicine, including the treatment of women's diseases, with his subordinate Chen Mingzhe.[65] In 1854, Gong produced an edition of the Bamboo Grove text *Transmitted Secrets of Women's Medicine (Nüke michuan)*, appending to it a fertility formula that he had personally found effective. Like the medical books discussed earlier, this prescription had also been transmitted from official to official: it had originally been held by the family of official Wang Maocun, who shared it with a second official, Zhu Yungu, who in turn gave it to Gong.[66] The practice of appending material was so routine, in fact, that Ye Feng specifically asked his readers to refrain from doing so when they reprinted *Easy Childbirth*, lest they obscure the recommendations of the original text. But while his readers complied with Ye Feng's general request to reprint

Easy Childbirth, they enthusiastically ignored his admonition not to append anything.

The size and complexity of these medical addenda could range from a couple of handy formulas to whole pages of new text or even entire chapters taken from other works. At the upper end of this continuum, the act of reprinting overlapped with the act of authorship, as knowledgeable writers essentially composed their own texts by collecting and organizing important quotations from existing works, often condensing or simplifying them. These amateur compilations could be highly eclectic, incorporating whatever information the author considered useful. An illustrative example is the *Edited Essentials of Medicine for Women (Nüke jiyao)*, compiled in 1823 by Shaoxing native Zhou Jichang.[67] Holder of a county-level *zhusheng* degree, Zhou was one of the many literati from Shaoxing who made their living as government secretaries *(muyou)* when they were unable to advance in the examinations.[68] Zhou Jichang was a legal expert, assisting the magistrate of Cixi County (Zhejiang Province) with the numerous civil and criminal cases that district officials were expected to investigate and adjudicate. In his spare time, Zhou studied medical texts and dispensed medical advice, ultimately composing his own work on women's medicine. Of the eight chapters in Zhou Jichang's work, one consisted entirely of material attributed to the Bamboo Grove Monks and another was a condensed version of the *Treatise on Easy Childbirth*. Similarly, when Governor Pan Wei wrote his *Essential Outline of Medicine for Women (Nüke yaolue, 1877)*, he included extracts from the *Treatise on Easy Childbirth* along with lore from the Qian family of Shaoxing, a lineage of hereditary *fuke* experts (discussed in chapter 6), all combined with teachings from the eminent physicians Xu Dachun and Chen Nianzu, as well as the famous Ming loyalist and scholar-official Fu Shan.

Another common format was the book of "tested prescriptions" *(yanfang)*, composed of formulas gathered from hither and yon that people could use at home to relieve mundane and unusual illnesses. A famous example was the *New Compilation of Tested Prescriptions (Yanfang xinbian, 1846)* by Hunan native Bao Xiang'ao.[69] Bao was in government service of some sort, for the signature line of his authorial preface said that he wrote it at the yamen of Wuxuan County in Guangxi Province. While some modern biographical dictionaries have interpreted this to mean he was a government official,[70] Bao does not mention any title or official post, and it is likely that he, like Ye Feng and Zhou Jichang, was also an administrative secretary. In any case, Bao did not consider himself to be a doctor, instead portraying himself as a collector of medicinal remedies. In his youth, Bao explained, he had developed a loathing for people "who had worthy remedies but kept them secret and were unwilling to disseminate them in the world."[71] Bao had vowed to spare no effort to search out worthy recipes and make them broadly known. *New Compilation of Tested Prescriptions,* he explained, represented twenty years' worth of collecting, and it included formulas gleaned from medical books as well as remedies "passed on to me by friends and relatives." While Bao does not identify his source texts, large portions of his chapter on menstrual ailments are identical to analogous sections of the Bamboo Grove Monastery works.

Despite the broad variety of amateur medical activities, such texts were unified by a common set of goals: to simplify medical knowledge and publicize effective healing techniques. In this way people did not have to rely on doctors, and even people without any background in medicine could treat themselves. Ye Feng, for example, pointed out that the many existing works on childbirth were too abstruse and thus hard for the uninitiated to understand. His simple treatise would thus rectify a glaring lacuna in the literature:

> Beginning with the *Childbirth Treasury* [ninth century] and such books, each era has presented its explanations on the matter of childbirth. Their methods of protecting the fetus, approaching labor, and regulating postpartum are all extremely refined and thorough, and it seems that nothing has been left out. So why listen to more words today? Just consider that some [books] concentrate exclusively on remedies and drugs but do not explain the rationale behind them. Some touch on things in a general way without thoroughly discussing their meanings. A person who is not already well versed in these issues will not find it easy to understand and employ [these books], and in pressing situations it will be extremely difficult to obtain results.[72]

The Legitimacy of the Scholarly Amateur

The wide production and circulation of dosing guides and household manuals bespoke the importance of self-treatment as a strategy for preventing and curing disease. The legitimacy of publications authored by literate male medical amateurs, furthermore, was bolstered by their allusion to norms of Confucian benevolence. In contrast to venal doctors, amateurs were honest and impartial, desiring only to help the sick, particularly those too poor to have ready access to doctors or the expensive medicines they prescribed.[73] Unlike doctors, amateurs were not concerned about establishing their authority as experts or making a name for themselves. One could therefore trust that their assessments were based on objective interpretation of facts, rather than any desire to display their technical virtuosity or demonstrate the efficacy of a proprietary therapeutic approach. Ye Feng's preface to *Easy Childbirth* incorporated such rhetoric, explaining that he was simply transmitting well-established medical lore in accessible form and not trying to promote doctrinal innovations: "I have deliberately arranged and clarified the material in compliance with the ideas of the ancients, without inventing any unusual sayings."[74] This rhetorical contrast between bad doctors and good scholar-amateurs notably lay at the heart of a preface that the Zhejiang surveillance commissioner Li Keqiong wrote for Zhou Jichang's *Edited Essentials of Medicine for Women* in 1824. Contemporary doctors were often poorly educated and ignorant of medical principles, Li Keqiong said. "They carelessly try this and that," he complained, "and if they are lucky and hit the target, then they boast and brag, considering themselves to be good doctors." More troublesome, he suggested, they championed their own therapeutic school as a means of acquiring a competitive advantage, even when these methods were not appropriate to the illness at hand. "If it is not a case of them favoring purgatives and damaging original qi," he said, "then it is a case of them favoring tonics and provoking an excess of latent heteropathy." Another problem was the practitioners who possessed a few secret formulas that they applied in all cases. In short, one could not rely on doctors.[75]

By contrast, Li Keqiong had the highest praise for Zhou Jichang, whom he described by evoking the old analogy likening the good healer and the wise official. Li pointed out that in medicine, as in law, it was important to investigate matters thoroughly and objectively. Judgments had to be formulated on the basis of actual circumstances, never swayed by one's personal preferences, prejudices, or wishful thinking. Zhou Jichang's legal work was successful because he possessed all the crucial moral and intellectual endowments that also qualified him to be an effective doctor—diligence, perspicacity, and equanimity:

> Mr. Zhou administers law, and at the beginning he was not known for medicine. But the essence of medicine is truly the same as that of the tribunal. Medicine has its prescriptions, just as the tribunal has its laws. In medicine one cannot apply prescriptions on the basis of forced diagnoses, just as in the tribunal one cannot apply the law according to altered facts. Therefore those who are doctors must analyze the circumstances and consider the minute details [of the illness] before using drugs, just as those

who manage the tribunal must seek out the facts from beginning to end, investigating all circumstances in detail before pronouncing a judgment. One must not be conceited about one's abilities, nor be carried away by emotion, nor shirk from vexations, nor fear difficulties, but manage affairs by seeking truth and clarity, smoothly and fairly bringing the matter to a close. The tribunal is like this, and medicine is also like this. Therefore when the sick encounter Mr. Zhou, they are cured, just as when litigants appear before Mr. Zhou they obtain justice.[76]

In chapter 1, we saw that literate doctors evoked the values of the Confucian scholar—learning, morality, and benevolence—to argue that they should be esteemed above other practitioners. Li Keqiong's preface, however, located these virtues in the figure of the learned amateur, whom he now used to criticize the pretensions of doctors. Doctors were incapable of putting aside their self-interest, Li Keqiong suggested, while only men like Zhou Jichang were truly concerned with truth and helping others. Of course, not every doctor was bad, but other preface writers also shared Li Keqiong's view that capable healers were hard to find. Under these circumstances, self-dosing with the aid of a reliable book was preferable to risking one's life and health by engaging charlatans or incompetents. Thus the preface writer Lu Yuan praised a Bamboo Monastery work by pointing out that it would "allow those in the world who fear the errors of quack doctors to know that, if they have such-and-such a syndrome, they can use such-and-such a formula."[77] Another preface writer, Luo Shanqing, also explained that such handbooks would allow one to "forgo seeking a doctor [keyi bu qiu yi] by matching the symptoms and following the formula."[78] And a good book of remedies was also useful in those situations when no practitioner was available at all. Wu Ziqing expressed a standard concern when he said, "In deserted corners and remote areas, how can one find a good doctor? When one is in a rushed panic in the middle of the night, it is difficult to search for medicine at a moment's notice. Truly this is lamentable."[79]

Concerns about obtaining proper and effective medical care took on special significance in the case of women. As we saw in chapter 1, medical writers had historically emphasized that women were more sickly and harder to treat than men.[80] Curing women's diseases therefore required an especially high degree of medical skill, and the frequency and severity of female disorders also meant women were especially susceptible to quack practitioners. Of course, not all Chinese accepted this picture of female sickliness, and we also saw that heuristic medical texts after the seventeenth century presented a more optimistic alternative that argued that the diseases of men and women were essentially the same, save for disorders of menstruation, pregnancy, and childbirth. Some writers also used this perspective to argue that ensuring women's health was just a matter of knowing the right treatments to use in these special cases. Zhou Jichang, for example, averred that female ailments fell into predictable and easily defined categories: menstrual irregularity and complications associated with pregnancy and childbirth. Such cases required little more than making a diagnosis and applying the appropriate remedy.[81] One preface writer went as far as to say that women's reproductive diseases were the easiest to treat of all women's ailments. In most cases of illness, he said, it was necessary to take the patient's pulse in order to determine the correct course of treatment. However, for women suffering from "the ailments of pregnancy, postpartum, regulating menses, bringing about conception, abnormal discharges, and diseases of the breast," one could understand the true nature of the disease simply by asking about the history of the illness.[82]

Despite differing views on the complexity of women's illnesses, even writers like Pan Wei, who felt that "women's medicine is nothing more than regulating menses and producing children,"[83] accepted the idea that treating women patients was particularly troublesome because gender segregation and female modesty prevented male doctors from carrying out a thorough medical examination. For those who felt that women's disorders were dangerous and difficult, therefore, books containing "wondrously effective" formulas and easily accessible medical knowledge were a godsend. As preface writer Chen Qirong affirmed, as long as people had a copy of the Bamboo Grove book at home, "then there will be no ailment of women's medicine that is difficult to treat."[84] With prescription books, women did not have to compromise their modesty or risk a doctor's incorrect diagnosis. Instead, they could treat themselves or be advised by a male family member.[85] Likewise, preface writers who thought women's illnesses were largely the same as men's also valued formula books, because they allowed for easy treatment of those few problems particular to women. In sum, suspicion of doctors and faith in the catholic abilities of learned men combined to imbue amateur medical texts with legitimacy.

MEDICAL MERIT PUBLISHING

We have seen that amateurs printed and distributed works that they considered to be therapeutically useful. Alongside these medical considerations, the proliferation of popular medical works was also spurred by moral and religious considerations. In particular, disseminating medical information was a widely recognized form of philanthropy that allowed one to demonstrate personal virtue and concern for humanity. Of the thirty-seven men who wrote prefaces for different editions of the Bamboo Grove texts, for example, fully twenty-three expressed a general wish "to benefit the world" by making useful knowledge widely available. Indeed, the virtuous man had a moral imperative to disseminate useful medical information, an idea reiterated in Ye Feng's preface to *Easy Childbirth*. Since *Easy Childbirth* would help eliminate the curse of difficult labor, Ye pointed out, each reader must circulate the text as widely as his personal circumstances permitted: "To know [about this text] and not speak of it is a wrongdoing. To hear of it and not disseminate it is likewise wrong. Anyone who values life and sees this book ought to disseminate it widely. Those who have the resources should have woodblocks cut for broad circulation. Those who lack the resources should write out several copies by hand or orally transmit it to several people, each according to his abilities."[86]

Ye Feng also used Confucian morality to underscore his point. While his treatise on childbirth might be only a "trifle," he reminded his readers of this teaching from the *Analects:* "Do not refrain from doing a good deed just because it is a minor affair."[87] In a similar vein, other preface writers quoted Fan Zhongyan's analogy between a good doctor and a good official to explain that distributing medical works was consistent with the virtues of humanity and benevolent government. Printing medical texts could also be a way of demonstrating filial piety, and a would-be philanthropist on his deathbed might charge a son, nephew, or grandson with publishing some worthy medical text that he had not succeeded in publishing himself.[88]

But while many writers spoke in general terms about doing good, others explicitly spoke about obtaining divine rewards. People had long believed that one could acquire earthly benefits or ensure a happy afterlife by performing good deeds, and the writings of Yuan Huang (*jinshi* [palace graduate] degree of 1586) stimulated an expanded and more systematic approach to such pursuits. The seventeenth and eighteenth centuries, in particular, witnessed a publishing boom in "ledgers of merit and demerit" that taught readers how to calculate the number of points that would be earned or deducted for various deeds, including the charitable distribution of medical texts. And while Yuan Huang had addressed the aspirations of the scholar-official elite, a new genre of ledgers emerged after the seventeenth century that also spoke to the needs of the lower classes. As Cynthia Brokaw shows, these detailed a wide array of possible rewards so that "those who had neither hope of nor desire for success in the examinations could find some goal more suitable to their station and situation."[89] Brokaw explains that these new ledgers embodied their elite authors' anxieties about maintaining social order at a time when rebellions and local disturbances were frequent and respect for traditional hierarchies seemed to be eroding. By persuading Chinese of all classes to behave in the manner befitting their status, ledgers could provide a valuable tool for promoting harmony and social cohesion.

The history of the Bamboo Grove texts and *Easy Childbirth* shows that this broadened model of merit accumulation continued to be commonplace throughout the late imperial era, and that it also helped to encourage popular medical publishing. The religious connotations associated with each set of authors—monks and a lay Buddhist—likely enhanced their appeal as merit texts. But the Bamboo Grove Monastery texts and *Treatise on Easy Childbirth* were also ideally suited to merit publishing by a wide range of individuals, being relatively short (and therefore less costly to produce), written in an easy-to-use format, and aimed at a wide readership. Many editions bear the notation "printed for free distribution" *(yinsong)*, and append the names of sponsors who paid for the work's publication. These indicate that a broad range of people participated in printing these works. Women as well as men could donate money to republish popular *fuke* texts, and two Bamboo Grove texts published in 1826 and 1890 list several married women who sponsored 10 to 140 copies of the text, which they presumably distributed to friends and relatives.[90] Altogether, the 1890 edition names forty people who printed or distributed a total of more than 4,000 copies. As for the *Treatise on Easy Childbirth*, individuals commonly printed between 20 and 100 copies, but some people also printed 1,000 or more copies on their own—an indication perhaps of wealth, devoutness, or desperation. It was also common for groups of friends or relatives to pool their funds to produce a print run of respectable size. One edition of the *Treatise on Easy Childbirth* produced in Hangzhou, for example, listed the names of twenty-three people who repeatedly reprinted the text between 1877 and 1884, producing a total of 3,550 copies. This included a consortium of sixteen people who together produced 600 copies.[91]

Thus, while book merchants and publishing shops did brisk business

selling medical texts to aspiring doctors, they also made money by printing medical works for charitable distribution by would-be philanthropists. Many editions of the Bamboo Grove Monastery texts and *Easy
Childbirth* include advertisements for the print shop where the books
were produced, with some explicitly encouraging "kind gentlemen" *(shan
jun)* to go to the shop and commission another print run.[92] The Zhang
Hongmao Engraving Shop, for example, included a notice addressed to
"gentlemen who delight in acts of goodness and wish to print and distribute this book," informing them how much it would cost to reprint
Easy Childbirth on lesser and superior grades of paper.[93] Such exhortations apparently even came from the spirit world. Kui Yutian, vice prefect of an unidentified jurisdiction, went to a spirit-writing session with
some friends. The local divinity advised them to publish medical books
if they wanted to reap heavenly reward and gave highly specific instructions, saying, "There is the *Good Prescriptions for Women from the Bamboo Grove Monastery* in two fascicles. The wood blocks are kept in the
Zhang Longwen Studio engraving shop. Why don't you gentlemen all
exert yourselves to circulate it?"[94]

In the case of *Easy Childbirth*, furthermore, it is clear that merit accumulation was a driving force behind the text's wide circulation. As early
as 1762, for example, preface writer Qiao Guanglie observed that people
who wanted to acquire merit "would print works such as the *Treatise
on Easy Childbirth*," and therefore there were numerous copies of that
work in circulation.[95] The title page for a mid-nineteenth-century edition even baldly stated: "Those who reprint and distribute this work will
increase their merit a hundredfold" (figure 3).[96] One writer, exhorting
people to circulate the *Treatise on Easy Childbirth*, cited teachings from
the *Tract on Action and Response (Ganying pian)*, the text that Cynthia
Brokaw has described as a primer for merit accumulation.[97] Some editions of the *Treatise on Easy Childbirth* even included the *Tract on Action and Response* as an appended chapter.[98] Particularly revelatory are
the appendices to some nineteenth-century editions of *Easy Childbirth*
that describe how people benefited from publishing—or simply vowing
to publish—the text. One obvious reward was the birth of sons, and as
one editor reminded his readers, "It has always been the case that people
who accumulate merit will obtain descendants."[99] Such beneficiaries included the elderly Zhu Qixian, who promised to publish one thousand
copies of *Easy Childbirth* and was rewarded with two sons in a row.[100]
Another author recounted in 1888 how a friend of his had fathered three
sons after printing the text.[101] And when Wang Yuwen's wife was vom-

iting blood in the throes of a difficult labor, her husband vowed to print one thousand copies of the text. She was then safely delivered of a son.[102] Other benefits could accrue as well, and the publishing history of *Easy Childbirth* meshes with Brokaw's observation that, "while success in the examinations remains one of the most popular rewards in the later ledgers [of merit accumulation], long life, cure of sickness, and rescue from natural disaster became alternative forms of recompense."[103] Thus Shen Qiwan of Hangzhou was cured of an intractable phlegm illness, and Wang Xueli of Shandong obtained a cure for his father's consumption after each reprinted *Easy Childbirth*.[104] Song Er'rui of the lower Yangzi region was caught in a life-threatening storm at sea, but the winds calmed down after he vowed to print three thousand copies. Lin Rujin of Fujian printed *Easy Childbirth* on an ongoing basis, with the result that during a neighborhood fire his house was spared.[105] In addition to specific benefits, merit publishing could also guarantee general well-being, and others explained that they printed the *Treatise on Easy Childbirth* "to preserve safety and health" or to ensure that "my requests will certainly be answered."[106] One edition of *Easy Childbirth* held by the Shanghai Library today comes from a batch of one hundred copies that Li Heli distributed in order to maintain "family purity and business prosperity."[107] Notably, one did not have to actually print the text before obtaining the benefit. In many cases, simply vowing to publish it would be enough to acquire heavenly reward, and people were serious about fulfilling their promises. For example, the middle-aged "Lay Buddhist Yuyin" (Yuyin jushi) vowed in 1882 to publish one thousand copies if he were granted a son. He obtained one after publishing the first two hundred copies, but continued to honor his promise and, by the summer of 1884, had printed a sixth and final batch of texts.[108]

In some instances, the publication of *Easy Childbirth* was overtly linked to Buddhist beliefs. For example, some of the people who reprinted the text signed themselves "Buddhist Believer" *(xinshi)*.[109] Testimonies in a 1902 edition also tell how the deity Guanyin personally instructed a petitioner to publish the *Treatise on Easy Childbirth* and was responsible for granting the request of another.[110] But belief in merit accumulation is best understood as a broad cultural phenomenon that was simultaneously nurtured by Daoist, Buddhist, and Confucian values.[111] One late imperial writer even used medical merit publishing to disparage Buddhist funerary practices. Weng Linzhong, an imperial envoy, charged that the popular Buddhist customs of holding feasts and burning grave goods on behalf of deceased parents were useless. The only true way to serve

翻刻印送
者功百倍

達生編

板藏江西省城
甲戌坊一黎磨

Figure 3. The title page of this cheaply printed edition of the *Treatise on Easy Childbirth* promises readers that their merit will increase a hundredfold if they reprint and redistribute the book. Such beliefs in merit accumulation were an important factor in the circulation of this text. Jizhai jushi, *Dasheng bian* (1715; Nanchang: Yili zhai woodblock edition [c. 1850], ST no. 440243), in the collection of the Shanghai Library. Courtesy of the Shanghai Library.

one's parents, Weng told his readers, was to perform good deeds, especially publishing meritorious books *(shanshu)*, thereby "bringing fame
to yourself and honor to your family, glorifying your ancestors, and
benefiting your descendants." Accordingly, from 1895 to 1896, Weng
himself printed and distributed 1,250 copies of a Bamboo Grove text.[112]
Finally, the fact that medical merit publishing was a routine part of Qing
culture is perhaps best illustrated by the case of a prominent midwife who
republished *Easy Childbirth.*[113] On the face of it, this appears to be a
counterintuitive act, for *Easy Childbirth* portrayed midwives as ignorant
meddlers and advocated curtailing their authority in the birthing room
(to be discussed further in chapter 5). But one can assume that midwives
pursued merit accumulation as frequently as did other folk, and reprinting *Easy Childbirth* would have been an obvious way to obtain concrete
benefits while also endowing a midwife with an air of benevolence.

CONCLUSION

Erudite physicians such as Xu Dachun saw medical amateurs as a thorn
in the side. Without a thorough understanding of the principles of medicine, he cautioned, these people would only cause harm in their attempts
to treat illness. Yet the people who sponsored, compiled, and distributed
popular medical works were equally adamant that an amateur armed with
the right book of remedies could obtain results equal or even superior to
those provided by a professional healer. The skepticism that doctors and
their potential clients felt toward one another reflected a larger set of debates about the nature of medical efficacy itself. Was the ability to heal a
function of the physician's learned insights into the myriad transformations of yin and yang, or could it be obtained primarily through practical experience? Did the power of medicine rely on the skill of the prescription writer, or was efficacy inherent in the remedy itself? Literate
doctors used medical case history narratives *(yi'an)* to demonstrate that
only a trained master of doctrine, diagnosis, and prescription could as-
sure a cure.[114] But the literate medical amateurs who sponsored popular
medical handbooks demonstrated their confidence in the innate power of
"tested prescriptions" *(yanfang),* proven formulas that had stood the test
of time. Whether a person was learned or ignorant, noble or mean, anyone who could "match the symptoms and administer the recipe" *(dui
zheng tou fang)* would be able to use these methods to cure disease.

The proliferation of medical handbooks also attested to a deep confidence in the layperson's ability to assess medical knowledge based on personal experience. Formulas might be considered worthy because they had been tested over time by medical lineages, but also because the handbook writer himself had used them successfully to treat friends and relatives. Ye Feng expressed typical sentiments when he wrote that his book on childbirth "was created on the basis of firsthand experiences obtained throughout time and all places; moreover, these are things that the body has experienced, the eyes have witnessed, the mouth has taught, and the ear has heard. In a thousand attempts, not one failed."[115] Ironically, educated physicians' attempts to enhance the status of medicine by embracing literati norms actually reinforced the legitimacy of the amateur. If being a scholar-gentleman was the key qualification to be a doctor, then it followed that any scholar-gentleman already possessed the fundamental qualifications for practicing medicine. Anyone who had access to medical literature was equipped to develop his or her own opinions on what remedies were effective. Furthermore, amateurs like Jizhai could claim to be completely selfless and disinterested. While even scholarly physicians had to fight to establish their reputations and make a living, the amateur medical hobbyist was able to set aside all concerns with self-promotion and concentrate instead on healing. Finally, faith in amateur healing was abetted by the common belief that one could benefit society (and therefore oneself) by disseminating works on medicine. The very act of medical merit publishing presumed that the layperson was qualified to judge who was a legitimate healer and what constituted proper modes of healing. And in distributing meritorious texts like those attributed to the Bamboo Grove Monastery monks, medical publishers readily promoted healers whom learned doctors would have disparaged.

These first two chapters have shown that judgments about proper and effective treatment for women were shaped by broader norms and dynamics both within and outside the medical sphere. In particular, the multipolar nature of medical knowledge and the expansion of print culture enabled a variety of practitioners and constituencies to shape the written discourse on women's illnesses. But as we shall see, perceptions of women's reproductive illnesses also grew out of a concrete material reality: the observation that childbearing could be accompanied by an array of discomforts and disorders that ranged from the troublesome to the potentially fatal. Did the ability to treat these female diseases reside in the mastery of a specialized repertoire of recipes for a relatively discrete number of disorders? Were the permutations of *fuke* as subtle and innumerable as those of other classes of illness? Were women actually more difficult to cure than men or not? The way in which a person answered these questions could mean the difference between health and debility. The following chapters examine the intellectual convergences and cleavages that arose as doctors sought to apply their knowledge to the management of specific female ailments.

CHAPTER 3

Function and Structure in the Female Body

By the time she was twenty-two years old, Ms. Cheng had given birth to five children. For the next eight years after that, however, she stopped menstruating entirely and was unable to conceive.[1] To restore her fertility, her family hired a succession of *fuke* experts who administered "thousands of doses of medicines" in a fruitless attempt to cure what they believed to be a case of stagnated Blood. Finally, Ms. Cheng was examined by one of her husband's senior kinsmen, the eminent doctor Sun Yikui (fl. late sixteenth century).[2] Sun declared that the previous doctors had all misdiagnosed Ms. Cheng's problem. She was not suffering from stagnated Blood, he said, but rather from "spleen dampness engendering phlegm, [causing] fat to fill up the womb." As proof, he pointed out that except for the worrisome fact that she had stopped menstruating, Ms. Cheng showed no apparent signs of illness. She was plumper than before, ate and drank twice as much as she previously had, and was in better spirits than ever. Furthermore, while internal stagnations of Blood were accompanied by hardness in the abdomen, Ms. Cheng's belly was soft. Taking her pulse, Sun Yikui also found that while it was large and vigorous, it was characterized by a "loose" quality *(huan)* typical in cases of internal dampness and impaired spleen.[3] The proper course, Sun concluded, was to concurrently harmonize the spleen and dissipate the accumulated phlegm and fat. Once the fat blocking Ms. Cheng's womb was gone, her menses would again flow of their own accord, and once her spleen's ability to properly transform food and drink into qi was restored, future meals would no longer "engender phlegm nor abet fat." Six months after following Sun's advice, Ms. Cheng indeed began to menstruate again, and she subsequently gave birth to three more children, two sons and a daughter.

Sun Yikui's case records were published by 1599 and continued to be an important reference for later doctors.[4] For example, Wei Zhixiu's 1770 collection of medical case records used Ms. Cheng's story to help readers understand the many causes that could underlie "blocked menses" *(jingbi)*, a potentially debilitating and even fatal malady.[5] For the historian, Ms. Cheng's case is the ideal point of departure for examining a question at the heart of any study of late imperial *fuke:* how did male doctors of this time envision and define the female reproductive body? The crux of Sun Yikui's narrative is the contrast between two alternate explanations for Ms. Cheng's infertility: one constructed around pathological Blood, and the other around a physically clogged womb. The first emphasized the vital flows and transformative energies that enabled conception and gestation, while the second foregrounded the physical bodily space wherein these transformations occurred. These alternate explanations were never mutually exclusive but instead defined a range of possibilities that doctors had to negotiate when deciding how to treat an apparent malfunction of the female reproductive system. Sun's narrative thus reiterated a lesson that his readers would all have learned at some point: to successfully manage female fertility, the doctor needed to be cognizant of all possible dysfunctions of Blood and womb and know how to distinguish among them.

This chapter analyzes how late imperial doctors understood Blood, womb, and the ensemble of bodily channels that linked these two elements and endowed the female body with its procreative potential. With this approach, I depart from the conventional wisdom that says Chinese doctors were uninterested in bodily structure, and that the womb was irrelevant to understandings of the female body. To be sure, Chinese medical thinkers did not pursue bodily knowledge via dissection or anatomical studies, and doctrinal innovations always focused on understanding the dynamic relations and transformations of yin and yang in the body. It is also true that medical discussions about women's bodies focused on the behavior of Blood, and that the female womb was never a focus of gender discourse as it was in the history of Western medicine. Furthermore, while Chinese *fuke* works routinely mention the womb, they contain only a few sustained discussions of the nature of the womb itself. Unlike Blood, whose protean nature made it an obvious focus for investigation and therapeutic manipulation, the womb seems to have been largely taken for granted as a relatively stable object whose range of functions and pathological states were more narrowly defined. But fully understanding the intellectual architecture of *fuke* requires us to acknowledge what Chinese writers took for granted: that Blood health and womb health were both essential for successful childbearing. Indeed, the two were intertwined: the womb was a key node in the network of channels through which Blood flowed to enable menstruation, conception, and pregnancy, while the overall state of qi and Blood in the body at large directly affected the womb's ability to fulfill its gestative functions. In sum, while the explicit focus of medical theorizing about women's bodies was the nature and behavior of Blood, doctors also recognized that female reproductive health depended on the state of the womb.

While modern guides to traditional Chinese medicine routinely point out the existence of older textual descriptions of the womb,[6] this chapter is the first sustained study of how medical writers imagined the womb's role in the female reproductive body. Analyzing late imperial discourses of Blood and womb health also helps us to understand one of the distinctive aspects of late imperial *fuke*: the increasing subordination of female difference to a master narrative of bodily androgyny. As we saw in chapter 1, late imperial doctors diminished the scope of female exceptionality even as they sought better ways of managing those illnesses still recognized as unique to women. So too, after the early seventeenth century, doctors came to accept the idea that both men and women had "wombs," even while they recognized that the female womb alone could produce babies. As a result, while the womb was irrelevant in explicit epistemological discussions of male and female difference, it remained an important consideration when managing the reproductive health of actual women. To illustrate this point, I begin by examining the key components of the female reproductive body as described in medical works. I then look more closely at two therapeutic areas in which discussions of Blood and womb interaction were particularly salient: menstrual health and infertility.

BLOOD, VESSELS, WOMB

The problem of female Blood has been amply studied by historians of medicine and gender, and for good reason—it is the element that receives the most explicit, sustained attention in medical discussions of women's diseases.[7] As we saw in chapter 1, Chinese medical thinkers explained all matter, energy, and transformative potential in the cosmos as different manifestations of qi. Within the human body, the yang form of this cosmic qi was also called qi, while the yin form was called Blood. Late imperial doctors took it for granted that this Blood represented the "refined qi of water and grain" *(shui gu zhi jingqi)*, produced through the spleen and stomach's transformation of food and drink.[8] Once produced, Blood's ability to fulfill its functions also depended heavily on three other organs: the kidney, which regulated water and produced reproductive essence; the liver, which stored Blood; and the heart, which governed the circulation of Blood. As the yin aspect of bodily qi, Blood was present in both men and women and it played the same general role. Both male and female reproductive seed were formed out of Blood, for example.[9] But Blood had a particular importance for female reproductive health. Descending into the lower part of the body, Blood became menses, the clearest sign of a woman's ability to procreate and the material basis of her generative powers. Upon conception, this Blood would be retained within the body to nourish the unborn child. After childbirth, Blood would rise to the breasts and manifest itself as breast milk.[10] Thus when Qing doctors pointed out that women's diseases were the same as men's, save for "ailments of menstruation, pregnancy, and the postpartum period," they essentially focused on those functions that implicated Blood in its distinctly female forms.

On a doctrinal level, this affinity between Blood and femaleness owed much to intellectual models established during the Song dynasty. As Charlotte Furth has shown, the idea that "women are governed by Blood" became the organizing principle for literate Song dynasty *fuke*. At the same time, menstruation became the principal bodily feature that marked female distinctiveness, and "regulating menses" *(tiaojing)* was now understood as the key to ensuring female fertility.[11] In therapeutic terms as well, Song medicine favored remedies that acted directly on Blood. These doctrinal orientations were modified after the thirteenth century, when the center of innovation shifted to medical masters who sought to discern which bodily dynamics were the most crucial in determining health and disease writ large. Whether they emphasized the importance of spleen and stomach function or worried about yin deficiency and yang surplus as the primary cause of illness, these competing doctrinal currents also presented explanations of female illness that shifted attention away from Blood specifically and toward the universal dynamics of bodily function in which Blood health was implicated. Building on these perspectives, *fuke* texts of the late sixteenth and early seventeenth centuries significantly narrowed the range of ailments gendered as female.[12]

But the Song legacy in *fuke* persisted in important ways. First, doctors continued to cite the idea that Blood was central to female reproductive health. Thus, although there were now many competing strategies to address pathologies of Blood, these did not discredit the basic analogy that linked men to qi and women to Blood. Second, the importance of Blood continued to be embedded in the very format of Qing *fuke* texts, which conventionally began with a chapter on "menstruation" *(jingmai)* or "regulation of menses" *(tiaojing)*.[13] As the eighteenth-century editor of the *Imperial Encyclopedia*'s section on women's diseases affirmed, "Menstruation is the foundation for women" *(jingmai wei furen zhi ben)*.[14] At the most basic level, the problem of regulating menses focused on the properties of the menstrual flow itself. Normal menses were red, flowed smoothly and moderately, and came once a month at the same time. Any irregularities in the timing, consistency, color, and quantity of this flow required medical intervention.[15] Heuristic works like the imperially commissioned *Golden Mirror* of 1742 provided extensive lists of pathological permutations: Menses could come early or late, or sometimes early then late. Deep red or purple-black menses indicated pathogenic heat, a yellowish discharge resembling water in which rice had been washed indicated dampness, and pale red menses meant depletion. Dull-colored clots in the menses arose from coldness, while glossy lumps pointed to heat.[16] Such catalogs were echoed and complemented by popular medical texts whose graphic and earthy language underscored how distressing these conditions must have been for the women concerned. Eighteenth-century gynecological works attributed to the Bamboo Grove Monastery monks, for example, describe menses that resemble "the pith of fish brains" or "slices of beef membrane," menses that form lumps like "the white part of scallions," or menses that stink "like something rotting during a summer month."[17]

Such perturbations of fluid and flow were disturbing enough in and of themselves, but menstrual irregularity was also worrisome because it was often a symptom of a broader disorder. Given the similarities between some of these descriptions and what today's medicine would identify as internal vaginal or cervical infections (including sexually transmitted diseases), it is unsurprising that Chinese medical writers would perceive abnormal vaginal discharges to be potentially dangerous. The *Golden Mirror* warned, for example, that copious menstrual flows which stank like excrement and filth *(hui)* or raw meat might signal a fatal internal "rupture" or putrefaction in the viscera.[18] But even when not life-threatening, menstruation-related ailments could be profoundly debilitating. In its entry for late menses, the Bamboo Grove Monastery's *New Book on Childbearing* describes a pattern of illness marked by pain, nausea, and impaired vision: "Description of symptoms: when menses come, they resemble water leaking into a house. Her head reels and she is unable to see clearly. She has pain in her lower abdomen, and at the same time she has white vaginal discharges. Inside her throat there is a stink like the odor of fish. She is nauseated and vomits."[19]

In sum, the imperative to "regulate menses" did not focus just on the menstrual flow itself but addressed a woman's physical and emotional well-being during the period of time surrounding menses. In a healthy woman, menstruation should provoke no bodily distress. But in a sickly woman, menses might be accompanied by symptoms such as vomiting and loose bowels, heart palpitations, fainting, fever, loss of appetite, constipation, or difficult urination.[20] Pain could occur before, during, or following menses, and be experienced in the lower abdomen, waist, ribs, or even the entire body. Any of these symptoms could signal a pathological imbalance rooted in carelessness prior to or during the menstrual flow. Menstrual pain, for example, was closely linked to stagnation of Blood, which if untreated could lead to a potentially fatal blockage of the flow altogether.[21] Doctors treating cases of menstruation-related pain had to carefully consider all possible signs to determine correctly the location and underlying cause of the stagnation. Thus when the physician Shen Youpeng treated Dai Liting's wife in 1759, he took note of the fact that she had abdominal pains before and after menses, with the pain spreading from her abdomen all the way to her right foot, all accompanied by outbreaks of red splotches over her body.[22]

Broadly speaking, late imperial doctors recognized two types of Blood dysfunction that could cause menstrual irregularity. First, menstrual ailments could arise from insufficiency in the overall economy of bodily vitalities. Illness in the organs responsible for producing and regulating Blood, for example, could result in scanty or ailing Blood that would in turn produce irregular flows. Similarly, even if the menstrual flow itself was otherwise unremarkable, the movement of Blood at this time and its expulsion as menses could exacerbate existing deficiencies, and these in turn might make the woman vulnerable to other forms of illness. Second, as menstrual Blood itself moved through the body, it could be directly affected or "seized" by pathological influences that would cause it to stagnate or flow incorrectly, thus leading to stopped menses or some other disorder. This also spoke to broader concerns about blockage in the channels closely associated with Blood-governing viscera, blockages that could arise from stagnations of female Blood specifically or of qi generally. A case involving the niece of Shen Youpeng illustrates how doctors negotiated between these two points of reference. Widowed at an early age, and constitutionally frail, Shen's niece habitually lost her voice during her menstrual period. Shen began by giving her drugs intended to bolster kidney and yin, a strategy that assumed her illness was rooted in a preexisting depletion exacerbated by menstruation. But when these drugs made his niece worse, Shen adopted the opposite tack, treating her illness as a case of pathological cold and stagnation in the heart and kidney channels. Using drugs to dispel cold and build up yang, he quickly cured her and ultimately prevented her illness from recurring.[23]

The Vessels of the Body

When doctors thought about the ways in which Blood flow could be stymied, they also considered the health or pathology of the bodily pathways through which it flowed. Literate medicine identified a network of channels running throughout the human body, channels that served as conduits for the flow of qi in its various manifestations, including Blood. These were known as the "twelve channels" *(shi'er jing)* and "eight singular vessels" *(qijing bamai),* and the ability to read their states and harmonize their conditions was a central component of Chinese diagnostics and therapeutics.[24] Each of the twelve channels ran through a regular depot or palace organ and was matched with another channel in a yin-yang pair. The eight singular vessels intersected with the twelve channels and with each other to form a bodywide circulation network. However, unlike the twelve channels, they were not associated with any of the regular depot or palace organs, nor were they paired with any other channel. These circulation channels were found in men and women alike and played analogous roles. But just as Blood took on special significance in a woman's body, two of these vessels, the thoroughfare *(chongmai)* and the controller *(renmai),* were particularly important for female reproductive health.

Classical commentaries explained that the graph "controller" *(ren)* in "controller vessel" *(renmai)* had originally been written with a homonymous character that meant "pregnant" or "conception" *(ren).*[25] This semantic connection between female fertility and the thoroughfare and controller vessels was also reinforced by the canonical description of sexual maturation from the *Yellow Emperor's Inner Classic, Basic Questions*, an account that often appeared at the beginning of Qing *fuke* works. According to the *Basic Questions*, sexual maturation in both boys and girls began with the maturation of the kidney, the organ that produced all reproductive essences. The specific manifestations of sexual maturity, however, were associated with different components of the male and female bodies. "When a girl is fourteen," the classic said, "she comes into her prenatal vitalities *[tiangui]*, her controller vessel moves and her thoroughfare vessel is abundant; her menses flow regularly and she is able to bear children."[26] The corresponding description of a boy's sexual maturation explains that, "when he is sixteen, his kidney qi is abundant and he comes into his prenatal vitalities. His seminal essence overflows and drains; he is able to unite yin and yang and so beget young." Here we see that a girl's sexual maturation involved bodily structures—the controller and thoroughfare vessels—that play no role in boys. By contrast, the analogous physical structures implicated in male sexual maturity appear to be the testicles and penis, implied in the phrase "he is able to unite yin and yang": in other words, he is able to physically penetrate the woman and ejaculate. Wang Bing (fl. ca. 751–62), whose version of the *Basic Questions* formed the foundation of the received text used by Qing doctors, further underscored the special role of controller and thoroughfare channels for women by explaining that "the thoroughfare vessel is the sea of Blood, and the controller vessel is master of the womb *[baotai]*."[27] Because the thoroughfare and controller vessels were the specific origin of female reproductive power, pathology in these two vessels was an important cause of female infertility. As the eighteenth-century physician Xu Dachun taught his readers, "whoever wants to treat women's diseases must first clearly understand the thoroughfare and controller vessels."[28]

Scattered passages in the *Basic Questions* spoke of "vessels" or "channels" of the womb *(baomai, baoluo)* that were governed by the heart or tied to the kidney. Blockage of these circulation tracts would produce ailments such as stopped menses or loss of voice during pregnancy.[29] While the *Basic Questions* did not give a specific name to these, a common explanation by late imperial times was that the womb vessels were in fact the thoroughfare and controller vessels, two circulation tracts that had a special relationship with the womb.[30] This interpretation owed much to classical medical accounts that identified the origin point of the controller and thoroughfare vessels as a spot near the genitals or as a center of generative energy located in the lower abdomen. One passage from the *Basic Questions,* for example, identified the origin of the controller vessel as a spot beneath "the middle extremity" *(zhongji)* and above the pubic hair line.[31] In Han-dynasty texts, this "middle extremity" referred to the area around the navel, where sexual energy accumulated during intercourse and whence it was dispersed through the body at orgasm.[32] Another ancient explanation specified that the controller vessel arose from the perineum. But the classical description most frequently cited in Qing *fuke* texts came from the *Yellow Emperor's Inner Classic, Divine Pivot,* which stated that "the thoroughfare and controller vessels both arise from within the *bao [bao zhong].*"[33] As we shall see, in descriptions of women's bodies this *bao* was understood to refer to the childbearing organ.

The Fetal Abode: The Womb as a Female Organ

Late imperial medical writers and their readers recognized that women had a unique organ in their lower abdomens that served as a repository and gateway for menses, received semen during intercourse, and held and nourished the unborn child. Chinese medical literature throughout the ages also recommended dozens of formulas that would treat female infertility by addressing pathologies of this organ, which could be cold, depleted, afflicted with pain, or stopped up with noxious substances.[34] The English translation that best captures the semantic flexibility and variability of the various Chinese terms for the childbearing organ is "womb," a term historically used to refer to the uterus but also to the belly in general, a hollow cavity, and figuratively to a "place or medium of conception and development."[35] For ease of discussion, I use "womb" as the default translation.

The earliest known medical discussion of the womb appears in the texts of the *Yellow Emperor's Inner Classic,* which used the term *bao.* During the centuries when these texts were being written down, the various uses of *bao* included specific references to "the child's birth wrapping" *(er sheng guo)* or "fetal garment" *(tai zhi yi),* as well as metaphorical descriptions of "an open expanse in the abdomen for the fetus" *(fu zhong tai lang kong kuang).*[36] This term *bao* was thus semantically flexible, and depending on context it could equally well refer to what modern anatomy would call a placenta or a uterus.[37] In medical discussions of women's ailments, however, this term was understood to refer to the childbearing organ located within the lower abdomen. Compounds based on *bao* are prominent among the terms for *womb,* and include "womb palace" *(baogong)*,[38] "womb-fetus" *(baotai)*, and "womb organ" *(baozang)*.

Besides variants on *bao*, the most common term was *zigong*, literally "child palace," now the modern Chinese term for the anatomical uterus. Also of great antiquity, the term *child palace* has been traced to the *Divine Husbandman's Classic of Materia Medica (Shennong bencao jing*, first or second century C.E.), which described fluorite *(zishiying)* as a standard drug for treating infertility due to "wind coldness in the child palace."[39] More so than *bao*, *child palace* evoked the discrete physical boundaries of the childbearing organ. Descriptions of prolapsed wombs, for example, employed the term *child palace* and its variants, describing this as an object resembling "conjoined alms bowls," an "eggplant," or even "a pig's belly."[40] Related terms like "child intestine" *(zichang)* and "childbirth intestine" *(chanchang)*[41] also emphasized both its gestative functions and its material form as a hollow organ in the lower abdomen. Other compounds that incorporated the concepts of children, childbirth, and palaces included "child organ" *(zizang)*, "child chamber" *(zishi)*,[42] "childbirth palace" *(chan'gong)*,[43] and "palace organ" *(gongzang)*.[44] All these terms circulated in late imperial texts, and writers borrowed freely from earlier authors without attempting to impose a standardized terminology. In short, the womb's place in the female body was taken as a given, even while there was little interest in articulating womb-centered medical doctrines. Finally, we should note the existence of compounds containing the word *Blood (xue)*, such as "Blood chamber" *(xueshi)* and "Blood organ" *(xuezang)*, which in context clearly referred to a generative space in women, but emphasized its function as a reservoir for Blood, rather than as a space for the child. Such terms overlapped conceptually with "Blood sea" *(xuehai)*, which was also another term for the thoroughfare vessel.

An early attempt to understand the womb's function appears in the *Basic Questions'* discussion of "unusual palace organs" *(qi heng zhi fu)*. Internal evidence from the *Inner Classic* texts and other early medical works shows that dissections of dead bodies had been performed on various occasions in antiquity, and a central issue for these early writers was how to classify and rank the internal bodily structures that they observed.[45] The *Inner Classic* categorized internal organs into two types: *zang* and *fu*. The exact definitions of these categories, as well as which organs should be assigned to which category, was still in flux during this early period.[46] In general, however, the terms *zang* and *fu* evoked metaphors of political and economic administration, with the *zang* organs serving as "depots" for storing the body's vitalities and the *fu* as "palaces," or administrative centers, in charge of transforming food, water, and air into vital essences and energies, circulating them through-out the body, and disposing of turbid essences. The depot organs were the heart, lungs, kidneys, liver, and spleen, considered to be the most vi-tal organs. The organs consistently categorized as palace organs included the stomach, large intestine, small intestine, triple burner, and bladder.[47] As the *Basic Questions* noted, however, a number of organs did not fit neatly into this schema. These were the brain, marrow, bones, pulse ves-sels, gall bladder, and the "womb of woman" *(nüzi bao)*. The *Basic Ques-tions* finessed the issue by classifying them as "unusual palace organs" whose fundamental characteristics and functions were distinct from the "transmitting and transforming" *(chuan hua)* nature of the regular palace organs.[48] Whereas regular palace organs were formed by the qi of Heaven, these were formed by the qi of Earth. And whereas the reg-ular palace organs "drain but do not store," the unusual palace organs "store but do not drain." The womb's unique function made it especially anomalous. Regular palace organs received and transmitted vital essences to the other parts of the body, but the womb alone took these vitalities and created a baby. As Wang Bing's eighth-century commentary ex-plained, "Although the womb retains and emits [in the manner of a reg-ular palace organ], what it receives and retains is essence and qi, and what it emits has been metamorphosed into something with a form and ap-pearance."[49] The seventeenth-century physician Zhang Jiebin echoed Wang in his own famous commentary on the *Inner Classic* texts, noting that the womb was unusual because "it receives and emits essence and qi to form a fetus."[50] Because of this, Chen Shiduo (fl. 1687–94) even suggested that the womb should be classified as a depot organ, namely, one whose basic function was to store.[51]

In addition to the question of how to situate the womb within the hi-erarchy of bodily organs, doctors disagreed as to the womb's actual shape. Such discussions grew out of a perennial question: what determined the sex of the unborn child? By the late imperial period, there were three main explanations in circulation, each with a long history, and all of which were routinely summarized in heuristic works on women's ill-nesses.[52] The first attributed the sex of the baby to the relative strength and timing of male and female orgasms during intercourse. Both men and women emitted reproductive essences during orgasm, and if the male essence dominated, a boy would form, whereas if the female prevailed, a girl would form. A second set of theories attributed sex determination to the day that conception took place relative to the end of the woman's menstrual cycle, with boys forming on days when yang influences dominated and girls forming on days when yin influences were strongest. Finally, a third model said that sex was determined by the side of the mother's body on which the conceptus lodged. The *Classic of Sagely Benefaction* (*Shengji jing*, 1118), authored by Emperor Huizong of the Song dynasty, had spoken in general terms of qi circulating on the mother's left (yang) side and forming boys, or on the right (yin) side and forming girls.[53] But the influential fourteenth-century physician Zhu Zhenheng linked sex selection to the very shape of the womb itself. Any well-read late imperial doctor would have been familiar with Zhu's explanation that the womb had two branching "pathways" *(qi)*: "Yin and yang have sexual intercourse, and the fetal conception then coalesces. The place where it is stored is called the child palace [*zigong*]. The place where [the child palace] is connected [to the body] is below, and above there are two pathways, one leading to the left and the other to the right."[54]

One can only speculate what Zhu based this description on. The description of a womb that is attached "below" with two pathways "above" suggests direct visualization of the womb and Fallopian tubes within the abdomen. Since there is no evidence of any dissection during Zhu's era, such an observation might have been made from an opportunistic encounter with an opened female corpse.[55] It is also possible that Zhu got his information from a midwife, who would have been called upon not only to attend women in labor but also to examine female corpses for signs of foul play.[56] But what exactly might this midwife have observed? One scholar has suggested that Zhu's description was based on a prolapsed uterus, but the physical structure of the uterus is such that the Fallopian tubes would not be seen in a case of prolapse.[57] A third possibility is that Zhu (or his informant) did in fact observe a prolapsed womb with two discernable subsections, the result of a common deformity of the female genital tract. As explained by modern biology, the two Müllerian ducts that develop into the upper vagina, cervix, and uterus may fail to fuse properly during fetal gestation. The result can be a uterus with a long central septum that partitions it into two chambers, a bicornuate ("two-horned") uterine body, or a double uterus (with double cervixes).[58] In milder cases, such women can still menstruate, become pregnant, and give birth. In some cases as well, the shape of the internal genitals are detectable through manual palpation, and thus also could have been discerned by a midwife while she inspected the "childbirth gate," broke the amniotic sac of a mother in labor, or examined the genitals of a female corpse.

Whatever its original source, late imperial works continued to mention Zhu Zhenheng's description of the womb and his accompanying explanation that these two branches of the womb determined the fetus's sex: "When [male] essence dominates [female] Blood [during intercourse], then yang is the ruler, and qi is received in the left child palace and a male takes form. When essence does not dominate Blood, then yin is the ruler, and qi is received in the right child palace and a female takes form."[59] Hermaphrodites, Zhu further explained, formed when deficiencies in male and female reproductive essences prevented this process from being properly completed. In such cases, "yin and yang become mutually muddled, and neither one is master of the other. Then they cannot adhere to the left or to the right, but the qi is received between the two branches [of the womb]."[60] In sum, the dominance of yin or yang at the time of conception provided the initial force for producing a male or female fetus, but it was also important that the fetus lodge on the correct side of the womb, receiving yang (male) influences on the left and yin (female) influences on the right. Zhu's explanations resonated with long-standing beliefs that the fetus's sex was not fixed until the end of the third month of pregnancy, and that one could "turn a girl into a boy" (zhuan nü wei nan) by surrounding the mother with objects gendered as male or defined as yang.[61] His theories also echoed the underlying rationale of copulatory techniques where men tried to select the sex of their child by ejaculating to the left or the right.[62]

A dissenting opinion, however, came from Zhang Jiebin (1563–1640), whose chapters on women's illnesses critiqued Zhu Zhenheng's teachings. Zhang conceded that it was not entirely unreasonable to presume that the womb had a dual structure. After all, seeds were composed of two halves and men had two testicles. But Zhang was highly skeptical of the idea that a fetus's position in the womb would influence its sex. It was impossible to verify this belief, he pointed out, because the gate of the womb opened and closed according to its own logic, and one could never be sure whether any given attempt to "shoot to the left or right" had truly hit its mark.[63] Xiao Xun, who was heavily influenced by Zhang Jiebin, dismissed Zhu Zhenheng's views of the womb altogether. In his 1684 work, Canonical Teachings on Medicine for Women (Nüke jinglun), Xiao averred that the womb was shaped like "two bowls joined together" and had no branching pathways. To speak of a left and right womb was thus tantamount to saying that there were two wombs, and that was clearly ridiculous.[64] Whatever their views on its shape, medical doctors recognized the womb as a distinctive feature of the female body. Beginning in the seventeenth century, however, learned doctrine explicitly subordinated this female womb to a universalistic model of human reproductive function: both men and women had wombs, it was just that the female womb produced babies. This de-exoticization of female anatomy was part of the universalizing trend that also inspired late imperial writers to promote the idea that "the illnesses of women are no different from those of men" (discussed in chapter 1).

FROM GATE OF BIRTH TO GATE OF LIFE

The writings of Zhang Jiebin occupied a pivotal historical position in this epistemological transition. A native of Shanyin County, Shaoxing Prefecture, Zhang Jiebin was descended from a family that had distinguished itself in military service during the early Ming. His father was an advisor to a high-ranking official, and his position allowed the young Zhang Jiebin to meet numerous talented scholars and expert practitioners of various arts.[65] Zhang developed a particularly keen interest in military and medical affairs after early exposure to these subjects, among others. When Zhang Jiebin was in his early teens, his father was posted to Beijing, giving the youth the opportunity to study with the famous physician Jin Ying.[66] Zhang's adult life was spent largely in the military, which took him throughout northern China and into Korea. Stymied in his efforts to make a name for himself there, however, he returned to his home county and devoted himself to medicine, for which he had already developed a substantial reputation.

Zhang Jiebin had come of age at a time of great medical ferment, as literate doctors vied to construct new intellectual currents by expanding, revising, or rejecting doctrines articulated by the famous masters of the Jin-Yuan period.[67] Historians of medicine have conventionally classified Zhang as a partisan of the "supplementing through warmth" intellectual current *(wenbu pai)*, which countered Zhu Zhenheng's earlier teachings by arguing that yang—not yin—was most likely to be deficient and in need of supplementing.[68] But Zhang was also famous as the author of *The* Inner Classic *Explicated by Topic (Leijing,* 1624), a detailed commentary on the texts of the *Yellow Emperor's Inner Classic (Basic Questions* and the *Divine Pivot)* that arranged and discussed their content under twelve broad thematic rubrics. Zhang further augmented this work with two companion volumes, the *Illustrated Supplement to "The* Inner Classic *Explicated by Topic" (Leijing tuyi),* which employed illustrations to further elucidate important points, and the *Appended Supplement to "The*

Inner Classic *Explicated by Topic" (Leijing fuyi)*, which elaborated Zhang's own medical philosophy and doctrinal interpretations. It was in these two adjunct works that Zhang presented the idea of an androgynous womb.

Zhang Jiebin's interest in the womb grew out of his larger mission to systematize existing medical knowledge and achieve an ever more perfect synthesis between medical doctrine and Neo-Confucian cosmology. Zhang elaborated this guiding philosophy in the opening chapter of his *Appended Supplement*, where he argued that mastery of the *Classic of Changes (Yijing)* was essential for doctors.[69] This ancient philosophical work, one of the "five classics" studied by all Chinese literati, was recognized as a literal map to the workings of the universe. In its sixty-four hexagrams composed of solid (yang) and broken (yin) lines, it symbolically encapsulated all the possible patterns of transformation that animated the cosmos, transformations that were marvelous in their variability yet knowable to those who could discern their organizing principles. In an essay titled "The Meaning of Medicine and the *Changes" (Yi yi yi)* Zhang Jiebin told his readers that understanding the human body and understanding the cosmos constituted a single, indivisible enterprise:

> [The word] *changes* means "transformation," which encompasses the wondrousness of yin and yang's active and quiet states. *Medicine* means "judgment," which unites with the dynamics of yin and yang's waning and waxing. Although yin and yang are already thoroughly discussed in the [*Yellow Emperor's*] *Inner Classic,* there is no account of their transformations that is superior to the *Classic of Changes.* I therefore say, Heaven and man share a single principle, which is yin and yang. Medicine and the *Changes* share a common origin, which is alteration and transformation. How could it be that medicine and the *Changes* would not be joined by a single, indivisible principle? How could it be possible to know medicine without knowing the *Changes?*[70]

Zhang's claim that "medicine means judgment" echoed a common saying in late Ming medical writings.[71] It meant that the hallmark of the superior doctor was his ability to quickly and correctly assess the variables at work in any given case of illness. But expert judgment required more than just the accumulation of technical knowledge. It also required sincerity of intent, concentration of will, and wholehearted dedication to correct action. To cultivate such a mind-set, furthermore, meant committing oneself to the Neo-Confucian enterprise of "investigating things to extend knowledge to the fullest" *(gewu zhizhi)*. In sum, when Zhang Jiebin said that judgment was united with yin and yang, he portrayed the practice of medicine as nothing less than the conscious application of human will to discerning the transformations of yin and yang within the human body. For this reason, it was essential to study the *Classic of Changes* alongside the *Yellow Emperor's Inner Classic*. But one could not accurately discern these universal cosmic principles if one's understanding of the body were plagued by inconsistencies. These were the concerns that led Zhang Jiebin to tackle one of the important doctrinal questions of his time: what exactly was the life-gate *(mingmen)*, and which internal organ, if any, did it correspond to?

Chang Chia-feng has shown that medical writers after the fourteenth century came to define the life-gate as the seat of primordial qi and thus the original source of all reproductive and generative vitality.[72] It became crucially important to determine the location of the life-gate within the body, for only then would doctors know which channels and acupuncture points could be used to diagnose or treat its associated ailments. Chief among these was smallpox, understood to be a kind of "fetal poison" *(taidu)* that had lodged in the life-gate during gestation and could break free in response to environmental stimuli. Historical debates over the life-gate's location highlight a fundamental challenge in classical Chinese medicine—how to map paradigms of qi flow and function onto observable bodily structures, and how to integrate body parts into a doctrinal framework structured around yin-yang dualism. Intertwined with the life-gate question was the problem of defining the kidney, which was the only organ to comprise two separate morphological entities. Did both of these things together constitute a single kidney? Or was one of them the kidney and the other something else? The prevailing explanation, elaborated in the *Classic of Difficult Issues* (*Nanjing*, compiled in the first century C.E.), was that "the one on the left is the kidney, and the one on the right is the life-gate. The life-gate is where essence and psyche reside, and the place to which original qi is tied. In men it stores [seminal] essence; in women it binds the womb."[73]

In his *Appended Supplement*, however, Zhang Jiebin rejected the explanation of the right kidney on the grounds that the life-gate was actually the womb itself. He elaborated his arguments in a lengthy essay that set forth his beliefs on the characteristics of the triple burner *(sanjiao)*, pericardium vessel *(baoluo)*, and life-gate *(mingmen)*, three crucial bodily components whose precise form, location, and interrelations were much debated.[74] For Zhang, the existence of competing explanations represented a form of intellectual chaos that contravened the regularity of the cosmos. "When one considers the governing principle of the cosmos *(li),*" he pointed out, "there cannot be two different explanations. So how can one tolerate such confusion?"[75] Concerning the life-gate, Zhang pointed out that the *Inner Classic* had never differentiated between the function of the two kidneys, nor had it associated the term *life-gate* with either of them.[76] He also criticized the right-kidney explanation for introducing unacceptable discrepancies into the known function of the two parts of the kidney, which he clearly believed had to serve parallel functions. "If the right kidney is the life-gate and men use it to store seminal essence, then what do they store in the left kidney?" Zhang asked. "If women use [the life-gate] to bind the womb, then how is it that the womb ultimately would be bound only to the right kidney? Because of this, one cannot eradicate all doubts."

In his quest for answers, Zhang consulted not only medical texts but also foundational works of "internal alchemy" *(neidan)*, a mode of Daoist self-cultivation.[77] In contrast to "external alchemy" *(waidan)*, which sought to create elixirs of immortality by chemically transforming material substances, internal alchemy sought to create a state of enlightenment that would return the adept to the primordial unity of the cosmos, allowing rebirth in the form of an immortal fetus.[78] In practical terms, the techniques of inner alchemy featured meditative and breathing practices through which the adept would identify, accumulate, circulate, fuse, and refine the physical and psychic vitalities within the body, passing through stages of intensifying purity that would ultimately lead back to a "moment of eternity, the moment when the world was born, before the division into two [yin and yang]."[79] The inner alchemy texts that Zhang consulted thus provided many descriptions of the bodily gates, passes, and reservoirs through which these vitalities would flow and collect. After extensive review, Zhang concluded that the only explanation that could reconcile these various descriptions was that the life-gate was in fact the "child palace" *(zigong)*.[80] This was the place where menses arose and where the fetus grew until birth. At the same time, however, Zhang constructed an expansive definition of "child palace" that cast it as a reservoir of primordial cosmic vitality located in the lower abdomen. In sum, while Zhang implicitly acknowledged that the term *child palace* commonly referred to the female gestative organ, he also argued that an analogous structure existed in men:

> If we carefully interpret all these sayings, there are some tacit convergences. Now the so-called child door *[zihu]* is the same as the child palace *[zigong]*, which is the same as the center of the jade room *[yufang zhi zhong]*. The popular name for this is the *child intestine [zichang]*. It is located in front of

the rectum and behind the bladder, right between the pass-origin [guan-yuan] and the qi ocean [qihai] acupoints. Men's essence and women's Blood are both stored here, and children are produced from this place. Therefore, in actuality *child palace* is also a term that can be generally used for both men and women.

This is where the masters of the Dao store the prenatally endowed primordial qi of the true one, and it is the foundation for the nine return-ings and the seven sending backs. Therefore they call it the cinnabar field. Medical experts identify this as the place whence the flourishing of the thoroughfare and controller vessels arises, so that the menses descend. Therefore they call it the Blood chamber [xueshi]. Ye Wenshu says that when people first receive life, they are within the fetal wrapper [baotai]. They breathe along with their mother, [thereby] receiving qi and coming to completion. When it is time to be born, a bit of primordial divine qi collects beneath the umbilicus, and they can breathe on their own. Now the exhalation of qi is linked to the heavenly root, and the inhalation of qi is linked to the earthly root. The generation of people solely takes qi as the first principle. Therefore this [child palace] is also called the sea of qi [qihai]. Although the names are different, in actuality they are all a single child palace.[81]

Zhang's description of the life-gate is clearly derived from the mor-phology of the uterus. Note, for example, that the life-gate's position in the body, as described here, also coincides with the position of the uterus: between the rectum and bladder and about two inches *(cun)* below the navel (between the *guanyuan* and *qihai* points on the controller vessel).[82] This physical similarity is even clearer in the "Diagram of the Inner Land-scape" *(Neijing tu)* that Zhang provided in his *Illustrated Supplement.*[83] Such diagrams, which showed the general shape and relative position of internal body parts, were among the charts that adepts of inner alchemy used to envision the circulation of vital forces within the body, and they also appear in medical discussions of human body structure.[84] A typical example from the sixteenth century, published in Li Chan's *Introduction to Medicine* (*Yixue rumen*, 1575), appears as figure 4. But in the caption accompanying his own version of the inner landscape, Zhang Jiebin ar-gued that the older versions were wrong. One of their "great failings" *(da shi)*, he said, was that they did not depict the "child palace life-gate" *(zigong mingmen)*. To rectify this, Zhang inserted a new body part into his version of the inner landscape, labeled the "life-gate." Drawn in the form of a rounded chamber, it was located under the large intestines, be-tween the bladder and the rectum (figure 5). Visually as well as textu-ally, this life-gate matches the anatomical position and shape of the uterus, and Zhang's illustration even includes a delineating line resembling the

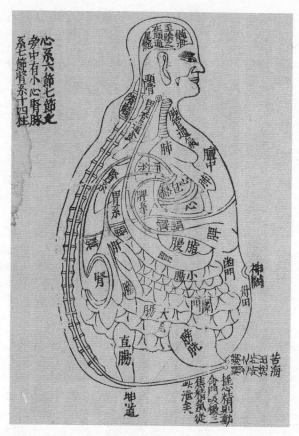

Figure 4. Diagram of internal organs from Li Chan,
An Introduction to Medicine (Yixue rumen) (1575;
Japanese woodblock edition of 1666 reprinted under
the title *Igaku nyūmon*), in the rare books collection of
the Harvard-Yenching Library. Courtesy of the Harvard-
Yenching Library, Harvard University.

cervix. Furthermore, Zhang added a new tubular pathway leading from
the kidney down to the life-gate. This visually reinforced his argument
that the life-gate served as a reservoir for reproductive vitalities generated
by the kidney, as well as being a pictorial echo of the *Inner Classic*'s description of "womb vessels" being tied to the kidney. Finally, Zhang depicted the "pathway of essence" *(jingdao)* as a vagina-like passage leading downward from the life-gate to the exterior of the body. This
corrected another supposed error of the ancient diagrams, namely, that
they "have the pathway of essence going along the spine and crossing

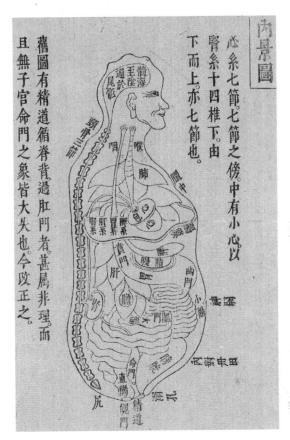

Figure 5. Diagram of internal organs from Zhang
Jiebin, *Illustrated Supplement to "The* Inner Classic
Explicated by Topic" (Leijing tuyi) (1624 wood-
block edition), in the rare books collection of the
Harvard-Yenching Library. Courtesy of the Harvard-
Yenching Library, Harvard University.

the anus, which is truly without reason." Li Chan, for example, had depicted essence leaving the body via a channel that began in the brain,
tunneled through the backbone, crossed the rectum, and ended below
the urinary aperture. But Zhang truncated this channel at the tailbone
and instead attached his pathway of essence to the womblike life-gate.

It must be emphasized that despite these feminine features, Zhang's
diagram was not intended to represent a female body. Instead, this diagram expresses pictorially what his essay explained verbally—that "child
palaces" are found in both men and women, and both male and female

bodies have the same basic structure. To make the case for uterine androgyny, Zhang repeatedly emphasized the womb's role as a reservoir for generative and gestational forms of qi. The term *child palace* could be used for both men and women because "men's essence and women's Blood are both stored here." Zhang also equated it to the cinnabar field, "where the masters of the Dao store the prenatally endowed primordial qi of the true one," and pointed out that it was also the same as the Blood chamber and the sea of qi. This focus on vitalities also allowed Zhang to resolve an issue that had been only awkwardly addressed in the *Inner Classic*—how to integrate the female womb into the yin-yang schema of the body. Zhang's solution was that the child palace–cum–life-gate did not actually represent a separate organ. Instead, it was an extension of the kidney, and Zhang explained that "the child palace is the palace where the kidney stores its essence."[85]

For Zhang, these descriptions of gates and reservoirs corresponded to tangible bodily structures. One could equate the child palace to the life-gate, he explained, because there was an actual gate there, one that governed the ingress and egress of reproductive essences that would ultimately form a child. Although it could be palpated only in women, its existence was equally unequivocal in men:

> In the lower part of the child palace there is a gate. In women, one can feel it with one's hand. Ordinary people call this the gate of childbirth *(chanmen)*. In men, one can discern the sensation of a gate shutting at the time of ejaculation. Now allow me to ask, "What is this place?" The guest said, "Could it be anything but the life-gate?" I reply, "It is thus."
> Permit me again to explain in full. Now at the beginning, when the form of the body has not been generated and at the time that the father and mother have intercourse, the man's bestowing [that is, yang essence] comes out from this gate, and the woman's regulating [that is, yin essence] goes in through this gate. And when the primordial qi of the fetus is adequate, it also comes out from this place. All of this going out and coming in takes place through this gate.[86]

In sum, Zhang Jiebin took the physical features of a uniquely female organ—the womb—and generalized it to all bodies, male and female. Envisioned both as a reservoir and gate, the womb could now be incorporated into a broader discourse of generative vitalities. Subsequently, Zhang's revised image of the inner landscape circulated widely during the late imperial period, both under Zhang's name and as part of Li Zhongzi's frequently reprinted medical textbook, *Essential Readings in Medical Learning (Yizong bi du,* 1637).[87] By the mid-eighteenth century, the

Golden Mirror's discussion of sex selection reiterated Zhang's views on the androgyny of the womb and Xiao Xun's views of its supposed shape: "The cinnabar field is the life-gate. In the man it is called the chamber of essence *(jingshi)*, and in women it is called the child palace. Its shape resembles a joined bowl, and there are not two branches that it can be divided into. References to 'left and right' would mean that there are two child palaces. Such teachings are particularly unusual."[88] In effect, then, the *Golden Mirror* simultaneously presented the womb as both a universal organ and one that took a particular morphological form in women. As we shall see in the next section, this female womb continued to occupy a salient place in late imperial understandings of female infertility.

FERTILITY AND CONCEPTION

Doctors recognized three broad categories of illness that directly impaired a woman's ability to conceive: menstrual irregularity, "girdle discharges" *(daixia,* namely, pathological vaginal flows),[89] and internal accumulations. In their discussion of these problems, furthermore, they routinely employed metaphors that portrayed the womb as a passageway or receptacle for Blood, and as a crucible or microenvironment for the transformation of seed into a child. Such metaphors notably appear in the *Golden Mirror*'s chapters on women's diseases, both in the opening entries on general principles and in the explanations of specific female ailments. The very first entry in the *Golden Mirror*'s section on *fuke* affirmed that women's diseases were fundamentally no different from those of men, with the exception of those associated with childbearing (discussed in chapter 1). Immediately following this affirmation of the fundamental homology of the sexes, however, the *Golden Mirror* provided more details on the distinctive features of women. In its second entry, which explicated the *Inner Classic*'s canonical description of female sexual maturation, the *Golden Mirror*'s commentary highlighted the physicality of the female reproductive network. In addition to reiterating older explanations that equated a woman's thoroughfare and controller vessels with her womb, the *Golden Mirror* suggested that a girl's sexual maturity involved reproductive vitalities flowing into her very womb:

> The phrase "when she is fourteen, the prenatal vitalities arrive" means that the moving qi of the prenatal vital fluids *arrives within the female womb [nüzi bao]*. The thoroughfare vessel is the sea of Blood, and the controller vessel is master of the fetal wrapper *[baotai]*. The thoroughfare and controller both arise from within the womb *[bao zhong]*. It is for this

reason that, when the controller vessel is open to circulation and the great thoroughfare vessel flourishes, then the monthly affair comes down according to schedule. Therefore she can produce children.[90]

The third essay in this opening chapter discussed the main causes of childlessness in women. Here we see that the womb, as a receptacle for female Blood, could also be a locus of pathology and its ailments could impair conception. In considering the causes of female infertility, therefore, the *Golden Mirror* gave equal rhetorical weight to the three interlinked bodily components of vessels, Blood, and womb:

[Verses] Inability to conceive is caused by injury to the controller and
    thoroughfare vessels,
Irregular menses, girdle discharges, menses that leak or gush;
Some cases arise from accumulated Blood, heat and cold in the womb,
Or phlegmy liquid and fatty membranes sickening the child palace.

[Commentary]: When women do not conceive, it is because the controller and thoroughfare vessels are injured. The *Classic* says, when a girl is twice seven, she comes into her prenatal vitalities, the controller vessel opens, the great thoroughfare vessel flourishes, and the monthly affair descends according to the time. Therefore she can bear children. But if heteropathy from the "three causes" injures her thoroughfare and controller vessels, then this will generate illnesses such as irregular menses, red and white discharges, dribbling menses, or gushing menses. In some cases [failure to conceive] is caused by retained Blood accumulating in the womb so that new Blood cannot complete its conception [into a fetus]. In some it is because the womb is cold or hot and cannot regulate Essence to complete the conception. In some it is because [the woman's] body is plump with copious phlegm, so that fatty membrane blocks up the inside of the uterus and she cannot conceive. In all cases it is proper to investigate the causes carefully and regulate according to the syndrome. Then conception will come about on its own.[91]

In sum, the three opening essays of the *Golden Mirror*'s *fuke* chapters framed the problem of menstrual disorders and infertility in terms of the interdependent relationship among Blood, vessels, and womb. Consistent with the "same as men" view of female illness, it rhetorically foregrounded the thoroughfare and controller vessels, channels of qi flow present in all bodies. At the same time, however, the concrete manifestations of pathology were conditioned by the particular functions and structures of the female body, presenting as retained or corrupted female reproductive essence (Blood) and a dysfunctional womb that could be blocked, too cold, or too hot. In the *Golden Mirror*'s subsequent dis-

cussions of the specific illnesses associated with childlessness, the interconnectedness of these three aspects continued to be a salient theme.

Womb as Passage and Receptacle

When the *Golden Mirror* talked of heteropathy from the "three causes"
injuring a woman's vessels, it essentially divided menstrual ailments into
three categories. The first were illnesses provoked by "external" factors
(wai yin), namely, climatic influences that breached the physical boundaries of the body to produce internal disharmonies. By contrast, menstrual ailments caused by "internal" factors *(nei yin)* arose from pent-up
and excessive emotions that produced stagnations of qi and thus impaired
the circulation of Blood. Finally, a third category of diseases arose from
factors that were "neither internal nor external" factors *(bu nei wai yin)*,
but which provoked a deficiency of Blood itself: dysfunction of the spleen
and stomach (which produced Blood), unregulated sexual desire and sexual activity, and frequent childbirth and breastfeeding.[92] It was in the category of externally provoked menstrual ailments that uterine morphology played an important role. The danger posed by external pathological
factors was twofold. First, Blood was a fluid whose behavior was directly
influenced by the prevailing temperature and climate: "When Heaven and
Earth are warm and harmonious, then the menses will be calm and tranquil. If Heaven is wintry and Earth is frozen, then the menses will congeal and stagnate. If Heaven is sweltering and Earth is hot, then the
menses will boil up and overflow. When a sudden wind bursts forth, then
the menses are whipped up into waves."[93]

Second, the womb was an opening through which pernicious climatic
influences could easily enter the body. As the *Golden Mirror* elaborated,
externally generated illnesses also arose when "the heteropathy of the
six climatic influences enters into the womb *(bao zhong)*, causing damage to the thoroughfare and controller vessels."[94] Having struck the vessels, these six climatic influences—wind, cold, summer heat, damp, dry-
ness, fire—would provoke pathology in the Blood that flowed through
them. Beyond the obvious danger of menstrual irregularity, other outcomes
included white and red "girdle discharges" *(bai dai, hong dai)*, noxious
flows that modern medicine would consider to be the result of vaginal or
uterine infections.

There was ample precedent for the *Golden Mirror*'s concern that
pathogens would enter the body via the womb, for it was widely recog-

nized as a passageway into the body. A graphic illustration of this idea is Song Ci's famous forensic medicine manual of 1247, reprinted in revised form throughout the late imperial period, which instructed that "in holding an inquest on a woman who has no apparent injuries, the vagina must be examined lest a knife have been inserted there to penetrate the vitals inside of the stomach."[95] Less violent, but still worrisome, Sun Simiao's seventh-century discussion of women's special ailments pointed out that illness could enter via the female genitals, either when women engaged in "sexual intercourse before vaginal wounds and sores have healed," or when "wind enters from below, causing [one of] the twelve chronic illnesses"[96] as women used the privy (and the logic of this description will be immediately apparent to any woman who has ever squatted over an outdoor latrine). Chen Ziming, similarly, had discussed the problem of menstrual irregularity caused by wind lodging in the womb and damaging the thoroughfare and controller vessels.[97] And as we saw earlier, Zhang Jiebin depicted the womb as a tangible gateway. These were but some of the many descriptions that portrayed the womb as a physical passageway into the body's interior.

These perceptions of the womb as a vulnerable aperture were undoubtedly reinforced by the medical belief that the womb opened and closed according to the woman's menstrual cycle. Conception, many said, would occur only during days that the womb was open and thus able to receive male semen. A typical description is found in Wan Quan's 1549 text on multiplying descendants, cited as an important medical reference by the *Imperial Encyclopedia* of 1725: "When the menses have not yet begun flowing, the sea of Blood is full, the child palace is not yet open, and it cannot receive [male] essence and form a pregnancy. When the menses have finished flowing, then the child palace is open, and the sea of Blood is cleansed, and then it is able to receive essence."[98]

Repeating common wisdom, Wan Quan pointed out that intercourse on the first, third, and fifth days following the cessation of menses would produce boys, while intercourse on the second, fourth, and sixth days would produce girls. On the seventh day, however, "the child palace again closes and is unable to conceive." Promoting fertility thus required one to simultaneously read the correct state of Blood (had menses actually stopped yet?) and the condition of the womb (open or closed?). To be sure, some skeptics pointed out that people had conceived even when they did not have intercourse at the supposedly correct moment. Nevertheless, the idea that the womb opened to allow conception continued to shape medical understandings of the female body.[99]

A womb that opened to emit menses and receive semen was also vulnerable to invading pathogens, and doctors suggested that the menstrual period could be just as dangerous as the period immediately following childbirth, a time when women were assumed to be at their weakest and most vulnerable. First, both were times when the womb was open, and both involved the loss of Blood and bodily fluids, which created or exacerbated the danger of depletion. Such concerns were clearly present, for example, in the *Golden Mirror*'s discussion of the many kinds of female abdominal swelling caused by invasions of cold wind: "These illnesses all arise because people do not know how to take proper precautions and avoidances after childbirth or during menstruation; and therefore coldness in the form of wind attacks from the outside, and the heteropathic and the orthopathic mutually mix and congeal within the abdomen."[100] Furthermore, the menstrual and postpartum periods were both transition periods when old Blood had to be cleansed away and new Blood produced. But this cycle was also vulnerable to interruption, and any disruption of this free flow was potentially dangerous. As Xu Dachun noted, "The Blood associated with menstruation and producing children easily congeals and stagnates."[101]

Of the many places where Blood stagnation could occur, the "gate of the womb" *(baomen)* was particularly troublesome, for an obstruction in the opening through which menses flowed could set off a vicious cycle of escalating pathology: blocked menses provoked additional illness, and additional illness exacerbated menstrual blockage. The locus classicus for discussions of the womb-gate was Zhang Ji (fl. 196–219), whose writings on "cold damage disorders" and pharmacology had become a pillar of learned medicine during the Northern Song (960–127).[102] Beginning around the seventeenth century, scholarly doctors also argued that Zhang Ji should be considered one of the founding sages of medicine, an argument that formed part of a broader attempt to elevate the status of medicine by positing an ancient intellectual lineage dating back to the Han dynasty.[103] His influence is particularly visible in the *Golden Mirror*, whose first twenty-five chapters *(juan)* consist of Zhang's works with commentaries. These included Zhang's *Essentials of the Golden Cabinet (Jinkui yaolue)*, where he discussed three categories of women's diseases: pregnancy, postpartum, and "unclassified diseases" *(zabing)*, a rubric that included menstrual ailments and internal accumulations. When Zhang Ji described the basic causes of "unclassified" female ailments, he notably identified the womb as a critical site of pathology: "The diseases of women arise because depletion, accumulated coldness, and congealed qi bring about the many forms of menstrual cessation, even to the extent that over the course of years, Blood is cold and accumulates and congeals in the gate of the womb *(baomen)*."[104]

Although the term *bao* was semantically flexible, such descriptions also show that the term *baomen* ("gate of the womb") was understood in concrete terms as the physical mouth to a female reproductive organ. Xu Bin's commentary of 1671 on Zhang Ji's *Golden Cabinet* similarly underscored the physicality of the womb-gate. "The 'gate of the womb' means the gate through which the child palace opens into the genitals *[yin zhong]*," Xu Bin explained. "It is the passageway for the menstrual waters."[105] The specific structure of women's bodies was also one possible explanation for why women's diseases were different from men's. This is suggested in the *fuke* section of the *Formulas for Universal Benefit (Puji fang,* ca. 1390), a massive collection of ancient and contemporary remedies compiled under the leadership of Zhu Xiao, fifth son of the founding emperor of the Ming dynasty.[106] In its discussion of noxious vaginal discharges, *Formulas for Universal Benefit* suggested that the unique physical components of the female body—the womb and its mouth—produced a uniquely female pattern of illness: "Question: Being struck by wind heteropathy is something that all people can suffer. How is it that only women have these illnesses [girdle discharges]? Reply: Although men and women have the same five depot organs and six palace organs, there are subtle differences between them. It is because women have a womb-gate and a child organ. When the wind coldness strikes these, then they become ill [in this way]. In men, it manifests itself in other illnesses."[107]

Besides directly impairing the egress of menstrual fluids, any pathogen that entered the womb could readily continue to the thoroughfare and controller vessels and thence to the rest of the body, setting off a cascade of illnesses. Conversely, damage to the thoroughfare and controller vessels from any cause would readily afflict the womb, making it even more vulnerable to existing pathogens. In practical terms, therefore, illness in one component was inseparable from illness in another. Accordingly, the *Golden Mirror* pointed out that girdle discharges arose when "the controller and thoroughfare vessels are injured by toil, wind heteropathy enters into the womb, and the Blood receives the heteropathic influence."[108] But the problem went beyond direct harm to Blood: the interconnectedness of all bodily channels and organs meant that a heteropathic influence that initially entered via the female reproductive system could manifest itself as illness in one of the internal organs. Since these organs were responsible for producing and governing Blood and qi, their illnesses could also produce noxious vaginal discharges. In such cases, the color and consistency of the discharge would indicate which organ was ailing. As the *Golden Mirror* explained, a greenish-blue vaginal discharge indicated that the liver was afflicted by wind and damp, a red discharge signaled heat and damp in the heart, and so on.[109] Female genital flows, in other words, could be rooted in many different bodily structures, and the *Golden Mirror* taught its readers to distinguishing between vaginal discharges that originated in the womb and those that originated elsewhere. For example, a putrid and fetid discharge indicated "a transformation of corrupted Blood, and is an illness located within the womb," whereas a puslike discharge had nothing to do with stagnated Blood but instead revealed the presence of an internal abscess. If the "urinary aperture" *(niaoqiao)* was obstructed and the vaginal discharge resembled water in which rice had been washed, then this was a sign that the pathology was located in the bladder. "But if there is no obstruction of the urinary aperture and it comes out from the essence aperture [that is, the vagina] or resembles starch, then this is an illness of white ooze *(bai yin)* within the womb."[110] Finally, the etiology of the discharge could also be determined by perceived sensations within the womb: "If girdle discharges are accompanied by heat and pain within the womb, then this is a case of heat dampness. If there is cold and pain within the womb, then this is a case of cold dampness.[111] Overall, such discussions highlighted the significance of the womb as a site of female pathology, and the need to consider its state during diagnosis.

While any of the six climatic influences could engender female illness, heat and cold were a special concern. The problem of heat notably appeared in a category of female illness known as "heat entering the Blood chamber *[re ru xueshi]*," a form of "wind strike" illness *(zhongfeng)* that manifested itself in fever, incoherent babbling, and hallucinations.[112] In late imperial times, the problem of heat entering the Blood chamber encompassed cases of pathogenic heat invading the body from without as well as excessive heat generated within the body itself as a result of excessive anger. Notably, heat was also one of the injurious forces that often entered the womb following childbirth.[113] But much more than heat, cold was a major preoccupation, for there was a deep metaphorical association between cold and stagnation. The seventeenth-century physician Xu Bin repeated accepted wisdom when he explained: "When qi is hot then it circulates, and when it is cold then it congeals. When cold qi congeals, stagnates, and accumulates, then it coagulates *[jie]*. 'Coagulates' means it does not disperse. When Blood encounters cold qi and does not circulate, then the menstrual fluids cease."[114]

Such was the danger posed by cold that one topical subsection *(men)* of the *Golden Mirror* notably identified ten distinct patterns of internal swellings in women that were all "caused by wind cold attacking after birth or during menses." These were differentiated by whether they primarily implicated Blood or qi, which viscera they afflicted, whether the internal mass was hard and fixed or soft and amorphous, and the patterns of pain that accompanied the swelling. Chief among these were the five "accumulations" *(ji),* which were forms of Blood illness *(xuebing)* that could be located in one or another of the five depot organs, and the six "conglomerations" *(ju),* which were forms of qi illness *(qibing)* associated with the six palace organs. There were also seven types of "verifiable masses" *(zheng)* caused by concentrations of qi that formed well-defined, stationary lumps in the abdomen, and eight types of "deceptive masses" *(jia)* resulting from accumulations of Blood that alternately coalesced and dispersed, without a clearly defined shape or location.[115] "Obstructions" *(pi)* arose from blockages in the channels of qi flow. "Stagnant Blood" *(yu xue)* referred to a condition where accumulations of Blood inside the abdomen had not yet formed hard lumps, whereas persistent stagnation would lead to a form of abdominal distention known as "Blood *gu*" *(xuegu).*[116] While the *Golden Mirror* usually speaks in general terms of "wind cold attacking from the outside," wind is frequently assumed to enter through a specific orifice. One cause of "verifiable masses," for example, was eating cold or raw food, an instance where pathogenic cold essentially enters via the mouth.[117] Likewise, discussions of "wind coldness lodging in the Blood chamber" or in "the womb" pointed to the female genitals as another entry point for pathology. A womb seized by cold could lead to stagnant Blood, for example, as well as to three types of tense, painful, and swollen protuberances surrounding the umbilicus, ranging in severity from finger-sized to the size of arms *(bi).*[118] "Mountainous swelling" *(shan),* for example, manifested itself as a high protuberant swelling with pain in the lower abdomen, waist, and flanks, and it was frequently caused by "wind cold and wintry dampness lodging in the gate of the womb and the Blood chamber."[119]

Womb as Container

As is clear from the examples above, concerns about pathology entering through the womb easily merged into concerns about pathology seizing the womb itself. In this way, the metaphor of womb as aperture also pointed to the importance of the womb as a container. A fertile womb was both open and empty, and blockage of the womb was an important cause of female infertility. Again, this view of the womb was intertwined with understandings of the menstrual cycle. Doctors explained the origins of the menstrual flow by likening it to the waxing and waning of the moon, and the rising and falling of the tide.[120] Menstruation occurred because Blood surged and swelled in response to these environmental forces, overflowing and spilling out in a monthly flow. Menstruation was also envisioned as a cycle of regeneration, when old Blood was voided, making room for the new Blood that would be produced to take its place. Li Gao (1180–1251), revered by late imperial physicians as one of the four masters of the Jin-Yuan period, described this cycle in his explanation of sex determination. In the first two days after menses ended, Li taught, "the sea of Blood has just been cleansed" and yin Blood would be relatively weak. Intercourse at this time would produce boys. By the third through fifth days, however, Blood would be flourishing and strong enough to prevail over semen, and intercourse would produce girls.[121] Sun Yikui's advice for begetting sons rested on a similar view of Blood exchange. The man should "cast into the vacuity" *(tou xu),* Sun counseled, meaning that one should synchronize intercourse with the moment that "the old [Blood] has been eliminated and the new [Blood] is starting to be generated."[122] The womb and its associated vessels constituted the space in which the exchange of new Blood for old occurred. But the stagnation or other pathology that blocked the mouth of the womb could also fill up the womb itself, occupying the space needed both for the menstrual exchange and for conception. As the *Golden Mirror* explained, conception would be impeded when "retained Blood accumulates in the womb and new Blood cannot bring about pregnancy."[123] Besides Blood, other bodily substances could fill the womb and impair fertility. The *Golden Mirror* was among many late imperial texts to cite Zhu Zhenheng's teaching that infertility in plump women was often due to excess fat blocking the mouth of the womb.[124] Indeed, this had been the problem with Ms. Cheng, whom we met at the beginning of this chapter: her fat-filled womb had prevented her from menstruating for eight years.

Womb as Crucible and Field

When the *Golden Mirror* taught that that women would fail to become pregnant if "the womb is either cold or hot and cannot regulate essence to bring the conception to fruition," it also focused attention on the female womb as a crucible or a field, an organ that simultaneously provided the site and transformative catalyst for gestation while also serving as the environment that would nurture the child.[125] Again, Blood and womb function were inseparable: weak Blood (as a bodily vitality) would impair the womb's ability to transform Blood (as female seed). While the metaphor of the womb as gate and receptacle emphasized the harm wreaked by invasion and blockage, the metaphor of the womb as a crucible or field focused on the problems of depletion and debility.

Since at least the seventh century, doctors had explained the dynamics of human gestation by pointing out that "yang bestows and yin transforms *(yang shi yin hua)*."[126] This meant that the man's body (yang) was responsible for planting the seed, and the woman's body (yin) took charge of gathering the seed, activating its transformation into a fetus and nurturing it until birth. Thus Zhu Zhenheng explained that thin women who had trouble conceiving tended to be suffering from a deficiency, such that "the womb is without Blood and the qi of essence cannot collect."[127] But insufficiency in the mother's qi or Blood could also lead to miscarriage even if conception had occurred. In an early discussion of this problem, Chao Yuanfang's seventh-century treatise explained: "If Blood and qi are vacuous and injured, and the child organ [womb] is occupied by wind cold, then Blood and qi will be insufficient and thus unable to nourish the fetus. Therefore it will bring about miscarriage."[128] Jiang Guan's medical case collection of 1549 told of a woman who believed that she was in her final month of pregnancy and sought some medicine to ensure an easy delivery. Several days later, however, she gave birth not to a child but to "half a bucketful of white worms." Because the woman's qi was too weak, Jiang explained, male and female essences were unable to complete their transformation into a fetus. As a result, the seed that should have metamorphosed into a child degraded into a "rotten and filthy accumulation."[129] Yan Chunxi was among the later physicians who continued to take it for granted that deficient uterine vitalities would subvert proper fetal development. In a discussion of weird and corrupted fetuses, Yan explained that these often arose from inadequacies in the "fundamental qi of the womb" *(zigong zhen qi)*.[130] Even though conception had occurred, Yan said, "yang is vacuous and yin cannot transform, therefore [the fetus] is ultimately unable to take shape. So each time that the time for birth arrives, what comes out are bloody lumps and bloody sacs." To avoid such illnesses, Yan counseled, one could try to correct the woman's deficiencies before conception by administering warming and replenishing medicines.

The many recognized causes of infertility thus included insufficient or defective reproductive essence (semen for him, Blood for her) as well as the inability of the sexual organs (penis and womb) to perform their allotted functions. Whereas deficient vitality in a man might lead to erectile or ejaculatory dysfunction, deficiency in women could produce a form of reproductive impotence centered on the womb. A standard reference on this problem was Chen Shiduo's seventeenth-century discussion of the six male and ten female causes of infertility.[131] If a man's seminal essence was cold, Chen explained, then "the woman's womb cannot retain it, and before a month has passed [the conceptus] will drop out." Similarly, scanty seminal essence would be so weak and thin that it would dribble out of the womb's "wide open" mouth as soon as it was ejaculated. Excessive dampness would also result in impure seminal essence, so that even if conception and birth occurred the child would die young. In addition to these malfunctions of male seed, male sexual performance depended on well-regulated yang forces—qi and fire—and imbalances here would prevent him from completing intercourse satisfactorily. More than simply attaining ejaculation, successful intercourse required that the male and female orgasms occur close enough together for the partners' released essences to mingle. But a man's pent-up liver qi and insufficient pericardium fire would cause impotence, so that "he cannot achieve an erection, or else when he approaches the oven the flame has already blown out, and when faced with the ramparts the spear topples." Weak yang qi caused the man to ejaculate prematurely, before the woman's Blood could arrive to mingle with his seminal essence, whereas excessive ministerial fire would excessively prolong intercourse and prevent the release of male seed until long after the woman's Blood had dispersed.

Chen Shiduo's longer list of female inadequacies reflected the more complicated female role in conception and gestation. Obstructed liver qi, he noted, would impair the woman's sexual enjoyment, and the female orgasm needed for conception would not occur. If her ministerial fire was exuberant, the excessive heat in the body would also prevent the growth of a child just as "land that has been consumed by fire and burned dry also suffers difficulty in getting grass and trees to grow." The remaining eight causes all involved forms of uterine dysfunction: the womb being too weak to support the weight of a fetus, the womb being too weak to transform seed, or womb pathology that created a hostile environment for the fetus. In several cases, the incompetence of the womb was rooted in some underlying weakness of channels, qi, Blood, or organs. Thus Chen noted that a cold womb "kills things," so that "even if the hot male essence is injected into it, how would it be able to swallow it without spitting it out?" Weakness of kidney water would cause the womb to become "parched and dried up," so that the fetus would dry up and fall out. If a woman suffered from concurrent vacuity of qi and Blood, then "the womb will drop down and be unable to rise and lift up and miscarriage will be unavoidable." Exuberant phlegm would produce excessive fat in the woman's lower body, so that "the uterus shrinks inward, and it is difficult for it to receive essence." In such cases, even if the man "engages the battle and shoots his essence straight in, dampness arises from the bladder, and inevitably one worries that [essence] will be washed away." Similarly, stagnation in the bladder that inhibited its ability to transform away water might also cause its dampness to seep into the womb and prevent conception. Although the thoroughfare and controller vessels were a chief focus of medical concern, other vessels could also be implicated, and here Chen identified the belt vessel *(daimai)* as an important source of uterine energy.[132] Deficiency and coldness of spleen and stomach could deplete the belt vessel, which would in turn prevent the womb from fulfilling its function. Obstructions in the waist and umbilicus would also cause distress in the belt vessel, with the result that "the womb has no force, so how can it carry the load of anything?" Finally, Chen worried about internal accumulations of Blood "between the controller and governor vessels" (that is, in the center of the abdomen) that would obstruct the entry of male essence, a description that reiterated the womb's function as a gate and receptacle.

CONCLUSION

Just as a feng shui master's reading of qi in a given landscape depends on the form and relative position of the objects that occupy it, so too, late imperial doctors assumed that the flow of qi and Blood throughout the body was patterned according to a given schema of bodily components. Thus while female Blood may have been the focus of medical theorizing, understandings of Blood health in women were inseparable from doctors' awareness of the distinctly female bodily structures through which Blood flowed. This exploration of the female body also invites us to reconsider a long-standing analytical narrative about the epistemological orientations of classical Chinese medicine, namely, that the Chinese were interested in "function, not structure." To be sure, the Chinese never shared the historical European obsession with anatomical investigation and dissection.[133] Modern scholars have explained this by pointing out that the aim of Chinese medicine was to understand the patterns of qi flow and metamorphosis in the human body, patterns that transcended the tangible features of the body's physical components. Thus, the prevailing narrative explains, when Chinese medical texts say the "*shen* produces semen," they are not necessarily concerned with the physical structure that modern medicine identifies as the "kidneys," but rather with a system of functions attributed to that organ. Indeed, Manfred Porkert's early interpretations eschewed the word *organ* altogether when speaking of the Chinese body, preferring instead to speak of "orbs of functions" that were only "coincidentally and vaguely" associated with observable internal structures.[134] For this reason English language literature on Chinese medicine frequently capitalizes the names of organs (for example, Kidney, Lung, Liver) or employs phrases such as "the hepatic system" or "Stomach visceral system" to emphasize that the referents of these terms in Chinese medicine are substantively different from those assigned by anatomical science. In sum, the "function, not structure" explanation has assumed that the physical morphology of the body was unimportant to the development of Chinese medical thought, and an influential commentator has wondered whether we can even speak of a Chinese medical "body" at all.[135]

Such explanations, however, grew out of twentieth-century efforts to make "traditional Chinese medicine" relevant to a biomedical world. In particular, the early generations of modern interpreters wanted to emphasize that the Chinese medical system could still be rational and effective even if it was based on ideas not substantiable by laboratory science. But while the "function, not structure" narrative provides a convenient entry point for cross-cultural comparisons, it is ultimately of limited utility for plumbing the historical deep structure of Chinese medical thought. To fully appreciate Chinese views on their own terms, we need to take seriously the numerous descriptions of bodily morphology that appear in Chinese medical texts. A famous passage from the *Divine Pivot*, for example, celebrated the perfect correspondence between the shape, number, and types of human body parts and the structure of Heaven and Earth.[136] Thus the twelve "terrestrial branches" *(dizhi)* used to mark periods of time and calculate cosmic patterns found their expression in the human body's ten toes plus genital organs (associated with earth because they were located in the lower half of the body). A man counted his penis and testicles to add up to twelve, while a woman made up the extra two branches by the fact that her womb could carry a child. Bodily structure was also important in externally applied therapies. Medical writers notably documented the crucial spots on the body where a practitioner could insert needles or could apply the heat of burning mugwort to cure illness, and they taught readers how to locate these points by describing their position relative to the bones, creases, and swellings of the body. Awareness of human morphology similarly shaped the organizational structure of therapeutic texts where a common format was to categorize illnesses and their cures according to the part of the body that was afflicted.[137] And as we saw earlier, a core theme of medical theorizing was how to clarify the relationship between the body's observed structures and its posited functions. Commentaries on the *Classic of Difficult Issues* notably sought to explain those internal features of the body that seemed anomalous given the assumed regularity of the cosmic patterns that shaped all creation. Why, for example, were the heart and lung situated above the diaphragm when other vital organs were not? How might the doctrine of yin-yang and the five phases be used to explain why the liver had two main lobes?[138]

Such examples suggest that a more fruitful approach to investigating Chinese medical thought would be to ask, "How did perceptions of function and structure mutually shape one another?" Put another way, how did medical thinkers conceptualize the body's dynamic and morphological components and the relationship between them? Such questions provide productive points of cross-cultural comparison while fully acknowledging the complete range of Chinese approaches to the body. For example, both the Chinese and the ancient Greeks focused on menstruation as the marker of femaleness, but they located this female function in a very different set of bodily components.[139] The authors of the Hippocratic corpus taught that menstruation was made possible by the "spongy" and "porous" nature of female flesh, which retained and stored blood more readily than male flesh.[140] Chinese *fuke*, by contrast, focused on Blood's origins in qi and worried about the state of the channels and gateways that it flowed through. Perceptions of structure and function, in other words, were never considered in isolation but rather developed in conversation with one another. Furthermore, the case of women's reproductive ailments illuminates how complex these systems of meaning could be. Even as elite medical doctrine subsumed the female womb into a rhetoric of bodily universality, the treatment of female diseases still assumed that women's bodies had special morphological features and functions. The dynamic functions of qi and Blood in women, in other words, were inevitably patterned by the physical layout of the female body, and the womb was a key node in the system of hydraulic flows that enabled female fertility. As we shall see in the next chapter, the metaphor of the womb as a crucible and field also overlapped with a related metaphor that depicted the pregnant female body as a vine, tree, or agricultural environment that had to be carefully regulated for the fruit to ripen properly.

CHAPTER 4

An Uncertain Harvest

Pregnancy and Miscarriage

Ms. Huang had suffered five miscarriages in a row, each time in the third month of pregnancy.[1] Now pregnant for the sixth time, she started to bleed and another miscarriage seemed imminent. Unlike during her previous pregnancies, however, she had to face the situation without her husband's support. Chen Nianzu (1753–1823) was the grandson of a doctor and an aspiring scholar, studying medicine while striving for examination success. He would receive the *juren* degree in 1792 and later win praise for his meritorious service as magistrate of Wei County in Zhili Province, where he personally formulated and distributed medicine to victims of a devastating epidemic that followed the floods of 1801. Chen would also later achieve fame as the author of influential medical primers and textbooks, eminent enough to merit a biographical entry in the official history of the Qing dynasty *(Qingshi gao)*.[2] Even at an earlier stage in his life, Chen Nianzu was confident that he knew how to manage his wife's difficulties. In each of Ms. Huang's previous pregnancies, he had dosed her according to the teachings of the famous fourteenth-century medical master Zhu Zhenheng, using a fire-dispersing and cooling combination of atractylodes rhizome *(baizhu)* and scutellaria *(huangqin)* to prevent miscarriage.[3] During Ms. Huang's sixth pregnancy, however, Chen Nianzu was away in the provincial capital taking the civil service examinations. In his absence, Chen's widowed mother consulted one of her late husband's kinsmen. This relative employed a pharmacological strategy contrary to that of Chen Nianzu, prescribing a formula laden with warming and Blood-moving drugs. One dose of the formula halted the signs of miscarriage, and subsequent doses at ten-day intervals allowed Ms. Huang to weather the critical period.

When Chen Nianzu finally returned home, he found his wife safely in her sixth month of pregnancy. Upon reading his relative's formula, he was shocked and dismayed. Not only did its ingredients gainsay his beliefs on the proper treatment of pregnant women, but Chen concluded that he himself had caused Ms. Huang's earlier miscarriages by giving her the wrong drugs: "Sighing, I said, 'Psoralea fruit is recorded in the *Materia Medica* as something that causes miscarriage. Furthermore [my kinsman's recipe] combines it with the warming properties of deer antler gelatin and eucommia, assisted by the [Blood] moving effects of lovage. And yet it has proven to be this effective. Supposing I had been at home. It is certain that I would have argued against this recipe and again provoked a miscarriage through the use of atractylodes and scutellaria.' "[4]

Some years later, Chen incorporated his wife's story into a guide for aspiring doctors, his *Essentials of Medicine for Women (Nüke yaozhi)* of 1803, where he used Ms. Huang's miscarriages to illustrate the principles of pregnancy care. Because of his wife's experiences, Chen related, he had tempered his earlier confidence in the formulas favored by Zhu Zhenheng: "After this, whenever I encountered symptoms of leaking fetus and impending miscarriage, I did not dare to exclusively follow the method of cooling the Blood." More profoundly, Chen revised his views on the dynamics of pregnancy itself. Whereas Zhu Zhenheng sought to counter what he saw as an inherent human preponderance toward excess fire, Chen Nianzu now argued that fire was the very thing that sustained pregnancy. It was for this reason that his cooling recipe had failed to prevent Ms. Huang's miscarriages while his relative's heating drugs had worked. Drawing on ancient explanations of the body's function, Chen pointed out that fetal development was dependent on the primordial fire of the life-gate *(mingmen)*, the part of the body that bound the womb. He further bolstered this point with agricultural metaphors that likened the woman's body to a fruiting plant: "[The fetus] can be compared to a fruit that is set in the spring and grows in the summer. If during the spring and summer there suddenly arises unseasonably cold weather or a chilling wind, then this causes the fruit to turn yellow and drop. Just use remedies that greatly replenish and greatly warm, allowing the womb to regularly obtain warm qi, and then the fetus will grow daily of its own accord until it is completely formed."[5]

The case of Ms. Huang and Chen Nianzu's change of heart speak to persistent questions in the history of *fuke:* what was the best way to guarantee a healthy and successful pregnancy? Which were the key dynamics governing gestation, and what remedies were most appropriate when things went wrong? Medical schools today teach that stress and infection are significant precipitating factors for miscarriage. A modern clinician might therefore note that many of the drugs prescribed both by Chen and his kinsman have vasodilative and antibiotic properties, and she might speculate about their relative ability to address Ms. Huang's specific risk factors.[6] But when Chen Nianzu and his readers thought about pregnancy, they drew on conceptual frameworks that explained gestation in terms of the balance of yin and yang forces within the woman's body and their effect on the interplay between maternal and fetal qi. These frameworks notably assumed that maintaining pregnancy and preventing miscarriage lay squarely within the realm of human control. While farmers could only pray for good weather to ripen their crops, a well-informed woman could directly regulate her qi—and that of her fetus—through personal regimens and medical recipes. At the same time, however, a woman's unhealthy behavior or improper use of drugs could readily destabilize her qi and the qi of her fetus, leading to a wide range of harmful or unusual outcomes: miscarriage, premature births, extra-long pregnancies, and corrupted fetuses. In sum, medical writers like Chen Nianzu saw gestation as both a mundane and highly vulnerable process whose successful outcome could not be taken for granted.

Such perspectives certainly owed much to the material and technological conditions of late imperial China, which meant that doctors and families had limited information on the actual state of the unborn fetus. As in other societies of the time, for example, it was impossible to directly view or monitor the contents of a woman's belly during gestation. Doctors also recognized that the signs of pregnancy could manifest themselves differently in different women, not to mention that the common discomforts of pregnancy could mimic other maladies and vice versa. But Ms. Huang's case also underscores another important factor: the existence of a medical discourse of childbearing whose organizing metaphors underscored the mutability and unpredictability of pregnancy itself. Medical writers could articulate female reproductive functions in terms of the relation between yin and yang, and this focused attention on the many ways in which imbalances of bodily vitalities could impair the normal course of pregnancy. They could equally well draw on agricultural metaphors that likened human gestation to the germination of seeds or the ripening of fruits, all subject to the vagaries of climate and terrain. In the case of Ms. Huang, Chen Nianzu shifted from an emphasis on yin-yang to an explicitly agricultural view. In other contexts, however, these metaphors could also be mutually reinforcing.

To explain how late imperial doctors negotiated these intellectual resources in the management of female reproductive health, this chapter focuses on two interlinked challenges that lay at the heart of effective care: accurately diagnosing pregnancy and preventing miscarriage. Imagine, for example, a woman with a swollen belly and stopped menses: was she pregnant or merely suffering from accumulated, blocked-up Blood? Or the supposedly pregnant woman who nevertheless continued to "menstruate"—was this an unusual pregnancy or one in danger of miscarriage? Or the woman who had been "pregnant" for seventeen months—was this a case of demonic invasion or just impaired fetal development? As I will show, classical medicine recognized all of these as possibilities. In this context, the Chinese medical preoccupation with regulating the behavior of pregnant women is best understood as an attempt to ensure the successful completion of a process that was highly contingent and easily subverted.

ASSESSING PREGNANCY

It is difficult to imagine a society where expectant mothers could avoid being showered with well-meaning advice. So too in China, medical texts throughout the centuries specified careful regimens for pregnant women. They described the fetus's development in each month of gestation and taught women how to regulate their diet, behavior, and emotions to promote the health of the unborn child and ensure its safe birth.[7] And while Chinese doctors emphasized that pregnancy itself was not a disease, they also portrayed it as a time when women were routinely vulnerable to illness. Medical writers thus identified a slew of ailments that a pregnant woman might suffer and that required treatment lest they harm her or her child. These mnemonic verses from the *Golden Mirror* of 1742 provided a concise summary of the main ailments, ranging from morning sickness (*ezu,* literally "noxious blockage") to corrupted fetuses:

> The illnesses of pregnancy and gestation comprise noxious blockage,
> Womb blockage, swelling and fullness, dashing qi, vexation, dangling,
> Seizures, coughing, turned bladder and dripping urine,
> Exuberant menses, fetal leaking and distressed fetus,

Halfling births, dead fetuses, and fetuses that do not grow,
Child muteness, parched organs, ghost fetuses and the like.
For other ailments, consult the sections on the signs and treatments of the
  various diseases.
What you must know is how to vigilantly watch over the fetus's primor-
  dial qi.[8]

Some of the illnesses in Qing texts might strike modern observers as
fanciful and imagined: accounts of babies crying within the womb, for
example, or a woman losing her voice as a result of pregnancy. Other
ailments would be familiar: vomiting and nausea, swelling of the lower
legs, and rarer complications signaled by dizziness, fainting, and seizures.
Chinese descriptions of "child seizures" *(zixian)*, for example, are strik-
ingly similar to modern medical descriptions of complications from
preeclampsia (pregnancy-induced hypertension). Discussions of "how to
determine whether the mother and child will live or die" also underscored
the fact that some complications of pregnancy could prove fatal if left
untreated.[9] The existence of such diseases, so threatening to the well-being
of the mother and the welfare of the family, made the management of
pregnancy a central concern for literate male doctors.

Pregnancy Tests

To successfully protect fetal qi and manage pregnancy, one first needed
to determine whether a woman was in fact pregnant or whether her perceived bodily changes were caused by some malady. Medical experts like
Chen Nianzu could refer to an ancient repertoire of pregnancy tests. These
fell into two categories: palpating the woman's pulse to see if it revealed
any of the physiological changes that were unique to pregnancy, and administering drugs that would provoke certain physical sensations in a
pregnant woman. The content and underlying rationale of these tests remained constant in medical literature produced from the seventh to nineteenth centuries, with different works varying from one another primarily
in their level of detail. Three passages from the *Yellow Emperor's Inner
Classic, Basic Questions* formed the textual basis for discussions of using pulse lore to ascertain pregnancy.[10] As a general principle, the classic explained, one could know that a woman was pregnant if "she suffers from bodily ailments, yet her pulse shows no sign of heteropathy."[11]
Later commentaries explained that such "illnesses" included signs such
as nausea and cessation of menses, which would be accompanied by a
pathological pulse if caused by illness rather than pregnancy. Elsewhere,

the *Basic Questions* noted that the specific interplay of yin and yang and Blood and qi that was required for human reproduction would produce a characteristic pulse pattern in pregnant women. Described as "striking yin and salient yang" *(yin bo yang bie)*, this was a pulse that dashed against the doctor's fingers, particularly at the *chi* point.[12] Finally, two organs played leading roles in nourishing the fetus: the heart (which governed Blood) and kidney (which governed essence). The pregnant woman's pulse would therefore reveal hyperactivity in the meridians that passed through these organs.[13] Later writers, most notably Chao Yuan-fang (fl. 605–16) and Chen Ziming (ca. 1190–1270), elaborated on these early, terse accounts. Chao explained that a different maternal meridian was responsible for nourishing the fetus during each of its ten months of gestation and suggested that these would produce distinct pulse patterns at each stage of pregnancy.[14] Chen Ziming's discussion of pregnancy pulses incorporated a set of mnemonic verses designed to help doctors remember all the key variations.[15] These passages were frequently cited by later writers and constituted the core of a rich pulse lore that in principle allowed one to determine how long a woman had been pregnant, the sex and number of her fetuses, and whether the unborn child(ren) was in danger of miscarriage or would come to term.

Whereas pulse lore was the domain of trained practitioners, other methods relied entirely on the woman's own perceptions. Learned and vernacular medical works alike included herbal formulas that would provoke a reaction in a pregnant woman but none in a woman who was not pregnant. A well-known method was to take a potion of ground, raw Sichuanese lovage root *(chuanxiong)* mixed into a thick broth made from stewed mugwort leaves *(ai)*. This formula was to be administered to a woman whose menses had stopped for three months. If the woman felt a "slight movement" in her belly after ingesting it, then she was pregnant. The origins of this formula are undetermined, but during the Song dynasty Chen Ziming incorporated it into the literate corpus. Thereafter the formula appeared regularly in the prescription books and *fuke* literature of the Yuan, Ming, and Qing dynasties, often as the only drug-based test that was mentioned.[16] During the Ming, authors such as Wang Kentang (1549–1613) and Wu Zhiwang (d. 1629) added a few more formulas to the repertoire. These included a combination of Shaanxi lovage *(quenao xiong)* with angelica *(danggui)* that would cause fetal motion in a pregnant woman but had the added benefit of clearing away obstruction in a woman who was simply suffering from stagnation.[17] A less gentle method was one that included honey locust fruit *(zaojiao)* and would induce vomiting if the woman were carrying a child.[18] If these tests were inconclusive, one could also employ a decoction of mugwort leaves that would provoke stomach pains in pregnant women.[19]

Doctors recognized, however, that these tests could prove inconclusive or misleading. Wang Kentang, for example, had noted that pulse readings allowed one to correctly assess the woman's condition in "eight or nine times out of ten."[20] This may be read as an optimistic affirmation of the high level of accuracy of pulse lore, but it also acknowledged that this diagnostic method was routinely inconclusive. One reason was that different women had different constitutions, and these innate variations meant that the most common symptoms of pregnancy did not manifest themselves equally in all individuals. Thus Yan Chunxi noted that "women who are pregnant will inevitably suffer from morning sickness after the first forty days have passed."[21] Yet alongside this confident pronouncement, he also recommended using drugs and pulse lore to ascertain pregnancy in a woman who had *not* developed morning sickness.[22] The first trimester of a suspected pregnancy, in particular, was notoriously difficult to diagnose, and medical texts counseled that drug-based tests were useful only after the woman's menses had stopped for three months.[23] False positives were also possible: Wu Zhiwang noted that the honey locust formula would induce vomiting in women with weak stomachs even if they were not pregnant.[24] The difficulty of diagnosis could also extend through the midpoint of the suspected pregnancy. The *Golden Mirror,* for example, explained how to distinguish between pregnancy and illness in a woman whose menses had already stopped for five months. The editors recommended checking the woman's breasts for signs. "If the breasts are large, protuberant, and contain milk, then she is pregnant," they explained. If not, then the woman was suffering from some ailment.[25]

The ambiguity of signs meant that even for trained and highly experienced doctors, the certainty of a diagnosis of pregnancy was only relative, not absolute. Such ambiguity was entirely typical of all societies prior to the advent of modern chemical pregnancy tests—and especially ultrasound—in the twentieth century.[26] Today, we are so accustomed to visualizing and monitoring fetal development before birth that the fetus has acquired an identity independent of the mother, constituting a distinct social actor with presumed rights and privileges. Some expectant parents even distribute high-quality, ultrasound portraits of their fetuses to friends and family.[27] In the annals of human history, however, this casual knowledge of the unborn is anomalous. Barbara Duden has shown, for example, that in eighteenth-century Germany, pregnancy could not be objectively confirmed during gestation. This does not gainsay the fact that doctors and women routinely made reasoned judgments about pregnancy based on educated interpretation of well-known bodily signs. However, it was only after the unseen entity emerged from inside the woman's body that they knew for certain whether her symptoms had indeed been caused by a growing baby or by some other "fruit of the womb."[28] In other words, Duden points out, pregnancy could be confirmed only "in retrospect," when the invisible being inside the mother at last became visible. What Duden terms the lack of "security in the knowledge of pregnancy" persisted despite the achievements of Renaissance anatomists and their successors, for while Western scholars amassed a wealth of knowledge about the body's structure, full knowledge of its most basic functions— including reproduction—remained tantalizingly elusive.[29] As one nineteenth-century British obstetrics textbook wryly remarked, "The most certain mode of knowing whether a woman is in a state of gestation or not is by waiting until the term of nine months is complete."[30]

It is hardly surprising, therefore, that Chinese doctors of this time also had to carefully negotiate a range of possibilities when treating women who might or might not be pregnant. The contingent nature of any diagnosis of pregnancy is exemplified by the narrative below, drawn from a nineteenth-century compendium of cases apocryphally attributed to the famous physician Xu Dachun (1693–1771):

> A woman aged twenty-seven years. Her menses had not flowed for three months. Some suspected blocked menses, and I was asked to take her pulse [diagnose her condition]. Her pulse was rapid, dashing yet harmonious, and the pulse at the *chi* point was slippery and urgent. I said, "This is not a case of trifling illness; this is a pregnancy." I directed her to take Lovage-Angelica Decoction, and there was a slight movement in her belly, which indicated that a fetus was present. As it turns out, after several months had passed, she indeed gave birth to a son.[31]

Taken at face value, this story describes a skillful expert whose informed judgment prevailed over the claims of less-informed people. At a deeper level, however, it also underscores the limits of the physician's knowledge. In this case, the doctor used not one but two pregnancy tests. He first took his own reading of the woman's pulse and found that it matched the classical "pulse of pregnancy": slippery, rapid, dashing against the doctor's fingers, and without any signs of bodily disharmony. He also double-checked his pulse reading by administering drugs to test for the presence of a fetus. This added the woman's own sensations to his trained observations and increased his confidence in his diagnosis of pregnancy. Nevertheless, the narrator still found it necessary to conclude his narrative by informing the reader that the woman did ultimately give birth to a boy. In the mind of the reader and the doctor, therefore, the birth of the child was the final—and indispensable—piece of evidence that the original diagnosis of pregnancy had been correct.

True Pregnancy and Its Imposters

The challenge of correctly determining pregnancy was further compli-cated by the fact that many ailments could mimic pregnancy. Partic-ularly troublesome was that the most obvious signs of pregnancy—cessation of menses and a swelling abdomen—could equally well indicate a pathological stagnation of Blood. This notably included "blocked-up menses" *(jingbi)*, where the woman simply did not menstruate. But over-lapping with menstrual dysfunction was a wide variety of other types of Blood or qi stagnation that could produce abdominal masses and im-peded menstrual flow.[32] There were three forms in particular that doc-tors warned were most often confused with pregnancy: intestinal spread-ing *(changtan)*, stony accumulation *(shijia)*, and ghost fetus *(guitai)*.[33] Modern medicine would equate these with ovarian growths and molar pregnancies. Late imperial medical writers, however, explained them as the result of depletion and external invasion. Intestinal spreading and stony accumulation were first discussed in *The Yellow Emperor's Inner Classic, Divine Pivot (Lingshu jing)*, which explained that these arose when heteropathic influences entered the woman's body.[34] Intestinal spreading was caused by cold qi lodging in the abdomen outside the in-testines, restraining defensive qi and causing it to stagnate. This stagnated qi then produced a fleshy lump that grew larger by the day. Stony accu-mulation, by contrast, arose when cold qi lodged in the mouth of the womb. Besides obstructing the flow of qi, this prevented Blood from leav-ing the womb. As a result, waste Blood accumulated inside the womb, creating an abdominal mass that also grew larger with time. Ghost fe-tus, which first appeared in the medical literature in the seventh century, was historically attributed to demonic invasion. If a woman's vitalities were too weak to ward off external heteropathy, then malevolent spirits *(gui)* could invade her body and deposit their essence within her womb. Outwardly, one would see the woman's menses stop and her belly swell, while inwardly her womb would be nurturing loathsome creatures and noxious accumulations, products of the ghostly seed.

Although earlier explanations of these types of false pregnancy focused on the problem of external invasion, it became common by the late imperial period to define them as arising from internally generated disharmonies within the female body. During the Ming, for example, doctors started to portray ghost fetus as a form of internal accumulation caused by immoderate female lust or brooding.[35] Barbara Duden has noted that, in eighteenth-century Germany, views of false pregnancy—mola, mooncalves, and other weird fruits—were characterized by a belief in the "polymorphous potency" of the womb.[36] By contrast, the late imperial Chinese discourse of false pregnancy increasingly focused on the myriad potentialities of Blood, which could coalesce into humans as well as monsters or inanimate lumps. These associations between false pregnancy and wayward Blood became especially strong beginning in the eighteenth century, when a variety of medical works described intestinal spreading, stony accumulation, and ghost fetus as rooted in menstrual disorder. The *Golden Mirror,* for example, classified stony accumulation as a form of "stopped menses due to stagnant Blood."[37] And while the ancient classics spoke simply of stagnation located in the woman's abdomen or womb, Qing popular medical texts also described intestinal spreading and stony accumulation as illnesses of the menstrual period itself, arising when cold qi entered the body during or after menstruation.[38]

While false pregnancies might be mistaken for true ones, the opposite problem could also arise, and the medical case literature included many examples of pregnancy being diagnosed as something else. Zhang Congzheng (ca. 1156–1228), for instance, reported the case of a forty-year-old woman who was actually pregnant, but who believed that her discomforts were simply due to aging.[39] Ming and Qing medical texts likewise reported cases in which a true pregnancy was misdiagnosed as consumption *(lao).*[40] Finally, beyond the problem of distinguishing between pregnancy and illness, there was an additional challenge rooted in the very dynamics of reproduction itself: even in cases of true pregnancy, the fetus could become corrupted, die within the womb, or suffer from arrested development. Classical explanations of fetal development taught that, once conception had taken place, two additional conditions had to be met for the fetus to develop properly: (1) both paternal and maternal vitalities had to be sufficiently vigorous so that the commingled Blood and essence could accomplish its transformation into a fetus, and (2) maternal vitalities had to flow smoothly in sufficient quantities to nourish the "fetal qi" that governed the unborn child's development. As we saw in chapter 3, for example, doctors had long worried that deficient uterine qi would prevent proper fetal development following

conception. The problem of verifying pregnancy thus extended well beyond the initial challenge of determining whether a woman had conceived, for it also required one to ascertain whether the fetus was still viable at any given stage of a suspected pregnancy. A well-known ailment
that embodied this problem was "the fetus does not grow" *(tai bu zhang)*.
Early discussions linked it primarily to the danger of miscarriage, and
this association continued to appear in texts throughout the late imperial period.[41] Beginning in the Ming, however, writers also increasingly
associated arrested fetal development with unusually long pregnancies.
As a result, the challenges of managing pregnancy were also complicated
by the variable length of gestation itself.

Ten Months or More?

Chinese doctors had long agreed that the usual human gestation period
was ten months, but from at least the seventh century they also taught
that true pregnancies could last substantially longer.[42] A standard reference was Yang Zijian (fl. eleventh century), whose treatise on the "ten
kinds of childbirth" stated that some women went into labor at seven,
eight, or nine months, while others had pregnancies that could go as long
as four or five years before the child was born.[43] Such beliefs were by no
means unique to China. Lindsay Wilson, for example, has analyzed a
number of paternity-dispute cases from Enlightenment France in which
doctors and jurists argued that extraordinarily long pregnancies were indeed possible, and that a child born long after a man's death could still
be considered his legitimate heir.[44] Sharia law likewise acknowledges the
concept of a "sleeping embryo" whose gestation can take up to five years
to complete.[45] To be sure, the historical lack of reliable pregnancy tests
helped create an ambiguous temporal space that allowed great flexibility in the recognized length of a given woman's pregnancy. As Laura
Gowing has shown for seventeenth-century England, the unreliability of
pregnancy tests meant that there was no social convention of women seeking medical confirmation of pregnancy, and therefore no moment at which
a woman would be expected to announce her pregnancy.[46] But perception is only part of the story. In the case of China, we see that the explanatory frameworks of classical medicine defined pregnancy in such a
way that allowed delayed birth to be one among several possible outcomes.

Late imperial Chinese doctors understood unusually long pregnancies
and premature births as two sides of the same coin, both being possible

manifestations of deficient or unruly maternal Blood and qi. As Yu Tuan (1438–ca. 1517) explained, pregnant women could experience ailments or injuries that were not severe enough to cause miscarriage yet still depleted Blood and qi enough to inhibit fetal development. The precipitating conditions included "exuberant fetus" *(shengtai)*, in which a woman continued to menstruate despite being pregnant, and "leaking fetus" *(loutai)*, in which a woman experienced copious bleeding halfway through gestation as a result of some shock to her controller vessel *(renmai)*. Yu reported that he had seen cases of pregnancy lasting anywhere from twelve to twenty-five months as a result of such illnesses. Long pregnancies were quite common, he averred, and therefore "those studying [medicine] must not be ignorant of this."[47] Zhang Jiebin later integrated the problem of extralong pregnancies into an etiological framework centered on internal disharmony. The fundamental cause of arrested fetal growth, he said, was deficiency of qi and Blood, and this could arise in many ways.[48] Disorders of spleen and stomach could interfere with the mother's ability to take nourishment, resulting in vacuity in the thoroughfare and controller vessels. Pent-up anger could also cause contrary flow of liver qi, impairing the liver's ability to regulate Blood and thus depriving the fetus of nourishment. Likewise, illnesses of cold or heat could inhibit fetal growth by consuming or weakening Blood and qi. Ultimately, Zhang implied that almost any malady that provoked a significant maternal disharmony could lead to retarded fetal development. Faced with a "fetus that does not grow," the practitioner thus had to determine the cause of the root illness and then "replenish or stabilize, warm or clear away heat, simply adjusting the strategy to the illness." Once the root problem was rectified, the fetus would then grow on its own, being born on time in some cases and born late in others. The only instance in which no treatment was available was if a woman's Blood and qi were exhausted because of her advanced age. Whether such a pregnancy would be successfully accomplished, Zhang observed, "is up to Heaven, and not something that humans can influence through their will."[49]

To be sure, not all medical thinkers gave equal credence to this problem, and a notable skepticism appeared in Xiao Xun's *Canonical Teachings on Medicine for Women* (*Nüke jinglun*, 1684). Xiao argued that superlong pregnancies were so rare that doctors did not have to worry about them. "If we talk about two- or four-year pregnancies," Xiao stated, "these are extraordinary births and not common. Can they still be called 'pregnancies'?"[50] Such stories were unsubstantiated, he said, so "one may disregard them." But the belief that a true pregnancy could last for years continued to be a staple of the medical literature, and physicians continued to elaborate on the etiology of delayed births. Yan Chunxi, for example, pointed out that fetal growth could be impeded even when the mother's natural constitution was vigorous and flourishing.[51] Such cases, he posited, arose from weakness in the father's seminal essence. But whether the root of the problem lay in the maternal or paternal vitalities, Yan said, therapy should focus on increasing the mother's qi, specifically the spleen qi. He explained this strategy with reference to the five phases, the conceptual system that classical medicine combined with yin and yang to explain the dynamic interrelations between different bodily phenomena. The spleen was associated with the phase of earth, and Yan noted that all living things received their nourishment from the earth. Therefore, as a matter of general principle, "for the fetus to grow and flourish, everything relies on the mother's spleen-earth being able to circulate qi to the child."[52] Wang Shixiong (1808–68) also explained that leakage of Blood during pregnancy could result in pregnancies lasting as long as "thirty or forty months," and he testified that he personally knew of a family in which three children had all been born after pregnancies lasting one or two years.[53]

Such explanations were all the more compelling because they were reinforced by observed reality. Chinese doctors had long taught that impaired fetal development could produce a "withered fetus" *(kutai)*, and their descriptions match what modern medicine calls fetus papyraceous (mummified fetus)—namely, a fetus that dies in utero without being expelled from the mother's body and becomes desiccated and flattened. Such dead fetuses may have been failed singletons or dead twins, and can be retained inside the womb until they are expelled with later, live births. Even with today's routine use of monitoring technology, such fetal deaths can escape medical attention, and cases of fetus papyraceous continue to be documented.[54] While it is impossible to know how often dried-out fetuses presented themselves in China, they were certainly a feature of the medical literature. Yan Chunxi, for example, cited the case of a woman who had produced a "withered and white fetus" after a thirteen-month pregnancy.[55] Wang Shixiong recounted a similar case involving a woman who had been pregnant for seventeen months before consulting a doctor. The doctor suspected that the fetus had died inside her and prescribed large doses of salvia root *(danshen)*, known for its ability to expel stagnations of Blood. After twenty days of treatment, she delivered a "dried-out" fetus.[56]

The reality of such anomalies resonated with explanatory frameworks of human reproduction, reinforcing the belief that corrupted or unusual pregnancies could readily result from malfunction of bodily organs or the impaired state of maternal qi and Blood. In such contexts, furthermore, cosmologically oriented explanatory frameworks articulated in terms of yin and yang were also reinforced by agricultural metaphors that explained human development in terms of the growth of plants.[57] As discussed earlier, classical medicine defined the human body as a microcosm of the universe, governed by the same forces of creation and maturation. In discussions of conception and pregnancy, this also manifested itself in metaphors likening the female body to a plant or the earth, and the child to her fruit. As Yan Chunxi explained, for example, "Land that is lean and scanty" could still "bear fruit" if properly irrigated, and similarly a woman with a weak constitution could still bear children if she were adequately fortified.[58] By the same token, it was possible that maternal vacuity could deprive the fetus of nourishment enough to stunt its development, but not enough to provoke miscarriage. Arrested fetuses, Yan explained, were exactly like a fruit that became "dried and withered on the branch." They could be corrected if treated early enough with medicines to increase Blood and qi. But "if one fails to irrigate and nourish it at an early stage, then the withering and parching will run their complete course, and there will be nothing that can be done."[59]

Thus, regardless of how unusual one considered long pregnancies to be, the perceived duration of gestation per se was not a conclusive sign as to whether a pregnancy was genuine. A case of "weird fetus" from Wei Zhixiu's case anthology underscores this point. Here the physician Qian Guobin (Ming dynasty) examined the wife of a farmworker who had been "pregnant" for eighteen months, during which her belly continually swelled. Qian palpated her pulse and found it to be "floating then deep, long then short, coming and going, starting and stopping, and was not the same at any point." In light of these pulse signs, he explained, "I knew that it was phlegm and not a fetus."[60] In other words, Qian's judgment that there was no fetus was based on the woman's pathological pulse, not on the extraordinary length of her supposed "pregnancy." Such beliefs were taken seriously outside medical circles as well. An 1803 legal handbook for government officials, for example, warned that it was possible for a chaste widow to give birth to her late husband's child even long after his death. The handbook cited the case of Ms. Ma, who gave birth four years after her husband died. Her father-in-law denounced her as an adulteress before the tribunal. Nevertheless, Ms. Ma ultimately convinced the court that the child was indeed her husband's progeny, and that its delayed development was simply the result of her emotional shock at her husband's death. In his analysis of the case, Matthew Sommer notes that "the widow's reputation for chastity [was] even enhanced" by the court's finding, since the prolonged pregnancy demonstrated the depth of the woman's feeling for her late husband.[61] The Qing dynasty literatus Zhou Lianggong recounted a similar case involving the widow of Zhu Peng, who claimed to be carrying her dead husband's child.[62] When she did not go into labor at the expected time, her husband's younger brother lodged a complaint against her at the departmental yamen, charging that she had deceived his family. Her mother-in-law, however, swore that the widow's pregnancy was genuine. Without any conclusive evidence of adultery, the prefect could only order the family to await the birth of the child before pursuing the case further. Ultimately, the widow gave birth to a son after a total of fifty-six months. Although the woman's neighbors were amazed by the child's tardy birth, none of them seem to have challenged the belief that a "pregnancy" could last for more than four and a half years.

Since unusually long pregnancies were within the realm of the possible, doctors had to tread carefully when treating women who were in the end stages of a suspected pregnancy. Another of Qian Guobin's cases anthologized by Wei Zhixiu suggests that doctors commonly erred on the side of assuming a woman was indeed pregnant, even if other signs inclined them to be skeptical. In this case, Qian Guobin examined a woman who had been pregnant for twenty months. Although Qian suspected that there was something abnormal about her condition, he still did not dare to use abortifacients. The case ultimately resolved itself when the woman passed a large quantity of gas, and the "fetus" subsequently dissipated on its own.[63] Judgments about long pregnancies were also colored by the recognition that an abnormally long "pregnancy" was a classic symptom of ghost fetus and other pseudopregnancies, noxious accumulations, and demonic infestations.[64] The possible conditions that mimicked long pregnancy notably included poisoning by *gu*, a demonic seed that malefactors concocted by distilling the essence of poisonous insects and other vermin. A person wishing to acquire another person's wealth or bring him misfortune and death could do so by placing *gu* poison in the victim's food or possessions.[65] Medical thinkers recognized many different manifestations of *gu* poisoning, some resembling demonic possession and others resembling infestation by worms. Since the array of possible symptoms associated with *gu* poisoning included abdominal swelling, *gu* was a possible explanation for an apparent pregnancy that did not resolve itself as expected. So, for example, during the fifty-six months that Zhu Peng's widow was with child, she was given medicines to expel *gu*. This treatment was ineffective, for the widow was genuinely pregnant. The converse situation appeared in a famous case by the doctor Zhou Hanqing (Ming dynasty). Zhou's patient, "the wife of a Mr. Ma" (Mashi fu), had been pregnant for fourteen months without giving birth. Zhou correctly diagnosed her as suffering from *gu* infestation and prescribed purgatives. The woman was cured after she voided "things resembling goldfish" from her body.[66]

SECURING THE FETUS

Late imperial writers envisioned pregnancy as a fluid and mutable process whose status could only be imperfectly monitored. As we shall see, the same factors that allowed for the possibility of long pregnancies also fostered a discourse where miscarriage was defined as an ever-present danger. Medical writers used several different terms to describe pregnancies where the fetus failed to complete its gestation. The most general term spoke of "sinking," "dropping," or "falling" fetuses *(duotai)*. Writers also spoke of "small births" *(xiaochan)* or "half-births" *(banchan)* in distinction to full-term births, which they called "great births" *(dachan)* or "correct births" *(zhengchan)*. In principle, such terms were supposed to distinguish between failed pregnancies according to how developed the fetus was at the time. In practice, however, they were often used interchangeably, and there was a continuum between what today would be called a miscarriage, a premature birth, and an intrauterine death. The *Imperial Encyclopedia,* for example, cited the teachings of the government official and medical expert Wang Lun *(jinshi* of 1484), who used the term *half-births* to refer to failed pregnancies in the third, fifth, and seventh month of gestation.[67] In some cases, dead fetuses would be retained within the mother, and discussions of miscarriage thus also explained how to tell if the fetus had truly died and needed to be expelled with drugs.

A woman's innate constitution *(bingfu),* endowed at conception, might predispose her to vacuity or other imbalance that made it difficult to sustain a pregnancy; likewise middle-aged women with declining vitalities would find it difficult to carry a child to term. But explanations of miscarriage almost always portrayed it as the result of human error, ignorance, or negligence, triggered by acquired illnesses or specific actions on the part of the woman or her family members: mistakes in diet and drink, bending or stretching the body in an awkward position, taking inappropriate medicines, overwork, injury from falling or being beaten or jostled, uncontrolled emotions, or excessive or overly vigorous sexual intercourse. Any of these could provoke an imbalance or deficiency in maternal vitalities and deprive the fetus of the nourishment it needed. The uterine environment could also be degraded by excesses of heat or cold (whether climatic or caused by medicines), which would blight the fetus just as inclement weather would blight a growing fruit. Finally, physical damage to the womb or other uterine inadequacy would weaken it or cause it to open, thus allowing the child to drop out. Once a miscarriage occurred, furthermore, the woman would be prone to miscarriage in subsequent pregnancies.

Beyond the disappointment of a failed pregnancy, miscarriage could seriously harm a woman's health or even lead to her death, and throughout the literate medical corpus, writers warned that "miscarriage is a more serious matter than full-term birth" *(xiaochan zhong yu dachan)*. To illustrate this point, they routinely evoked the image of a tree whose fruit had been broken from its branches. Wei Yilin's 1337 text, *Efficacious Prescriptions from a Hereditary Medical Family (Shiyi dexiao fang)* provides a particularly graphic example of this well-known agricultural metaphor of miscarriage: "The ailment of half-birth is not like proper birth. Proper birth resembles the behavior of the ripe chestnut in the fruit world. Its husk opens on its own, and neither [tree nor fruit] is harmed. But half-birth can be compared to hacking off a green chestnut, breaking its husk into little bits, and damaging its membranes in order to extract the kernel."[68] Indeed, the violence done to the green chestnut had a physical counterpart in the woman's body. As Wei Yilin explained, the fetus fell out because "the woman's fetal organ is injured and the bindings of her womb are severed" *(taizang shang sun, baoxi duan qu)*.[69] In his 1684 compendium of essential teachings on women's medicine, Xiao Xun quoted a similar description from the official and medical educator Wang Haogu (thirteenth century), who further recommended that women who suffered miscarriages should be given medicines to regrow "skin and flesh" *(jirou)*.[70]

In sum, doctors took the prevention of miscarriage very seriously, for it affected both the viability of the immediate pregnancy and the woman's continued health. Since miscarriage was almost always the result of human action, furthermore, the converse was also true: that people could actively prevent miscarriage through proper prophylaxis. This belief underlay the concept of *antai,* "securing the fetus," a central pillar in Chinese medical approaches to managing pregnancy. The basic meaning of *an* is "quiet, tranquil, peaceful," and thus also "to make something quiet, tranquil, or peaceful." Related to this is a set of meanings that invoke the idea of making something "fixed" or "secure" or "safe."[71] The term *antai* notably appears in the name of pharmaceutical formulas used during pregnancy, and it is also used as a verb phrase to explain the effect of medicines in general, as in "use this formula and the fetus [tai] will be secure [an]." A close synonym for *antai* was *gutai,* where the verb *gu* referred to making the fetus "firm," "stable," and thus not easily miscarried. In translating *antai* as "securing the fetus," I thus eschew an earlier interpretation which claimed that *antai* aimed to "tranquilize" or "sedate" the fetus.[72] This previous interpretation owed much to the observation that *antai* medicines were used to treat an ailment of pregnancy called *taidong,* literally "the fetus moves." As I show in the next section, however, Chinese doctors did not consider fetal movement per se to be pathological. Instead, when read in proper context, it is clear that *taidong* is best understood as "fetal displacement," focused on an ensemble of specific symptoms—abdominal pain, bleeding—that were widely recognized precursors to impending miscarriage or early labor. Thus *antai* was not about eliminating fetal movement, but rather about "securing" the fetus to prevent it from being ripped off the maternal branch.

Fetal Movement and Fetal Displacement

Learned and popular texts alike depicted fetal movement as a normal and expected part of gestation that could even be used to discern the fetus's sex. Male fetuses were yang, female fetuses were yin, and this determined their position in the womb as well as the location and timing of their movements. Zhang Jiebin, for example, pointed out that boys began moving earlier than girls:

> Fetuses are divided into male and female, and thus their development can be tardy or quick. The body has yin and yang, and thus the fetus is carried in the womb facing toward or away from [the mother]. If it is male, then it moves at three months, because the nature of yang is to be early. If it is a female, then it moves at five months, because the nature of yin is to be tardy. A female fetus is carried with its back toward the mother, therefore the mother's belly feels soft. The male fetus is carried with its face toward the mother, therefore the mother's belly feels hard.[73]

The nineteenth-century handbook *A Secret Book of Childbearing* (*Taichan mishu*), attributed to the Qian family of Shaoxing, made similar points in its discussion of the fetus's development in each month of gestation, noting that the baby's sex determined how it would move at given points in the pregnancy: "In the seventh month, it moves its right hand (if it is a boy, then it moves on the mother's left, and if it is a girl it moves on the mother's right). In the eighth month, it moves its left hand (if it is a boy, then it moves on the mother's right, and if it is a girl, then it moves on the mother's left). In the ninth month, it turns its body three times. In the tenth month, it reaches completion."[74]

Not only was fetal movement normal and expected, but also the absence of fetal movement was considered positively pathological, indicative of arrested fetal development or even fetal death. Wei Yilin, for example, warned that if fetal qi was not properly stabilized and nourished, this could lead to "withered and parched" *(wei zao)* fetuses that did not grow properly. Even after ten months of pregnancy, the child would lack the strength "to turn and move."[75] The eighteenth-century physician Shen Yaofeng likewise provided advice on what to do if "the fetus is sick and does not move *(tai bing bu dong)*": "If you wish to know whether [the fetus] is alive or dead, have someone feel [the woman's belly]. If it resembles an overturned basin, then the fetus is a boy. If it there are irregular protrusions from the elbow and neck, it is a girl. If it is cold, then it is dead. If it is warm, then it is alive."[76] In his annotations to Shen Yaofeng's book, Wang Shixiong also appended the case of a woman who was delivered of a dead and withered fetus after a seventeen-month gestation.[77] The woman reported that all fetal movement had ceased after the fifth month and Wang estimated that the fetus's death had probably occurred at about this time.

These examples show that the illness term *taidong* was not a literal description of fetal motion in general, but instead referred to the perception that the fetus was about to be dislodged or expelled from the woman's body before the proper time had come. Thus doctors could worry about *taidong* as early as the second or third month of pregnancy, well before any actual fetal movement would have been discernable.[78] "Fetal displacement" best embodies this Chinese medical understanding of *taidong*, conveying the sense that some factor external to the fetus has provoked fetal distress that is severe enough to provoke miscarriage or otherwise threaten the viability of the pregnancy. In this context we can understand why writers could counsel the use of "fetus-securing" *(antai)* medicines from the very beginning of a suspected pregnancy as a way of ensuring its successful completion. During the first three months the pregnancy was especially vulnerable, doctors taught, for the form of the child had not yet stabilized, and it was still highly malleable. One standard description of fetal development, dating from at least the eleventh century, likened the one-month fetus to a bead of dew and the two-month fetus to a peach blossom, implicitly underscoring the evanescent nature of the early conceptus.[79] As the editors of the *Imperial Encyclopedia* warned, "When the fetus has first congealed, it disperses easily," and they thus advised against using pinellia rhizome *(banxia)* in remedies for morning sickness because "its properties are fetus-displacing *[dong tai]*."[80]

Besides a general sensation that the fetus might "drop," the symptoms that commonly accompanied fetal displacement included acute and unremitting abdominal pain, continual bleeding from the vagina, fever, headache, vomiting, and dizziness.[81] Fetal displacement was also routinely described as arising from the woman's own unhealthy behavior or from some injury to the woman—such as an injury sustained by falling from a high place or by being hit and beaten.[82] To properly manage the situation, furthermore, doctors needed to distinguish between different forms of threatened miscarriage. The *Golden Mirror* of 1742, for example, provided this advice on how to distinguish between "fetal displacement" and another malady of pregnancy, "fetal leaking": "Fetal displacement *[taidong]* and fetal leaking *[tailou]* both involve downward bleeding [from the vagina]. But in fetal displacement there are abdominal pains, and in fetal leaking there are no abdominal pains. Therefore, for fetal displacement it is proper to promote qi circulation, and for fetal leaking it is proper to clear away heat."[83]

Because Chinese doctors saw miscarriage and premature birth as two points on a continuum, the threat of fetal displacement and the need to secure the fetus could continue throughout a pregnancy. Wang Lun repeated common wisdom when he pointed out that women who miscarried *(duo)* once would tend to miscarry again in subsequent pregnancies. To prevent such recurrences, Wang Lun advised the use of medicines to "nourish qi and Blood and secure the fetus's primordial qi *[gu taiyuan]*" at key junctures throughout the pregnancy:

> After two and a half months [of pregnancy], use ten-and-some doses of medicine to secure the fetus, so as to prevent miscarriage from occurring in the third month. After four and a half months [of pregnancy], again administer eight to nine doses to prevent miscarriage and allow her to pass through the fifth month. Then use medicine again at six and a half months to prevent miscarriage in the seventh month. Then when she

reaches the ninth month, administer ten-and-some doses of Zhu Danxi's
Easy Birth Powder [dasheng san], and this will preserve her without
worry.[84]

Treating the Mother, Treating the Child

Beyond its therapeutic meaning of "securing the fetus" in cases of threatened miscarriage, antai was also used in a much broader sense, as shorthand for ensuring maternal and fetal health during pregnancy. Pan Wei,
for example, used the term antai in place of the more common term taiqian (literally, "before the fetus") as a chapter heading for the section on
pregnancy in his 1877 work, Essential Outline of Medicine for Women.[85]
Similarly, A Secret Book of Childbearing opened its section on pregnancy
by reminding its readers what steps were necessary to "replenish the
mother and secure the fetus."[86] Such usage reflected the prevailing belief
that protecting the mother's health and preventing miscarriage were inseparable issues. Not only did maternal imbalance cause fetal distress,
but also injury or illness in the fetus could be transmitted to the mother.
Particularly worrisome were cases of excessive or apparently pathological fetal movement: besides being a sign of some disharmony, fetal hyperactivity could distress the mother. Successful management of pregnancy required one to determine correctly if a particular case of maternal
illness originated with the woman or with the fetus. The Golden Mirror set forth conventional wisdom when it distinguished between fetal-
securing strategies that targeted the fetus and those that targeted the
mother:

> The principle of securing the fetus [antai] involves two methods. It is im-
> portant to distinguish carefully whether it is the mother who is sick or the
> fetus who is sick, then carry out the treatment. Whenever it is because the
> mother's illness results in fetal displacement, merely treat the mother. When
> the mother is secure, then the fetus will be secure of its own accord. If it is
> because the fetus is sick, and there is jostling around [chudong] that causes
> the mother to fall ill, then it is proper merely to secure the fetus. When the
> fetus is secure then the mother will recover on her own.[87]

But although there was a heuristic distinction between illnesses that
originated in the fetus and those that originated in the mother, doctors
placed the primary emphasis on the state of the mother. In practical terms,
this was undoubtedly because it was possible to directly observe the
mother's condition, while the state of the fetus was hidden from view. In
etiological terms, however, medical writers also taught that all illnesses

of the fetus could ultimately be traced to maternal imbalances, whether arising because of her natural constitution, illness predating pregnancy, or behavior during pregnancy. In some cases, maternal imbalances went undetected until the fetus became ill. In others, there was some direct injury to the fetus or fetal wrapper, such as that caused by sexual intercourse during pregnancy.[88] Although such actions might not originally harm the mother, the resultant fetal pathology would make her ill. In short, the paired concepts of "fetal displacement" and "securing the fetus" provided a kind of shorthand for identifying and treating a wide variety of linked maternal and fetal ailments and imbalances. In this context we can fully appreciate the medicalization of pregnancy, manifested in the dozens of ailments that medical writers identified as requiring intervention. Besides advocating a careful preventative regimen, doctors believed that an impending miscarriage or preterm birth could be halted with timely pharmaceutical intervention.

But which medicines were most appropriate? Returning to the case of Chen Nianzu's wife, Ms. Huang, we find a disagreement between those who would use cooling medicines and those who would use heating ones. The differences in these perspectives arose not only from different views of the human body but also from different views of the reproductive functions of women and the extent to which they differed from men. As doctors tried to discern which strategies were the most useful, they drew, to differing extents, on metaphors of yin-yang and agricultural production.

A Killing Frost

Chinese philosophy taught that women were yin, the principle associated with the cosmic realm of Earth and the nurturing powers of the terrestrial sphere. Men were yang, associated with Heaven and the initiation of life. The association of woman with Earth was thus an integral pattern of the cosmos. Medical discussions of fertility and pregnancy underscore the fact that this rhetorical equation of women with Earth was much more than an explanatory analogy, for they portrayed conception and childbirth as the human version of agricultural production. Such perspectives notably shape Sun Yikui's discussion of promoting fertility. Here Sun describes female reproductive essence (that is, Blood) as the soil that would receive and transform male seed. "There are four aspects to the way of planting sons [zhongzi]," Sun explained. "The first is called 'selecting the ground.' The second is called 'nourishing the seed.' The third is called 'taking advantage of the season.' The fourth is called 'casting

into the vacuity.' What does this mean? The ground is the mother's
essence. The seed is the father's essence. The season is the time when the
two essences meet through sexual congress. Vacuity means the beginning
of the time when the old is eliminated and the new is being generated."[89]

Another standard reference that equated female fertility and that of
the earth was Wan Quan's advice that regulating menses was the key to
successful childbearing. Unless a woman's menses were properly regulated, Wan Quan warned, she would be infertile, and having intercourse
with such a woman was "vainly using force [to cultivate] useless soil."[90]
As we saw in chapter 3, furthermore, medical texts frequently described
the womb as a field or ecosystem whose state would either nurture life
or kill it. Of primary importance was water, for the womb needed adequate irrigation if the seed was to grow. This concern with water also
emphasized the role of the kidney. As the organ both associated with the
phase of water and defined as the source of reproductive essence, the
kidney was an important irrigator of the womb. Thus, Chen Shiduo explained, "weak kidney water" would cause early termination of pregnancy just as drought would kill crops: "In cases of weak kidney water,
the child palace is parched and dried up. When grain sprouts lack mois-
ture from rain and dew, they similarly become withered and yellow. Thus
one will inevitably mourn a miscarriage."[91]

Chen Xinlan, the grandson of physician Chen Nianzu, used similar
logic to explain the efficacy of "Pills for Responsive Intercourse, with
added ingredients" (jiawei jiaogan wan), a fertility formula. In an annotation to his grandfather's text on women's medicine, Chen Xinlan
noted that this remedy's primary ingredients would ensure the proper
balance between water (kidney) and earth (spleen) in the female body:
"When water and earth are regulated with respect to one another, then
the grasses and trees are generated. When the spleen [associated with the
phase of earth] and kidney [associated with the phase of water] are harmonized with respect to one another, then the fetal qi forms. The ingredient dodder seed [tusizi] can make complete the qi of water and earth,
therefore we select it as the sovereign drug [jun]. Angelica can irrigate
the womb when it is dry and parched, and therefore we select it as the
emissary drug [shi]."[92]

Chen Xinlan's rich description is notable for its synthesis of five phase
doctrine with agricultural and political metaphors that depict the water-
ing of the womb as an act of governance. A woman's spleen and kidney
must be regulated because they are her body's earth and water, and their
condition will determine her ability to conceive. The "emissary" drug an-

gelica serves as the agent of the sovereign drug dodder seed, dispatched to the womb to assist in regulating water and earth. Chen's description of female earth and water thus portrayed them as having an actual material referent in the woman's body. This materiality of female bodily earth was also consistent with other well-known descriptions, such as Chen Shiduo's warning about the problems of too much water in the womb. Chen Shiduo's description in 1687, later also anthologized in the *Imperial Encyclopedia,* pointed out that stagnation in the bladder could cause dampness to seep into the womb and prevent conception. So even if the man were able to deposit his seed, Chen said, "dampness arises from the [woman's] bladder, and there is inevitably the worry of flooding."[93]

Besides ensuring the fertility of the soil and appropriate irrigation levels, one also needed to promote a temperate climate. But how did one know if the temperature of any given womb was indeed too hot or too cold? This was the problem that Chen Nianzu addressed in the story of his wife's repeated miscarriages, and his discussion shows how different explanatory frameworks could be used to support opposing therapeutic approaches. Specifically, Chen's narrative reveals an important tension between agricultural metaphors of human reproduction and explanations articulated in terms of the body's yin and yang vitalities. To be sure, the metaphorical association of women with Earth was itself a outgrowth of yin-yang thinking. However, the language of agriculture also privileged certain yin-yang interpretations over others. The case of Chen Nianzu's wife shows that agricultural metaphors reinforced those medical explanations that focused on cold as the root cause of infertility and miscarriage. Germination and growth occurred in the warm seasons, and a frost would kill the fruit. As with fruit, so with fetuses, and Chen Shiduo pointed out that "the channel of the fetal wrapper *[baotai zhi mai]* is where things are received. If it is warm, then it produces things, and if it is cold then it kills things."[94] Such statements contributed to the long-standing belief (discussed in chapter 3) that coldness in the womb was a main cause of disease and childlessness. The rhetoric of agricultural production thus supported the use of warming formulas to facilitate conception and preserve pregnancy.[95]

The climato-agricultural metaphor of human gestation was quite old, and during the fourteenth century Zhu Zhenheng tried to refute it with his innovative doctrine of yin and yang. Some people, he noted, favored warming remedies to promote fertility, based on the assumption that "the qi of spring is warm and harmonious, and the myriad things erupt into life. The winter qi is cold and bleak, and the myriad things die away."[96]

But Zhu charged that such people were ignorant, failing to recognize the fundamental dynamics of illness and health. For Zhu Zhenheng, it was obvious that yang tended to be excessive while yin tended to be deficient. This imbalance was the inevitable result of human activity, which simultaneously arose from and stimulated ministerial fire. The exuberance of fire not only tilted the body's balance toward yang but also potentially consumed yin. In this situation, the use of warming and heating drugs would only exacerbate existing imbalances. As for miscarriage, Zhu explained that most cases were caused by excessive internal fire coupled with depletion. "Heat and fire consume things," he explained. "This is the self-so way of creation and transformation [zaohua ziran]." So claiming, he specifically criticized the seventh-century teachings of Chao Yuanfang, who had maintained that "the fetus falls because wind cold damages the child organ." To hold to such explanations, Zhu claimed, "is to fail to grasp the nature of the illness."[97] The appropriate way to secure the fetus, he affirmed, was to use cooling drugs. To illustrate this point, he recounted the case of "Master Jia's wife" (Jiashi fu), who had repeatedly miscarried because of depletion of Blood, the yin form of bodily qi:

> Whenever she got pregnant, she would inevitably miscarry around the third month. I read her pulse and found that the left hand pulse was large but without strength, and when I palpated deeply it was rough. Thus I knew she was lacking in Blood. Because she was a young woman, it was just necessary to replenish her center qi, and this would allow her Blood to flourish of its own accord. At the time it was the beginning of summer, so I instructed her to make a concentrated decoction of atractylodes [baizhu] and use it to wash down a qian worth of scutellaria powder [huangqin]. She took some thirty to forty doses and, subsequently, was completely secure and gave birth.[98]

Zhu Zhenheng was prominent among the medical masters of the Jin and Yuan dynasties whose teachings inspired numerous doctrinal currents in Ming and Qing medicine. Throughout the late imperial period, furthermore, his dictum to cool during pregnancy remained highly influential.[99] Doctors regularly cited Zhu's saying that "during pregnancy one ought to clear away fire and replenish Blood," and the eighteenth-century physician Xu Dachun remarked on the widespread assumption that cooling drugs were the most appropriate treatment during pregnancy.[100] It was therefore not surprising that Chen Nianzu should initially use Zhu Zhenheng's cooling combination of atractylodes and scutellaria to try to prevent his wife's repeated miscarriages. When those remedies failed, however, Chen looked to agricultural metaphors for explanations. Human babies, like fruits, needed warmth to ripen, and the use of cooling drugs to bolster yin would only chill the bud.

CONCLUSION

We have seen that late imperial doctors assigned primary importance to human agency in the outcome of a pregnancy. While proper behavior would ensure the successful birth of a healthy child, a wide array of transgressions in maternal behavior, posture, diet, or mental state could bring a pregnancy to an abrupt end. Accordingly, medical books overflowed with advice and restrictions for the pregnant woman. Early analyses of these teachings discerned in them the heavy hand of Confucian patriarchy and suggested that doctors' desire to monitor and regulate pregnant female bodies was but another manifestation of men's desire to control women.[101] This view has since been mitigated by later scholarship demonstrating that men, as much as women, were exhorted to practice self-restraint, moderation, and cultivation of healthful habits.[102] Such injunctions, furthermore, were the medical expression of broader norms of self-discipline and regulation that permeated Chinese culture. Whether in the form of the scholar-official trying to cultivate humaneness *(ren),* the practitioner of esoteric arts seeking unity with the Dao, or the Buddhist adept striving to attain nirvana, the core Chinese philosophies taught that self-mastery was a supreme virtue. Restrictions on women's behavior, in short, were a general extension of broader social ideals of morality and order applicable to all people.

In this chapter I have also argued that the material conditions of late imperial China profoundly shaped the context in which people worried about maternal behavior. Patriarchy notwithstanding, male doctors were motivated by the practical challenges of pregnancy care: ensuring the health of the mother during a time when debilitating complications could arise, and ensuring the viability of the fetus when its true state could only be partially discerned. Framing these material issues was a multilayered repertoire of explanatory models, where agricultural metaphors of human reproduction alternated with the language of yin and yang. These could be used in complementary or contradictory ways, but the overall effect was to depict pregnancy as a routine yet highly precarious process. Not only could a woman's illness threaten the viability of her pregnancy, but also the premature termination of her pregnancy could threaten her future health. The desire to successfully negotiate these tensions between certainty and contingency, coupled with the high perceived cost of failure, profoundly shaped the male medical preoccupation with supervising the gestative body. But there was an additional, pressing concern beyond preventing a failed pregnancy. By the eighteenth century, promoting a woman's health during pregnancy had become an increasingly indispensable strategy for preventing difficult childbirth. A fruit that had properly matured, doctors taught, would fall easily and spontaneously from the stem.

CHAPTER 5

"Born Like a Lamb"

The Discourse of Cosmologically Resonant Childbirth

Zhang Baohua's wife had been in labor for three days, and still the baby would not come out.[1] Anyone who knew her medical history would have been filled with despair. In each of her previous pregnancies, Mrs. Zhang had gone into labor in the eighth month of pregnancy, suffering for several excruciating days until she finally delivered a baby who died within the week. Now again, she had gone into labor in her eighth month. She must have been attended by a highly regarded midwife, for she had married into a prominent family: her father-in-law was a *jinshi* degree holder who had served the former Ming dynasty as an imperial censor and as vice minister for the central agency that maintained state pasturages and horse-drawn vehicles.[2] But although the midwife declared that the child's head was "at the gate," it remained inside its mother.

At this point, the Zhang family made an urgent appeal to Ye Feng, a scholar of modest achievements who was also something of a medical expert. Zhang Baohua and Ye Feng were both natives of Huoshan County in Anhui Province, and they had undoubtedly become acquainted through local literati networks. Around 1707, Ye Feng had first learned of Mrs. Zhang's earlier difficulties, and he had told her husband to consult him the next time she was about to give birth. The following year, he responded to the family's summons. En route to their home, he met a carriage hastening to fetch Mrs. Zhang's parents so they could bid their daughter a deathbed farewell. But when Ye Feng arrived, he took her pulse and declared that the time for birth had not truly arrived. Immediately he ordered her to lie quietly, gave her medicines to stabilize the fetus, and forbade anyone to disturb her further. "The next morning," Ye recalled, "the master of the house came out, smiling without speaking." Upon questioning, Ye learned that the mother was well and the baby's head was no longer to be seen. Four months later, after a full twelve months of gestation, Mrs. Zhang was safely delivered of a son. In gratitude, the family declared that Ye Feng was the boy's "father."

Several years after these events, Ye Feng composed what was to become one of the most famous and widely circulating medical works of the late imperial period, the *Treatise on Easy Childbirth* (*Dasheng bian*, 1715). Writing under the pseudonym Lay Buddhist Jizhai (Jizhai jushi), Ye recounted the story of Zhang Baohua's wife to prove his main argument: that childbirth was an intrinsically easy *(yi)* process that became difficult only because of human ignorance and error. In her case, he explained, the earlier instances of "difficult childbirth" had actually all been cases of false labor where people had tried to extract the baby by force, and only Mrs. Zhang's youth and strong constitution had allowed her to survive. By contrast, her last labor was ultimately successful because it was allowed to follow its own rhythms. Based on his personal observations of this and numerous other cases, Ye Feng declared that the key to safe and successful delivery could be summed up in just a few words: "sleep, endure the pain, delay approaching the birthing tub." Put another way, the mother should conserve her stamina, avoid assuming the birthing posture until the very last minute, and avoid any special measures to facilitate or expedite birth. When the correct moment for birth had arrived, the child would leave its mother's body as easily as "a ripe melon drops from the stem" *(gua shu di luo)*. Active attempts to facilitate birth not only were unnecessary but also could cause fatal complications.

On a superficial level, Ye Feng's ideas resemble what twenty-first-century observers might call "natural childbirth," but to use this term would be misleading and anachronistic. Instead, Ye Feng's beliefs are best described as "cosmologically resonant childbirth," rooted in the belief that human birth was the mundane reiteration of an irresistible, cosmic dynamic: the unceasing generation of life. Just as the cosmos generated the "myriad things" *(wanwu)* spontaneously and easily, so too human birth was meant to be easy. The task for humans, therefore, was to understand the cosmic principles *(li)* that governed birth so that one could avoid interfering with them. Ye Feng saw himself as a medical reformer, and indeed no other writer before or after him advocated such a strongly noninterventionist approach. And yet, Ye Feng's views were also very

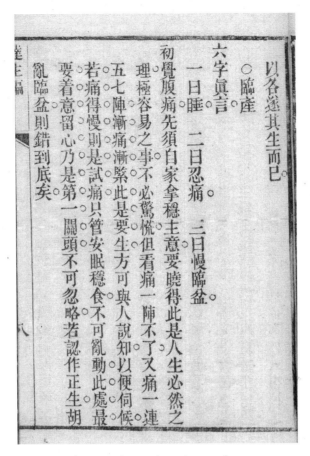

以各遂其生而已。

○臨產

六字眞言

一曰睡。二曰忍痛。三曰慢臨盆。

初覺腹痛先須自家拿穩主意要曉得此是人生必然之
理極容易之事。不必驚慌。但看痛一陣不了又痛一連
五七陣漸痛漸緊。此是要生方可與人說知。以便伺候。
若痛得慢則是試痛只管安眠穩食不可亂動此處最
要着意留心乃是第一關頭不可忽略若認作正生胡
亂臨盆則錯到底矣。

Figure 6. This page from a late-nineteenth-century
expanded edition of *Treatise on Easy Childbirth* presents its pithy, six-character slogan for ensuring safe
childbirth, instructing women to "sleep, endure the
pain, delay approaching the birthing tub." Jizhai jushi,
Zengguang Dasheng pian (Zhenjiang [Jiangsu]: Shanhua tang, 1888), in the personal collection of the
author.

much a product of his age. In chapter 2, we saw that the wide textual
dissemination of the *Treatise on Easy Childbirth* owed much to the dynamics of popular publishing and lay philanthropy. But the pursuit of
merit alone does not explain *Easy Childbirth*'s appeal, or why literate
male medical experts widely incorporated its teachings and cases into their
own pedagogical works. This chapter shows that the medical legitimacy

of *Easy Childbirth* owed much to the fact that it essentially crystallized a set of optimistic perspectives that had become increasingly salient in late imperial doctors' views of childbirth. In earlier chapters, we saw that the expansion of internally oriented, universalistic etiological frameworks over the course of the fourteenth to sixteenth centuries allowed doctors to reduce the significance of female bodily difference. These developments also nurtured a more benign view of childbirth. Eschewing harsh drugs and heroic manual interventions, medical writers increasingly argued that safe delivery was simply a matter of protecting the woman's vitalities so that the innate dynamics of birth could properly unfurl.

Easy Childbirth was simultaneously a product and a promoter of such reorientations. Ye Feng's doctrine of cosmologically resonant birth was based on ideas that had already been circulating in the literate medical corpus for centuries, albeit in diffuse form. But while earlier writers had seen easy birth as an exception, Ye argued that it was the norm. To understand how he constructed this view, it is necessary to examine the ways in which *Easy Childbirth* built on changing medical opinions in three key therapeutic areas: the use of birth-expediting medicines, management of fetal malpresentation, and assessment of whether a woman was truly in labor. By Ye Feng's lifetime, medical writers were promoting birth-expediting medicines that focused more on regulating maternal vitalities than on purging stagnation. Doctors also had increasing confidence that the child's position in the womb could be corrected by orally ingested drugs to boost qi and Blood, thus making fetal version (manipulation) unnecessary. Finally, a clear precedent had emerged for erring on the side of nonintervention when the signs of labor were ambiguous.

The currency of these ideas provided the raw material for *Easy Childbirth* while also creating a receptive intellectual environment that permitted its teachings to spread. During the late imperial period, therefore, the premise that easy birth was both attainable and normal became a salient reference point for medical thinkers as they articulated the challenges of preventing and managing complications of childbirth. Equally significant, the prevalence of this idea reinforced the gendered division of labor between male physicians and female midwives. Male doctors argued that their insights into the innate ease of childbirth made them superior to midwives, who believed that active intervention was required. This discursive link between practical obstetrics and inferior medical knowledge helped to turn male doctors' interest away from the actual management of childbirth and toward a broader concern with regulating female reproductive health.

DIMENSIONS OF COSMOLOGICALLY RESONANT BIRTH

The Judeo-Christian tradition depicts the travail of childbirth as Eve's punishment for original sin. Physical anthropologists explain the relative difficulty of human birth as the price that we pay for walking upright: the pelvic structure that evolved to support walking produced a birth canal that changes shape from top to bottom, compelling the baby to rotate first one way, then the other, as it leaves the mother's body. Indeed, some have postulated that the presumed inability of the human female to give birth without assistance may have spurred the very formation of human society.[3] Late imperial Chinese medical texts similarly echo these depictions of childbirth as a time of unavoidable suffering and danger. They discussed numerous complications of childbirth in graphic terms: protracted labors that lasted for several days, retained placentas, unborn children dying and rotting inside the mother's belly, all situations in which the mother's life could be lost in an instant. Alongside such descriptions, writers recommended a welter of ritual charms, geomantic and hemerological measures, and medicinal decoctions that could be used to protect the woman in childbirth and speed her labor, all of which suggested that childbirth was intrinsically polluting, dangerous, and prone to complication. Medical experts repeatedly emphasized that women and their families "absolutely must not panic" as childbirth approached, and they advised householders to resist the ministrations of midwives who would carry out all sorts of interventions. Such warnings bespeak a widespread and persistent perception that childbirth represented a kind of medical emergency that required meticulous oversight.

It was exactly these sorts of perceptions that Ye Feng sought to refute, and he rooted his arguments in the philosophical substrate of Chinese culture. "The great virtue of Heaven and Earth is called 'generating life' " *(tiandi zhi da de yue sheng)*, he pointed out, quoting a famous line from the "Great Commentary" *(Xici)* to the *Classic of Changes (Yijing)*, the canonical text that described all the possible transformations of yin and yang in the cosmos.[4] Here the word *virtue (de)* referred to the observable manifestation of being in accordance with the cosmic Way *(dao)*. To say that the "great virtue" of Heaven and Earth was "generating life" meant that creation and growth were the most basic expressions of the cosmos's essential nature. Therefore, Ye affirmed, it was wrong to suppose that birth was meant to be dangerous. Human childbirth was simply a reiteration of the cosmos's most fundamental dynamic, and like other forms of cosmic generation, it was also meant to be easy *(yi)*. Animals and plants did not need midwives, Ye Feng observed, so why should people? "In the generation of other things, there is never any case of difficulty. Therefore, the sprouts of grasses and trees come according to the season, the nestlings of the wild duck come out according to the day. And when was there ever an additional agent guiding them? These things came about as a result of their self-so nature *[ziran er ran]*, without needing any compulsion."[5]

Here it is important to emphasize that "easy birth" *(yi sheng, yi chan)* never meant painless childbirth—indeed, we shall see later that Ye Feng and other writers viewed pain as an inevitable and even necessary part of labor. Instead, when they spoke of easy birth, they envisioned a labor that was free from complications: simple, spontaneous, and smooth. "Easy" childbirth was thus the opposite of "difficult childbirth" *(nan-chan)*, the standard term used for an obstructed or prolonged labor. And childbirth was so inherently easy, Ye suggested, that not even conscious will was necessary. "The generation [of life] is a self-so principle *[ziran zhi li]* of Heaven and Earth," he pointed out, "like the eye seeing and the ear hearing, the hand grasping and the foot treading. It is exceedingly harmonious and exceedingly easy *[yi]*. One does not need to compel it with force."[6] Ye Feng's use of the phrase "self-so principle" *(ziran zhi li)* would have held deep philosophical significance for his readers. Originating in Daoism, where it constituted a "core value," the idea of "self-so" *(ziran)* undergirded Chinese explanations of existence and change in the universe. Liu Xiaogan has identified three interrelated meanings of the term as used in the canonical Daoist text *The Classic of the Way and Its Virtue (Daodejing)*, all of which are relevant to Ye Feng's arguments.[7] One usage of *self-so* referred to the spontaneous, primordial state of a given thing, "a state that exists and develops without any need for outside input." A second usage referred to the preservation of this primordial state free from outside attempts to change it: "[Self-so] in this sense is the continuation of an original state or the maintenance of a spontaneous state." Finally, *self-so* referred to the ineluctable tendency of all things to follow their own proper course of transformation and development. Thus it described "the sustained and continuing inertial tendency of a primordial and spontaneous state." All of these shades of meaning were present in Ye's discussion of the "self-so principle" of childbirth, which emphasized that birth was a self-driven, self-sufficient, and self-correcting dynamic.

Since the basic essence of the cosmos was to generate life effortlessly, Ye Feng argued, childbirth must also be a "fundamentally easy" matter.[8]

He signaled this belief in the very title of his work, which alluded to the miraculous easy birth of Lord Millet (Hou Ji), mythic founder of the Zhou dynasty. All educated Chinese knew "Birth of the People" *(Sheng min)*, a poem from the *Classic of Odes (Shijing)* that was part of the scholar's canon. These ancient verses recounted how the childless woman Jiang Yuan ultimately conceived Lord Millet after assiduously performing fertility rituals and sacrifices. As a further mark of divine favor, the gods granted her an utterly effortless labor, and Lord Millet was born "with no bursting, no rending, no injury, and no harm" to his mother.[9] Soon afterward, Jiang Yuan abandoned her son on a road. Later commentators speculated that Jiang Yuan did so because her son's birth was so extraordinarily easy that she became frightened.[10]

The *Odes* described Lord Millet's easy birth with the phrase *xian sheng ru da*. Ancient and modern commentators alike have argued over how to interpret this phrase, but one standard gloss was: "Her firstborn *[xian sheng]* came like *[ru]* a lamb *[da]*." The rationale was that, while human birth was difficult, sheep gave birth easily, and therefore Lord Millet's miraculous birth was as easy as that of a lamb.[11] Ye Feng's preface explicitly quoted from this legend, pointing out that, if people followed his recommendations when managing childbirth, then "in all cases *xian sheng ru da*."[12] Simultaneously, Ye Feng incorporated the story of Lord Millet into the very title of his childbirth text, which he coined from key words in the *Odes* narrative, reversing *sheng* and *da* to form the *dasheng* treatise. This wordplay had ample precedent, for the renowned physician Zhu Zhenheng (1282–1358) had earlier invented "*dasheng* powder" *(dasheng san)*, a medicinal formula for preventing difficult labor.[13] The seventeenth-century doctor Zhang Jiebin explained that the name of Zhu's formula referred to Lord Millet's birth, and that several doses of this formula in the last month of pregnancy would allow "birth to occur easily *[yi-chan]*."[14] Thus, although the Chinese characters for *dasheng* literally mean "attaining childbirth," the translation that best captures Ye Feng's intent is "easy birth." We must also note that when Ye Feng appropriated the phrase *dasheng*, he actually subverted the original implications of the legend. The *Odes* depicted Lord Millet's easy birth as a miracle bestowed by the gods. Ye Feng, by contrast, insisted that easy birth was the normal order of things, and that ensuring easy delivery was solely a matter of human will.

It would be erroneous to conclude that Ye Feng was a starry-eyed naïf. He did in fact admit that in some instances difficult labor would result even when the mother had followed his teachings faithfully. But his fundamental aim was to combat the idea that childbirth was a dangerous emergency requiring early and active intervention. To this end, he insisted that cases of difficult labor were exceptional. Furthermore, he explained that such cases arose from some injury or transgression occurring during pregnancy that had damaged the mother or fetus. Overall then, he implied that such exceptions did not disprove the intrinsic ease of childbirth:

> In some cases [of difficult labor] it is because the mother's body is too vacuous and does not nourish the fetus sufficiently, so that Blood and qi are not complete. Or the mother became ill with a cold damage disorder, after which heat toxin injured the fetus. There are also cases where the husband and wife share a chamber too often and the fire of lust injures the fetus. In some cases it is because during ordinary times she eats peppers, ginger, deep-fried or broiled foods, and the fire toxin from these hot things injures the fetus. In addition, there is injury from falling and beatings. All these can lead to difficult labor and frequently to the fetus dying within the belly. Other than these, there will be no cases of difficult labor.[15]

Historical Precedents

Ye Feng claimed that he was "reverently observing the ideas of the ancients, organizing and clarifying them without inventing unusual doctrines."[16] The authors whose "guiding teachings" he cited notably included Chen Ziming, author of *Comprehensive Compendium of Good Formulas for Women* (1237). And indeed, the idea that childbirth replicated the "great virtue of Heaven and Earth" appears in medical discussions at least as far back as Chen Ziming's text. But like many medical writers before and after him, Ye Feng used tradition selectively, citing the authority of former worthies to justify new ideas. When we compare the two authors, we find that Chen Ziming's text subordinated the idea of birth's cosmological resonance to a broader rhetoric that depicted birth as destabilizing, polluting, and inherently dangerous. Ye Feng, by contrast, rejected the beliefs and practices associated with birthing pollution and elevated the ideal of cosmologically resonant birth to a guiding principle.

Chen Ziming's *Comprehensive Compendium of Good Formulas for Women* was intended as a master synthesis of best medical practices as they then existed.[17] Here we see that doctors of the time took a triple-pronged approach to preventing and managing difficult labor. First, they employed hemerological, geomantic, and ritual techniques to ensure that the act of giving birth did not violate cosmic harmony, offend any deities, or expose the woman to inauspicious forces or malevolent spirits. Second, they assumed male physicians needed to know how to correct a baby's position in the womb, even if these manipulations were generally carried out by a female birth attendant. Third, alongside these older ritual and manual interventions, male physicians deployed an array of pharmacological techniques meant to regulate and replenish qi and Blood, a drug-based strategy shaped by the doctrines of systems of correspondence medicine. These different approaches also reflected different assumptions about the dangers of childbirth. While ritual and geomantic practices portrayed birth as a polluting and inherently dangerous disturbance to cosmic order, discussions of malpresentation and the use of drugs allowed for the possibility that childbirth was a cosmologically resonant process that would go smoothly in the absence of error.

Three essays in Chen Ziming's compendium contain early formulations of the ideal of easy birth that Ye Feng would later expand into a central tenet. The first was a preface that Zhou Ting composed in 897 for his expanded version of Zan Yin's famous mid-ninth-century text, *Childbirth Treasury (Chanbao)*.[18] Zhou Ting began by lamenting that people did not know how to properly nourish their vitalities, "so that before their Heaven-allotted years have come to an end, they have been snatched away by disease." This observation echoed the central idea set forth in the opening essays of the Yellow Emperor's *Basic Questions*, namely, that people would naturally live long and healthy lives if only they harmonized themselves with the innate dynamics of the cosmos.[19] Similarly, Zhou Ting suggested that childbirth would be trouble-free in the absence of mistakes. Citing the *Classic of Changes*, he pointed out, "The great virtue of Heaven and Earth is called 'generating life.' Therefore we know that reproduction is the foundation for everything within Heaven and Earth. So how could it be that childbearing would endanger people's lives?" Analogous perspectives appeared in a second essay, namely, Chen Ziming's own discussion of the six causes of difficult birth. Here he explained that a healthy woman would always give birth easily. "In women, Blood is the controlling element," Chen began, reiterating the guiding principle of Song dynasty *fuke*. "As long as qi flows smoothly, then Blood will flow smoothly. If the fetal qi is secure *(an)*, then the dynamics of childbearing will be harmonious."[20] The ideal of smooth childbirth likewise frames a third essay, the "Ten Forms of Childbirth" *(Shichan lun)* ascribed to Yang Zijian (fl. ca. 1100).[21] Yang discussed var-

ious situations in which birth could become difficult and require intervention. But he opened his discussion with this description of "correct
childbirth" *(zhengchan),* thereby establishing trouble-free labor as the
normative point of reference:

> In correct childbirth, the woman fulfills her complete ten months of preg-
> nancy, and yin and yang qi are sufficient. Suddenly she has waves of pain
> in the waist and abdomen, followed by an immediate sinking down of the
> fetal qi. When things arrive at the point where the pains in the navel and
> abdomen are at their most extreme, there is also heavy pain within the
> waist, and the birth path protrudes, then the starchy waters burst and
> Blood descends, and the child is subsequently born. This is what we call
> correct childbirth.[22]

In short, correct childbirth was simple and straightforward, the signs
of progressing labor appearing in orderly and predictable fashion, and
the child coming out without any complications. By definition, then, any
form of protracted labor or labor accompanied by maternal and fetal illness was a deviation from the norm, caused by mistakes made during
pregnancy or labor. The most general problem was failure to regulate
a woman's qi and Blood, and *Comprehensive Compendium of Good Formulas* identified numerous bad habits and pernicious practices that
would lead to maternal disharmony and thus complications of childbirth.
Chen Ziming was particularly concerned with the self-indulgent and
indolent lifestyles of rich women, which caused maternal qi to become
lethargic, thereby preventing the innate ease of birth from asserting itself:

> The rich families of our day generally coddle their pregnant mothers, fear-
> ing only that they will overexert themselves. Therefore they become afraid
> to come and go, and only ever sit or lie down. Never do they consider that
> this causes qi to be closed up and prevents it from being loose and nimble.
> Then Blood stagnates and does not flow freely, and the fetus cannot turn
> and move. This causes childbearing to lose its proper dynamic, and there
> will inevitably be difficulties at the time of birth, even to the extent that the
> child is suffocated to death.[23]

Other harmful practices included sexual intercourse during pregnancy,
which could injure the unborn baby. The male and female essences emitted during sexual intercourse might also become "corrupted" and "stagnant" and collect in the womb. If these engorged the baby, so that "the
baby is big when the mother is small," then difficult labor would result.[24]
It was also dangerous to alarm the mother as birth neared. If one allowed
her to be engulfed by birth attendants and a flurry of chaotic activity, then
fright and worry would cause her qi to congeal and stagnate, impeding

birth.[25] Like qi, Blood could also become chaotic or depleted, with tragic results. Chen Ziming and Yang Zijian both noted that failure to regulate the temperature of the birthing room during especially hot or cold weather would destabilize maternal Blood. Cold could provoke Blood stagnation and thus obstruct delivery, while overheated Blood would rise upward in the body and provoke fever, headache, and dizziness. Unresolved, it also readily turned into "Blood swooning" *(xueyun)*, a potentially dangerous postpartum ailment characterized by mental derangement or loss of consciousness. And even if a woman came through childbirth safely, she could commit other errors that would produce chronic and dangerous depletions and make subsequent births difficult. Zhou Ting, for example, warned that women who breastfed their own children did so at the cost of their own health.[26] Repeated childbearing itself also depleted a woman's vitalities, making proper regulation even more challenging and crucial. Zhou Ting additionally highlighted the danger posed by incompetent or unscrupulous doctors. Skillful use of medicinal remedies would produce wondrous results, he said, but doctors who used drugs inappropriately or indiscriminately would end up exacerbating the disorder and killing their female patients. Greedy doctors who balked at treating poor women were also culpable in their deaths. Described in this way, the complications of childbirth were analogous to other diseases that arose through human error.

But while Song dynasty doctors affirmed that preventing human error could prevent difficult labor, they also assumed that error was difficult to avoid, and Chen Ziming portrayed childbirth as something that routinely required medical intervention. In the larger context of Chen Ziming's text, furthermore, references to childbirth's innate ease were subordinated to concerns about childbirth as a polluting and potentially disruptive event. Chen Ziming took it for granted that prophylactic measures were essential for placating gods, avoiding baleful influences, and reconciling possible incompatibilities between a woman's horoscope and the date of her delivery. Even Zhou Ting, who affirmed that "the great virtue of Heaven and Earth is called 'generating life,' " assumed that one had to make provisions for the "pollution" *(hui)* of childbirth. He further advised that when the woman entered her final month of pregnancy, she should post on her wall the birthing charts that would teach her how to properly situate and orient herself in the birthing room and to avoid fetus-killing demons.[27] The coexistence of these seemingly contradictory views in Song medicine—one affirming that birth was fundamentally easy, the other warning that it was inevitably dangerous—reflects the fact that the Song was an important transition period in the expansion of literate approaches to women's diseases. As discussed in chapter 1, it was during this era that male doctors were expanding the ambit of scholarly medicine, using yin-yang and five phases doctrine to create a new way of explaining women's reproductive problems. At the same time, however, Chen Ziming and others still saw older ritual precautions as essential for managing childbirth, and Charlotte Furth has shown that Song male doctors did not reject rituals so much as try to ensure their proper use.[28]

Over the next several centuries, the leading edge of medical innovation sought ever finer understandings of the internal bodily patterns responsible for illness. Ritual practices thus became increasingly marginalized in the literate *fuke* tradition. At the same time, medical writers paid greater attention to the ways in which the state of a woman's qi and Blood could affect the difficulty or ease of her labor. In the pages of *Easy Childbirth,* these two tendencies merged as Ye Feng used the ideal of easy birth to reject any role for fate or spirits in the outcome of labor. "Childbirth is not an illness," Ye Feng said, "but difficult childbirth is something that people are afflicted with. When human afflictions cannot be eradicated, then people blame the matter on Heaven. But what fault could there be with Heaven?"[29] People had only themselves to blame if things went badly, he emphasized, for all instances of difficult birth arose from "errors in the human realm damaging [the Way of] Heaven."[30] By way of proof, he also referred to the widely held belief that women who secretly gave birth to illegitimate children did not suffer difficult labor.[31] Some believed that this was due to divine intervention, Ye Feng said, but this was untrue. Instead, he asserted that secret births were easy because the mothers tried to hide their condition until the last possible minute, thus ensuring that no one would interfere with the birthing process: "So the only thing they can do is to endure the pain to the full limit of their ability, and when the pain reaches the point where it can no longer be borne, [the child] easily comes out. The principle behind this is exceedingly clear. What doubt can there be?"[32]

In response to the widespread view that childbirth required active intervention, therefore, Ye Feng emphatically and repeatedly declared that attempts to facilitate childbirth would do more harm than good. Central to his arguments was a rejection of the two most common forms of intervention: the manual manipulation of the baby, and the use of birth-expediting drugs. Ye Feng's views were heir to changing medical opinions on these two issues.

RESOLVING MALPRESENTATION

A guiding assumption of *Easy Childbirth* was that the baby was a self-propelled being endowed with the ability to "tunnel" or "bore" *(zuan)* its own way out of the mother's body. Ye Feng made this point by likening the human baby to young plant shoots breaching the surface of the earth or baby birds pecking their way out of the egg, both of which happened spontaneously without active assistance.[33] So that no one could possibly mistake his meaning, Ye also underscored his arguments with the earthiest of analogies. Some people, he noted, argued that one had to exert oneself in order to pass a bowel movement, so why not during childbirth? Ye Feng countered that "excrement is a lifeless thing that inevitably requires human effort [to expel]. [But] a child is able to turn and move on its own, and one must wait until it turns itself."[34] Trying to push the baby out any earlier was therefore futile. "This would be like passing a bowel movement before the time has arrived," Ye Feng said. "Even if one uses force, it cannot come out. And how much more is this true for [expelling] a person?"[35] Like a seed or a chick, the child alone would determine the time of its birth. As we saw in chapter 4, Chinese doctors all accepted that the usual term of gestation was ten months, but medical explanations of fetal development also allowed for the possibility of much longer pregnancies. These teachings, too, shaped Ye Feng's argument that one must never rush childbirth: "The ancients say there were people not born until after three or four years," he noted. "This is merely because the child was unwilling to come out. If it is unwilling to come out, who can force it; and if it wants to come out, who can resist it?"[36] Any attempt to expel the child from the womb before the right time was like "pulling sprouts to help them grow" and tantamount to "cutting open an egg to extract the chick, or splitting the cocoon to take out the pupa."[37] Even if the child survived, it would be sickly and difficult to rear.

Ye's faith in the self-driven nature of birth was inseparable from his belief that the root cause of difficult labor was the mother trying to push the baby out before the correct time had arrived. While other writers took a less monocausal view, medical texts since at least the seventh century had warned that laboring too early was a potentially deadly error.[38] Trying to push the baby out too soon would exhaust the mother, leaving her vulnerable to heteropathic influences. It could also cause the waters of the womb to break too early, so that the birth canal would become "dried up and rough" and make birth difficult when the child was actually ready to come out. Most dangerous, however, pushing too early was a direct cause of fetal malpresentation. Medical writers throughout the centuries all accepted the premise that the child rotated into the correct head-down position during labor. Pushing too early would therefore cause the baby to become stuck in midrotation and prevent it from attaining the correct posture for delivery. An early mention of this problem appeared in Chao Yuanfang's *Master Chao's Treatise on the Origins and Manifestations of the Myriad Diseases* (610), but the standard reference was Yang Zijian's detailed essay on the ten types of childbirth.[39] Yang introduced the general problem of women pushing too early under the rubric of "injurious birth" *(shangchan)*, then went on to detail three specific kinds of malpresentation that were directly caused by this error: "transverse" *(hengchan)*, where the child's hand or buttock presented first, "upside-down" *(daochan)*, where the foot came out first, and "tilted" *(pianchan)*, where the child was head-down but had its head stuck in a tilted position. Yang Zijian presented fetal version as the principal means of resolving malpresentation, and although these interventions were to be carried out by the birthing attendant, male doctors of the time were clearly expected to be familiar with the procedures. Yang's description of transverse presentation shows how detailed these manipulations could be: "Have the mother lie quietly on her back, and have the birth attendant push [the baby] back in. The method for pushing a baby: first push on its body, causing it to straighten upward. Then gradually insert your hand and use your middle finger to rub its shoulder, pushing it upward and rectifying [its position]. Then gradually work the finger over to grasp the child's ear and rectify [the head]. The mother must be lying down on her back. Then push the baby straight upward and steadily correct its position."[40]

Like other Qing authors, Ye Feng's description of the different forms of malpresentation essentially just repeated Yang Zijian's essay. Where Ye differed from Yang Zijian, however, was in advocating a minimally interventionist approach for resolving malpresentation. If the mother had mistakenly pushed too early and caused the child to be stuck, he counseled, the only proper course of action was to restore the mother's bodily vitalities through a combination of sleep and replenishing drugs. Any physical handling of the baby was to be kept to a minimum. In cases of transverse and reversed birth, for example, Ye recommended the following: "Urgently order her to sleep quietly, and administer a large dose of Ligusticum-Angelica Decoction with Added Ingredients. Press gradually on the [baby's] hands and feet to make them go back inside, and let [the mother] sleep one night, and birth will occur of its own accord."[41]

To properly contextualize Ye's willingness to rely on birth's innate dynamics, we must realize that doctors had long been concerned about the risks of fetal version. Yang Zijian himself had repeatedly emphasized that only a clever birth attendant could successfully turn an incorrectly positioned baby. "But if the birth attendant does not have skilled and nimble hands," he warned, "one cannot rely on this method, for fear that giving free rein to that person's stupidity will cause injury to life."[42] Yang does not suggest what to do if a skilled birth attendant could not be found. In a later commentary on Yang Zijian's essay, however, Lou Ying (1332–1400) suggested that it might be better to let things take their own course, and he noted examples where babies had been safely born even when their positions were left uncorrected:

> As for reversed birth, people today frequently deliver the child in the foot-down position without any harmful aftereffects, and the mother and child are both preserved. So one does not necessarily have to rely on the method of pushing the foot back up. Furthermore, in cases of obstructed labor, it frequently happens that the umbilical cord is wrapped around the crown of the child's head, but the child's head has already come out of the gate of birth [i.e., the cord is now wrapped around the child's neck]. The birth attendant can manually lift the cord over the top of the baby's head and then deliver [the child]. There are also cases where the cord is wrapped around the baby's crown, but the child and the placenta come out together of their own accord [ziran], all without obstruction. So one does not inevitably have to use the method of resolving obstructed labor by unhooking the cord from within the gate of birth.[43]

But scattered in Song dynasty texts was another possibility: that one could resolve malpresentation with drugs. This approach was rooted in an alternate etiology for malpresentation, one that attributed it to dysfunctional maternal qi and Blood that impaired the baby's ability to achieve the proper position. A work attributed to the eleventh-century childbirth expert Guo Jizhong, for example, had noted that accumulations of waste Blood within the womb would impede the child's movements. Guo thus envisioned malpresentation in terms of a temporary obstruction that could be resolved with drugs to eliminate the accumulated Blood: "What causes difficult birth? Next to the fetus, there are lumps [of Blood] that have formed into Child Pillows. At the time when the child wants to be born, the pillows break and the waste Blood envelops the child, therefore labor is difficult. Merely administer Powder to Conquer Metal to clear away the waste Blood, and the child will be born of its own accord. Cases of reversed birth or transverse birth can also all be treated this way."[44]

In his commentary on Guo Jizhong's teachings, the etiological au-

thority Chen Yan (courtesy name Wuze) (fl. 1161–74) disagreed that
Blood lumps were the sole contributor to difficult labor, and he reminded
his readers of the dangers of pushing too early. Yet Chen Yan also agreed
that fetal malpresentation could be resolved with medical formulas. In
cases where the child's hand or foot came out first, he said, one should
simply irritate the appendage with a needle, "causing it to retract inward
of its own accord." The next step was a remedy to stabilize the mother's
Blood, after which the child "will turn of its own accord and be born."[45]

Besides stagnant or deficient Blood, vacuity of maternal qi was another factor that could cause malpresentation. Since the child drew its
vitality from the mother, maternal depletion could make the child too
weak to rotate inside her womb. Yang Zijian's discussion of "upside-
down birth" *(daochan),* for example, had described it as an instance of
vacuity compounded by pushing too early. "Upside-down birth," Yang
said, "is when the maternal and fetal qi are insufficient, and at the key
juncture things are not secure. She uses force too early, causing the child
to be unable to turn back around and align itself for birth. Then it can
only go straight down and it reveals its foot first."[46] During the fifteenth
and sixteenth centuries, medical writers continued to expand the idea that
maternal imbalance was an important cause of malpresentation, and that
fetal position could therefore be corrected with drugs. As Yu Tuan (1438–
ca. 1517), pointed out, the key to safe childbirth was careful regulation
of maternal qi. Only then would the fetus have the strength to rotate into
the head-down position. Here Yu elaborated on the earlier teachings of
Zhu Zhenheng (courtesy name Danxi), who had previously identified
vacuity, not repletion, as the chief cause of difficult birth:

> Zhu Danxi says that when women suffer difficult birth, it is all because
> they were unable to be prudent during the eighth or ninth month, with the
> result that qi and Blood became vacuous. What is the meaning of this?
> Answer: In general when a woman becomes pregnant, it is greatly improper
> for her to share a bed with her husband. People today are not familiar with
> this principle, to the extent that they still engage in bedchamber affairs
> during the eighth or ninth month. Now, as soon as emotions and desires
> are aroused, then qi and Blood are accordingly consumed. The fetus de-
> pends entirely on qi and Blood for its growth and nourishment, and when
> qi and Blood are deficient, then the fetal qi is emaciated and weak.
>   When the days and months [of pregnancy] are fulfilled, the child is like
> someone waking from a dream, and it wishes to be born. Then it is able
> to break open the fetal wrapper *[bao],* search for its pathway, and come
> out. After the wrapper is broken, the starchy fluids within it will gush out
> below. [A baby] with robust fetal qi will then turn its body over and follow
> the fluids out, and this will be an easy birth. But if the fetal qi is fatigued

and weak, then it is like someone who has yet to awake from sleep. In turning its head, it will be delayed and slow, and it will not be able to follow the waters out. Once the womb's starchy waters are dry, the corrupted Blood will block up the pathway of birth. As a result, the child will have no direction in which to go, and transverse birth or upside-down birth will result.[47]

In this passage, the contrast with Song-era teachings is striking: whereas earlier texts focused on difficult labor as a physical obstruction, Yu Tuan cast difficult birth as a case of qi debility impairing the natural process of birth. For example, Chen Ziming had also forbidden intercourse during pregnancy, but he did so on the grounds that male and female ejaculates would cause the fetus and placenta to become bloated and physically obstruct the birth canal. Yu Tuan, by contrast, worried that sexual arousal would deplete qi and Blood and thus deplete the baby's source of nourishment. Yang Zijian's earlier discussion of malpresentation highlighted the problem of the mother's pushing too early, but Yu Tuan depicted deficient qi as the main problem that might prevent the fetus from completing its rotation. Overall, then, Yu Tuan assigned the fetus the leading role in managing its own birth, and he concurrently expanded the ways in which malfunction of Blood and qi could lead to difficult labor. By redefining fetal malpresentation as a result of internal bodily disharmonies, doctors like Yu Tuan also expanded the range of obstetrical ailments amenable to drug therapy. This in turn helped to promote the use of medicinal formulas where manual manipulation had once been the technique of choice. This trend can be discerned in Li Chan's sixteenth-century textbook for aspiring doctors, *An Introduction to Medicine* (*Yixue rumen*, 1575). When Li Chan reproduced Yang Zijian's treatise on the ten types of childbirth, he added his own recommendations for medicinal formulas to each of Yang's explanations of how to manually reposition a baby.[48]

By the time Ye Feng was formulating his views, therefore, the belief that one could resolve malpresentation by regulating maternal qi and Blood had become prominent in the medical literature. Yu Tuan and Li Chan's teachings on the subject were sufficiently well-regarded to be anthologized in the chapters on childbirth in the Qing *Imperial Encyclopedia*, for example, and we may assume that Ye Feng was familiar with them as well. Ye's faith that fetal version was unnecessary was thus broadly consistent with the view that that drugs were an effective way to manage malpresentation. Ye Feng's innovation, however, was to elevate what had originally been an alternative or adjunct method to the

therapeutic strategy of first choice. To be sure, Ye Feng did mention "guiding" the child's hands or feet back into the mother's body in cases of
malpresentation, but this was a far cry from the detailed manipulations
that Yang Zijian had recommended. Nor did Ye Feng see this as a particularly difficult proposition, provided the woman was able to conserve
her energies. To those who worried that a baby's hands or feet could not
be put back into its mother's body, Ye assured them that "as long as [the
mother] is willing to sleep, there is no reason that one would be unable
to guide [them] back inside."[49] Fundamentally, then, Ye asked his readers to trust that the innate dynamic of birth, properly protected, would
be self-correcting as well as self-driven.

BIRTH-EXPEDITING MEDICINES

Ye's criticism of fetal manipulation was implicitly aimed at the midwives
who performed these procedures, as well as at the families who listened
to the midwives' advice. His attack on birth-expediting medicines, by comparison, was a sweeping criticism of lay people and therapeutic experts
of both genders. Ye Feng's objection to birthing drugs was twofold: the
medicines used to assist birth were largely dangerous or ineffective, and
even the effective ones were used indiscriminately and inappropriately.

> Someone asked, "As the time of birth approaches, there are many tested
> remedies. Can one also use them?" I say, "Do not use them." Among the
> extraordinary formulas of the past, none was more popular than pills of
> rat liver and rabbit brain. Of those remedies in wide circulation today,
> none is more widely used than Elixir for Returning Life [huisheng dan].
> I am not saying that these should not be used because they are ineffective.
> It is simply that they are generally unnecessary. Now if one does not use
> force, does not meddle, and furthermore assists [the process of birth] with
> the method of sleep, then the baby will be born on its own. So why would
> there be any need to use medicine? Even if there is a case that does not go
> smoothly, the best strategy is to sleep.[50]

Ye Feng warned that these birthing medicines were composed of ingredients that consumed and dispelled qi while breaking up Blood. Their
immediate and lingering effects thus posed a real threat to the woman's
health both during and after childbirth. More broadly, he portrayed the
use of birth-expediting medicines as inseparable from the erroneous view
that childbirth was an extraordinary event requiring heroic measures. For
example, when he criticized the errors made by rich families, Ye bemoaned
the chaos that inevitably ensued the moment the mother appeared to go

into labor. The household would erupt in a frenzy of noisy activity, and the midwives would invariably tell the mother to bear down before the proper time had arrived. "Then, once they have caused the labor to become protracted, they recklessly administer extraordinary remedies and costly medicines one after the other," Ye Feng recounted.[51] In other words, birth-expediting medicines became necessary only because people had already bungled things. But if people just respected the natural dynamic of childbirth, then drugs were utterly superfluous, and Ye Feng cited his own empirical observations as proof: "In my spare time, I managed affairs by carrying out this principle. In a hundred attempts, there was not a single failure, and in most of these cases it was unnecessary to employ drugs."[52]

In order to convince his readers that birth was a naturally easy process, Ye Feng forcefully repeated that it was harmful to use birth-expediting medicines. He did, however, allow for the use of drugs that would replenish and preserve the mother's qi and Blood in cases where she was clearly exhausted. Furthermore, Ye emphasized, since birth was an ordinary event, any medicines that might be used should also be "extremely ordinary medicines"[53] These notably included decoctions of lovage and angelica, which could bolster the strength of mother and child in cases of malpresentation. At first glance, Ye Feng's recommendation that replenishing medicines could be used to assist birth may seem to contradict his blanket condemnation of birth-expediting medicines. But he was actually making a subtle distinction between different kinds of birthing therapies, a distinction that resonated with larger trends in fourteenth- to seventeenth-century medicine: the rejection of birth-expediting drugs that attacked stagnation in favor of drugs that nurtured maternal vitalities. Thus, while no other late imperial author seemed to share Ye's optimism that a woman in labor would actually be able to sleep, many would have been sympathetic to the idea that gentle replenishing drugs were the most effective means to facilitate labor.

Speeding Birth in the Song Dynasty

When Ye criticized the use of rabbit-based pills and "unusual drugs," he targeted medicines that had long been a standard part of the literate repertoire. Again, Chen Ziming's *Comprehensive Compendium of Good Formulas* provides a useful point of reference for understanding the historical changes embodied in Ye's arguments. Thirteenth-century doctors recommended the routine and prophylactic use of two categories of medicines to prevent difficult labor and ensure easy birth *(yichan)*: medicines designed to make the fetus slim and slippery *(huatai, shoutai)*, and those designed to expedite and hasten labor *(cuisheng)*. Women were counseled to take these drugs as they entered the final month of gestation, or in some cases even during the last trimester of pregnancy.[54] The rhetoric of fetal slimming and lubricating portrayed the fetus as a potential locus of surfeit and stagnation, and it conceptualized difficult childbirth in terms of a physical blockage that needed to be expelled. One formula, for example, promised that it could "shrink" *(suo)* a fetus that was too "fat" *(fei)*.[55] Accordingly, formulas to slim the fetus relied heavily on drugs that consumed qi and broke up stagnation. One staple was the mature fruit of the bitter orange *(zhike)*, the main ingredient in two of Chen Ziming's favored formulas: Bitter Orange Powder *(zhike san)* and Divine Bedchamber Pills *(shenqin yuan)*.[56] But blockage during labor could also arise from insufficient lubrication, and thus "slippery fetus" medicines also sought to promote the flow of bodily fluids. Chen Ziming's methods for making the fetus slippery included drugs perceived to have a diuretic effect.[57] These included plantain seed *(cheqianzi)*, which the *Classic of Odes* had long ago described as an effective remedy for difficult labor.

In addition to the routine use of fetal-slimming and lubricating medicines during the last month of pregnancy, Song-era doctors recommended the use of birth-expediting *(cuisheng)* medicines as soon as the child had assumed the head-down position and was pressing against the "gate of birth" *(chanmen)*.[58] In normal cases, birth-expediting medicines were used both to prevent difficult childbirth and to positively encourage swift labor. They were also the standard pharmacological response to obstructed or protracted labor. Chen Ziming thus listed some two dozen formulas and simples (remedies composed of a single ingredient) that could be used to expedite labor. Like fetal-slimming formulas, these also relied on drugs that dispersed stagnation. One important ingredient was frankincense *(ruxiang)*, an "aromatic" *(xiang)* drug valued for its ability to clear away stagnant and obstructed qi and Blood.[59] But Chen's birth-expediting repertoire also notably included substances that appear to have been chosen for their magical resonance as much as any perceived pharmaceutical properties. These included sloughed snakeskin *(shetui)*, which evoked the image of something squirming out from a narrow place. Drugs derived from the body parts of rabbits were also favored, including rabbit brain, rabbit blood, rabbit pelts, and rabbit hair. Modern science would explain that the hormones in the pituitary gland of the rabbit can induce uterine contractions, but the literate doctors of imperial China favored the use of rabbit for its association with speed.[60]

Replenishing Formulas for Birth

Ye Feng's objections to rabbit-based drugs and other birthing medicines show that these methods continued to be a staple in the late imperial medical repertoire. By Ye's lifetime, however, there was also a significant body of opinion against these older approaches. A main concern was that the qi-consuming effects of fetal-slimming formulas would injure mothers who were actually suffering from depletion. An early note of caution had in fact been sounded by Yan Yonghe (ca. 1206–68). Even though Yan recommended the routine use of fetal-slimming medicines during the final month of pregnancy, he warned that Bitter Orange Powder was inappropriate in cases of weak fetal qi.[61] But it was Zhu Zhenheng's fourteenth-century teachings that provided the doctrinal underpinnings for a sustained critique of Song birthing medicines.[62] Like Chen Ziming, Zhu identified stagnation as the root cause of difficult childbirth. But while Chen Ziming traced stagnation in birthing women to excess, Zhu attributed it to deficiency. "The cause of difficult childbirth is lack of prudence [bu jin] in the eighth or ninth month of pregnancy," Zhu explained. "Because qi and Blood become depleted, qi and Blood likewise congeal and stagnate, so that they cannot circulate."[63] Zhu Zhenheng thus criticized the use of Bitter Orange Powder on the grounds that its qi-consuming properties would only exacerbate preexisting maternal vacuities. The standard description of the formula explained that it had been used to great effect by Princess Huyang (Huyang gongzhu) of the Eastern Han dynasty, but Zhu pointed out that a formula compounded for one person could not be universally effective for all.[64] In fact, Zhu himself had seen cases where the use of Bitter Orange Powder had created problems for women. This included one of his own kinswomen, who had suffered so greatly from a difficult labor that she aborted her subsequent pregnancies to avoid giving birth again.[65] After contemplation, Zhu realized that a pampered aristocrat like Princess Huyang would have had a classic case of replete qi, which is why a qi-consuming drug like bitter orange was effective for her. His own kinswoman, however, suffered from the opposite problem, namely, depletion. Thus, Zhu Zhenheng explained, "the proper course was to replenish the maternal qi, then the child would be healthy and easily born." The next time his kinswoman became pregnant, Zhu treated her from the fifth month onward with medicines to replenish maternal qi, and in the end she easily gave birth to a son.

Whereas Zhu Zhenheng questioned the appropriateness of specific birth-expediting formulas, other doctors worried that birth-expediting

medicines in general encouraged people to interfere inappropriately with
the natural progression of labor. An early reference to this concern appears in Chen Ziming's *Comprehensive Compendium of Good Formulas.*
Quoting the ninth-century *Childbirth Treasury,* Chen warned, "Childbirth has its own time; therefore one must not compel it with birth-
expediting or fetus-lubricating medicines."[66] But Chen Ziming used this
quotation to criticize people who would try to manipulate the time of a
child's birth so that it would be born on an auspicious day or during a
favorable alignment of cosmic forces. His statement was not a criticism
of birthing medicines per se, but rather an assertion that the norms of
scholarly medicine should take precedence over ritual and hemerological beliefs. Beginning in the sixteenth century, however, we find doctors
arguing that expediting medicines are fundamentally unnecessary because
birth is intrinsically easy. In his *Introduction to Medicine* (*Yixue rumen,*
1575), Li Chan presented themes that later became central to *Easy Childbirth:* "At ten months, qi is full, the fetus's primordial qi is sturdy and
strong. Suddenly the abdomen hurts, or in some only the waist hurts, and
in a short while the child is born. What need is there to expedite it? This
is the Heaven-endowed, wondrous nature of easy birth."[67] Several decades
later, Zhang Jiebin (1563–1640) reiterated these arguments, emphasizing his point by likening babies to fruits. "During pregnancy, the fetus's
primordial qi is completed, the months are accomplished, and then it is
born," he said. "There is a time for its ripening and falling, and it is not
something that can be expedited."[68]

Such criticisms did not mean that "birth-expediting" medicines ever
went out of fashion, and we continue to find a range of opinions throughout the late imperial period, from those of doctors who inveighed against
the use of fetal slimming and birth-expediting remedies, to those of others who felt it was appropriate to use these remedies routinely.[69] But the
teachings of Li Chan and Zhang Jiebin show that skepticism toward these
medicines had now become an important theme in literate medicine. Both
Li Chan and Zhang Jiebin intended their works to be authoritative accounts of correct medical learning that would enhance the intellectual
status of medicine and facilitate the education of aspiring medical practitioners.[70] Their statements on the natural ease of childbirth thus legit-
imized a medical viewpoint that subsequently found popular currency
in Ye Feng's noninterventionist tract. During the Song dynasty, doctors
had portrayed birth-expediting medicines as routine, even necessary, pro-
phylactics that were universally applicable. But by the late sixteenth century, writers criticized birth-expediting medicines on the grounds that

birth was a naturally easy process. When they did allow for the use of birth-expediting medicines, it was as a remedy for specific complications of childbirth, not as an all-purpose treatment. Li Chan explained, for example, that medicines to expedite birth were necessary only if the mother had borne down too early, causing the child to get stuck. He also identified different forms of careless behavior during pregnancy or early labor that could cause complications in childbirth by provoking deficiency, surfeit, or blockage of maternal vitalities. These would be rectified by different formulas, depending on the root cause. Difficult labor was therefore to be treated like any other disease, with the remedy carefully tailored to the situation at hand.[71]

Zhang Jiebin went even further, promoting a new pharmacological logic for birth-expediting medicines that embodied the basic assumptions of cosmologically resonant childbirth. Presaging Ye Feng's arguments by several decades, Zhang Jiebin pointed out that birthing medicines were not only ineffective but also frequently harmful, consuming the mother's qi and Blood and thereby subverting the natural course of labor:

> Whether [birth] is difficult or easy depends on whether Blood is flourishing or vacuous, and not on the lubricating and diuretic effects of drugs. Now if Blood is copious, then there is moisture, and birth is inevitably easy. If Blood is lacking, then there is roughness, and birth is inevitably difficult. Therefore, prior to birth the only proper approach is to build up and nurture qi and Blood as the main principle, thereby establishing her condition ahead of time. . . .
>
> If one is ignorant of this and excessively employs slippery and diuretic drugs, or if the time of birth is not yet near and she is without fire or stagnation, and yet one recklessly uses drugs that clear away fire, circulate qi, impel downward, or are bitter and cold in nature, then in all cases this will inevitably cause a hidden injury. Constructive qi departs, dispersing the true yin, and this often leads to Blood being damaged and qi submerged. Contrary [to one's intent] there will be great harm when birth approaches.[72]

As a general principle, Zhang affirmed that " 'expediting birth' consists of nothing more than assisting her Blood and qi and guiding them."[73] Such assistance, furthermore, should be limited to helping the mother regain her strength in cases of prolonged labor. It was absolutely wrong to try to speed up a normal delivery, and Zhang rejected the use of "medicines to make qi move and lead Blood out." Trying to bring the baby down before its time, he said, was like plucking at petals to help a flower bloom or pulling on sprouts to help them grow.[74] Thus, although Zhang Jiebin recommended some formulas that could facilitate birth, his

favored remedies embodied a therapeutic strategy that was opposite to
the one espoused by Chen Ziming and Song dynasty *fuke*. The difference
between their strategies is illustrated by a description Wang Kentang
(1549–1613) wrote of the five principal pharmacological approaches for
expediting a difficult birth: "Slippery drugs are used to promote flow and
clear away obstruction in cases of impediments and stagnation; bitter
drugs are used to expel in cases of closed-up blockages; aromatic drugs
are used to bore open and drive out Blood. In cases of stagnant qi, make
qi circulate. In cases where the womb waters break first and she is exhausted, then stabilize Blood."[75]

The first four kinds of drugs all speak to a shared strategy of attacking blocked accumulations of Blood and qi. The last kind of drug points
to a different strategy, namely, preserving the proper flow and amplitude
of Blood throughout the duration of a labor, especially a lengthy one.
Chen Ziming's birth-expediting formulas relied on the former approach,
notably deploying slippery and aromatic drugs to disperse and expel various kinds of stagnation. Although Chen Ziming also recognized the utility of Blood-stabilizing medicines, he used these much less often. Zhang
Jiebin, by contrast, relied heavily on drugs to nurture Blood and hardly
ever used the antistagnation ingredients favored by Chen Ziming.[76] Thus
in pharmacological as well as textual terms, Zhang Jiebin defined the prevention of difficult labor as a matter of protecting the mother's Blood
and qi. Writing almost a century later, Ye Feng took these ideas to their
obvious extreme, rejecting all birth-expediting drugs while also recommending medicines to preserve a woman's vitalities.

ERRING ON THE SIDE OF NONINTERVENTION

As we saw in chapter 4, Chinese medical thinkers believed that the length
of a pregnancy could vary depending on the mother's constitution or circumstances. In addition to complicating doctors' attempts to judge the
status of a suspected pregnancy, this belief also framed the way in which
they thought about managing delivery. How could one tell whether any
given pregnancy had finally reached its natural conclusion? More specifically, how did one know whether a woman was truly in labor? Particularly difficult were cases where the woman experienced signs of labor
but the child had still not been born after a prolonged period of time.
Here the observer had to distinguish among three possible scenarios:
was this a false labor, an obstructed labor, or an unusually slow but otherwise normal labor? Each scenario required a distinct approach, and judg-

ing wrongly could lead to the death of the mother, the child, or both. The medical literature described many diagnostic signs that people could use to assess the true state of a woman's apparent labor, but it also acknowledged that these signs could be ambiguous or of varying utility depending on the case. In practical terms, therefore, one was always potentially confronted with having to decide whether to err on the side of intervention, or on the side of letting things take their own course.

For Ye Feng, nonintervention was the obvious choice. Since birth would always occur easily when the time was ripe, the failure of the baby to emerge was the definitive sign that the correct time had not actually come. Modern readers may see this as a circular argument, but for Ye Feng it proceeded in linear fashion from a fixed and incontrovertible truth: that childbirth embodied the irresistible procreative urge of the cosmos. To be sure, human discernment of these cosmic principles could be imperfect, but the principles themselves were eternal. In cases of diagnostic and therapeutic uncertainty, therefore, the "great virtue of Heaven and Earth" represented a stable point of reference against which families or healing consultants should make their judgments. For this reason, Ye Feng argued that seemingly protracted births were simply instances where the baby was not ready to be born. This principle was of course epitomized by the case of Zhang Baohua's wife, who gave birth easily once her pregnancy had reached its twelfth month. Although Ye Feng's views were much more noninterventionist than those of his predecessors and near contemporaries, his beliefs were nevertheless well grounded in literate medical teachings and the accumulated observations of eminent doctors. This will become clear as we look at the ways in which doctors of the past tried to read the signs of birth and wrestle with ambiguous cases.

Reading the Signs of Childbirth

When Ye Feng first examined Zhang Baohua's wife, he used her pulse signs to determine whether her labor was a true one. Beginning with the imperial physician Wang Shuhe's *Classic of the Pulse* (*Maijing*, ca. 280), doctors had recognized a distinctive pulse pattern that signaled the end of pregnancy and the onset of labor, the so-called *li jing*.[77] Although there was some debate over the precise quality of this pulse, doctors agreed that the characters *li jing* meant "to depart from the usual." Some described it as an erratic pulse "without any regularity in its amplitude, sometimes like a sparrow pecking or water leaking through a roof," and the *Golden Mirror* explained that "when the fetus moves within, the pulse is disordered without."[78] For his part, Wang Kentang had argued that the distinctive feature of the *li jing* was that it pointed to a sudden change in the woman's body. Under normal circumstances, such a pulse could indicate illness, but when accompanied with abdominal pains it pointed to the conclusion of pregnancy: "For example, yesterday the pregnant woman had a floating and replete pulse on the left, as if pregnant with a boy, but today her pulse is floating [as if pregnant with a girl]. This is a pulse that has departed from the usual and also one that is different from the day before. If furthermore her abdomen hurts, then you can know that she is about to give birth."[79]

To master pulse reading techniques required hands-on training under the tutelage of an experienced doctor, and Ye Feng did not discuss these skills in *Easy Childbirth*, a text aimed at householders. Instead, he assigned primary importance to the problem of correctly distinguishing between true and false labor pains. If one mistook false pains for real ones, then the mother would try to push the baby out too soon, thus resulting in a difficult delivery. Conversely, Ye asserted, as long as one read the signs correctly, birth would be easy. In focusing on pain, Ye Feng essentially diminished the importance of several other bodily signs that had long been used to assess whether a woman was in labor. To appreciate the way in which he did this, it is helpful to refer again to Yang Zijian's canonical description of *zhengchan*, or "correct childbirth": "In correct childbirth, the woman fulfills her complete ten months of pregnancy, and yin and yang qi are sufficient. Suddenly she has waves of pain in the waist and abdomen, followed by an immediate sinking down of the fetal qi. When things arrive at the point where the pains in the navel and abdomen are at their most extreme, there is also heavy pain within the waist, and the birth path protrudes, then the starchy waters burst and Blood descends, and the child is subsequently born."[80]

In this particular passage, the *zhengchan* carries the meaning of "correct birth," namely, the opposite of the obstructed births or births accompanied by illness that Yang Zijian goes on to discuss. But the term *zhengchan* also comprised the meaning of "the true time for delivery"—that is, a true labor (the pregnancy had genuinely run its course) as opposed to a false labor. This usage appears, for example, in Yang Zijian's description of "injurious childbirth" *(shangchan)* from pushing too early. Here he says that that false labor pains are "not *zhengchan*," meaning that they do not signal a true labor. This usage is also frequently seen in later medical literature, including Lou Ying's well-known Ming-dynasty commentary on Yang Zijian. In his remarks on the dangers of pushing too early, Lou listed a number of manifestations that were "not signs of true labor" *(fei zhengchan zhi hou).*[81] For example, if the fetus had not yet dropped down, if the birth canal was not protruding, if Blood and fluids had not come out, if there was no pain in the waist, then the time for birth had not actually arrived. In sum, the signs that Yang Zijian described as characterizing a smooth labor could also serve to distinguish a real labor from a false one.

Of all these known signs, Ye Feng chose to focus on pain, a bodily sign that could vary according to intensity, frequency, and location. For male medical experts, the challenge of distinguishing between different types of pain was twofold: first, did the pattern of pain indicate that this was a true labor; and second, did the pattern of pain indicate that the moment for the baby to leave the mother's body had arrived? Such distinctions broadly correspond to what modern obstetrics defines as the first and second stages of labor, the former characterized by the effacement and dilatation of the cervix and the latter by the expulsion of the baby. Chinese texts, however, framed the progress of labor in temporal rather than anatomical terms: had the pregnancy reached its own natural limit (which could be shorter or longer than the canonical ten months)? If so, had the baby completed its head-down rotation so that it was ready to be born? In practical terms, furthermore, ascertaining the baby's readiness to emerge was the key issue, for trying to push it out at any earlier moment could lead to complications. Thus the problem of distinguishing between false and true labor overlapped with the problem of determining whether or not it was too soon for the mother to bear down.

False Pains and False Waters

Chinese medical experts had long recognized that women often experienced laborlike pains during the last months of pregnancy, a phenomenon corresponding to what modern obstetricians refer to as Braxton-Hicks contractions of the uterine muscles. Yang Zijian had called these pains "testing the month" *(shiyue),* a phrase that defined them as a kind of practice labor: "Nowadays there are cases where one month before the [expected time of] birth, the navel and abdomen suddenly begin to hurt. It seems as if she is about to give birth, and yet nothing happens. This is called 'testing the month,' and it is not true childbirth."[82]

Historical discussions of a related problem known as "teasing pains" *(nongtong)* show that there could also be a conceptual overlap between false labor pains and the pains in the early stages of a true labor. In his thirteenth-century discussion of difficult birth, Chen Ziming provided this description of "teasing pains": "When she first enters the time of birth *(lin chan)*, she has abdominal pains that start and stop."[83] Chen Ziming saw "teasing pains" as signaling the onset of true labor, but not the moment of birth. He therefore warned against reckless and ignorant midwives who would seize this opportunity to begin "testing the waters" *(shi shui)* by poking the amniotic sac, for if the waters broke too early, the birth canal would become dried out and impede delivery when the time for delivery arrived. Later writers, however, used the term "teasing pains" to refer to false labor pangs during the end stages of pregnancy. Lou Ying, for example, described them as something that occurred "before the ten months [of pregnancy] have been completed," and he included these in his list of things that should be clearly distinguished from true labor.[84] When Li Chan said that these pains occurred in women with "weak bodies and anxious dispositions," he also implied that they were false labor signs arising from an underlying deficiency.[85] But although there was some semantic flexibility, doctors like Zhang Jiebin continued to describe a temporal continuum of misleading pains, distinguished by how close to the time of expected labor they occurred. Here Zhang distinguished between two patterns of false labor pains, which he called "teasing the fetus" *(nongtai)* and "testing the month" *(shiyue):* "A pregnant woman has reached the time for birth and suddenly her abdomen hurts intermittently, sometimes for one or two days, sometimes for two or three days; there is a little flow of fetal waters, but the abdominal pains are not close together. These are called 'teasing the fetus.' It is not the actual birth. Also there are cases where a month or half-month beforehand, the abdomen suddenly hurts as if she is going to give birth, but she does not. This is called 'testing the month' and it is also not childbirth."[86]

Besides noting the pattern and timing of any apparent birth pains, it was also important to verify their location in the woman's body. Doctors taught that only pains in the waist indicated true labor, and these could also signal whether the precise moment for birth had indeed arrived. Lou Ying specified, for example, that it was not "correct childbirth" if the woman felt severe pain in the abdomen but not in the waist.[87] Li Chan went as far as to warn against taking action when "the navel and abdomen both hurt, and the child begins to show its crown, but yet the waist does not hurt."[88] The significance of waist pains arose directly from the perceived structure of the female reproductive system. As Zhang Jiebin explained, "The kidney is tied to the waist, and the womb is tied to the kidney."[89] Since the womb and waist were essentially connected, pain that extended to the mother's waist was a reliable sign that the child was ready to come out.

Another sign that required careful interpretation was the breaking of the woman's waters. Doctors recognized that labor could become difficult if the waters broke too early and the mother got "dried out." At the same time, however, they disagreed whether discharges of fluid indicated that birth was truly imminent. Lou Ying, for example, cautioned that, if "the starchy fluids and Blood have come out, but the abdomen does not hurt," then this was a false labor.[90] Yu Tuan was among those who noted that there could be false waters analogous to false pains: "If the abdominal and waist pains are not severe, and there is only a little bit of fluid dripping out, this is called 'trial fluids' *(shijiang)*. These are not the true starchy fluids that are within the womb. Moreover, it is proper to put one's mind at ease and wait. One absolutely must not lightly summon the midwife to deliver the child."[91] But the challenge of distinguishing between true and false signs of labor was also complicated by beliefs in the cosmological resonance of childbirth, and the question here was whether a ripe melon could ever fail to fall. During the eleventh century, Yang Zijian taught that an otherwise correct birth could become protracted, even if the right time for delivery had arrived. In such cases, it was imperative to carry out an "expedited birth" *(cuichan)*:

> Expedited birth refers to cases where the woman is going to give birth, the starchy waters have broken and Blood has come out, there are jolts of pain in the navel and abdomen and the pain is extreme, the waist is heavy and the birth canal protrudes, and one already sees the signs of correct birth, but the child still does not come out. Then one can use medicines to expedite the birth. There are cases where this has endured for several days, the mother is suffering greatly, and one has already clearly ascertained that these are the signs of true birth, but the child is having difficulty being born. One can also use medicines to assist the mother's orthopathic qi, and make the child be born swiftly. This is called expedited birth.[92]

The individual variations in each pregnancy, however, meant that it was not so easy to distinguish between false labors and true labors that were not progressing. Lou Ying's account of his own grandson's birth epitomizes the difficulties in judgment that could arise:

> My son's wife experienced pain in both the waist and abdomen during the month prior to birth. All signs appeared to indicate that birth was imminent, and her pains were severe, but during the midmorning hours it would stop slightly. Things continued like this for more than ten days. Seeing that nothing came out, and having read [Yang Zijian's discussion of injurious

birth], we subsequently used several doses of fetus-securing formula with added Ginseng-Atractylodes Powder and nourished her with the flavor of meat. In this way, she calmly recovered and was without pain. Moreover, after another twenty-some days she delivered a son. At that [earlier] time, if one had acted recklessly, chaotically using force and administering medicines to expedite birth, then the situation would have immediately turned perilous.[93]

In this case, the observable signs had all indicated that Lou Ying's daughter-in-law was truly in labor. After all, it was not unheard of for babies to be born a month early. But the family's knowledge that it was dangerous to inappropriately expedite birth, joined with their observation that the labor was not progressing, ultimately led them to conclude that the correct time for birth had not in fact arrived. Faced with ambiguous signs, Lou's family chose to err on the side of nonintervention—correctly, as it turned out. By giving the mother fetus-stabilizing and qi-augmenting drugs, they positively helped the pregnancy come to its natural conclusion. Thus while Yang Zijian taught that even a genuine labor could become protracted, Lou's account supports an opposite view: protracted birth meant that the correct time had not actually arrived.

Later writers continued to negotiate between these two poles. Yu Tuan, for example, urged intervention when all the signs of true labor were present but the child had not yet been born. As discussed earlier, Yu Tuan believed that the baby itself broke the placental wrapper, allowing the fluids inside the womb to gush out. But while the breaking of the waters was a sign that the baby was truly ready to be born, weak babies might also be unable to turn and follow the waters out. Thus, Yu Tuan counseled medical intervention in all cases where the waters had broken but the child was tardy in emerging. To do nothing in such cases was tantamount to "sitting with one's hands up one's sleeves, awaiting death."[94] Particularly dangerous were cases where the fetus had died inside the mother, for its poisonous qi could lead to the woman's agonizing demise. For his part, Zhang Jiebin provided only a qualified view of nonintervention. On the one hand, he acknowledged the ambiguity of signs and suggested that the onset of a true labor was not necessarily accompanied by the waters breaking. At the same time, however, he agreed that one should pharmacologically assist the child if the waters had broken and the baby had still not come out after an hour or two. "Now, the starchy waters are there to nourish the child's life," Zhang explained, "and when the starchy waters are dried and it is not born, this inevitably means that the fetus's primordial qi lacks strength. The longer one tarries, the drier it will be, and the more deficient its strength will definitely become. Therefore it is proper to quickly expedite it."[95]

The foregoing discussion shows that, by the time that Ye Feng wrote his treatise, male medical writers had been wrestling for some time with how to resolve the potential ambiguities surrounding childbirth. Intervening too early would cause dangerous obstructions, but failure to intervene in time could also prove fatal. In response to these complexities, Ye Feng chose to err on the side of nonintervention. His dictum to "sleep, endure the pain, and delay approaching the birthing tub" meant that in the face of any apparent birthing pain—whether a "trial pain" or pain in the early stages of a true labor—the only appropriate course of action was to watch, wait, and protect the mother's stamina. Under no circumstances should one actively try to facilitate the baby's birth:

> When the woman begins to feel abdominal pains, she must first hold these ideas firmly in her own mind. She must realize that [giving birth] is the self-so principle of human generation. It is an exceedingly easy matter, and there is no need to panic. But when she feels a bout of pain that does not stop, and that is followed by several successive waves of pain, *gradually increasing in the intensity of pain and gradually coming closer together, then this means the child is about to be born.* Then one can notify people to come and wait on her.
>
> If the pains come slowly, then these are trial pains, and the only thing to do is to rest quietly and eat calmly. One must not recklessly take action. *At this point, it is exceedingly crucial to be extremely attentive and careful.* This is the first critical juncture, and one must not take things lightly. If one takes it to be a proper birth and recklessly approaches the birthing tub, then this will be an utter error.[96]

In response to imagined skeptics who asked whether the mother could be allowed to exert any effort at all, Ye Feng allowed that there was a brief moment when it was not positively forbidden. That was the moment when the child was actually ready to leave the mother's body, which one could determine by a careful reading of signs. At that point, the mother could bear down, but for no longer than the time it took to drink a small cup of tea: "If the child is truly pressing on the gate of childbirth, the bones and joints of the entire body are loose, the front of the chest sinks down, the waist and abdomen are unusually heavy and sinking, she has the need to urgently defecate and urinate at the same time, and she sees bursts of sparks before her eyes, *then this is the true time.* It is proper to approach the tub at this time and use a bout of force. The mother and child will separate, and what difficulty could there be?"[97]

Despite this apparent concession to common sentiment, Ye Feng insisted overall that it was best to refrain from any effort whatsoever. There was no harm in mistaking the signs of real labor for false pains, for the child would come out on its own when the time was ripe regardless of whether anyone helped it. The worst that could happen, he said, was that the child would "fall out into [the mother's] trousers or be born on the bed."[98] But in his discussion of "trial pains," Ye Feng pointed out that those who tried to expedite a false labor ran a high risk of killing the mother, the child, or both: "They carelessly [make her] approach the tub, and for an entire day she sits upright without being allowed to sleep or lie down. In some cases they grasp her about the waist and rub her belly. In some cases they use a hand to pull or use medicines to attack, absolutely determined to extract the child. As for the mother, nine will die and one will live, while out of ten babies, nine will die. The tragedy is indescribable."[99]

Again, we must note that Ye Feng was not ignorant of the real difficulties that might arise. He did admit that there were occasionally situations where the child's strength was exhausted so that it did not come out even when "the fruit has reached its proper time." But he insisted that the best approach was still to have the mother rest and thereby replenish maternal and fetal energies: "It is proper to have the woman go to bed and sleep quietly, so that the child inside the belly will also sleep quietly. In a while it will regain its strength, and it will come out of its own accord."[100] For Ye Feng, then, the sole purpose of medical intervention was to bolster the woman's qi and Blood, allowing her to maintain control over herself while awaiting the child's arrival. Given the ambiguity of birthing signs and the potential dangers in active intervention, relying on cosmic principle became a justifiable therapeutic option.

GENDER AND CHILDBIRTH

Ye Feng distilled out older ideas about the innate ease of birth and expanded them into a firmly noninterventionist credo. In formulating his ideas, he also evoked established strategies for managing childbirth by regulating a woman's vitalities so that her childbearing powers could operate unimpeded. These conceptual resonances between Ye's work and broader currents in learned medicine also help explain why contemporary and later medical authors incorporated Ye Feng's teachings into their own works even when they did not completely share his noninterventionist stance. In chapter 3, I recorded the details of *Easy Childbirth*'s wide circulation. It is also worth noting here that Wei Zhixiu included the story of Zhang Baohua's wife and another of Ye's cases in his *Continuation of the* Cases from Famous Doctors, Arranged by Category (ca. 1770). *Easy Childbirth* was also praised and cited in Chen Nianzu's *Essentials of Medicine for Women* (*Nüke yaozhi*, 1803), a popular textbook for aspiring doctors. The ubiquity of *Easy Childbirth* meant that the doctrine of cosmologically resonant childbirth was a salient characteristic of eighteenth- and nineteenth-century medicine, shaping the intellectual parameters of how male doctors thought about the challenges of ensuring safe delivery.

The prominence of this idea also helps explain the gendered patterns of childbirth practice in late imperial China. While medical texts routinely presented advice for preventing and managing the complications of childbirth, these discussions were markedly shorter, less detailed, and less systematic compared to their lengthy and exhaustive descriptions of the ailments of menstruation, pregnancy, and postpartum. Even works with *childbirth (chan)* in the title might present only a perfunctory mention of labor. And in childbirth, as with other female ailments, the male physician's interventions consisted almost entirely of orally ingested pharmaceutical formulas, occasionally supplemented by acupuncture or externally applied plasters and medicinal washes. To the extent that Qing medical texts discussed the problem of how to physically extract the child from the mother's body, they generally just cited Yang Zijian's eleventh-century treatise. Thus the late imperial period witnessed a consistent division of labor between female midwives, who managed the physical aspects of birth, and the male physician, who would be called only in an emergency and then was primarily responsible for administering drugs. As Charlotte Furth points out, Chinese male doctors' interest in the hands-on aspects of delivery seems to have declined steadily after the thirteenth century.[101] During the late seventeenth century, Xiao Xun's compendium of classical teachings on women's medicine even suggested that Yang Zijian's treatise on the ten types of childbirth was largely irrelevant for male physicians. Xiao listed only two types of labor as being "within the doctor's [sphere] of using drugs to regulate and protect." These were cases when birth occurred during severely cold weather or overly hot weather. In such instances, drugs could be used to prevent climatic extremes from stagnating or dissipating the laboring mother's Blood and qi. As for the other categories discussed by Yang Zijian, including various forms of malpresentation, Xiao pointed out that "these are all the affair of the mother in labor and the midwife."[102]

One reason for this lack of male interest in obstetrics was undoubt-

edly the educated Chinese doctor's disdain for manual techniques, something that seems to have become more pronounced during the Qing, as
elite doctors became ever more concerned with constructing a gentlemanly identity. Another contributing factor was certainly the prevailing
norms of gender segregation and the historical association of childbirth
with the female sphere. But the broad issues of gentlemanly snobbery
and desire to protect female modesty were hardly foreign to western Europe at that time, where a growing cohort of male doctors nevertheless
pursued an active role in obstetrics. All this suggests that we must look
for additional historical factors to explain late imperial Chinese perspectives. A previously unexamined but crucial factor, I propose, is the relationship between medical definitions of childbirth and the professional
and social aspirations of male practitioners.

Medical historians have amply shown that European male practitioners used obstetrics as a way to both further their careers and consolidate
their medical authority. In Great Britain, for example, male surgeons
scrambling to establish a foothold in the highly competitive medical
marketplace pursued obstetrics as a valuable stratagem for building up
their clientele.[103] "Man midwives" further justified their activities by
pointing out that their knowledge of human anatomy and physiology—
derived from study in medical schools—made them superior to practitioners without similar training. These, notably, included female midwives
and other women whose attendance at medical schools was curtailed or
prohibited altogether. Extending male control over obstetrics was thus
part of a broader movement to strengthen the professional privileges of
male doctors with a particular kind of medical education. Furthermore,
the ascendance of man-midwifery was abetted by a particular medical
definition of difficult childbirth, one that portrayed it as a mechanical
and structural problem rooted in defective female pelvic anatomy. The
historical thrust of European male-directed obstetrics, therefore, was to
seek ever more effective ways of physically extracting the baby from the
mother's body, whether by developing better techniques to grasp, manipulate, or dismember the baby, or by developing different ways of opening up the mother's abdomen or pelvis.[104]

In comparison, the manual work of delivering babies offered no professional or social benefits to late imperial Chinese male healers. Quite
the contrary, for the rhetoric of cosmologically resonant childbirth essentially defined practical obstetrics as an inferior form of medical practice, one rooted in an imperfect understanding of the human body. Instead, the claimed superiority of Chinese male doctors came from their

awareness that childbirth was self-driven and spontaneously easy, and they derided female midwives for believing that birth required active management and intervention. The best way to manage a difficult labor, the Chinese male physician declared, was to prevent it from happening in the first place.

These beliefs animated the preface that literatus and medical expert Zhang Yuesun wrote in 1830 to his own work on pregnancy and childbirth. Here Zhang affirmed the superiority of prevention in no uncertain terms, a belief that sprang from his faith in the innate ease of birth.[105] In words that echoed the *Treatise on Easy Childbirth* (which he also cited in the body of his book), Zhang Yuesun's preface asserted: "Difficulty in labor is caused by people themselves, and it is not the fundamental nature of things." The ancients gave birth easily, he said, because they knew how to control their actions and desires during pregnancy. Later generations, however, wantonly flouted the proper regimens, leading to an increase in the incidence of difficult labor. This spurred people to employ birthing drugs and midwives, but these measures just compounded the problem. Once a protracted labor had reached a certain point, furthermore, there were few good options available. As Zhang Yuesun noted, it was supremely inhumane for midwives to dismember unborn babies, "yet bystanders do not regard this as wrong, and the household heads do not resent this. Why not? Because doctors have no methods for rescuing them, so that one can only look to the wives and grannies for aid." The best way to manage such calamities, Zhang emphasized, was to keep them from happening at all:

> If you want to make boiling water cool down, stirring it up is not as good as taking it off the fire. If you want to make a bowstring firm, joining the ends of a broken one together is not as good as avoiding breakage in the first place. If you want to safely manage difficult birth, treating it with medicine is not as good as preventing things from reaching that point.
>
> If one does not investigate the root [causes of the problem] but equates them with the end results, failing to halt the former and trying to rescue the situation from the latter, then even a good official will be unable to govern and a good doctor will be unable to obtain results.[106]

Although only in his early twenties, Zhang Yuesun spoke with the moral authority of a man belonging to an eminent family of scholars and talented women, as well as with the confidence of an experienced healer who had been studying medicine since childhood.[107] No rational person would try to cool down boiling water by stirring it while the pot was still on the stove, and only those with divine assistance could ever expect a mended bowstring to perform adequately.[108] Zhang's analogies thereby portrayed prevention as a self-evident, superior strategy, and ex post facto intervention as a fool's errand. Furthermore, when he evoked the old trope likening medicine to government service, Zhang gendered the preventative strategy as a distinctly male one: just as the wise (male) official knew how to prevent social unrest by promoting the welfare of the people, the wise (male) doctor knew how to prevent difficult labor by regulating the woman's health in the period leading up to birth. So whereas European male doctors criticized midwives for their ignorance of anatomy, Chinese male doctors excoriated midwives for their ignorance of cosmic principles.

To be sure, the general idea that midwives did not know how to respect the innate rhythms of birth was an old one in China. It already appears in medical writings of the seventh and eighth centuries, and Chen Ziming's thirteenth-century textbook repeated what were obviously common complaints: midwives induced premature rupture of the amniotic sac by "testing the waters" with their hands, so that the birth canal was dried up by the time birth began, and they ordered the mother to "sit on the rushes" and bear down before the proper time had arrived, thus interfering with labor.[109] Zhang Congzheng (ca. 1156–1228) famously told of a woman harmed by the joint efforts of three midwives. "Two of them pulled hard on the woman's arms," Zhang related, "and one of them braced her head against the woman's abdomen and also used both hands to grasp [the mother's] waist with great force." These efforts to physically squeeze the baby out killed it in utero and provoked a grave illness in the mother. But such heroic exertions were unnecessary, Zhang lamented, because "when the melon is ripe, the stalk breaks."[110] Late imperial writers continued to repeat these criticisms. However, their concerns were now also integrated into an explicitly gendered rhetoric of medical authority that portrayed the application of cosmological principles to childbirth as a male approach and manual intervention as a female one. A treatise on childbirth by Chen Zhidao (fl. 1600?) even blamed the prevalence of difficult labor on female ignorance. The fundamental nature of birth was to be easy, he said, so why did difficult labor arise? "The reason is because the matter [of childbirth] belongs to the inner quarters," Chen affirmed, "and although the principle [of easy birth] is recorded in books, who in the female sphere has ever heard of or practiced it?"[111] If one were lucky, Chen Zhidao said, the midwife would know how to respect the innate rhythm of the birth at hand and would deliver the baby safely. But these skills arose from happenstance, Chen emphasized, and "not because she is knowledgeable about the principles."

These observations thus drew a contrast between male knowledge derived from scholarly cultivation and female knowledge based on custom and experience. They also implied that male expertise was the only viable solution to problems created by female ignorance. In this way, discernment of the cosmic principles patterning childbirth became the crux of the male physician's claim to superiority over the midwife. A case from Xu Dachun, relating how he managed the protracted labor of a kinsman's wife, shows how male doctors could deploy this epistemological authority in a therapeutic setting. The poor woman had been in labor for two days when the midwife declared that nothing more could be done. At that moment, Xu Dachun happened to be visiting his kinsman, who was the woman's uncle-in-law. Xu offered to see what he could do, and they hurried to the woman's home in a nearby lane. Arriving on the scene, Xu Dachun found that her womb waters had dried up. Although the woman was now too exhausted to speak, the midwife still urged her to keep trying to push the baby out. Upon taking the woman's pulse, however, Xu judged that she was actually experiencing a false labor: "I said, 'Fear not, this is a case of "testing the fetus" [shitai]. The time for birth has not yet arrived, so do not force her. Help her [onto the bed] and have her lie quietly. After another month, she will go into labor, her birth will definitely be smooth, and moreover, she will give birth to a boy.' "[112]

The woman's family did not know what to think, and the midwife was incredulous. "What kind of person is this, to talk so big?" she scoffed. "I have been delivering babies for several decades, and I have never seen anyone in this kind of situation successfully give birth." Undaunted, Xu prescribed a formula to nourish the woman's Blood and secure the fetus. "After one dose," he recalled, "all signs of labor ceased." A little over a month later, the woman indeed went into labor, delivering a son with the utmost ease.

Asked to explain his seemingly miraculous predictions, Xu explained that the woman's false labor had originally been caused by a disharmony in maternal vitalities, such as might be provoked by exposure to cold wind or overwork. In such cases, the fetus would drop down, producing symptoms that resembled impending childbirth. But the pulse readings had told Xu Dachun that her gestation was not yet complete, and the relative vigor of her left pulse had told him the child was a boy. Furthermore, since the fetus had been already dislodged during the first attempt to push it out, it naturally followed that the real delivery would proceed easily. Xu Dachun brushed aside the praise that his diagnosis had been like that of a divinity *(shen)*, pointing out that "this is an extremely obvious principle; it is just that people are unable to see it for themselves." But the tone and structure of the case narrative belied Xu's modesty, presenting his actions as a virtuosic performance by a supremely insightful male literatus-physician. Although his diagnosis provoked disbelief on the part of the woman's family and the midwife alike, Xu Dachun was able to prevail, thanks to his ability to read the pulse and his knowledge of the fundamentally self-correcting dynamics of childbirth. Ever the gentleman, he maintained an assured and calm demeanor that contrasted sharply with the midwife's futile instructions and her blustery response when challenged. Xu Dachun thereby showed how male scholarly knowledge could trump a midwife's years of hands-on experience when it came to caring for women in childbirth.

Despite their sometimes scathing criticisms of midwives, however, male doctors never sought to take over the actual management of labor themselves, and they assumed that midwives would continue to be a standard presence in the birthing room. Even a noninterventionist like Ye Feng acknowledged that, "since there are such people [as midwives], it is not possible to not use them."[113] But male medical thinkers did aim to make the midwife's role largely superfluous. Chen Zhidao, who blamed midwives for complicating labor, notably addressed himself to husbands who could then explain things properly to their wives.[114] By teaching householders about the true nature of birth, he and other male authors sought to undermine the midwife's power to define the proper management of labor and thus curb the source of her authority over the parturient woman and her family. As Ye Feng put it, if one engaged a midwife, "it must be you using her, and not her using you."[115] Furthermore, he insisted that the midwife's role was to be strictly limited to catching the baby and putting it on the bed. To support his argument, Ye Feng pointed out that the various terms for "midwife" all described her as a granny who "received" *(jie)* or "collected" *(shou)* the baby. Under no circumstances, therefore, should the midwife be allowed to actively assist the birth, not least because the innately easy nature of birth made such assistance entirely unnecessary.[116]

These male criticisms of midwives owed much to long-standing anxieties about the potentially corrupting influence of the various female experts and "grannies" who serviced the women of the inner quarters.[117] But worries about midwives also echoed the broader repertoire of criticisms leveled against supposedly incompetent medical practitioners in general. In chapter 2, we saw that people who published popular medical handbooks frequently justified the need for these books by pointing out that one could not rely on doctors. Similarly, praise for the cosmologically resonant approach to childbirth was often coupled with fears about possible abuses by birthing attendants. One common stereotype notably described midwives in the same terms as quack doctors in general: they did not understand the true nature of the illnesses they claimed to treat, and they were more concerned with displaying their skills and collecting their fees than with the well-being of their patients. Ye Feng developed these points with particular detail:

> In general, this type of person is frequently stupid and ignorant of the proper principles. As soon as they come in the door, they do not ask if the birth is early or tardy, and they do not ask if [the melon] is green or ripe. They just order [the woman] to sit on the grass and exert herself, and they inevitably say that the child's head has already arrived [at the gate of birth]. Some will order that the mother's waist be kneaded and her belly rubbed. Some insert their hands into the birth gate to investigate, frequently causing injury. In general their concern is to display their virtuosity and diligence, and they refuse to be calm and quiet. Furthermore, there is a class of crafty and evil women who seek profits by "hoarding rare goods until the prices go up." The disaster is indescribable.[118]

Ye Feng's remark about "hoarding rare goods" referred to the fear that a midwife would pretend that she was unable to help, until the family beseeched her with promise of great rewards. A related stereotype was the midwife whose "help" constituted the most extreme form of intervention: dismembering the unborn child to extract it from the birth canal. Such tragedies provided an ideal straw man that male scholar-doctors could use to assert their superiority with respect to the midwife. This dynamic is exemplified by Wang Shixiong's account of Shi Qiutao's wife, who had experienced two protracted labors in a row. Both had ended with "the midwife rashly employing lethal techniques, extracting the child by cutting it up."[119] Commenting on this case, Wang Shixiong emphasized that every birth was unique, varying according to women's circumstances and innate constitutions. He cited the adage that "ten children will be born in ten different ways," and he emphasized that one should not jump to panicked conclusions when a birth appeared to be impeded. Some births simply took longer than others. Thus, Wang instructed, "if the child's body is properly aligned downward, then even if the hours and days grow long there is no need for alarm, and one can simply wait quietly with a calm mind." As proof, he cited the case of Licentiate Shi Pusheng of Guiji County (Shaoxing Prefecture), who was born after thirteen days of labor, without harm to either child or mother. Unfortunately, Wang said, "the common people of this world are ignorant of this principle," leaving them vulnerable to bad midwives: "As soon as they perceive the slightest difficulty, they start to panic. An evil midwife will deliberately intimidate [the family] so that they do not dare to object to her plans. In a desire to obtain heavy recompense, she wields the knife and delivers the baby by cutting it up. After she collects her fee and leaves, there are cases where the mother subsequently dies. But that rash person does not know that she injured [the mother] through her techniques and, furthermore, brags about the excellence of her skills."[120]

In Wang's account, the manual techniques used by the midwife symbolized both her lack of knowledge and her lack of morals. By contrast, the male doctor's textual learning gave him access to pharmaceutical techniques that were more humane. Dismembering an unborn child was the cruelest of all cruel acts, Wang suggested, precisely because there were safer, alternative therapies that people could use if only they possessed the requisite knowledge: "If it happens that the child cannot come out, there are all kinds of methods to regulate and treat according to the illness signs. If the child dies within the belly, there are also medicines that can bring it down. In the remedy books that have existed since antiquity, one never hears of cases where infants seeking to be rescued are condemned to be cut up into pieces."[121]

And what kind of knowledge would enable a mother and her baby to escape the knife? For Ye Feng, the answer was clear: one needed to understand that childbirth was a self-so, cosmologically resonant process. Armed with this insight, Ye Feng himself had prevented a midwife from cutting off an unborn child's hand when she was unable to resolve a transverse presentation. Following his own advice, Ye Feng ordered the parturient woman to lie quietly, and he administered some replenishing drugs. "The next morning the child was born," he reported, "and the mother and child were both safe."[122]

CONCLUSION

It is tempting to dismiss anti-midwife stories as misogynistic slander or the inevitable expression of a literate gentleman's snobbish disdain for unlettered manual practitioners. A consideration of the material conditions of childbirth prior to the twentieth century, however, suggests an additional dimension to the story. Objectively speaking, before the development of safe cesarean sections, the physical destruction of an unborn child could be the only feasible way to resolve an intractable labor. Such techniques were a standard part of Euro-American obstetrical practice and also used by foreign doctors in China who treated cases of difficult birth among Chinese women. An illustrative example appears in a report filed in 1898–99 by James H. McCartney, a medical officer assigned to the Imperial Maritime Customs Administration in Chongqing. McCartney criticized Chinese midwives who "invariably pull off an arm in their frantic efforts to deliver" cases of shoulder presentation. But when summoned to resolve a case of difficult birth where the midwife had already dismembered the baby, McCartney himself amputated the child's other arm in order to extract it.[123] Western contemporaries of McCartney also reported performing craniotomies on Chinese babies.[124] This operation, in which the unborn child's skull was perforated and crushed to facilitate extraction, had long been a staple of Euro-American obstetrics, and its relative merits as an emergency intervention continued to be discussed in Western textbooks well into the twentieth century.[125]

The heartrending measures that might be required to resolve an obstructed labor thus served as the material point of reference against which Chinese literate male doctors sought improved and less destructive alternatives for solving obstetrical problems. They found an appealing answer in the discourse of cosmologically resonant childbirth, which promised both that things would go well by default, and that mild, replenishing drugs would rectify the situation if things happened to go wrong. Thus, while their European contemporaries sought to wrest actual obstetrical practice away from midwives, Chinese male doctors projected their authority in epistemological terms. They pursued this goal by subordinating the specific problem of difficult labor (the province of midwives) to the larger one of regulating female reproductive health (the province of male doctors), and they concurrently denigrated the utility of manual methods while elevating that of drugs. As a result, the discourse of cosmologically resonant childbirth provided an important intellectual resource that male doctors could use to legitimate themselves as superior overseers of women's gestational bodies. It also meant that practical obstetrics would continue to be tangential to the professional strategies and self-identities of literate Chinese physicians.

CHAPTER 6

To Generate and Transform

Strategies for Postpartum Health

Three decades after the death of his wife, Ms. Wei, magistrate Xu Lian still lamented her untimely demise.[1] Soon after giving birth in 1813, Ms. Wei had fallen ill and was diagnosed as suffering from an internal stagnation of Blood. We have no description of her precise symptoms, but diagnoses of Blood stagnation were common in cases of postpartum abdominal pain, especially when accompanied by distension or hardness in the lower abdomen and apparent obstructions in the flow of postpartum discharges.[2] The doctor was emphatic: breaking up the accumulated Blood was the only way to cure her. He prescribed zedoary rhizome *(ezhu)* and bur-reed rhizome *(jingsanleng)*, two stagnation-dispersing drugs commonly used in such cases.[3] After taking the medicine, however, Ms. Wei became mentally confused and began to babble. The doctor responded by increasing the dosage, explaining that the first prescription had been "too weak to overcome the illness." But this only caused Ms. Wei's condition to deteriorate. As Xu Lian recounted, "Her qi reversed upward with violent desertion," meaning that symptoms of illness intensified in the upper regions of her body, her mental derangement increased, and her vital signs abruptly ceased.

At the time, Xu Lian had no medical expertise and accepted the explanation that Ms. Wei's illness was simply incurable. "But still, I ached with grief," he recalled, and thereafter he began a concerted study of medical literature. His investigations ultimately convinced him that his wife had fallen victim to the belief that one should treat postpartum stagnation by attacking Blood. But this belief was completely wrong, Xu Lian averred, as ill-advised as "trying to manage stagnant water by splashing it up to make it flow." Xu pointed out that the body's Blood was animated by qi, just as water in a cauldron was made to bubble by a cooking flame. Regulating qi was thus the proper way to regulate Blood, whereas drugs that directly targeted Blood would only provoke a deadly dissipation of qi. Unfortunately, Xu Lian said, contemporary "practitioners of childbirth medicine" *(ye chanke zhe)* clung to the misguided strategy of dispersing Blood, with the result that they "killed" *(sha)* their patients. To help prevent such tragedies, Xu Lian decided in 1842 to print and distribute an eighteenth-century manuscript on postpartum ailments, the *Childbirth Treasury (Chanbao)* compiled in 1728 by one Ni Zhiwei. Although we have scant information about Ni, we know he was a Zhejiang native like Xu Lian.[4] It was from Ni Zhiwei's book, Xu Lian explained, that he had learned about the proper remedy for postpartum stagnation. This was Generating and Transforming Decoction *(shenghua tang)*, a supplementing and regulating formula composed of warming drugs. Ni Zhiwei had recommended it for a wide array of postpartum diseases, and Xu attested that he had used variants of this formula to successfully treat his own female relatives. By broadening the circulation of Ni's book, Xu Lian said, he hoped to help more people—including childbirth doctors—learn the proper way to treat the illnesses of newly birthed women.

Xu Lian was not alone in his enthusiasm for Generating and Transforming Decoction or in his belief that it represented a superior strategy for treating postpartum ailments. Records of this once-obscure formula had started circulating in China in the early seventeenth century, and by Xu Lian's time Generating and Transforming Decoction was promoted in both popular manuals and heuristic medical works alike. Xu Lian himself was a *jinshi* degree holder from Hangzhou, an elite scholar from the most politically influential and economically developed region of late imperial China.[5] During a government career that took him to some of the most difficult districts in the empire, he would also acquire a reputation as an incorruptible official and tireless dispenser of justice. On the basis of Xu Lian's influential collection of legal cases, Pierre-Étienne Will has called him "one of the most important legal specialists of the nineteenth century."[6] Xu also produced four medical works, including an edition of Song Ci's renowned thirteenth-century manual on forensic medicine, *The Washing Away of Wrongs (Xiyuan jilu)*.[7] Xu Lian's medical activities were thus framed by the concerns of the scholar-official and learned medical amateur. By the nineteenth century, the endorsements of Xu Lian and other medical authors, practitioners, and patients had established Generating and Transforming Decoction as a staple of both expert and lay practice. Today, practitioners of TCM gynecology continue to use Generating and Transforming Decoction as a standard remedy for numerous postpartum illnesses, particularly those in which Blood stagnation is implicated.[8]

How did this once-obscure remedy become a prominent part of the literate medical repertoire? The answers provide an intimate look at the continuities and changes in late imperial conceptions of the parturient body while also showing how these were affected by larger medical developments. The popularity of Generating and Transforming Decoction owed much to the convergence of several sociomedical dynamics. The first was a widespread cultural consensus that the period following childbirth was a particularly dangerous time for women. The ever-present possibility of illness or death, starkly illustrated by the case of Ms. Wei, motivated people to seek out new remedies. This notably included Generating and Transforming Decoction, a warming remedy that promised to simultaneously generate new Blood and transform away the old. Second, the expansiveness and diversity of Qing medical publishing facilitated the wide circulation of Generating and Transforming Decoction in different textual genres, allowing it to appeal to amateurs and expert healers alike. Finally, its appeal for learned doctors lay in its apparent ability to resolve a long-standing dilemma in postpartum care: how to effectively address the twin postpartum dangers of stagnation and vacuity. Ironically, while Xu Lian and other advocates of Generating and Transforming Decoction praised it as superior to older, cooling therapies, beginning in the nineteenth century this formula was criticized by doctors who felt it was inappropriately warming. As we examine these changing and conflicting views of Generating and Transforming Decoction, we will see that debates over which postpartum drugs to use were intertwined with debates over the nature of childbirth as well as with larger contests for intellectual authority in Chinese medical circles.

FRAMING "POSTPARTUM"

When people in late imperial China thought about the potential complications of childbirth, they worried not only about the immediate ease or difficulty of labor but also about the woman's health in the period following delivery. A deeply rooted custom that embodied this concern was "doing the month" *(zuoyue)* after childbirth. During this period, women were to remain secluded at home, sheltered from the harmful influences of weather, demon, and human alike. Ideally they would rest in bed, exempt from household duties, and supplement their strength while family members plied them with foods and drugs that were seen as "warming" and fortifying. Women were also forbidden to wash their hair or bodies, or otherwise do anything that would expose them to cold or drafts. Besides facilitating the mother's recovery, this seclusion would confine the pollution of birth within the woman's home, so that neither she nor her child would incur the wrath of offended gods.[9] The idea that one ought to "do the month" still shapes present-day postpartum practices in Chinese cultures, so much so that modern researchers once speculated that this elevated level of attention to the new mother might shield Chinese women from postpartum depression.[10] As we shall see, some prominent medical writers criticized the salient features of these vernacular practices, in particular the idea that the postpartum woman always required warming. Nevertheless, the underlying logic of doing the month was broadly reinforced by the frameworks of literate medicine, which similarly depicted the postpartum period as a time of great vulnerability. While the actual delivery of the baby hovered at the margins of male physicians' practice, the care of postpartum illnesses was a core concern for them, and texts on women's diseases routinely included a detailed section on "after birth" *(chanhou).*

Medical writers conventionally spoke of an "after birth" period that began once the child left the mother's body and lasted for one hundred days after that (considerably longer than the vernacular "month" of seclusion).[11] Discussions of postpartum care set forth detailed restrictions governing a woman's diet, behavior, and sexual activity during this period, and also explained how to manage the illnesses that might arise. Some of the numerous ailments classified as postpartum overlapped with complications of labor and delivery, such as retained placenta and postpartum hemorrhage. Another category of illness was that of physical injuries to the female genitals and reproductive organs. These included lacerations of the perineum, genital contusions, prolapse of the uterus, and vaginal "protrusions" *(yinting).* The lactating breast was likewise a site of illness, and doctors worried about scanty and blocked milk, as well as breast sores, swellings, and fevers associated with breastfeeding. Besides these, there were numerous disturbances of the bodily system that were understood to be direct results of childbearing or of the by-products of childbearing. As we shall see, doctors disagreed as to whether the act of giving birth inevitably left the woman in a pathological state of imbalance. But even those who saw childbirth itself as a benign event agreed that the physical and mental exertion of labor consumed qi and Blood. Furthermore, the Blood retained during pregnancy to nourish the child now constituted a waste product that had to be eliminated from the body. Postpartum ailments of all kinds were thus commonly attributed either to a deficiency of Blood and qi or to a stagnation of "noxious dew" *(elu)* and "corrupt Blood" *(baixue)*.

The illnesses rooted in Blood and qi pathologies encompassed a wide range of physical and mental disturbances: fevers and chills, severe headaches and abdominal pains, sudden copious bleeding, constipation and impaired urination, nausea and loss of appetite, seizures and convulsions, fainting and mental stupor, emotional derangement and manic or violent outbursts, vomiting and diarrhea, and gasping for breath. These also included diseases described as "fatal illnesses" *(sizheng)*, "illnesses that cannot be treated" *(bu zhi zhi zheng)*, and "illnesses where one cannot save the afflicted person" *(bu jiu zhi zheng)*.[12] Doctors still suggested possible remedies, of course, but the idea that some postpartum illnesses were untreatable spoke to the pessimistic prognosis that routinely accompanied them. Among the deadliest were the "three dashings" *(san chong)* of postpartum Blood that failed to drain properly from the vagina and instead reversed course to strike against the vital organs. As Yan Chunxi explained, "corrupted Blood dashing into the heart" would provoke an ensemble of uninhibited and erratic behaviors.[13] In mild cases, the woman "sings and dances, chats and laughs, or gets angry and scolds, now sitting up, now lying down." Severe cases were characterized by more alarming forms of derangement, as the woman "climbs over walls and onto rooftops, bites and hits, utters vulgarities, and calls out the names of Buddhas and divinities." Such cases had a high mortality rate: "it is difficult to save even one out of ten people." Only slightly less fatal was Blood dashing into the lung, which would manifest itself in a red face and vomiting, with the woman "appearing to be at the point of death." In such cases, one could hope to save perhaps one or two patients out of ten. Finally, Blood dashing into the stomach would provoke feelings of suffocating fullness in the stomach region, accompanied by "vomiting and nausea, abdominal fullness and distention with pain." Out of ten women afflicted with this illness, Yan estimated, "five will die, and five will live."

Material Dimensions of Postpartum Disease

In general, then, medical discussions of postpartum took place within a broad societal consensus that childbirth was depleting, and that the period following birth was a dangerous passage. To ignore the proper regulations was to flirt with disaster, and even if the woman did not immediately fall ill she risked being plagued with chronic disease and reproductive maladies for the rest of her life. But if these frameworks had explanatory power, it was also because they resonated with observed material phenomena. While a thorough comparison of late imperial and biomedical disease descriptions is beyond the scope of this study, we can note that the symptoms described by Yan Chunxi are also found in Western medical literature of the past and present. Postpartum mania, for example, can arise when pregnancy triggers a latent mental illness. Eclampsia (pregnancy-induced hypertension) can cause convulsions, babbling, and mental stupor. Jerky "dancing" accompanied by death suggests damage to the central nervous system or cardiovascular system, such as that rooted in a previously dormant streptococcal infection (rheumatic fever) or preexisting damage from rheumatic heart disease. Similarly, congestive heart failure could be a possible explanation for a fatal postpartum illness characterized by a red face. Finally, abdominal fullness with pain and vomiting suggests a postpartum infection.[14] For the time being, such retrospective diagnoses must remain tentative and speculative. However, they usefully remind us that the typical repertoire of postpartum ailments discussed in late imperial Chinese medical texts included conditions that their contemporaries in other societies would also have recognized as potentially dangerous complications of childbirth. As for modern medical textbooks, they speak of a "deadly triad" of diseases—"hypertensive disorders, hemorrhage and infection"—that are still responsible for most cases of maternal injury, illness, and death.[15] These nosological classifications are a far cry from late imperial Chinese rubrics such as "Blood swooning" *(xueyun)*, "wind strike" *(zhongfeng)*, and "internal accumulations" *(jiju)*, but the signs of postpartum illness described in Chinese texts would have signaled danger in any language.

Deadly Convulsions

The issue of postpartum infection provides a particularly illuminating case study of the material challenges that Chinese doctors and women faced in the preantibiotic, prevaccine age. Chinese medical writers had long worried about a postpartum pattern of muscular spasms and rigidity that clearly overlaps with the modern disease of maternal tetanus. Tetanus is caused by *Clostridium tetani* bacilli, which live in soil and animal feces and can enter the body through an open wound. As they multiply, they produce a toxin that causes severe muscle rigidity and muscular spasms that can be strong enough to fracture bones and rupture tendons. The classic symptoms of tetanus include spasms of the facial and back muscles, "lockjaw," and hyperextended arching of the back (opisthotonus). Cardiac arrest and respiratory failure can also ensue, and modern mortality rates range from 31 to 50 percent, depending on the age of patient and the severity of the infection.[16] *Maternal tetanus* refers to cases caused by bacteria entering genital wounds caused by childbirth, and it is still a significant cause of death in lesser-developed countries today where the tetanus vaccine is not widely used.[17]

The earliest discussion of postpartum muscular disorders appeared in the writings of Zhang Ji (ca. 150–219), who spoke of a postpartum ailment called *chi,* a term that referred to a pattern of wind illnesses that could manifest itself as muscle rigidity, spasms, and convulsions, as well as muscle weakness.[18] In late imperial editions of Zhang Ji's text, the term *chi* was often replaced by the term *jing,* suggesting that later doctors saw these terms as effectively synonymous.[19] The term *jing* first appears in the constituent texts of the *Yellow Emperor's Inner Classic.* The *Basic Questions* described *jing* as a disease characterized by rigidity of the neck and caused by dampness. The *Divine Pivot* also discussed *jing* together with "seizures" *(xian)* and "twisting spasms" *(chi)* in its description of the main diseases of the foot lesser yin channel. Such disorders were potentially incurable, and their yang manifestation was distinguished by rigid, backward arching: "When it is a yang illness, then the person bends backward from the waist and cannot bend forward. If it is a yin illness, then [he] cannot lift his head up. . . . If the tendons contort and twist, and the twisting is extremely frequent, then this is a fatal illness that cannot be treated."[20] In later texts, the term *jing* became the standard term for a pattern of muscular rigidity and convulsions or spasms characterized by the body being "pulled backward like a horn bow" *(jiaogong fan zhang).* The "horn bow" was the traditional Chinese archery bow, the belly of which was reinforced with animal horn.[21] Just as a bow is forced to bend contrary to its resting state when the archer strings it or draws back the bowstring, so too the sufferer's body would be forced backward, gripped by contractile forces beyond her control. Although Chinese authors pro-

Figure 7. The Scottish anatomist and surgeon Sir Charles Bell (1774–1842) created this image of a soldier suffering from tetanus following the Battle of Corunna in 1809. Bell's original painting, titled *Opisthotonus (Tetanus)*, is in the collection of the Royal College of Surgeons of Edinburgh. The image subsequently circulated as an engraving in the multiple editions of Bell's *Anatomy and Philosophy of Expression as Connected with the Fine Arts*. This image comes from the John Murray edition published in London in 1847. Wellcome Library, London.

vide only a verbal description of this condition, an early-nineteenth-century British illustration of a soldier convulsed by tetanus can provide a reliable representation of what they had in mind (figure 7). While the Yellow Emperor's *jing* was not specifically associated with women, *jing* and other similar illnesses became a specific concern in women's medicine.

Historically, Chinese writers ascribed these kinds of convulsive illnesses to invasions of pathogenic wind, and descriptions of *jing* and *jing*-like "backward arching" were also conflated with illnesses known as "childbirth wind" (*rufeng*, literally "birthing-mat wind," after the rush mats used during childbirth) and "postpartum windstrike" *(chanhou zhongfeng)*. In late imperial texts, the standard description of this condition mentioned not only the convulsive arching of the back but also the jaw being clenched shut and spasms in the hands and feet. This relatively detailed description of childbirth wind from 1830 thus describes a constellation of symptoms that had been known for centuries: "The illness signs of [postpartum] windstrike are that the tongue is cold, the lips are tense, and the fingers jerk. In severe cases the teeth are clenched tightly, the hands and feet spasm, the back and neck are forcedly rigid, the entire body is heavy and either hurts or itches, she gags while staring fixedly ahead, [and] she arches backward like a horn bow. The name of this is 'childbirth wind.' This is caused by depletion [allowing] wind coldness and damp [to penetrate] and by injury from overexertion."[22]

To be sure, other illnesses can produce postpartum seizures and convulsions, but tetanus was undoubtedly prominent among the various ailments classified as postpartum windstrike.[23] Particularly telling are the similarities between the symptoms of "childbirth wind" and another Chinese illness category called "wound wind" (po shang feng, literally "breakage and injury wind"). The name of this illness referred to the fact that it was caused by pathogenic wind entering the body as a result of an injury to the skin or flesh. In some cases, doctors explained, excessive blood loss weakened the body's defenses and made it vulnerable to noxious influences. But wound wind was also specifically understood as a case of pathogenic wind entering via the wound itself, and its typical symptoms included the clenching of the jaw, muscle rigidity and "backward arching."[24] Here the correspondence with tetanus is clear. Furthermore, descriptions of postpartum wind imply that childbirth wind does not strike immediately after delivery but only after a woman's carelessness has had the time to generate pathology. This suggests that there was an incubation period preceding the eruption of severe symptoms, again consistent with the course of a bacterial infection. In addition, a standard cause of childbirth wind was engaging in sexual intercourse too soon after childbirth, an observation consistent with the fact that postpartum infections frequently arise in the woman's genital tract.[25]

It seems likely, in fact, that Chinese postpartum restrictions originally arose as a direct response to such infections. We can discern this connection, for example, in the seventh-century medical writings of Sun Simiao, who warned that failure to observe postpartum prohibitions would inevitably lead to childbirth wind. Put another way, postpartum restrictions were the only way to prevent potentially fatal illnesses from arising: "During the hundred days after the woman gives birth, it is of the utmost importance that [these regulations be observed] with reverence and concern. Do not indulge desires and violate [behavioral regulations] or immediately engage in bedroom activities. *If there is any violation, then inevitably [she will contract a condition where] her body arches backward and is forcedly rigid, like a horn bow being pulled backward.* The name of this is 'childbirth wind,' and it is a sign that she has violated [the regulations]."[26]

Sun added that, once the illness had progressed to the arched-back stage, the woman's life was like "a candle flickering in the wind," and even those rich enough to summon a phalanx of famous doctors could not expect a cure. Heuristic texts of the Qing continued to repeat similar warnings. Wei Zhixiu, for example, included this account in his collection of cases: "Wang Kentang [1549–1613] treated a woman on the seventh day after she gave birth. During her recuperation, she had failed to observe the proper [behavior]. Her pores were not closed, and she happened to encounter cold wind, which invaded her body. She had a fever, headache, her eyes were rolled back in her head, and her hands and feet were spasming. This is called childbirth wind."[27]

Childbirth wind was explained in terms of a woman's bodily depletion and invasion of external influences. But late imperial medical texts also discussed other types of illnesses that similarly suggest bacterial infections of varying intensity. These notably include illnesses attributed to stagnant or impeded postpartum Blood, especially those involving fevers and abdominal pains.[28] Another illustrative example from Wei Zhixiu's anthology is this account of a woman suffering from postpartum flows of genital pus:

> Sun Wenyuan [Sun Yikui] treated the wife of a Mr. Wen. Some fifty days after giving birth, her right flank became so distended and painful that no one could touch her. She had red and white vaginal discharges that greatly resembled pus, along with fever and constipation. Sun diagnosed her, saying, "This is a case where noxious dew was not completely eliminated, and the Blood has transformed into pus. She must be treated at once. I have seen many women suffering from this. If the treatment is not successful and the accumulation lasts for a prolonged time, then it becomes toxic. In some cases, it forms intestinal abscesses. In some cases the internal poison seeps out through [the skin of] the waist. All these are disasters caused by stagnated Blood."[29]

These horrific symptoms would have sounded sadly familiar to Wei Zhixiu's European contemporaries. As Irvine Loudon shows, eighteenth-century European doctors were preoccupied with "puerperal fever," a category of postpartum disease that they attributed to causes as diverse as retained blood, female irritability, putrid matter, and stagnant air.[30] Modern medicine defines puerperal fever as a bacterial infection originating in the vaginal tract (most commonly due to streptococcus), and it was the leading cause of maternal death prior to the development of antibiotics in the mid-twentieth century. If the scope of the infection were limited, the woman's immune system would be able to overcome it. However, an infection that spread to the rest of abdomen sentenced the woman to an excruciating death from peritonitis, internal gangrene, and septicemia (blood poisoning). Puerperal fever became a particularly lethal

Figure 8. Woman suffering from "shallow and deep abscesses of the postpartum period" (Wu Qian, ed., *Yuzuan yizong jinjian* [Imperially compiled golden mirror of medical learning] [Beijing: Wuying dian, 1742]). Internal abscesses of this kind were commonly attributed to waste Blood stagnating inside the woman following childbirth. Beginning in the seventeenth century, Generating and Transforming Decoction *(shenghua tang)* joined the repertoire of remedies meant to prevent and treat such illnesses. Image from an edition catalogued as Neifu (1739), in the rare books collection of the Harvard-Yenching Library. Courtesy of the Harvard-Yenching Library, Harvard University.

problem in Europe after maternity hospitals began to proliferate in the eighteenth century. Rates of infection in hospital births were up to twenty times higher than in births outside, for medical staff unwittingly carried bacteria on their hands from the postmortem rooms to the birthing wards, where they would infect one woman after another during vaginal examinations. Statistically speaking, even in the worst hospitals, the numerical majority of women would pass through childbirth without serious problem.[31] But there were no reliable cures or universally accepted preventive measures for puerperal fever, and with fatality rates as high as 80 percent, doctors and women alike viewed it as a fearsome disease. Similarly, while the majority of women in late imperial China probably survived childbirth without serious problems, the uncertainly of cure, the potential for horrific suffering, and the potential devastation to the family meant that the danger of postpartum illnesses loomed large in the imagination.[32] The biological realities of these infections and other potential complications thus served as important points of reference that shaped the literate Chinese discourse of female debility after childbirth.

DEFINING THE POSTPARTUM BODY

As they sought to promote postpartum well-being, medical experts and amateurs alike agreed that prevention and careful regulation were crucial. They disagreed, however, as to which therapeutic strategies were most appropriate and effective. To understand these disagreements, we should first note that doctors' judgments were framed by two competing epistemological impulses within learned medicine itself. The first was the quest for ever-more-systematized medical knowledge, embodied in attempts to classify illnesses according to rubric and to define the main mechanisms of pathology that governed each rubric. In the case of postpartum care, this systematizing impulse emphasized the common mental and physical states of women who had just given birth, and it justified treating all postpartum bodies as fundamentally alike. At the same time, however, the norms of learned medicine taught the superior doctor to eschew rote approaches to diagnosis and treatment. Skilled practitioners, by definition, were those who understood the potential uniqueness of each case and used their superior knowledge of yin and yang to identify the illness's true root cause as well as its transformations over time. One could not always assume that the recent experience of giving birth was the most important factor in a postpartum woman's illness.

In sum, medical debates over correct postpartum treatment simultaneously took place on two epistemological levels: deciding what general rule should govern postpartum treatment, and judging whether a given case proved the rule or was an exception to it. During the late imperial period, furthermore, debates over the specific causes of postpartum illness revolved around three intersecting sets of binaries. First, did the act of giving birth itself inevitably leave the woman in a state of sickliness, or was it simply a mundane—albeit vulnerable—stage in the cycle of generation? Second, if birth created a pathological imbalance in women, was it most likely to be rooted in stagnation and excess or in depletion and vacuity? Third, if a woman was suffering from postpartum stagnation or depletion, was this pathology most likely associated with excessive heat or excessive coldness in the maternal body? These were the problems that had occupied medical writers for centuries, and the answers they gave directed their choice of drugs.

Before we explore how these tensions played out in the history of Generating and Transforming Decoction, it will be useful to examine how doctors dealt with the linked questions of whether the postpartum state was an inherently pathological one, and whether postpartum women inevitably required medical intervention. In chapter 5, we examined the idea that childbirth replicated cosmogenesis and was therefore meant to be trouble-free. In the writings of Zhang Congzheng (ca. 1156–1228), Zhu Zhenheng (1281–1358), and Zhang Jiebin (1563–1640), we can see that doctors employed similar themes to argue that birth did not necessarily cast women into a state of pathology. Zhang Congzheng and Zhu Zhenheng were two of the Jin and Yuan dynasty masters whose teachings undergirded the multiple doctrinal currents that proliferated during the Ming and Qing. It is hard to imagine two doctors whose therapeutic approaches were more diametrically opposed than Zhang Congzheng, famous for his advocacy of purgatives, and Zhu Zhenheng, who emphasized supplementing the body's vulnerable yin. But both men sought to modify the widely held view that childbirth was intrinsically destabilizing, and that the postpartum woman always needed to be given certain drugs and food. Citing the idea that childbirth replicated cosmogenesis, Zhang and Zhu argued against rote therapeutic approaches to postpartum care.

In *How Scholars Serve Their Relatives (Rumen shi qin)*, Zhang Congzheng included a long essay about the ways in which the incorrect use of drugs could cause illness and even death. Here he complained about doctors who did not carefully examine the root causes of their patients' maladies but instead dispensed stock remedies based on simplistic under-

standings of the illness at hand. In this context Zhang Congzheng criticized doctors who always assumed that childbirth itself inevitably produced a deficiency of Blood and qi that manifested itself in pathological
cold.[33] These inferior practitioners, Zhang wrote, "consider it expedient
to use warming and heating remedies to nourish Blood and supplement
the vacuity, and only ever treat it as a case of cold." Zhang rejected this
approach, however, on the grounds that childbirth recapitulated the natural dynamic of the cosmos. The very fact that birth had successfully occurred proved that the woman's yin and yang vitalities were in harmony.
Just as plants did not germinate or fruit in cold weather, so too the woman
would not have been able to conceive and carry the child to term if she
were indeed suffering from cold:

> Pregnancy in a woman resembles the gestation of [the myriad] things [of
> the cosmos] by Heaven and Earth. These things are generated after yin and
> yang are harmoniously joined. Likewise, humans are conceived after yin
> and yang are harmoniously joined. If there were a preponderance of yin or
> of yang, then how could conception occur? How is this any different from
> the case of grains and fruits? If water is scarce and does not come in due
> season, then although the flower has set a fruit, it will wither and drop off.
> So again, how is this different from a pregnancy in which the fetus is not
> nourished [and thus miscarries]? Eighteen days after autumn begins in the
> seventh month, the blades of grass will not form, and this can be attributed
> to the cold weather. And yet people will contrarily say that a woman is
> cold after she has completed her ten months of pregnancy and given birth
> without difficulty.[34]

Besides drawing on agricultural analogies, Zhang also compared the
gestation of a child to the firing of bricks.[35] The kiln had to be heated
for bricks to form, and it did not cool down immediately after the bricks
were taken out. Likewise, he suggested, the warmth required for the successful gestation of a child would linger after its birth. To assume that
the postpartum woman was cold was therefore wrong, and the use of
heating drugs was equally misguided.

Zhu Zhenheng too suggested that postpartum women were not inherently ill. His work *Fully Deploying the Formulary of the Imperial Pharmacy Service (Jufang fahui,* 1347) is an extended criticism of uncritical
dosing practices. Whereas Zhang Congzheng had sought to discredit the
rote use of heating drugs, Zhu Zhenheng suggested that one might not
even need to use postpartum medicines at all. "Some say," Zhu noted,
"that in women who have just given birth, the good Blood is already damaged and the stagnated Blood still remains." Thus, people commonly used

heating and purging drugs to expel congealed blood. But Zhu Zhenheng disapproved, and he articulated his point with a citation from the *Classic of Changes (Yijing)* that celebrated the life-giving powers of *kun,* the purest yin of the cosmos. Zhu thereby portrayed the female body as the human expression of *kun,* whose interactions with cosmic yang enabled all things to be created. Since childbirth replicated cosmogenesis, it followed that the postpartum state was not inherently pathological. Administering medicines was thus unnecessary, and all that was required was for the woman to carefully regulate her behavior following delivery: " 'How great is the fundamental nature of *kun!* The myriad things are provided their births by it.' This is the constant principle. In women who have just given birth, the good Blood is not necessarily damaged, the polluted Blood has not necessarily accumulated, and the organs are not necessarily cold. So why employ drugs? If one increases one's vigilance as to regulating and taking precautions in eating and drinking, sleeping and rising, then what illnesses would there be?"[36]

In the early seventeenth century, Zhang Jiebin expanded this relatively benign view of childbirth, going so far as to propose that the loss of Blood during birth might even constitute a return to bodily harmony. He made this point as part of his detailed criticism of the twin assumptions that postpartum women were always suffering from vacuity, and that this vacuity was inevitably rooted in the loss of Blood and qi during labor.[37] While Zhang Jiebin acknowledged that syndromes of postpartum vacuity were common, he also pointed out that these syndromes had different causes and forms. In some instances, vacuity in one aspect of the body might even be accompanied by repletion in another. Furthermore, Zhang affirmed, some postpartum illnesses were caused by factors unrelated to vacuity, and others were positively rooted in repletion. Overall, he emphasized that postpartum ailments were marked by the same variety of causes as any other class of ailments, and the fact that a woman had just given birth should be only one factor among many in the doctor's diagnosis. Zhang's belief that that childbirth was not inherently depleting is exemplified in his exposition of "postpartum syndromes without vacuity." Here he explained that, in healthy women with no history of illness, the accumulation and stoppage of bodily vitalities during pregnancy in fact constituted a surplus and thus a departure from bodily harmony. It was this surplus that provoked ailments such as distention and vomiting, for example. In such cases, the expulsion of blood and fluids during childbirth represented the elimination of a retained bodily surplus rather than the depletion of bodily vitalities. Instead of debilitating the woman, childbirth positively restored her to equilibrium:

> There are cases where the woman had no prior illness, or she is in the prime of her youth, or she has the kind of constitution that can endure hardship, poverty, and toil. These kinds of women were originally without any insufficiency. Then one day, they became pregnant. Into an abdomen that had been without illness, this thing was inserted, causing qi and Blood to become stopped up and blocked, resulting in distention and vomiting. These are all illnesses caused by something being added so that there is surplus. Then when she is about to give birth, it starts to become unblocked and nimble. That which was retained is eliminated, and thus she returns to her old self. These kinds of births are extremely frequent among ordinary people. So how could they ultimately cause vacuity?[38]

Since childbirth was not depleting for such women, Zhang counseled, if they happened to show signs of vacuity after birth then the doctor should consider the role of internal injury or external pathogens. Otherwise, one could trust that the woman's vitalities would rapidly return to equilibrium without active intervention.

By arguing that childbirth was not inherently pathological, doctors like Zhang Jiebin drew a rhetorical boundary between themselves and less able practitioners who would treat postpartum diseases in rote fashion. Furthermore, their view that the postpartum state was fundamentally benign contrasted sharply with the ritual and popular practices that treated childbirth as an unavoidably polluting event whose danger had to be properly mitigated. The seventeenth-century sectarian religious tracts examined by Daniel Overmyer, for example, repeated the popular belief that women would be punished in the "Pool of Blood" after death, "condemned to suffering in purgatory because of pollution caused by blood from childbirth."[39] Such pollution beliefs also shaped the practices associated with doing the month, which assumed that danger and illness would ensue unless proper precautions were taken. Read against this backdrop, then, the belief that childbearing was inherently harmonious constituted the hallmark of educated male doctors and a cultural resource that they used to assert the superiority of scholarly medicine over other practices. By the late imperial period, for example, doctors could cite the warnings of both Zhu Zhenheng and Zhang Jiebin, who criticized the popular custom of giving postpartum women generous quantities of fortifying food in an attempt to rebuild their supposedly depleted bodies. Such customs, as mentioned earlier, were part of the tradition of doing the month. But Zhu Zhenheng pointed out that the practice of eating chicken and ham would actually cause illness, because chicken was hard to digest and ham produced heat. It was best instead to avoid such meats and eat only "light and bland foods."[40] Zhang Jiebin's description of postpartum illnesses similarly expressed his worry about repletion syndromes caused by "internal injury" from overeating after labor, when "people were afraid that [a woman] had become exhausted through toil and so compelled her [to eat], causing [the food] to be stopped and stored up without dispersing."[41]

In sum, while literate medicine shared broader cultural concerns about postpartum vulnerability, it also allowed for the possibility that childbirth was simply a mundane passage in a woman's cycle of fertility. Within this framework doctors negotiated the primary dynamics that could be at work—depletion/vacuity, stagnation/repletion, cold/heat—and debated what kind of therapies were most appropriate: replenishing, purging, warming, cooling. Beginning in the seventeenth century, a new postpartum remedy entered the fray: Generating and Transforming Decoction, a warming formula whose advocates claimed it could simultaneously address depletion and stagnation.

THE HISTORY OF GENERATING AND TRANSFORMING DECOCTION

All available evidence indicates that Generating and Transforming Decoction first originated among practitioners in northern Zhejiang province. The earliest textual reference to this formula appears in Zhang Jiebin's didactic treatise *The Complete Works of Jingyue,* compiled near the end of his life, sometime between 1624 and 1640. Zhang listed 186 formulas used to treat women's ailments, including Generating and Transforming Decoction, which he identified as a proprietary formula "transmitted down through the generations of the Qian family of Shaoxing."[42] This was certainly the Qian family of Shanyin County (Shaoxing Prefecture), a medical lineage famous in late imperial times for their expertise in treating the ailments of "childbearing" *(taichan).* The Qian family traced their medical practice back to the Northern Song and were among the longest-lived *fuke* lineages in China.[43] As a fellow native of Shanyin and himself a practicing doctor, Zhang Jiebin would have known of the Qians. Some of the family members would have been his contemporaries, and they were prominent enough to merit inclusion in county gazetteers. The 1671 *Gazetteer of Shanyin County (Shanyin xianzhi),* for example, lauded four generations of Qian family doctors for their medical abilities, literary activities, and moral rectitude.[44] The names of later descendants are absent from subsequent gazetteers, suggesting that the family's earlier prominence had become attenuated. However, anecdotal evidence suggests that the Qian family's medical reputation continued to flourish. In 1877, for example, the Suzhou scholar-official Pan Wei compiled a gynecological text that used as its main sources "the secret prescriptions and books of Fu Qingzhu, Xu Lingtai, Chen Xiuyuan, and Master Qian of Yue [Shaoxing]."[45] Any nineteenth-century reader with the slightest knowledge of medical matters would have immediately recognized the first three names as the courtesy names of renowned, learned doctors of the late Ming and Qing: Fu Shan, Xu Dachun, and Chen Nianzu. Each had also written a famous work on *fuke*. For the Qians to be mentioned in the same breath as these eminent figures suggests that their medical lore continued to be highly valued even if individual family members did not attract special notice.

Although Zhang Jiebin described Generating and Transforming Decoction as the Qian family's proprietary formula, it appears that other northern Zhejiang doctors were also using it around the same time. One nineteenth-century account even suggested that the Qian family ancestor originally obtained the formula from a Shan Nanshan, also a native of Shaoxing Prefecture."[46] Little else is known about Shan, but it appears that his original name was Shan Yangxian, and he was the purported author of various treatises on childbirth-related illnesses.[47] While none of these survive as independent texts, portions of Shan's writings are preserved in other works, notably Xiao Xun's *Canonical Teachings on Medicine for Women* (1684). Xiao Xun, a native of Jiaxing County (also in northern Zhejiang), was a medical practitioner of some erudition who also compiled works on medical theory, pulse lore, and pharmacopoeia.[48] Xiao cited Shan Yangxian as the source of Generating and Transforming Decoction, and he praised this formula to his readers, recommending it as the principal remedy for postpartum ailments.[49]

In the figures of Zhang Jiebin, the Qian family, Shan Yangxian, and Xiao Xun, Generating and Transforming Decoction's history during the seventeenth century was closely linked to northern Zhejiang doctors. Subsequently, the decoction became incorporated into an ever-wider range of medical literature as an array of healers from other geographical areas also began to promote its use. Heuristic works of the eighteenth century that featured Generating and Transforming Decoction included Yan Chunxi's *Essential Teachings on Childbearing*, and the imperial medical bureau's *Golden Mirror,* where it was recommended as the principal treatment for postpartum abscesses caused by waste Blood.[50] In addition to its mention in these works aimed at expert healers and doctors-in-training, the formula for Generating and Transforming Decoction also began to circulate widely in popular medical handbooks. These notably included Lay Buddhist Jizhai's *Treatise on Easy Childbirth* of 1715 (*Dasheng bian,* discussed in chapters 2 and 5) and the corpus of texts attributed to the monks of the Bamboo Grove Monastery (discussed in chapter 2). The monks' 1771 compendium, *A New Book on Childbearing*, even claimed that Generating and Transforming Decoction was the monks' own proprietary formula.[51] After midcentury, the formula also began circulating in published texts attributed to the Qian family itself. It appears that the Qian family played no role in publishing these works, however, which usually appeared under the title *A Secret Book of Childbearing (Taichan mishu)* and claimed to reveal the Qians' proprietary teachings for the benefit of the public.[52] *A Secret Book* was first printed in 1759, and the earliest surviving printed edition was produced in 1796. Versions of *A Secret Book* eventually circulated throughout the Jiangnan region, as well as further afield in Beijing and Hunan, Guizhou, and Yunnan Provinces.[53]

Finally, during the nineteenth century the place of Generating and Transforming Decoction in the Chinese pharmacological pantheon was cemented with its inclusion in *Fu Qingzhu's Medicine for Women (Fu Qingzhu nüke),* which modern TCM textbooks consider to be one of the great works of Chinese *fuke.* Fu Qingzhu was the courtesy name of Fu Shan (1607–84), a native of Shanxi Province who was a renowned literatus and calligrapher.[54] Fu was acclaimed for his high ethical standards, his intellectual brilliance, and his steadfast refusal to serve either the corrupt Ming court or the foreign Qing dynasty. *Fu Qingzhu's Medicine for Women* was first printed in 1827, and more than seventy different editions were produced between 1827 and 1900.[55] The last fascicle of this work, titled "Treatise on Postpartum Illnesses" *(Chanhou bian),* recommended Generating and Transforming Decoction as the primary formula for postpartum ailments.[56] By the Republican era, medical writers generally cited Fu Shan as the source of this formula, and many modern scholars have followed suit.[57] However, it is almost certain that Fu Shan played no part in developing this formula. There is textual evidence, for example, that Fu did not even write the fascicle on postpartum diseases attributed to him, and in any case knowledge about the formula was already circulating during Fu's youth.[58] Nevertheless, Fu Shan's prestige and the popularity of *Fu Qingzhu's Medicine for Women* provided an important vehicle for legitimating and disseminating Generating and Transforming Decoction throughout the empire.

Association with Fu Shan conferred a sterling scholarly pedigree on this formula. Simultaneously, association with famous medical lineages like the Qian family and Bamboo Grove Monastery monks or with literate amateurs like Lay Buddhist Jizhai gave Generating and Transforming Decoction the patina of a mystical secret formula and a time-tested remedy collected by upper-class philanthropists. The publication history of this decoction thus illuminates the multilayered social and medical dynamics that allowed new techniques to be legitimated and integrated into practice. But if people reprinted this formula, it was because they also thought it was therapeutically valuable. Generating and Transforming Decoction promised an easy solution to long-standing challenges in postpartum care.

Medical Rationales

Different works varied in the prominence that they assigned to Generating and Transforming Decoction as a postpartum remedy. Some, such as Zhang Jiebin's compendium and the *Golden Mirror*, recommended it for specific complications of the postpartum period. But many other works, popular and heuristic alike, described it as an all-purpose prophylactic and tonic for postpartum illnesses. The overarching virtue of Generating and Transforming Decoction, according to its advocates, was its ability to simultaneously create new Blood ("generating") while dispersing the old Blood ("transforming"). Yan Chunxi's description was typical in its praise:

> I have investigated all the prescriptions for women who have just given birth, and none can compare to Generating and Transforming Decoction as the most marvelous formula for postpartum. The lovage, angelica, and peach pit in this recipe warm the center and make Blood circulate, and they are good at eliminating the old Blood and swiftly generating the new Blood. They are assisted by charred black ginger and charred licorice, which lead the first three drugs into the lung and liver. In the midst of circulating there is replenishing, and in the midst of transforming there is generating. Therefore it is called "generating and transforming," with the name of the formula established on the basis of its effects.[59]

Generating and Transforming Decoction thus promised an elegant resolution to a long-standing debate about the treatment of postpartum ailments: should one should give priority to attacking stagnation, or should one should first redress vacuity and depletion? Such debates were never just academic, for the fate of women like Xu Lian's wife hung in the balance. Both approaches had their proponents, and both were supported by ample doctrinal precedents. During the thirteenth century, Chen Ziming had given priority to preventing and attacking internal stagnations of Blood after childbirth. While Chen Ziming certainly recognized that women were prone to vacuity after childbirth, his chief concern was that the "noxious dew" and other harmful by-products of birth would stagnate or flow recklessly inside the woman's body, causing a multitude of illnesses. Accordingly, Chen recommended several preventative methods aimed at directing, moving, and breaking up Blood. During the first three days after giving birth, he counseled, the woman should lie on her back in bed with her knees bent, and her belly should be regularly stroked from top to bottom during that time. This would facilitate the elimination of noxious dew and prevent it from being impeded inside the woman's body. Chen also recommended administering vinegar mixed with ink *(cu mo)* to break up stagnations of Blood. Another technique with similar effect was to fumigate the woman's room with vinegar or burning lacquer, meant to prevent Blood from flowing recklessly in the woman's body.[60] The use of these pungent and acrid remedies echoed Song dynasty birth-expediting remedies, which used bitter and fragrant drugs to bore through and clear away blockages within the womb.

Countering this focus on stagnation was a strategy that prioritized the problem of postpartum depletion. In the earliest systematic medical discussion of postpartum illness, Zhang Ji (ca. 196–219) had spoken of the "three illnesses" *(san bing)* that commonly afflicted postpartum women: *chi* (later conflated with "childbirth wind," discussed earlier), *yu mao* ("stagnant accumulation with dizziness," characterized by mental confusion, dizziness, and fainting), and constipation.[61] The phrase "three illnesses" did not mean that Zhang Ji recognized only three postpartum maladies. Indeed, he discussed about a dozen other postpartum disorders, most of them being different types of abdominal pain caused by factors such as stagnant Blood. But the rubric of "three illnesses" focused attention on the harm of depletion, which Zhang depicted as the chief underlying cause of postpartum disease.[62] Although the visible manifestations of the "three illnesses" were quite different, Zhang attributed them all to the depletion of Blood and bodily fluids. Blood vacuity and copious sweating made postpartum women extremely susceptible to pathogenic wind, which caused convulsions. Copious sweating exacerbated the weakness engendered by loss of Blood during childbirth, and this resulted in dizziness. Finally, the loss of bodily fluids also left the stomach parched, causing constipation. In sum, Zhang Ji defined childbirth as an inherently exhausting, depleting, and destabilizing process for the woman, which made her vulnerable to pernicious external influences.

When late imperial doctors discussed the problem of postpartum vacuity, however, they most often cited Zhu Zhenheng (1281–1358). His oft-quoted dictum on postpartum ailments stated that, "after childbirth, the proper course is to first greatly supplement qi and blood. Even if there are signs of other illnesses, these are to be addressed afterward" *(chanhou dang da bu qi xue wei xian, sui you zazheng yi mo zhi zhi).*[63] Zhu's advocacy of postpartum supplementation grew out of his belief that bodily yin always tended to be deficient. Furthermore, his postpartum strategies specifically sought to discredit two other therapeutic approaches that Zhu believed would irreparably damage women's vitalities: the use of drugs to break up or attack Blood, and the use of drugs to purge and expel heteropathic influences. Broadly speaking, Zhu Zhenheng emphasized the need for flexibility in treating postpartum women—even purgatives could have their place, if used correctly. But "supplement first" became Zhu's therapeutic hallmark, and many later doctors adopted it as standard operating procedure for postpartum care.

Despite Zhu's influential criticisms of it, however, the strategy of attacking postpartum stagnation continued to be widely used. The continued coexistence of the antistagnation and "supplement first" approaches may be explained by the fact that neither was obviously superior to the other in practice. As Chinese physicians noted, each approach promised certain benefits, but each also had the potential to provoke harmful side effects and fatal complications. It was widely acknowledged that breaking up, moving, and eliminating Blood might cause already-depleted bodily vitalities to be consumed even further. Strong purgatives to eliminate blockages of Blood, for example, could provoke deadly postpartum hemorrhages. As Yan Chunxi explained:

> Now when it comes to prescriptions for expelling stagnation, one may not use harsh drugs even in syndromes of repletion. How much more true this is for the great depletion of the postpartum period, when one worries that there is nothing to exert mastery over Blood [because qi is deficient]. As soon as these medicines exert their force, [the situation] then turns into a [Blood] collapse that cannot be halted. The depletion readily becomes a "stripping away" *[tuo]*, and the dynamic resembles that of water that is poured out and cannot be easily gathered up again.[64]

But the "supplement first" approach also carried its own risks. When Yan Chunxi's own wife fell ill after giving birth, for example, the attending doctor rejected Yan's explicit instructions to give her strong qi-supplementing drugs. Yan's contemporaries would have immediately understood the rationale behind this refusal—the doctor feared that drugs to increase qi and Blood would engender a pathological surplus that could produce stagnations or impede the elimination of noxious dew. Such concerns were well known, and late imperial doctors frequently criticized their competitors for following Zhu Zhenheng's "supplement first" teaching too slavishly. A prominent critic was Zhang Jiebin, who framed his own discussion of postpartum illnesses as a direct refutation of Zhu's teachings. Zhang explained that he had originally followed Zhu Zhenheng's dictum to supplement first, but had abandoned it after meeting with too many cases of failure.[65] Wei Zhixiu's collection of case records similarly include several episodes where the "supplement first" approach made the patient sicker. In one case, a kinswoman of Sun Yikui (fl. late sixteenth century) became ill after a miscarriage, developing an aversion to cold and experiencing pain and bloating in her lower abdomen. The family had consulted "a specialist who was mired in [Zhu Zhenheng] Danxi's saying that after birth one must greatly supplement qi and Blood," and he had treated her on the assumption that she was suffering from postpartum depletion with pathological cold. However, Sun explained, her illness was actually caused by retention of noxious dew complicated by internal heat. It was for this reason that the specialist's medicines failed to cure the patient, instead provoking severe bouts of bloody diarrhea.[66] Shen Shiyu, a near contemporary of Sun Yikui, had a similar experience with one Yuan Lingmo's daughter, who developed a fever soon after giving birth.[67] The first doctor to treat her observed that she was young and thin, and he also "revered Zhu Danxi's method of greatly supplementing after birth." However, his drugs only intensified the patient's illness, Shen Shiyu explained, because Yuan's daughter was actually suffering from stagnant Blood compounded by internal wind cold. And the case of Chen Ao's wife showed that the "supplement first" approach could prove fatal.[68] A week after giving birth, Chen's wife developed abdominal pain and fever. Her family consulted a doctor, who diagnosed vacuity and prescribed large doses of ginseng, pointing out that "this is exactly what [Zhu] Danxi meant when he said that after birth it is proper to greatly supplement qi and Blood." Unfortunately, the root cause of Chen's wife's illness was stagnant Blood. Once she had taken the medicine, "her pain became intense, her facial skin darkened, she began gasping for breath, and she died."

Warming versus Cooling Medicines

The twin dangers of postpartum stagnation and depletion presented practitioners and their clients with a therapeutic dilemma. As Yan Chunxi summed it up: "If one focuses only on dissipating [stagnations], then new Blood will not be generated, and if one focuses only on generating, then the old Blood will contrarily stagnate."[69] The problem of managing stagnation and depletion was further complicated by the challenge of determining whether heat or cold was preponderant in any given case. Doctors recognized several ways in which these dynamics could intersect, and each required a distinct strategy. For example, vacuity could engender either excess heat or excess cold, depending on whether the body's yin or yang was primarily afflicted. Likewise, impeded discharge of noxious dew could be rooted either in stagnant blockage (linked to excess, cold, or congelation) or to fluids being dried up by heat. Interweaving these issues were disagreements over the fundamental nature of the postpartum body: was it inherently cold (which would require the use of warming drugs) or inherently warm (which would call for cooling therapies)? Again, doctors seeking guidance in the works of their predecessors would find ample doctrinal precedence for both the heating and cooling approaches.

As noted earlier, the popular custom of doing the month promoted the use of warming foods and avoidance of cold in the period following childbirth. The assumption that postpartum women required warming had also long been a staple of the literate medical tradition. Again, Chen Ziming was an important reference. As discussed earlier, Chen Ziming's main concern was to prevent stagnations of postpartum blood, and this led him to favor heating and blood-moving remedies. The most important was Black Divinity Powder *(heishen san),* which notably had been listed in the *Formulary of the Imperial Pharmacy Service for Benefiting the People in an Era of Great Peace* (*Taiping huimin hejiju fang,* 1110), a government compilation of all remedies sold by the retail outlets of the imperial pharmacy service.[70] Black Divinity Powder was known for its ability to treat postpartum ailments rooted in stagnant Blood, thanks to its combination of drugs that were hot or warming, and/or acted on Blood: black beans *(heidou),* prepared (cooked) rehmannia *(shudi),* angelica *(danggui),* cinnamon bark *(rougui),* dried ginger *(ganjiang),* licorice *(gancao),* white peony root *(shaoyao),* and cattail pollen *(puhuang).*[71] Chen Ziming recommended Black Divinity Powder as an all-purpose prophylactic that should be administered immediately after birth.[72] While he acknowledged that replenishing formulas were also useful after birth, Chen cautioned that these were to be used sparingly and only as an adjunct to heating and antistagnation remedies. Otherwise, they would engender excess blood and provoke stagnation.[73] The formulas that fell into Chen Ziming's cautious-use category included Four Ingredients Decoction *(siwu tang),* which I discuss later.

Chen Ziming's reliance on heating and Blood-moving remedies was consistent with his overarching concern about the dangers of Blood stagnation after birth, and it was reinforced by the view that the vacuity provoked by childbirth left the postpartum woman in a state of cold. But while Black Divinity Powder occupied a privileged place in the Song government's medical repertoire, other contemporaries portrayed it as a symbol of uncritical postpartum care. As we saw earlier, Zhang Congzheng used the idea that childbirth reiterated cosmogenesis, to attack what he saw as the uncritical and harmful use of heating drugs in the postpartum period.[74] In this context, Zhang also specifically criticized the common use of Black Divinity Powder. It would not cure the woman, he said, but instead would produce a pathogenic excess of heat that would readily turn fatal. Zhu Zhenheng articulated this concern about heating drugs with a new level of etiological sophistication. Since the human body was prone to deficient yin, he warned against drugs that would consume yin and increase bodily yang by augmenting fire and heat. In response to an imagined interlocutor who claimed that it was reasonable to use warming drugs as a general course of treatment for women, Zhu countered that "women take Blood as the leader. Blood belongs to yin, and it easily becomes deficient. Those medicines that are not good at regulating will be unable to preserve [the patient]."[75] As for postpartum ailments, Zhu also specifically rejected the use of Black Divinity Powder.[76]

Zhu Zhenheng's influence on later doctors certainly contributed to the subsequent diminution of Black Divinity Powder's place in the medical repertoire. Although Ming-Qing writers continued to quote Chen Ziming's discussion of Black Divinity Powder, they notably diluted its therapeutic relevance by presenting it side by side with Zhu Zhenheng's criticism of such formulas.[77] The editors of the *Imperial Encyclopedia* downgraded Black Divinity Powder even further. Although they cited Chen's various teachings on postpartum treatments, they omitted his essay praising Black Divinity Powder, and they listed the formula only in the repertoire of remedies at the end of the postpartum section. By contrast, the *Imperial Encyclopedia* gave pride of place to Four Ingredients Decoction. Neither heating nor purging, it was known for its Blood-replenishing and -regulating drugs and had long been an all-purpose prescription for a wide range of female ailments. The editors of the *Imperial Encyclopedia* underscored the importance of Four Ingredients Decoction for postpartum care by putting it first in the section on postpartum formulas.[78] The usual method for treating postpartum diseases, they explained, was to add and subtract from this basic remedy, and they included a lengthy list of ailments that it would cure. So whereas Chen Ziming presented Black Divinity Powder as the master formula and listed Four Ingredients Decoction as an auxiliary to be used in certain cases, the *Imperial Encyclopedia* presented Four Ingredients Decoction as the master postpartum remedy, with Black Divinity Powder as the auxiliary. A decade and a half later, when Wu Qian and his team of imperial physicians compiled the *Golden Mirror*, they made no mention of Black Divinity Powder at all in their discussions of postpartum treatment.

In sum, over the course of the seventeenth and eighteenth centuries, Black Divinity Powder lost its status as a postpartum cure-all, although it was sometimes recommended as a specific remedy for resolving difficult labor.[79] It also seems to have lost its unique identity as a medicinal formula during this time. The names of Chinese medical formulas are generally descriptive and use common words, such as Four Ingredients Decoction. But famous formulas retain their integrity because there is a textual consensus on what combination of drugs these names refer to. It is therefore significant that, during the early 1600s, three distinct formulas circulated under the name Black Divinity Powder. One of these used the recipe originally given by Chen Ziming, but the other two were completely different.[80] The continued confusion was such that, during the eighteenth century, Yan Chunxi even included an explanatory discussion of the discrepancies between these different versions.[81]

But medical change is never unidirectional. Even as Zhu Zhenheng and others sought to marginalize the heating remedy Black Divinity Powder, other doctors began to articulate new rationales for using warming formulas in the postpartum period. Of particular concern was the danger that postpartum coldness would cause stagnation. Indeed, this was the central argument that proponents of Generating and Transforming Decoction used to promote it as a superior alternative to Four Ingredients Decoction. The problem with the latter, these doctors pointed out, was that it contained two cooling drugs—prepared rehmannia and white peony root—that would cause Blood stagnation and exacerbate depletion in the postpartum woman. As Shan Yangxian explained, "Rehmannia root has a stagnating nature, and white peony's sour and cold properties attack the qi of generation."[82] By contrast, Shan said, Generating and Transforming Decoction was superior because it omitted both of these cooling drugs and replaced them with ingredients to warm the body's interior. To appreciate the novelty of this critique, we must understand that many of Shan Yangxian's predecessors and contemporaries would have shared his concerns over the postpartum use of rehmannia and especially of white peony. Where they differed, however, was over the question of how best to counteract the drugs' cooling tendencies. Some believed that these ingredients could be sufficiently counterbalanced by other drugs, or that their cool nature could be mitigated through extra processing. Shan Yangxian and other proponents of Generating and Transforming Decoction, in contrast, felt that such measures were ineffective, and they sought to contraindicate these drugs altogether in the postpartum period.

Yan Chunxi provided a detailed discussion of these arguments in an essay titled "Why Four Ingredients Decoction Is Inappropriate for Postpartum Treatment." He started by refuting the common belief that warming drugs could balance the coldness of rehmannia and peony, and he asserted that, while Four Ingredients Decoction was a valuable formula for women most of the time, it should not be used after childbirth:

> For treating the ailments of postpartum, the ancient recipes mostly consist of Four Ingredients Decoction with added and subtracted ingredients. Why is this? They consider that in this prescription there is the acrid warmth of lovage and angelica, assisted by the wintry coolness of rehmannia and peony. Warmth and coolness balance one another, and one could say that there is nothing to worry about. But people do not realize that, although Four Ingredients Decoction is a marvelous remedy for the all the various illnesses of women, it is profoundly inappropriate to use it in the postpartum period.[83]

Yan emphasized that the cooling properties of peony were well known, to the extent that older books of medical prescriptions had all recommended that the drug be stir-fried in wine—a heating substance—prior to using it in postpartum prescriptions. Some even added charred ginger to offset its cooling properties. Such measures would supposedly make white peony safe for postpartum use and enable women to benefit from its ability to concentrate dispersed yin qi. But for Yan Chunxi, the very need for such precautions proved that cooling drugs were simply inappropriate for postpartum women. He thus interdicted the use of white peony altogether in the first few days after birth, while reluctantly permitting its use in the days thereafter as long as it was "thoroughly

processed in wine and assisted by other medicines." Rehmannia, however, was not to be used in either of its two common forms. Raw rehmannia *(shengdi)* was overly cooling, while prepared rehmannia *(shudi)* was
profoundly stagnating, and, again, the other drugs in Four Ingredients
Decoction were simply insufficient to counteract their effects:

> The raw rehmannia in Four Ingredients Decoction is even more cooling
> [than white peony]. It goes directly to the portion of Blood and also injures
> the spleen and the stomach, and its harm is even more profound. Some say
> to replace it with prepared rehmannia, [which will] supplement and increase
> the true yin, and they call this highly appropriate. However, they do not
> consider that the nature of prepared rehmannia is stagnating, and it will
> cause Blood to be even more stagnant and less lively. Even though there is
> lovage and angelica to counteract and curb [the stagnation, because they
> nourish and enliven Blood], the circulation and movement will still be
> slight. So it is still inappropriate for someone who has just given birth.[84]

Generating and Transforming Decoction, by contrast, contained no
dangerously cooling ingredients. More to the point, its wondrous efficacy directly resulted from its pairing of warming drugs with supplementing ones. As Yan Chunxi explained, "Strong supplementers will impart great vigor and widely clear away obstructions, and warm drugs
that promote circulation will produce flowing and spreading and prevent congealing and impeding."[85] Put another way, the dissipating effect
of warmth would prevent the stagnant surpluses that might otherwise
result from the use of supplementing agents. In effect, then, Generating
and Transforming Decoction combined Chen Ziming's strategy of preventing stagnation through heat with Zhu Zhenheng's emphasis on supplementing qi and Blood. In so doing, it also created a new rationale for
the use of heating drugs in the postpartum period.

This enthusiasm for Generating and Transforming Decoction was also
consistent with new pharmacological approaches to regulating bodily vitalities. The sixteenth and seventeenth centuries witnessed the emergence
of a new intellectual current *(xuepai)* in medicine known as the "supplementing through warmth" *(wenbu)* approach. Its advocates agreed
with Zhu Zhenheng's basic idea that yin tended to be deficient, but they
argued that this deficiency could not be corrected by bolstering yin directly as Zhu had advocated. They pointed out that, because yin followed
yang, the proper way to boost yin was by augmenting yang. In therapeutic terms, this meant using warming, yang-supplementing formulas
instead of cooling, yin-supplementing ones. By the time the formula for
Generating and Transforming Decoction started to circulate in the med-

ical literature of the seventeenth century, the supplementing-through-warmth approach was well rooted in the medical landscape. In fact, the author who first published the formula for Generating and Transforming Decoction was Zhang Jiebin, a well-known proponent of supplementing through warmth. While discussions of this decoction did not explicitly mention the issue of warming supplements, the influence of this doctrine can be discerned in Ni Zhiwei's eighteenth-century text, the very one that introduced magistrate Xu Lian to Generating and Transforming Decoction. In his opening essay, "General Discussion of Postpartum Treatment," Ni Zhiwei began by quoting Zhu Zhenheng's dictum that one must replenish after childbirth. He then recommended Generating and Transforming Decoction for the various postpartum maladies. So while Zhu Zhenheng himself would have cautioned against a warming remedy such as this decoction, Ni now portrayed it as the ideal way to carry out Zhu's "supplement first" approach to postpartum care.[86]

In earlier writings, the idea that one could simultaneously address postpartum stagnation and vacuity had almost never been discussed, except to be dismissed as a practical impossibility. Zhu Zhenheng, for example, openly doubted that a single formula could simultaneously supplement and dispel stagnation.[87] So why did late imperial doctors start to see this as a feasible strategy? It is difficult to identify direct causal factors, but this faith in Generating and Transforming Decoction was consistent with other developments in learned medicine that fostered a more benign view of female reproductive function. As we saw in the previous chapter, the doctrine of cosmologically resonant childbirth depicted human birth as the recapitulation of cosmogenesis. Everything would go right unless people positively committed some error. This optimism was also echoed in rhetoric surrounding Generating and Transforming Decoction. The Chinese name of this recipe, *shenghua tang,* ostensibly referred to the formula's action on Blood, to "generate" *(sheng)* and "transform" *(hua).* But the phrase *shenghua* was also laden with centuries of philosophical and cosmological resonance, for it was the standard phrase used to describe the ineluctable creative impulse of the cosmos. Zhang Jiebin, for example, had explicitly invoked the innate nature of *shenghua* to explain how the loss of Blood during childbirth could actually represent a return to equilibrium for women of sturdy constitution: "That which was eliminated is something that ought to have been eliminated, and that which should be generated will be swiftly generated. Before many days have passed, [equilibrium] will certainly already have been restored. This is the self-so principle of generation and transformation [*shenghua ziran zhi li*]. How could it be that childbirth always causes vacuity?"[88]

If a postpartum woman was not necessarily ill, recovery from birth would happen as spontaneously as any other form of cosmogenesis. So while a formula name like "Black Divinity Powder" suggested divine intervention in female health, and "Four Ingredients Decoction" pointed to the skill of the pharmacologist, "Generating and Transforming Decoction" framed the postpartum state as a mundane stage in the universal cycle of reproduction. To be sure, the frequent, prophylactic use of Generating and Transforming Decoction assumed that the postpartum woman needed special regulation. But while older medical approaches focused only on expelling pathogens or on supplementing insufficiencies, Generating and Transforming Decoction confidently proclaimed its ability to do both at the same time, pharmacologically recapitulating the self-driven cyclical dynamics of cosmogenesis that would naturally restore the postpartum woman to equilibrium.

CHILDBIRTH IN A TIME OF CHOLERA

We have seen that advocates of Generating and Transforming Decoction promoted it as superior to Four Ingredients Decoction. Their arguments drew on ancient concerns with the behavior of female Blood, and they were also influenced by changing views of the relative utility of warming or cooling medicines. By the nineteenth century, Generating and Transforming Decoction was so widely used that this formula itself came under attack as a symbol of unthinking and inferior medical care. A leading critic was the eminent physician Wang Shixiong (1808–68), who charged that the indiscriminate use of this decoction had been harming women "for centuries."[89] Besides adding an important dimension to the history of debates over postpartum remedies, Wang's concerns illuminate how doctors' efforts to understand nongestational ailments could also influence specific approaches to the female body.

Wang Shixiong's criticism of Generating and Transforming Decoction—and the allegedly ignorant people who employed it—was fundamentally an attack on the belief that postpartum bodies were inherently cold. As we have seen, the idea that women needed warming after birth was supported by many educated doctors, and it also lay at the heart of popular practices associated with doing the month. Wang Shixiong, however, believed that the greatest threat to postpartum women was not cold, but heat: women who had just given birth tended to have a preponderance of yang, and the use of a warming remedy like Generating and Trans- forming Decoction would exacerbate this imbalance. In fact, he charged, many of the commonly seen postpartum ailments were actually caused by the inappropriate use of this decoction:

> It is the popular custom to value Generating and Transforming Decoction for all postpartum ailments, employing this fixed and inflexible prescription to treat the varying illnesses of the multitudes. In cases where the person's body is cold, it will certainly produce wondrous results. But if the person has Blood heat, or has been concurrently afflicted by warm or hot influ- ences, then as soon as this is administered, acute cases will transform into a swarm of illnesses, and chronic cases will gradually develop into childbed debility [rusun]. People only know that these are commonly seen illnesses, and they do not realize that half of these arise from the harmful effects of Generating and Transforming Decoction.[90]

In general terms, Wang's concern with pathogenic postpartum heat owed much to Zhu Zhenheng's teachings on the body's tendency toward yin depletion and the danger posed by excessive yang. He also agreed with Zhu's idea that postpartum women needed replenishing drugs.[91] But Wang Shixiong's medical perspectives were also shaped by his attempts to understand a major medical problem of his day: the seasonal epidemics of southern China, and specifically the etiological category known as "warm factor illnesses" (wenbing). Doctors had long considered warm factor illnesses as a subcategory of the "cold damage disorders" studied by Zhang Ji during the Han dynasty. As Marta Hanson has shown, how- ever, over the course of the eighteenth and nineteenth centuries, educated southern Chinese physicians became increasingly convinced that the "cold damage" doctrine was of limited utility in explaining the diseases of southern bodies.[92] In the sultry climes of the south, it was pathogenic heat itself—not a transfigured form of pathogenic cold—that was the root cause of seasonal epidemics. These southern physicians eventually artic- ulated a new intellectual current that elevated "warm factor illnesses" into an independent and influential etiological doctrine. The development of these ideas was also spurred by the arrival in China of epidemic cholera, which spread from India in the early nineteenth century and roiled the world in successive pandemics. Historians concur that epidemic cholera established itself in China in 1820–21, and the disease continued to be a global health problem for the rest of the century.

Wang Shixiong's writings played a key role in the consolidation of the warm factors medical current during the nineteenth century, and historians also conventionally credit him with producing the first specialized text on epidemic cholera, the *Treatise on Huoluan (Huoluan lun)* first published in 1839 and reedited in 1863.[93] Chinese doctors had historically recognized two diseases that seemed similar to cholera, namely, *huoluan*, a cholera-like illness characterized by "sudden uproar" of the bowels, and *sha*, meaning "acute outbreak."[94] Wang Shixiong and others argued over whether the epidemics of the 1820s and after represented an entirely new disease or simply a variant form of *huoluan* or *sha*. What was beyond dispute, however, was the disease's virulence and horrific death tolls, reported by Chinese and foreign observers alike.[95] Wang's experiences with *huoluan* shaped his views of Generating and Transforming Decoction in two important ways. First, he deplored the rote approach to healing illnesses that it embodied. To be sure, Chinese doctors routinely lamented the fact that their inferior competitors treated disease by mechanically applying standard formulas, and thus Wang was repeating a common trope. But the imperative to diagnose carefully took on special importance for Wang, who was acutely concerned with the many forms that epidemic disease could take. Second, Wang's concern with the problem of pathogenic heat as a cause of seasonal epidemics fed his conviction that pathogenic heat presented the gravest danger to postpartum women. Two discussions of postpartum illness that appear in Wang Shixiong's *Treatise on Huoluan* show how Wang melded these strains of thought together.

In a long section titled "Mengying," meaning "dream images" or "illusory scenes," Wang recounted more than fifty cases of *huoluan* from his own practice. He meant this title phrase as a reference to the inherent difficulty of diagnosing and treating *huoluan*. Not only were the signs of illness often misleading, but they could also transform their appearance and nature during the course of treatment. So even while he presented his experiences as useful guidelines, Wang emphasized that doctors would face a constantly shifting array of ambiguous signs: "The way in which this illness transforms and hides itself is like the cunning machinations of an enemy. Things seem to be a certain way, but actually are not. Or you will think that something is not so when actually it was. It takes myriad forms and appearances; one is unable to assess the clues, and one errs as to the bodily channels. These I append as illusory scenes."[96]

The cases that Wang placed in this section included a long account of an epidemic outbreak of 1844.[97] This outbreak began during the last third of the fifth lunar month (the summer) with a spell of unusually severe heat. "Great numbers of people were dying in the roads," Wang recalled, and attempts to treat them with conventional warming remedies did not help. The reason, Wang explained, was that their illnesses were not actually caused by coldness or damp, as the "cold damage" doctrine would claim. Instead, they had been "struck by summer heat," and the use of warming drugs had fatally augmented this heat. Among the victims was Wang's own sister-in-law, who felt a slight pain in her abdomen after lunch one day. Mistakenly believing that she had caught a chill, she dosed herself with hot wine (a doubly-heating remedy because alcohol was itself a heating drug). She subsequently fell into a frenzied confusion and was dead by sunset, blood flowing out of her nose and mouth. Clearly, one had to beware mistaking an illness caused by heat for one caused by cold, a principle that applied not only to epidemics but also to postpartum ailments. Continuing his account of this deadly season, Wang Shixiong lamented that numerous women had succumbed to pathogenic heat following childbirth:

> During this time, women who had just given birth were dying in especially high numbers. This was because yin Blood had been greatly lost and the summer heat easily invaded them, yet ignorant people did not know how to properly manage matters in accordance with the season. They still locked the windows and doors shut, enclosed the [woman] with screens and curtains, surrounded her with attendants, and gave her sugared wine to drink. Likewise, medical hacks did not investigate the incompatibilities between the season and the person's constitution, and when they took action it was to administer Generating and Transforming Decoction. Even though the signs of [pathological] heat were already apparent, they still erroneously believed the popular teaching that after birth it is proper to warm, and they did not know the flexible method of composing the formula according to the illness signs. The result was that [women] everywhere fell dead like so many cups being knocked over.[98]

While no one was immune to diseases of pathogenic heat, Wang's account depicted postpartum women as particularly vulnerable. First, the depletion of childbirth did not make a woman cold but rather left her hot. Furthermore, whenever a woman gave birth during the summer, the doctor had to consider the possibility of illness arising from summer heat. While Yang Zijian (eleventh century) had long ago identified the dangers associated with giving birth in excessively hot weather, Wang now integrated this problem into the broader category of illnesses caused by pathogenic heat. A third risk factor was the practices associated with doing the month, specifically those meant to shield a newly birthed mother from cold. Wang deplored the fact that, even during the summer, people stifled newly delivered mothers inside closed rooms and under heavy blankets, further plying them with warming drugs, drinks, and foods. But these naive attempts to protect the mother from cold and Blood stagnation ultimately sentenced her to death from a pathogenic excess of heat. Finally, the mistakes committed by family members were exacerbated by the errors of incompetent doctors, who uncritically prescribed Generating and Transforming Decoction.

At one level, such comments simply reiterated well-known criticisms about the harmful effects of common postpartum regimens. The *Imperial Encyclopedia,* for example, had included Liu Wansu's criticism of "popular" *(su)* measures designed to warm the postpartum woman's body and shield her from all cold.[99] Liu pointed out that the loss of bodily fluids during birth made the postpartum woman prone to yin vacuity. Adding heat to a body in which yang was already dominant would therefore induce illnesses of heat. But popular practices were uninformed by the medical classics and the principles of "creation and transformation" *(zaohua)* and, thus, were unable to distinguish the transformations of yin and yang in different illness manifestations. As a result, Liu Wansu said, people ignored the danger of postpartum heat and instead assumed that all postpartum ailments were rooted in cold and required heating remedies. The result, of course, was to create a preponderance of heat. "They erroneously use heating medicines and do not let the woman drink water even when she suffers vexatious thirst," Liu said. "Their basic intentions are kind, but they cause much harm."

But Wang Shixiong's concerns about postpartum practices were also significantly shaped by his experiences with *huoluan.* It was not simply that the practices associated with doing the month embodied an erroneous view of the postpartum body. They also directly contravened Wang's specific recommendations for protecting oneself against *huoluan.* In his *Treatise on Huoluan,* Wang Shixiong set out twelve guidelines for preventing and managing cases of this disease. His overall thrust was that one should use medicine with the greatest caution while avoiding heat and seeking out coolness. For example, Wang interdicted warming foods, and he positively enjoined people to ensure that their dwellings were well ventilated, with windows and doors left open.[100] All these recommendations would have been violated by popular postpartum customs. Wang's eleventh guideline for *huoluan* also specifically addressed the problems of postpartum women. Here he reiterated his view that the depletion of childbirth produced an excess of heat. "After childbirth," he explained, "yin Blood has been completely evacuated, orphan yang stands alone, the viscera are burning, and the channels and vessels are boiling."

Furthermore, he continued, women who gave birth during hot weather might also be afflicted by a warm factor disorder, and thus the doctor had to carefully distinguish what kind of heat was at work. In sum, Wang's effort to master *huoluan* led to an intense concern with issues of differential diagnosis, as well as to an emphasis on the problem of pathogenic heat, and both perspectives infused his views of postpartum care. For both of these reasons, he deplored the widespread use of Generating and Transforming Decoction. While Wang did acknowledge that there might be some postpartum women who were genuinely suffering from cold, such cases were the exception and could be identified only by means of careful inspection. By no means should one administer warming medicines just because the woman had given birth:

> Not only must her lips not touch Generating and Transforming Decoction, but sugared wine is also forbidden. If she has no abdominal pains, and you have not yet investigated whether or not she has *sha,* then only Six-One Powder is the efficacious medicine that can address both. If it is clear that she has *sha* or *huoluan,* treat her according to the usual methods. If the heat toxin is very deep, then one must not hesitate to use cooling and transforming drugs. If there are no signs of vacuity, then do not blindly use supplementing drugs on the grounds that she has just given birth. If there is no symptom of cold, then do not blindly give warming drugs just because she has given birth.[101]

CONCLUSION

The history of Generating and Transforming Decoction highlights the divergences and commonalities in late imperial Chinese views of childbearing women. Pollution beliefs and popular custom assumed that the postpartum body was sui generis. Depleted, stagnant, cold, and contaminated, it required immediate and continual prophylaxis and protection. The fact that a woman had just given birth thus outweighed any other factors that might be affecting her health. To a large extent, literate medicine shared these concerns with postpartum vulnerability. But physicians also recognized a wider range of subtler possibilities that had to be properly negotiated if a cure was to be achieved. The textual canon pointed out that childbirth was not inherently pathological, and that a fluid array of factors could underlie postpartum disease. Educated male doctors seeking to bolster their medical authority deplored those who would cling to stereotyped assumptions about the postpartum body, prescribing certain drugs just because a woman had given birth.

Beyond the immediate issue of health care for women, the story of

Generating and Transforming Decoction also provides insight into the social and intellectual substructures that shaped Chinese medical thought and its development over time. We have seen that this decoction appealed to a broad constituency of medical practitioners and laypeople, and that this appeal was both promoted and embodied by the proliferating medical literature of the day. While a Qing imperial doctor might recommend it specifically as a treatment for Blood stagnation, another healer might use it as a master formula for most postpartum illnesses, and lay people could recommend it to their friends as a time-tested, efficacious nostrum. But its appeal also grew out of its pharmacological properties, which allowed the practitioner to treat postpartum vacuity and stagnation together, thus reconciling the disparate teachings of ancient medical masters. Partisans of warming remedies could also employ Generating and Transforming Decoction instead of Four Ingredients Decoction. And as Wang Shixiong's criticisms of Generating and Transforming Decoction show, its widespread use was also promoted by the popular custom of doing the month, which taught that the postpartum body should be kept warm. By examining how these intellectual, material, and social dynamics alternately contradicted and reinforced each other, we can attain a fuller understanding of the various strategies that people in late imperial China deployed to ensure women's reproductive health.

Epilogue

Body, Gender, and Medical Legitimacy

On the first day of the third month of 1919, Mrs. Meng died in childbirth. She had gone into labor at dawn, and by afternoon the attending midwife declared that the birth was hopelessly obstructed. The family then summoned a doctor of Western medicine, who tried to deliver the child, but to no avail. By evening, both mother and baby were dead.[1]

The incident made a deep impression on Qiu Qingyuan (1873–1947), a friend of the Meng family. A native of Shaoxing, Qiu was a doctor and publisher and a leader in efforts to preserve and modernize Chinese medical practices.[2] These efforts had their roots in the upheavals of the preceding century, when Great Britain's decisive victory over China in the Opium War of 1839–42 inaugurated an era of foreign imperialist expansion in China. The latter's subsequent inability to resist these growing pressures eventually led Chinese elites to reevaluate the cultural underpinnings of their society.[3] In the wake of the Opium War, for example, a series of unequal treaties with Great Britain, France, the United States, Russia, and others forced the Qing government to open more and more ports to international trade and to permit Christian missionaries to travel freely in the interior of the county. The foreign powers demanded that China abandon the rhetoric of the tribute system and establish diplomatic relations with them on a basis of equality, even as they declared that their own nationals would not be subject to Chinese law. The Anglo-French expeditions of 1858–60, culminating in the destruction of the Summer

Palace and the occupation of Beijing, also signaled that the world order had irrevocably changed.

As the devastating civil conflict of the Taiping Rebellion (1851–64) came to an end, Chinese statesmen and intellectuals turned their attention to a wide range of self-strengthening initiatives. Even as they reaffirmed Confucian norms of public service and individual moral cultivation, they intensified and expanded earlier initiatives to adopt useful ideas from abroad. Whether building arsenals or translating works on Western sociopolitical thought, establishing military academies or sending students to Europe and the United States, these reformers aimed to revive China's strength and prosperity. By century's end, however, the foreign powers were competing to acquire territorial leaseholds in China, provoking fears that the empire was about to be cut up like a melon. Most humiliating, the ranks of the imperialists now included the Japanese, whom the Chinese had historically regarded as inferiors. But Japan's victory in the Sino-Japanese War of 1894–95 seemed to suggest that Japan had successfully modernized in response to Western pressures, while China had not.

The foreign scramble for concessions in 1897–98, the abortive Hundred Days' Reform of 1898, and the failed antiforeign Boxer Uprising of 1900 convinced many that the Qing court was hopelessly conservative and corrupt, fuelling a revolutionary movement that saw overthrowing the dynasty as the only way to preserve the country. An uprising in October 1911, supported by civilian officials and military commanders alike, led to the emperor's abdication in February 1912 and the establishment of a republican government. Thus did China's imperial age come to an end. But foreign pressures, along with intensifying calls for Chinese political and cultural reform, continued unabated. Soon after Mrs. Meng's death in childbirth, Chinese students marched in mass demonstrations to protest the Treaty of Versailles that ended World War I and awarded German leaseholds in China to Japan. This "May Fourth Movement" launched an era of iconoclastic attacks against China's indigenous traditions—including medicine—which leading reformers had already denounced as an embarrassment and an obstacle to modernization and national strengthening.

In this time of political and social transformation, Qiu Qingyuan and others insisted on the continued relevance of Chinese medical traditions, even as they sought to remake them among modern lines. By undertaking this critical reevaluation themselves, proponents of national medicine *(guoyi)* sought to defend their patrimony from reformers who would eliminate it all together. And so in 1919, Qiu was in the midst of producing a multivolume series of medical texts under the collective title *The Hundred Masters of National Medicine (Guoyi baijia)*. A first installment had already been published the year before by his Shaoxing Medical Journal Society. At that time, a colleague from the society had suggested that Qiu also include a work on pregnancy and postpartum treatment attributed to the Qing dynasty doctor Shan Nanshan (discussed in chapter 6). Other medical practitioners had been utilizing the methods in this text with great success, he said.[4] But Qiu Qingyuan was then studying a work on Western obstetrics *(chanpoxue)*, and he was skeptical that Chinese medicinal remedies could be useful during labor.[5]

He had a change of heart, however, after hearing about two friends whose wives had experienced difficult labor within two weeks of each another. The first was Mrs. Meng, the very woman who was treated according to Western methods and died. Although Qiu does not specify the techniques used, his readers would have assumed that the doctor had used obstetrical instruments or attempted some kind of emergency surgical procedure. The other woman was Mrs. Chen, who endured a protracted labor that lasted for four and a half days. During this time, she was dosed with one of the formulas that appeared in Shan Nanshan's book. Although her unborn child died, Ms. Chen herself recovered her health after few days. For Qiu Qingyuan, the lesson was clear: Chinese *fuke* had therapeutic value after all, and he should have published Shan Nanshan's work when he first learned of it. Ashamed of his earlier disdain, he now hastened the book into print. "Because I was prejudiced, I buried this old book for several months," he confessed in an afterword that he wrote for the text. "During these several months, how many Mrs. Mengs met an early death because they were unable to obtain the prescriptions in this book? My culpability is very deep."[6]

Qiu Qingyuan's initial ambivalence toward Shan Nanshan's text was emblematic of his time, when Chinese society as a whole was seeking a new cultural consensus. There was enough opposition against Chinese medicine for its critics to launch a vigorous, although unsuccessful, attempt in 1929 to ban its practice altogether. For their part, defenders of Chinese medicine showcased its virtues while criticizing the innate shortcomings of Western "science."[7] On the subject of reproductive medicine, they also made their case by employing older tropes of medical authority and therapeutic efficacy. During the Qing, learned male doctors had equated literate classical medicine with the use of drugs, and midwifery with the use of manual techniques. Qiu Qingyuan's account of Mrs.

Meng's death now projected this analogy onto a comparison of Chinese and Western techniques, implicitly using it to underscore the superiority of indigenous pharmacological therapies (Shan Nanshan's formulas) over foreign manual techniques (obstetrical instruments). Similar rhetoric informed the views of Feng Shaoqu, another physician involved in "national medicine" circles. A few years after the failed attempt to outlaw Chinese medicine, Feng published a manuscript by the Song family of Ningbo, a famous lineage of *fuke* practitioners.[8] In his editorial preface of 1933, Feng argued that, although "Western medicine slanders Chinese medicine, saying it is not in accordance with science *[kexue]*," the reverse was actually true. Western medicine was unscientific, he claimed, because it failed to respect the natural patterns that governed the human body. "When Western medicine treats diseases," Feng Shaoqu said, "it always goes contrary to the self-so nature of things *[ziran]*. Even if the treatment produces a cure, the original Heaven-endowed functions of the human body *[renshen tianfu zhi benneng]* are already lost." And nowhere was this unscientific, antinature orientation of Western medicine more clearly seen than in its approach to childbirth, which relied on surgical instruments to prematurely extract the child from its mother's womb:

> Western-style childbirth medicine has refined and excellent instruments and adroit surgical skills. I deeply admire them. But often they do not understand what the illnesses of pregnancy and postpartum consist of. Some are dazzled by money, while others cherish their time, and before the time for "the melon to ripen and drop" arrives [i.e., the proper time of birth], they have already recklessly used surgical methods to make [the baby] come out. Women in childbirth who have undergone Western surgical techniques must then have surgery the next time they give birth. The result of this is that humankind's original ability to give birth will be reduced day by day.

In Feng's description, the complaints that Chinese male doctors had historically directed against midwives were now projected onto Western doctors: whether out of ignorance or cunning, they violated the innate rhythms of birth. To underscore the limitations of Western medicine, Feng Shaoqu also pointed out that birth was meant to be easy, and here he echoed the animal analogies that had figured so prominently in the *Treatise on Easy Childbirth*. "One never hears of dogs, cats, cows, or sheep dying from difficulties in giving birth," Feng said. "And even if there are some cases, these are only one or two out of ten thousand." The failure of Western medicine to understand these basic truths, he implied, made it inferior to Chinese medicine. Indeed, Feng Shaoqu affirmed, it was Chinese medicine that was "scientific" precisely because, "in all respects, it

takes accordance with nature as its main principle" *(chuchu yi heyu ziran wei zhu)*. So even if Western medicine could provide new surgical
methods, Feng said, "this is nothing more than 'virtue increasing by one
foot, while vice increases by ten.' " In fact, Western medicine's ignorance
of the human body meant that it could not even achieve the most basic
goal of the Chinese physician: preventing miscarriage. As Feng Shaoqu
pointed out, "Among those who call themselves 'Doctorates in Obstetrics' *[chanke boshi]*, not one knows the methods for sustaining a pregnancy." His readers would have understood, furthermore, that there was
more at stake than simply the survival of a medical system. Looming over
the discussion was the issue of national and racial survival and how best
to use medicine to improve the Chinese body politic.[9] If Western medicine destroyed the innate ability of Chinese women to give birth, where
would China's future strength come from?

PATTERNS OF LATE IMPERIAL MEDICINE FOR WOMEN

During the Qing, literate doctors had promoted the ideal of cosmologically resonant childbirth as a way to save women's lives. In Feng Shaoqu's
critique of Western obstetrics, it was now yoked to the cause of saving
China. Feng's use of this rhetoric is an illuminating example of how older
ideas were reconfigured to new contexts, and it also testifies to the deeply
rooted nature of late imperial medical perspectives. In particular, we see
the persistence of what I have argued is a distinctive feature of Qing *fuke,*
namely, a more optimistic and benign view of female reproductive function and bodily difference. This view is most clearly seen in the discourse
of cosmologically resonant childbirth, but it also manifested itself in many
other subtle ways as well.

Everyone took it for granted that women had illnesses that men did not,
and medical concerns over the state of womb and Blood bespeak an ac-
knowledgment of the distinct physical endowments that shaped women's
experiences of reproductive illness and health. Discussions of pregnancy
and the postpartum period likewise show that late imperial medical writers continued to recognize therapeutic challenges unique to the female
body. But as learned male doctors sought to expand their epistemological authority over women's illnesses, they also increasingly foregrounded
the workings of a universal, cosmological body where male and female
were but two inflections of a single whole. Turning away from models
of female pollution and innate debility, they instead affirmed the power
of human agency to ensure optimal reproductive health in women. In-

fertility, difficult pregnancy, death in childbirth or after delivery—all these could be prevented if only women learned to protect their essential vitalities through emotional and physical discipline. In this enterprise, the wise male physician would be their natural guide.

This more optimistic view of the female reproductive body, rooted in mastery of the medical and scholarly classics, undergirded literate doctors' claims to be superior to other practitioners, especially female midwives. And yet, these rhetorical sallies never produced any institutional or social changes in the gendered organization of birth in the late imperial period. It is only during the Republican era that we find concerted attempts to reform midwifery, whether by the Nationalist government or by individual physicians. Even here, however, reform efforts were directed at improving the skills of traditional midwives and training new ones, rather than at replacing midwives with another kind of practitioner. Beyond the fact that families preferred the experienced "grannies," the relatively tiny number of Western-trained physicians available in a country as populous as China meant that midwives continued to be indispensable as service providers.[10] As for the late imperial period, male rhetoric against midwives did not diminish the essentially pluralistic and multipolar nature of healing or the central role of women in overseeing delivery. The continued frustration that male doctors expressed over the supposed misdeeds of midwives is, in fact, evidence of the midwife's constant presence in the birthing room.[11]

We should also note that male doctors competed with each other as much as—if not more than—they did with female healers. Whether seeking to preserve a pregnancy, salvage a seemingly hopeless labor, or prevent postpartum illness, literate physicians continually debated among themselves as to the correct approach to take. These doctrinal contests, furthermore, were framed by intramedical contests for status. The reputation of the scholarly male physician came from his ability to articulate a therapeutically efficacious interpretation of medical cosmology, one that would attract disciples and supporters. In this struggle for epistemological authority, his key rivals were other learned male doctors. As we have repeatedly seen, even if literate doctors all agreed that an inspired mastery of yin and yang was essential for proper diagnosis and cure, they could deploy yin and yang frameworks in different and conflicting ways. For example, the idea that pregnancy resembled agricultural production was predicated on the ancient correspondences between cosmic yin, the realm of earth, and human women. Viewed from one perspective, this meant that the growth of fetuses, like the growth of plants, required warmth. But concerns about yin could also focus attention on the relative balance of yin and yang forces within the body itself, and Zhu Zhenheng's influential yin-bolstering doctrine warned that augmenting heat (yang) would cause miscarriage.

Debates over postpartum drugs similarly revolved around competing ways to apply yin and yang frameworks to the gestative body. For example, did the depletion of childbirth tend to result in a preponderance of cold (rooted in vacuity of yang) or a preponderance of heat (vacuity of yin)? Getting the answer right in any given case could mean the difference between recovery or death. Finally, as male doctors sought to assert their epistemological authority over birth itself, they wrestled with a question that has faced all healers: when to intervene and how? Here the study of yin and yang guided the physician toward a model of cosmogenesis in which birthing interventions were fundamentally unnecessary. Just as the continual mingling of cosmic yin and yang produced the myriad things spontaneously, so too the congress of human yin (female Blood) and yang (male essence) should generate life with self-so ease.

The history of *fuke* also emphasizes the broader diversity of healing practice in late imperial China. Although learned doctors used their classical training to claim superior medical knowledge, the routinization of the norms of scholarly medicine in late imperial times diluted their claims to special authority. The proliferation of medical literature and the philanthropic impulse to disseminate medical works as widely as possible helped to promote amateur medical connoisseurship and authorship. The knowledge in these popular medical works, along with folk practices like doing the month, also constituted a resource that allowed people to ignore or refute physicians' judgments. Thus although the works of literate physicians dominate China's recorded history, these practitioners themselves enjoyed no privileged position of power in the medical marketplace. Indeed, the medical plurality of late imperial China was reinforced by continual skepticism toward self-proclaimed medical experts. Childbearing women potentially faced serious or even fatal ailments, and reliable cures were not always forthcoming. In the final analysis, the health of women was simply too important to entrust solely to doctors.

Gender and the Body

But even if scholarly physicians did not always receive the deference they sought, their records are essential landmarks in the late imperial medical landscape. An important historical question is how literate medicine understood the body that it sought to protect and heal. In the case of *fuke*, we must also ask how Chinese medicine defined the female sex and how it assigned gendered meanings to the bodies of women. The division of humankind into yin and yang—woman and man—was a basic fact, as obvious as the many other binaries that patterned the universe: earth and heaven, night and day, moon and sun. So what did it mean in this context to say that men as well as women had wombs, or that the diseases of men and women were alike except those related to childbearing?

Charlotte Furth has suggested that there was a tension between the idealized "androgynous" body of classical doctrine (what she calls "the body of generation") and the gendered childbearing body of *fuke* ("the body of gestation"). The androgyny of the classical body, Furth explains, comes from its simultaneous embrace of yin and yang, the binary pair that "name the 'feminine' and 'masculine' as aspects of all bodies and of the cosmos at large."[12] The fundamental androgyny of this "normative medical body of the Yellow Emperor" could, however, be compromised to a lesser or greater degree, depending on context and historical era.[13] In particular, Furth proposes that the development of *fuke* in the Song dynasty was rooted in an epistemological shift "from homology to difference." As she elaborates: "Song medical thinkers in developing *fuke* started out with the androgynous body of yin and yang, and the model of gender homology in males and females. In theory, Blood was simply bodily *qi* in its yin aspect, the same in all bodies. However, when doctors theorized that 'in women Blood is the leader,' in fact they produced gender difference."[14] Overall, Furth's analysis suggests that androgyny and difference were two points on a spectrum of gender along which Chinese medical thought could position itself differently at different points in time. Similarly, she implies that they were in opposition to one another, noting for example that, "in the history of tensions between the spheres of generation and those of gestation, we can see how bodily androgyny was challenged by female difference."[15]

But I suggest an alternate way of conceptualizing the relationship between androgyny and gender difference in Chinese medical thought, one that squares the circle by arguing that Chinese medical cosmology saw the human body as simultaneously sexless and sexed. Rather than as two points on a spectrum, Chinese medical doctrine saw androgyny and gender difference as two sides of a single coin. Although it may sound paradoxical, this perspective is consistent with a fundamental characteristic of Chinese philosophical thought: the simultaneity of unity and duality, and indeed the simultaneity of unity and multiplicity. The starting assumption for Neo-Confucian inquiry into the natural world was that the Great Ultimate *(taiji)* of the cosmos was divided and subdivided into yin and yang aspects. In the human realm, this division between yin and yang manifested itself in the distinction between female and male. Furthermore, the universe could not function without the existence of these distinctions. After all, it was the division of the Great Ultimate into yin and yang that allowed these opposite yet mutually generating forces to combine and give birth to the "myriad things" *(wanwu)*. Likewise, it was the division of humans into "women" and "men" that allowed them to couple and produce children. The universe, in short, was patterned by the primordial unity of phenomena that also needed to be distinct from one another. Insofar as medical doctrine was concerned, this meant that male and female bodies were part of a single inalienable whole, yet the observable differences between the sexes also constituted a phenomenon that required attention and study.

To further describe this simultaneity of unity and multiplicity in the classical medical body, I borrow the terminology of linguistics. "Inflectional morphology" is the process by which units of meaning (lexemes) take on different structural forms (inflections) during use, changing their morphological manifestations depending on grammatical context. For example, the lexeme "think" in English can be inflected as "thinks," "thinking," or "thought." In languages that inflect verbs, furthermore, these marked forms are frequently derived from an unmarked "infinitive" verb form that is then "conjugated" according to tense, person, number, mood, and so forth. Thus the French infinitive verb *parler* (to speak) becomes *parles* (you speak), *parlaient* (they were speaking), and *parlerons* (we will speak).[16] Inflectional morphology is thus predicated on the coexistence of unity (of lexical meaning) and multiplicity (of forms). Despite their different appearances, furthermore, there is no inherent tension between these forms of the verbs, simply differing contexts in which each form is appropriate. So rather than describe the Chinese doctrinal body as androgynous, which defines it in terms of possessing male and female attributes, I instead call it an infinitive body, one that serves as the basis for all human bodies, to be conjugated into male and female, young and old, robust and delicate, Southern and Northern, depending on circumstance.[17]

The conjugation of this infinitive body began from the moment that male and female seed intermingled, gaining in semantic relevance as the fetal form stabilized. As soon as the midwife looked between the newborn's legs and announced its sex, the child's future social role would be clear. For the learned doctor, then, the question was not whether men and women had bodily differences (because clearly they did) but rather how to explain those differences in terms of universal principles. In practical terms, he also had to understand how much significance to assign these differences during diagnosis and therapy. Fluent and sophisticated language use requires one to master the patterned transformations of lexical units. Similarly, effective medical care was a form of epistemological eloquence: knowing what corporeal inflection was appropriate to what context. Women did in fact differ from men, but when did those differences count? Was the fact that a woman had just given birth more important than her innate constitution? Was it always true that pregnant women should not be given cooling drugs? The doctor's virtuosity in treating women's diseases depended on his ability to correctly conjugate for sex difference in any given situation.

The concept of the infinitive body also suggests alternate interpretations of Chinese medical history. Rather than being a departure from androgyny, for example, Song dynasty *fuke* can be seen as an essential step toward understanding the multiple inflections of the infinitive body. After all, the development of "childbirth medicine" was part of a larger intellectual initiative in which multiple new subfields of medicine were created and organized around specific populations (including children) or specific ailments and therapies. To be sure, as Furth points out, Song medicine produced no "medicine for men" that focused equal attention on male bodies. But consider that the authors of Song medicine were men, and that the traditional caregivers for women were other women. The special attention that male physicians gave to women's bodies was thus an attempt to project authority over an area of practice that had previously lain largely outside their purview. Viewed in this context, Song male doctors did not produce gender difference so much as produce a new way of explaining gender differences that were already presumed to exist and that already patterned therapy. Furthermore, as Song male doctors applied the language of cosmological correspondences to the gestational illnesses of women, they also introduced ideas that allowed female bodies to be increasingly de-exoticized. The noxious "girdle discharges" specific to women were now reimagined as perturbations of Blood, a yin form of qi present in all bodies. Social customs were now identified as a significant cause of women's presumed sickliness, thereby diluting an earlier emphasis on the innately pathological nature of female childbearing functions. Finally, even while they observed ancient rituals to mitigate the supposed danger and pollution of childbirth, Song doctors also proposed that "the great virtue of Heaven and Earth is called generating life," and that human reproduction should reiterate the ease of cosmogenesis.

In subsequent centuries, the intellectual vanguard was occupied by doctors who developed universally applicable doctrines that would explain all forms of human disease. Was it true that women's gestational problems were rooted in cold and wind striking Blood? An innovator like Zhu Zhenheng did not need to write specialized works on *fuke* to answer these questions, because he could refine his knowledge of women's bodies by refining his knowledge of the infinitive body. In Zhu's doctrines, for example, the human body's tendency to suffer from yin vacuity now also served as an explanation for miscarriage and difficult labor. As more and more scholars entered medicine, mastery of the Neo-Confucian-inspired works of physicians like Zhu Zhenheng became central to their self-identity and medical legitimacy. Furthermore, as these learned male practitioners pursued ever more perfect applications of cosmology to medicine, they also increasingly argued that the seemingly unique aspects of the female body were but a variation of the infinitive body. These developments were epitomized by Zhang Jiebin's sixteenth-century argument that the womb was the female version of a procreative space that existed in all bodies, a formulation that became accepted elite doctrine by the eighteenth century.

At the same time, Qing *fuke* witnessed the full maturation of the idea that women's illnesses were fundamentally no different from those of men, except for those conditions pertaining to childbirth. And even in those special cases, one could not assume that the woman's gestational state was the most important factor in any medical situation. After all, everyone knew that pregnancy and childbirth affected different women in different ways. Variations in women's innate constitutions meant that pregnancy tests could be unreliable. Some pregnancies would last for the canonical ten months, while others would be premature or unusually long. Some women would be dangerously depleted by childbirth, while others would be restored to a state of yin-yang harmony. So while the subfield of "medicine for women" provided a useful way to classify medical knowledge and promote its intellectual development, the skilled doctor still had to be constantly aware of the individual variations present in the bodies of different women.

Finally, it is worth recalling the perceived material realities of sickness and death that the gender rhetoric, doctrinal arguments, and therapeutic innovations of late imperial Chinese medicine all sought to address. Women died in childbirth. Men did not. The technological resources of world medicine before the twentieth century, furthermore, meant that the options for successful intervention were limited and the consequences of failure were all too familiar. These problems thus loomed large in the minds of parturient women, their families, and medical experts. Whatever their differences of opinion over therapy and prevention, therefore, they were unified by the desire to protect women's health as they performed that most crucial human function: giving birth to the next generation.

Notes

ABBREVIATIONS

Published Sources

FSYJ   Guo Aichun, ed., *Zhongguo fensheng yiji kao* (A study of Chinese medical texts by province) (Tianjin: Tianjin kexue jishu chubanshe, 1987).

GJTS   Chen Menglei et al., comps., *Gujin tushu jicheng* (A compendium of ancient and modern texts and illustrations, also known as the *Imperial Encyclopedia*) (Beijing: Neifu, 1726–28; reprint, Chengdu: Zhonghua shuju and Bashu shushe, 1986). In my page citations, the number preceding the colon refers to the separately numbered *juan* of the "Section on Arts and Techniques" *(yishu dian)*.

LDYJ   He Shixi, *Zhongguo lidai yijia zhuanlu* (Biographical records of medical experts throughout Chinese history) (Beijing: Renmin weisheng chubanshe, 1991).

LHML   Zhongguo zhongyi yanjiuyuan tushiguan, ed., *Quanguo zhongyi tushu lianhe mulu* (Union catalog of Chinese medicine books in Chinese libraries) (Beijing: Zhongyi guji chubanshe, 1991).

SKQS   *Siku quanshu* (Complete library of the four treasuries) (Wenyuange edition, 1782; facsimile reprint published Taipei: Taiwan shangwu yinshuguan, 1986; electronic version published Hong Kong: Chinese University of Hong Kong and Digital Heritage Publishing, 1998).

YJDCD   Zhongguo yiji dacidian bianzuan weiyuanhui, *Zhongguo yiji daci-*

dian (Comprehensive dictionary of Chinese medical texts) (Shanghai: Shanghai kexue jishu chubanshe, 2002).

YJTK   Yan Shiyun, ed., *Zhongguo yiji tongkao* (A comprehensive study of Chinese medical texts) (Shanghai: Shanghai zhongyi xueyuan chubanshe, 1990–94).

YZJJ   Wu Qian, ed., *Yuzuan yizong jinjian* (The imperially compiled golden mirror of medical learning) (Beijing: Wuying dian, 1742). Reprinted in *SKQS*.

ZBYS   Qiu Qingyuan [Jisheng], ed., *Zhenben yishu jicheng* (Collection of precious medical works) (Shaoxing, 1936; facsimile reprint, Shanghai: Shanghai kexue jishu chubanshe, 1986.

Library Abbreviations

To allow greater precision in distinguishing among multiple woodblock editions of pre-twentieth-century medical texts attributed to Jizhai jushi (Lay Buddhist Jizhai) and the Zhulinsi seng (Bamboo Grove Monastery monks), I've included in their bibliographic citations an abbreviation derived from the name of the library that owns the text and the accession or registration number of the text. For example, CM no. 193780 refers to an edition of *Zhulinsi sanchanshi nüke sanzhong* owned by the Zhongguo zhongyi kexue yuan, and the first fascicle of this text bears the registration number 193780.

(BH)   Zhongguo guojia tushuguan (National Library of China, Beihai branch, Beijing)

(CM)   Zhongguo zhongyi kexue yuan (China Academy of Chinese Medical Sciences, Beijing)

(CS)   Zhongguo kexueyuan (Chinese Academy of Sciences, Beijing)

(PU)   Beijing xiehe yixueyuan (Peking Union Medical College, Beijing)

(ST)   Shanghai tushuguan (Shanghai Library)

(SY)   Shanghai zhongyiyao daxue (Shanghai University of Traditional Chinese Medicine and Materia Medica)

(ZJ)   Zhejiang zhongyiyao yanjiuyuan (Zhejiang Research Academy for Traditional Chinese Medicine and Materia Medica, Hangzhou)

INTRODUCTION

1. In Chinese sources that do not provide a married woman's full name, the woman is conventionally identified in one of two ways. The first is to use the woman's natal surname, plus the suffix *shi,* meaning "person of this family." Yan Chunxi, for example, refers to his wife as "Shen *shi.*" In such cases, I refer to the woman as "Ms. Natal Surname." The second is to refer to the woman as "the

wife of So-and-So." In such cases, I refer to the woman in question as "Mrs. So-and-So."

All translations from Chinese texts are mine, unless otherwise noted. The main narrative describing Ms. Shen's illness and death are related in Yan Chunxi, *Taichan xinfa* (Essential teachings on childbearing), comp. ca. 1725, author's preface dated 1730. I quote from the modern critical edition, by Tian Daihua and Guo Junshuang, of the Yongzheng-era woodblock edition, published in *Nüke jiyao, taichan xinfa* (Beijing: Renmin weisheng chubanshe, 1988), 372–73. The book bears a preface dated 1725 by the Hubei native Gong Jianyang, a *jinshi* degree holder and imperial censor. While Gong speaks of the book being complete in 1725, Yan Chunxi's own authorial preface is dated 1730. For information on Ms. Shen's miscarriages, see Yan, *Taichan xinfa*, 192–93. I have derived my description of Yan's motivations and medical background from his own comments as well as from Gong Jianyang's preface. See also the modern editors' preface to this edition.

2. Yan was "recommended and recruited" *(jianbi)* for office, and he held the formal designation of *gongsheng* (tribute student). He was appointed Surveillance Vice Commissioner for the Left River Circuit *(zuojiang fenxun dao)* in Guangxi Province in 1725, serving until 1737. As far as I have been able to determine, this was the only ranked position he held in the government. See Wang Zhefu, ed., *Qianlong Xuanhua fuzhi* (Gazetteer of Xuanhua Prefecture from the Qianlong reign) (1757; reprint, Shanghai: Shanghai shudian chubanshe, 2006), 26:19a; and Xie Qikun, ed., *Guangxi tongzhi* (Gazetteer of Guangxi Province) (1800; facsimile reprint, Taipei: Wenhai chubanshe, 1966), 33:10b. I have translated his degree status and official title according to Charles O. Hucker, *A Dictionary of Official Titles in Imperial China* (Stanford: Stanford University Press, 1985). For tribute students and office via recommendation *(jianju)* in the Qing, see also Benjamin A. Elman, *A Cultural History of Civil Examinations in Late Imperial China* (Berkeley: University of California Press, 2000).

3. Yan describes dissolving a pill of "childbirth elixir" *(taichan jindan)* into the ginseng decoction. Although I have not been able to conclusively identify the compound that he used, it may have been akin to a formula by this name that first appeared in Li Wenbin's *Xian nian ji* (Collection of formulas selected by immortals), first published in 1754. For this attribution, see the entry for *taichan jindan* in Zhongyi dacidian bianji weiyuanhui, ed., *Zhongyi dacidian: Fangji fence* (Comprehensive dictionary of Chinese medicine: Volume on medicinal formulas) (Beijing: Renmin weisheng chubanshe, 1983), 374.

4. For a discussion of these laws in the Ming and Qing, see Yüan-ling Chao, "Medicine and Society in Late Imperial China: A Study of Physicians in Suzhou" (PhD diss., University of California, Los Angeles, 1995), 140–44. See also the entry for *yongyi shangsha ren* in the *Daqing lüli* (Great Qing Code with substatutes) (1740; reprinted in *SKQS*), 26:35a.

5. There are forty-seven Qing editions of this work listed in Zhongguo zhongyi yanjiuyuan tushiguan, ed., *Quanguo zhongyi tushu lianhe mulu* (Union catalog of Chinese medicine books in Chinese libraries) (Beijing: Zhongyi guji chubanshe, 1991), hereafter *LHML*.

6. Charles E. Rosenberg, "Framing Disease: Illness, Society, and History," in *Framing Disease: Studies in Cultural History,* ed. Charles E. Rosenberg and Janet Golden (New Brunswick, N.J.: Rutgers University Press, 1992), xiii–xxvi.

7. Here I borrow the analytical perspectives of Shigehisa Kuriyama in *The Expressiveness of the Body and the Divergence of Greek and Chinese Medicine* (New York: Zone Books, 1999).

8. A useful overview of the high Qing is Susan Naquin and Evelyn S. Rawski, *Chinese Society in the Eighteenth Century* (New Haven, Conn.: Yale University Press, 1987). Of the numerous other excellent studies of this period that one could cite, my historical summary here has been influenced most by Benjamin A. Elman, *From Philology to Philosophy: Intellectual and Social Aspects of Change in Late Imperial China* (Cambridge, Mass.: Harvard University Press, 1984); Susan Mann, *Precious Records: Women in China's Long Eighteenth Century* (Stanford: Stanford University Press, 1997); and Cynthia J. Brokaw and Kai-wing Chow, eds., *Printing and Book Culture in Late Imperial China* (Berkeley: University of California Press, 2005).

9. For an overview of this idea as expressed in the teachings of Xunzi, see Philip J. Ivanhoe, "Early Confucianism and Environmental Ethics," in *Confucianism and Ecology,* ed. Mary Evelyn Tucker and John Berthrong (Cambridge, Mass.: Harvard University Press, 1998), 59–76.

10. This passage originated with Chen Wuze, as quoted in Chen Ziming, *Furen daquan liangfang* (Comprehensive compendium of good formulas for women) (comp. 1237, rev. ca. 1265; modern critical edition of Yuan dynasty Qinyou shutang edition by Yu Ying'ao et al., Beijing: Renmin weisheng chubanshe, 1992), 286. My rendering of Mencius's quotation is adapted from James Legge, trans., *The Works of Mencius (Mengzi)*, 2nd ed. (Oxford: Clarendon Press, 1895), bk. 4, pt. 1, chap. 26.

11. Xiao Xun, preface to *Nüke jinglun* (Canonical teachings on medicine for women) (1684; modern punctuated edition published Shanghai: Shanghai weisheng chubanshe, 1957). The sixth classic, not mentioned in Xiao's description, was the *Classic of Music (yuejing)*, which was dropped from the canon as an individual work in the second century C.E. in order to bring the number of texts into conformity with the cosmological five phases *(wu xing)*. See Michael Nylan, *The Five "Confucian" Classics* (New Haven, Conn.: Yale University Press, 2001), 21, 33.

12. The earliest text we have is the *Taichan shu* (Book on childbearing), a silk manuscript excavated from the Mawangdui tombs near Changsha, Hunan. This work notably describes the care of the unborn fetus during pregnancy, as well as methods for selecting a placenta burial site. It is estimated to date from at least 188 B.C.E., if not substantially earlier. See Donald Harper, *Early Chinese Medical Literature* (London: Keegan Paul, 1998), 27–28. For a discussion of key developments in medicine for women in the Han through Tang dynasties, see the essays by Robin D. S. Yates, Sabine Wilms, and Jen-der Lee in *Medicine for Women in Imperial China,* ed. Angela Ki Che Leung (Leiden: Brill, 2006). For the history of *fuke* from the Song to the Ming dynasties, see Charlotte Furth, *A Flourishing Yin: Gender in China's Medical History, 960–1665* (Berkeley: University of California Press, 1999), 110.

13. See the *LHML*. A useful reference that describes the history and content of these extant books is Zhongguo yiji dacidian bianzuan weiyuanhui, *Zhong-guo yiji dacidian* (Comprehensive dictionary of Chinese medical texts) (Shang-hai: Shanghai kexue jishu chubanshe, 2002), hereafter *YJDCD*. A modern collection that consists of the reprinted prefaces to extant medical books (including works on women's medicine) is Yan Shiyun, ed., *Zhongguo yiji tongkao* (A comprehensive study of Chinese medical texts) (Shanghai: Shanghai zhongyi shueyuan chubanshe, 1990–94), hereafter *YJTK*. For medical works that are no longer extant, but whose titles are recorded in gazetteers, see also Guo Aichun, ed., *Zhong-guo fensheng yiji kao* (A study of Chinese medical texts by province) (Tianjin: Tianjin kexue jishu chubanshe, 1987), hereafter *FSYJ*.

14. For this characterization of the book market and late imperial reader-ship, I have relied on Cynthia J. Brokaw, *Commerce in Culture: The Sibao Book Trade in the Qing and Republican Periods* (Cambridge, Mass.: Harvard University Press, 2007).

15. Paul U. Unschuld and Zheng Jinsheng, "Manuscripts as Sources in the History of Chinese Medicine," in *Medieval Chinese Medicine: The Dunhuang Medical Manuscripts,* ed. Vivienne Lo and Christopher Cullen (Abingdon, U.K.: Routledge Curzon, 2005), 19–44.

16. Furth, *Flourishing Yin.*

17. Francesca Bray, *Technology and Gender: Fabrics of Power in Late Im-perial China* (Berkeley: University of California Press, 1997).

18. Volker Scheid, *Chinese Medicine in Contemporary China: Plurality and Synthesis* (Durham, N.C.: Duke University Press, 2002).

19. *YZJJ,* 44:1a.

CHAPTER 1. LATE IMPERIAL *FUKE* AND THE LITERATE MEDICAL TRADITION

1. Wei Zhixiu, *Xu mingyi lei'an* (A continuation of the *Cases from Famous Doctors, Arranged by Category*) (ca. 1770; reprinted in *SKQS*, 34:11b–12b. Un-less otherwise noted, all my translations of Wei's work are of this eighteenth-century edition, to be distinguished from a revised version produced in 1853 by Wang Shixiong. For the latter version, see Wang Shixiong, ed., *Xu mingyi lei'an* (A continuation of the *Cases from Famous Doctors, Arranged by Category*), by Wei Zhixiu (editor's preface dated 1853, first published 1863; modern critical edition of Zhuyi tang woodblock edition of 1863 published Beijing: Renmin weisheng chubanshe, 1997). While Wei's original does not give the doctor's name, I have accepted Wang Shixiong's later interpretation that the doctor in this case is in fact Wei Zhixiu. See Wang, ed., *Xu mingyi lei'an,* 25:779.

There are three good reasons for accepting Wang's attribution. First, the case follows the known textual pattern of Wei's compendium. We know that Wei Zhixiu included his own case records in his collection, and these usually appeared unattributed at the end of each section. In the instances where Wei placed his cases in the middle of a section, he identified himself by name. Second, Wei's col-lection is the only place that I have been able to find this case, suggesting that it came from his own experiences rather than another doctor's text. Finally, Wang

Shixiong's attribution of this case was the product of intensive study into Wei Zhixiu's opus. While revising Wei's *Xu mingyi lei'an,* in fact, Wang also produced the *Liuzhou yihua liangfang* (Medical discussions and worthy prescriptions from Master Liuzhou), the core of which consisted of Wei's original case annotations to the *Xu mingyi lei'an.* See Wang Shixiong, comp., *Liuzhou yihua liangfang* (Medical discussions and worthy prescriptions from Master Liuzhou) (1851; critical edition of 1918 Jiguge lithographic edition reprinted in Wang Shixiong, *Wang Shixiong yixue quanshu* [The complete collection of Wang Shixiong's medical books], Beijing: Zhongguo zhongyiyao chubanshe, 1999). For Wang Shixiong's reading notes and his assessment of Wei's book, see also Wang's preface to *Xu mingyi lei'an;* Wang Shixiong, *Gui yan lu* (Records of returning to the inkstone) (author's first preface dated 1857; reprinted with author's new preface dated 1862; critical edition of 1918 Jiguge lithographic edition reprinted in Wang Shixiong, *Wang Shixiong yixue quanshu*), 421–23; and *YJDCD,* 2:1330.

2. Wei Zhixiu, courtesy name Yuheng, was a native of Qiantang County, Hangzhou Prefecture, Zhejiang Province. Official histories described him as a "commoner," namely, someone not from a scholar-official background. He reportedly supported himself in his youth by working in a money-lending shop, studying medicine and literature at night. Some sources also state that he came from a family with a tradition of medical practice. His literary contacts notably included the poet, historian, and painter Hang Shijun (1696–1773), who wrote in praise of Wei's medical case collection, and the eminent bibliophile Bao Tingbo (1728–1814), who published a collection of Wei's poems as well as Wei's recension of Jiang Guan's *Mingyi lei'an* (Cases from famous doctors, arranged by category). Bao was also a leading contributor of books to the *SKQS* and likely played a part in bringing Wei's works to the attention of the editors. For details on Wei and his texts, see Chen Qiong et al., comps., *Minguo Hangzhou fuzhi* (Gazetteer of Hangzhou Prefecture from the Republican period) (1922; reprint, Shanghai: Shanghai shudian, 1993), 150:15b; He Shixi, *Zhongguo lidai yijia zhuanlu* (Biographical records of medical experts throughout Chinese history) (Beijing: Renmin weisheng chubanshe, 1991, hereafter *LDYJ*), 3:370; *YJDCD,* 2:1331, and the modern editorial preface to Wang Shixiong, ed., *Xu mingyi lei'an,* 3–5. For Bao Tingbo and Hang Shijun, see their entries in Arthur W. Hummel, ed., *Eminent Chinese of the Ch'ing Period* (Washington, D.C.: Library of Congress, 1943).

3. Wei's formula consisted of raw rehmannia root *(shengdi),* achyranthis root *(niuxi),* motherwort *(yimu),* safflower *(honghua),* peach pit paste *(taoren ni),* tail of angelica root *(danggui wei),* salvia root *(danshen),* and cockleshell *(walengzi).* The first ingredient served to "cool" Blood and would address the fever, while the remaining ingredients were commonly known for their ability to break up accumulated Blood and promote circulation. While the case narrative does not explain the family's reluctance to use these drugs, their rationale would have been evident to any contemporary reader. For medical debates over purging stagnation versus replenishing Blood in the postpartum period, see chapter 6.

4. These statistics come from *YJDCD,* 2:1331. While *YJDCD* gives the date of compilation for *Xu mingyi lei'an* as 1774, all other sources that I have seen give it as 1770. The actual date of completion is probably somewhere in between, as Wei had just completed a major annotation project around 1770, namely, a

reedition of Jiang Guan's *Mingyi lei'an*. For Wei's involvement in this latter work, see the prefaces in Jiang, *Mingyi lei'an* (Cases from famous doctors, arranged by category) (comp. 1549; first ed. 1591; annot. Wei Zhixiu and republished by Bao Tingbo in 1770; reprint, Taipei: Hongye shuju, 1994).

5. See the editorial synopsis of the *SKQS* edition of Wei, *Xu mingyi lei'an;* and Wang Shixiong's preface to his edition of *Xu mingyi lei'an*.

6. For the history of the medical case history genre, its narrative conventions, and epistemological functions, see the following chapters in Charlotte Furth, Judith T. Zeitlin, and Ping-chen Hsiung, eds., *Thinking with Cases: Specialist Knowledge in Chinese Cultural History* (Honolulu: University of Hawai'i Press, 2007): Furth, "Producing Medical Knowledge through Cases: History, Evidence, Action," 125–51; Hsiung, "Facts in the Tale: Case Records and Pediatric Medicine in Late Imperial China," 152–68; and Zeitlin, "The Literary Fashioning of Medical Authority: A Study of Sun Yikui's Case Histories," 169–202. Another helpful study is Christopher Cullen, "*Yi'an* (Case Statements): The Origins of a Genre of Chinese Medical Literature," in *Innovation in Chinese Medicine*, ed. Elisabeth Hsu (Cambridge: Cambridge University Press, 2001), 297–323.

7. See, for example, *YZJJ*, 47:2a–b.

8. Here I adopt Volker Scheid's translation of *xuepai*. *Currents of Tradition in Chinese Medicine: 1626–2006* (Seattle: Eastland Press, 2007). Accounts of the main historical currents and their representative figures are Qiu Peiran and Ding Guangdi, eds., *Zhongyi gejia xueshuo* (The teachings of famous Chinese medical experts) (Beijing: Renmin weisheng chubanshe, 1992); and Paul U. Unschuld, *Medicine in China: A History of Ideas* (Berkeley: University of California Press, 1986). An essential case study of a major current in late imperial medicine is Marta Hanson, "Inventing a Tradition in Chinese Medicine: From Universal Canon to Local Medical Knowledge in South China, the Seventeenth to the Nineteenth Century" (PhD diss., University of Pennsylvania, 1997).

9. For descriptions of different healing modalities and their development during different periods of Chinese history, see Unschuld, *Medicine in China: A History of Ideas*. Western interest in and misinterpretation of these practices is examined in Linda Barnes, *Needles, Herbs, Gods, and Ghosts: China, Healing, and the West to 1848* (Cambridge, Mass.: Harvard University Press, 2005).

10. Helpful studies of female participation in healing are Charlotte Furth, *A Flourishing Yin: Gender in China's Medical History, 960–1665* (Berkeley: University of California Press, 1999); Angela Ki Che Leung, "Women Practicing Medicine in Premodern China," in *Chinese Women in the Imperial Past: New Perspectives*, ed. Harriet T. Zurndorfer (Leiden: Brill, 1999), 101–34; Zheng Jinsheng, "Female Medical Workers in Ancient China," in *Current Perspectives in the History of Science in East Asia*, ed. Yung Sik Kim and Francesca Bray (Seoul: Seoul National University Press, 1999), 460–66; Victoria B. Cass, "Female Healers in the Ming and the Lodge of Ritual and Ceremony," *Journal of the American Oriental Society* 106, no. 1 (January–March 1986): 233–40. The history of male complaints about the "six grannies" is examined in Leung. Cass points out that in the case of medical women at court, there was the real concern that midwives and the like would become embroiled in palace intrigues.

11. Quoted in Cass, "Female Healers," 237.

12. Dorothy Ko, *Teachers of the Inner Chambers: Women and Culture in Seventeenth-Century China* (Stanford: Stanford University Press, 1994), 225.

13. Susan Mann, *The Talented Women of the Zhang Family* (Berkeley: University of California Press, 2007), 42.

14. Zeng Jifen, *Testimony of a Confucian Woman: The Autobiography of Mrs. Nie Zeng Jifeng, 1852–1942*, trans. and annot. by Thomas L. Kennedy (Athens: University of Georgia Press, 1993), 101–2.

15. Furth, *Flourishing Yin*, chap. 8.

16. Zhang Yuanduan, preface dated 1921 to *Huayunlou yi'an* (Medical cases from the Pavilion of Flowery Rhymes) by Gu Dehua (mid-nineteenth century, reprinted in *ZBYS*), vol. 12.

17. Gu Dehua's father, Gu Kaijun, was a departmental vice magistrate with a volume of poetry to his credit. Dehua's own poetry was titled *Shi-style Poems from the Pavilion of Flowery Rhymes*. See Li Mingwan and Tan Junpei, eds., *Tongzhi Suzhou fuzhi* (Gazetteer of Suzhou Prefecture from the Tongzhi reign) (1882; reprint, Nanjing: Jiangsu guji chubanshe, 1991), 136:47a; *FSYJ*, 495, 719, 740. See also Gu Dehua's entry in Hu Wenkai, *Lidai funü zhuzuo kao* (Study of women authors throughout history) (Shanghai: Shanghai guji chubanshe, 1984), 807.

18. Zeng Yi is not related to Zeng Jifen. I estimate her date of birth based on the prefaces to her 1907 works, which state that she was in her fifty-fourth year in 1906. Zeng Yi, preface dated 1906 to her *Yixue pian* (A treatise on medicine) in *Guhuanshi yixue pian* (A treatise on medicine from the Delighting in Antiquity Studio) (Changsha: n.p., 1907). Zeng Yi's father, the Sichuan native Zeng Yong, and one of her brothers both held the *jinshi* degree, and two other brothers were county officials. Zeng Yi's own husband (and cousin) was the son of Yuan Jimao, a *jinshi* scholar and secretary in the Ministry of Justice *(xingbu)* who earned an entry in the Qing dynastic history's section on "loyal and righteous officials." *Qingshi gao* (Draft history of the Qing dynasty) (1927; reprint, Beijing: Zhonghua shuju, 1977), 490:13544. Zeng Yi's mother, Zuo Xijia, was the granddaughter of Zuo Fu, who served as governor of Hunan during the Qianlong reign, and the daughter of Zuo Ang, who held various midlevel official posts, including that of vice prefect of Fengyang Prefecture in Anhui. Zuo Xijia and one of her sisters were both accomplished and renowned poets and painters, and after her husband died fighting the Taiping rebels, Xijia sold her own paintings to support the family. Her fortitude and chaste widowhood earned Xijia a place among the "virtuous women" immortalized by the Huayang County gazetteer. Subsequently, Zeng Yi and her own sister Yan also became skilled painters and writers in their own right. Altogether, the women of the Zuo and Zeng families produced several volumes of poetry. For information on the members of the Zeng and Zuo families, see Lin Sijin, ed., *Huayang xianzhi* (Gazetteer of Huayang County) (1934; reprint, Taipei: Taiwan xuesheng shuju, 1967), 15:1a–4b (Zeng Yong) and 19:4b–6b (Zuo Xijia), and their entries in the following biographical dictionaries: Yu Jianhua, *Zhongguo meishujia renming cidian* (Dictionary of Chinese artists) (Shanghai: Shanghai renmin meishu chubanshe, 1981), 1082; Hu, *Lidai funü zhuzuo kao;* and Yuan Shaoying and Yang Guizhen, eds., *Zhongguo funü mingren cidian* (Dictionary of famous Chinese women) ([Changchun:] Beifang funü ertong chubanshe, 1989), 563.

19. Zeng Yi, preface, *Yixue pian*. Additional descriptions of her medical activities are Tu Kuixian, "Qingdai nüzhongyi Zeng Yi ji qi 'Yixue bian' jianjie" (A brief introduction to the Qing dynasty woman doctor of Chinese medicine, Zeng Yi, and her work "Treatise on Medicine"), *Zhongyi zazhi* (April 1981): 69; Hu Guojun, "Zeng Yi nüyi wannian yixue yishi" (An anecdote about the female doctor Zeng Yi's medicine late in life), *Sichuan zhongyi* (October 1985): 6–7; and Xin Fu, "Lidai Shuyi kao—Chengdu nüyijia Zeng Yi zhuanlue" (Researches into Sichuan doctors throughout history—a general biography of the Chengdu female doctor Zeng Yi), *Chengdu zhongyi xueyuan xuebao* (March 1980): 65.

20. This epidemic occurred during the Tongzhi reign (1862–74). Zhang Baixi, preface dated 1906 to *Nüxue pian* (A treatise on female education), by Zeng Yi, in *Guhuanshi yixue pian* (A treatise on medicine from the Delighting in Antiquity Studio) (Changsha: n.p., 1907).

21. Zeng, *Yixue pian*. In 1933, the Suzhou National Medicine Society put out an edition of this text that treated Zeng Yi's original topical chapters as separate works, publishing them under the collective title *The Complete Medical Books of Female Scholar Zeng (Zeng nüshi yixue quanshu).*

22. See the entries for Wang Zhu and Wang Hengqi in *FSYJ*, 1:721 (daughter), 1:495, 719, 740 (father) and *LDYJ*, 1:102 (daughter), 1:32 (father). Wang Zhu reportedly coauthored three titles with one Qian Dazhi, a *jiansheng* (National University student by purchase) from Jiading County. He is also said to have transmitted his learning to a Cheng Yaotian. Little else is known about these men, however; nor do their medical works appear to be extant.

23. Introduction to Kang-i Sun Chang and Haun Saussy, eds., *Women Writers of Traditional China: An Anthology of Poetry and Criticism* (Stanford: Stanford University Press, 1999), 4.

24. Kang-i Sun Chang, "Ming and Qing Anthologies of Women's Poetry and Their Selection Strategies," in *Writing Women in Late Imperial China,* ed. Ellen Widmer (Stanford: Stanford University Press, 1997), 147–70. For the valorization of the female poet, see also Ko, *Teachers of the Inner Chambers,* 59–64.

25. Ellen Widmer, *The Beauty and the Book: Women and Fiction in Nineteenth-Century China* (Cambridge, Mass.: Harvard University Asia Center and Harvard University Press, 2006).

26. For late imperial debates over whether education and virtue were truly compatible in a woman, see Susan Mann, *Precious Records: Women in China's Long Eighteenth Century* (Stanford: Stanford University Press, 1997), chap. 4; and Ko, *Teachers of the Inner Chambers,* chap. 4.

27. Robyn Hamilton, "The Pursuit of Fame: Luo Qilan (1755–1813?) and the Debates about Women and Talent in Eighteenth-Century Jiangnan," *Late Imperial China* 18, no. 1 (June 1997): 39–71.

28. This imagery also appeared in the titles and prefaces to some female-authored poetry anthologies, suggesting that the "verses saved from burning" would have been sacrificed to female modesty if not for the exhortation of others. See, for example, Sun Chang, "Ming and Qing Anthologies," 169. An early example of women burning poems in the tenth century appears in Wilt Idema and Beata Grant, *The Red Brush: Writing Women of Imperial China* (Cambridge, Mass.: Harvard University Asia Center, 2004), 164–65.

29. For the publication history of Tan Yunxian's work, see Furth, *Flourishing Yin,* 289. For the publication history of Zeng Yi's book, see Duan Fang, preface dated 1907 to Zeng, *Yixue pian,* and Zhang, preface dated 1906 to Zeng, *Nüxue pian.*

30. Zeng, *Nüxue pian,* and *Zhongkui lu* (Records on feeding a household), in *Guhuanshi yixue pian* (A treatise on medicine from the Delighting in Antiquity Studio) (Changsha: n.p., 1907).

31. Zhang, preface dated 1921 to *Huayunlou yi'an.*

32. Monica H. Green, ed. and trans., *The Trotula: An English Translation of the Medieval Compendium of Women's Medicine* (Philadelphia: University of Pennsylvania Press, 2001).

33. Taylor points out that the term *traditional Chinese medicine* did not even exist until 1955, when it was coined—in English—to promote indigenous Chinese practices to a global audience. Taylor, *Chinese Medicine in Early Communist China, 1945–1963: A Medicine of Revolution* (London: RoutledgeCurzon, 2005), 82–86. The idea that one could even speak of a "Chinese medicine" was the result of Chinese modernization efforts of the late nineteenth century, efforts that called for a reevaluation of indigenous practices in comparison to new medical learning from abroad. See Bridie Andrews, "The Making of Modern Chinese Medicine, 1895–1937" (PhD diss., Cambridge University, 1996); Sean Hsiang-lin Lei, "When Chinese Medicine Encountered the State: 1910–1949" (PhD diss., University of Chicago, 1999); Ralph Croizier, *Traditional Medicine in Modern China* (Cambridge, Mass.: Harvard University Press, 1968). Also illuminating are Volker Scheid's detailed case studies of doctors associated with the Menghe medical current. Scheid highlights the diverse ways that practitioners and educators articulated the meaning of modernity and tradition in their efforts to define the proper relationship between Chinese and Western medicine; see *Currents of Tradition.*

34. The contentious relationship between adherents of different "currents of learning" *(xuepai)* in medicine is well documented in the literature. For details on leading figures, see Qiu and Ding, eds., *Zhongyi gejia xueshuo.* Not only did doctors argue over broad issues of doctrine, but they also disagreed about the ways to treat specific classes of ailments. See, for example, Ling Yunpeng, "Luetan zhongyi waike xuepai" (A general discussion of different intellectual currents in the treatment of external ailments in traditional Chinese medicine), *Jiangsu zhongyi* (May 1964): 5–6.

35. For the history of the received text of the *Suwen,* see Paul U. Unschuld, *Huang Di Nei Jing Su Wen: Nature, Knowledge, Imagery in an Ancient Chinese Medical Text* (Berkeley: University of California Press, 2003), chaps. 3 and 4. Details on extant editions are also given in Nathan Sivin, "Huang Ti Nei Ching," in *Early Chinese Texts: A Bibliographical Guide,* ed. Michael Loewe (Berkeley: Society for the Study of Early China and the Institute of East Asian Studies, University of California, Berkeley, 1993), 196–215.

36. Sivin explains that, while the phrase "Yellow Emperor's Inner Classic" has historically been affixed to four different medical texts, "since the Northern Song it has been used as a collective title" for the *Suwen* (Basic Questions) and the *Lingshu* (Divine Pivot), also referred to as the *Lingshu jing* (Divine Pivot Classic). Sivin, "Huang Ti Nei Ching," 196. While the origins of the *Lingshu* are still

unclear, Paul Unschuld believes that an early version was circulating by the third century, albeit under various names. The textual history of the *Lingshu jing* stabilized after Song Shi's recension was published under the current title in 1155. See Unschuld, *Huang Di Nei Jing Su Wen,* 3–7; and Sivin, "Huang Ti Nei Ching," 203–4.

37. Unschuld, *Medicine in China: A History of Ideas.*

38. For details, see Nathan Sivin, *Traditional Medicine in Contemporary China* (Ann Arbor: Center for Chinese Studies, University of Michigan, 1986), 47–52.

39. For a detailed account of different historical interpretations of qi and its manifestations in the body, see ibid., chaps. 2 and 4. Charlotte Furth examines female Blood and its relationship to qi and to male semen in "Blood, Body, and Gender: Medical Images of the Female Condition in China," *Chinese Science* 7 (1986), 44–46.

40. Asaf Goldschmidt, "The Transformations of Chinese Medicine during the Northern Song Dynasty (A.D. 960–1127): The Integration of Three Past Medical Approaches into a Comprehensive Medical System Following a Wave of Epidemics" (PhD diss., University of Pennsylvania, 1999).

41. Furth's study of "granny healers" in the Ming notes that the male practitioner's use of drugs contrasted with the manual healing techniques that were the hallmark of lower-level and female practitioners. *Flourishing Yin,* chap. 8. The medical cases recorded by male doctors likewise show that they typically used drug-based therapies. See ibid., chap. 7; Joanna Grant, *A Chinese Physician: Wang Ji and the "Stone Mountain Medical Case Histories"* (London: RoutledgeCurzon, 2003).

42. See Catherine Despeux, "The System of the Five Circulatory Phases and the Six Seasonal Influences *(wuyun liuqi),* a Source of Innovation in Medicine under the Song," in *Innovation in Chinese Medicine,* Needham Research Institute Series 3, ed. Elisabeth Hsu (Cambridge: Cambridge University Press, 2001), 121–66; Marta Hanson, "Robust Northerners and Delicate Southerners: The Nineteenth-Century Invention of a Southern Medical Tradition," *positions* 6, no. 3 (1998): 515–50.

43. For an analysis of this dynamic in twentieth-century TCM, see Judith Farquhar, *Knowing Practice: The Clinical Encounter of Chinese Medicine* (Boulder, Colo.: Westview Press, 1994).

44. See, for example, Xiao Xun's preface to his *Nüke jinglun* (Canonical teachings on medicine for women) (1684; modern punctuated edition published Shanghai: Shanghai weisheng chubanshe, 1957).

45. E. T. C. Werner, *A Dictionary of Chinese Mythology* (Shanghai: Kelly and Walsh, 1932), 377.

46. Paul U. Unschuld, trans. and annot., *Nan-ching: The Classic of Difficult Issues: With Commentaries by Chinese and Japanese Authors from the Third through the Twentieth Century* (Berkeley: University of California Press, 1986), 13. Song dynasty commentators and their successors considered the *Nanjing* to be a commentary on the *Yellow Emperor's Inner Classic.* Unschuld argues, however, that it should be considered a seminal and innovative work in its own right. For Bian Que as the author of this text, see Unschuld, *Nan-ching,* 32–33.

47. Although early texts used the term *below the girdle* as a general term for

the ailments of women, beginning in the Song its semantic scope was restricted to refer just to noxious vaginal discharges. For details on this semantic shift, see Furth, *Flourishing Yin;* and Sabine Wilms, "The Female Body in Medieval China" (PhD diss., University of Arizona, 2002).

48. Sima Qian, *Shiji* (Records of the historian) (second to first century B.C.E.; reprinted in *SKQS*), 150:9a. Handan is located in present-day southern Hebei Province. Luoyang, in present-day Henan Province, was the capital of the Eastern Zhou Dynasty. Xianyang, in present-day Shaanxi Province, was the capital of the Qin dynasty.

49. Qi Zhongfu, preface to *Nüke bai wen* (One hundred questions about medicine for women) (1279; facsimile reprint of 1735 woodblock edition, Shanghai: Shanghai guji shudian, 1983).

50. A notable reference to Bian Que is the title of Zhao Xianke's work on women's medicine, *Handan yigao* (A bequeathed draft from Handan), compiled around 1617. *LHML* lists a woodblock edition of 1796 as the earliest extant version. Other notable references to Bian Que and Handan are Xiao, author's preface to *Nüke jinglun,* and Wang Kentang, preface dated 1607 to his *Nüke zhunsheng,* as reprinted in *YJTK,* 3:3839–40.

51. Robin Yates, "Medicine for Women in Early China: A Preliminary Survey," in *Medicine for Women in Imperial China,* ed. Angela Ki Che Leung (Leiden: Brill, 2006), 19–73. The earliest known written references to childbirth appear on the inscribed oracle bones that rulers of the Shang dynasty used for divination during the fourteenth through eleventh centuries B.C.E. Jen-der Lee has argued, however, that it was only in the Tang dynasty that medical writers began to define fertility and reproduction as specifically female medical problems. "Han Tang zhijian qiuzi yifang shitan, jian lun fuke lanshang yu xingbie lunshu" (Reproductive medicine in late antiquity and early medieval China: Gender discourse and the birth of gynecology), *Zhongyang yanjiuyuan lishi yuyan yanjiusuo jikan* 68, no. 2 (1997): 283–367. For later periods, see the works of Furth, particularly *Flourishing Yin.* A detailed history of salient developments from antiquity to the Qing is Ma Dazheng, *Zhongguo fuchanke fazhan shi* (The history of the development of gynecology and obstetrics in China) (n.p.: Shanxi kexue jiaoyu chubanshe, 1992).

52. The issue of Tang-Song periodization is a major theme of the collected articles in Leung, ed., *Medicine for Women.*

53. Wilms, "Female Body in Medieval China"; and Leung, ed., *Medicine for Women.*

54. Jen-der Lee, "Childbirth in Early Imperial China," in *Medicine for Women in Imperial China,* ed. Angela Ki Che Leung (Leiden: Brill, 2006), 108–78.

55. My discussion of Song medicine here draws heavily on Chen Yuan-peng, "Liangsong de 'shangyi shiren' yu 'ruyi'—Jianlun qi zai Jin Yuan de liubian ("Elites who esteemed medicine" and "Confucian doctors" in the Northern and Southern Song dynasties, with a discussion on their spread and transformation during the Jin and Yuan dynasties) (Master's thesis, Taiwan National University, 1996); Goldschmidt, "Transformations of Chinese Medicine"; and TJ Hinrichs, "The Medical Transforming of Governance and Southern Customs in Song Dynasty China (960–1279 C.E.)" (PhD diss., Harvard University, 2003). For Song

fuke, see Furth, *Flourishing Yin.* A helpful study that contextualizes Song developments in larger historical scope is Angela Ki Che Leung, "Medical Learning from the Song to the Ming," in *The Song-Yuan-Ming Transition in Chinese History,* ed. Paul Jakov Smith and Richard von Glahn (Cambridge: Harvard University Press, 2003), 374–98.

56. Goldschmidt, "Transformations of Chinese Medicine," 209–20.

57. Medical historians have translated the term *ke* both as "department" and "curriculum." I prefer the translation "curriculum" in this context because it emphasizes the division of knowledge into distinct fields and better reflects the way in which the term *ke* was generally used in medical circles.

58. A classic study of Tang government medicine and medical examinations is Joseph Needham, *Science and Civilisation in China,* vol. 4, pt. 6: "Medicine," with the collaboration of Lu Gwei-Djen, ed. Nathan Sivin (Cambridge: Cambridge University Press, 2000). For an overview of government medical divisions in other eras, see the section for each dynasty in Fu Weikang, *Zhongguo yixueshi* (A history of medicine in China) (Shanghai: Shanghai zhongyi xueyuan chubanshe, 1990); and Gong Chun, *Zhongguo lidai weisheng zuzhi ji yixue* (Health organizations and medical education throughout Chinese history) (N.p.: Weishengbu kejiaosi, 1983). For Song medical education and the increased importance of drug-based therapies, see also Goldschmidt, "Transformations of Chinese Medicine"; and TJ Hinrichs, "Medical Transforming of Governance."

59. Qi Zhongfu, preface to *Nüke bai wen.*

60. Despeux, "System of the Five Circulatory Phases," 121. For the development of a pharmacology of systematic correspondences, see Unschuld, *Medicine in China: A History of Ideas,* and Unschuld, *Medicine in China: A History of Pharmaceutics* (Berkeley: University of California Press, 1986).

61. For the original quotation from the *Inner Classic* with ancient and modern commentaries, see Ha Xiaoxian, *Neijing fuke jiwen jiyi* (Compilation of gynecological discussions from the *Neijing,* with collected commentaries) (Beijing: Zhongguo yiyao keji chubanshe, 1992), 2–4.

62. Furth, *Flourishing Yin,* chap. 2.

63. *Da Qing huidian* (Collected statutes of the Qing dynasty) (1818; reprint, Taipei: Wenhai chubanshe, 1991), 64:26a.

64. *Qingchao xu wenxian tongkao* (A Continuation of the *General History of Institutions and Critical Examination of Documents and Studies for the Qing Dynasty*) (1921; reprint, Shanghai: Commercial Press, 1936), 128:8886–87.

65. In a previous study, I examined a group of 278 Qing dynasty practitioners listed in the medical biographies section of gazetteers from four northern Zhejiang prefectures: Hangzhou, Jiaxing, Shaoxing, and Ningbo. Tallying just the practitioners explicitly described as being particularly skilled in a subfield of medicine, and omitting those mentioned only as "carrying on the profession" of an ancestor with specialized skills, I found that 53 of 278 doctors identified as Qing figures (close to one-fifth) were identified as experts in a subfield of medicine. Only one of these 53 had ever held a government medical post, showing that specialization was routine in the medical population at large. Yi-Li Wu, "Transmitted Secrets: The Doctors of the Lower Yangzi Region and Popular Gynecology in Late Imperial China" (PhD diss., Yale University, 1998), chap. 2.

66. Yan Chen et al., comps., *Tongxiang xianzhi* (Gazetteer of Tongxiang County) (1887; reprint, Taiwan: Chengwen chubanshe, 1970), 15:6b.

67. Tang Xuchun, *Shangyu xianzhi* (Gazetteer of Shangyu County) (1891; reprint, Taipei: Chengwen chubanshe, 1970), 40:9a.

68. Zhao Weiyu, ed., *Guangxu Jiaxing xianzhi* (Gazetteer of Jiaxing County from the Guangxu reign) (1908; reprint, Shanghai: Shanghai shudian, 1993), 27:19a.

69. Wei Zhixiu, *Xu mingyi lei'an* (A continuation of the *Cases from Famous Doctors, Arranged by Category*) (ca. 1770; reprinted in *SKQS*), 32:30a–b. This case is undated and unattributed, indicating the narrator is likely Wei himself. Wang Shixiong's medical cases also include numerous instances where the name of the medical discipline is used as way of referring to the practitioner. For example, "doctors of external ailments" *(waike)* appear in Wang Shixiong, *Wangshi yi'an xubian* (A second collection of medical cases by Master Wang), comp. Zhang Hong et al. (prefaces dated 1850; critical edition of 1918 Jiguge lithographic edition reprinted in Wang Shixiong, *Wang Shixiong yixue quanshu* (The complete collection of Wang Shixiong's medical books) (Beijing: Zhongguo zhongyiyao chubanshe, 1999), 1:290, 4:324, 5:332, 8:348.

70. Ch'iu Chung-lin, "Mingdai shiyi yu fuzhou xian yixue" (Lineages of doctors and local medical institutions in the Ming Dynasty), *Hanxue yanjiu* 22, no. 2 (2004): 327–59.

71. Ping-ti Ho, *The Ladder of Success in Imperial China: Aspects of Social Mobility, 1368–1911* (New York: Columbia University Press, 1962), chap. 2 generally, and especially pp. 55–56.

72. Numerous examples of famous Ming dynasty doctors from Suzhou who had hereditary medical specialties appear in Ch'iu Chung-lin, "Ruyi, shiyi yu yongyi: Mingdai dianji zhong duiyu yizhe de pinglun" (Scholar-physicians, hereditary doctors, and bad doctors: Assessments of medical practitioners in Ming-era records), in *Ming ren wenji yu mingdai yanjiu xueshu yantaohui* (Conference on Ming literati collections and Ming studies) (Taipei: Zhongguo Mingdai yanjiu xuehui, 2001), 7–9.

73. For the role of noncourt doctors in caring for imperial patients during the Qing, see Chang Che-chia, "The Therapeutic Tug of War: The Imperial Physician-Patient Relationship in the Era of Empress Dowager Cixi (1874–1908)" (PhD diss., University of Pennsylvania, 1998).

74. Chen et al., comp., *Minguo Hangzhou fuzhi*, 149:9b–10a.

75. A handwritten manuscript copy of Chen Wenzhao's version of Chen Yi's book is currently held by the library of the Shanghai University of Traditional Chinese Medicine and Materia Medica. A modern reprint was produced under the title *Chen Su'an fuke bujie* (Chen Su'an's medicine for women, with supplements and commentary) (Shanghai: Shanghai kexue jishu chubanshe, 1983).

76. Zhu Xuzeng, *Kaiyouyi zhai dushu zhi* (Record of books read at the There Is Benefit in Reading Studio) (Woodblock edition, 1880), 4:9b–10a. Zhu, a native of Nanjing, served as magistrate in various jurisdictions in Hubei, Shandong, and Gansu, and as prefect of Taiping Prefecture in Guangxi. The Zhu family included other prominent and successful officials as well: Xuzeng's father was circuit intendant in Zhili, and his son Guizhen obtained the *jinshi* degree and held

various positions in the central and local governments, serving lastly as governor of Canton. Zhu probably wrote this description of the Chens in the early nineteenth century, since he died in 1824. Hummel, ed., *Eminent Chinese of the Ch'ing Period,* 186. Although the fan described by Zhu no longer exists, twentieth-century descendants of the Chen family donated a similar fan to the Tongxiang County Public Health Bureau, bearing the inscription "A palace fan bestowed by the emperor, women's medicine transmitted by the ancestors" *(qinsi gongshan, zuchuan nüke).* See Wu, "Transmitted Secrets," 50.

77. Li Jianmin, "Zhongguo gudai 'jinfang' kaolun" (Jinfang: The transmission of secret techniques in ancient China), *Zhongyang yanjiuyuan lishi yuyan yanjiusuo jikan* 68, pt. 1 (1997): 117–66. Li finds that, during the Han, writers distinguished between *jinfang* (secret techniques passed down from master to disciple, under oath of strictest secrecy) and *mifang* (methods that people had acquired and then kept secret). After the Song dynasty, however, these terms were increasingly used interchangeably.

78. Xu Dachun, *Yixue yuanliu lun* (Treatise on the origins of medicinal learning) (1757; reprinted in *SKQS*), 1:39b. I have also referred to a translation given in Xu Dachun, *Forgotten Traditions of Ancient Chinese Medicine,* annot. and trans. Paul U. Unschuld (Brookline, Mass.: Paradigm Publications, 1990), 159–61.

79. A notable example of secret formulas in Chinese literature is the episode in *Dream of the Red Chamber* where Xue Baozhai explains the daunting process for concocting "Cold Fragrance Pills," a remedy "supposedly handed down from the Immortals of the Islands." Cao Xueqin, *Honglou meng* (Dream of the red chamber) (ca. 1760), trans. David Hawkes and John Minford as *The Story of the Stone* (Harmondsworth: Penguin, 1973–1986), 1:168–69. Xu Dachun claimed that such beliefs were fed by the fantasies of the rich and powerful, who sought elixirs of immortality *(changsheng fang)* and rewarded those doctors who were crafty enough to humor them. *Shenji chuyan* (Humble opinions on the prudent management of illness) (1767; modern critical edition of Master Cai's Hanxu ge woodblock edition of 1838 reprinted in *Xu Lingtai yixue quanshu* [The complete medical works of Xu Lingtai] Beijing: Zhongguo zhongyiyao chubanshe, 1999), 367.

80. Local histories used the appellation "Guo the childbirth doctors" (*Guo yichan,* literally "Guo who treats ailments of childbirth") to refer to specific members of a family, but also as a shorthand for the family as a whole. See, for example, Wei Yuan, ed., *Kangxi Qiantang xianzhi* (Gazetteer of Qiantang County from the Kangxi reign) (1718; reprint, Shanghai: Shanghai shudian, 1993), 26:17b–18a.

81. Ma Rulong, ed., *Hangzhou fuzhi* (Gazetteer of Hangzhou Prefecture) (1686), 32:10a–b.

82. The 1718 Qiantang County gazetteer, however, says that a Guo family doctor was among several imperial doctors who followed the Song court to Hangzhou after the fall of the Northern Song. Wei, ed., *Kangxi Qiantang xianzhi,* 26:17b–18a.

83. For the various late imperial iterations of this legend, including the claim that the Daoist immortal Lü Dongbing was the source of the peony formulas, see Wu, "Transmitted Secrets," 37–42.

84. These figures are derived from Ma, ed., *Hangzhou fuzhi* and entries for Guo family members in *LDYJ* and *YJTK*.

85. Wu, "Transmitted Secrets," 42–43.

86. Furth, *Flourishing Yin,* chap. 8.

87. Jiang Fengqing et al., eds., *Jiashan xianshi* (Gazetteer of Jiashan County) (1892; reprint, Taipei: Chengwen chubanshe, 1970), 26:4a–b.

88. A valued adviser of Emperor Xuanzong (r. 712–56), Song Jing also served at various times as the chief minister of the Board of Punishments and the Board of Personnel, as well as the director of the Chancellory. Biography of Song Jing, in *Jiu Tangshu* (Old history of the Tang dynasty) (945; reprint, *SKQS*), 96:12a–21b.

89. Song Lin'gao, preface to his *Siming Songshi nüke mishu* (A secret book of women's medicine from Master Song of Siming) (reprint, Shanghai: Wanyou shuju, 1932). While this edition provides no date for Song Lin'gao's preface, a date of 1612 appears in the preface as reprinted in *YJTK*, 3:3845–46.

90. Contemporary female descendants include the TCM gynecology practitioners Song Lili and Song Guoying. For additional details on the Song family history, see Wu, "Transmitted Secrets," chap. 6.

91. Volker Scheid also finds that aspiring doctors would agree to uxorilocal marriage to the daughters of influential medical families as a way of gaining entrée into powerful medical networks. See *Currents of Tradition,* 80, 104.

92. Jiang et al., eds., *Jiashan xianshi,* 26:4a–b.

93. Song Lin'gao, preface to *Siming Songshi nüke mishu.*

94. The numerous analyses of medical specialization in Europe and North America and the intellectual and institutional factors that precipitated and accompanied these changes include Stanley Joel Reiser, *Medicine and the Reign of Technology* (Cambridge: Cambridge University Press, 1978); Paul Starr, *The Social Transformation of American Medicine* (New York: Basic Books, 1982); William G. Rothstein, *American Medical Schools and the Practice of Medicine* (New York: Oxford University Press, 1987); Charles E. Rosenberg, ed., *The Origins of Specialization in American Medicine* (New York: Garland, 1989); Charlotte G. Borst, *Catching Babies: The Professionalization of Childbirth, 1870–1920* (Cambridge, Mass.: Harvard University Press, 1995); and John Harley Warner, *Against the Spirit of System: The French Impulse in Nineteenth-Century American Medicine* (Princeton, N.J.: Princeton University Press, 1998).

95. While some scholars have translated *ruyi* as "Confucian physician," this rendering is problematic because it suggests that a *ruyi* was defined by allegiance to Confucianism as opposed to other systems of thought, a culturally irrelevant label in a society where religious and philosophical eclecticism was the rule. "Scholar-physician" more closely cleaves to the intent of the Chinese original, which emphasizes that it was the moral and intellectual formation derived through study and application of the Confucian classics that distinguished the *ruyi* from other practitioners. My discussion here has also been much influenced by the excellent account of the history of scholarly medicine in Scheid, *Currents of Tradition,* chap. 2.

96. For Fan's role in reforming government medical schools, see Goldschmidt, "Transformations of Chinese Medicine," 209–12.

97. Asaf Goldschmidt, "Huizong's Impact on Medicine and on Public Health," in *Emperor Huizong and Late Northern Song China: The Politics of Culture and the Culture of Politics,* ed. Patricia Ebrey and Maggie Bickford (Cambridge, Mass.: Harvard University Asia Center, 2006).

98. Robert P. Hymes, "Not Quite Gentlemen? Doctors in Sung and Yuan," *Chinese Science* 8 (1987): 9–76; and Ch'iu, "Mingdai shiyi yu fuzhou xian yixue."

99. Wu, "Transmitted Secrets," 26–27, 280–82.

100. Yüan-ling Chao, "The Ideal Physician in Late Imperial China: The Question of *Sanshi,*" *East Asian Science, Technology, and Medicine,* no. 17 (2000): 66–93.

101. Although historical demographers disagree about the precise timing of this population growth, it is accepted that the Chinese population increased from around one hundred million in the year 1500 to around three hundred million in 1800. See, for example, James Z. Lee and Wang Feng, *One Quarter of Humanity: Malthusian Mythology and Chinese Realities, 1700–2000* (Cambridge, Mass.: Harvard University Press, 1999), 6; and Willard J. Peterson, "Introduction: New Order for the Old Order," in *The Cambridge History of China,* vol. 9, pt. 1: *The Ch'ing Dynasty to 1800,* ed. Willard J. Peterson (Cambridge: Cambridge University Press, 2002), 5.

102. Benjamin Elman's exhaustive study estimates that during the Qing, only 1.5 percent of candidates would pass the county-level licentiate examinations, and that only about 1.5 percent of eligible county licentiates would then pass the provincial-level examinations. *A Cultural History of Civil Examinations in Late Imperial China* (Berkeley: University of California Press, 2000), 143–44 and 662–65 (tables 3.3, 3.4, 3.5, 3.6).

103. Li Chan, *Yixue rumen* (An introduction to medicine) (1575; modern edition of 1575 woodblock edition reprinted in *Zhonghua yishu jicheng* [Collection of Chinese Medical Books], vol. 26, Beijing: Zhongyi guji chubanshe, 1999), 12.

104. Scheid, *Currents of Tradition,* 33.

105. Ch'iu, "Mingdai shiyi yu fuzhou xian yixue." For more examples of and details on the routine overlap of scholarly and hereditary modes of medical identity and knowledge transmission, see Wu Yiyi, "A Medical Line of Many Masters: A Prosopographical Study of Liu Wansu and His Disciples from the Jin to the Early Ming," *Chinese Science* 11 (1993–94): 36–65; Wu, "Transmitted Secrets"; Chao, "Ideal Physician"; and Scheid, *Currents of Tradition.*

106. Wu, "Transmitted Secrets," 31–33, 40.

107. Chao, "Ideal Physician," 80.

108. Yüan-ling Chao, "Lineages and Schools: Zhang Zhongjing and *Sidajia* in Ming and Qing" (paper presented at the Tenth International Conference on the History of Science in East Asia, Shanghai, China, 2002).

109. Angela Ki Che Leung, "Medical Instruction and Popularization in Ming-Qing China," *Late Imperial China* 24, no. 1 (2003): 130–52.

110. A revelatory case study of this integration of Neo-Confucian cosmology into medicine is Charlotte Furth, "The Physician as Philosopher of the Way: Zhu Zhenheng (1282–1358)," *Harvard Journal of Asiatic Studies* 66, no. 2 (December 2006): 423–59. Particularly important is Furth's account of how Zhu Zhenheng articulated his innovative doctrines on Princely and Ministerial Fire

by reading the *Yellow Emperor's Inner Classic* through the lens of Zhou Dunyi's interpretation of the *Classic of Changes* (*Yijing*).

111. Quotations from Zhang Danian, *Key Concepts in Chinese Philosophy* (New Haven, Conn.: Yale University Press, 2002), 27. My discussion of Neo-Confucian concepts has also relied on Philip J. Ivanhoe, "Neo-Confucian Philosophy," in *Routledge Encyclopedia of Philosophy*, ed. Edward Craig (London: Routledge, 1998), 6:764–76; Wing-tsit Chan, *A Sourcebook in Chinese Philosophy* (Princeton, N.J.: Princeton University Press, 1963), 588–92; and Wing-tsit Chan, ed., *Chu Hsi and Neo-Confucianism* (Honolulu: University of Hawai'i Press, 1986).

112. *YZJJ, fanli* (paginated separately), 1:5a. The phrase *yizong* in the title of this work means "medical clan," implying the existence of a body of ancestral knowledge from which all properly trained physicians would claim intellectual descent. Marta Hanson has persuasively argued that the title should be translated as the "Golden Mirror of the Orthodox Lineage of Medicine," since this work was meant to set forth standards of correct practice as embodied in the teachings of certain medical masters over others. "The *Golden Mirror* in the Imperial Court of the Qianlong Emperor," *Early Science and Medicine: Special Issue: Science and State Patronage in Early Modern East Asia* 8, no. 2 (May 2003): 111–47. However, the English word *orthodoxy* tends to evoke an institutionally rooted effort to enforce conformity and suppress deviance, something that did not exist in the Chinese medical context. Since the metaphor of a "golden mirror" already refers to a standard of learning to be followed as a model, I have chosen to translate the title of this work more neutrally.

113. Sun Simiao, *Beiji qianjin yaofang* (Essential prescriptions worth a thousand golds for managing urgent situations) (651; reprinted in *SKQS*), 2:1a–b. Here I have borrowed liberally from the translations by Furth, *Flourishing Yin*, 71–72; and Wilms, "Female Body in Medieval China," 116–18.

114. *YZJJ*, 44:1a–b.

115. Hanson, "Golden Mirror."

116. To explain the *Golden Mirror*'s importance at court, Chang Che-chia points out that maximizing reliability and legitimacy was particularly crucial in the fraught world of imperial medicine. Physicians outside the government sometimes accused court doctors of cleaving too inflexibly to the *Golden Mirror*. But in the dangerous event that government physicians were accused of giving incorrect treatment to their imperial patients, they could argue quite literally that they had gone by the book. "Therapeutic Tug of War," 48–52.

117. Cynthia J. Brokaw, *Commerce in Culture: The Sibao Book Trade in the Qing and Republican Periods* (Cambridge, Mass.: Harvard University Press, 2007), 431–32.

118. Zhang Jiebin's writings on *fuke* appear in his *Jingyue quanshu* (The complete works of Jingyue) (comp. ca. 1624–40; reprinted in *SKQS*). The dating of this text is uncertain, however. The LHML claims that *Jingyue quanshu* was compiled in 1624, while the YJDCD claims that it was compiled around 1636. A preface by Zhang Jiebin's grandson Lin Riwei states that the text was compiled in the last years of Zhang's life, well after Zhang's *Leijing* texts of 1624. In any case, Lin Riwei tells us that *Jingyue quanshu* was not published until 1700, which was long after Zhang's death in 1640. See Lin's preface to *Jingyue quanshu*.

119. Sun's full essay on female sickliness is reproduced in Chen's section on "seeking descendants." *Furen daquan liangfang* (Comprehensive compendium of good formulas for women) (comp. 1237; revised ca. 1265; modern critical edition of Yuan dynasty Qinyou shutang edition by Yu Ying'ao et al., Beijing: Renmin weisheng chubanshe, 1992), 288.

120. Quoted in ibid., 64–65. For Kou's contributions to the larger medical changes of the Song, see Goldschmidt, "Transformations of Chinese Medicine," 169–72.

121. Quoted in Chen, *Furen daquan liangfang*, 64–65.

122. For examples of male doctors treating female patients, see Furth, *Flourishing Yin;* and Grant, *Chinese Physician.* When Xue Ji redacted Chen Ziming's *Furen daquan liangfang,* he modified Kou's essay by adding a description of his own experiences that both supported and belied the supposed inability to examine women properly and its negative effect on therapy. When called to treat the "mother of Prefectural Licentiate Xue Daofu," Xue initially is able to take her pulses on both wrists and ascertain the history of her illness. Based on this initial inspection, he believes that her disease cannot be cured. When he is allowed to also inspect the color of her eyeballs, however, Xue changes his mind about the prognosis and is ultimately able to cure her. *Jiaozhu furen liangfang* (The edited and annotated *Good Prescriptions for Women*) (1547; modern critical edition of Ming dynasty edition reprinted in *Xue Lizhai yixue quanshu* [The complete medical works of Xue Lizhai], Beijing: Zhongguo zhongyiyao chubanshe, 1999), 796. Compare to Chen, *Furen daquan liangfang*, 64–65.

123. Furth, *Flourishing Yin,* chap. 4.

124. Chen, *Furen daquan liangfang*, 63; compare to Xue, *Jiaozhu furen liangfang,* 796.

125. Xue, *Jiaozhu furen liangfang,* 888. Compare to Chen, *Furen daquan liangfang,* 288–90. By my count, Chen's original includes 353 characters, while Xue's redaction comprises 60 characters.

126. Wu Zhiwang, preface to *Jiyin gangmu* (A comprehensive guide to benefiting yin) (1620; modern critical edition by Li Mingjian et al. of 1620 woodblock edition published Beijing: Renmin weisheng chubanshe, 1996), reprinted in *YJTK,* 3:3850.

127. Furth, *Flourishing Yin,* 165–69.

128. Zhang, *Jingyue quanshu,* 38:1a–b. *Zazheng* is sometimes literally translated as "miscellaneous diseases" but is better understood as "illnesses which do not fall under a specified category." Since Zhang goes on to point out that these *za zheng* are discussed under their own sections, it is especially clear that *za zheng* here refers not to "miscellaneous" illnesses but rather to illnesses that do not fall under one of the nine categories of special female illnesses.

129. The locus classicus for the phrase "thirty-six diseases" is Zhang Ji, *Jinkui yaolue* (Essentials of the golden cabinet) (ca. 200 C.E., reprinted in *Zhongyi ba da jingdian quanzhu* [The eight great classics of Chinese medicine, complete and annotated], ed. Shang Zhijun and Zhai Shuangqing [Beijing: Huaxia chubanshe, 1994]), 369, 392. Zhang uses this phrase in a discussion of the diseases of viscera and channels as well as in his discussion of women's ailments. However, the earliest description of what the thirty-six diseases of women actually consisted

of is Chao Yuanfang, *Chaoshi zhubing yuanhou lun* (Master Chao's treatise on the origins and manifestations of the myriad diseases) (comp. 610; revised 1026–27; ed. Wang Jichuan and Fang Kuang [Ming]; reprinted in *SKQS*), 38:12b–13a. For a discussion of how Chao's list was then taken up by Sun Simiao, see Wilms, "Female Body in Medieval China," 354–56. While there was some later fluidity in how medical texts described these thirty-six illnesses, doctors agreed that they were rooted in pathologies of menstrual blood. See, for example, Chen Yan's discussion of this issue in *Sanyin jiyi bingzheng fang lun* (Treatise on the manifestations and treatment of diseases caused by the three factors) (comp. 1174; reprinted in *SKQS*), 18:11a–b.

130. See, for example, Chen, *Furen daquan liangfang,* 63–64.

131. Wei Yilin, *Shiyi dexiao fang* (Efficacious prescriptions from a hereditary medical family) (1337; reprinted in *SKQS*), 14:1a–b

132. Zhang, *Jingyue quanshu,* 38:1b–2b.

133. Ibid.

134. Paul U. Unschuld, "Prolegomena," in Xu Dachun, *Forgotten Traditions of Ancient Chinese Medicine,* annot. and trans. Unschuld (Brookline, Mass.: Paradigm Publications, 1990), 2–5.

135. Chinese doctors distinguished between internal masses that had a well-defined shape and mass, and those whose forms were more illusive and indistinct. These were referred to by the term *zhengjia,* literally the "verifiable" and "illusory" accumulations. These are discussed further in chapter 3 of this book.

136. Xu, *Yixue yuanliu lun,* 2:43a–b.

137. Both books were included in the *SKQS* and also appear to have been frequently reprinted on their own. For example, *LHML* lists twenty-four editions of Xu's work dated between 1757 and 1900, in addition to many other "Qing editions" whose dates cannot be confirmed.

138. Wang, ed., *Xu mingyi lei'an,* 23:705. One study claims that there were more than seventeen different editions of this work later produced. See the modern editor's preface to *Xu mingyi lei'an,* 3–5. While the *LHML*'s listings do not explicitly distinguish between copies of Wei's original and Wang's revision of the *Xu mingyi lei'an,* the dates, publishing houses, and number of *juan* ascribed to each allow us to reasonably identify eight editions of Wang's version produced between 1863 and 1900.

139. Zhou Jichang, author's preface dated 1823 to *Nüke jiyao* (Edited essentials of medicine for women) (Kuizhaolou woodblock edition, 1865).

140. Pan Wei's medical philosophy is described by a writer who identifies himself only as "Huyuan yuke" (The Guest Residing in Hu Garden). Preface dated 1877 to *Nüke yaolue* (Essential outline of medicine for women), in *Weiyuan yixue liu zhong* (Six medical works from Weiyuan) (Hubei Fanshu woodblock edition, 1877).

141. See, for example, the range of prefaces to *fuke* works reprinted in *YJTK,* 3:3785–4017.

142. For Wang Ji's view of men, see Grant, *Chinese Physician,* chap. 4. For Ming dynasty *yangsheng,* see Furth, *Flourishing Yin,* chap. 6.

143. Ko, *Teachers of the Inner Chambers,* 72.

144. Ibid., 110–12.

145. Furth, *Flourishing Yin,* 178–82.

146. Catherine Despeux finds that, although precursors to *nüdan* can be dated to the twelfth century, texts dedicated to female alchemy began to circulate only in the eighteenth century. Elena Valussi, by contrast, believes that the *Qingjing yuanjun kunyuanjun* of 1683 can be called the first *nüdan* text. Despeux, *Immortelles de la Chine ancienne: Taoïsme et alchémie féminine* (Puiseaux: Pardes, 1990); and Elena Valussi, "Beheading the Red Dragon: A History of Female Inner Alchemy in Late Imperial China" (PhD diss., School of Oriental and African Studies, University of London, 2003).

CHAPTER 2. AMATEUR AS ARBITER

1. Wu Yu was a native of Renhe County. These events are narrated in Wu Yu's 1793 preface to *Taichan xinshu* (A new book on childbearing), attrib. Zhulinsi seng (Bamboo Grove Monastery monks), attrib. specifically to Master Jingguang, Master Lunying, and Master Xueyan (comp. ca. 1771; recopied with preface dated 1793; printed 1886; reprinted in *ZBYS,* vol. 8). This modern reprint, like the woodblock versions that I have examined, gives no signature or date line for the first preface to this work, a preface that predates Wu Yu. However, this preface appears in a manuscript version held by the library of the Zhejiang zhongyiyao yanjiusuo, and there it is dated 1771. See Zhulinsi seng (Bamboo Grove Monastery monks), attrib., *Jikun yulin Zhulin nüke* (Women's medicine from the Bamboo Grove to benefit females and raise children) (Qingbai daoren hand-copied manuscript, 1891, ZJ no. 4880).

2. What little biographical information I have on Cao Binggang comes from the preface he wrote for his reprint of Wu Yu's text. This preface is reprinted as an afterword in Zhulinsi seng, *Taichan xinshu,* 173. A native of Renhe County, Cao Binggang was the son-in-law of Chen Zhenfu, a prefect and medical expert who claimed descent from the Fujianese physician Chen Nianzu. Cao himself also studied medicine with his father-in-law. He describes obtaining the Bamboo Grove book from the family collection of one Wu Youyun. While I have not been able to identify Wu Youyun, it seems probable that he was related to Wu Yu.

3. The discussions of the Bamboo Grove Monastery in this chapter are quoted or adapted from my earlier article "The Bamboo Grove Monastery and Popular Gynecology in Qing China," *Late Imperial China* 21, no. 1 (June 2000): 41–76. I thank Johns Hopkins University Press for granting me permission to reuse this material.

4. Many have argued convincingly that medicine as a remunerative occupation was becoming increasingly professionalized in the Ming and Qing. But unlike European professions, where occupational identity was constructed around sociolegal institutions, Chinese professions were defined by expert practice and cultural norms. See Paul Unschuld, *Medical Ethics in Imperial China: A Study in Historical Anthropology* (Berkeley: University of California Press, 1979); Yüanling Chao, "The Ideal Physician in Late Imperial China: The Question of *Sanshi,*" *East Asian Science, Technology, and Medicine,* no. 17 (2000): 66–93; Charlotte Furth, "Producing Medical Knowledge through Cases: History, Evidence, Action," 125–51; Ping-chen Hsiung, "Facts in the Tale: Case Records and Pedi-

atric Medicine in Late Imperial China," in *Thinking with Cases,* ed. Charlotte Furth, Judith T. Zeitlin, and Ping-chen Hsiung (Honolulu: University of Hawai'i Press, 2007), 152–68.

5. Two important case studies of this phenomenon are Yüan-ling Chao, "Medicine and Society in Late Imperial China: A Study of Physicians in Suzhou" (PhD diss., University of California, Los Angeles, 1995); and Volker Scheid, *Currents of Tradition in Chinese Medicine: 1626–2006* (Seattle: Eastland Press, 2007).

6. Xu Dachun, *Yixue yuanliu lun* (Treatise on the origins of medical learning) (1757; reprinted *SKQS*), 2:62a–63b. I have also drawn on Paul Unschuld's translation in Xu Dachun, *Forgotten Traditions of Ancient Chinese Medicine,* annot. and trans. Unschuld (Brookline, Mass.: Paradigm Publications, 1990), 380–82.

7. A lively survey of the many ways in which medical consumers criticized doctors and used different strategies to test their abilities is Chang Che-chia, "The Therapeutic Tug of War: The Imperial Physician-Patient Relationship in the Era of Empress Dowager Cixi (1874–1908)" (PhD diss., University of Pennsylvania, 1998), chap. 3.

8. Wang Dejun, preface dated 1826 to *Nüke mifang* (Secret prescriptions of women's medicine), attrib. Zhulinsi seng (Bamboo Grove Monastery monks) (Beijing: Wenrui Studio woodblock edition, 1826, BH no. 117/857). Wang's preface lists the surnames of "colleagues" who helped pay for the text's publication. One of these colleagues appears to have been Han Ximen, who is also named in the list of sponsors appended to the text. There Han is identified as a company commandant, serving either with the Beijing city guards or on special transport duty.

9. Xu, *Yixue yuanliu lun,* 2:53a–54a. I have drawn on Paul Unschuld's translation in Xu, *Forgotten Traditions,* 359–60.

10. Susan Mann, *The Talented Women of the Zhang Family* (Berkeley: University of California Press, 2007), 24.

11. TJ Hinrichs, "The Medical Transforming of Governance and Southern Customs in Song Dynasty China (960–1279 C.E.)" (PhD diss., Harvard University, 2003), 111–12.

12. Joseph McDermott, "The Ascendance of the Imprint in China," in *Printing and Book Culture in Late Imperial China,* ed. Cynthia J. Brokaw and Kai-wing Chow (Berkeley: University of California Press, 2005), 86.

13. See Lucille Chia, "Of Three Mountains Street: The Commercial Publishers of Ming Nanjing," in *Printing and Book Culture in Late Imperial China,* ed. Cynthia J. Brokaw and Kai-wing Chow (Berkeley: University of California Press, 2005), 107–51; and Cynthia J. Brokaw, *Commerce in Culture: The Sibao Book Trade in the Qing and Republican Periods* (Cambridge, Mass.: Harvard University Press, 2007).

14. Angela Ki Che Leung, "Medical Instruction and Popularization in Ming-Qing China," *Late Imperial China* 24, no. 1 (2003): 130–52; Charlotte Furth, Judith T. Zeitlin, and Ping-chen Hsiung, eds., *Thinking with Cases: Specialist Knowledge in Chinese Cultural History* (Honolulu: University of Hawai'i Press, 2007).

15. Leung, "Medical Instruction and Popularization." He Zhongling has also

identified the flourishing of popular medical texts as a characteristic of the Qing. "Wanqing Sichuan pujilei yizhu de chansheng he yingxiang" (The production and influence of popular medical texts in late Qing Sichuan), *Zhonghua yishi zazhi* 24, no. 1 (January 1994): 20–22.

16. Unless otherwise noted, this historical summary is derived from Zhang Zonghai et al., eds., *Xiaoshan xianzhi gao* (Draft gazetteer of Xiaoshan County) (1935; reprint, Taipei: Chengwen chubanshe, 1970), 8:7a–b; and Zhejiangsheng zhongyiyao yanjiusuo, ed., *Xiaoshan Zhulinsi fuke mifang kao* (Investigation into the secret prescriptions of medicine for women from the Bamboo Grove Monastery of Xiaoshan) (Shanghai: Shanghai kexue jishu chubanshe, 1959). The latter source contains lengthy citations from two temple genealogies (now lost), namely, *The Successive Generations of the Bamboo Grove Monastery* of 1680 and *The Genealogy of the Monastery of Benevolent Aid*, originally compiled in 1782 and revised during the Guangxu reign as *Continued Genealogy of the Monastery of Benevolent Aid*. As of 1959, both documents were housed in the library of the Zhejiang Province Research Institute for Traditional Chinese Medicine and Pharmacology (Zhejiangsheng zhongyiyao yanjiusuo). During April and July 1995, I made exhaustive inquiries, both within the Zhejiang Research Institute and at government offices in Xiaoshan, but the documents could not be located. It is believed that the documents were destroyed or lost during the Cultural Revolution.

17. The temple genealogies, however, list the names of only about half of the hundred-plus generations of these monks. There are also a few monks mentioned in outside sources who do not appear in the genealogies. For details, see Yi-Li Wu, "Transmitted Secrets: The Doctors of the Lower Yangzi Region and Popular Gynecology in Late Imperial China" (PhD diss., Yale University, 1998), appendix B.

18. Wang Honglie, "Chongjian beiji" (Memorial tablet for the rebuilding of the temple), reproduced in Zhang Zonghai et al., eds., *Xiaoshan xianzhi gao* (Draft gazetteer of Xiaoshan County) (1935; reprint, Taipei: Chengwen chubanshe, 1970), 8:7a.

19. Xihu Chunyai shi (Master Spring Cliffs of the West Lake), preface dated 1795 to *Nüke michuan* (Transmitted secrets of medicine for women), attrib. Zhulinsi seng (Bamboo Grove Monastery monks) (Hangzhou: Zhou Zonglong woodblock edition, 1854, ZJ no. 4845).

20. Zhang Yao and Ma Jixing have both analyzed the typology of these texts and their filiation. See Zhang Yao, "Xiaoshan Zhulinsi nüke yiji yuanliu chu tan" (A preliminary study of the medical literature pertaining to the treatment of women's disorders at the Bamboo Grove Monastery of Xiaoshan) (Master's thesis, Zhongguo zhongyi yanjiu yuan, yishi wenxian yanjiu suo, 1987); and Ma Jixing, *Zhongyi wenxian xue* (The study of Chinese medical literature) (Shanghai: Shanghai kexue jishu chubanshe, 1990). For another interpretation of this corpus, see Wu, "Transmitted Secrets."

21. See Xihu Chunyai shi, preface to *Nüke michuan* (ZJ no. 4845); Mozhi zhuofu (The Stupid Man Who Doesn't Know Anything), preface dated 1771 to *Jikun yulin Zhulin nüke* (Women's medicine from the Bamboo Grove to benefit females and raise children), attrib. Zhulinsi seng (Qingbai daoren hand-copied manuscript, 1891, ZJ no. 4880); Chang Maolai, preface dated 1852 to *Zhulinsi*

nüke michuan (Transmitted secrets of medicine for women from the Bamboo Grove Monastery), attrib. Zhulinsi seng (Bamboo Grove Monastery monks) (Kaifeng: Zhang Longwen Studio Engraving Shop woodblock edition, 1852, CM no. 203569); Chen Shouchun, "Zhulinsi fuke shilue" (A general history of the Bamboo Grove Monastery's medicine for women), in *Xiaoshan wenshi ziliao xuanji* (Selected documents on the history of Xiaoshan), ed. Zhongguo renmin zhengzhi xieshang huiyi, Xiaoshanshi weiyuan hui, wenshi ziliao gongzuo wei-yuanhui (Historical Documents Working Committee of the Xiaoshan City Com-mittee of the People's Political Consultative Conference) (Xiaoshan: n.p., 1988), 1:87–103.

22. The earliest preface found in any of the Bamboo Grove Monastery texts is the 1771 preface (to *Jikun yulin Zhulin nuke,* ZJ no. 4880) attributed to Mozhi zhuofu. This suggests that the Bamboo Grove works were already being com-piled by the late eighteenth century. The earliest known printed work was *Ningkun miji* (A secret book for female tranquility), compiled by a Tian Litang, based primarily on Bamboo Grove lore and published in 1786. See Ma, *Zhongyi wenxian xue;* Zhang, "Xiaoshan Zhulinsi."

23. *LHML* lists sixty-five Qing editions, i.e., books published under differ-ent titles in different years; this does not include editions published as part of larger literary collections. The most comprehensive study of the extant Bamboo Grove texts is Zhang, "Xiaoshan Zhulinsi," which identifies eighty-eight distinct editions. Whatever the exact number, the texts clearly circulated widely during the Qing.

24. Although the nominal status of district jailer was relatively low, lower literati still saw this post as a path to social power and influence. See Susan Naquin and Evelyn S. Rawski, *Chinese Society in the Eighteenth Century* (New Haven, Conn.: Yale University Press, 1987), 117. It is reasonable to assume that all pref-ace writers were men, although in some cases their identities cannot be conclu-sively determined.

25. Zhulinsi seng (Bamboo Grove Monastery monks), attrib., *Fuke mifang, taichan husheng pian* (Secret prescriptions of women's medicine, discussion of childbearing and ensuring birth) (Zhili Provincial Administration Office wood-block edition, 1888, CM no. 167192).

26. Zhulinsi seng (Bamboo Grove Monastery monks), attrib., *Zhulinsi nüke zhengzhi* (Treatments for women's illnesses from the Bamboo Grove Monastery) (Shanghai: Haihe Pavilion Bookstore, 1895; reprinted with preface dated 1915, CM no. 167198).

27. Pan Wei was appointed provincial administration commissioner of Hu-bei in 1877 and subsequently served as governor of Hubei from 1878 to 1879, governor of Jiangxi from 1882 to 1884, and governor of Guizhou from 1885 to 1891. See Cao Yunyuan and Li Genyuan, comps., *Wuxian zhi* (Gazetteer of Wu County) (1933; reprint, Nanjing: Jiangsu guji chubanshe, 1991), 66b:40a–b; *Qingshi gao* (Draft history of the Qing dynasty) (1927; reprint, Beijing: Zhonghua shuju, 1977), 204:7884–86, 7892–96. His most eminent relative was his grand-father's first cousin Pan Shi'en, who served as president or vice president of five different imperial ministries from 1801 to 1831. See Arthur W. Hummel, ed., *Eminent Chinese of the Ch'ing Period* (Washington, D.C.: Government Printing

Office, 1943), 607–9; Pan Wei, *Nüke yaolue* (Essential outline of medicine for women), in *Weiyuan yixue liu zhong* (Six medical works from Weiyuan) (Hubei Fanshu woodblock edition, 1877). A recent study of the history of the Pan lineage is Yongtao Du, "Translocal Lineage and the Romance of Homeland Attachment: The Pans of Suzhou in Qing China," *Late Imperial China* 27, no. 1 (June 2006): 31–65. Chinese bibliographies attribute fifteen medical works to Pan. In about two-thirds of these, Pan simply revised existing books by famous medical authors. Most of these were originally popularly oriented works, including recipe books, manuals on health-preservation exercises, and general treatises aimed at the medical student or layperson. See works cited in Shanghai tushuguan, ed., *Zhongguo congshu mulu* (1959; reprint, Shanghai: Shanghai guji chubanshe, 1983), 3:547; and *LHML*, 1067. Pan's popularizing bent also led him to "edit and supplement" three works by the Fujianese physician Chen Nianzu, himself an influential medical popularizer of the late nineteenth century. These included Chen's *Yixue yitong* (Medicine made easy), which Chinese medical historians consider to be one of the most important Qing-era popular medical texts. See Li Jingwei and Li Zhidong, *Zhongguo gudai yixueshi* (A history of ancient medicine in China) (Shijia zhuang: Hebei kexue jishu chubanshe, 1990), 339. For a discussion of Pan's works on "guarding life" *(weisheng)*, see Ruth Rogaski, *Hygienic Modernity: Meanings of Health and Disease in Treaty-Port China* (Berkeley: University of California Press, 2004), chap. 2.

28. Zhulinsi seng, *Zhulinsi nüke zhengzhi* (CM no. 167198).

29. Zhulinsi seng (Bamboo Grove Monastery monks), attrib., *Zhulin fuke michuan* (Transmitted secrets of women's medicine from the Bamboo Grove) (Hangzhou: Gu Haizhou woodblock edition, 1890, with handwritten material added in 1892, ST no. 482812). Pan Yantong (courtesy name Yiqin) was a native of Nanhai County, Guangdong Province. For his biography, see Zheng Ying et al., eds., *Nanhai xianzhi* (Gazetteer of Nanhai County) (1910; reprint Taipei: Chengwen chubanshe, 1974), 14:20b–22a.

30. In the *Water Margin*, for example, the monks of the Waguan Monastery were unrepentant womanizers who drove away their abbot after he tried to curtail their misbehavior. These monks were in turn dispossessed by a Daoist priest in collusion with an itinerant Buddhist monk, the latter of whom also kept a female lover. See Shi Nai'an and Luo Guanzhong, attrib., *Shuihu zhuan* (Water margin) (14th c.; modern reprint Changsha: Yuelu shushe, 2008), chap. 6. Suspicions about monastic impropriety have persisted in modern times. Writing in 1983, Chinese physician Dong Hao noted that some of his contemporaries still suspected that the Bamboo Grove Monastery monks engaged in "irregular behavior" in their gynecological practice. Dong dismissed such suspicions as feudalistic thinking. Dong Hao, "Xiaoshan Zhulinsi fuke mifang guangfan chuanbo de wojian," *Weishengzhi jianxun*, no. 5 (October 1983): 12–13.

31. Xihu Chunyai shi, preface to *Nüke michuan* (ZJ no. 4845). Unfortunately, the writer does not specify the name of this magistrate, or the year in which these events occurred. This appears to have been a temporary setback, since later sources still speak of the Bamboo Grove monks as belonging to a monastery.

32. Song Chun, preface to *Fuke mifang, Taichan husheng pian* (Secret prescriptions of women's medicine, discussion of childbearing and ensuring birth),

attrib. Zhulinsi seng (Bamboo Grove Monastery monks) (Zhili Provincial Administration Office woodblock edition, 1888, CM no. 167192). The Kangxi dictionary (Kangxi zidian [Dictionary of the Kangxi reign] [1716; facsimile reprint, Beijing: Zhonghua shuju, 1992]) defines the word ban as "female pollution" (furen wu), and says it refers to things such as menses and miscarriage.

33. Xihu Chunyai shi, preface to Nüke michuan (ZJ no. 4845). Liao Yuqun also interprets the sources to mean that the monks relied heavily on their book of remedies, and that their practices historically consisted of "giving medicine" (gei yao) rather than "composing prescriptions" (shu fang). Liao Yuqun, "Xiaoshan Zhulinsi nüke kaolue" (Outline of inquiries into the practice of women's medicine at the Xiaoshan Bamboo Grove Monastery), Zhonghua yishi zazhi 16, no. 3 (1986): 159–61.

34. Yu Zan, preface dated 1876 to Fuke mifang (Secret formulas of women's medicine), attrib. Zhulinsi seng (Bamboo Grove Monastery monks) (Gu Haizhou woodblock edition, 1890, BH no. 117/857.3).

35. Wu, preface to Taichan xinshu.

36. Yu, preface to Fuke mifang (BH no. 117/857.3.)

37. Song, preface to Fuke mifang, taichan husheng pian (CM no. 167192).

38. This discussion is based on Arthur Kleinman's framework of "explanatory models" as elaborated in Patients and Healers in the Context of Culture: An Exploration of the Borderland between Anthropology, Medicine, and Psychiatry (Berkeley: University of California Press, 1980).

39. A modern formulation of the same issue is whether a specific drug actually works or merely induces a placebo effect in the patient.

40. For a quick reference guide to biochemical analyses of the active ingredients in traditional herbal ingredients, see Hong-yen Hsu et al., Oriental Materia Medica: A Concise Guide (Long Beach, Calif.: Oriental Healing Arts Institute, 1986). A comprehensive compilation of case studies in which Bamboo Grove Monastery formulas were used successfully is Zhou Mingdao et al., Xiaoshan Zhulinsi fuke pingshi (An assessment and explanation of medicine for women from the Bamboo Grove Monastery of Xiaoshan) (Xiaoshan: Xiaoshanshi zhongyi xuehui, 1992).

41. Paul Demiéville, "Byō," in Hobogirin: Dictionnaire encyclopédique du bouddhisme d'après les sources chinoises et japonaises, ed. Demiéville (Tokyo: Maison franco-japonaise, 1929; reprint, Paris: Librairie d'Amérique et d'Orient, 1974), 3:224–65. Religious beliefs were also enmeshed in Chinese views of the body and its functions. According to Daoist teachings, for example, each part of the human body was inhabited by a different god. Kristofer Schipper, The Taoist Body, trans. Karen C. Duval (Berkeley: University of California Press, 1993), chap. 6.

42. One edition of Transmitted Secrets of Women's Medicine from the Bamboo Grove Monastery appended seven formulas and healing techniques that had been revealed during a "spirit-writing" (luan bi) divination session. Strangely enough for a book on women's medicine, the appended remedies included treatments for things such as insect bites, choking on fish bones, difficult urination, and choleric ailments. See Zhulinsi seng (Bamboo Grove Monastery monks), attrib., Zhulinsi nüke michuan (Transmitted secrets of women's medicine from the

Bamboo Grove Monastery) (Kaifeng: Zhang Longwen Zhai Engraving Shop woodblock edition, 1852; reprinted with a new preface dated 1864, CM no. 167188), appendix 3a–4b. Another belief was that water from a temple well or ashes from its incense burners had medicinal properties. One present-day *fuke* practitioner in Shanghai, whose family also claimed an inherited expertise in gynecology, told me that his forebears started practicing gynecology out of pity for the women who ingested as medicine the incense ashes from a local temple. Cai Xiaomin, interview by author, August 10, 1993, Shanghai.

43. People of all social strata worshipped these gods, although with different motives. Yüan-ling Chao has shown, for example, that the Yuan-dynasty government promoted the cults of certain medical gods in order to impose medical orthodoxy on popular beliefs. "Patronizing Medicine: The *Sanhuang miao* (Temple of the Three Emperors) in Late Imperial China" (paper presented at the American Historical Association Annual Meeting, New York, January 2–5, 1997). See also the practices that Paul Katz has documented for the cult of Marshal Wen, a major plague-fighting deity who was worshipped throughout Zhejiang. *Demon Hordes and Burning Boats: The Cult of Marshal Wen in Later Imperial Chekiang* (Albany: State University of New York Press, 1995).

44. For Bixia yuanjun, see Brian Dott, "Ascending Mount Tai: Social and Cultural Interactions in 18th Century China" (PhD diss., University of Pittsburgh, 1999), especially chap. 3. Details on the Guanyin fertility cult appear in Chünfang Yu, "A Sutra Promoting the White-Robed Guanyin as Giver of Sons," in *Religions of China in Practice,* ed. Donald S. Lopez Jr. (Princeton, N.J.: Princeton University Press, 1996), 97–105. For fertility goddesses specific to southern China and Taiwan, see James L. Watson's discussion of the cult of Tian Hou, the "Empress of Heaven." Best known as the patron goddess of fishermen, Tian Hou had special significance for her female devotees who sought her in curing gynecological and obstetrical problems. "Standardizing the Gods: The Promotion of T'ien Hou ('Empress of Heaven') along the South China Coast, 960–1960," in *Popular Culture in Late Imperial China,* ed. David Johnson et al. (Berkeley: University of California Press, 1985), 292–325.

45. The story appears in the preface to *Fenglinsi taichan* (The Phoenix Grove Monastery's book on producing children) (hand-copied manuscript, n.d., SY no. 96432). This gynecological text is identical to some editions of the Bamboo Grove Monastery texts. The preface also states that the Bamboo Grove Monastery monks originally obtained their medical knowledge from the Phoenix Grove Monastery, but I have seen no information in other sources to confirm or refute this.

46. Wang Honglie, quoted in Zhang et al., eds., *Xiaoshan xianzhi gao,* 8:7a. For Wang Honglie's biographical information, see Liu Yan, ed., *Xiaoshan xianzhi* (Gazetteer of Xiaoshan County) (1693), 19:8b. Wang seems to have taken a certain interest in the Bamboo Grove Monastery. Besides the memorial tablet, he wrote an essay titled "Zhulinsi fuke xingshuai kao" (Investigation into the rise and decline of women's medicine at the Bamboo Grove Monastery). For details, see Zhou Mingdao, "Xiaoshan Zhulinsi nüke shixi bukao" (Supplementary investigations into the transmission of women's medicine by the generations of the Bamboo Grove Monastery of Xiaoshan), *Zhejiang zhongyi xueyuan xuebao* (December 1981): 43.

47. See listings in *LHML*. The actual number of editions in circulation was certainly higher. The *Zhongguo congshu zonglu*, for example, lists four additional editions not included in *LHML*.

48. See Guo Qianyi, preface dated 1895 to *Jisheng ji* (Collection on benefiting life), as reprinted in *YJTK*, 4:4005; and Deng Boting, preface dated 1790 to *Taichan mishu* (Secret book of childbearing), as reprinted in *YJTK*, 3:3823–24.

49. The *LHML* lists seventy-seven different Qing editions, comprising editions of Tang's original text as well as editions of two different expanded nineteenth-century versions of Tang's original text. The third *juan* of this work, titled "Approaching the Birthing Tub," begins with several pages that are a distillation of the first *juan* of the *Treatise on Easy Childbirth*, including the story of Zhang Baohua's wife. See, for example, Tang Qianqing, *Dasheng yaozhi* (Essentials of fecundity) (1762; Yangzhou: Weiyang wencheng tang woodblock edition, 1857).

50. Typical was a 1767 preface that one Wan Mianqian wrote in praise of the *Transmitted Family Knowledge about Childbirth (Chanbao jiachuan)*. Wan noted that *Easy Childbirth* was the best of the specialized works on childbearing then in circulation, but that *Transmitted Family Knowledge about Childbirth* was "even more clear and comprehensive." Wan Mianqian, preface dated 1767 to *Chanbao jiachuan*, as reprinted in *YJTK*, 3:3908.

51. For the English translation, see William Lockhart, trans., "A Treatise on Midwifery: A New Edition Published in the Fifth Year of Taou Kwong (1825)," *Dublin Journal of Medical Science* 20, no. 60 (1842): 333–69. Another English-language synopsis was published several decades later in Preston Maxwell and J. L. Liu, "Ta Sheng P'ien: A Chinese Household Manual of Obstetrics," *Annals of Medical History* 5, no. 2 (Summer 1923): 95–99. The Russian, German, and Polish versions were translations of the Manchu version. See Helmut Walravens, "Medical knowledge of the Manchus and the *Manchu Anatomy*," *Etudes mongoles et sibériennes* 27 (1996): 359–60. The Manchu version in question was *Baochan dasheng bian*, an undated woodblock edition with bilingual Chinese and Manchu title, text in Manchu, published by "[Minister] Fu of the Lifan yuan," in the collection of the Institute of Oriental Studies, Academy of Sciences, St. Petersburg, Russia. I am indebted to Marta Hanson for bringing this to my attention and for providing me with copies of this text as well as other information on the Manchu editions of the *Dasheng bian*. For a discussion of how Manchu-language medical texts served as a vehicle for transmitting Chinese medical knowledge to Russia, see Hanson, "The Significance of Manchu Medical Sources in the Qing," in *Proceedings of the First North American Conference on Manchu Studies* (Portland, Oregon, May 9–10, 2003), vol. 1: *Studies in Manchu Literature and History*, ed. Stephen Wadley, Carsten Naeher, and Keith Dede (Wiesbaden: Harrassowitz Verlag, 2006), 131–75.

52. According to the *LHML*, five different versions of *The Medical Books of Chen Xiuyuan* circulated, each containing a different number of texts. The texts and their first dates of publication are *The Medical Books of Chen Xiuyuan, Forty-eight Titles* (1905), *The Medical Books of Chen Xiuyuan, Fifty Titles* (1905), *The Medical Books of Chen Xiuyuan, Seventy Titles* (1907), *The Medical Books of Chen Xiuyuan, Seventy-two Titles* (1915), and *The Medical Books of Chen*

Xiuyuan, Sixty Titles (1919). The wide circulation of this work is evident when we consider that the collection of forty-eight titles was reprinted thirteen times between 1905 and 1955, and the collection of seventy-two works was reprinted nine times between 1915 and 1955.

53. Chen Nianzu, *Nüke yaozhi* (Essentials of medicine for women) (comp. 1803; first ed. 1841; reprinted in *Chen Xiuyuan yishu qishi'er zhong* [The medical books of Chen Xiuyuan, seventy-two titles], Shanghai: Shanghai Shudian, 1988). Chen's words of praise were also cited by Pan Wei, *Nüke yaolue,* 20a.

54. Quoted in Angela Ki Che Leung, "Women Practicing Medicine in Premodern China," in *Chinese Women in the Imperial Past: New Perspectives,* ed. Harriet T. Zurndorfer (Leiden: Brill, 1999), 114.

55. Yu Songyun, *Kexue de Dasheng bian* (A scientific *Treatise on Easy Childbirth*) (Shanghai: Zhongde yiyuan chubanshe, 1933). Yu was the principal of the Sino-German Advanced Professional School of Midwifery in Shanghai (Zhongde gaoji zhuchan shiye xuexiao).

56. Yang Chongrui, "Zhongguo fuying weisheng gongzuo" (The work of maternal and infant care in China), *Zhongguo yixue zazhi* 27, no. 5 (May 1941): 280–91. A 1917 graduate of the Peking Union Medical College, Yang Chongrui notably served as head of the First National Midwifery School, which was founded in 1929 under the direct supervision of the Ministry of Health. A few years later, she was appointed to concurrently head the Department of Maternity and Child Health. See Ka-che Yip, *Health and National Reconstruction in Nationalist China: The Development of Modern Health Services, 1928–1937* (Ann Arbor, Mich.: Association for Asian Studies, 1995), 120–122, 193. Yang continues to be remembered as a pioneering figure in promoting maternal health. See the collection of essays in Yen Renyin, ed., *Yang Chongrui boshi danchen bainian jinian* (A commemoration of the hundredth anniversary of the birth of Dr. Yang Chongrui) (Beijing: Beijing yike daxue and Zhongguo xiehe yike daxue, 1990).

57. Luo Yuankai, ed., *Zhongyi fuke xue* (TCM gynecology) (Beijing: Renmin weisheng chubanshe, 1994), 13.

58. Jizhai jushi [Ye Feng], author's preface dated 1715 to *Dasheng bian* (Treatise on easy childbirth) (1715; Du Fei, ed., 1727; reprinted with preface dated 1767 in *Yilin zhiyue* [Pointing the moon out to doctors], ed. Wang Qi, Hangzhou: Baohu lou woodblock edition). Emphasis mine. Except where otherwise noted, all of my quotations are based on this 1767 edition, which appears to be one of the earliest extant editions of the *Treatise on Easy Childbirth.* Special thanks to Qiu Jian for expediting me a copy of this text from the library of the Zhongguo zhongyi kexue yuan. Because people did not always write new prefaces when reprinting the *Treatise,* and because it was common to reuse old title pages from earlier editions, it is impossible to conclusively verify the actual date of the many extant editions of the *Dasheng bian.* Nevertheless, the core content of this work was extremely stable over time, and this particular edition is an entirely representative early exemplar. For comparison purposes, I have also translated this edition with reference to a woodblock edition produced by Wen Huide in 1830 owned by the University of Michigan and a lithographic edition that circulated widely in various editions of *The Medical Books of Chen Xiuyuan (Chen Xiu-*

yuan yishu) starting in 1905. See Jizhai jushi [Ye Feng], *Dasheng bian* (Treatise on easy childbirth) (1715; reprinted in *Chen Xiuyuan yishu qishi'er zhong* [The medical books of Chen Xiuyuan, seventy-two titles], Shanghai: Shanghai shu-dian, 1988).

59. Jia Zhizhong and Yang Yanfei have proposed that Jizhai may have been the Ming-Qing scholar official Zhang Zhao (b. 1625), but their analysis is deeply flawed. Jia and Yang start with the assumption that there were only two individuals in all of China in the late Ming and early Qing who used *Jizhai* as a sobriquet, an assumption based on their perusal of modern dictionaries of sobriquets. Their choice of Zhang Zhao, furthermore, stems from the fact that he is the only one of these two whose life history does not positively rule him out (notably, Jia and Yang fail to identify Ye Feng as a possible candidate). The authors admit that the evidence for Zhang Zhao having ever engaged in medical activities is circumstantial at best. Furthermore, they acknowledge that Zhang would not have been alive in 1715, the date of Jizhai's preface. They unconvincingly try to finesse this discrepancy by arguing that there could have been a typographical error in the date of the preface so that the work was completed in 1679 rather than 1715. Jia and Yang, "*Dasheng bian* ji qi zuozhe" (The "Treatise on Easy Childbirth" and its author), *Zhonghua yishi zazhi* 26, no. 2 (1996): 103–5.

60. I have reconstructed this history of the Ye family from biographical information provided in various editions of Huoshan County gazetteers about Ye Feng, his son Ye Dashou, his grandmother Ms. Wang, and his niece Ms. Feng. For the most comprehensive accounts, see Gan Shan et al., eds., *Huoshan xianzhi* (Gazetteer of Huoshan County) (1776; reprint, Taipei: Chengwen chubanshe, 1985), 5 (pt. 1): 20b for Ye Dashou; 6 (pt. 9): 4a–5a for Ye Feng; 6 (pt. 12): 52b–53a for Ms. Feng; and 8 (pt. 2): 102a–103a for Ms. Wang. The detail that Ye Feng was a younger brother appears in the entry for Ms. Feng in Qin Dazhang, ed., *Huoshan xianzhi* (Gazetteer of Huoshan County) (1905; reprint, Taipei: Chengwen chubanshe, 1974), 12:8b.

61. It is likely that Ye Feng stayed in his secretarial position from at least 1715 (when *Easy Childbirth* was written) until 1720, when he asked the Jiangxi Provincial Educational Commissioner Wang Sixun to write a biographical account of his paternal grandmother, Ms. Wang. Wang Sixun's account of Ms. Wang is reproduced in Gan et al., eds., *Huoshan xianzhi* 8 (pt. 2): 102a–103a.

62. See Gan et al., eds., *Huoshan xianzhi,* 8 (pt. 1): 98a–99a, for Ye Feng's essay about Men Yuying, the magistrate who defended Huoshan against bandits in 1648; and 8 (pt. 2), 32b–33a for Ye's poem on the "heavenly lake of Yueding."

63. Biography of Ye Feng, in Gan et al., eds., *Huoshan xianzhi,* 6 (pt. 9): 4a–5a.

64. Gong Chunpu's title is given as *tun sima,* literally the "vice commandant of a military settlement," and by context it is clear that he is serving in Haiyan County. See Chen Mingzhe, preface dated 1854 to *Nüke michuan* (Transmitted secrets of medicine for women), attrib. Zhulinsi seng (Bamboo Grove Monastery monks) (Hangzhou: Zhou Zonglong woodblock edition, 1854, ZJ no. 4845).

65. Ibid.

66. Gong Chunpu, "appended record" (undated) to *Nüke michuan* (Transmitted secrets of medicine for women), attrib. Zhulinsi seng (Bamboo Grove

Monastery monks) (Hangzhou: Zhou Zonglong woodblock edition, 1854, ZJ no. 4845), 62a–b.

67. Zhou Jichang, *Nüke jiyao* (Edited essentials of medicine for women) (1823; Kuizhaolou woodblock edition, 1865).

68. Information on Zhou Jichang's scholarly and medical background is given in Zhang Jiuzhao, preface dated 1823 to *Nüke jiyao* (Edited essentials of medicine for women), by Zhou Jichang (1823; Kuizhaolou woodblock edition, 1865). For the *muyou* and their social status, see Kenneth E. Folsom, *Friends, Guests, and Colleagues: The Mu-fu System in the Late Ch'ing Period* (Berkeley: University of California Press, 1968). For the preponderance of secretaries from Shaoxing, see James Cole, *Shaohsing: Competition and Cooperation in Nineteenth-Century China* (Tucson: University of Arizona Press, 1986).

69. Zeng Jifen reported, for example, that Bao Xiang'ao's *Yanfang xinbian* was widely used, and that she herself consulted it when making medicines to treat her mother's chronic illnesses. Zeng, *Testimony of a Confucian Woman: The Autobiography of Mrs. Nie Zeng Jifeng, 1852–1942*, trans. and annot. Thomas L. Kennedy (Athens: University of Georgia Press, 1993), 64.

70. Li Jingwei ed., *Zhongyi renwu cidian* (A dictionary of eminent figures in Chinese medicine) (Shanghai: Shanghai cishu chubanshe, 1988), 642; Li Yun, ed., *Zhongyi renming cidian* (A biographical dictionary of Chinese medicine) (Beijing: Guoji wenhua chubanshe, 1988), 915.

71. Bao Xiang'ao, preface to *Yanfang xinbian* (A new compilation of tested remedies) (first ed. 1846; expanded and ed. Mei Qizhao, [Hangzhou]: Zhejiang sheng cheng dongbizhai kezidian, 1878; modern critical edition published Beijing: Renmin weisheng chubanshe, 1990).

72. "General meaning" *(dayi)*, in Jizhai jushi, *Dasheng bian,* 1:1a (paginated separately).

73. A particularly detailed description of these difficulties is found in Bao Xiang'ao's preface to his *Yanfang xinbian.*

74. Jizhai jushi, author's preface dated 1715, *Dasheng bian.*

75. Li Keqiong, preface dated 1824 to *Nüke jiyao* (Edited essentials of medicine for women), by Zhou Jichang (1823; Kuizhaolou woodblock edition, 1865).

76. Ibid. This equation of law and medicine was in fact an important element in the development of the medical case study as a literary genre. See Furth, Zeitlin, and Hsiung, eds., *Thinking with Cases,* especially Furth, introduction (1–27), "Producing Medical Knowledge" (125–51), and Zeitlin, "The Literary Fashioning of Medical Authority" (169–202).

77. Lu Yuan, preface dated 1872 to *Fuke michuan, jushi zhibao* (Transmitted secrets of women's medicine, the greatest treasure for those residing at home), attrib. Zhulinsi seng (Bamboo Grove Monastery monks) (woodblock edition, afterword dated 1872, SY no. 64223).

78. Luo Shanqing, preface dated 1825 to *Ningkun miji* (A secret book for female tranquility), attrib. Zhulinsi seng (Bamboo Grove Monastery monks) (Guang Tongji woodblock edition, preface dated 1876, CS no. 454/6019).

79. Wu Ziqing, undated preface (probably 1801) to *Ningkun miji* (A secret book for female tranquility), attrib. Zhulinsi seng (Bamboo Grove Monastery monks) (Guang Tongji woodblock edition, preface dated 1876, CS no. 454/6019).

80. See also Charlotte Furth's discussion of these issues in "Blood, Body, and Gender: Medical Images of the Female Condition in China," *Chinese Science* 7 (1986): 48–51.

81. Zhou Jichang, author's preface dated 1823 to his *Nüke jiyao* (Edited essentials of medicine for women) (1823; Kuizhaolou woodblock edition, 1865).

82. Tiexiao daoren (Iron-Reverent Follower of the Way), preface dated 1854, "revised following divination" in 1864, to *Zhulinsi nüke michuan* (Transmitted secrets of women's medicine from the Bamboo Grove Monastery), attrib. Zhulinsi seng (Bamboo Grove Monastery monks) (Kaifeng: Zhang Longwen Zhai Engraving Shop woodblock edition, 1852; reprinted with a new preface dated 1864, CM no. 167188).

83. Pan Wei, preface dated 1886 to *Zhulinsi nüke zhengzhi* (Treatments for women's illnesses from the Bamboo Grove Monastery), attrib. Zhulinsi seng (Bamboo Grove Monastery monks) (Shanghai: Haihe Pavilion Bookstore, 1895, reprinted with preface dated 1915, CM no. 167198).

84. Chen Qirong, preface dated 1873 to *Guyue Zhulinsi fuke mifang, neifu xiao'er yingyan jingfeng fang* (Secret prescriptions of medicine for women from the Bamboo Grove Temple of ancient Yue, with appended tested prescriptions for treating windfright in children), attrib. Zhulinsi seng (Bamboo Grove Monastery monks) (Tangshan: Minghua Lithographic Printing Shop, lithograph edition, 1885, BH no. 117/857.4).

85. Pan Wei clearly felt that men were responsible for ensuring the health of women in their families. He related how he had long wanted to compile and publish a text on women's medicine, since "this would enable a copy to be placed in the homes where there are women, allowing the men to freely investigate [the women's illnesses] in detail and use medicine according to the illness, thus enabling them to save women from their illnesses." Pan Wei, preface to *Zhulinsi nüke zhengzhi* (CM no. 167198).

86. Jizhai jushi, author's preface to *Dasheng bian*.

87. "Compilation principles" *(fanli)*, in Jizhai jushi, *Dasheng bian*, 1:3b.

88. See, for example, Chen Qirong, preface to *Guyue Zhulinsi fuke mifang* (BH no. 117/857.4). For other examples, see Wu, "The Bamboo Grove Monastery."

89. Cynthia Brokaw, *The Ledgers of Merit and Demerit: Social Change and Moral Order in Late Imperial China* (Princeton, N.J.: Princeton University Press, 1991), 103–9 and 173–75 (the quotation is from p. 173). A description of how to earn merit through the dissemination of medical information appears in the ledger text translated in Cynthia Brokaw, "Supernatural Retribution and Human Destiny," in *Religions of China in Practice*, ed. Donald S. Lopez Jr. (Princeton, N.J.: Princeton University Press, 1996), 423–36.

90. See Zhulinsi seng (Bamboo Grove Monastery monks), attrib., *Nüke mifang* (Secret prescriptions of women's medicine) (Beijing: Wenrui Studio woodblock edition, 1826, BH no. 117/857); and Zhulinsi seng, attrib., *Zhulinsi nüke mifang* (Secret prescriptions of women's medicine from the Bamboo Grove Monastery) (Yizheng Hall woodblock edition, 1890, SY no. 60373).

91. Jizhai jushi [Ye Feng], *Dasheng bian* (1715; Hangzhou: Fuyunde Engraving Shop woodblock ed., 1878, ST no. 108207).

92. See, for example, Zhulinsi seng, *Nüke mifang* (BH no. 117/857). Those

who commissioned these publications, however, intended them for charitable distribution. There may have been a secondary market for Bamboo Grove texts that had originally been distributed gratis: although the vast majority of Bamboo Grove preface writers obtained the book through a friend or colleague, a couple of writers do mention purchasing Bamboo Grove books in stores.

93. Jizhai jushi [Ye Feng], *Dasheng bian* (1715; Hefei: Zhang Hongmao Engraving Shop woodblock edition, n.d., ST no. 090492).

94. Xinshi lianhua shanren (The Mountain Dweller with a Lotus Flower Heart), afterword dated 1864 to *Zhulinsi nüke michuan* (Transmitted secrets of women's medicine from the Bamboo Grove Monastery), attrib. Zhulinsi seng (Bamboo Grove Monastery monks) (Kaifeng: Zhang Longwen Zhai Engraving Shop woodblock edition, 1852; reprinted with a new preface dated 1864, CM no. 167188).

95. Qiao Guanglie, preface dated 1762 to *Zengbu dasheng yaozhi* (The essentials of fecundity, expanded and supplemented), as reprinted in *YJTK*, 3:3922.

96. Jizhai jushi [Ye Feng], *Dasheng bian* (1715; Nanchang: Yili zhai woodblock edition [c. 1850], ST no. 440243).

97. Brokaw, *Ledgers,* 35–36. The medical text in question is Jizhai jushi [Ye Feng], *Zengguang Dasheng pian* (The expanded *Treatise on Easy Childbirth*) (Zhenjiang [Jiangsu]: Shanhua tang, 1888; personal collection of author).

98. Mao Xianglin, preface dated 1852 to *Zengzhu Dasheng bian* (The expanded and annotated "Treatise on Easy Childbirth") as reprinted in *YJTK*, 3:3885.

99. Jizhai jushi, *Zengguang Dasheng pian* (1888). As Brokaw notes, the link between merit and sons was also explicitly promoted by Yuan Huan. See Brokaw, *Ledgers,* 61, 73, 78n50.

100. Jizhai jushi, *Dasheng bian* (ST no. 108207).

101. Jizhai jushi, *Zengguang Dasheng pian* (1888).

102. Jizhai jushi, *Dasheng bian* (ST no. 108207).

103. Brokaw, *Ledgers,* 172.

104. Jizhai jushi, *Dasheng bian* (ST no. 108207).

105. Ibid.; and Jizhai jushi [Ye Feng], *Dasheng bian* (1715; Renyu Hall woodblock ed., 1902, ST no. 440635).

106. Jizhai jushi, *Dasheng bian* (ST no. 108207).

107. Jizhai jushi [Ye Feng], *Dasheng bian* (1715; n.p., preface dated 1809, woodblock edition, ST no. 440260).

108. Jizhai jushi, *Dasheng bian* (ST no. 108207).

109. See, for example, the signature line of Li Heli on the last page of the second *juan* of Jizhai jushi, *Dasheng bian* (ST no. 440260). Another example is the signature line printed on the inside back cover of Jizhai jushi [Ye Feng], *Dasheng bian* (1715; n.p., woodblock ed., 1839, ST no. 539001). The *Hanyu dacidian* (Comprehensive dictionary of the Chinese language [Shanghai: Hanyu dacidian chubanshe, 1990–94]) defines *xinshi* as a male lay Buddhist or, more broadly, as someone who manifests belief in Buddhism by donating money for religious works.

110. Jizhai jushi, *Dasheng bian* (ST no. 440635) 2:13a–b.

111. Brokaw, *Ledgers.*

112. Weng Linzhong, afterword dated 1896 to *Nüke mifang* (Secret prescriptions of women's medicine), attrib. Zhulinsi seng (Bamboo Grove Monastery monks) (Wenlin Hall woodblock edition, 1896, ZJ no. 4883)

113. This episode appears in Leung, "Women Practicing Medicine in Premodern China."

114. Furth, "Producing Medical Knowledge."

115. "General intent" *(da yi)*, in Jizhai jushi, *Dasheng bian,* 1:3a (paginated separately).

3. FUNCTION AND STRUCTURE IN THE FEMALE BODY

1. Sun Yikui, *Sunshi yi'an* (The medical cases of Master Sun), comp. Yu Huang et al. (1599; modern critical edition reprinted in Sun Yikui, *Sun Yikui yixue quanshu* [The complete medical works of Sun Yikui], ed. Han Xuejie et al., Beijing: Zhongguo zhongyiyao chubanshe, 1999), 824–25. A condensed version of this case was reprinted in Wei Zhixiu, *Xu mingyi lei'an* (A continuation of the *Cases from Famous Doctors, Arranged by Category*) (ca. 1770; reprinted in *SKQS*), 1:8b–9a.

2. Sun Yikui is known to have lived during the period bracketed by the reigns of the Ming dynasty's Jiajing and Wanli emperors (1522–1619). For his biography, see Sun Yikui, *Sun Yikui yixue quanshu* (The complete medical works of Sun Yikui), ed. Han Xuejie et al. (Beijing: Zhongguo zhongyiyao chubanshe, 1999), 841. The term that Sun uses to refer to Ms. Cheng's husband is *zuzhi sun,* literally the "grandson of my clan nephew." According to the *Hanyu dacidian,* a clan nephew is the son of a male relative with whom one shares the same great-great-grandfather (i.e., the son of one's fourth cousin). In English, a clan nephew would thus be one's fourth cousin once removed, and a clan nephew's grandson would be one's fourth cousin thrice removed. For simplicity, I have described Sun as the husband's "senior kinsman." *Hanyu dacidian* (Comprehensive dictionary of the Chinese language) (Shanghai: Hanyu dacidian chubanshe, 1990–94).

3. The *huan* pulse is one that has a relaxed quality to it, and modern reference works translate this into English as a "moderate" pulse. See, for example, Nigel Wiseman and Feng Ye, *A Practical Dictionary of Chinese Medicine* (Brookline, Mass.: Paradigm Publications, 1998), s.v. "Huan." However, the *huan* pulse can denote either pathology or harmony, depending on the particular case at hand. Since Sun is clearly using it here to diagnose spleen dampness, I have translated it with the word *loose,* which carries more of a pathological tint than the term *moderate.*

4. Although standard reference works such as *LHML* list the earliest extant edition of Sun's case records as bearing the publication date of 1573, I have relied on Judith Zeitlin's dating of this text, which is based on an analysis of the prefaces and the dates of the cases recorded in the text. "The Literary Fashioning of Medical Authority: A Study of Sun Yikui's Case Histories," in *Thinking with Cases,* edited by Charlotte Furth, Judith T. Zeitlin, and Ping-chen Hsiung (Honolulu: University of Hawai'i Press, 2007).

5. Wei, *Xu mingyi lei'an,* 31:8b–9a. For an analysis of blocked menses in literate Chinese medicine, see Francesca Bray, "A Deathly Disorder: Understand-

ing Women's Health in Late Imperial China," in *Knowledge and the Scholarly Medical Traditions,* ed. Don Bates (Cambridge: Cambridge University Press, 1995), 235–50.

6. See Ha Xiaoxian, *Neijing fuke jiwen jiyi* (Compilation of gynecological discussions from the *Neijing,* with collected commentaries) (Beijing: Zhongguo yiyao keji chubanshe, 1992), 28; and Luo Yuankai, ed., *Zhongyi fuke xue* (TCM gynecology) (Beijing: Renmin weisheng chubanshe, 1994), 10–11.

7. Charlotte Furth, "Blood, Body, and Gender: Medical Images of the Female Condition in China," *Chinese Science* 7 (1986): 48–51.

8. *YZJJ,* 44:5a.

9. Ibid.

10. The earliest description that I have found of this congruence between Blood and breast milk is in the writings of Chao Yuanfang (fl. ca. 605–16). The explanation that Blood "ascends as breast milk, and descends as menses" appears throughout Chao's discussion of women's ailments, including menstrual ailments and vaginal discharges, diseases of pregnancy, and disorders of lactation following birth. Chao Yuanfang, *Chaoshi zhubing yuanhou lun* (Master Chao's treatise on the origins and manifestations of the myriad diseases) (comp. 610; revised 1026–27; edited by Wang Jichuan and Fang Kuang [Ming]; reprinted in *SKQS*), *juan* 37, 38, 41, 42, 44.

11. Charlotte Furth, *A Flourishing Yin: Gender in China's Medical History, 960–1665* (Berkeley: University of California Press, 1999), chap. 2.

12. Ibid., chaps. 4 and 5.

13. See, for example, *YZJJ, juan* 44.

14. *GJTS,* 402:55412. The GJTS editors used the phrase "menstruation is the foundation for women" as the title for an excerpt from Zhang Jiebin. In so doing, they actually altered the title of Zhang's original essay, which had simply been titled "The Origins of Menses" *(Jingmai zhi ben).* Zhang, *Jingyue quanshu* (The complete works of Jingyue) (comp. ca. 1624–40; reprinted in *SKQS*), 38:2b.

15. Doctors did recognize that some women might menstruate at intervals other than once a month, which they attributed to variations in individual constitutions. The *YZJJ,* for example, mentioned women who menstruated every two months, every three months, once a year, or even never, yet who were still healthy and fertile. *YZJJ,* 44:3a–b. This suggests that doctors perceived pathology as, above all, a matter of irregularity rather than the specific length of the cycle.

16. *YZJJ,* 44:5b–6b.

17. In this discussion I have compared two versions of the Bamboo Grove works: Zhulinsi seng (Bamboo Grove Monastery monks), attrib., *Taichan xinshu* (A new book on childbearing), attrib. specifically to Master Jingguang, Master Lunying, and Master Xueyan (comp. ca. 1771; recopied with preface dated 1793; printed 1886; reprinted in *ZBYS*), vol. 8; and Zhulinsi seng, attrib., *Ningkun miji* (A secret book for female tranquility) (preface dated 1786; 1795 edition reprinted in *Zhulinsi nüke er zhong* [Two books on medicine for women from the Bamboo Grove Monastery], Beijing: Zhongyi guji chubanshe, 1993). The quotations appear in *Taichan xinshu* 3:31–32 and *Ningkun miji,* 6–7.

18. *YZJJ,* 44:6a.

19. Zhulinsi seng, *Taichan xinshu,* 3:27. A similar passage is in Zhulinsi seng,

Ningkun miji, 1:2. In some editions, the phrase "pain in the lower abdomen" *(xiaofu)* is replaced by "pain on urination" *(xiaobian).* See Zhulinsi seng (Bamboo Grove Monastery monks), attrib., *Fuke mifang* (Secret prescriptions of women's medicine) (Li Guangming studio woodblock edition; preface dated 1866; facsimile reprint, Beijing: Zhongguo shudian, 1987), 1b.

20. For examples, see *YZJJ,* 44:8a–b; and Zhulinsi seng, *Ningkun miji,* 7–14.

21. For blocked menstruation see Bray, "Deathly Disorder."

22. Shen Yaofeng [Shen Youpeng], *Nüke jiyao* (Edited essentials of medicine for women) (comp. mid-eighteenth century; ed. and published by Wang Shixiong, 1850; modern critical edition by Li Guangwen, Huang Shuzhen, and Li Zhulan, published in *Nüke jiyao, taichan xinfa,* Beijing: Renmin weisheng chubanshe, 1988), 19. Note that this modern edition is published under the author's courtesy name, Shen Yaofeng.

23. Ibid., 19.

24. Other English translations that have been used for these circulation channels are "tracts" and "meridians" and "pulse vessels." For simplicity, I have adapted the translations used in contemporary TCM. However, it must be noted that the precise Chinese medical understanding of these circulation channels has changed over time. Unschuld shows that the doctrine of the circulation channels was first articulated during the second century B.C.E. But the theory of the extraordinary vessel is still rudimentary in the *Yellow Emperor's Inner Classic* and was fully articulated only in the *Classic of Difficult Issues.* For the early history of pulse vessel theory, see also Li Jianmin, *Si sheng zhi yu: Zhou-Qin-Han maixue zhi yuanliu* (The boundary between life and death: The origins of meridian theory in the Zhou, Qin, and Han dynasties) (Taipei: Institute of History and Philology, Academia Sinica, 2000), 264–74; Vivienne Lo, "The Influence of Nurturing Life Culture on the Development of Western Han Acumoxa Therapy," in *Innovation in Chinese Medicine,* Needham Research Institute Series 3, ed. Elisabeth Hsu (Cambridge: Cambridge University Press, 2001), 19–50; and Elisabeth Hsu, "Pulse Diagnostics in the Western Han: How *Mai* and *Qi* Determine *Bing,*" in *Innovation in Chinese Medicine,* Needham Research Institute Series 3, ed. Hsu (Cambridge: Cambridge University Press, 2001), 51–92. A summary description of how eighteenth-century doctors understood these is found in *YZJJ,* 84:1a. Finally, most English language sources use the translation "extraordinary vessels" for *qijing bamai.* However, Paul Unschuld, citing ancient commentaries, has cogently argued that the *qi* in *qimai* refers to the single, unpaired nature of these vessels, rather than to their being "unusual," and that these should be properly called the "single-conduit vessels." Following Furth, *Flourishing Yin,* I use the translation "singular," which implies both the unique and extraordinary.

25. See Sun Yikui, *Yizhi xuyu* (Additional discussions on the meaning of medicine) (1573; reprinted in *SKQS*), 2:68:5–7; Xiao Xun, *Nüke jinglun* (Canonical teachings on medicine for women) (1684; modern punctuated edition published Shanghai: Shanghai weisheng chubanshe, 1957), 1:3; as well as the commentaries listed in Paul U. Unschuld, trans. and annot., *Nan-ching: The Classic of Difficult Issues: With Commentaries by Chinese and Japanese Authors from the Third through the Twentieth Century* (Berkeley: University of California Press, 1986), 329.

26. Texts that opened with the *Suwen*'s description of sexual maturation notably include the *fuke* sections of the *GJTS* and the *YZJJ*. In rendering this passage, I have borrowed Charlotte Furth's translation, with some modifications. *Flourishing Yin*, 45. Unless otherwise stated, I employ the text of the *Suwen* reprinted in Shandong zhongyi xueyuan and Hebei yixue yuan, eds., *Huangdi neijing suwen jiaoshi* (The *Yellow Emperor's Inner Classic, Basic Questions*, annotated and explicated) (Beijing: Renmin weisheng chubanshe, 1993).

27. For the text with Wang Bing's annotations, see *Huangdi neijing suwen* (The Yellow Emperor's inner classic, basic questions) (originally compiled first century C.E.; reprinted in *SKQS*), 1:4b. For the history of Wang Bing's redaction of the *Inner Classic*, see Paul U. Unschuld, *Huang Di Nei Jing Su Wen: Nature, Knowledge, Imagery in an Ancient Chinese Medical Text* (Berkeley: University of California Press, 2003), 39–66.

28. Xu Dachun, *Yixue yuanliu lun* (Treatise on the origins of medical learning) (1757; reprinted in *SKQS*), 2.43b.

29. *Suwen* 33 ("Ping rebing lun") says that "the womb vessel *[baomai]* belongs to the heart and runs as a channel into the womb." *Suwen* 47 ("Qibing lun") says that the womb channel *(baoluo)* is connected to the kidney. Shandong Zhongyi xueyuan and Hebei yixue yuan, eds., *Huangdi neijing suwen jiaoshi*, 436, 607.

30. See, for example, Zhu Xiao, ed., *Puji fang* (Formulas for universal benefit) (1390; reprinted in *SKQS*), 331:1a. During the movement to standardize and modernize Chinese medicine in the early twentieth century, this also became a standard explanation for the "vessels of the womb." Xie Guan, *Zhongguo yixue dacidian* (A comprehensive dictionary of Chinese medicine) (preface dated 1926; facsimile reprint, Beijing: Zhongguo shudian, 1988), 1938.

31. *Suwen* 60 ("Gukong lun"), in Zhongyi xueyuan and Hebei yixue yuan, eds., *Huangdi neijing suwen jiaoshi*, 741.

32. Vivienne Lo has also suggested that the middle extremity was conceptually conflated with the womb itself. See "Influence of Nurturing Life Culture," 45–46.

33. The *Huangdi neijing lingshu* (The Yellow Emperor's inner classic, divine pivot), was also known as the *Lingshu jing* (Classic of the divine pivot). For the original quotation, see *Lingshu jing* (earliest published recension dated 1155; reprinted in *SKQS*), 1:2b. The Qing sources that adopted the *Lingshu jing*'s description of the thoroughfare and controller vessels notably included the *GJTS* and the *YZJJ*. See, for example, the description given by Li Wen in the *YZJJ*: "The controlling vessel is in charge of the womb *[baotai]*, and the thoroughfare vessel is the Blood Sea. The two meridians arise in the womb palace *[baogong]* and come out from the perineum *[huiyin,* literally "convergence of yin"]." *YZJJ*, 23:28b–30a. Likewise, when the editors of the *GJTS* cited the *Inner Classic*'s account of female sexual maturation, they added the note that the thoroughfare and controller vessels arose in the lower abdomen, "within the womb" *(bao zhong)*. *GJTS*, 404:55434.

34. An early example is found in Sun Simiao, who observed that women would be unable to conceive if there was noxious, corrupted Blood inside their wombs. Sun recommended a decoction of saltpeter *(poxiao)* and seventeen other

ingredients to cleanse the womb. See "Poxiao dang bao tang" (Saltpeter decoction to wash the womb), in his *Beiji qianjin yaofang* (Essential prescriptions worth a thousand golds for managing urgent situations) (651; reprinted in *SKQS*), 2:4a–b. An extensive collection of formulas meant to address womb pathology can be found in the *fuke* sections of Zhu, ed., *Puji fang*.

35. See, for example, the usages given in the *Oxford English Dictionary*.

36. These definitions are collected in the *Kangxi zidian* (Dictionary of the Kangxi reign) (1716; facsimile reprint, Beijing: Zhonghua shuju, 1992), 979. The glosses I quote come from the *Shuowen jiezi* (first century C.E.) and the *Zhuangzi* (compiled on the basis of texts ranging from the third century B.C.E. to the third century C.E.; see Michael Loewe, ed., *Early Chinese Texts: A Bibliographical Guide* [Berkeley: Society for the Study of Early China and the Institute of East Asian Studies, University of California, Berkeley, 1993], 56–57). For additional etymological discussion, see Morohashi Tetsuji, *Dai Kanwa jiten* (Great Chinese dictionary) (Tokyo: Taishūkan shoten, 1986). The word *bao* was also pronounced "pao" in antiquity, and in some cases it was used to write the homonymous word *pao* meaning "bladder." This usage appears in the name of a well-known ailment of pregnancy, *zhuan bao*, literally meaning "turned bladder," which refers to difficult urination caused by the pressure of the expanding womb on the urinary bladder. Generally, however, medical texts from the *Inner Classic* onward refer to the bladder as the *pangguang*.

37. Pharmacological literature used the term *bao* when talking about the medicinal uses of human placenta. See Li Shizhen, *Bencao gangmu* (A classification of materia medica) (comp. 1552–78; preface dated 1590, ed. and republished by Wu Shuchang in 1655, reprinted in *SKQS*), 52:36b–39b.

38. Although the terms *bao* and *zigong* have both been dated to the Han, the term *baogong* appears to be a later term. The earliest reference I have found for it is Chen Ziming's *Furen daquan liangfang* (Comprehensive compendium of good formulas for women) (comp. 1237; revised ca. 1265; modern critical edition of Yuan dynasty Qinyou shutang edition by Yu Ying'ao et al., Beijing: Renmin weisheng chubanshe, 1992).

39. Cited in Ha, *Neijing fuke jiwen jiyi*, 28.

40. A typical example is Wei, *Xu mingyi lei'an*, 25:629.

41. A relatively obscure variation, which is used in descriptions of prolapsed uterus. See, for example, Li, *Bencao gangmu*, 22:9a.

42. A relatively obscure variation. Xu Bin, *Jinkui yaolue lunzhu* (*Essentials of the Golden Cabinet*, discussed and annotated) (1671; reprinted in *SKQS*), 20:1b.

43. See, for example, Zhu, ed., *Puji fang*, 328:19a, 332:42b, 332:66a.

44. A relatively obscure variation. Ibid., 336:30a.

45. Li Jianmin suggests that those engaged in such dissections sought to obtain information about the dimensions of the circulation tracts as well as about the body's internal organs. Li, *Si sheng zhi yu*. See also the historical overview of dissection given in Catherine Despeux, "The Body Revealed: The Contribution of Forensic Medicine to Knowledge and Representations of the Skeleton in China," in *Graphics and Text in the Production of Technical Knowledge in China:*

The Warp and the Weft, ed. Francesca Bray, Vera Dorofeeva-Lichtmann, and Georges Metailie (Leiden: Brill, 2007), 635–84.

46. Unschuld, *Huang Di Nei Jing Su Wen,* 129–41.

47. Paul Unschuld notes the existence of several competing categorization schema in the *Suwen,* and the status of the gall bladder was ambiguous. Here Qi Bo identifies it as an unusual palace organ, but elsewhere it is categorized as one of six regular palace organs. Ibid., 136–41. In later texts the pericardium was added as a sixth depot *(zang)* organ.

48. *Suwen* 11, "Wuzang bielun" ("Additional discussion of the five depot organs"). See Shandong zhongyi xueyuan and Hebei yixue yuan, eds., *Huangdi neijing suwen jiaoshi,* 162–65; and Ha, *Neijing fuke jiwen jiyi,* 26–30.

49. *Suwen* 11. For Wang's commentary, see *Huangdi neijing suwen,* 3:21.

50. Zhang Jiebin, *Leijing* (The *Inner Classic* explicated by topic) (1624; reprinted in *SKQS*), 4:11a.

51. Quoted in Ha, *Neijing fuke jiwen jiyi,* 28–30.

52. In compiling this analysis, I have drawn on the overviews in Xiao, *Nüke jinglun,* 2:10–14; and *GJTS, juan* 404 ("Begetting Heirs"), passim, and *YZJJ,* 44:25a–27b.

53. Quoted in Xiao, *Nüke jinglun,* 2:10.

54. Zhu Zhenheng, *Gezhi yulun* (Additional discourses on extending knowledge through the investigation of things) (comp. ca. 1347; modern critical edition of Yuan dynasty woodblock edition reprinted in Zhu Zhenheng, *Danxi yiji* [The collected medical works of Danxi], Beijing: Renmin weisheng chubanshe, 1993), 27. Although Zhu Zhenheng did not date his own preface to *Gezhi yulun,* its approximate date of completion can be estimated from a preface that Song Lian wrote for it in 1347. For the text of Song's preface, see *YJTK* 2:2396–97.

55. For example, Wang Qingren's (1768–1831) iconoclastic investigations into bodily anatomy in the nineteenth century were conducted on exposed corpses in graveyards. For a sample translation from Wang's *Yilin gaicuo* (Correcting the errors of physicians) of 1830 and a general description of his activities, see Paul U. Unschuld, *Medicine in China: A History of Ideas* (Berkeley: University of California Press, 1986), 212–15.

56. Forensic medicine manuals instructed midwives to examine the external and internal genitals of female corpses for various reasons, most notably to see if they were virgins, if they had recently given birth, or if any foreign object had been inserted inside their vaginas. See Brian E. McKnight, introduction to *Xiyuan jilu* (The washing away of wrongs), by Song Ci, 1247, trans. Brian E. McKnight (Ann Arbor: Center for Chinese Studies, University of Michigan, 1981), 11–12, 28. For a discussion of doctors and midwives exchanging information during the Song, see Furth, *Flourishing Yin,* 119–21.

57. Detailed anatomical descriptions and illustrations of uterine prolapse and uterine inversion from British midwifery texts of the seventeenth to twentieth centuries make this clear. While there are Chinese medical descriptions of prolapsed uteruses that describe the uterus as a body with two branches, it is clear that these "two branches" cannot refer to the Fallopian tubes, and most likely reflect some genital abnormality of the woman in question.

58. I am indebted to Ronald Cyr for bringing this to my attention. According to Cyr, he encounters a patient with bicornuate uterus every few years in his own gynecological practice. Cyr, personal communication. For a modern textbook description, see James R. Scott et al., eds., *Danforth's Obstetrics and Gynecology*, 6th ed. (Philadelphia: J. B. Lippincott, 1990), 48–51. According to *Danforth's*, these "anomalies of internal development are quite common."

59. Zhu, *Gezhi yulun*, 27.

60. Ibid., 26–27.

61. For an early discussion of the mutable state of the fetus in the third month and the methods for "changing a girl into a boy," see Chao, *Chaoshi zhubing yuanhou lun*, 41:2b–3a, 6b. Common techniques included placing axes and bows under the pregnant woman's bed and wearing sachets of realgar *(xionghuang)*, a drug whose Chinese name translates literally as "male yellow." Medicinal decoctions could also be used.

62. Zhang Jiebin refers to these sexual techniques when he discusses Zhu Zhengheng's description of the womb. Zhang, *Jingyue quanshu*, 39:65a–b.

63. Ibid.

64. Xiao, *Nüke jinglun*, 2:14.

65. For details of Zhang Jiebin's life, see the many sources cited in *LDYJ*. 2:703–5, as well as Zhang, *Zhang Jingyue yixue quanshu* (The complete medical works of Zhang Jingyue), ed. Li Zhiyong (Beijing: Zhongguo zhongyiyao chubanshe, 1999), 1863–64. His father's employer was the Marquis for Pacification of the Western Regions *(dingxi hou)*, a position held for generations by the Jiang family of Jiangdu County, one of the counties encompassed by the city of Yangzhou. For the names of Jiang family men who held ths title from 1438 to 1640, see *Qinding xu wenxian tongkao* (Imperially compiled continuation of the *General History of Institutions and Critical Examination of Documents and Studies*) (compilation commissioned in 1747; reprinted in *SKQS*), 209:48b–49a.

66. The sources disagree as to whether Zhang was thirteen or fourteen when he moved to Beijing. Although all accounts describe Jin Ying as a "famous doctor" *(mingyi)* of the time, little information remains about him now other than that he was Zhang Jiebin's teacher. See, for example, *LDYJ*, 2:38.

67. Zhang, *Zhang Jingyue yixue quanshu*, 1861–63.

68. Qiu Peiran and Ding Guangdi, eds., *Zhongyi gejia xueshuo* (The teachings of famous Chinese medical experts) (Beijing: Renmin weisheng chubanshe, 1992).

69. Zhang Jiebin, *Leijing fuyi* (Appended supplement to *"The* Inner Classic *Explicated by Topic"*) (1624; reprinted in *SKQS*), *juan* 1.

70. Ibid., 1:8a–b.

71. My discussion of medical judgment relies on Charlotte Furth, "Producing Medical Knowledge through Cases: History, Evidence, Action," in *Thinking with Cases,* edited by Furth, Judith T. Zeitlin, and Ping-chen Hsiung (Honolulu: University of Hawai'i Press, 2007), 143–45.

72. See Chang Chia-feng, "Dispersing the Foetal Toxin of the Body: Conceptions of Smallpox Aetiology in Pre-Modern China," in *Contagion: Perspectives from Pre-Modern Societies,* ed. Lawrence I. Conrad and Dominik Wujastyk (Aldershot, U.K.: Ashgate, 2000); and Chang Chia-feng, "Shenghua zhi yuan yu

liming zhi men: Jin Yuan Ming yixue zhong de 'mingmen' shitan" (The gate of life: The conceptions of *mingmen* in traditional Chinese medicine in the Jin, Yuan, and Ming periods), *Xin shixue* 9, no. 3 (1998): 1–48.

73. See the thirty-sixth difficult issue. This description also appears in the thirty-ninth difficult issue. My translation here is adapted from Unschuld, trans. and annot., *Nan-ching*, 382–86 and 399–402.

74. For different interpretations of the triple burner through time, see ibid., thirty-first difficult issue, 347–57. For a discussion of the belief that the triple burner "has a name but no form," see also the thirty-eighth difficult issue, 394–98.

75. Zhang, *Leijing fuyi*, 3:1b.

76. Ibid., 3:5b.

77. Ibid., 3:6a–8a. Besides citing the *Huangting jing* (Scripture of the Yellow Court), Zhang also quotes a commentary to this work by Bai Lizhong (also known as Liangqiuzi, fl. 729). Other authors and works that he cites include Zhao Yizhen (d. 1382, also known as Yuanyangzi); and Chen Zhixu (1289—after 1335, also known as Shangyangzi), *Jindan dayao* (Essentials of golden cinnabar). All of these authors were also included in the *Zhengtong Daozang* (Daoist Canon, compiled during the Zhengtong reign). For more information on these authors and their works, see the discussions of them scattered through the essays in Livia Kohn, ed., *Daoism Handbook* (Leiden: Brill, 2004), especially Fabrizio Pregadio and Lowell Skar, "Inner Alchemy," 466–97. Isabelle Robinet also discusses Chen Zixiu and inner alchemy in *Taoism: Growth of a Religion*, trans. Phyllis Brooks (Stanford: Stanford University Press, 1997), 225–27.

78. Robinet, *Taoism*, chap. 8, esp. 216–18.

79. Ibid., 219.

80. Zhang, *Leijing fuyi* 3:7a–b.

81. Ibid.

82. The *guanyuan* point was three *cun* below the umbilicus, and the *qihai* point was one *cun* below the umbilicus. See Zhang Jiebin, *Leijing tuyi* (Illustrated supplement to "*The* Inner Classic *Explicated by Topic*") (1624; reprinted in SKQS), 8:30b–33a.

83. Ibid., 3:60a.

84. A comprehensive study of diagrams used for internal visualization is Catherine Despeux, *Taoïsme et corps humain: Le xiuzhen tu* (Paris: Guy Tredaniel, 1994).

85. Zhang, *Leijing fuyi*, 3:8b.

86. Ibid., 3:7b.

87. The *LHML* identifies thirty-two distinct Ming and Qing editions of Li's *Yizong bi du* produced before 1900. See, for example, Li Zhongzi, *Yizong bi du* (Essential readings in medical learning) (1637; modern critical edition reprinted in *Li Zhongzi yixue quanshu* [The complete medical works of Li Zhongzi], ed. Bao Laifa et al., Beijing: Zhongguo zhongyiyao chubanshe, 1999), 88.

88. *YZJJ*, 45:25b–26b.

89. I have adopted the translation of *girdle discharges* from Sabine Wilms, "The Female Body in Medieval China" (PhD diss., University of Arizona, 2002).

90. *YZJJ*, 44:1a–2a. Emphasis added.

91. Ibid., 44:2a–b.

92. Ibid., 44:4a–5a. The concept of the "three causes" was famously elaborated in Chen Yan's *Sanyin jiyi bingzheng fang lun* (Treatise on the manifestations and treatment of diseases caused by the three factors) (comp. 1174; reprinted in *SKQS*) and became one of the many schema that doctors used to classify diseases.

93. Ibid., 44:4a–b, quoting the *Inner Classic*.

94. Ibid.

95. Song, *Xiyuan jilu*, 63. In his notes to this translation, McKnight notes that "it seems highly probable that such deaths followed attempted abortions."

96. Sun, *Beiji qianjin yaofang*, 2:1b.

97. Chen, *Furen daquan liangfang*, 13.

98. Wan Quan, *Guangsi jiyao* (Essentials of fecundity), as quoted in *GJTS*, 404:55439. A native of Luotian County in Hubei Province, Wan Quan was a county degree holder descended from a medical family with a transmitted expertise in pediatric diseases. While modern biographical dictionaries also label Wan Quan a specialist in pediatrics, he clearly saw himself as possessing broad qualifications, writing medical works on cold damage disorders, nurturing life *(yangsheng)*, multiplying descendants *(guangsi)*, and women's diseases, as well as pediatrics. *LDYJ*, 2:802–3. For Wan Quan's extant medical works, see *LHML*.

99. Xiao Xun was one of the skeptics. *Nüke jinglun*, 2:12. Chen Nianzu, however, was among many who repeated the conventional wisdom that "on the seventh day [after menses], the womb is already closed and even if sexual relations occur she will not conceive." *Nüke yaozhi* (Essentials of medicine for women) (comp. 1803; first ed. 1841; reprinted in *Chen Xiuyuan yishu qishi'er zhong* [The medical books of Chen Xiuyuan, seventy-two titles], Shanghai: Shanghai Shudian, 1988), 1:483.

100. *YZJJ*, 45:14a

101. Xu, *Yixue yuanliu lun*, 2:43a–b.

102. For Zhang Ji and Song dynasty medicine, see Asaf Goldschmidt, "The Transformations of Chinese Medicine during the Northern Song Dynasty (A.D. 960–1127): The Integration of Three Past Medical Approaches into a Comprehensive Medical System Following a Wave of Epidemics" (PhD diss., University of Pennsylvania, 1999).

103. Yüan-ling Chao, "Lineages and Schools: Zhang Zhongjing and *Sidajia* in Ming and Qing" (paper presented at the Tenth International Conference on the History of Science in East Asia, Shanghai, China, 2002).

104. Zhang Ji, *Jinkui yaolue* (Essentials of the golden cabinet) (ca. 200 C.E.; reprinted in *Zhongyi ba da jingdian quanzhu* [The eight great classics of Chinese medicine, complete and annotated], ed. Shang Zhijun and Zhai Shuangqing, Beijing: Huaxia chubanshe, 1994), 392. My interpretation relies heavily also on Xu, *Jinkui yaolue lunzhu*, and Zhongguo zhongyi yanjiu yuan, ed., *Jinkui yaolue yuyi* ("The Essentials of the Golden Cabinet," translated into modern Chinese) (Beijing: Renmin weisheng chubanshe, 1959).

105. Xu, *Jinkui yaolue lunzhu*, 22:8a–9b.

106. See the editorial synopsis *(tiyao)* of this work at the beginning of the *SKQS* edition of Zhu, ed., *Puji fang*. The work is 426 *juan* long.

107. Ibid., 331:2a.

108. *YZJJ*, 45:7a.

109. Ibid.

110. Ibid., 45:7b–8a. White ooze was conceptualized as corrupted female essence, produced as a result of frustrated female desire.

111. Ibid., 45:8b–9a

112. Zhongyi dacidian bianji weiyuanhui, ed., *Zhongyi dacidian: Fuke erke fence* (Comprehensive dictionary of Chinese medicine: Volume on gynecology and pediatrics) (Beijing: Renmin weisheng chubanshe, 1981), 149.

113. See, for example, Chen, *Furen daquan liangfang*, 401; and Xu Dachun, *Lantai guifan* (Standard criteria of the orchid dais) (1764; reprinted in *SKQS*), *juan* 8.

114. Xu, *Jinkui yaolue lunzhu*, 22:8a–9b.

115. *YZJJ*, 45:13a–b. The illness term *zheng* was written with the word for "evidence" *(zheng)* coupled with the illness radical, whereas the term *jia* consisted of a word meaning "false" coupled with the illness radical. The standard etymological explanation was that *zheng* accumulations had a "verifiable" shape, whereas *jia* accumulations did not.

116. The character for *gu* is composed of the character *chong* (bug, worm, noxious creature) repeated three times over the character *min* (dish, plate). Frédéric Obringer has studied one of the best-known meanings of *gu*, which refers to a kind of poison manufactured by distilling the vile essences of noxious insects. *L'aconit et l'orpiment: Drogues et poisons en Chine ancienne et médiévale* (Paris: Fayard, 1997). In the medical literature, however, the term *gu* is also regularly used to refer to various forms of abdominal distention, appearing in compounds such as qi *gu*, water *gu*, Blood *gu*, and stony *gu*. Within discussions of female diseases, furthermore, it is not uncommon for "Blood *gu*" to appear in lists of conditions linked to pathological accumulations of Blood. For examples, see Chen, *Furen daquan liangfang*, 62, 652–53.

117. For the discussion of "food *zheng*" and "Blood *zheng*" see *YZJJ*, 45:14b–15a.

118. Ibid., 45:17b.

119. Ibid., 45:17b, 18b–19a.

120. See, for example, Zhang, *Jingyue quanshu*, 38:2b–4a; and *YZJJ*, 44:2b–3a.

121. Li Gao, *Lanshi micang* (Stored secrets from the orchid chamber) (comp. thirteenth century; first ed. 1276; reprinted in *SKQS*), 3:68a. Li Gao's original comment appeared in a discussion of the causes of skin eruptions and rashes in children, but later works regularly integrated it into explanations of promoting fertility and conception. See, for example, Zhu, *Gezhi yulun*, 26–27; Xiao, *Nüke jinglun*, 2:10.

122. Sun, *Yizhi xuyu*, 2:12a. For some reason, when Xiao Xun quotes this teaching he attributes it to Wang Kentang, but I have not been able to find it in Wang's work. The association with Wang may also suggest that this saying had become sufficiently well known that people had grown careless about its attribution. See Xiao, *Nüke jinglun*, 2:5.

123. *YZJJ*, 44:2a–b.

124. For Ming-Qing authors who cited Zhu's teaching that fat women suf-

fered from blocked-up wombs, see Wu Zhiwang, *Jiyin gangmu* (A comprehensive guide to benefiting yin) (1620; modern critical edition by Li Mingjian et al. of 1620 woodblock edition published Beijing: Renmin weisheng chubanshe, 1996), 334, 338–39; Xiao, *Nüke jinglun*, 2:8–9; and Chen, *Nüke yaozhi*, 1:482.

125. The quotation appears in *YZJJ*, 44:2a–b.

126. The earliest medical example of this citation that I have found dates from the seventh century. See Chao, *Chaoshi zhubing yuanhou lun*, 41a.

127. Zhu Zhenheng, attrib., *Jinkui gouxuan* (Drawing out the subtleties of the *Golden Cabinet*), comp. Dai Yuanli (comp. between 1368 and 1398; modern critical edition of Shenxiu tang woodblock edition of the Ming, published in Zhu Zhenheng, *Danxi yiji* [The collected medical works of Danxi] Beijing: Renmin weisheng chubanshe, 1993), 160.

128. Chao, *Chaoshi zhubing yuanhou lun*, 41:11b–12a.

129. Jiang Guan, *Mingyi lei'an* (Cases from famous doctors, arranged by category) (comp. 1549; first ed. 1591; annot. Wei Zhixiu and republished by Bao Tingbo in 1770; reprint, Taipei: Hongye shuju, 1994), 11:331. The name of the doctor in this case is not specified. Jiang's book lists it soon after a case attributed to Zhu Zhenheng, which seems to suggest that it might come from Zhu, but none of Zhu's extant works include this narrative. Since Jiang made a point of naming his sources when he cited cases from other authors, and since he also included some of his own cases in this work, the most reasonable conclusion is that this case comes from Jiang's own medical practice.

130. Yan Chunxi, *Taichan xinfa* (Essential teachings on childbearing) (comp. ca. 1725; author's preface dated 1730; modern critical edition of Yongzheng-era woodblock edition by Tian Daihua and Guo Junshuang, reprinted in *Nüke jiyao, taichan xinfa*, Beijing: Renmin weisheng chubanshe, 1988), 290. The term *zhenqi*, literally "genuine qi" had two main referents. One was the prenatal or "original" qi with which a person was endowed at conception *(yuanqi)*. The other, less common usage, was the "orthopathic" qi *(zhengqi)* that protected and nourished the body—that is, the opposite of the heteropathic qi *(xieqi)* that provoked illness. I have chosen the translation "fundamental qi" as a way of semantically suggesting both interpretations without favoring either. For ancient glosses of this term, see *Hanyu dacidian*, 2:147, and Xie, *Zhongguo yixue dacidian*, 2:2237.

131. Chen Shiduo, *Shishi milu* (Secret records of the stone chamber), as quoted in the section on infertility in *GJTS*, 404:55440–41.

132. Chen's concern with the belt vessel appears to derive from an older model of female bodily function. For a discussion of how Song doctors envisioned the link between different vessels and female gestational vitality, see Furth, *Flourishing Yin*, 75.

133. While anatomical descriptions from medical texts of the first and second centuries B.C.E. show that human dissection was not unknown in ancient China, there was never anything resembling the European culture of dissection, where doctors, natural scientists, and artists actively sought to view and document the physical structures that lay hidden under the human skin. For a discussion of the anatomical descriptions in the *Huangdi neijing suwen*, see Ilza Veith, *Huang-ti Nei-ching: The Yellow Emperor's Classic of Internal Medicine*,

new ed. (1956; reprint, Berkeley: University of California Press, 1972); Unschuld, *Huang Di Nei Jing Su Wen;* and Li, *Si sheng zhi yu.*

134. Manfred Porkert, *The Theoretical Foundations of Chinese Medicine: Systems of Correspondence* (Cambridge, Mass.: MIT Press, 1974), 107.

135. Nathan Sivin, "Why Didn't the Chinese Have Bodies?" *Chinese Studies Association of Australia Newsletter* (University of New South Wales, Sydney) (November 18, 1999): 1–5.

136. *Lingshu jing,* 10:11b–12b. The Han dynasty philosopher Dong Zhongshu (ca. 179–104 B.C.E.) even used this correspondence to argue that humans were the noblest of all life-forms. *Chunqiu fanlu,* translated in Patricia Ebrey, ed., *Chinese Civilization: A Sourcebook,* 2nd ed. (New York: Free Press, 1993), 58.

137. Arranging information according to body parts was in fact the standard format in treatises on "skin and flesh diseases" (*waike,* literally "external" diseases). For a typical example, see the *YZJJ.* But this classificatory schema was also used in a more general way, as in Bao Xiang'ao, *Yanfang xinbian* (A new compilation of tested prescriptions) (first ed. 1846; expanded and ed. Mei Qizhao, [Hangzhou]: Zhejiang sheng cheng dongbizhai kezidian, 1878; modern critical edition reprint, Beijing: Renmin weisheng chubanshe, 1990). Charlotte Furth has also documented this format being used in medical case collections. "Producing Medical Knowledge through Cases: History, Evidence, Action," in *Thinking with Cases,* edited by Furth, Judith T. Zeitlin, and Ping-chen Hsiung (Honolulu: University of Hawai'i Press, 2007).

138. Unschuld, trans. and annot., *Nan-ching,* 395–98. See the thirty-second and forty-first difficult issues.

139. According to Lesley Dean-Jones, "Menstrual blood is the linchpin of both the Hippocratic and the Aristotelian theories on how women differed from men. Whether a woman was healthy, diseased, pregnant, or nursing, in Classical Greece her body was defined scientifically in terms of blood-hydraulics." *Women's Bodies in Classical Greek Science* (Oxford: Clarendon Press, 1994), 225.

140. Ibid., 55–58.

4. AN UNCERTAIN HARVEST

1. The account of his wife's miscarriages is found in Chen Nianzu, *Nüke yaozhi* (Essentials of medicine for women). The text was originally compiled in 1803, and the earliest printed version was published in 1841 with annotations by Chen's sons and grandsons. I have used the edition reprinted in *Chen Xiuyuan yishu qishi'er zhong* (The medical books of Chen Xiuyuan, seventy-two titles) (Shanghai: Shanghai shudian, 1988), 492. While Chen does not tell us the date of this case, it would have been in or before 1792, the year he received his *juren* degree. And while the original case does not give the name of Chen Nianzu's wife, Ms. Huang's name and identity is provided in the county gazetteer for Changle County, where she is listed among the rolls of "chaste and filial" women. Meng Zhaohan, ed., *Minguo Changle xianzhi* (Republican-era gazetteer of Changle County) (1917, reprint Shanghai: Shanghai shudian chubanshe, 2000), 29 *(shang):* 26b. For other biographical information on Chen Nianzu, see Meng,

ed., *Minguo Changle xianzhi* 14 *(shang):* 66b; 14 *(xia):* 35a; 24:26a. See also *LDYJ,* 2:454–56.

2. *Qingshi gao* (Draft history of the Qing dynasty) (1927; reprint, Beijing: Zhonghua shuju, 1977), 502:13872.

3. While atractylodes itself is a warming and qi-replenishing drug, medical convention regarded this particular combination of herbs as a cooling formula, with the active ingredient being the fire-dispersing ingredient scutellaria. An important eighteenth-century reference to Zhu Zhenheng's use of this drug combination for securing the fetus is *GJTS,* 405:55458.

4. Chen, *Nüke yaozhi,* 492.

5. Ibid.

6. According to modern laboratory findings, atractylodes, scutellaria, psoralea fruit, eucommia bark, and lovage all have hypotensive, vasodilative, or sedative properties, while scutellaria, psoralea, and lovage additionally demonstrate antibacterial or antiviral properties. See Dan Bensky and Andrew Gamble, *Chinese Herbal Medicine: Materia Medica,* rev. ed. (Seattle: Eastland Press, 1993); Hong-yen Hsu et al., *Oriental Materia Medica: A Concise Guide* (Long Beach, Calif.: Oriental Healing Arts Institute, 1986).

7. This discussion of assessing true and false pregnancy is closely adapted from Yi-Li Wu, "Ghost Fetuses, False Pregnancies, and the Parameters of Medical Uncertainty in Classical Chinese Gynecology," *Nan Nü: Men, Women, and Gender in Early and Imperial China* 4, no. 2 (2002): 170–206. My thanks to Brill for allowing me permission to reuse this material.

8. *YZJJ,* 46:1a.

9. For a typical example, see ibid., 46:17a–b.

10. For the original text with modern and ancient commentaries, see Shandong zhongyi xueyuan and Hebei yixue yuan, eds., *Huangdi neijing suwen jiaoshi* (The *Yellow Emperor's Inner Classic, Basic Questions,* annotated and explicated) (Beijing: Renmin weisheng chubanshe, 1993).

11. Ibid., 509–22.

12. Ibid., 121. Various commentators advanced different interpretations of what the "yin" and "yang" referred to, but they agreed that this pulse was marked by unusual forcefulness.

13. Shandong zhongyi xueyuan and Hebei yixue yuan, *Huangdi neijing suwen jiaoshi,* 252. There was some discrepancy between different editions of the classic, but the most frequently cited version explained that, "in women, if the Hand Lesser Yin meridian moves in an extreme way, then she is pregnant." Later writers argued that this phrase should be properly understood as referring to both the Foot Lesser Yin and Hand Lesser Yin meridians. For a seventeenth-century discussion of the debates, see Xiao Xun (fl. ca. 1660), *Nüke jinglun* (Canonical teachings on medicine for women) (1684; modern punctuated edition published Shanghai: Shanghai weisheng chubanshe, 1957), 2:29.

14. Chao Yuanfang, *Chaoshi zhubing yuanhou lun* (Master Chao's treatise on the origins and manifestations of the myriad diseases) (comp. 610; rev. 1026–27; ed. Wang Jichuan and Fang Kuang [Ming]; reprinted in *SKQS*), 41:1a–5b.

15. Chen Ziming, *Furen daquan liangfang* (Comprehensive compendium of good formulas for women) (comp. 1237; rev. ca. 1265; modern critical edition

of Yuan dynasty Qinyou shutang edition by Yu Ying'ao et al., Beijing: Renmin weisheng chubanshe, 1992), 319–21.

16. Ibid., 322. See also Wei Yilin (1277–1347), *Shiyi dexiao fang* (Efficacious prescriptions from a hereditary medical family) (1337; reprinted in *SKQS*), 14:6b,

17. Wang Kentang, *Zhengzhi zhunsheng* (Guidelines for treating illness) (comp. ca. 1597–1607, reprinted in *SKQS*), 64:29b–30b. This work was also frequently referred to as *Liuke zhengzhi zhusheng* (Guidelines for treating illnesses in six subdivisions) because it comprised six distinct component works, for which I have used the dates of completion cited by the editors of the SKQS. Wang's work on women's medicine was completed in 1607 and also circulated separately under the name *Nüke zhengzhi zhunsheng* (Guidelines for treating women's illnesses).

18. Ibid., 64:29b–30b.

19. Wu Zhiwang, *Jiyin gangmu* (A comprehensive guide to benefiting yin) (1620; modern critical edition by Li Mingjian et al. of 1620 woodblock edition published Beijing: Renmin weisheng chubanshe, 1996), 368.

20. Wang, *Zhengzhi zhunsheng*, 64:29b–30b.

21. Yan Chunxi, *Taichan xinfa* (Essential teachings on childbearing) (comp. ca. 1725; author's preface dated 1730; modern critical edition of Yongzheng-era woodblock edition by Tian Daihua and Guo Junshuang, reprinted in *Nüke jiyao, taichan xinfa*, Beijing: Renmin weisheng chubanshe, 1988), 176–77.

22. Ibid.

23. See, for example, Chen, *Furen daquan liangfang*, 322.

24. Wu, *Jiyin gangmu*, 239.

25. *YZJJ*, 45:28b.

26. The earliest chemical test for pregnancy that measured hormone levels in a woman's urine was developed in 1928. See Michael J. O'Dowd and Elliot E. Phillipp, *The History of Obstetrics and Gynaecology* (New York: Parthenon, 1994), 86; and Harold Speert, *Obstetrical and Gynecologic Milestones Illustrated* (New York: Parthenon, 1996), 222–27.

27. Recent studies of the independent identity of the fetus and its gendered social implications notably include Lynn M. Morgan and Meredith W. Michaels, eds., *Fetal Subjects, Feminist Positions* (Philadelphia: University of Pennsylvania Press, 1999). Advertisements for intrauterine fetal "portraits" also routinely appear in magazines aimed at expectant parents. For reportage on this modern phenomenon, see Sam Lubell, "The Womb as Photo Studio," *New York Times*, September 23, 2004; and Marc Santora, "Fetal Photos: Keepsake or Health Risk?" *New York Times*, May 14, 2004, both at www.nyt.com, accessed January 5, 2007.

28. My ideas on the historicity of the fetus draw heavily on the works of Barbara Duden. See her *The Woman beneath the Skin: A Doctor's Patients in Eighteenth-Century Germany*, trans. Thomas Dunlap (Cambridge, Mass.: Harvard University Press, 1991), especially 160–70; *Disembodying Women: Perspectives on Pregnancy and the Unborn*, trans. Lee Hoinacki (Cambridge, Mass.: Harvard University Press, 1993); "The Fetus on the 'Farther Shore': Toward a History of the Unborn," in *Fetal Subjects, Feminist Positions*, ed. Lynn M. Morgan and Meredith W. Michaels (Philadelphia: University of Pennsylvania Press, 1999), 13–25; and "The History of Security in the Knowledge of Pregnancy" (seminar pa-

per delivered as part of "Women's Health: Historical Perspectives and Policy Dilemmas," lecture series at University of Michigan, Ann Arbor, March 19, 1999).

29. For example, the human ovum was not isolated until 1827, and it was only in 1840 that scientists confirmed that ovulation occurred monthly, rather than in response to coitus. O'Dowd and Phillipp, *History of Obstetrics*, 256–57. During the late nineteenth and early twentieth centuries, doctors also continued to debate whether ovulation and menstruation were causally linked. See Emil Novak, *Menstruation and Its Disorders* (New York: D. Appleton, 1921), 74–76.

30. James Blundell, *The Principles and Practice of Obstetrics* (London: E. Cox, 1834), quoted in Ann Oakley, *The Captured Womb: A History of the Medical Care of Pregnant Women* (Oxford: Basil Blackwell, 1984), 17.

31. The case appears in Xu Dachun, attrib., *Nüke yi'an* (Medical cases on medicine for women), which first appeared in *Xu Lingtai yishu quanji* (The complete medical works of Xu Dachun) a collection of sixteen works that was first printed in 1855. I have used a modern reprint of an 1893 edition; reprinted in *Xu Dachun yishu quanji* (Beijing: Renmin weisheng chubanshe, 1988), 2:1858. Although this collection of women's cases was attributed to Xu Dachun, it actually comprises cases from various anonymous and named doctors, including famous practitioners of the Jin through Ming dynasties such as Zhang Congzheng, Li Gao, and Wang Ji. The identity of the doctor in this case is not given, and I have not been able to find it in any other extant medical works. It is thus reasonable to assume that it represents the experiences of some nineteenth-century practitioner.

32. Chinese medical writers throughout the centuries noted cases of internal accumulations being mistaken for pregnancy and vice versa. See, for example, Zhang Congzheng, *Rumen shi qin* (How scholars serve their relatives) (comp. between 1224 and 1231; reprinted in *SKQS*), 8:7a–8a; Wei Zhixiu, *Xu mingyi lei'an* (A continuation of the *Cases from Famous Doctors, Arranged by Category*) (ca. 1770; reprinted in *SKQS*), 32:24a–25a; and Shen Yaofeng [Shen Youpeng], *Nüke jiyao* (Edited essentials of medicine for women) (comp. mid-eighteenth century; ed. and published by Wang Shixiong, 1850; modern critical edition by Li Guangwen, Huang Shuzhen, and Li Zhulan, published in *Nüke jiyao, taichan xinfa,* Beijing: Renmin weisheng chubanshe, 1988), 62. For a scholarly analysis of the similarities between blocked menses and true pregnancy and the implications of diagnostic ambiguity, see Francesca Bray, "A Deathly Disorder: Understanding Women's Health in Late Imperial China," in *Knowledge and the Scholarly Medical Traditions,* ed. Don Bates (Cambridge: Cambridge University Press, 1995).

33. Xiao Xun, for example, grouped intestinal spreading, stony accumulation, and ghost fetus together as three types of false pregnancies arising from stagnated qi or Blood, and warned that not only did they resemble pregnancy, but they also superficially resembled one another. *Nüke jinglun,* 4:37–38.

34. *Lingshu jing* (The Yellow Emperor's inner classic, divine pivot) (earliest published recension dated 1155; reprinted in *SKQS*), 9:1a–2a.

35. For details, see Wu, "Ghost Fetuses."

36. Duden, "The Fetus on the 'Farther Shore,'" 14.

37. *YZJJ,* 44:32a–b

38. For a fuller discussion, see Wu, "Ghost Fetuses."

39. Zhang, *Rumen shi qin,* 7:20a–b.

40. For examples, see Jiang Guan, *Mingyi lei'an* (Cases from famous doctors, arranged by category) (comp. 1549; first ed. 1591; annot. Wei Zhixiu and republished by Bao Tingbo in 1770; reprint, Taipei: Hongye shuju, 1994), 11:326; and Shen, *Nüke jiyao,* 43.

41. Chen, *Furen daquan liangfang,* 378–80.

42. The earliest discussion of this phenomenon that I have found is in Chao, *Chaoshi zhubing yuanhou lun,* 42:12a–b.

43. Quoted in Chen, *Furen daquan liangfang,* 463.

44. Lindsay Wilson, *Women and Medicine in the French Enlightenment: The Debate over* Maladies des Femmes (Baltimore: Johns Hopkins University Press, 1993), 59.

45. The "sleeping embryo" theory was cited by a Nigerian appeals court as one of several reasons it was overturning a lower court's sentence that an alleged adulteress be stoned to death. Somini Sengupta, "Facing Death for Adultery, Nigerian Woman Is Acquitted," *New York Times,* September 26, 2003, p. A3.

46. Laura Gowing, "Secret Births and Infanticide in Seventeenth-Century England," *Past and Present* 156, no. 1 (1997): 87–115.

47. Yu Tuan, *Yixue zheng chuan* (The orthodox transmission of medical learning) (1515; modern critical edition of 1604 Japanese reprint of 1531 woodblock ed., Shanghai: Huiwentang shuju, Republican period), 1:13a. A medical case involving a twenty-seven-month pregnancy appears in Wei, *Xu mingyi lei'an,* 32:25b:594.

48. Zhang Jiebin, *Jingyue quanshu* (The complete works of Jingyue) (comp. ca. 1624–40; reprinted in *SKQS*), 38:54a–55a. See Wu, *Jiyin gangmu,* 348–49.

49. Zhang, *Jingyue quanshu,* 38:55a.

50. Xiao, *Nüke jinglun,* 4:32–34.

51. Yan, *Taichan xinfa,* 287–88.

52. Ibid., 287.

53. See Wang Shixiong's commentary in Shen, *Nüke jiyao,* 57; and his commentary on the case from Qian Guobin in Wang Shixiong, ed., *Xu mingyi lei'an* (A continuation of the *Cases from Famous Doctors, Arranged by Category*), by Wei Zhixiu (editor's preface dated 1853, first published 1863; modern critical edition of Zhuyi tang woodblock edition of 1863 published Beijing: Renmin weisheng chubanshe, 1997), 24:750.

54. For a photograph of a mummified twin, see Samuel J. Cameron et al., *A Glasgow Manual of Obstetrics* (London: Edward Arnold & Company, 1924), 413–14. I thank Ronald Cyr for sharing with me his extensive collection of historical and contemporary images and articles on fetus papyraceous.

55. Yan, *Taichan xinfa,* 287–88.

56. See Wang Shixiong's commentary in Shen, *Nüke jiyao,* 71. Wang attributes this case to one "Xu Guqing." This may be a reference to Xu Ning, courtesy name Guqing, a Qing-era doctor from Anhui known for his skills in massage therapy. *LDYJ,* 2:536–537. Although we have few details about Xu himself, his case seems to have circulated widely in medical circles, for Yan Chunxi also cites a version of it. Yan, *Taichan xinfa,* 288.

57. A helpful analysis of plant metaphors in Chinese medicine is Shigehisa

Kuriyama, "Visual Knowledge in Classical Chinese Medicine," in *Knowledge and the Scholarly Medical Tradition,* ed. Don Bates, 205–34 (Cambridge: Cambridge University Press, 1995).

58. Yan, *Taichan xinfa,* 288.

59. Ibid.

60. Wei, *Xu mingyi lei'an,* 32:48b.

61. Matthew Sommer, "The Uses of Chastity: Sex, Law, and the Property of Widows in Qing China," *Late Imperial China* 17, no. 2 (1996): 116.

62. Quoted in Qian Yuanming, ed., *Jingshi baijia yilu* (Medicine-related passages from the Confucian classics, official histories, and writings of the hundred masters) (Guangzhou: Guangdong keji chubanshe, 1986), 728.

63. Wei, *Xu mingyi lei'an,* 32:49a. See also Charlotte Furth's discussion of the way in which the sixteenth-century physician Cheng Maoxian negotiated ambiguous pregnancies. *A Flourishing Yin: Gender in China's Medical History, 960–1665* (Berkeley: University of California Press, 1999), 255–256.

64. See, for example, the discussion in Fu Shan, attrib., *Fu Qingzhu nüke* (Fu Qingzhu's medicine for women) (preface dated 1827; published in *Fu Qingzhu nan, nüke* [Fu Qingzhu's medicine for men and medicine for women]; preface dated 1881; reprint, Shanghai: Qixin shuju, n.d.; facsimile reprint, Beijing: Zhongguo shudian, 1985), 1:7b.

65. Frédéric Obringer shows that early understandings of *gu* focused on afflictions from worms, winds, excessive heat, or the ghosts of dismembered criminals. By the fourth century, however, we find textual discussions of people deliberately manufacturing *gu* to poison or curse others, and by the seventh century the classic descriptions of how to manufacture *gu* with worms and insects were fully elaborated. *L'aconit et l'orpiment: Drogues et poisons en Chine ancienne et médiévale* (Paris: Fayard, 1997), 239–42.

66. The case appears in Zhou Hanqing's biography in *Mingshi* (History of the Ming dynasty) (1739; reprinted in *SKQS*), 299:6a–7a; and was also later anthologized in Wei, *Xu mingyi lei'an,* 32:48a.

67. Wang Lun, *Mingyi zazhu* (The writings of enlightened doctors on various topics) (1502), as quoted in *GJTS,* 406:55460.

68. Wei, *Shiyi dexiao fang,* 14:3a

69. Ibid.

70. Wang Haogu, courtesy name Haicang, as quoted in Xiao, *Nüke jinglun,* 4:27. For Wang's biographical information, see *LDYJ,* 1:79–81.

71. See, for example, the entry for *an* in the *Kangxi zidian* (Dictionary of the Kangxi reign) (1716; facsimile reprint Beijing: Zhonghua shuju, 1992).

72. Charlotte Furth, "Concepts of Pregnancy, Childbirth, and Infancy in Ch'ing Dynasty China," *Journal of Asian Studies* 46, no. 1 (1987): 13.

73. Zhang, *Jingyue quanshu,* 38:37b.

74. *Taichan mishu* (A secret book of childbearing) (Luo Ruilin woodblock edition, 1879, PU no. CM/25a/C538s2), 1:20b.

75. Wei, *Shiyi dexiao fang,* 14:11b.

76. Shen, *Nüke jiyao,* 69.

77. See Wang Shixiong's annotations in ibid., 71–72.

78. *Taichan mishu* (PU no. CM/25a/C538s2), 1:2a.

79. This description comes from a work titled the "Treatise on the Five Depot Organs" *(Wuzang lun)*, attributed to the famous Indian Buddhist doctor Jivaka (Chinese name Qipo). Paul Demiéville notes, however, that the content of this work appears to be entirely Chinese. "Byō," in *Hobogirin: Dictionnaire encyclopédique du bouddhisme d'après les sources chinoises et japonaises,* ed. Paul Demiéville (Tokyo: Maison franco-japonaise, 1929; reprint, Paris: Librairie d'Amérique et d'Orient, 1974), 263. Works attributed to Jivaka were already circulating in the Sui dynasty, and a formula attributed to him was included in Sun Simiao's *Beiji qianjin yaofang.* However, the earliest mention I have found of the "Treatise on Five Depot Organs" is Wang Yaochen et al., *Chongwen zongmu* (Bibliographic catalog of the Academy for Veneration of Literature) (1041; reprinted in *SKQS*), 7:11a; and the earliest extant citation of this description of gestation that I have been able to locate is Chen, *Furen daquan liangfang,* 304. For a discussion of Indian influence on Chinese medicine, see Li Jingwei and Lin Zhaogeng, eds., *Zhongguo yixue tongshi, gudai juan* (A comprehensive history of Chinese medicine: The ancient period) (Beijing: Renmin weisheng chubanshe, 2000), 286–87; Paul U. Unschuld, *Medicine in China: A History of Ideas* (Berkeley: University of California Press, 1986), chap. 6.

80. *GJTS*, 405:55452.

81. See, for example, Shen, *Nüke jiyao,* 68–69; and *Taichan mishu* (PU no. CM/25a/C538s2), 1:3a.

82. A notable example is Li Chan's discussion of *taidong,* quoted in the *GJTS* section on pregnancy, 405:55462. For the original, see Li Chan, *Yixue rumen* (An introduction to medicine) (1575; modern edition of 1575 woodblock edition reprinted in *Zhonghua yishu jicheng* [Collection of Chinese Medical Books], vol. 26, Beijing: Zhongyi guji chubanshe, 1999), 537. See also *Taichan mishu* (PU no. CM/25a/C538s2), 1:5a.

83. *YZJJ*, 23:3b, citing a commentary by "Master Fang." I have not been able to identify the original author.

84. Wang, *Mingyi zazhu,* as quoted in *GJTS*, 406:55460.

85. Pan Wei, *Nüke yaolue* (Essential outline of medicine for women), in *Weiyuan yixue liu zhong* (Six medical works from Weiyuan) (Hubei Fanshu woodblock edition, 1877).

86. *Taichan mishu* (PU no. CM/25a/C538s2), 1:1a.

87. *YZJJ*, 45:30b–31a.

88. An example of such concerns is Yan Yonghe, *Jisheng fang* (Prescriptions for benefiting life) (comp. 1253), as quoted in *GJTS*, 405:55456–57.

89. Sun Yikui, *Yizhi xuyu* (Additional discussions on the meaning of medicine) (1573; reprinted in SKQS), 2:12a–b. This passage was also included in Xiao's *Nüke jinglun,* 2:5, although Xiao attributes the quotation to Wang Kentang.

90. Wan Quan, *Furen mike* (Secrets of medicine for women) (1549), as quoted in *GJTS*, 404:55440.

91. Chen Shiduo, *Shishi milu* (Secret records from the stone room) (1687), as quoted in *GJTS*, 404:55441.

92. Chen, *Nüke yaozhi,* 1:486. The use of political metaphors—sovereigns, ministers, emissaries—to describe the hierarchical importance of drugs in a formula dates from the *Huangdi neijing.* Unschuld translates *shi* as "aide." See *Med-*

icine in China: A History of Ideas, 115. I have chosen a more politically literal translation of *shi,* however, following Hucker's translation of the term as "sent as a representative," or more broadly, a centrally dispatched "commissioner." Charles O. Hucker, *A Dictionary of Official Titles in Imperial China* (Stanford: Stanford University Press, 1985).

93. Chen, *Shishi milu,* as quoted in *GJTS,* 404:55441.

94. Ibid.

95. Numerous examples of such formulas can be found among the fertility formulas collected in the *GJTS.* Out of forty-two formulas, thirteen are described as directly correcting some pathology of the womb, and in most cases the perceived problem is coldness in the womb. *GJTS,* 404:55441–47.

96. Zhu Zhenheng, *Gezhi yulun* (Additional discourses on extending knowledge through the investigation of things) (comp. ca. 1347; modern edition of Yuan dynasty woodblock edition, reprinted in Zhu Zhenheng, *Danxi yiji* [The collected medical works of Danxi], Beijing: Renmin weisheng chubanshe, 1993), 33.

97. Ibid., 24. For the original passage from Chao, see *Chaoshi zhubing yuanhou lun,* 41:11b–12a.

98. Zhu, *Gezhi yulun,* 24.

99. See, for example, the citations of Zhu Zhenheng that appear in the *fuke* sections of the *GJTS.*

100. Xu Dachun, *Yixue yuanliu lun* (Treatise on the origins of medical learning) (1757; reprinted in *SKQS*), 2:44a.

101. Charlotte Furth, "Blood, Body, and Gender: Medical Images of the Female Condition in China," *Chinese Science* 7 (1986): 48–51; Angela Ki Che Leung, "Autour de la naissance: La mère et l'enfant en Chine aux XIVe et XVIIe siècles," *Cahiers internationaux de sociologie* 76 (1984): 51–69.

102. The late fifteenth- and sixteenth-century preoccupation with male self-restraint and the dangers of sexual incontinence is well documented in Furth, *Flourishing Yin,* chap. 6; and Joanna Grant, *A Chinese Physician: Wang Ji and the "Stone Mountain Medical Case Histories"* (London: RoutledgeCurzon, 2003), chap. 4.

5. "BORN LIKE A LAMB"

1. The events of this case are based on the account in Jizhai jushi [Ye Feng], *Dasheng bian* (Treatise on easy childbirth) (1715; Du Fei, ed., 1727; reprinted with preface dated 1767 in *Yilin zhiyue* [Pointing the moon out to doctors], ed. Wang Qi, Hangzhou: Baohu lou woodblock edition; in the library of the Zhongguo zhongyi kexue yuan), 13a–b. I have reconstructed the approximate date of events based on Ye's comment that the child in question was already eight *sui* (approximately seven years old) at the time he recorded this story, which would have been no later than 1715.

2. Ye Feng describes the father-in-law only as "His Excellency Zhang [Zhang Gong], native of Huoshan and former *qing* of the Court of the Imperial Stud *[taipu].*" According to Charles Hucker, the term *qing* can refer to either a chief minister or vice minister. *A Dictionary of Official Titles in Imperial China* (Stan-

ford: Stanford University Press, 1985). The clues we have allow us to identify Zhang Baohua's father as Zhang Sunzhen, a native of Huoshan and *jinshi* of 1628 who held the position of vice minister *(shao qing)* of the Court of the Imperial Stud and that of imperial censor charged with overseeing Shanxi Province. For Zhang Sunzhen's degrees, titles, and official positions, see Gan Shan et al., eds., *Huoshan xianzhi* (Gazetteer of Huoshan County) (1776; reprint, Taipei: Chengwen chubanshe, 1985), 6 (pt. 4): 1a; and Jueluo shilin, ed., *Shanxi tongzhi* (Gazetteer of Shanxi Province) (1734; reprinted in SKQS): 79:68a.

3. Sarah Bunney, "On the Origins of the Midwife," *New Scientist* (May 22, 1993): 18.

4. For the original quotation in context, see Richard John Lynn, trans., *The Classic of Changes: A New Translation of the I Ching as Interpreted by Wang Bi* (New York: Columbia University Press, 1994), 77. My translation and interpretation of the quotation rely on Lynn and on Victor Mair, trans., *The Tao Te Ching* (New York: Bantam Books, 1990), 130–35.

5. Jizhai jushi, *Dasheng bian,* 1:4a.

6. Ibid.

7. Liu Xiaogan, "An Inquiry into the Core Value of Laozi's Philosophy," in *Religious and Philosophical Aspects of the Laozi*, ed. Mark Csikszentmihalyi and Philip J. Ivanhoe (Albany: State University of New York Press, 1999). The quotations here all come from Liu, 232–33.

8. Jizhai jushi, *Dasheng bian,* 1:4b.

9. Bernhard Karlgren, trans., *The Book of Odes* (Stockholm: Museum of Far Eastern Antiquities, 1950), 200–201.

10. David R. Knechtges, "Questions about the Language of *Sheng min,*" in *Ways with Words: Writing about Reading Texts from Early China*, ed. Pauline Yu, Peter Bol, Stephen Owen, and Willard Peterson (Berkeley: University of California Press, 2000), 22.

11. Karlgren presents an alternate interpretation by glossing this line as: "the first-born then came forth." *Book of Odes,* 200–201. The issue of how to gloss *da* continues to occupy scholars today. Stephen Owen, "Interpreting *Sheng min,*" in *Ways with Words: Writing about Reading Texts from Early China*, ed. Pauline Yu, Peter Bol, Stephen Owen, and Willard Peterson (Berkeley: University of California Press, 2000), 28–29. The majority of interpreters, however, continue to gloss *da* as "lamb."

12. Jizhai jushi, preface dated 1715, *Dasheng bian.*

13. Zhu Zhenheng, *Gezhi yulun,* 25.

14. Zhang Jiebin, *Jingyue quanshu* (The complete works of Jingyue) (comp. ca. 1624–40; reprinted in *SKQS*), 61:14a–b.

15. Jizhai jushi, *Dasheng bian,* 1:10b.

16. "Da yi" (main meaning), in Jizhai jushi, *Dasheng bian,* 1:1a (paginated separately).

17. For the history of this text, see the modern editors' introduction to Chen Ziming, *Furen daquan liangfang* (Comprehensive compendium of good formulas for women) (comp. 1237; revised ca. 1265; modern critical edition of Yuan dynasty Qinyou shutang edition by Yu Ying'ao et al., Beijing: Renmin weisheng

chubanshe, 1992); and Charlotte Furth, *A Flourishing Yin: Gender in China's Medical History, 960–1665* (Berkeley: University of California Press, 1999), chap. 2.

18. As quoted in Chen, *Furen daquan liangfang,* 441–42. Zan Yin was a physician active during the Dazhong reign of the Tang dynasty (847–59). Later writers routinely described Zan Yin's *Childbirth Treasury* as a foundational work of medicine for women. See, for example, Chen Ziming's own preface to *Furen daquan liangfang,* as well as the editorial description that opens the *SKQS* edition of Chen Ziming's work. Although Zan Yin's original text was lost in China after the Song dynasty, *fuke* texts continued to cite extant passages from the book. During the nineteenth century, a Japanese copy of what was determined to be a Northern Song edition was brought back to China and widely reprinted. See Okanishi Tameto, *Song yiqian yiji kao* (Research on medical works before the Song dynasty) (Taipei: Guting shuwu, 1969), 3:1080; *YJDCD,* 2:833.

19. Shandong zhongyi xueyuan and Hebei yixue yuan, eds., *Huangdi neijing suwen jiaoshi* (The *Yellow Emperor's Inner Classic, Basic Questions,* annotated and explicated) (Beijing: Renmin weisheng chubanshe, 1993), 1–50.

20. Chen, *Furen daquan liangfang,* 461.

21. One standard account dates the *Shichan lun* to 1098, while other sources suggest that Yang lived during the Southern Song dynasty (1127–79); depending on his longevity, however, these are not necessarily mutually exclusive claims. For additional details on Yang's elusive biography, see He Shixi, *Zhongguo lidai yijia zhuanlu* (Biographical records of medical experts throughout Chinese history) (Beijing: Renmin weisheng chubanshe, 1991), 3:34–35; Okanishi, *Song yiqian yiji kao,* 1086–87; and Furth, *Flourishing Yin,* 117–19.

22. Quoted in Chen, *Furen daquan liangfang,* 463. Although one might also translate *zhengchan* as "normal labor," I prefer "correct" because Yang Zijian's overall concern is to elucidate "correct" versus "incorrect" permutations of labor, rather than "normal" versus "abnormal" forms.

23. Ibid., 461.

24. Ibid.

25. While Chen Ziming's text does not detail why a chaotic birthing environment will cause difficult labor, his contemporary and later readers would have been familiar with explanations like that given by Xu Shuwei (1079–ca. 1154): "If there is a case of childbirth where the child has not come down for several days, and taking birth-expediting medicines has not been effective, this is definitely due to sitting on the grass too early, so that the heart became frightened and qi congealed and did not circulate. The *Classic* says: Fear causes qi to descend and essence to become timid. When it becomes timid, then the Upper Burner closes up. When it closes up, then qi returns. When it returns, then the Lower Burner becomes distended, and then the qi does not circulate." Quoted in Xiao Xun, *Nüke jinglun* (Canonical teachings on medicine for women) (1684; modern punctuated edition published Shanghai: Shanghai weisheng chubanshe, 1957), 5:3.

26. Quoted in Chen, *Furen daquan liangfang,* 441.

27. Ibid., 443.

28. Furth, *Flourishing Yin,* chap. 3.

29. Jizhai jushi, preface, *Dasheng bian.*

30. Jizhai jushi, *Dasheng bian*, 1:4a.

31. The idea that secret births were always easy appears as early as Wang Tao's (ca. 670–755) *Waitai biyao* (Secret essentials from the imperial palace), which also explains this phenomenon in terms of birth being left alone to follow its own rhythms. Like the later Song dynasty texts, however, such affirmations of birth's innate ease were subordinated to a larger discourse of danger and pollution, and "doctors, households, and birth assistants were all deeply convinced that childbirth involved supernatural forces." See Jen-der Lee, "Childbirth in Early Imperial China," in *Medicine for Women in Imperial China,* ed. Angela Ki Che Leung (Leiden: Brill, 2006), 136, 168. Chen Ziming also referred to the belief that secret births were easy. However, he used it to buttress his argument that the presence of too many people in the birthing room could cause difficult labor by emotionally agitating the mother or exposing her to pollution from outside. Chen, *Furen daquan liangfang,* 461–62.

32. Jizhai jushi, *Dasheng bian*, 1:8a.

33. Ibid., 1:4a, 7a.

34. Ibid., 1:6a.

35. Ibid., 1:6b.

36. Ibid., 1:7b.

37. Ibid., 1:7a,12b.

38. For a detailed discussion of this issue in seventh- and eighth-century texts, see Lee, "Childbirth in Early Imperial China."

39. Chao Yuanfang, *Chaoshi zhubing yuanhou lun* (Master Chao's treatise on the origins and manifestations of the myriad diseases) (comp. 610; revised 1026–27; ed. Wang Jichuan and Fang Kuang [Ming]; reprinted in *SKQS*), 43:13a–b. For Yang Zijian, see Chen, *Furen daquan liangfang,* 463–68.

40. Quoted in Chen, *Furen daquan liangfang,* 465–66.

41. Jizhai jushi, *Dasheng bian*, 1:8a.

42. Quoted in Chen, *Furen daquan liangfang,* 466.

43. Lou Ying, *Yixue gangmu* (Outline of medical learning) (comp. 1389; published 1565; modern reprint of 1565 woodblock edition published in *Zhonghua yishu jicheng* [Collection of Chinese medical books], vol. 24, Beijing: Zhongyi guji chubanshe, 1999), 999–1000.

44. As quoted in Chen, *Furen daquan liangfang,* 477–78; compare to Guo Jizhong, attrib., *Chanyu baoqing ji* (Precious and felicitous collection of teachings on childbearing) (comp. ca. 1109, reprinted in *SKQS*), 2:2b. As with many early authors, Guo Jizhong's biographical particulars are difficult to confirm, and there are no extant copies of his contemporary work. All accounts place him in the first half of the eleventh century, however. The standard information on his life and work comes from a preface that one Li Shisheng wrote for the *Chanyu baoqing ji*, with a date of 1109. Li possessed a text on childbirth that he said "had medical teachings but no prescriptions." At some point, Guo Jizhong expanded that work by incorporating his own formulas into it. Later writers frequently attributed the work to Guo despite evidence of its mixed authorship, and that is how it is usually catalogued in modern works. The passage that Chen Ziming attributes to Guo Jizhong, for example, actually comes from the part of the text that likely predated Guo Jizhong's involvement. For more details on the

history of this work, see the editorial summary in the SKQS edition, as well as the sources cited in Okanishi, *Song yiqian yiji kao,* 3:1088; and *LDYJ,* 2:363.

45. As quoted in Chen, *Furen daquan liangfang,* 478; compare to Guo, attrib., *Chanyu baoqing ji,* 2:3a. Chen Yan was famous as the author of the *Sanyin jiyi bingzheng fang lun* (Treatise on the manifestations and treatment of diseases caused by the three factors) (comp. 1174; reprinted in *SKQS*), which classified illnesses according to three types of causes: internal factors (emotional excess), external factors (climatic excesses), and neither internal nor external factors (including diet and lifestyle). At some undetermined point, Chen Yan wrote a number of commentaries to Guo Jizhong's *Chanyu baoqing ji,* which were subsequently incorporated into standard editions of the text itself.

46. Quoted in Chen, *Furen daquan liangfang,* 466.

47. Yu Tuan, *Yixue zheng chuan* (The orthodox transmission of medical learning) (1515; modern critical edition of 1604 Japanese reprint of 1531 woodblock edition, Shanghai: Huiwentang shuju, Republican period), 1:13b. Yu Tuan also gives a variant of this description of childbirth in his discussion of postpartum illnesses, 7:30a.

48. Li Chan, *Yixue rumen* (An introduction to medicine) (1575; modern critical edition of 1575 woodblock edition reprinted in *Zhonghua yishu jicheng* [Collection of Chinese Medical Books], vol. 26, Beijing: Zhongyi guji chubanshe, 1999), 541–42.

49. Jizhai jushi, *Dasheng bian,* 1:8a.

50. Ibid., 1:9b. Emphasis in original. Also see the discussion of this issue at 1:1b.

51. Ibid., 1:2a–2b.

52. Ibid., 1:4b.

53. Ibid., 1:1b.

54. See, for example, Chen, *Furen daquan liangfang,* 444; Qi Zhongfu, *Nüke bai wen* (One hundred questions about medicine for women) (1279; facsimile reprint of 1735 woodblock edition, Shanghai: Shanghai guji shudian, 1983), 2:53a; Yan Yonghe, *Jisheng fang* (Prescriptions for benefiting life) (comp. 1253; expanded 1267; reprinted in *SKQS*), 7:3a–b.

55. Chen, *Furen daquan liangfang,* 445.

56. Ibid., 444–47. The fruit of the bitter orange could be used in either its immature form *(zhishi)* or its ripe form. Both had the same basic properties, but the ripe fruit was milder in nature and thus more suited for weaker patients or for prolonged use. For details of the effects of bitter orange as explained by commentators across the ages, see Li Shizhen, *Bencao gangmu* (A classification of materia medica) (comp. 1552–78; preface dated 1590, ed. and republished by Wu Shuchang in 1655, reprinted in *SKQS*), 36:16a–21b; and Zhejiang xinyi xueyuan, ed., *Zhongyao dacidian* (Comprehensive dictionary of Chinese drugs) (Shanghai: Shanghai kexue jishu chubanshe, 1977), 2:1507.

57. Chen Ziming, *Furen daquan liangfang,* 446.

58. Ibid., 444.

59. Li, *Bencao gangmu,* 34:48b–52b; Zhejiang xinyi xueyuan, ed., *Zhongyao dacidian,* 1:1379–81.

60. For snakeskin and rabbit parts, see Chen, *Furen daquan liangfang,* 472–

73. The belief that objects associated with speed can be used medicinally to expedite birth appears in Xiao, *Nüke jinglun,* 5:9.

61. Yan, *Jisheng fang,* 7:3a–b.

62. For Zhu Zhenheng's influence on Ming *fuke,* see Furth, *Flourishing Yin,* chap. 4.

63. The problem of maternal carelessness in the eighth or ninth month appears in Zhu Zhenheng, attrib., *Jinkui gouxuan* (Drawing out the subtleties of the *Golden Cabinet*), comp. Dai Yuanli (comp. between 1368 and 1398; modern critical edition of Shenxiu tang woodblock edition of the Ming published in *Danxi yiji* [The collected medical works of Danxi], Beijing: Renmin weisheng chubanshe, 1993), 3:162. For carelessness in the ninth and tenth months, see Zhu Zhenheng, attrib., *Danxi xinfa* (The essential methods of Danxi), comp. Yang Xunshi (first published between 1450 and 1456; modern critical edition of 1481 woodblock edition edited by Cheng Chong published in *Danxi yiji*), 5:440. Both of these works were written by Zhu Zhenheng's disciples after his death on the basis of his unpublished writings. See Ma Jixing, *Zhongyi wenxian xue* (The study of Chinese medical literature) (Shanghai: Shanghai kexue jishu chubanshe, 1990), 192–93.

64. Medical discussions of a childbirth formula known as Bitter Orange Powder or Bitter Orange Potion (because the powdered drugs were mixed into hot water) routinely describe how it was used successfully by a Princess Huyang. Thus while Zhu Zhenheng's text refers only to a "potion for slimming the fetus," his description of the formula's effect and his mention of Princess Huyang shows that he is in fact referring to Bitter Orange Powder. Chen Ziming's description of this formula calls it "Bitter Orange Powder for Making the Fetus Slippery." Princess Huyang (Huyang gongzhu) was the elder sister of Liu Xiu, the founder of the Eastern Han dynasty who ruled as Emperor Guangwu from 25 to 57 C.E. She was a central figure in two famous stories showcasing upright government officials of the dynasty: Song Hong, whom she admired but who declined to leave his wife to marry her, and Dong Xuan, who killed one of the princess's servants while trying to arrest him for murder. For the official biographies of these two men, see *Hou Hanshu* (History of the later Han) (445; reprinted in *SKQS*), 56:11a–14a and 107:2b–4b.

65. Zhu Zhenheng, *Gezhi yulun* (Additional discourses on extending knowledge through the investigation of things) (comp. ca. 1347; modern critical edition of Yuan dynasty woodblock edition reprinted in Zhu Zhenheng, *Danxi yiji* [The collected medical works of Danxi], Beijing: Renmin weisheng chubanshe, 1993), 24–25. Also cited in *GJTS* 408:55500. Zhu uses the word *chu* (jostle, strike) to describe the measures his cousin took to "get rid of" *(qu)* fetuses, so she may also have deliberately engaged in the various behaviors that women were taught to avoid during pregnancy for fear of provoking miscarriage. These included reaching up or over with the arms, climbing up to high places, falling down, or lifting heavy objects. She may have equally well used abortifacients. For the historical use of drug-based abortifacients in Chinese medicine, see Furth, *Flourishing Yin;* and Francesca Bray, "A Deathly Disorder: Understanding Women's Health in Late Imperial China," in *Knowledge and the Scholarly Medical Traditions,* ed. Don Bates (Cambridge: Cambridge University Press, 1995).

66. Chen, *Furen daquan liangfang,* 444.

67. Li, *Yixue rumen,* 541.

68. Zhang, *Jingyue quanshu,* 39:1b–2a.

69. See, for example, a late-eighteenth-century text attributed to the Bamboo Grove Monastery monks, which warned readers against using birth-expediting formulas that "expel Blood, consume qi, or contain aromatics and rodents." Zhulinsi seng (Bamboo Grove Monastery monks), attrib., *Taichan xinshu* (A new book on childbearing), attrib. specifically to Master Jingguang, Master Lunying, and Master Xueyan (comp. ca. 1771; recopied with preface dated 1793; printed 1886; reprinted *ZBYS*), 8:137.

70. For the history of model medical curricula for aspiring doctors, see Angela Ki Che Leung, "Medical Instruction and Popularization in Ming-Qing China," *Late Imperial China* 24, no. 1 (2003): 130–52.

71. For example, Li Chan recommended Perilla Potion *(zisu yin)* for cases where the mother became frightened, causing her upper burner to close and qi to accumulate in the Lower Burner. And for those with a surfeit of qi, "use bitter orange and licorice powder to slim the fetus; for those with deficient qi, use Easy Birth Powder *[dasheng san].*" *Yixue rumen,* 541.

72. Zhang, *Jingyue quanshu,* 39:1a–b

73. Ibid., 39:1b–2a.

74. Ibid., 39:2a.

75. Wang Kentang, *Zhengzhi zhunsheng* (Guidelines for treating illness) (comp. ca. 1597–1607; reprinted in *SKQS*), 67:54a.

76. For the birthing formulas recommended by Zhang, see his *Jingyue quanshu,* 39:1a–2b.

77. The earliest known description of this pulse of childbirth is Wang Shuhe, *Maijing* (Classic of the pulse) (ca. 280; modern reprint Beijing: Kexue jishu wenxian chubanshe, 2001), 150. Wang Xi, better known by his courtesy name Wang Shuhe, was an imperial physician during the Western Jin dynasty (265–316). In addition to his authorship of the *Pulse Classic,* which synthesized earlier and contemporary pulse teachings, Wang is renowned for his editorial reconstitution and expansion of Zhang Ji's *Shanghan lun* (Treatise on cold damage disorders). At some point during the Six Dynasties period (220–589), one Gao Yangsheng attached Wang Shuhe's name to a work called *Secrets of the Pulse (Maijue),* whose description of the *li jing* circulated widely thereafter. This is the version quoted, for example, in Chen, *Furen daquan liangfang,* 482–84. But much of the confusion surrounding the *li jing* can also be traced to Gao Yangsheng's text, which introduced significant discrepancies into the descriptions of this pulse. For example, Wang's original described the pulse of childbirth as "floating," whereas the Gao version said it was "deep, fine, and slippery." To further complicate matters, the *Nanjing* described an abnormal pulse called the *li jing* (not specifically associated with childbirth) that was distinguished by its frequency of beat. For late imperial attempts to sort out these conflicting descriptions, see Wang, *Zhengzhi zhunsheng,* 67:46a–b; Zhang, *Jingyue quanshu,* 38:34b; *YZJJ,* 34:68a. For details on Wang Shuhe and the pulse works associated with him, see Ma, *Zhongyi wenxian xue,* 114; Fu Weikang, *Zhongguo yixueshi* (A history of medicine in China) (Shanghai: Shanghai zhongyi xueyuan chubanshe, 1990), 109;

Dai Qizong, *Maijue kanwu* (Correcting the errors of the *Secrets of the Pulse*) (first ed. 1523; reprinted in *SKQS*); *YJDCD*, 1:202.

78. *YZJJ*, 34:68a.

79. Wang, *Zhengzhi zhunsheng*, 67:46a. For the association of different pulses with the gender and number of the child, see Wang, *Maijing*, 149.

80. Chen, *Furen daquan liangfang*, 463.

81. Lou, *Yixue gangmu*, 999. Other prominent works that cite Lou Ying's commentary are Sun Yikui, *Chishui xuanzhu* (Pearls of wisdom from the Crimson Sea) (first ed. 1584; modern critical edition of 1596 edition reprinted in Sun Yikui, *Sun Yikui yixue quanshu* (The complete medical works of Sun Yikui), ed. Han Xuejie et al. (Beijing: Zhongguo zhongyiyao chubanshe, 1999); and Wang, *Zhengzhi zhunsheng*.

82. Quoted in Chen, *Furen daquan liangfang*, 463.

83. Ibid., 462.

84. Lou, *Yixue gangmu*, 999.

85. Li, *Yixue rumen*, 541.

86. Zhang, *Jingyue quanshu*, 39:4a.

87. Lou, *Yixue gangmu*, 999.

88. Li, *Yixue rumen*, 541.

89. Zhang, *Jingyue quanshu*, 39:4b.

90. Lou, *Yixue gangmu*, 999.

91. Yu, *Yixue zheng chuan*, 7:3a.

92. Quoted in Chen, *Furen daquan liangfang*, 464.

93. Lou, *Yixue gangmu*, 999–1000.

94. Yu, *Yixue zheng chuan*, 7:30a.

95. Zhang, *Jingyue quanshu*, 39:6b.

96. Jizhai jushi, *Dasheng bian*, 1:5a. Emphases in original.

97. Ibid., 1:7a. Emphasis in original.

98. Ibid., 1:13a.

99. Ibid., 1:12a–b.

100. Ibid., 1:7b.

101. Furth, *Flourishing Yin*.

102. Xiao, *Nüke jinglun*, 5:7–8.

103. A classic study of obstetrics in the professional strategies of male British doctors is Irvine Loudon, *Medical Care and the General Practitioner, 1750–1850* (Oxford: Clarendon Press, 1986). See also Ornella Moscucci, *The Science of Woman: Gynaecology and Gender in England, 1800–1929* (Cambridge: Cambridge University Press, 1990).

104. Besides cesarean section, another often-used but controversial technique was symphysiotomy, where the doctor severed the pubic symphysis in an attempt to enlarge the pelvic outlet. An illuminating discussion of obstetrical surgeries and the way in which male doctors selected among them during the late nineteenth and early twentieth centuries is Judith Walzer Leavitt, "The Growth of Medical Authority: Technology and Morals in Turn-of-the-Century Obstetrics," *Medical Anthropology Quarterly* 42, no. 2 (Summer 2002): 181–214.

105. Zhang Yuesun, *Chanyun ji* (Collected teachings on childbirth and pregnancy) (comp. 1830; first ed. 1845). To understand Zhang's work in general, I

have relied on a reprint published in *ZBYS*, vol. 8. Although the *ZBYS* edition does not include Zhang Yuesun's authorial preface of 1830, the preface is reprinted in *YJTK*, 3:3970–71.

106. Zhang, author's preface to *Chanyun ji*, as reprinted in *YJTK*, 3970–71.

107. An eloquent account of Zhang Yuesun's birth in 1807, his scholarly formation, office holding, and medical training is given in Susan Mann, *The Talented Women of the Zhang Family* (Berkeley: University of California Press, 2007). In a tragic irony, Zhang Yuesun's own wife died in childbirth fourteen years after this preface was written.

108. The metaphor of rejoining a snapped bowstring referred to something that could be done only through magical means. Ancient legend had it that the immortals of the Western Seas made a divine glue from the beaks of the phoenix and the horns of the *qilin* that was so effective it could be used to join broken bowstrings and broken sword blades back together again. The joined spots would henceforth be unbreakable. *Hanyu dacidian* (Comprehensive dictionary of the Chinese language) (Shanghai: Hanyu dacidian chubanshe, 1990–94), 9:1048.

109. Lee, "Childbirth in Early Imperial China," 165–67; and Chen, *Furen daquan liangfang*, 462.

110. Zhang Congzheng, *Rumen shi qin* (How scholars serve their relatives) (comp. between 1224 and 1231; reprinted in *SKQS*), 7:14a–b.

111. Chen Zhidao, author's preface (n.d.) to *Baochan wanquan shu* (A book on complete protection during childbearing), as reprinted in *YJTK*, 3:3847. The only extant copy of this work is an edition dated 1613. Biographical dictionaries identify Chen Zhidao as a Ming dynasty figure from Qiyang County, Hubei Province. See *LDYJ*, 2:457.

112. Xu Dachun, *Huixi yi'an* (Medical cases from Huixi) (n.d., annot. version by Wang Shixiong published 1855; modern critical edition reprinted in *Xu Lingtai yixue quanshu* [The complete medical works of Xu Lingtai], Beijing: Zhongguo zhongyiyao chubanshe, 1999), 393.

113. Jizhai jushi, *Dasheng bian*, 1:8b.

114. Chen, author's preface to *Baochan wanquan shu*, reprinted in *YJTK*, 3:3847.

115. Jizhai jushi, *Dasheng bian*, 1:9a.

116. Ibid.

117. Furth, *Flourishing Yin*, chap. 8.

118. Jizhai jushi, *Dasheng bian*, 1:9b.

119. Wang Shixiong, *Wangshi yi'an sanbian* (A third collection of medical cases by Master Wang), comp. Xu Ranshi (prefaces dated 1854; critical edition of 1918 Jiguge lithographic edition reprinted in *Wang Shixiong yixue quanshu* [The complete collection of Wang Shixiong's medical books], Beijing: Zhongguo zhongyiyao chubanshe, 1999), 2:380–81. I have translated the narrative with reference to another version of this case presented in Wang Shixiong, *Qianzhai jianxiao fang* (Simple and efficacious methods from Qianzhai) (prefaces dated 1853; critical edition of 1918 Jiguge lithographic edition reprinted in *Wang Shixiong yixue quanshu*), 495–96.

120. Wang, *Wangshi yi'an sanbian*, 2:380–81.

121. Ibid., 2:381.

122. Jizhai jushi, *Dasheng bian* 1:13b. An 1830 edition of *Dasheng bian* further contains an explicit warning against "evil women who want to use a knife to cut off the hand" in cases of transverse presentation. Jizhai jushi [Ye Feng], *Dasheng bian* (Treatise on easy childbirth) (1715; Taiyuan: Wen Huide woodblock edition, 1830), 2:9b.

123. China Imperial Maritime Customs, *Medical Reports* (Shanghai) 57 (October–March 1898–99): 6–7.

124. For examples, see China Imperial Maritime Customs, *Medical Reports* (Shanghai) 47–48 (October–March 1893–94): 4, 9.

125. A 1924 textbook written by doctors at the Glasgow University Hospital, for example, noted that, although cesarean section was now safe enough that it was no longer a measure of last resort, there were still cases where it was too dangerous to use and should be contraindicated. Situations where craniotomy was preferred to cesarean section included those where "the genital canal is known to be infected or where contamination is suspected." Samuel J. Cameron et al., *A Glasgow Manual of Obstetrics* (London: Edward Arnold & Company, 1924), 517.

6. TO GENERATE AND TRANSFORM

1. This account of events and all direct quotations come from Xu Lian, preface dated 1842 to *Chanbao* (Childbirth treasury), by Ni Zhiwei (comp. 1728; reprinted in *ZBYS*), 8:1–2. At the time he wrote the preface to Ni's work, Xu Lian was serving as the magistrate of Pingdu Department in Shandong Province.

2. Xu Lian describes his wife's condition as a "stagnation" *(yuzhi)*. In the context of Ms. Wei's illness, contemporary readers would have understood that this referred specifically to a stagnation of Blood. For a typical description of the symptoms of stagnated Blood, see the *YZJJ*'s section on postpartum ailments, which identified stagnant Blood as an immediate cause of pain in the "heart and stomach," the upper and lower abdomen, the flanks, and the waist. *YZJJ*, 47:9b–13a.

3. For the properties of these drugs, see Li Shizhen, *Bencao gangmu* (A classification of materia medica) (comp. 1552–78; preface dated 1590; ed. and republished by Wu Shuchang in 1655; reprinted in *SKQS*), 14:58a–62b (note that *ezhu* is listed here under its alternate name of *pengzhurong*). Scholars agree that the first printed edition of Li Shizhen's magisterial work appeared in the 1590s, but they disagree as to whether it appears in 1593 or 1596. See *YJDCD*, 1:262. For the filiation of this work's numerous reprints, see Ma Jixing, *Zhongyi wenxian xue* (The study of Chinese medical literature) (Shanghai: Shanghai kexue jishu chubanshe, 1990), 284–90. Unless otherwise noted, I have adapted common English names from Dan Bensky and Andrew Gamble, *Chinese Herbal Medicine: Materia Medica*, rev. ed. (Seattle: Eastland Press, 1993).

4. Xu Lian's preface to Ni's work says that Ni Zhiwei used the courtesy name Peiyu and the sobriquet Fengbin. Qiu Qingyuan's editorial synopsis says that Ni was a native of Pujiang County (Zhejiang Province). See the prefatory material in Ni Zhiwei, *Chanbao* (Childbirth treasury) (comp. 1728; reprinted in *ZBYS*), vol. 8.

5. A native of Haining County in Hangzhou Prefecture, Xu Lian attained the

jinshi degree in 1833. *Ming-Qing jinshi timing beilu suoyin* (An index to rosters of *jinshi* degree holders in the Ming and Qing) (Taipei: Wen shi zhe chubanshe, 1982). Other biographical details cited here come from *FSYJ*, 1:1190–91.

6. Pierre-Étienne Will, "Developing Forensic Knowledge through Cases in the Qing Dynasty," in *Thinking with Cases: Specialist Knowledge in Chinese Cultural History*, edited by Charlotte Furth, Judith T. Zeitlin, and Ping-chen Hsiung (Honolulu: University of Hawai'i Press, 2007), 64.

7. There are four distinct medical works attributed to Xu Lian in *FSYJ*, 1190, 2539, 2541, 2546, 2560. These all appear to be works by other authors that he edited or annotated. Besides Ni Zhiwei's *Childbirth Treasury*, they include an undated work on diseases of the skin and flesh *(waike)*, a work on throat diseases from 1807, and his *Xiyuan lu xiangyi* (Explanation of the meaning of *The Washing Away of Wrongs*), dated 1845. For more information on his books on throat diseases and forensic medicine, both of which are still extant, see *YJDCD*, 2:1103–4, 1460. Pierre-Étienne Will also describes Xu Lian's contributions to late imperial studies of the human skeleton in "Developing Forensic Knowledge," 90. For a history of the original *Xiyuan jilu* and its relation to ideals of good governance, see Joseph Needham, *Science and Civilisation in China*, vol. 4, pt. 6: "Medicine," with the collaboration of Lu Gwei-Djen, edited by Nathan Sivin (Cambridge: Cambridge University Press, 2000), 175–200; as well as Song Ci, *Xiyuan jilu* (The washing away of wrongs) (1247; trans. Brian E. McKnight, Ann Arbor: Center for Chinese Studies, University of Michigan, 1981).

8. See, for example, Luo Yuankai, ed., *Zhongyi fuke xue* (TCM gynecology) (Beijing: Renmin weisheng chubanshe, 1994); and Nigel Wiseman and Feng Ye, *A Practical Dictionary of Chinese Medicine* (Brookline, Mass.: Paradigm Publications, 1998). Chinese doctors have also reported success using Generating and Transforming Decoction to treat ailments such as retained placenta and excessive bleeding after miscarriage or abortion. See Wang Yanrong et al., "Jiawei shenghuatang zhiliao taipan tuimo canliu 34 li tihui" (Our experiences in using "Generating and Transforming Decoction with added ingredients" to treat 34 cases of retained and damaged placenta), *Henan zhongyi* 13, no. 4 (1993): 185–86; and Zhao Kaiyuan and Yang Jinmin, "Shenghuatang jiajian zhiliao taipan taimo canliu 56 li" (Using "Add-and-Subtract Generating and Transforming Decoction" to treat 56 cases of retained or damaged placenta), *Zhongyi zazhi*, no. 3 (1993): 1.

9. For twentieth-century views of birth pollution, see Emily Ahern, "The Power and Pollution of Chinese Women," in *Women in Chinese Society*, ed. Margery Wolf and Roxane Witke (Stanford: Stanford University Press, 1975).

10. Studies carried out during the 1980s initially concluded that women in Chinese societies did not suffer from postpartum depression. The attention and pampering they received while doing the month, it was postulated, prevented women from suffering postpartum depression. This narrative circulated both in scholarly journals and in the popular press. See, for example, Leu Chin-ai, "Postpartum Bliss," *Free China Review* 44, no. 4 (1994): 52. These findings have been challenged by recent studies showing that Chinese women actually do suffer from postpartum depression, and at rates comparable to those of Euro-Americans. Shu-Shya Heh, Lindsey Coombes, and Helen Bartlett, "The Association between De-

pressive Symptoms and Social Support in Taiwanese Women during the Month," *International Journal of Nursing Studies* 41, no. 5 (2004): 573–79; Dominic T. S. Lee et al., "A Psychiatric Epidemiological Study of Postpartum Chinese Women," *American Journal of Psychiatry* 158, no. 2 (February 2001): 220–26.

11. Sun Simiao, for example, forbade sexual intercourse during the first one hundred days after childbirth. *Beiji qianjin yaofang* (Essential prescriptions worth a thousand golds for managing urgent situations) (651; reprinted in *SKQS*), 4:1b–2a. For a description of postpartum care up to the hundredth day and a discussion of the necessary prohibitions, see also Chen Ziming, *Furen daquan liangfang* (Comprehensive compendium of good formulas for women) (comp. 1237; rev. ca. 1265; modern critical edition of Yuan dynasty Qinyou shutang edition by Yu Ying'ao et al., Beijing: Renmin weisheng chubanshe, 1992), 485–87. For the present-day definition of the postpartum period, see Luo, ed., *Zhongyi fuke xue*, 256.

12. A particularly salient example is Chen Shiduo's discussion of postpartum ailments, in which he repeatedly states that many postpartum ailments were potentially fatal and untreatable. See Chen Shiduo, *Shishi milu*, as cited in *GJTS*, 411:55538–41.

13. Yan Chunxi, *Taichan xinfa* (Essential teachings on childbearing) (comp. ca. 1725; author's preface dated 1730; modern critical edition of Yongzheng-era woodblock edition by Tian Daihua and Guo Junshuang, reprinted in *Nüke jiyao, taichan xinfa*, Beijing: Renmin weisheng chubanshe, 1988), 358–59. While the problem of waste blood dashing against the heart was already being discussed during the eleventh century, the rubric of the three dashings seems to have developed substantially later. Modern reference works trace it to Zhang Lu's *Zhangshi yitong* (Master Zhang's book for understanding medicine fully), compiled by 1695. See Zhongyi dacidian bianji weiyuanhui, ed., *Zhongyi dacidian: Fuke erke fence* (Comprehensive dictionary of Chinese medicine: Volume on gynecology and pediatrics) (Beijing: Renmin weisheng chubanshe, 1981), 63, 108; *YJDCD* entry no. G0128. Zhang Lu (1617–99) was a literatus from Changzhou County (Jiangsu Province) who dedicated himself to medicine after the fall of the Ming. Zhang Lu is also the source cited by Yan Chunxi. However, the earliest published discussion that I have found of the three dashings appears in a work by Zhang Lu's second son, Zhang Zhuo, who may well have been drawing on knowledge originally articulated by his father or otherwise developed within the Zhang family. See Zhang Zhuo, *Shanghan jianzheng xiyi* (Explanation of cold damage disorders occurring simultaneously with other illnesses) (1667; reprinted in *SKQS*), 56b–57a. For biographical information on Zhang Lu and Zhang Zhuo, see He Shixi, *Zhongguo lidai yijia zhuanlu* (Biographical records of medical experts throughout Chinese history) (Beijing: Renmin weisheng chubanshe, 1991), 2:653, 685–86.

14. I am indebted to Timothy R. Johnson and Frank Anderson for suggesting possible biomedical correspondences for these symptoms. For nineteenth-century descriptions of "puerperal insanity" that bear a striking resemblance to Yan Chunxi's description of "waste Blood dashing into the heart," see William Thompson Lusk, *The Science and Art of Midwifery* (New York: D. Appleton, 1888), 708–10; and Richard C. Norris, ed., *An American Text-Book of Obstet-*

rics for Practitioners and Students (Philadelphia: W. B. Saunders, 1895), 797–99. Medicine today continues to consider pregnancy as a possible trigger for mental illness. See, for example, Harish Kalra et al., "Pregnancy-Induced Obsessive Compulsive Disorder: A Case Report," *Annals of General Psychiatry* 4 (2005): 12.

15. See, for example, Gary F. Cunningham et al., eds., *Williams Obstetrics,* 21st ed. (New York: McGraw Hill, 2001), 568.

16. "Tetanus," in Mark H. Beers et al., eds., *The Merck Manual of Medical Information, Second Home Edition* (New York: Pocket Books, 2003), 1114–15; and *Infectious Diseases,* vol. 1: *Bacterial,* PDxMD Medical Conditions Series (Philadelphia: Elsevier Science, 2003), 608–10.

17. Although statistics vary, a frequently quoted figure is that maternal tetanus still accounts for some thirty thousand deaths per year worldwide. A standard account of the problem is Vincent Fauveau et al., "Maternal Tetanus: Magnitude, Epidemiology, and Potential Control Measures," *International Journal of Gynecology and Obstetrics* 40 (1993): 3–12. In 1999, the United Nations Children's Fund, the World Health Organization, and the United Nations Population Fund announced an initiative to eliminate maternal and neonatal tetanus by 2005, a goal that has yet to be achieved. See *Maternal and Neonatal Tetanus Elimination by 2005: Strategies for Achieving and Maintaining Elimination,* UNICEF, WHO, UNFPA, November 2000, www.unfpa.org/upload/lib_pub_file/155_filename_matetanuseng.pdf, accessed May 26, 2009.

18. I have employed the original text and modern explications from Zhongguo zhongyi yanjiuyuan, ed., *Jinkui yaolue yuyi* ("The Essentials of the Golden Cabinet," translated into modern Chinese) (Beijing: Renmin weisheng chubanshe, 1959), 219–20. For the usages of *chi,* see the sources cited in *Hanyu dacidian* (Comprehensive dictionary of the Chinese language) (Shanghai: Hanyu dacidian chubanshe, 1990–94), 8:312.

19. See, for example, *YZJJ,* 23:12. Xie Guan also noted that the term *chi* was conflated with *jing,* meaning "spasms, convulsions." *Zhongguo yixue dacidian* (A comprehensive dictionary of Chinese medicine) (preface dated 1926; facsimile reprint, Beijing: Zhongguo shudian, 1988), 3:2652.

20. *Lingshu jing* (The Yellow Emperor's inner classic, divine pivot) (earliest published recension dated 1155; reprinted in *SKQS*), 4:3b–4a.

21. Stephen Selby, *Chinese Archery* (Hong Kong: Hong Kong University Press, 2000), 91–101, 165.

22. Zhang Yuesun, *Chanyun ji* (Collected teachings on childbirth and pregnancy) (comp. 1830; first ed. 1845; reprinted in *ZBJS*), 8:54–55.

23. Conditions with symptoms known to resemble tetanus include epilepsy, hypocalcemia, and bacterial meningitis. *Infectious Diseases,* 595–96.

24. The *YZJJ,* for example, discusses wound wind under two rubrics. The section on "wind damage" emphasizes the role of blood loss in making the person vulnerable to wind, and describes clenched teeth and stiffness in the jaw as characteristics signs of the early stages of this disease. The section on "external diseases" (i.e., ailments of skin and flesh, including externally inflicted injuries) emphasizes the wound site as an entry point for pathogenic wind, and describes lockjaw and backward arching as standard symptoms of mild and severe cases of wound wind, respectively. See *YZJJ,* 39:24b–25b and 75:23a–25a.

25. Modern doctors identify infection of the female genital tract as the most common cause of postpartum infection. Estimated rates of infection today range from 1 to 8 percent of all deliveries. David C. Jones, "Postpartum Emergencies," in *Handbook of Obstetric and Gynecologic Emergencies,* 3rd ed., ed. Guy I. Benrubi (Philadelphia: Lippincott Williams & Wilkins, 2005), 199.

26. Sun, *Beiji qianjin yaofang,* 3:31. Emphasis added.

27. Wei Zhixiu, *Xu mingyi lei'an* (A continuation of the *Cases from Famous Doctors, Arranged by Category*) (ca. 1770; reprinted in *SKQS*), 36:2a.

28. See, for example, Yan Chunxi's discussions of abdominal pain due to Blood lumps. Yan, *Taichan xinfa,* 395–96 and 400–401.

29. Wei, *Xu mingyi lei'an,* 34:16a–16b.

30. Irvine Loudon, *The Tragedy of Childbed Fever* (Oxford: Oxford University Press, 2000).

31. To explain why women continued to go to these hospitals despite the higher rates of puerperal fever, Loudon points out that, "even in the worst years in the worst maternity hospitals, the majority of the women survived. A mortality rate as high as 500 per 10,000 (or 5 per cent) was terrible from the obstetrician's point of view, but it meant that 95 percent of the woman entered the hospital, had their babies, and in most cases returned home none the worse for a hospital delivery." Ibid., 69.

32. Although we do not have reliable maternal mortality statistics for the Qing, there is no reason to assume that rates of death were significantly different from those in Europe at the time. For a discussion of maternal death in an earlier era, see Jen-der Lee, "Childbirth in Early Imperial China," in *Medicine for Women in Imperial China,* ed. Angela Ki Che Leung (Leiden: Brill, 2006), 110.

33. Zhang Congzheng, *Rumen shi qin* (How scholars serve their relatives) (comp. between 1224 and 1231; reprinted in *SKQS*), 1:49b–50b. For Zhang's biographical information, see He, *Zhongguo lidai yijia zhuanlu,* 2:737–42.

34. Zhang, *Rumen shi qin,* 1:49b–50b.

35. Ibid. Helen King has found that the metaphor of woman as oven was common in Greek medicine, but this is the only example I have seen of it in the Chinese literature. *Hippocrates' Woman: Reading the Female Body in Ancient Greece* (London: Routledge, 1998).

36. Zhu Zhenheng, *Jufang fahui* (Fully deploying the formulary of the Imperial Pharmacy Service) (comp. 1347; modern critical edition of Yuan dynasty woodblock edition reprinted in *Danxi yiji* [The collected medical works of Danxi], Beijing: Renmin weisheng chubanshe, 1993), 65. I have taken this translation of the *Yijing* quotation from Richard John Lynn, *The Classic of Changes* (New York: Columbia University Press, 1994), 143.

37. Zhang Jiebin, *Jingyue quanshu* (The complete works of Jingyue) (comp. ca. 1624–40; reprinted in *SKQS*), 39:20b–24a.

38. Ibid., 39: 21a–b.

39. Daniel L. Overmyer, *Precious Volumes: An Introduction to Chinese Sectarian Scriptures from the Sixteenth and Seventeenth Centuries* (Cambridge, Mass.: Harvard University Press, 1999), 245.

40. Zhu, *Jufang fahui,* 66. The word Zhu uses for "ham" is *huoyan,* literally "fire salt."

41. Zhang, *Jingyue quanshu,* 39:23b.

42. Ibid., 61:15a–17b. This is the first mention of Generating and Transforming Decoction that I have been able to find, and my findings agree with those of Zhongyi dacidian bianji weiyuanhui, ed., *Zhongyi dacidian: Fangji fence* (Comprehensive dictionary of Chinese medicine: Volume on medicinal formulas) (Beijing: Renmin weisheng chubanshe, 1983); and Zhao Cunyi, *Zhongyi gufang fang ming kao* (A study of the names of ancient Chinese medical formulas) (Beijing: Zhongguo zhongyiyao chubanshe, 1994).

43. A typical description of Qian family practices appears in the appendix to Zhulinsi seng (Bamboo Grove Monastery monks), attrib., *Zhulinsi nüke mifang* (Secret prescriptions of women's medicine from the Bamboo Grove Monastery) (N.d., woodblock edition, CM no. 193396). As of 1994, a descendant of the Qian lineage was still practicing medicine in Shaoxing. For full details on the Qians, see Yi-Li Wu, "Transmitted Secrets: The Doctors of the Lower Yangzi Region and Popular Gynecology in Late Imperial China" (PhD diss., Yale University, 1998).

44. Gao Dengxian, ed., *Shanyin xianzhi* (Gazetteer of Shanyin County) (1671), 37:15a–b.

45. Pan Wei, *Nüke yaolue* (Essential outline of medicine for women), in *Weiyuan yixue liu zhong* (Six medical works from Weiyuan) (Hubei Fanshu woodblock edition, 1877).

46. Chen Caizhong, preface dated 1856 to *Taichan zhinan* (A compass for childbearing), by Shan Nanshan (n.d., reprinted in *Guoyi baijia qi zhong* [Seven works from the myriad masters of national medicine], ed. Qiu Qingyuan [Shaoxing]: Shaoxing yiyao xuebao lead plate edition, 1918).

47. Tamba no Mototane identifies this doctor as Shan Nanshan, original name Yangxian, and notes that his work relied heavily on Generating and Transforming Decoction. See *Iseki ko* (Study of medical books) (1819; facsimile edition of 1831 manuscript copy reprinted Tokyo: Kokuhon shuppansha, 1933–35), 2895. For Shan Yangxian's native place, see Shan Yangxian, *Taichan quanshu,* appended to *Nüke jiyao* (Edited essentials of medicine for women), by Zhou Jichang (1823; Kuizhaolou woodblock edition, 1865).

48. *LDYJ,* 3:293–94.

49. Xiao Xun, *Nüke jinglun* (Canonical teachings on medicine for women) (1684; modern punctuated edition published Shanghai: Shanghai weisheng chubanshe, 1957), 5:8, 25–26.

50. The *YZJJ* discusses postpartum abscesses in two different sections: the section on postpartum ailments, and the section on ailments of skin and flesh *(waike)*. For the postpartum discussion, see *YZJJ,* 48:14a–b.

51. Zhulinsi seng (Bamboo Grove Monastery monks), attrib., *Taichan xinshu* (A new book on childbearing), attrib. specifically to Master Jingguang, Master Lunying, and Master Xueyan (comp. ca. 1771; recopied with preface dated 1793; printed 1886; reprinted in *ZBYS*), 8:61.

52. These also occasionally appeared under the title *Golden Needle of Childbearing (Taichan jinzhen). Golden needle* was a term meaning "divinely imparted secret knowledge" or "secret techniques." Altogether, some thirty Qing dynasty editions of *A Secret Book* are still extant. Although the prefaces to these works

clearly state that they contain the Qian family's knowledge, study of these editions has been complicated by the fact that modern reference works and Chinese library catalogs have often attributed these texts to various authors besides the Qians. For example, the *LHML* attributes them to Chen Hu'an (*LHML* entry no. 7022). Internal evidence from the texts themselves, however, suggests that Chen was simply a link in the transmission of the work. *Secret Book* has also been attributed to Chen Shiduo, who appended it to his treatise on medical diagnosis, *Bianzheng lu* (Differentiation of symptoms) (see *LHML* entry no. 11663). There is no evidence that Chen Shiduo actually wrote this text, however. Finally, there is a work titled *A Secret Book of Childbearing* attributed to Zhu Zhenheng. Liu Shijue has determined, however, that this was based on Qian family medical practices and falsely attributed to Zhu. Liu, "Danxi zhushu bianwei" (Distinguishing the false among the books authored by Zhu Danxi), *Zhonghua yishi zazhi* 23, no. 2 (1993): 106–9.

53. We have a surviving preface for *Secret Book* dated 1752, but the text does not appear to have been published at this time. See *YJTK*, 3:3946. He Rong claims to have published an edition in 1759. See his preface dated 1809 to *Taichan mishu* (A secret book of childbearing) (Shancheng tang woodblock edition, CM no. 192855). For information on the 1796 edition, see *LHML* entry no. 7022. For information about the geographical distribution of this text, see the preface by He Rong, and also that of Qian Xizuo, to *Taichan mishu* (undated woodblock edition, CM no. 167460).

54. See Fu Shan's biography in Arthur W. Hummel, ed., *Eminent Chinese of the Ch'ing Period* (Washington, D.C.: Government Printing Office, 1943).

55. See the *LHML* for details on these editions. For a modern English translation aimed at American practitioners of TCM, see Fu Shan, *Fu Qing-zhu's Gynecology*, trans. Yang Shou-zhong and Liu Da-wei (Boulder, CO: Blue Poppy Press, 1995).

56. See the section titled "Chanhou bian," in Fu Shan, attrib., *Fu Qingzhu nüke* (Fu Qingzhu's medicine for women) (preface dated 1827; published in *Fu Qingzhu nan, nüke* [Fu Qingzhu's medicine for men and medicine for women], preface dated 1881; reprint, Shanghai: Qixin shuju, n.d.; facsimile reprint, Beijing: Zhongguo shudian, 1985), 1:5a.

57. Zhao Cunyi has criticized the fact that medical writers have traditionally attributed the formula to Fu. See *Zhongyi gufang fang ming kao*, 128–29. Republican-era scholars who cite Fu include Xie, *Zhongguo yixue dacidian;* and Liu Houkun, "Du *Shenghua pian* shu hou" (After reading the book *Treatise on Generating and Transforming*), *Funü yixue zazhi*, no. 11 (n.d.): 7. For a modern Chinese textbook of TCM gynecology that cites Fu Shan as the originator of Generating and Transforming Decoction see Luo, ed., *Zhongyi fuke xue*, 202.

58. Scholars still disagree as to whether Fu even wrote *Fu Qingzhu's Gynecology* at all, and some have suggested that Fu's name was falsely used to lend greater prestige to a text by someone else. And even scholars who accept Fu's authorship in general acknowledge that the style of the "Treatise on Postpartum Illnesses"—where Generating and Transforming Decoction appears—differs markedly from the preceding fascicles and was likely written by a different au-

thor. Ma Dazheng gives an overview of the main arguments in *Zhongguo fuchanke fazhan shi* (The history of the development of gynecology and obstetrics in China) (N.p.: Shanxi kexue jiaoyu chubanshe, 1992), 272–73. See also Lü Zhi, "Zaitan Fu Shan yixue zhuzuo de zhenwei" (Revisiting the issue of whether Fu Shan's medical books are genuine or fake), *Zhejiang zhongyi zazhi* no. 3 (1986): 137–39. Finally, Zhao Cunyi points out that Fu Shan would have been about seventeen years old when Zhang Jiebin's *Regulations for Women* first recorded Generating and Transforming Decoction. At that age, Fu was hardly likely to be an expert in women's diseases. Zhao, *Zhongyi gufang fang ming kao*, 129.

59. Yan, *Taichan xinfa*, 353

60. Chen, *Furen daquan liangfang*, 485–87.

61. Zhongguo zhongyi yanjiu yuan, ed., *Jinkui yaolue yuyi*, 219–20.

62. Ibid., 220.

63. Zhu Zhenheng, attrib., *Danxi xinfa* (The essential methods of Danxi), comp. Yang Xunshi (first published between 1450 and 1456; modern critical edition of 1481 woodblock edition, ed. Cheng Chong, published in *Danxi yiji* [The collected medical works of Danxi], Beijing: Renmin weisheng chubanshe, 1993), 442. As cited in this reprint, the entire original quotation says, "After birth, one must not let vacuity arise. It is proper to first greatly replenish qi and blood; and even if there are other symptoms, these are to be treated afterward." To show how Zhu's teachings were generally used in late imperial times, however, I give the quotation as it is usually phrased in Ming-Qing texts.

64. Yan, *Taichan xinfa*, 352–53. *Tuo* literally means to "strip away" or "to shed." The modern TCM translation of *tuo* is "desertion." See Wiseman and Feng, *Practical Dictionary of Chinese Medicine*, 124. Here I have used a more literal translation to reflect the semantic nuance of Yan Chunxi's description, in which he worries about drugs that cause qi and Blood to be entirely stripped or drained from the body.

65. Zhang, *Jingyue quanshu*, 39:20b–21b.

66. Wei, *Xu mingyi lei'an*, 35:22b–23b.

67. Ibid., 36:10b–11b. Shen Shiyu, courtesy name Mingsheng, lived during the late Ming and early Qing. A native of Huating (now Shanghai), he later moved to Suzhou. Shen wrote a medical book that was published in 1661 and two additional works no longer extant. See Li Jingwei ed., *Zhongyi renwu cidian* (A dictionary of eminent figures in Chinese medicine) (Shanghai: Shanghai cishu chubanshe: 1988), 294.

68. Wei, *Xu mingyi lei'an*, 34:15b. Neither Wei Zhixiu's original nor Wang Shixiong's later redaction of this collection gives the identity of the doctor in this case.

69. Yan, *Taichan xinfa*, 352–53.

70. For a history of the Song government pharmacy service in the context of Song dynasty pharmacological practices, see Asaf Goldschmidt, "The Transformations of Chinese Medicine during the Northern Song Dynasty (A.D. 960–1127): The Integration of Three Past Medical Approaches into a Comprehensive Medical System Following a Wave of Epidemics" (PhD diss., University of Pennsylvania, 1999), chap. 3, especially 147–50, 164–67.

71. Some texts also referred to this formula as Black Gold Powder, and the standard description touted it as a cure-all for the "eighteen ailments of postpartum." These included ailments such as postpartum dizziness, dry mouth with a stifled feeling in the chest, various forms of chills and fever, abdominal distention, hallucinations, inability to speak, different types of abdominal pains accompanied by diarrhea or other ailments, all-over body aches, sudden and heavy bleeding from different bodily orifices, respiratory ailments (coughing, gasping), and being struck by wind. See Chen, *Furen daquan liangfang*, 489–90.

72. Ibid., 488.

73. Ibid.

74. Zhang, *Rumen shi qin*, 1:49b–50b.

75. Zhu, *Jufang fahui*, 65.

76. Ibid., 65–66.

77. For example, when Xue Ji redacted Chen Ziming's discussion of postpartum care, he appended a lengthy quotation from Zhu Zhenheng that criticized Chen's use of heating drugs and formulas like Black Divinity Powder. Xue, *Jiaozhu furen liangfang* (The edited and annotated *Good Prescriptions for Women*) (1547; modern critical edition of Ming dynasty edition reprinted in *Xue Lizhai yixue quanshu* [The complete medical works of Xue Lizhai], Beijing: Zhongguo zhongyiyao chubanshe, 1999), 498. Similarly, Wu Zhiwang's famous *Jiyin gangmu* also printed Chen Ziming's essay together with Zhu Zhenheng's criticisms of warming remedies. Wu, *Jiyin gangmu* (A comprehensive guide to benefiting yin) (1620; modern critical edition by Li Mingjian et al. of 1620 woodblock edition published Beijing: Renmin weisheng chubanshe, 1996), 559–62, 564. For more details on how these Ming doctors used Zhu Zhenheng's teachings to revise Song dynasty *fuke*, see Charlotte Furth, *A Flourishing Yin: Gender in China's Medical History, 960–1665* (Berkeley: University of California Press, 1999), chaps. 4 and 5.

78. *GJTS*, 412:55542.

79. Zhang Jiebin, for example, recommended Chen's version of Black Divinity Powder as a formula that could be used during childbirth for bringing down a retained placenta. *Jingyue quanshu*, 39:19b–20b and 39:10a. Yan Chunxi similarly recommended it for expelling a dead fetus or for managing cases of difficult birth arising from corrupted Blood. *Taichan xinfa*, 333, 337.

80. For versions of Black Divinity Powder that differed significantly from the one given by Chen Ziming, see Wang Kentang, *Zhengzhi zhunsheng* (Guidelines for treating illness) (comp. ca. 1597–1607; reprinted in *SKQS*), 68:41a–b; Wu, *Jiyin gangmu*, 612; and Zhang, *Jingyue quanshu*, 54:70a–b.

81. Yan, *Taichan xinfa*, 333.

82. As quoted in Xiao, *Nüke jinglun*, 5:25. The book that Xiao Xun attributes to Shan Yangxian, the *New Book of Obstetrical Treasures (Chanbao xinshu)*, is no longer extant, at least under that name. However, we have a surviving chapter from another work attributed to Shan Yangxian, *A Complete Book of Producing Children (Taichan quanshu)*, which was incorporated into Zhou Jichang's *Essentials of Medicine for Women (Nüke jiyao)*. My discussion of Shan Yangxian's teachings come from a comparison of the material attributed to him in these two works. See similar comments in Shan, *Taichan quanshu*, 4a.

83. Yan, *Taichan xinfa,* 351.

84. Ibid.

85. Ibid., 352.

86. Ni, *Chanbao,* 1–2.

87. Zhu, *Jufang fahui,* 65–67.

88. Zhang, *Jingyue quanshu,* 39:21b.

89. Wang Shixiong, *Wangshi yi'an* (Master Wang's medical cases), comp. Zhou Heng (preface dated 1843; critical edition of 1918 Jiguge lithographic edition reprinted in *Wang Shixiong yixue quanshu* [The complete collection of Wang Shixiong's medical books], Beijing: Zhongguo zhongyiyao chubanshe, 1999), 2:272. This was one of three collections of Wang's medical cases that were compiled during his lifetime by his friends and admirers on the basis of his records. Zhou Heng, for example, was a secretary with the government salt administration when he first met Wang in 1824, and he opened this case collection with the story of how Wang saved him from a potentially fatal depletion of yang qi. See Wang, *Wangshi yi'an,* 1:257; and the modern reprint editor's comments in *Wang Shixiong yixue quanshu,* 919. (Note on dates: both *YJDCD* and *LHML* claim that this text was first printed in 1839 as part of a collection titled *Qianzhai yishu sanzhong* [Three medical books from Qianzhai], a collection that included two compilations of Wang's medical cases and his *Huoluan lun,* or Treatise on *huoluan* [cholera]. *YJDCD* entry no. U0220; and *LHML* entry no. 11692. However, this date cannot be correct, because the medical cases include ones dating up through 1849. Although I have not been able to personally inspect the first edition of *Qianzhai yishu sanzhong,* it is highly likely that the date of 1839 was misattributed from older editorial material left attached to the *Huoluan lun* that bears Wang's preface of 1838 and was first published in 1839. For the early prefaces to the *Huoluan lun,* see *YJTK* 1:1741–46.)

90. Wang, *Wangshi yi'an,* 2:272.

91. For Wang Shixiong's discussion of Zhu Zhenheng, see *Wangshi yi'an,* 2:272; and Wang Shixiong, *Suixi ju chongding Huoluan lun* (Reedited Treatise on *Huoluan* from the Suixi residence) (first ed. 1839; rev. 1863, modern critical edition of Siming Lin Yanchun woodblock edition of 1887 reprinted in *Wang Shixiong yixue quanshu* [The complete collection of Wang Shixiong's medical books], Beijing: Zhongguo zhongyiyao chubanshe, 1999), 2:157.

92. For Wang Shixiong's influence on the "warm factors disorders" current, see Marta Hanson, "Inventing a Tradition in Chinese Medicine: From Universal Canon to Local Medical Knowledge in South China, the Seventeenth to the Nineteenth Century" (PhD diss., University of Pennsylvania, 1997), 308–10.

93. Ibid. Kim Taylor has argued that, although Wang's text on *huouan* was the earliest, another, slightly later text was actually far more influential at the time. The eventual renown of Wang's book, she suggests, was due more to his own fame as a doctor than to the text's inherent merits. "A Survey of the Impact of Epidemic Cholera on the Medical Community in Nineteenth-Century China" (paper presented at the "Rencontres et circulation des savoirs et des pratiques en médecine," Centre National de la Recherche Scientifique, Recherches épistémologiques et historiques sur les sciences exactes et les institutions scientifiques, Paris, December 3, 2002).

94. Taylor has shown that early attempts to explain epidemic cholera included explanations that it was actually *sha,* an ancient disease category. Taylor translates *sha* as "acute outbreak," and shows that Qing writers used this term to refer to a wide range of epidemic outbreaks, including diseases we would now refer to as plague, diphtheria, and cholera. Attention to *sha* increased during the cholera pandemics, and attempts to understand epidemic cholera were also complicated by uncertainty as to the precise relationship between *sha* and *huoluan.* Taylor, "Survey of the Impact of Epidemic Cholera," 8–10.

95. See ibid.; and Kerrie L. MacPherson, "Cholera in China, 1820–1930: An Aspect of the Internationalization of Infectious Disease," in *Sediments of Time: Environment and Society in Chinese History,* ed. Mark Elvin and Liu Ts'ui-jung (Cambridge: Cambridge University Press, 1998), 487–519.

96. Wang, *Suixi ju chongding Huoluan lun,* 3:178.

97. Ibid., 3:169. The fifth lunar month would correspond to late June or early July in the Gregorian calendar, thus being a time when southern China would already be expecting hot weather. While there are some inconsistencies in scholars' accounts of the number and timing of world cholera pandemics, the preponderance of evidence confirms that 1844 was indeed in the middle of such an outbreak. MacPherson, "Cholera in China," 489; Taylor, "Survey of the Impact of Epidemic Cholera," 3.

98. Wang, *Suixi ju chongding Huoluan lun,* 3:169.

99. *GJTS,* 410:55528.

100. Wang, *Suixi ju chongding Huoluan lun,* 2:155–57. See especially guidelines 2, 3, 7, and 11.

101. Wang, *Suixi ju chongding Huoluan lun,* 3:157.

EPILOGUE

1. This account comes from Qiu Qingyuan, afterword dated 1919 to *Taichan zhinan* (A compass for childbearing), by Shan Nanshan (n.d.; reprinted in *Guoyi baijia qi zhong* [Seven works from the myriad masters of national medicine], ed. Qiu Qingyuan, [Shaoxing]: Shaoxing yiyao xuebao lead plate edition, 1918). The two women in this account are identified as Meng *fu,* namely, "the wife of Meng," and Chen *fu,* "the wife of Chen."

2. For a detailed discussion of Qiu Qingyuan's opus and impact on Chinese medicine, see Bridie Andrews, "The Making of Modern Chinese Medicine, 1895–1937" (PhD diss., Cambridge University, 1996).

3. My description of these historical events relies on John K. Fairbank, ed., *The Cambridge History of China,* vol. 10: *Late Ch'ing, 1800–1911, Part 1* (Cambridge: Cambridge University Press, 1978); and John K. Fairbank and Kwang-ching Liu, eds., *The Cambridge History of China,* vol. 10: *Late Ch'ing, 1800–1911, Part 2* (Cambridge: Cambridge University Press, 1980).

4. Qiu Qingyuan, afterword dated 1919 to *Taichan zhinan.*

5. The term *chanpoxue* (midwife studies) was a neologism that referred to Western-style obstetrics. That this term was associated with foreign obstetrics is also seen, for example, in Zhang Yanzhao's 1906 preface to Zhou Jing's *Linchan xuzhi,* as reprinted in *YJTK,* 3:4010–11. *Chanpoxue* was a literal translation of

the English term *midwifery,* which had historically been used alongside *obstetrics* as a standard term for the science and business of delivering babies. This continued to be the case throughout the nineteenth and early twentieth centuries, even after male obstetricians began to consolidate their institutional power. Thus male medical practitioners could hold professorships of "midwifery" or be licensed in "midwifery." Indeed, as late as 1932, the British College of Obstetricians and Gynaecologists issued a report titled *Memorandum on the Training of Medical Students in Midwifery and Gynaecology.* See Ornella Moscucci, *The Science of Woman: Gynaecology and Gender in England, 1800–1929* (Cambridge: Cambridge University Press, 1990), 187, and chaps. 2 and 6 generally.

    6. Qiu Qingyuan, afterword dated 1919 to *Taichan zhinan.*

    7. For the tensions between traditional and scientific medicine in Republican China, see Ralph Croizier, *Traditional Medicine in Modern China* (Cambridge, Mass.: Harvard University Press, 1968); and Sean Hsiang-lin Lei, "When Chinese Medicine Encountered the State: 1910–1949" (PhD diss., University of Chicago, 1999). An essential study of how individual doctors and medical lineages sought to modernize Chinese medicine in response to the growing power of Western medicine is Volker Scheid, *Currents of Tradition in Chinese Medicine: 1626–2006* (Seattle: Eastland Press, 2007).

    8. *Siming Songshi jiachuan chanke quanshu miben* (The complete secret book of childbearing transmitted by the Song family of Siming), comp. and suppl. by Feng Shaoqu (Shanghai: Zhongxi shuju, 1934). Feng's connections to the national medicine movement can be seen in his affiliation with Dai Dafu (1887–1968), who wrote one of the other prefaces to this Song family work. During the 1920s, Dai trained at the Shanghai Technical College of Chinese Medicine (Shanghai zhongyi zhuanmen xuexiao), a school founded by Ding Ganren in 1916 with the aim of modernizing Chinese medicine and placing it on an equal footing with Western medicine. Dai himself was a member of the Shanghai Municipal Association of National Medicine and had also helped to establish the Shanghai Chinese Medicine Press *(Shanghai zhongyi shuju).* See Scheid, *Currents of Tradition,* 236, 329.

    9. The wide range of ways that medicine, disease, and national strength could intersect are exemplified by Ruth Rogaski, *Hygienic Modernity: Meanings of Health and Disease in Treaty-Port China* (Berkeley: University of California Press, 2004); Frank Dikötter, *Imperfect Conceptions: Medical Knowledge, Birth Defects, and Eugenics in China* (New York: Columbia University Press, 1998); and Hugh Shapiro, "The Puzzle of Spermatorrhea in Republican China," *positions* 6, no. 3 (1998): 551–96.

    10. For a comprehensive study of Republican-era midwifery reforms, see Tina Phillips, "Building the Nation through Women's Health: Modern Midwifery in Early Twentieth-Century China" (PhD diss., University of Pittsburgh, 2006). See also Ka-che Yip, *Health and National Reconstruction in Nationalist China: The Development of Modern Health Services, 1928–1937* (Ann Arbor, Mich.: Association for Asian Studies, 1995), passim, especially 134, 165–67. Not only did families prefer female midwives, but they also insisted on employing older women and were reluctant to trust the young female graduates of modern midwifery schools on the grounds that they lacked experience (12, 124). Graduates of the

Sino-German Advanced Professional School of Midwifery in Shanghai reported a similar prejudice. Zhongde gaoji zhuchan zhiye xuexiao, ed., *Zhongde gaoji zhuchan zhiye xuexiao shiwu zhou jinian kan* (A commemorative volume for the fifteenth anniversary of the Sino-German Advanced Professional School of Midwifery) (Shanghai: Zhongde gaoji zhuchan zhiye xuexiao, 1940).

11. An expanded discussion of this point appears in Angela Ki Che Leung, "Women Practicing Medicine in Premodern China," in *Chinese Women in the Imperial Past: New Perspectives,* ed. Harriet T. Zurndorfer (Leiden: Brill, 1999), 101–3.

12. Charlotte Furth, *A Flourishing Yin: Gender in China's Medical History, 960–1665* (Berkeley: University of California Press, 1999), 52.

13. Ibid., 302.

14. Ibid., 91.

15. Ibid., 58. Similarly, Furth observes elsewhere: "Narratives of separate prescriptions reveal tensions between the androgynous body of generation and a female gestational body" (302).

16. My discussion of these linguistic concepts relies on Geoffrey Finch, *Linguistic Terms and Concepts* (New York: St. Martin's Press, 2000), 92–93, 101; Victoria Fromkin, ed., *Linguistics: An Introduction to Linguistic Theory* (Oxford: Blackwell, 2000), 259–60; and Andrew Spencer, "Morphology," in *The Handbook of Linguistics,* ed. Mark Aronoff and Janie Rees-Miller (Oxford: Blackwell, 2003), 214–23.

17. Doctors viewed Southern and Northern Chinese bodies as qualitatively different, and the perceived inappropriateness of northern remedies for southern illnesses helped to spur the development of the *wenbing* intellectual current. See Marta Hanson, "Robust Northerners and Delicate Southerners: The Nineteenth-Century Invention of a Southern Medical Tradition," *positions* 6, no. 3 (1998): 515–50.

Glossary

ai 艾
an (secure) 安
antai 安胎
bai dai 白帶
baixue 敗血
bai yin 白淫
baizhu 白朮
ban (female pollution) 姅
banchan 半產
banxia 半夏
bao (womb) 胞
baogong 胞宮
baoluo 胞絡
baomai 胞脈
baomen 胞門
baotai 胞胎
baotai zhi mai 胞胎之脈
Bao Xiang'ao 鮑相璈
baozang 胞臟
bao zhong 胞中
Beiji qianjin yaofang 備急千金要方
bi (arm) 臂
Bian Que 扁鵲
Bian Shiying 邊石英
bingfu 稟賦
Bixia yuanjun 碧霞元君
bu jin 不謹

bu jiu zhi zheng 不救之證
bu nei wai yin 不內外因
bu tong 不同
bu zhi zhi zheng 不治之證
Cao Binggang 曹秉綱
chan 產
Chanbao 產寶
chanchang 產腸
chan'gong 產宮
Chang Sangjun 長桑君
changsheng fang 長生方
changtan 腸覃
chanhou 產後
chanhou bian 產後編
*chanhou dang da bu qi xue wei xian,
    sui you zazheng yi mo zhi zhi*
    產後當大補氣血為先,雖有雜證以
    末治之
chanhou zhongfeng 產後中風
chanke 產科
chanke boshi 產科博士
chanmen 產門
chanpoxue 產婆學
Chanyun ji 產孕集
Chaoshi zhubing yuanhou lun 巢氏
    諸病源候論
Chao Yuanfang 巢元方

311

Chen, Mrs. (patient) 陳婦
Chen Ao 陳鰲
Chen Chun 陳椿
Chen Dejie 陳德階
Chen Ding 陳鼎
Cheng, Ms. (patient) 程氏
Chen Gao 陳誥
Chen Hongdian 陳鴻典
Chen Hongxing 陳鴻興
Chen Jian 陳諫
Chen Jin 陳謹
Chen Jingfu 陳靜復
Chen Lin 陳林
Chen Mengxiong 陳夢熊
Chen Mingzhe 陳明哲
Chen Mo 陳謨
Chen Mushan 陳木扇
Chen Nianzu (Xiuyuan) 陳念祖
　(修園)
Chen Qingyin 陳清隱
Chen Qirong 陳起榮
Chen Shannan 陳山南
Chen Shiduo 陳士鐸
Chen Shiliang 陳仕良
Chen Sishu 陳司叔
Chen Weikang 陳惟康
Chen Weimei 陳維枚
Chen Wenfu 陳文甫
Chen Wenzhao 陳文昭
Chen Xiebiao 陳謝表
Chen Xinlian 陳心蘭
Chen Xiuyuan yishu 陳修園醫書
Chen Yan (Wuze) 陳言 (無擇)
Chen Yi 陳沂
Chen Yi'nan 陳宜南
Chen Yinchuan 陳引川
Chen Yinquan 陳引泉
Chen Yishan 陳以善
Chen Zhidao 陳治道
Chen Zhongchang 陳仲常
Chen Zi 陳鼏
Chen Ziming 陳自明
Chen Zuan 陳鑽
cheqian zi 車前子
chi (pulse point) 尺
chi (spasms, syn. with *jing*) 痓
chi (twisting spasms) 瘛

chongmai 衝脈
chuan hua 傳化
chuanxiong 川芎
chuchu yi heyu ziran wei zhu 處處
　以合於自然為主
chudong 觸動
Cixi 慈谿
cuichan 催產
cuisheng 催生
cun (inch) 寸
dachan 大產
Dai Liting 戴禮亭
daimai 帶脈
daixia 帶下
danggui 當歸
danshen 丹參
dao 道
daochan 倒產
Daodejing 道德經
Dasheng bian 達生編
dasheng san 達生散
Da sheng yaozhi 大生要旨
da shi 大失
de 德
Dingxi hou 定西侯
dong tai 動胎
dui zheng tou fang 對症投方
duo (miscarry) 墮
duotai 墮胎
duo yinde 多隱德
elu 惡露
erke zhuanjia 兒科專家
er sheng guo 兒生裹
ezhu 莪术
ezu 惡阻
Fa (family) 法
Fan Yuanpu 樊元圃
Fan Zhongyan 范仲淹
fei 肥
fei zhengchan zhi hou 非正產
　之候
Feng, Ms. (Guo family) 馮氏
Feng Shaoqu 馮紹蘧
Fenyang 汾陽
fu (palace organ) 腑
fuke 婦科
Fu Qingzhu nüke 傅青主女科

Furen daquan liangfang 婦人大全
   良方
furen sanshiliu bing 婦人三十六病
furen zhubing ben yu nanzi wu yi
   婦人諸病本與男子無異
Fu Shan (Qingzhu) 傅山 (青主)
fu zhong tai lang kong kuang
   腹中胎閬空曠
gancao 甘草
ganjiang 乾薑
Ganying pian 感應篇
Gaotan 高曇
gewu 格物
gewu zhizhi 格物致知
Gong Chunpu 龔春圃
gongzang 宮臟
gu (poison) 蠱
Guangping 廣平
guangsi 廣嗣
guanli 官吏
Guanyin 觀音
guanyuan 關元
gua shu di luo 瓜熟蒂落
Gu Dehua 顧德華
Guiji 會稽
guitai 鬼胎
guo Handan 過邯鄲
Guo Jizong 郭稽中
Guo Shaoqu 郭紹渠
Guo Shiyi 郭時義
guoyi 國醫
Guoyi baijia 國醫百家
Guo Yuan 郭遠
Guo Zhaoqian 郭昭乾
gutai 固胎
gu taiyuan 固胎元
Haichang 海昌
Haining 海寧
Haiyan 海鹽
hanxue 漢學
heidou 黑豆
heishen san 黑神散
hengchan 橫產
hong dai 紅帶
Hou Ji 后稷
huan (loose pulse) 緩
Huang, Ms. (Chen family) 黃氏

Huangdi neijing 黃帝內經
huangqin 黃芩
hua tai 滑胎
hui (filth) 穢
Huijisi 惠濟寺
huisheng dan 回生丹
Hu Jishi 胡吉士
huoluan 霍亂
Huoluan lun 霍亂論
Huoshan 霍山
Huoshan xianzhi 霍山縣志
Huyang gongzhu) 湖陽公主
ji (accumulation) 積
jia (illusory accumulation) 瘕
Jiading 嘉定
Jiang Guan 江瓘
Jiang Yuan 姜嫄
jiaogong fan zhang 角弓反張
jiaogu bu kai 交骨不開
Jiashi fu 賈氏婦
jiating jingji xue 家庭經濟學
jiawei jiaogan wan 加味交感丸
Jiaxing 嘉興
jie (coagulate) 結
jie (receive) 接
jiegan 節幹
jiju 積聚
Jikong 即空
jing (spasms) 痙
jingbi 經閉
jingdao 精道
jingmai (menses) 經脈
jingmai wei furen zhi ben 經脈為
   婦人之本
jing Qi-Huang 精岐黃
jingsanleng 荊三棱
jingshi 精室
Jingxian 靜嫻
Jingyue quanshu 景岳全書
Jinkui yaolue 金匱要略
Jinkui yaolue lunzhu 金匱要略論注
jinshi 進士
Jin Ying 金英
jirou 肌肉
Jisheng fang 濟生方
Jiyin gangmu 濟陰綱目
Jizhai jushi 疢齋居士

ju (conglomeration) 聚
Jufang fahui 局方發揮
jun (sovereign drug) 君
kaozheng 考證
kexue 科學
Kexue de Dasheng bian 科學的
　達生編
keyi bu qiu yi 可以不求醫
Kou Zongshi 寇宗奭
Kui Yutian 奎玉田
kun (female principle) 坤
kutai 枯胎
lao 勞
Leijing 類經
Leijing fuyi 類經附翼
Leijing tuyi 類經圖翼
li (principle) 理
Li Chan 李梴
Li Gao 李杲
Li Heli 李合利
Liji 禮記
li jing 離經
Li Keqiong 李可瓊
linchan 臨產
Lingshu jing 靈樞經
Lin Rujin 林如錦
Liu Wansu 劉完素
Li Zhongzi 李中梓
loutai 漏胎
Lou Ying 樓英
luan bi 鸞筆
Luo Qilan 駱綺蘭
Luo Shanqing 羅善慶
Lu Yuan 陸沅
Maijing 脈經
Mao, Ms. (Guo family) 毛氏
Mashi fu 馬氏婦
men (subsection) 門
Meng (Empress Dowager) 孟
Meng, Mrs. (patient) 孟婦
mengying 夢影
mifang 秘方
mingmen 命門
Ming Taizu 明太祖
mingyi 名醫
muyou 幕友
nanchan 難產

Nanchang 南昌
Nanjing 難經
neidan 內丹
neijing tu 內景圖
nei yin 內因
niaoqiao 尿竅
Ni Zhiwei 倪枝維
nongtai 弄胎
nongtong 弄痛
nüdan 女丹
nüke 女科
Nüke jinglun 女科經論
Nüke jiyao 女科輯要
Nüke yaolue 女科要略
Nüke yaozhi 女科要旨
Nüke zuanyao 女科纂要
nüwu 女巫
nüxue 女學
nüzi bao 女子胞
Pan Jingru 潘鏡如
Pan Wei 潘蔚
Pan Yantong 潘衍桐
pi (internal obstruction) 痞
pianchan 偏產
po shang feng 破傷風
puhuang 蒲黃
Puji fang 普濟方
qi 氣
qi (uterine branches) 歧
Qian (family) 錢
qian (male principle) 乾
qian (unit of weight) 錢
Qian Biyi 錢必宜
Qian E 錢萼
Qian Guobin 錢國賓
Qian Qingshi 錢清時
Qiantang 錢塘
Qiao Guangjie 喬光烈
qibing 氣病
Qi Bo 岐伯
qie (obtain by stealth) 竊
qie (palpate the pulse) 切
qihai 氣海
qi heng zhi fu 奇恒之腑
qijing bamai 奇經八脈
qing (emotion, cult of) 情
Qiu Qingyuan 裘慶元

qi xue 氣血

Qi Zhongfu 齊仲甫

Quanguo zhongyi tushu lianhe mulu 全國中醫圖書聯合目錄

quenao xiong 雀腦芎

ren (humaneness) 仁

ren (pregnant) 姙

renmai 任脈

renshen tianfu zhi benneng 人身天賦之本能

re ru xueshi 熱入血室

rougui 肉桂

ru (scholar) 儒

rufeng 蓐風

rusun 蓐損

ruxiang 乳香

ruyi 儒醫

san bing 三病

san chong 三衝

sanjiao 三焦

Sanyin jiyi bingzheng fanglun 三因極一病證方論

sha (acute outbreak) 痧

sha (kill) 殺

shan 疝

shangchan 傷產

shangchi shui 上池水

shan jun 善君

Shan Nanshan 單南山

shanshu 善書

Shan Yangxian 單養賢

Shanyin 山陰

Shanyin xianzhi 山陰縣志

Shaoxing 紹興

shaoyao 芍藥

shelie yishu 涉獵醫書

shen (divinity) 神

shen (kidney) 腎

Shen, Ms. (Yan family) 沈氏

shengdi 生地

sheng hua tang 生化湯

shenghua ziran zhi li 生化自然之理

Shengji jing 聖濟經

Sheng min 生民

shengsanzi 聖散子

shengtai 盛胎

shengyuan 生員

Shennong bencao jing 神農本草經

shenqin yuan 神寢圓

Shen Qiwan 沈其萬

Shen Shiyu 沈時譽

Shen Youpeng (Yaofeng) 沈又彭 (堯封)

shetui 蛇蛻

shi (emissary drug) 使

shi (replete) 實

Shichan lun 十產論

shi'er jing 十二經

Shiji 史記

shijia 石瘕

shijiang 試漿

Shi Jiefan 施介繁

Shijing 詩經

Shi Pusheng 施圃生

Shi Qiutao 施秋濤

shisan ke 十三科

Shishi milu 石室秘錄

shishui 試水

shitai 試胎

shiyi 世醫

Shiyi dexiao fang 世醫得效方

shiyue 試月

shou (collect) 收

shou tai 瘦胎

shudi 熟地

Shu Gui 敍珪

shui gu zhi jingqi 水穀之精氣

Siku quanshu 四庫全書

Sima Qian 司馬遷

siwu tang 四物湯

sizheng 死證

Song Chun 松椿

Song Ci 宋慈

Song Er'rui 宋爾瑞

Song Jing 宋璟

Song Lin'gao 宋林皋

Song si gongshan, nan du shiyi 宋賜宮扇, 南渡世醫

su 俗

Sunshi yi'an 孫氏醫案

Sun Simiao 孫思邈

Sun Yikui (Wenyuan) 孫一奎 (文垣)

Sun Yikui yixue quanshu 孫一奎醫學全書

suo 縮

Su Shi (Dongpo) 蘇軾 (東坡)

Tai (Mount) 泰山

tai bing bu dong 胎病不動

tai bu zhang 胎不長

taichan 胎產

Taichan mishu 胎產秘書

Taichan xinfa 胎產心法

Taichan xinshu 胎產新書

taidong 胎動

taidu 胎毒

tailou 胎漏

Taiping huimin hejiju fang 太平惠民
和劑局方

taiqian 胎前

taiyi ju 太醫局

taiyi shu 太醫署

taiyi yuan 太醫院

taizang shang sun, baoxi duan qu
胎臟傷損, 胞繫斷去

tai zhi yi 胎之衣

Tang Qianqing 唐千頃

Tang Yaoqing 湯瑤卿

Tan Jinzhang 談金章

Tan Yunxian 談允賢

tiandi zhi da de yue sheng 天地之大
德曰生

tiangui 天癸

tiaojing 調經

Tongxiang 桐鄉

tou xu 投虛

tuo 脫

tusizi 菟絲子

waidan 外丹

wai yin 外因

wang (looking) 望

Wang, Ms. (Ye family) 汪氏

Wang Bing 王冰

Wang Dejun 王德峻

Wang Haogu 王好古

Wang Hengqi 王恆其

Wang Honglie 王鴻烈

Wang Ji 汪機

Wang Kentang 王肯堂

Wang Lun 王綸

Wang Maocun 王茂村

Wang Shixiong 王士雄

Wang Shuhe 王叔和

Wang Xueli 王學立

Wang Yuwen 王欲文

wang zhi yi ming 罔知義命

Wang Zhu 王珠

Wan Quan 萬全

wanwu 萬物

Wei, Ms. (Xu family) 衞氏

wei ji 危疾

weisheng 衞生

Wei Yilin 危亦林

wei zao 痿燥

Wei Zhixiu 魏之琇

wen (asking) 問

wen (listening/smelling) 聞

wenbing 溫病

wenbu 溫補

wenbu pai 溫補派

Weng Linzhong 翁林忠

Wu, Ms. (Guo family) 吳氏

Wu Bai 吳柏

wu ru 吾儒

wu xing 五行

Wuxuan 武宣

Wu Yu 吳煜

wu yun liu qi 五運六氣

wu zang liu fu 五臟六腑

Wu Zhiwang 武之望

Wu Ziqing 吳子卿

xi (practice) 習

xian (seizures) 癇

xiang 香

xian sheng ru da 先生如達

xiaochan 小產

xiaochan zhong yu dachan 小產重
於大產

Xiaoshan 蕭山

Xiao Xun 蕭壎

Xici 繫辭

xinshi 信士

Xiyuan lu 洗冤錄

xu 虛

Xuanhua 宣化

Xu Bin 徐彬

Xu Dachun (Lingtai) 徐大椿 (靈胎)

xue 血

xuebing 血病

xuegu 血蠱
xuehai 血海
Xue Ji 薛己
xuepai 學派
xueshi 血室
xueyun 血暈
xuezang 血臟
Xu Lian 許槤
Xu mingyi lei'an 續名醫類案
Yan Chunxi 閻純璽
yanfang 驗方
Yanfang xinbian 驗方新編
yang chang you yu, yin chang bu zu
    陽常有餘, 陰常不足
Yang Chongrui 楊崇瑞
yangsheng 養生
yang shi yin hua 陽施陰化
yangyi 瘍醫
Yang Zijian 楊子建
Yan Yonghe 嚴用和
ye (profession) 業
ye chanke zhe 業產科者
Ye Feng (Weifeng) 葉風(維風)
Ye Mengyu 葉夢瑀
Ye Sheng 葉升
Ye Wanpu 葉完樸
Ye Wenshu 葉文叔
yi (easy) 易
yi (medicine) 醫
yi'an 醫案
yi bu san shi, bu fu qi yao 醫不三世,
    不服其藥
yichan 易產
yihu 醫戶
Yijing 易經
yin bo yang bie 搏陽別
yin song 印送
yinting 陰挺
yin yang 陰陽
yin zhong 陰中
yipo 醫婆
yiren 異人
yisheng 易生
Yixue rumen 醫學入門
Yixue yuanliu lun 醫學源流論
yi yi yi 醫易義
Yizong bi du 醫宗必讀

Yizong jinjian 醫宗金鑑
Yu, Ms. (Song family) 余氏
Yuan Huang 袁黃
Yuan Lingmo 袁令默
Yuan Xiang 袁祥
Yue 越
yufang zhi zhong 玉房之中
yu mao 鬱冒
Yu Songyun 余松筠
Yu Tuan 虞摶
yu xue 瘀血
Yuyin jushi 漁隱居士
Yu Zan 余贊
zabing 雜病
zang (depot organ) 臟
Zan Yin 昝殷
zaohua 造化
zaohua ziran 造化自然
zaojiao 皂角
zazheng 雜症
Zeng Guofan 曾國籓
Zeng Jifen 曾紀芬
Zeng Yi 曾懿
Zhang Baohua 張葆華
Zhang Congzheng 張從正
Zhang Ji (Zhongjing) 張機 (仲景)
Zhang Jiebin (Jingyue) 張介賓
    (景岳)
Zhang Juesun 張珏孫
Zhang Qi 張琦
Zhang Yuesun 張曜孫
zheng (syndrome) 症
zheng (verifiable accumulation) 癥
zhengchan 正產
zhike 枳殼
zhike san 枳殼散
zhongfeng 中風
zhongji (middle extremity) 中極
zhong ji (myriad illnesses) 眾疾
zhongzi 種子
Zhou Hanqing 周漢卿
Zhou Jichang 周紀常
Zhou Lianggong 周亮工
Zhou Ting 周頲
zhuanke 專科
zhuanmen fuke zhi yi 專門婦科
    之醫

zhuan nüke 專女科

zhuan nü wei nan 轉女為男

Zhulinsi 竹林寺

Zhulinsi nüke zhengzhi 竹林寺女科
　證治

Zhu Peng 朱鵬

Zhu Qixian 朱啟先

zhusheng 諸生

Zhu Xi 朱熹

Zhu Xiao 朱橚

Zhu Xuzeng 朱緒曾

Zhu Yungu 朱雲谷

Zhu Zhenheng (Danxi) 朱震亨
　(丹溪)

zichang 子腸

zigong 子宮

zigong zhen qi 子宮真氣

zihu 子戶

zimen 子門

ziran 自然

ziran er ran 自然而然

ziran zhi li 自然之理

zishi 子室

zishiying 紫石英

zixian 子癇

zizang 子臟

zuan 鑽

zuoyue 坐月

Bibliography

PRIMARY SOURCES IN CHINESE

Bao Xiang'ao. *Yanfang xinbian* (A new compilation of tested prescriptions). First edition 1846; expanded and edited by Mei Qizhao, [Hangzhou]: Zhejiang sheng cheng dongbizhai kezidian, 1878. Modern critical edition published Beijing: Renmin weisheng chubanshe, 1990.

Cao Xueqin. *Honglou meng* (Dream of the red chamber). Circa 1760. Translated by David Hawkes and John Minford as *The Story of the Stone*. 5 vols. Harmondsworth: Penguin, 1973–1986.

Cao Yunyuan and Li Genyuan, comps. *Wuxian zhi* (Gazetteer of Wu County). 1933. Reprint, Nanjing: Jiangsu guji chubanshe, 1991.

Chao Yuanfang. *Chaoshi zhubing yuanhou lun* (Master Chao's treatise on the origins and manifestations of the myriad diseases). Compiled 610; revised 1026–27; edited by Wang Jichuan and Fang Kuang (Ming). Reprinted in *SKQS*.

Chen Menglei et al., comps. *Gujin tushu jicheng* (A compendium of ancient and modern texts and illustrations, also known as the *Imperial Encyclopedia*). Beijing: Neifu, 1726–28. Reprint, Chengdu: Zhonghua shuju and Bashu shushe, 1986.

Chen Nianzu. *Nüke yaozhi* (Essentials of medicine for women). Compiled 1803; first edition 1841. Reprinted in *Chen Xiuyuan yishu qishi'er zhong* (The medical books of Chen Xiuyuan, seventy-two titles). Shanghai: Shanghai shudian, 1988.

Chen Qiong et al., comps. *Minguo Hangzhou fuzhi* (Gazetteer of Hangzhou Prefecture from the Republican period). 1922. Reprint, Shanghai: Shanghai shudian, 1993.

Chen Yan. *Sanyin jiyi bingzheng fang lun* (Treatise on the manifestations and treatment of diseases caused by the three factors). Compiled 1174. Reprinted in *SKQS*.

Chen Yi. *Chen Su'an fuke bujie* (Chen Su'an's medicine for women, with supplements and commentary). Compiled twelfth century; edited by Chen Wenzhao, Ming dynasty. Reprint, Shanghai: Shanghai kexue jishu chubanshe, 1983.

Chen Ziming. *Furen daquan liangfang* (Comprehensive compendium of good formulas for women). Compiled 1237; revised circa 1265. Modern critical edition of Yuan dynasty Qinyou shutang edition by Yu Ying'ao et al., Beijing: Renmin weisheng chubanshe, 1992.

Dai Qizong, *Maijue kanwu* (Correcting the errors of the *Secrets of the Pulse*). First ed. 1523. Reprinted in *SKQS*.

Da Qing huidian (Collected statutes of the Qing dynasty). 1818. Reprint, Taipei: Wenhai chubanshe, 1991.

Daqing lüli (Great Qing Code with substatutes). 1740. Reprinted in *SKQS*.

Fenglinsi taichan (The Phoenix Grove Monastery's book on producing children). Hand-copied manuscript, n.d. SY no. 96432.

Fu Shan, attrib. *Fu Qingzhu nüke* (Fu Qingzhu's medicine for women). Preface dated 1827. Published in *Fu Qingzhu nan, nüke* (Fu Qingzhu's medicine for men and medicine for women). Preface dated 1881. Reprint, Shanghai: Qixin shuju, n.d. Facsimile reprint, Beijing: Zhongguo shudian, 1985.

Gan Shan et al., eds. *Huoshan xianzhi* (Gazetteer of Huoshan County). 1776. Reprint, Taipei: Chengwen chubanshe, 1985.

Gao Dengxian, ed. *Shanyin xianzhi* (Gazetteer of Shanyin County). 1671.

Geng Weihu, ed. *Shimen xianzhi* (Gazetteer of Shimen County). 1821.

Gu Dehua. *Huayunlou yi'an* (Medical cases from the Pavilion of Flowery Rhymes). Compiled mid-nineteenth century. Reprinted in *ZBYS*, vol. 12.

Guo Aichun, ed. *Zhongguo fensheng yiji kao* (A study of Chinese medical texts by province). 2 vols. Tianjin: Tianjin kexue jishu chubanshe, 1987.

Guo Jizhong, attrib. *Chanyu baoqing ji* (Precious and felicitous collection of teachings on childbearing). Compiled circa 1109. Reprinted in *SKQS*.

Ha Xiaoxian. *Neijing fuke jiwen jiyi* (Compilation of gynecological discussions from the *Neijing*, with collected commentaries). Beijing: Zhongguo yiyao keji chubanshe, 1992.

Hou Hanshu (History of the later Han). 445. Reprinted in *SKQS*.

Huangdi neijing suwen (The Yellow Emperor's inner classic, basic questions). Originally compiled first century C.E. Reprinted in *SKQS*.

Jiang Fengqing et al., eds. *Jiashan xianshi* (Gazetteer of Jiashan County). 1892. Reprint, Taipei: Chengwen chubanshe, 1970.

Jiang Guan. *Mingyi lei'an* (Cases from famous doctors, arranged by category). Compiled 1549; first edition 1591; annotated by Wei Zhixiu and republished by Bao Tingbo in 1770. Reprint, Taipei: Hongye shuju, 1994.

Jiu Tangshu (Old history of the Tang dynasty). 945. Reprinted in *SKQS*.

Jizhai jushi [Ye Feng]. *Dasheng bian* (Treatise on easy childbirth). 1715. Du Fei, ed., 1727. Reprinted with preface dated 1767 in *Yilin zhiyue* (Pointing the moon out to doctors), edited by Wang Qi, Hangzhou: Baohu lou woodblock edition. In the library of the Zhongguo zhongyi yanjiuyuan. Unless otherwise noted, all citations are to this edition.

———. *Dasheng bian* (Treatise on easy childbirth). 1715. N.p., woodblock edition, preface dated 1809. ST no. 440260.

———. *Dasheng bian* (Treatise on easy childbirth). 1715. Taiyuan: Wen Huide woodblock edition, 1830. In the University of Michigan Harlan Hatcher Graduate Library, Special Collections.

———. *Dasheng bian* (Treatise on easy childbirth). 1715. N.p., woodblock edition, 1839. ST no. 539001.

———. *Dasheng bian* (Treatise on easy childbirth). 1715. Nanchang: Yili zhai woodblock edition [circa 1850]. ST no. 440243.

———. *Dasheng bian* (Treatise on easy childbirth). 1715. Hangzhou: Fuyunde Engraving Shop woodblock edition, 1878. ST no. 108207.

———. *Dasheng bian* (Treatise on easy childbirth). 1715. Renyu Hall woodblock edition, 1902. ST no. 440635.

———. *Dasheng bian* (Treatise on easy childbirth). 1715. Reprinted in *Chen Xiuyuan yishu qishi'er zhong* (The medical books of Chen Xiuyuan, seventy-two titles). Shanghai: Shanghai shudian, 1988.

———. *Dasheng bian* (Treatise on easy childbirth). 1715. Hefei: Zhang Hongmao Engraving Shop woodblock edition, n.d. ST no. 090492.

———. *Zengguang Dasheng pian* (The expanded *Treatise on Easy Childbirth*). Zhenjiang [Jiangsu]: Shanhua tang, 1888. Personal collection of author.

Jueluo Shilin, ed. *Shanxi tongzhi* (Gazetteer of Shanxi Province). 1734. Reprinted in SKQS.

Kangxi zidian (Dictionary of the Kangxi reign). 1716. Facsimile reprint, Beijing: Zhonghua shuju, 1992.

Li Chan. *Yixue rumen* (An introduction to medicine). 1575. Modern edition of 1575 woodblock edition reprinted in *Zhonghua yishu jicheng* (Collection of Chinese Medical Books), 33 vols. Beijing: Zhongyi guji chubanshe, 1999, vol. 26.

Li Gao. *Lanshi micang* (Stored secrets from the orchid chamber). Compiled thirteenth century; first edition 1276. Reprinted in *SKQS*.

Li Mingwan and Tan Junpei, eds. *Tongzhi Suzhou fuzhi* (Gazetteer of Suzhou Prefecture from the Tongzhi reign). 1882. Reprint, Nanjing: Jiangsu guji chubanshe, 1991.

Lingshu jing (The Yellow Emperor's inner classic, divine pivot). Earliest published recension dated 1155. Reprinted in *SKQS*.

Lin Sijin, ed. *Huayang xianzhi* (Gazetteer of Huayang County). 1934. Reprint, Taipei: Taiwan xuesheng shuju, 1967.

Li Shizhen. *Bencao gangmu* (A classification of materia medica). Compiled 1552–78; preface dated 1590; edited and republished by Wu Shuchang in 1655. Reprinted in *SKQS*.

Liu Yan, ed. *Xiaoshan xianzhi* (Gazetteer of Xiaoshan County). 1693.

Li Zhongzi. *Yizong bi du* (Essential readings in medical learning). 1637. Modern critical edition reprinted in *Li Zhongzi yixue quanshu* (The complete medical works of Li Zhongzi), edited by Bao Laifa et al. Beijing: Zhongguo zhongyiyao chubanshe, 1999.

Lou Ying. *Yixue gangmu* (Outline of medical learning). Compiled 1389; published 1565. Modern reprint of 1565 woodblock edition published in *Zhong-*

hua yishu jicheng (Collection of Chinese medical books), 33 vols. Beijing: Zhongyi guji chubanshe, 1999, vol. 24.

Ma Rulong, ed. *Hangzhou fuzhi* (Gazetteer of Hangzhou Prefecture). 1686.

Meng Zhaohan, ed. *Minguo Changle xianzhi* (Republican-era gazetteer of Changle County). 1917. Reprint, Shanghai: Shanghai shudian chubanshe, 2000.

Mingshi (History of the Ming dynasty). 1739. Reprinted in *SKQS*.

Ni Zhiwei. *Chanbao* (Childbirth treasury). Compiled 1728. Reprinted in *ZBYS*, vol. 8.

Pan Wei. *Nüke yaolue* (Essential outline of medicine for women). In *Weiyuan yixue liu zhong* (Six medical works from Weiyuan). Hubei Fanshu woodblock edition, 1877. In the library of Zhongguo zhongyi kexue yuan.

Qiantang xianzhi (Gazetteer of Qiantang County). Compiled 1609; published 1893. Reprint, Taipei: Chengwen chubanshe, 1975.

Qian Yuanming, ed. *Jingshi baijia yilu* (Medicine-related passages from the Confucian classics, official histories, and writings of the hundred masters). Guangzhou: Guangdong keji chubanshe, 1986.

Qin Dazhang, ed. *Huoshan xianzhi* (Gazetteer of Huoshan County). 1905. Reprint, Taipei: Chengwen chubanshe, 1974.

Qinding xu wenxian tongkao (Imperially compiled continuation of the *General History of Institutions and Critical Examination of Documents and Studies*). Compilation commissioned 1747. Reprinted in *SKQS*.

Qingchao xu wenxian tongkao (A continuation of the *General History of Institutions and Critical Examination of Documents and Studies for the Qing Dynasty*). 1921. Reprint, Shanghai: Commercial Press, 1936.

Qingshi gao (Draft history of the Qing dynasty). 1927. Reprint, Beijing: Zhonghua shuju, 1977.

Qiu Qingyuan [Jisheng], ed. *Zhenben yishu jicheng* (Collection of precious medical works). 14 vols. Shaoxing, 1936. Facsimile reprint, Shanghai: Shanghai kexue jishu chubanshe, 1986.

Qi Zhongfu. *Nüke bai wen* (One hundred questions about medicine for women). 1279. Facsimile reprint of 1735 woodblock edition, Shanghai: Shanghai guji shudian, 1983.

Shandong zhongyi xueyuan and Hebei yixue yuan, eds. *Huangdi neijing suwen jiaoshi* (The *Yellow Emperor's Inner Classic, Basic Questions,* annotated and explicated). 2 vols. Beijing: Renmin weisheng chubanshe, 1993.

Shanghai tushuguan, ed. *Zhongguo congshu mulu*. 1959. Reprint, Shanghai: Shanghai guji chubanshe, 1983.

Shan Nanshan. *Taichan zhinan* (A compass for childbearing). N.d. Reprinted in *Guoyi baijia qi zhong* (Seven works from the myriad masters of national medicine), edited by Qiu Qingyuan. [Shaoxing]: Shaoxing yiyao xuebao lead plate edition, 1918.

Shan Yangxian. *Taichan quanshu*. Appended to *Nüke jiyao* (Edited essentials of medicine for women), by Zhou Jichang. 1823. Kuizhaolou woodblock edition, 1865.

Shen Yaofeng [Shen Youpeng]. *Nüke jiyao* (Edited essentials of medicine for women). Compiled mid-eighteenth century. Edited and published by Wang Shixiong, 1850. Modern critical edition by Li Guangwen, Huang Shuzhen, and Li Zhulan, published in *Nüke jiyao, taichan xinfa*. Beijing: Renmin weisheng chubanshe, 1988.

Siku quanshu (Complete library of the four treasuries). Wenyuange edition, 1782. Facsimile reprint published Taipei: Taiwan shangwu yinshuguan, 1986. Electronic version published Hong Kong: Chinese University of Hong Kong and Digital Heritage Publishing, 1998.

Sima Qian. *Shiji* (Records of the historian). Second to first century B.C.E. Reprinted in *SKQS*.

Siming Songshi jiachuan chanke quanshu miben (The complete secret book of childbearing transmitted by the Song family of Siming), compiled and supplemented by Feng Shaoqu. Shanghai: Zhongxi shuju, 1934.

Song Lin'gao, ed. *Siming Songshi nüke mishu* (A secret book of women's medicine from Master Song of Siming). Preface dated 1612. Reprint, Shanghai: Wanyou shuju, 1932.

Sun Simiao. *Beiji qianjin yaofang* (Essential prescriptions worth a thousand golds for managing urgent situations). 651. Reprinted in *SKQS*.

Sun Yikui. *Yizhi xuyu* (Additional discussions on the meaning of medicine). 1573. Reprinted in *SKQS*.

———. *Chishui xuanzhu* (Pearls of wisdom from the Crimson Sea). First edition 1584. Modern critical edition of 1596 edition reprinted in Sun Yikui, *Sun Yikui yixue quanshu*.

———. *Sunshi yi'an* (The medical cases of Master Sun). Compiled by Yu Huang et al. 1599. Modern critical edition reprinted in Sun Yikui, *Sun Yikui yixue quanshu*.

———. *Sun Yikui yixue quanshu* (The complete medical works of Sun Yikui). Edited by Han Xuejie et al. Beijing: Zhongguo zhongyiyao chubanshe, 1999.

Taichan mishu (A secret book of childbearing). Preface dated 1809; Shancheng tang woodblock edition. CM no. 192855.

Taichan mishu (A secret book of childbearing). Luo Ruilin woodblock edition, 1879. PU no. CM/25a/C538s2.

Taichan mishu (A secret book of childbearing). Luo Wenhua Hall woodblock edition, Changsha: n.p., 1879. SY no. 09281.

Taichan mishu (A secret book of childbearing). Undated woodblock edition. CM no. 167460.

Tang Qianqing. *Dasheng yaozhi* (Essentials of fecundity). 1762. Yangzhou: Weiyang wencheng tang woodblock edition, 1857.

Tang Xuchun. *Shangyu xianzhi* (Gazetteer of Shangyu County). 1891. Reprint, Taipei: Chengwen chubanshe, 1970.

Wang Kentang. *Zhengzhi zhunsheng* (Guidelines for treating illness). Compiled circa 1597–1607. Reprinted in *SKQS*.

Wang Shixiong. *Suixi ju chongding Huoluan lun* (Reedited *Treatise on Huoluan* from the Suixi residence). First edition 1839; revised 1863. Modern critical edition of Siming Lin Yanchun woodblock edition of 1887 reprinted in Wang Shixiong, *Wang Shixiong yixue quanshu*.

———. *Wangshi yi'an* (Master Wang's medical cases). Compiled by Zhou Heng. Preface dated 1843. Critical edition of 1918 Jiguge lithographic edition reprinted in Wang Shixiong, *Wang Shixiong yixue quanshu*.

————. *Wangshi yi'an xubian* (A second collection of medical cases by Master Wang). Compiled by Zhang Hong et al. Prefaces dated 1850. Critical edition of 1918 Jiguge lithographic edition reprinted in Wang Shixiong, *Wang Shixiong yixue quanshu.*

————, comp. *Liuzhou yihua liangfang* (Medical discussions and worthy prescriptions from Master Liuzhou). 1851. Critical edition of 1918 Jiguge lithographic edition reprinted in Wang Shixiong, *Wang Shixiong yixue quanshu.*

————. *Qianzhai jianxiao fang* (Simple and efficacious methods from Qianzhai). Prefaces dated 1853. Critical edition of 1918 Jiguge lithographic edition reprinted in Wang Shixiong, *Wang Shixiong yixue quanshu.*

————, ed. *Xu mingyi lei'an* (A continuation of the *Cases from Famous Doctors, Arranged by Category*), by Wei Zhixiu. Editor's preface dated 1853; first published in 1863. Modern critical edition of Zhuyi tang woodblock edition of 1863 published Beijing: Renmin weisheng chubanshe, 1997. See also Wei Zhixiu.

————. *Wangshi yi'an sanbian* (A third collection of medical cases by Master Wang). Compiled by Xu Ranshi. Prefaces dated 1854. Critical edition of 1918 Jiguge lithographic edition reprinted in Wang Shixiong, *Wang Shixiong yixue quanshu.*

————. *Gui yan lu* (Records of returning to the inkstone). Author's first preface dated 1857. Reprinted with author's new preface dated 1862. Critical edition of 1918 Jiguge lithographic edition reprinted in Wang Shixiong, *Wang Shixiong yixue quanshu.*

————. *Wang Shixiong yixue quanshu* (The complete collection of Wang Shixiong's medical books). Beijing: Zhongguo zhongyiyao chubanshe, 1999.

Wang Shuhe. *Maijing* (Classic of the pulse). Circa 280. Modern reprint Beijing: Kexue jishu wenxian chubanshe, 2001.

Wang Yaochen et al. *Chongwen zongmu* (Bibliographic catalog of the Academy for Veneration of Literature). 1041. Reprinted in *SKQS.*

Wang Zhefu, ed. *Qianlong Xuanhua fuzhi* (Gazetteer of Xuanhua prefecture from the Qianlong reign). 1757. Reprint, Shanghai: Shanghai shudian chubanshe, 2006.

Wei Yilin. *Shiyi dexiao fang* (Efficacious prescriptions from a hereditary medical family). 1337. Reprinted in *SKQS.*

Wei Yuan, ed. *Kangxi Qiantang xianzhi* (Gazetteer of Qiantang County from the Kangxi reign). 1718. Reprint, Shanghai: Shanghai shudian, 1993.

Wei Zhixiu. *Xu mingyi lei'an* (A continuation of the *Cases from Famous Doctors, Arranged by Category*). Circa 1770. Reprinted in *SKQS.* See also Wang Shixiong, ed., *Xu mingyi lei'an.*

Wu Qian, ed. *Yuzuan yizong jinjian* (The imperially compiled golden mirror of medical learning). Beijing: Wuying dian, 1742. Reprinted in *SKQS.*

Wu Zhiwang. *Jiyin gangmu* (A comprehensive guide to benefiting yin). 1620. Modern critical edition by Li Mingjian et al. of 1620 woodblock edition. Beijing: Renmin weisheng chubanshe, 1996.

Xiao Xun. *Nüke jinglun* (Canonical teachings on medicine for women). 1684. Modern punctuated edition. Shanghai: Shanghai weisheng chubanshe, 1957.

Xie Qikun, ed. *Guangxi tongzhi* (Gazetteer of Guangxi Province). 1800. Facsimile reprint, Taipei: Wenhai chubanshe, 1966.

Xu Bin. *Jinkui yaolue lunzhu* (*Essentials of the Golden Cabinet,* discussed and annotated). 1671. Reprinted in *SKQS.*

Xu Dachun. *Yixue yuanliu lun* (Treatise on the origins of medical learning). 1757. Reprinted in *SKQS.*

———. *Lantai guifan* (Standard criteria of the orchid dais). 1764. Reprinted in *SKQS.*

———. *Shenji chuyan* (Humble opinions on the prudent management of illness). 1767. Modern critical edition of Master Cai's Hanxu ge woodblock edition of 1838 reprinted in *Xu Lingtai yixue quanshu* (The complete medical works of Xu Lingtai). Beijing: Zhongguo zhongyiyao chubanshe, 1999.

———, attrib. *Nüke yi'an* (Medical cases on medicine for women). 1893. Reprinted in *Xu Dachun yishu quanji.* Beijing: Renmin weisheng chubanshe, 1988.

———. *Huixi yi'an* (Medical cases from Huixi). N.d., annotated version by Wang Shixiong published 1855. Modern critical edition reprinted in *Xu Lingtai yixue quanshu* (The complete medical works of Xu Lingtai). Beijing: Zhongguo zhongyiyao chubanshe, 1999.

Xue Ji. *Jiaozhu furen liangfang* (The edited and annotated *Good Prescriptions for Women*). 1547. Modern critical edition of Ming dynasty edition reprinted in *Xue Lizhai yixue quanshu* (The complete medical works of Xue Lizhai). Beijing: Zhongguo zhongyiyao chubanshe, 1999.

Yan Chen et al., comps. *Tongxiang xianzhi* (Gazetteer of Tongxiang County). 1887. Reprint, Taiwan: Chengwen chubanshe, 1970.

Yan Chunxi. *Taichan xinfa* (Essential teachings on childbearing). Compiled circa 1725; author's preface dated 1730. Modern critical edition of Yongzheng-era woodblock edition by Tian Daihua and Guo Junshuang, reprinted in *Nüke jiyao, taichan xinfa.* Beijing: Renmin weisheng chubanshe, 1988.

Yan Shiyun, ed. *Zhongguo yiji tongkao* (A comprehensive study of Chinese medical texts). 4 vol., plus index. Shanghai: Shanghai zhongyi shueyuan chubanshe, 1990–94.

Yan Yonghe. *Jisheng fang* (Prescriptions for benefiting life). Compiled 1253, expanded 1267. Reprinted in *SKQS.*

Ye Feng. See Jizhai jushi.

Yu Songyun. *Kexue de Dasheng bian* (A scientific *Treatise on Easy Childbirth*). Shanghai: Zhongde yiyuan chubanshe, 1933.

Yu Tuan. *Yixue zheng chuan* (The orthodox transmission of medical learning). 1515. Modern critical edition of 1604 Japanese reprint of 1531 woodblock edition. Shanghai: Huiwentang shuju, Republican period.

Zeng Yi. *Nüxue pian* (A treatise on female education). In *Guhuanshi yixue pian* (A treatise on medicine from the Delighting in Antiquity Studio). Changsha: n.p., 1907.

———. *Yixue pian* (A treatise on medicine). In *Guhuanshi yixue pian* (A treatise on medicine from the Delighting in Antiquity Studio). Changsha: n.p., 1907.

———. *Zhongkui lu* (Records on feeding a household). In *Guhuanshi yixue pian* (A treatise on medicine from the Delighting in Antiquity Studio). Changsha: n.p., 1907.

Zhang Congzheng. *Rumen shi qin* (How scholars serve their relatives). Compiled between 1224 and 1231. Reprinted in *SKQS*.

Zhang Ji. *Jinkui yaolue* (Essentials of the golden cabinet). Circa 200 C.E. Reprinted in *Zhongyi ba da jingdian quanzhu* (The eight great classics of Chinese medicine, complete and annotated), edited by Shang Zhijun and Zhai Shuangqing. Beijing: Huaxia chubanshe, 1994.

Zhang Jiebin. *Leijing* (The *Inner Classic* explicated by topic). 1624. Reprinted in *SKQS*.

———. *Leijing fuyi* (Appended supplement to "*The* Inner Classic *Explicated by Topic*") 1624. Reprinted in *SKQS*.

———. *Leijing tuyi* (Illustrated supplement to "*The* Inner Classic *Explicated by Topic*"). 1624. Reprinted in *SKQS*.

———. *Jingyue quanshu* (The complete works of Jingyue). Compiled circa 1624–40. Reprinted in *SKQS*.

———. *Zhang Jingyue yixue quanshu* (The complete medical works of Zhang Jingyue). Edited by Li Zhiyong. Beijing: Zhongguo zhongyiyao chubanshe, 1999.

Zhang Yuesun. *Chanyun ji* (Collected teachings on childbirth and pregnancy). Compiled 1830; first edition 1845. Reprinted in *ZBJS*, vol. 8.

Zhang Zhuo. *Shanghan jianzheng xiyi* (Explanation of cold damage disorders occurring simultaneously with other illnesses). 1667. Reprinted in *SKQS*.

Zhang Zonghai et al., eds. *Xiaoshan xianzhi gao* (Draft gazetteer of Xiaoshan County). 1935. Reprint, Taipei: Chengwen chubanshe, 1970.

Zhao Weiyu, ed. *Guangxu Jiaxing xianzhi* (Gazetteer of Jiaxing County from the Guangxu reign). 1908. Reprint, Shanghai: Shanghai shudian, 1993.

Zheng Ying et al., eds. *Nanhai xianzhi* (Gazetteer of Nanhai County). 1910. Reprint, Taipei: Chengwen chubanshe, 1974.

Zhongde gaoji zhuchan zhiye xuexiao, ed. *Zhongde gaoji zhuchan zhiye xuexiao shiwu zhou jinian kan* (A commemorative volume for the fifteenth anniversary of the Sino-German Advanced Professional School of Midwifery). Shanghai: Zhongde gaoji zhuchan zhiye xuexiao, 1940.

Zhou Jichang. *Nüke jiyao* (Edited essentials of medicine for women). 1823. Kuizhaolou woodblock edition, 1865. In the library of Zhongguo zhongyi yanjiuyuan.

Zhulinsi seng (Bamboo Grove Monastery monks), attrib. *Taichan xinshu* (A new book on childbearing). Attrib. specifically to Master Jingguang, Master Lunying, and Master Xueyan. Compiled circa 1771; recopied with preface dated 1793; printed 1886. Reprinted in *ZBYS*, vol. 8.

———. *Ningkun miji* (A secret book for female tranquility). Preface dated 1786. 1795 edition reprinted in *Zhulinsi nüke er zhong* (Two books on women's medicine from the Bamboo Grove Monastery). Beijing: Zhongyi guji chubanshe, 1993.

———. *Nüke mifang* (Secret prescriptions of women's medicine). Beijing: Wenrui Studio woodblock edition, 1826. BH no. 117/857.

————. *Zhulinsi nüke michuan* (Transmitted secrets of women's medicine from the Bamboo Grove Monastery). Kaifeng: Zhang Longwen Studio Engraving Shop woodblock edition, 1852. CM no. 203569.

————. *Zhulinsi nüke michuan* (Transmitted secrets of women's medicine from the Bamboo Grove Monastery). Kaifeng: Zhang Longwen Zhai Engraving Shop woodblock edition, 1852. Reprinted with a new preface dated 1864. CM no. 167188.

————. *Nüke michuan* (Transmitted secrets of women's medicine). Hangzhou: Zhou Zonglong woodblock edition, 1854. ZJ no. 4845.

————. *Fuke mifang* (Secret prescriptions of women's medicine). Li Guangming studio woodblock edition; preface dated 1866. Facsimile reprint, Beijing: Zhongguo shudian, 1987.

————. *Fuke michuan, jushi zhibao* (Transmitted secrets of women's medicine, the greatest treasure for those residing at home). Woodblock edition, afterword dated 1872. SY no. 64223.

————. *Ningkun miji* (A secret book for female tranquility). Guang Tongji woodblock edition, preface dated 1876. CS no. 454/6019.

————. *Zhulinsi nüke mishu, Qian yichan shiyi zheng fang* (A secret book on women's medicine from the Bamboo Grove Monastery, Childbirth Doctor Qian's remedies for eleven illnesses). Beijing: Fuwen zhai engraving shop, 1877. ZJ no. 4888.

————. *Guyue Zhulinsi fuke mifang, neifu xiao'er yingyan jingfeng fang* (Secret prescriptions of medicine for women from the Bamboo Grove Temple of ancient Yue, with appended tested prescriptions for treating windfright in children). Tangshan: Minghua Lithographic Printing Shop, lithograph edition, 1885. BH no. 117/857.4.

————. *Fuke mifang, taichan husheng pian* (Secret prescriptions of women's medicine, discussion of childbearing and ensuring birth). Zhili Provincial Administration Office woodblock edition, 1888. CM no. 167192.

————. *Fuke mifang* (Secret prescriptions of women's medicine). Hangzhou: Gu Haizhou woodblock edition, 1890. BH no. 117/857.3.

————. *Zhulin fuke michuan* (Transmitted secrets of women's medicine from the Bamboo Grove). Hangzhou: Gu Haizhou woodblock edition, 1890, with handwritten material added in 1892. ST no. 482812.

————. *Zhulinsi nüke mifang* (Secret prescriptions of women's medicine from the Bamboo Grove Monastery). Yizheng Hall woodblock edition, 1890. SY no. 60373.

————. *Jikun yulin Zhulin nüke* (Women's medicine from the Bamboo Grove to benefit females and raise children). Qingbai daoren hand-copied manuscript, 1891. ZJ no. 4880.

————. *Zhulinsi nüke zhengzhi* (Treatments for women's illnesses from the Bamboo Grove Monastery). Shanghai: Haihe Pavilion Bookstore, 1895. Reprinted with preface dated 1915. CM no. 167198.

————. *Nüke mifang* (Secret prescriptions of women's medicine). Wenlin Hall woodblock edition, 1896. ZJ no. 4883.

————. *Zhulinsi nüke mifang* (Secret prescriptions of women's medicine from the Bamboo Grove Monastery). N.d., woodblock edition. CM no. 193396.

Zhu Xiao, ed. *Puji fang* (Formulas for universal benefit). 1390. Reprinted in *SKQS*.

Zhu Xuzeng. *Kaiyouyi zhai dushu zhi* (Record of books read at the There Is Benefit in Reading Studio). Woodblock edition, 1880.

Zhu Zhenheng. *Gezhi yulun* (Additional discourses on extending knowledge through the investigation of things). Compiled circa 1347. Modern critical edition of Yuan dynasty woodblock edition reprinted in Zhu Zhenheng, *Danxi yiji*.

———. *Jufang fahui* (Fully deploying the formulary of the Imperial Pharmacy Service). Compiled 1347. Modern critical edition of Yuan dynasty woodblock edition reprinted in Zhu Zhenheng, *Danxi yiji*.

———, attrib., Dai Yuanli, comp. *Jinkui gouxuan* (Drawing out the subtleties of the *Golden Cabinet*). Compiled between 1368 and 1398. Modern critical edition of Shenxiu tang woodblock edition of the Ming, published in Zhu Zhenheng, *Danxi yiji*.

———, attrib., Yang Xunshi, comp. *Danxi xinfa* (The essential methods of Danxi). First published between 1450 and 1456. Modern critical edition of 1481 woodblock edition, edited by Cheng Chong, published in Zhu Zhenheng, *Danxi yiji*.

———. *Danxi yiji* (The collected medical works of Danxi). Beijing: Renmin weisheng chubanshe, 1993.

OTHER SOURCES

Ahern, Emily. "The Power and Pollution of Chinese Women." In *Women in Chinese Society,* edited by Margery Wolf and Roxane Witke, 193–214. Stanford: Stanford University Press, 1975.

Andrews, Bridie. "The Making of Modern Chinese Medicine, 1895–1937." PhD diss., Cambridge University, 1996.

Barnes, Linda. *Needles, Herbs, Gods, and Ghosts: China, Healing, and the West to 1848.* Cambridge, Mass.: Harvard University Press, 2005.

Beers, Mark H., et al., eds. *The Merck Manual of Medical Information, Second Home Edition.* New York: Pocket Books, 2003.

Bensky, Dan, and Andrew Gamble. *Chinese Herbal Medicine: Materia Medica.* Revised edition. Seattle: Eastland Press, 1993.

Borst, Charlotte G. *Catching Babies: The Professionalization of Childbirth, 1870–1920.* Cambridge, Mass.: Harvard University Press, 1995.

Bray, Francesca. "A Deathly Disorder: Understanding Women's Health in Late Imperial China." In *Knowledge and the Scholarly Medical Traditions,* edited by Don Bates, 235–50. Cambridge: Cambridge University Press, 1995.

———. *Technology and Gender: Fabrics of Power in Late Imperial China.* Berkeley: University of California Press, 1997.

Brokaw, Cynthia J. *The Ledgers of Merit and Demerit: Social Change and Moral Order in Late Imperial China.* Princeton, N.J.: Princeton University Press, 1991.

———. "Supernatural Retribution and Human Destiny." In *Religions of China in Practice,* edited by Donald S. Lopez Jr., 423–36. Princeton, N.J.: Princeton University Press, 1996.

————. *Commerce in Culture: The Sibao Book Trade in the Qing and Republican Periods.* Cambridge, Mass.: Harvard University Press, 2007.

Brokaw, Cynthia J., and Kai-wing Chow, eds. *Printing and Book Culture in Late Imperial China.* Berkeley: University of California Press, 2005.

Bunney, Sarah. "On the Origins of the Midwife." *New Scientist* (May 22, 1993): 18.

Cai Xiaomin. Interview by author, August 10, 1993, Shanghai.

Cameron, Samuel J., Archibald N. McLellan, Robert A. Lennie, and John Hewitt. *A Glasgow Manual of Obstetrics.* London: Edward Arnold & Company, 1924.

Cass, Victoria B. "Female Healers in the Ming and the Lodge of Ritual and Ceremony." *Journal of the American Oriental Society* 106, no. 1 (January–March 1986): 233–40.

Chang Che-chia. "The Therapeutic Tug of War: The Imperial Physician-Patient Relationship in the Era of Empress Dowager Cixi (1874–1908)." PhD diss., University of Pennsylvania, 1998.

Chang Chia-feng. "Shenghua zhi yuan yu liming zhi men: Jin yuan ming yixue zhong de 'mingmen' shitan" (The gate of life: The conceptions of *mingmen* in traditional Chinese medicine in the Jin, Yuan, and Ming periods), *Xin shixue* 9, no. 3 (1998): 1–48

————. "Dispersing the Foetal Toxin of the Body: Conceptions of Smallpox Aetiology in Pre-Modern China." In *Contagion: Perspectives from Pre-Modern Societies,* edited by Lawrence I. Conrad and Dominik Wujastyk, 23–38. Aldershot, U.K.: Ashgate, 2000.

Chang, Kang-i Sun. "Ming and Qing Anthologies of Women's Poetry and Their Selection Strategies." In *Writing Women in Late Imperial China,* edited by Ellen Widmer and Kang-i Sun Chang, 147–70. Stanford: Stanford University Press, 1997.

Chang, Kang-i Sun, and Haun Saussy, eds. *Women Writers of Traditional China: An Anthology of Poetry and Criticism.* Stanford: Stanford University Press, 1999.

Chan, Wing-tsit. *A Sourcebook in Chinese Philosophy.* Princeton, N.J.: Princeton University Press, 1963.

————, ed. *Chu Hsi and Neo-Confucianism.* Honolulu: University of Hawai'i Press, 1986.

Chao, Yüan-ling. "Medicine and Society in Late Imperial China: A Study of Physicians in Suzhou." PhD diss., University of California, Los Angeles, 1995.

————. "Patronizing Medicine: The *Sanhuang Miao* (Temple of the Three Emperors) in Late Imperial China." Paper presented at the American Historical Association Annual Meeting, New York, January 2–5, 1997.

————. "The Ideal Physician in Late Imperial China: The Question of *Sanshi.*" *East Asian Science, Technology, and Medicine,* no. 17 (2000): 66–93.

————. "Lineages and Schools: Zhang Zhongjing and *Sidajia* in Ming and Qing." Paper presented at the Tenth International Conference on the History of Science in East Asia, Shanghai, 2002.

Chen Shouchun. "Zhulinsi fuke shilue" (A general history of the Bamboo Grove Monastery's medicine for women). In *Xiaoshan wenshi ziliao xuanji* (Selected documents on the history of Xiaoshan), edited by Zhongguo renmin zhengzhi xieshang huiyi, Xiaoshanshi weiyuan hui, wenshi ziliao gongzuo weiyuanhui (Historical Documents Working Committee of the Xiaoshan City Committee of the People's Political Consultative Conference), 1:87–103. Xiaoshan, n.p., 1988.

Chen Yuan-peng. "Liangsong de 'shangyi shiren' yu 'ruyi'—Jianlun qi zai Jin Yuan de liubian" ("Elites who esteemed medicine" and "Confucian doctors" in the Northern and Southern Song dynasties, with a discussion on their spread and transformation during the Jin and Yuan dynasties). Master's thesis, Taiwan National University, 1996.

Chia, Lucille. "Of Three Mountains Street: The Commercial Publishers of Ming Nanjing." In *Printing and Book Culture in Late Imperial China,* edited by Cynthia J. Brokaw and Kai-wing Chow, 107–51. Berkeley: University of California Press, 2005.

China Imperial Maritime Customs. *Medical Reports* (Shanghai). 1871–1910.

Ch'iu Chung-lin. "Ruyi, shiyi yu yongyi: Mingdai dianji zhong duiyu yizhe de pinglun" (Scholar-physicians, hereditary doctors, and bad doctors: Assessments of medical practitioners in Ming-era records). In *Ming ren wenji yu mingdai yanjiu xueshu yantaohui* (Conference on Ming literati collections and Ming studies). Taipei: Zhongguo Mingdai yanjiu xuehui, 2001.

———. "Mingdai shiyi yu fuzhou xian yixue" (Lineages of doctors and local medical institutions in the Ming Dynasty). *Hanxue yanjiu* 22, no. 2 (2004): 327–59.

Cole, James. *Shaohsing: Competition and Cooperation in Nineteenth-Century China.* Tucson: University of Arizona Press, 1986.

Croizier, Ralph. *Traditional Medicine in Modern China.* Cambridge, Mass.: Harvard University Press, 1968.

Cullen, Christopher. "*Yi'an* (Case Statements): The Origins of a Genre of Chinese Medical Literature." In *Innovation in Chinese Medicine.* Needham Research Institute Series 3, edited by Elisabeth Hsu, 297–323. Cambridge: Cambridge University Press, 2001.

Cunningham, Gary F., Norman F. Gant, Kenneth J. Leveno, Larry C. Gilstrap III, John C. Hauth, and Katharine D. Wenstrom, eds. *Williams Obstetrics.* Twenty-first edition. New York: McGraw Hill, 2001.

Dean-Jones, Lesley. *Women's Bodies in Classical Greek Science.* Oxford: Clarendon Press, 1994.

Demiéville, Paul. "Byō." In *Hobogirin: Dictionnaire encyclopédique du bouddhisme d'après les sources chinoises et japonaises,* edited by Demiéville, 224–65. Tokyo: Maison franco-japonaise, 1929. Reprint, Paris: Librairie d'Amérique et d'Orient, 1974.

Despeux, Catherine. *Immortelles de la Chine ancienne: Taoïsme et alchémie féminine.* Puiseaux: Pardes, 1990.

———. *Taoïsme et corps humain: Le xiuzhen tu.* Paris: Guy Tredaniel, 1994.

———. "The System of the Five Circulatory Phases and the Six Seasonal Influences *(wuyun liuqi),* a Source of Innovation in Medicine under the Song." In *Innovation in Chinese Medicine.* Needham Research Institute Series 3, edited by Elisabeth Hsu, 121–66. Cambridge: Cambridge University Press, 2001.

———. "The Body Revealed: The Contribution of Forensic Medicine to Knowledge and Representations of the Skeleton in China." In *Graphics and Text in the Production of Technical Knowledge in China: The Warp and the Weft*, edited by Francesca Bray, Vera Dorofeeva-Lichtmann, and Georges Metailie, 635–84. Leiden: Brill, 2007.

Dikötter, Frank. *Imperfect Conceptions: Medical Knowledge, Birth Defects, and Eugenics in China*. New York: Columbia University Press, 1998.

Dong Hao. "Xiaoshan Zhulinsi fuke mifang guangfan chuanbo de wojian." *Weishengzhi jianxun*, no. 5 (October 1983): 12–13.

Dott, Brian. "Ascending Mount Tai: Social and Cultural Interactions in 18th Century China." PhD diss., University of Pittsburgh, 1999.

Duden, Barbara. *The Woman beneath the Skin: A Doctor's Patients in Eighteenth-Century Germany*. Translated by Thomas Dunlap. Cambridge, Mass.: Harvard University Press, 1991.

————. *Disembodying Women: Perspectives on Pregnancy and the Unborn*. Translated by Lee Hoinacki. Cambridge, Mass.: Harvard University Press, 1993.

————. "The Fetus on the 'Farther Shore': Toward a History of the Unborn." In *Fetal Subjects, Feminist Positions*, edited by Lynn M. Morgan and Meredith W. Michaels, 13–25. Philadelphia: University of Pennsylvania Press, 1999.

————. "The History of Security in the Knowledge of Pregnancy." Seminar paper delivered as part of "Women's Health: Historical Perspectives and Policy Dilemmas," lecture series at University of Michigan, Ann Arbor, March 19, 1999.

Du, Yongtao. "Translocal Lineage and the Romance of Homeland Attachment: The Pans of Suzhou in Qing China." *Late Imperial China* 27, no. 1 (June 2006): 31–65.

Eberhard, Wolfram. *Dictionary of Chinese Symbols*. Hong Kong: Federal Publications, 1990.

Ebrey, Patricia, ed. *Chinese Civilization: A Sourcebook*. Second edition. New York: Free Press, 1993.

Elman, Benjamin A. *From Philology to Philosophy: Intellectual and Social Aspects of Change in Late Imperial China*. Cambridge, Mass.: Harvard University Press, 1984.

————. *A Cultural History of Civil Examinations in Late Imperial China*. Berkeley: University of California Press, 2000.

Farquhar, Judith. *Knowing Practice: The Clinical Encounter of Chinese Medicine*. Boulder, Colo.: Westview Press, 1994.

Fauveau, Vincent, Masuma Mamdani, Robert Steinglass, and Marjorie A. Koblinsky. "Maternal Tetanus: Magnitude, Epidemiology, and Potential Control Measures." *International Journal of Gynecology and Obstetrics* 40 (1993): 3–12.

Finch, Geoffrey. *Linguistic Terms and Concepts*. New York: St. Martin's Press, 2000.

Folsom, Kenneth E. *Friends, Guests, and Colleagues: The Mu-fu System in the Late Ch'ing Period*. Berkeley: University of California Press, 1968.

Fromkin, Victoria, ed. *Linguistics: An Introduction to Linguistic Theory*. Oxford: Blackwell, 2000.

Furth, Charlotte. "Blood, Body, and Gender: Medical Images of the Female Condition in China." *Chinese Science* 7 (1986): 43–66.

———. "Concepts of Pregnancy, Childbirth, and Infancy in Ch'ing Dynasty China." *Journal of Asian Studies* 46, no. 1 (1987): 7–35.

———. *A Flourishing Yin: Gender in China's Medical History, 960–1665.* Berkeley: University of California Press, 1999.

———. "The Physician as Philosopher of the Way: Zhu Zhenheng (1282–1358)." *Harvard Journal of Asiatic Studies* 66, no. 2 (December 2006): 423–59.

———. Introduction to *Thinking with Cases,* edited by Furth, Judith T. Zeitlin, and Ping-chen Hsiung, 1–27. Honolulu: University of Hawai'i Press, 2007.

———. "Producing Medical Knowledge through Cases: History, Evidence, Action." In *Thinking with Cases,* edited by Furth, Judith T. Zeitlin, and Ping-chen Hsiung, 125–51. Honolulu: University of Hawai'i Press, 2007.

Furth, Charlotte, Judith T. Zeitlin, and Ping-chen Hsiung, eds. *Thinking with Cases: Specialist Knowledge in Chinese Cultural History.* Honolulu: University of Hawai'i Press, 2007.

Fu Shan, attrib. *Fu Qing-zhu's Gynecology.* Translated by Yang Shou-zhong and Liu Da-wei. Boulder, Colo.: Blue Poppy Press, 1995.

Fu Weikang. *Zhongguo yixueshi* (A history of medicine in China). Shanghai: Shanghai zhongyi xueyuan chubanshe, 1990.

Goldschmidt, Asaf. "The Transformations of Chinese Medicine during the Northern Song Dynasty (A.D. 960–1127): The Integration of Three Past Medical Approaches into a Comprehensive Medical System Following a Wave of Epidemics." PhD diss., University of Pennsylvania, 1999.

———. "Huizong's Impact on Medicine and on Public Health." In *Emperor Huizong and Late Northern Song China: The Politics of Culture and the Culture of Politics,* edited by Patricia Ebrey and Maggie Bickford, 275–323. Cambridge, Mass.: Harvard University Asia Center, 2006.

Gong Chun. *Zhongguo lidai weisheng zuzhi ji yixue* (Health organizations and medical education throughout Chinese history). N.p.: Weishengbu kejiaosi, 1983.

Gowing, Laura. "Secret Births and Infanticide in Seventeenth-Century England." *Past and Present* 156, no. 1 (1997): 87–115.

Grant, Joanna. *A Chinese Physician: Wang Ji and the "Stone Mountain Medical Case Histories."* London: RoutledgeCurzon, 2003.

Green, Monica H., ed. and trans. *The Trotula: An English Translation of the Medieval Compendium of Women's Medicine.* Philadelphia: University of Pennsylvania Press, 2001.

Hamilton, Robyn. "The Pursuit of Fame: Luo Qilan (1755–1813?) and the Debates about Women and Talent in Eighteenth-Century Jiangnan." *Late Imperial China* 18, no. 1 (June 1997): 39–71.

Hanson, Marta. "Inventing a Tradition in Chinese Medicine: From Universal Canon to Local Medical Knowledge in South China, the Seventeenth to the Nineteenth Century." PhD diss., University of Pennsylvania, 1997.

———. "Robust Northerners and Delicate Southerners: The Nineteenth-Century Invention of a Southern Medical Tradition." *positions* 6, no. 3 (1998): 515–50.

———. "The *Golden Mirror* in the Imperial Court of the Qianlong Emperor." *Early Science and Medicine: Special Issue: Science and State Patronage in Early Modern East Asia* 8, no. 2 (May 2003): 111–47.

———. "The Significance of Manchu Medical Sources in the Qing." In *Proceedings of the First North American Conference on Manchu Studies* (Portland, Oregon, May 9–10, 2003). Vol. 1: *Studies in Manchu Literature and History,* edited by Stephen Wadley, Carsten Naeher, and Keith Dede, 131–75. Wiesbaden: Harrassowitz Verlag, 2006.

Hanyu dacidian (Comprehensive dictionary of the Chinese language). 12 vols. plus index. Shanghai: Hanyu dacidian chubanshe, 1990–94.

Harper, Donald. *Early Chinese Medical Literature.* London: Keegan Paul, 1998.

Heh, Shu-Shya, Lindsey Coombes, and Helen Bartlett. "The Association between Depressive Symptoms and Social Support in Taiwanese Women during the Month." *International Journal of Nursing Studies* 41, no. 5 (2004): 573–79.

He Shixi. *Zhongguo lidai yijia zhuanlu* (Biographical records of medical experts throughout Chinese history). 3 vols. Beijing: Renmin weisheng chubanshe, 1991.

He Zhongling. "Wanqing Sichuan pujilei yizhu de chansheng he yingxiang" (The production and influence of popular medical texts in late Qing Sichuan). *Zhonghua yishi zazhi* 24, no. 1 (January 1994): 20–22.

Hinrichs, T. J. "The Medical Transforming of Governance and Southern Customs in Song Dynasty China (960–1279 C.E.)." PhD diss., Harvard University, 2003.

Ho, Ping-ti. *The Ladder of Success in Imperial China: Aspects of Social Mobility, 1368–1911.* New York: Columbia University Press, 1962.

Hsiung, Ping-chen. "Facts in the Tale: Case Records and Pediatric Medicine in Late Imperial China." In *Thinking with Cases,* edited by Charlotte Furth, Judith T. Zeitlin, and Ping-chen Hsiung, 152–68. Honolulu: University of Hawai'i Press, 2007.

Hsu, Elisabeth, ed. *Innovation in Chinese Medicine.* Needham Research Institute Series 3. Cambridge: Cambridge University Press, 2001.

———. "Pulse Diagnostics in the Western Han: How *Mai* and *Qi* Determine *Bing.*" In *Innovation in Chinese Medicine.* Needham Research Institute Series 3, edited by Hsu, 51–92. Cambridge: Cambridge University Press, 2001.

Hsu, Hong-yen, et al. *Oriental Materia Medica: A Concise Guide.* Long Beach, Calif.: Oriental Healing Arts Institute, 1986.

Hucker, Charles O. *A Dictionary of Official Titles in Imperial China.* Stanford: Stanford University Press, 1985.

Hu Guojun. "Zeng Yi nüyi wannian yixue yishi" (An anecdote about the female doctor Zeng Yi's medicine late in life). *Sichuan zhongyi* (October 1985): 6–7.

Hummel, Arthur W., ed. *Eminent Chinese of the Ch'ing Period.* Washington, D.C.: Government Printing Office, 1943.

Hu Wenkai. *Lidai funü zhuzuo kao* (Study of women authors throughout history). Shanghai: Shanghai guji chubanshe, 1984.

Hymes, Robert P. "Not Quite Gentlemen? Doctors in Sung and Yuan." *Chinese Science* 8 (1987): 9–76.

Idema, Wilt, and Beata Grant. *The Red Brush: Writing Women of Imperial China.* Cambridge, Mass.: Harvard University Asia Center, 2004.

Infectious Diseases. Vol. 1: *Bacterial.* PDxMD Medical Conditions Series. Philadelphia: Elsevier Science, 2003.

Ivanhoe, Philip J. "Early Confucianism and Environmental Ethics." In *Confucianism and Ecology,* edited by Mary Evelyn Tucker and John Berthrong, 59–76. Cambridge, Mass.: Harvard University Press, 1998.

———. "Neo-Confucian Philosophy." In *Routledge Encyclopedia of Philosophy,* edited by Edward Craig, 764–76. London: Routledge, 1998.

Jiangsu xin yixueyuan, ed. *Zhongyao dacidian* (Comprehensive dictionary of Chinese materia medica). 3 vols. Shanghai: Shanghai kexue jishu chubanshe, 1998–2000.

Jia Zhizhong and Yang Yanfei. "*Dasheng bian* ji qi zuozhe" (The "Treatise on Easy Childbirth" and its author). *Zhonghua yishi zazhi* 26, no. 2 (1996): 103–5.

Jones, David C. "Postpartum Emergencies." In *Handbook of Obstetric and Gynecologic Emergencies.* 3rd ed., edited by Guy I. Benrubi, 199–213. Philadelphia: Lippincott Williams & Wilkins, 2005.

Karlgren, Bernhard, trans. *The Book of Odes.* Stockholm: Museum of Far Eastern Antiquities, 1950.

Kalra, Harish, Rajul Tandon, Jitendra Kumar Trivedi, and Aleksandar Janca. "Pregnancy-Induced Obsessive Compulsive Disorder: A Case Report." *Annals of General Psychiatry* 4 (2005): 12.

Katz, Paul. *Demon Hordes and Burning Boats: The Cult of Marshal Wen in Later Imperial Chekiang.* Albany: State University of New York Press, 1995.

King, Helen. *Hippocrates' Woman: Reading the Female Body in Ancient Greece.* London: Routledge, 1998.

Kleinman, Arthur. *Patients and Healers in the Context of Culture: An Exploration of the Borderland between Anthropology, Medicine, and Psychiatry.* Berkeley: University of California Press, 1980.

Knechtges, David R. "Questions about the Language of *Sheng min.*" In *Ways with Words: Writing about Reading Texts from Early China,* edited by Pauline Yu, Peter Bol, Stephen Owen, and Willard Peterson, 25–31. Berkeley: University of California Press, 2000.

Ko, Dorothy. *Teachers of the Inner Chambers: Women and Culture in Seventeenth-Century China.* Stanford: Stanford University Press, 1994.

Kohn, Livia, ed. *Daoism Handbook.* 2 vols. Leiden: Brill, 2004.

Kuriyama, Shigehisa. "Visual Knowledge in Classical Chinese Medicine." In *Knowledge and the Scholarly Medical Tradition,* edited by Don Bates, 205–34. Cambridge: Cambridge University Press, 1995.

———. *The Expressiveness of the Body and the Divergence of Greek and Chinese Medicine.* New York: Zone Books, 1999.

Leavitt, Judith Walzer. "The Growth of Medical Authority: Technology and Morals in Turn-of-the-Century Obstetrics, " *Medical Anthropology Quarterly* 42, no. 2 (Summer 2002): 181–214.

Lee, Dominic T. S., et al. "A Psychiatric Epidemiological Study of Postpartum Chinese Women." *American Journal of Psychiatry* 158, no. 2 (February 2001): 220–26.

Lee, James Z., and Wang Feng. *One Quarter of Humanity: Malthusian Mythol-*

ogy and Chinese Realities, 1700–2000. Cambridge, Mass.: Harvard University Press, 1999.

Lee, Jen-der. "Han Tang zhijian qiuzi yifang shitan, jian lun fuke lanshang yu xingbie lunshu" (Reproductive medicine in late antiquity and early medieval China: Gender discourse and the birth of gynecology). *Zhongyang yanjiuyuan lishi yuyan yanjiusuo jikan* 68, no. 2 (1997): 283–367.

———. "Childbirth in Early Imperial China." In *Medicine for Women in Imperial China,* edited by Angela Ki Che Leung, 108–78. Leiden: Brill, 2006.

Legge, James, trans. *The Works of Mencius (Mengzi).* Second edition. Oxford: Clarendon Press, 1895.

Lei, Sean Hsiang-lin. "When Chinese Medicine Encountered the State: 1910–1949." PhD diss., University of Chicago, 1999.

Leu Chin-ai. "Postpartum Bliss." *Free China Review* 44, no. 4 (1994): 52.

Leung, Angela Ki Che. "Autour de la naissance: La mère et l'enfant en Chine aux XIVe et XVIIe siècles." *Cahiers internationaux de sociologie* 76 (1984): 51–69.

———. "Women Practicing Medicine in Premodern China." In *Chinese Women in the Imperial Past: New Perspectives,* edited by Harriet T. Zurndorfer, 101–34. Leiden: Brill, 1999.

———. "Medical Instruction and Popularization in Ming-Qing China." *Late Imperial China* 24, no. 1 (2003): 130–52.

———. "Medical Learning from the Song to the Ming. In *The Song-Yuan-Ming Transition in Chinese History,* edited by Paul Jakov Smith and Richard von Glahn, 374–98. Cambridge, Mass.: Harvard University Press, 2003.

———, ed. *Medicine for Women in Imperial China.* Leiden: Brill, 2006.

Liao Yuqun. "Xiaoshan Zhulinsi nüke kaolue" (Outline of inquiries into the practice of women's medicine at the Xiaoshan Bamboo Grove Monastery). *Zhonghua yishi zazhi* 16, no. 3 (1986): 159–61.

Li Jianmin. "Zhongguo gudai 'jinfang' kaolun" (Jinfang: The transmission of secret techniques in ancient China). *Zhongyang yanjiuyuan lishi yuyan yanjiusuo jikan* 68, pt. 1 (1997): 117–66.

———. *Si sheng zhi yu: Zhou-Qin-Han maixue zhi yuanliu* (The boundary between life and death: The origins of meridian theory in the Zhou, Qin, and Han dynasties). Taipei: Institute of History and Philology, Academia Sinica, 2000.

Li Jingwei, ed. *Zhongyi renwu cidian* (A dictionary of eminent figures in Chinese medicine). Shanghai: Shanghai cishu chubanshe, 1988.

Li Jingwei and Lin Zhaogeng, eds. *Zhongguo yixue tongshi, gudai juan* (A comprehensive history of Chinese medicine: The ancient period). Beijing: Renmin weisheng chubanshe, 2000.

Li Jingwei and Li Zhidong. *Zhongguo gudai yixueshi* (A history of ancient medicine in China). Shijia zhuang: Hebei kexue jishu chubanshe, 1990.

Ling Yunpeng. "Luetan zhongyi waike xuepai" (A general discussion of different intellectual currents in the treatment of external ailments in traditional Chinese medicine). *Jiangsu zhongyi* (May 1964): 5–6.

Liu Houkun. "Du *Shenghua pian* shu hou" (After reading the book *Treatise on Generating and Transforming*). *Funü yixue zazhi,* no. 11 (n.d.): 7.

Liu Shijue. "Danxi zhushu bianwei" (Distinguishing the false among the books authored by Zhu Danxi). *Zhonghua yishi zazhi* 23, n. 2 (1993): 106–9.

Liu Xiaogan. "An Inquiry into the Core Value of Laozi's Philosophy." In *Religious and Philosophical Aspects of the Laozi,* edited by Mark Csikszentmihalyi and Philip J. Ivanhoe, 211–37. Albany: State University of New York Press, 1999.

Li Yang. "Chenshi fuke shijia" (The Chen family of hereditary experts in medicine for women). In *Tongxiang wenshi ziliao* (Historical materials on Tongxiang). Edited by Tongxiangxian zhengxie wenshi ziliao gongzuo weiyuanhui (Historical Documents Working Committee of the Tongxiang County Committee of the People's Political Consultative Conference), 4:183–86. Tongxiang: n.p., 1986.

Li Yun, ed. *Zhongyi renming cidian* (A biographical dictionary of Chinese medicine). Beijing: Guoji wenhua chubanshe, 1988.

Lockhart, William, trans. "A Treatise on Midwifery: A New Edition Published in the Fifth Year of Taou Kwong (1825)." *Dublin Journal of Medical Science* 20, no. 60 (1842): 333–69.

Loewe, Michael, ed. *Early Chinese Texts: A Bibliographical Guide.* Berkeley: Society for the Study of Early China and the Institute of East Asian Studies, University of California, Berkeley, 1993.

Loudon, Irvine. *Medical Care and the General Practitioner, 1750–1850.* Oxford: Clarendon Press, 1986.

———. *The Tragedy of Childbed Fever.* Oxford: Oxford University Press, 2000.

Lo, Vivienne. "The Influence of Nurturing Life Culture on the Development of Western Han Acumoxa Therapy." In *Innovation in Chinese Medicine.* Needham Research Institute Series 3, edited by Elisabeth Hsu, 19–50. Cambridge: Cambridge University Press, 2001.

Luo Yuankai, ed. *Zhongyi fuke xue* (TCM gynecology). Beijing: Renmin weisheng chubanshe, 1994.

Lusk, William Thompson. *The Science and Art of Midwifery.* New York: D. Appleton, 1888.

Lü Zhi. "Zaitan Fu Shan yixue zhuzuo de zhenwei" (Revisiting the issue of whether Fu Shan's medical books are genuine or fake) *Zhejiang zhongyi zazhi,* no. 3 (1986): 137–39.

Lynn, Richard John, trans. *The Classic of Changes: A New Translation of the I Ching as Interpreted by Wang Bi.* New York: Columbia University Press, 1994.

MacPherson, Kerrie L. "Cholera in China, 1820–1930: An Aspect of the Internationalization of Infectious Disease." In *Sediments of Time: Environment and Society in Chinese History,* edited by Mark Elvin and Liu Ts'ui-jung, 487–519. Cambridge: Cambridge University Press, 1998.

Ma Dazheng. *Zhongguo fuchanke fazhan shi* (The history of the development of gynecology and obstetrics in China). N.p.: Shanxi kexue jiaoyu chubanshe, 1992.

Ma Jixing. *Zhongyi wenxian xue* (The study of Chinese medical literature). Shanghai: Shanghai kexue jishu chubanshe, 1990.

Mann, Susan. *Precious Records: Women in China's Long Eighteenth Century.*
    Stanford: Stanford University Press, 1997.
————. *The Talented Women of the Zhang Family.* Berkeley: University of Cali-
    fornia Press, 2007.
Maternal and Neonatal Tetanus Elimination by 2005: Strategies for Achieving and
    Maintaining Elimination, UNICEF, WHO, UNFPA, November 2000. www
    .unfpa.org/upload/lib_pub_file/155_filename_matetanuseng.pdf, accessed
    May 26, 2009.
Maxwell, Preston, and J. L. Liu. "Ta Sheng P'ien: A Chinese Household Manual
    of Obstetrics." *Annals of Medical History* 5, no. 2 (Summer 1923): 95–99.
McDermott, Joseph. "The Ascendance of the Imprint in China." In *Printing and*
    Book Culture in Late Imperial China, edited by Cynthia J. Brokaw and Kai-
    wing Chow, 55–104. Berkeley: University of California Press, 2005.
Ming-Qing jinshi timing beilu suoyin (An index to rosters of *jinshi* degree hold-
    ers in the Ming and Qing). 3 vols. Taipei: Wen shi zhe chubanshe, 1982.
Morgan, Lynn M., and Meredith W. Michaels, eds. *Fetal Subjects, Feminist Po-*
    sitions. Philadelphia: University of Pennsylvania Press, 1999.
Morohashi Tetsuji. *Dai Kanwa jiten* (Great Chinese dictionary). Tokyo: Taishūkan
    shoten, 1986.
Moscucci, Ornella. *The Science of Woman: Gynaecology and Gender in England,*
    1800–1929. Cambridge: Cambridge University Press, 1990.
Naquin, Susan, and Evelyn S. Rawski. *Chinese Society in the Eighteenth Cen-*
    tury. New Haven, Conn.: Yale University Press, 1987.
Needham, Joseph. *Science and Civilisation in China.* Vol. 4, pt. 6: "Medicine,"
    with the collaboration of Lu Gwei-Djen, edited by Nathan Sivin. Cambridge:
    Cambridge University Press, 2000.
Novak, Emil. *Menstruation and Its Disorders.* New York: D. Appleton, 1921.
Norris, Richard C., ed. *An American Text-Book of Obstetrics for Practitioners*
    and Students (Philadelphia: W. B. Saunders, 1895.
Nylan, Michael. *The Five "Confucian" Classics.* New Haven, Conn.: Yale Uni-
    versity Press, 2001.
Oakley, Ann. *The Captured Womb: A History of the Medical Care of Pregnant*
    Women. Oxford: Basil Blackwell, 1984.
Obringer, Frédéric. *L'aconit et l'orpiment: Drogues et poisons en Chine anci-*
    enne et médiévale. Paris: Fayard, 1997.
O'Dowd, Michael J., and Elliot E. Phillipp. *The History of Obstetrics and Gy-*
    naecology. New York: Parthenon, 1994.
Okanishi Tameto. *Song yiqian yiji kao* (Research on medical works before the
    Song dynasty). 4 vols. Taipei: Guting shuwu, 1969.
Overmyer, Daniel L. *Precious Volumes: An Introduction to Chinese Sectarian*
    Scriptures from the Sixteenth and Seventeenth Centuries. Cambridge, Mass.:
    Harvard University Press, 1999.
Peterson, Willard J. "Introduction: New Order for the Old Order." In *The Cam-*
    bridge History of China. Vol. 9, pt. 1: *The Ch'ing Dynasty to 1800,* edited
    by Willard J. Peterson. Cambridge: Cambridge University Press, 2002.
Phillips, Tina. "Building the Nation through Women's Health: Modern Mid-

wifery in Early Twentieth-Century China." PhD diss., University of Pittsburgh, 2006.

Porkert, Manfred. *The Theoretical Foundations of Chinese Medicine: Systems of Correspondence*. Cambridge, Mass.: MIT Press, 1974.

Pregadio, Fabrizio, and Lowell Skar. "Inner Alchemy." In *Daoism Handbook*, edited by Livia Kohn, 466–97. Leiden: Brill, 2004.

Qiu Peiran and Ding Guangdi, eds. *Zhongyi gejia xueshuo* (The teachings of famous Chinese medical experts). Beijing: Renmin weisheng chubanshe, 1992.

Reiser, Stanley Joel. *Medicine and the Reign of Technology*. Cambridge: Cambridge University Press, 1978.

Robinet, Isabelle. *Taoism: Growth of a Religion*. Translated by Phyllis Brooks. Stanford: Stanford University Press, 1997.

Rogaski, Ruth. *Hygienic Modernity: Meanings of Health and Disease in Treaty-Port China*. Berkeley: University of California Press, 2004.

Rosenberg, Charles E., ed. *The Origins of Specialization in American Medicine*. New York: Garland, 1989.

———. "Framing Disease: Illness, Society, and History." In *Framing Disease: Studies in Cultural History*, edited by Charles E. Rosenberg and Janet Golden, xiii–xxvi. New Brunswick, N.J.: Rutgers University Press, 1992.

Rothstein, William G. *American Medical Schools and the Practice of Medicine*. New York: Oxford University Press, 1987.

Scheid, Volker. *Chinese Medicine in Contemporary China: Plurality and Synthesis*. Durham, N.C.: Duke University Press, 2002.

———. *Currents of Tradition in Chinese Medicine: 1626–2006*. Seattle: Eastland Press, 2007.

Schipper, Kristofer. *The Taoist Body*. Translated by Karen C. Duval. Berkeley: University of California Press, 1993.

Scott, James R., et al., eds. *Danforth's Obstetrics and Gynecology*. 6th ed. Philadelphia: J. B. Lippincott, 1990.

Selby, Stephen. *Chinese Archery*. Hong Kong: Hong Kong University Press, 2000.

Sengupta, Somini. "Facing Death for Adultery, Nigerian Woman Is Acquitted." *New York Times*, September 26, 2003, p. A3.

Shanghai tushuguan, ed. *Zhongguo congshu zonglu* (A general index to Chinese collectanea). Shanghai: Shanghai guji chubanshe, 1982.

Shapiro, Hugh. "The Puzzle of Spermatorrhea in Republican China." *positions* 6, no. 3 (1998): 551–96.

Sivin, Nathan. *Traditional Medicine in Contemporary China*. Ann Arbor: Center for Chinese Studies, University of Michigan, 1986.

———. "Huang Ti Nei Ching." In *Early Chinese Texts: A Bibliographical Guide*, edited by Michael Loewe, 196–215. Berkeley: Society for the Study of Early China and the Institute of East Asian Studies, University of California, Berkeley, 1993.

———. "Why Didn't the Chinese Have Bodies?" *Chinese Studies Association of Australia Newsletter* (University of New South Wales, Sydney), November 18, 1999.

Sommer, Matthew. "The Uses of Chastity: Sex, Law, and the Property of Widows in Qing China." *Late Imperial China* 17, no. 2 (1996): 77–130.

Song Ci. *Xiyuan jilu* (The washing away of wrongs). 1247. Translated by Brian E. McKnight. Ann Arbor: Center for Chinese Studies, University of Michigan, 1981.

Speert, Harold. *Obstetrical and Gynecologic Milestones Illustrated*. New York: Parthenon, 1996.

Spencer, Andrew. "Morphology." In *The Handbook of Linguistics*, edited by Mark Aronoff and Janie Rees-Miller, 213–37. Oxford: Blackwell, 2003.

Starr, Paul. *The Social Transformation of American Medicine*. New York: Basic Books, 1982.

Tamba no Mototane. *Iseki ko* (Study of medical books). 1819. Facsimile edition of 1831 manuscript copy reprinted Tokyo: Kokuhon shuppansha, 1933–35.

Taylor, Kim. "A Survey of the Impact of Epidemic Cholera on the Medical Community in Nineteenth-Century China." Paper presented at the "Rencontres et circulation des savoirs et des pratiques en médecine," Centre National de la Recherche Scientifique, Recherches épistémologiques et historiques sur les sciences exactes et les institutions scientifiques, Paris, December 3, 2002.

———. *Chinese Medicine in Early Communist China, 1945–1963: A Medicine of Revolution*. London: RoutledgeCurzon, 2005.

Tu Kuixian. "Qingdai nüzhongyi Zeng Yi ji qi 'Yixue bian' jianjie" (A brief introduction to the Qing dynasty woman doctor of Chinese medicine, Zeng Yi, and her work "Treatise on Medicine"). *Zhongyi zazhi* (April 1981): 69.

Unschuld, Paul U. *Medical Ethics in Imperial China: A Study in Historical Anthropology*. Berkeley: University of California Press, 1979.

———. *Medicine in China: A History of Ideas*. Berkeley: University of California Press, 1986.

———. *Medicine in China: A History of Pharmaceutics*. Berkeley: University of California Press, 1986.

———, trans. and annot. *Nan-ching: The Classic of Difficult Issues: With Commentaries by Chinese and Japanese Authors from the Third through the Twentieth Century*. Berkeley: University of California Press, 1986.

———. *Huang Di Nei Jing Su Wen: Nature, Knowledge, Imagery in an Ancient Chinese Medical Text*. Berkeley: University of California Press, 2003.

Unschuld, Paul U., and Zheng Jinsheng. "Manuscripts as Sources in the History of Chinese Medicine." In *Medieval Chinese Medicine: The Dunhuang Medical Manuscripts*, edited by Vivienne Lo and Christopher Cullen, 19–44. Abingdon, U.K.: RoutledgeCurzon, 2005.

Valussi, Elena. "Beheading the Red Dragon: A History of Female Inner Alchemy in Late Imperial China." PhD diss., School of Oriental and African Studies, University of London, 2003.

Veith, Ilza. *Huang-ti Nei-ching: The Yellow Emperor's Classic of Internal Medicine*. New ed. 1956. Reprint, Berkeley: University of California Press, 1972.

Walravens, Helmut. "Medical Knowledge of the Manchus and the *Manchu Anatomy*." *Etudes mongoles et sibériennes* 27 (1996): 359–60.

Wang Yanrong et al. "Jiawei shenghuatang zhiliao taipan tuimo canliu 34 li tihui" (Our experiences in using "Generating and Transforming Decoction with added ingredients" to treat 34 cases of retained and damaged placenta). *Henan zhongyi* 13, no. 4 (1993): 185–86.

Warner, John Harley. *Against the Spirit of System: The French Impulse in Nine-teenth-Century American Medicine.* Princeton, N.J.: Princeton University Press, 1998.

Watson, James L. "Standardizing the Gods: The Promotion of T'ien Hou ('Empress of Heaven') along the South China Coast, 960–1960." In *Popular Culture in Late Imperial China,* edited by David Johnson et al., 292–325. Berkeley: University of California Press, 1985.

Werner, E. T. C. *A Dictionary of Chinese Mythology.* Shanghai: Kelly and Walsh, 1932.

Widmer, Ellen. *The Beauty and the Book: Women and Fiction in Nineteenth-Century China.* Cambridge, Mass.: Harvard University Asia Center and Harvard University Press, 2006.

Wilkinson, Endymion. *Chinese History: A Manual, Revised and Enlarged.* Harvard-Yenching Institute Monograph Series, 52. Cambridge, Mass.: Harvard University Press, 2000.

Will, Pierre-Étienne. "Developing Forensic Knowledge through Cases in the Qing Dynasty." In *Thinking with Cases: Specialist Knowledge in Chinese Cultural History,* edited by Charlotte Furth, Judith T. Zeitlin, and Ping-chen Hsiung, 62–100. Honolulu: University of Hawai'i Press, 2007.

Williams, C. A. S. *Encyclopedia of Chinese Symbolism and Art Motives.* New York: Julian Press, 1960.

Wilms, Sabine. "The Female Body in Medieval China." PhD diss., University of Arizona, 2002.

———. " 'Ten Times More Difficult to Treat': Female Bodies in Medical Texts from Early Imperial China." In *Medicine for Women in Imperial China,* edited by Angela Ki Che Leung, 74–107. Leiden: Brill, 2006.

Wilson, Lindsay. *Women and Medicine in the French Enlightenment: The Debate over* Maladies des Femmes. Baltimore: Johns Hopkins University Press, 1993.

Wiseman, Nigel, and Feng Ye. *A Practical Dictionary of Chinese Medicine.* Brookline, Mass.: Paradigm Publications, 1998.

Wu, Yi-Li. "Transmitted Secrets: The Doctors of the Lower Yangzi Region and Popular Gynecology in Late Imperial China." PhD diss., Yale University, 1998.

———. "The Bamboo Grove Monastery and Popular Gynecology in Qing China." *Late Imperial China* 21, no. 1 (June 2000): 41–76.

———. "Ghost Fetuses, False Pregnancies, and the Parameters of Medical Uncertainty in Classical Chinese Gynecology." *Nan Nü: Men, Women, and Gender in Early and Imperial China* 4, no. 2 (2002): 170–206.

Wu Yiyi. "A Medical Line of Many Masters: A Prosopographical Study of Liu Wansu and His Disciples from the Jin to the Early Ming." *Chinese Science* 11 (1993–94): 36–65.

Xie Guan. *Zhongguo yixue dacidian* (A comprehensive dictionary of Chinese medicine). Preface dated 1926. Facsimile reprint, Beijing: Zhongguo shudian, 1988.

Xin Fu. "Lidai Shuyi kao—Chengdu nüyijia Zeng Yi zhuanlue" (Researches into Sichuan doctors throughout history—a general biography of the Chengdu female doctor Zeng Yi). *Chengdu zhongyi xueyuan xuebao* (March 1980): 65.

Xu Dachun. *Forgotten Traditions of Ancient Chinese Medicine.* Annotated and translated by Paul U. Unschuld. Brookline, Mass.: Paradigm Publications, 1990.

Yang Chongrui. "Zhongguo fuying weisheng gongzuo" (The work of maternal and infant care in China). *Zhongguo yixue zazhi* 27, no. 5 (May 1941): 280–91.

Yates, Robin D. S. "Medicine for Women in Early China: A Preliminary Survey." In *Medicine for Women in Imperial China,* edited by Angela Ki Che Leung, 19–73. Leiden: Brill, 2006.

Yen Renyin, ed. Yang Chongrui boshi danchen bainian jinian (A commemoration of the hundredth anniversary of the birth of Dr. Yang Chongrui). Beijing: Beijing yike daxue and Zhongguo xiehe yike daxue, 1990.

Yip, Ka-che. *Health and National Reconstruction in Nationalist China: The Development of Modern Health Services, 1928–1937.* Ann Arbor, Mich.: Association for Asian Studies, 1995.

Yu, Pauline, Peter Bol, Stephen Owen, and Willard Peterson, eds. *Ways with Words: Writing about Reading Texts from Early China.* Berkeley: University of California Press, 2000.

Yuan Shaoying and Yang Guizhen, eds. *Zhongguo funü mingren cidian* (Dictionary of famous Chinese women). [Changchun]: Beifang funü ertong chubanshe, 1989.

Yu, Chün-fang. "A Sutra Promoting the White-Robed Guanyin as Giver of Sons." In *Religions of China in Practice,* edited by Donald S. Lopez Jr., 97–105. Princeton, N.J.: Princeton University Press, 1996.

Yu Jianhua. *Zhongguo meishujia renming cidian* (Dictionary of Chinese artists). Shanghai: Shanghai renmin meishu chubanshe, 1981.

Zeitlin, Judith T. "The Literary Fashioning of Medical Authority: A Study of Sun Yikui's Case Histories." In *Thinking with Cases,* edited by Charlotte Furth, Judith T. Zeitlin, and Ping-chen Hsiung, 169–202. Honolulu: University of Hawai'i Press, 2007.

Zeng Jifen. *Testimony of a Confucian Woman: The Autobiography of Mrs. Nie Zeng Jifeng, 1852–1942.* Translated and annotated by Thomas L. Kennedy. Athens: University of Georgia Press, 1993.

Zhang Danian. *Key Concepts in Chinese Philosophy.* New Haven, Conn.: Yale University Press, 2002.

Zhang Yao. "Xiaoshan Zhulinsi nüke yiji yuanliu chu tan" (A preliminary study of the medical literature pertaining to the treatment of women's disorders at the Bamboo Grove Monastery of Xiaoshan). Master's thesis, Zhongguo zhongyi yanjiuyuan, yishi wenxian yanjiu suo, 1987.

Zhao Cunyi. *Zhongyi gufang fang ming kao* (A study of the names of ancient Chinese medical formulas). Beijing: Zhongguo zhongyiyao chubanshe, 1994.

Zhao Kaiyuan and Yang Jinmin. "Shenghuatang jiajian zhiliao taipan taimo canliu 56 li" (Using "Add-and-Subtract Generating and Transforming Decoction" to treat 56 cases of retained or damaged placenta). *Zhongyi zazhi,* no. 3 (1993): 1.

Zhejiangsheng zhongyiyao yanjiusuo, ed. *Xiaoshan Zhulinsi fuke mifang kao* (Investigation into the secret prescriptions of medicine for women from the Bamboo Grove Monastery of Xiaoshan). Shanghai: Shanghai kexue jishu chubanshe, 1959.

Zhejiang xinyi xueyuan, ed. *Zhongyao dacidian* (Comprehensive dictionary of Chinese drugs). Shanghai: Shanghai kexue jishu chubanshe, 1977.

Zheng Jinsheng. "Female Medical Workers in Ancient China." In *Current Perspectives in the History of Science in East Asia,* edited by Yung Sik Kim and Francesca Bray, 460–66. Seoul: Seoul National University Press, 1999.

Zhongguo yiji dacidian bianzuan weiyuanhui. *Zhongguo yiji dacidian* (Comprehensive dictionary of Chinese medical texts). Shanghai: Shanghai kexue jishu chubanshe, 2002.

Zhongguo zhongyi yanjiuyuan, ed. *Jinkui yaolue yuyi* ("The Essentials of the Golden Cabinet," translated into modern Chinese). Beijing: Renmin weisheng chubanshe, 1959.

Zhongguo zhongyi yanjiuyuan tushiguan, ed. *Quanguo Zhongyi tushu lianhe mulu* (Union catalog of Chinese medicine books in Chinese libraries). Beijing: Zhongyi guji chubanshe, 1991.

Zhonghua quanguo zhongyi xuehui Zhejiang fenhui and Zhejiang zhongyiyao yanjiusuo, eds. *Yilin huicui* (An assemblage of distinguished doctors). Hangzhou: Zhejiangsheng weisheng ting, 1981.

Zhongyi dacidian bianji weiyuanhui, ed. *Zhongyi dacidian: Fuke erke fence* (Comprehensive dictionary of Chinese medicine: Volume on gynecology and pediatrics). Beijing: Renmin weisheng chubanshe, 1981.

———. *Zhongyi dacidian: Fangji fence* (Comprehensive dictionary of Chinese medicine: Volume on medicinal formulas). Beijing: Renmin weisheng chubanshe, 1983.

Zhou Mingdao. "Xiaoshan Zhulinsi nüke shixi bukao" (Supplementary investigations into the transmission of women's medicine by the generations of the Bamboo Grove Monastery of Xiaoshan). *Zhejiang zhongyi xueyuan xuebao* (December 1981).

Zhou Mingdao et al. *Xiaoshan Zhulinsi fuke pingshi* (An assessment and explanation of medicine for women from the Bamboo Grove Monastery of Xiaoshan). Xiaoshan: Xiaoshanshi zhongyi xuehui, 1992.

Index

Note: Figures are indicated by the abbreviation *fig.* after the page number. Names in parentheses following personal names are either courtesy names or other names the person is known by.

abortion, 167, 293n65

acupuncture, 9, 25, 28, 99, 179

Additional Discourses on Extending Knowledge through the Investigation of Things (*Gezhi yulun*, Zhu Zhenheng), 41

advertisements, 78

"after birth" *(chanhou)*. *See* postpartum period

agricultural and nature metaphors: analysis of, 285–86n57; for easy childbirth, 151–52, 227–28; for human gestation and development, 122–23, 133, 142–44; for movements of child in labor, 159–60; for postpartum woman, 201; for promoting fertility, 141–42; for womb as crucible and field, 113–16. *See also* climatic influences

alchemy: internal *(neidan)* vs. external *(waidan)*, 100–101; textual tradition of female, 53, 257n146

amateurs, medical: attitudes toward, 56, 81–83; doctors distinguished from, 55–56, 72–74; legitimacy of, 72–75, 82; medical judgments made by, 57; medical texts by, 57–59, 67–75; merit of publishing by, 58, 75–81; motivations of, 188–90; portrayal

of doctors by, 75; prescription books of, 58, 71–75, 81–82, 267n69; texts used by, 54–55, 60. *See also* Bamboo Grove Monastery texts; scholar-physicians *(ruyi)*

Analects, 76

anatomy: European obsession with, 117, 280–81n133; forensic examination of, 108, 189; knowledge based on opportunistic observations, 95; midwives' examination of, 275n56; nineteenth-century investigations of, 275n55; pelvic structure and birth in, 151

Anderson, Frank, 299–300n14

Appended Supplement to "The Inner Classic Explicated by Topic" (*Leijing fuyi*, Zhang Jiebin): background of, 97–98; on life-gate *(mingmen)*, 99–104

authority of medical practitioners: amateurs' challenges to, 57; female knowledge of female body irrelevant to, 22; interpractitioner struggles over, 17–18; questions about, 16–17. *See also* legitimacy of medical practice

authorship: act of reprinting as overlapping with, 70–72; of Bamboo Grove Monastery texts, 60; of *Easy Child-*

authorship *(continued)*
  birth, 68–70, 266n59; of *Fu Qing-*
  zhu's Medicine for Women, disputed,
  206, 303–4n58; gendered patterns
  of, 19–22; of Qian family texts, 206,
  302–3n52

Bai Lizhong (aka Liangqiuzi), 277n77
Bamboo Grove Monastery (Zhulinsi):
  elite patronage of, 62–64; finances
  of, 65; legitimacy of, 64–66; location of, 59; origins of medical practice of, 59–60; reputation of, 54–
  55, 59–60, 66; suspicions about,
  63, 261n30; temple genealogies of,
  259n17
Bamboo Grove Monastery texts: on
  birth-expediting drugs, 294n69;
  circulation of, 54, 62, 268–69n92;
  context of, 55; earliest known, 60;
  efficacy of treatments in, 64–66;
  on Generating and Transforming
  Decoction, 206, 207; illustration of,
  61*fig.*; on menstrual irregularities,
  88–89; merit of publishing, 75–81;
  multiple editions and appendices of,
  60, 67–68, 70–71, 260n23, 264n49;
  perceived utility of, 74–75, 76; prefaces for, 62, 63–64, 260n22, 260n24;
  print shop advertisements in, 78.
  See also *New Book on Childbearing,*
  A (Taichan xinshu, Bamboo Grove
  Monastery monks); *Transmitted*
  Secrets of Women's Medicine from
  the Bamboo Grove; Treatise on Easy
  Childbirth (Dasheng bian, Jizhai
  jushi [Ye Feng])
bao, use of term, 92–93, 110, 274n36.
  See also womb
Bao Tingbo, 242n2
Bao Xiang'ao, 71–72, 267n69
Basic Questions (Suwen): authoritative
  version of, 27; as influence, 66; on
  living in harmony with cosmos, 155;
  origins of, 23; on palace organs,
  275n47; as part of *Yellow Emperor's*
  Inner Classic, 246–47n36; pregnancy
  tests in, 125; on sexual maturation,
  91, 273n26; on vessels and channels,
  91–92, 273n29; on womb's function,
  93–94. See also *Yellow Emperor's*
  Inner Classic (Huangdi neijing)
Bell, Charles, 195*fig.*
Bian Que: monks compared to, 65–66;
  as mythic ancestor of *fuke,* 26–27;
  references to, 248n50; secret medical
  methods of, 34

Bian Shiying, 62
birthing charts, 27, 157
birthing environment: excessively cold
  or hot weather and, 179, 220–21;
  recommendations for, 221–22;
  temperature of, 157; warnings
  against chaotic, 156, 164–65,
  290n25. *See also* childbirth (labor
  and delivery)
bitter orange *(zhike),* in birth-expediting
  medicines, 166–67, 292n56, 293n64,
  294n71
Bixia yuanjun (deity), 65
Black Divinity Powder *(heishen san),*
  211–13, 217, 305n71, 305n77,
  305n79
bladder, 143, 274n36. *See also* organs
Blood: breast milk congruent with, 87,
  271n10; channels and vessels of,
  90–92, 273n29, 273nn32–33; cooling vs. warming, debates on, 120–
  23, 141, 143, 144–45, 211–18; depletion and debility of womb and,
  114–16; effects of heat and cold on,
  111–12; false pregnancy and, 129;
  as female equivalent of semen, 53;
  formula for cooling and breaking
  up stagnation of, 242n3; life-gate
  (mingmen) and, 100–101; menstrual
  irregularities and, 89–90; in postpartum, 15–17, 200–204; shift in
  thinking about gender and, 46, 50;
  stagnation in womb of, 109–10;
  symptoms of stagnation of, 16,
  84; terms for womb linked to, 93;
  "three dashings" *(san chong)* of,
  192, 299n13, 299–300n14; understanding possible dysfunctions of,
  85–86; use of term, 24; vessels and
  womb interconnected with, 105–7,
  110–11, 116–17; women as ruled by,
  28–29, 87–88. *See also* depletion;
  menstruation; qi and Blood *(qi xue);*
  repletion; stagnation; vacuity;
  vessels; womb
body: focus on individual, 25; Northern
  vs. Southern, 309n17; primary
  dynamics of illness and cure located
  in, 23–24; religious beliefs in views
  of, 262n41; unity and multiplicity
  of (infinitive body), 231–34. *See also*
  female reproductive body; muscles;
  organs
book market, 44–45
Book of Rites (Liji), 40
Boxer Uprising (1900), 225
breastfeeding: Blood congruent with

breast milk, 87, 271n10; postpartum ailments and, 191–92; warning against, 157
breasts, signs of pregnancy in, 126
Brokaw, Cynthia, 77, 78, 79, 268n89
Buddhism: and fertility beliefs, 65; and *fuke*, 63; *Lotus Sutra* of, 66*fig.*; lay practitioners of, 269n109; medical activities and rituals of, 65–66; and merit accumulation, 79, 81

Cai Xiaomin, 263n42
Canonical Teachings on Medicine for Women (*Nüke jinglun*, Xiao Xun), 96, 131, 205
Cao Binggang, 55, 257n2
Cao Xueqin, 251n79
case collections, medical (*yi'an*). *See* medical texts
case studies: ambiguous pregnancies, 114, 127, 135; anomalous fetuses, 132, 133, 138; fetal or infant death during or following childbirth, 147, 182, 185, 187; impaired fertility, 84–85; long pregnancy, 133–34; maternal death in childbirth, 224, 226–27; maternal death in postpartum period, 1–2, 188; menstrual ailments, 89, 90; miscarriages, 54, 120–23, 141, 143, 144–45; postpartum illnesses, 1–2, 15–17, 188, 197, 210, 297n2; protracted labor, 147–49, 171, 175, 179, 183, 185, 186
Cass, Victoria B., 243n10
Chang Che-chia, 254n116
Chang Chia-feng, 99
Chang Sangjun, 34
Chao, Yüan-ling, 40, 263n43
Chao Yuanfang: on Blood and breast milk, 271n10; on deficiency of Blood, 114; on miscarriage, 144; on pulse patterns, 125; on pushing too early and fetal malpresentation, 160; on "thirty-six diseases" of women, 255–56n129
Chen family of Jiaxing: history of, 31, 33, 40; members of (table), 32
Chen, Mrs., 226
Chen Ao, 210
Cheng, Ms., 84–85
Chen Hu'an, 303n52
Chen Mingzhe, 70
Chen Nianzu (Xiuyuan): background of, 120, 281–82n1; changing medical views of, 122–23; compilations of texts by, 264–65n52; on *Easy*

Childbirth, 68, 179; on menses and fertility, 278n99; possible descendant of, 257n2; pregnancy tests available to, 124–25; reputation of, 205; on wife's miscarriages, 120–23, 141, 143, 144–45; work of, edited by others, 261n27; work of, in other compilations, 71
Chen Qirong, 75
Chen Shiduo: on infertility, 115–16; on kidneys, water, and miscarriage, 142, 143; on postpartum ailments, 299n12; on womb's function, 94; work attributed to, 303n52
Chen Shiliang, 31
Chen Wenzhao, 31
Chen Xinlan, 142–43
Chen Yan (Wuze), 46, 162, 278n92, 292n45
Chen Yi, 31
Chen Zhidao, 182–83, 184, 296n111
Chen Zhixu (aka Shangyangzi), 277n77
Chen Ziming: on behavior during pregnancy, 156–57, 163; on birth-expediting medicines, 165–66, 170; on birthing environment, 156–57, 290n25; on childbirth, 154–57, 168; on difficult births, 155, 167; on fetal-slimming medicines, 293n64; interventionist approach of, 157–58; midwives criticized by, 182; on postpartum ailments, 208; on postpartum treatments, 211–12, 213, 215, 305n77; on pregnancy tests, 125; on procreation, 6; on secret births as always easy, 291n31; synthesis of *fuke* knowledge by, 45–46; on "teasing pains" *(nongtong)*, 174; on womb as gateway for illness, 108; on women's diseases, 7, 29; Xue Ji's revision of, 46–47, 305n77
childbirth (labor and delivery): auspicious day for, 168; birth-expediting medicines used in, 153, 155, 164–70; Blood health and womb health essential for, 86; cholera epidemics and, 218–22; contradictory approaches to, 154–58, 175–77; "correct" form *(zhengchan)*, 155–56, 172, 290nn21–22; cosmological resonance of, 148–50, 149*fig.*, 151–58, 169, 171, 175, 179, 212; death in, 224, 226–27, 234–35; as depleting, 192, 193; difficult and lengthy cases, 147–50, 154, 155–56, 167, 171, 178–79, 183–84, 185–86, 226,

childbirth *(continued)*
288n1; debates over supposedly
pathological nature of, 200–204;
"doing the month" *(zuoyue)* after,
191, 203–4, 211; earliest known
written references to, 248n51; as
easy *(yi)* process, 13, 17, 148, 150,
151–54, 155–56, 158, 168; expedited type of, 175; as ex post facto
confirmation of suspected pregnancy, 127–28; false vs. true pains
of, 148, 172–78, 183–84; famous
text on, 67–68; fatal medical error
after, 1–3; fetal malpresentation in,
155, 160–64; gendered patterns
of practice surrounding, 179–86;
individual differences in, 185–86;
as inherently safe process, 4; interventionist approach to, 157–58,
176–77; literature of, 6–9; medical
definitions of, 180–81; midwives'
primary role in, 17; noninterventionist approach to, 67, 148–50, 149*fig.*,
164, 165, 168–69, 171–72, 173,
177–78; premature, 130, 139; prevention as key to managing complications of, 181–82; pulse readings
in, 171–73, 183–84, 294–95n77;
pushing only briefly during, 177;
pushing too early in, 159–60, 162,
172–73; reading signs of, 170–73;
resolving intractable labor, 180, 185,
186, 187, 297n125; secret births, as
always easy, 158, 291n31; terms for,
135; water breaking in, 159, 172,
174, 175, 176. *See also* birthing environment; placenta; *Treatise on Easy
Childbirth (Dasheng bian,* Jizhai
jushi [Ye Feng]); Western medicine
Childbirth Treasury (Chanbao, Zan Yin),
155, 168, 189, 290n18, 297n1
childbirth wind *(rufeng),* 195–97
childlessness. *See* infertility
children: movements of, in childbirth,
159–60; secret birth of illegitimate,
158, 291n31; skin eruptions on,
caused by "fetal poison" *(taidu),*
52–53, 99; specialization in medicine
for (pediatrics), 30. *See also* fetus
"child seizures" *(zixian),* 124
China. *See* Republic of China; *and
specific dynasties*
Ch'iu Chung-lin, 40, 250n72
cholera, 218–22, 307n97
Classic of Changes (Yijing): as essential
text for doctors, 98, 99; interpretations of, 253–54n110; medicine

linked to, 48; on yin and yang and
generating life, 151, 155, 202
Classic of Difficult Issues (Nanjing), 26,
99, 118, 294–95n77
Classic of Odes (Shijing), 7, 21, 153, 166
*Classic of Sagely Benefaction (Shengji
jing,* Song Emperor Huizong), 95
Classic of the Divine Pivot (Lingshu jing):
authoritative version of, 23; bodily
morphology descriptions in, 117–
18; on intestinal spreading and stony
accumulation, 128; on muscular
disorders, 194–95; use of title, 246–
47n36; on vessels of the body, 92,
273n33. *See also Yellow Emperor's
Inner Classic (Huangdi neijing)*
Classic of the Pulse (Maijing, Wang
Shuhe), 171, 294–95n77
*Classic of the Way and Its Virtue (Dao-
dejing),* 152
climatic influences: on Blood, 107; heat
and cold chief among, 111–12, 144–
45; posing danger during childbirth,
179, 220–21; on vessels, 107. *See
also* birthing environment
*Compiled Essentials of Medicine for
Women (Nüke zuanyao,* Wang
Hengqi), 20
*Complete Library of the Four Treasuries
(Siku quanshu),* 16
*Complete Works of Jingyue, The (Jingyue
quanshu,* Zhang Jiebin), 204–5
*Comprehensive Compendium of Good
Formulas for Women (Furen daquan
liangfang,* Chen Ziming), 29, 45,
154–57, 165–66, 168; as revised
by Xue Ji, 46–47, 305n77
*Comprehensive Guide to Benefiting Yin
(Jiyin gangmu,* Wu Zhiwang), 47
conception: *See* fertility and conception
Confucianism: behavioral exhortations
in, 145; as motivation in publishing, 76; reaffirmed after Taiping
Rebellion, 225; scholarly medical
ideal linked to, 37–39, 74. *See also*
cosmological frameworks; Neo-
Confucianism
consumption *(lao),* 129
*Continuation of the Cases from Famous
Doctors, A (Xu mingyi lei'an,* Wei
Zhixiu): background on, 241–42n1;
compilation of, 242–43n4; description of, 16–17; on lengthy labor
cases, 179; on men's and women's
illness as essentially the same, 50–
51; multiple editions of, 256n138
cosmological frameworks: and bodily

morphology, 117–19; body as governed by, 23–24; childbirth explained
in terms of, 148–50, 149*fig.*, 151–
58, 169, 171, 175, 179, 212; corrupted or unusual pregnancies explained by, 133; expansion of, 28–29;
fertility explained by, 141–42; five
phases *(wu xing)* as component of,
5, 24, 28–29; "generation and transformation" *(shenghua)* in, 216–17;
li and qi as central ideas in, 41; life-
gate *(mingmen)* in, 99–105; medicine integrated with, 18, 41, 51,
98–105, 253–54n110; midwives criticized for not understanding, 181–
83; postpartum period in, 201, 217;
procreation linked to, 6; secret medical methods and, 33–34, 251n79;
system of correspondences in, 23–
25; unity and multiplicity of classical
body in, 231–34; yin and yang/Earth
and Heaven in, 141–42. *See also* yin
and yang; *and specific religions*
"currents of learning" *(xuepai)*: interpractitioner struggles over, 17–18,
246n34; Scheid on, 243n8; "supplementing through warmth" *(wenbu)*,
97, 215–16; "warm factor illnesses"
(wenbing), 218–19
Cyr, Ronald, 276n58

Dai Dafu, 308n8
Dai Liting, 89
daily life: amateur practitioners' role
in, 55; merit accumulation in, 79,
81; self-diagnosing and -dosing in,
18, 55–57, 72–73. *See also* gender
segregation; midwives
Daoism: canon of, 277n77; on human
body, 262n41; qi in, 100–101, 104;
self-cultivation practices in, 100;
"self-so principle" *(ziran zhi li)* in,
152
Dean-Jones, Lesley, 281n139
deities: for fertility and women's problems, 263n44; healing and herbal
treatment linked to, 65–66, 265n43;
instructions for merit publishing
from, 79; of medical practitioners,
26; promotion of cults of medical,
263n43
Demiéville, Paul, 287n79
depletion: childbirth and, 157, 162, 163,
167, 193, 234; debates about, 2–3,
15, 92; factors in, 24, 43, 90, 109–
10; fetal development and, 131;
miscarriage due to, 144; postpartum,

193, 196–97, 200, 202–4, 208–11,
213–14, 218, 220, 221–22; signs
of, 88, 128; womb as crucible and,
114–16
Despeux, Catherine, 257n146
diagnosis: applying general principles in
flexible, 25, 199–204, 219, 222–23;
of case of blocked menses, 84–85;
elements of, 25; gender segregation
as problematic in, 45–51, 255n122;
by laypeople and medical amateurs,
55–56; of pregnancy, 124–28; reading state of channels and vessels in,
90–92. *See also* pulse lore
Ding Ganren, 308n8
*Divine Husbandman's Classic of Materia
Medica (Shennong bencao jing)*, 93
Divine Pivot Classic. See *Classic of the
Divine Pivot (Lingshu jing)*
Dong Hao, 261n30
Dong Xuan, 293n64
Dong Zhongshu, 281n136
*Dream of the Red Chamber (Honglou
meng,* Cao Xueqin), 251n139
drug-based therapies: for balancing water
and earth in female body, 142–43; in
Bamboo Grove Monastery texts, 60;
types used in pregnancy and childbirth, 165–66; for cleansing womb,
273–74n34; current understanding
of characteristics of, 122, 282n6;
divine and mysterious sources of, 14,
33–34, 64; efficacy and perception
of, 64–66, 262n39; for expediting
birth, 153, 155, 164–70; for fetal
malpresentation, 161, 162; gender
of practitioners using, 247n41; for
gu poisoning, 134–35; for infertility
treatment, 93; as key therapy, 2;
male practitioners' focus on, for
childbirth, 179; for miscarriages,
prevention and aftermath, 54, 120–
21, 136, 143–45, 282n3; naming of,
213; Northern vs. Southern differences in, 309n17; political metaphors for, 287–88n92; postpartum
uses of, 188–90, 200–204, 297n2;
for pregnancy, 121, 165–66; prescription books on, 58, 71–75, 81–
82, 267n69; refusal to take, 15, 46;
for regulating maternal and fetal qi,
122–23; to restart lochia, 242n3;
for "securing the fetus" *(antai)*, 137,
138–39, 140–41, 144–45, 175–76,
183–84; warming vs. cooling, debate
on, 120–23, 141, 143, 144–45, 211–
18. *See also specific texts*

drug-based therapies, specific: abortifacients, 293n65; bitter orange (zhike),
166–67, 292n56, 293n64, 294n71;
Black Divinity Powder (heishen san),
211–13, 217, 305n71, 305n77, 305n79;
fetal slimming and lubricating type,
166, 168, 170, 293n64; Four Ingredients Decoction (siwu tang), 212–
15, 217; ginseng, 2, 57, 176, 210,
239n3; herbal, as pregnancy tests,
124, 125–26; "peony formulas" of
Guo family, 34; peony, white (baishao), 213–15; purgatives, 2–3;
rabbit-based, 165, 166, 292–93n60;
rehmannia (shudi), 211, 213–15,
242n3. See also Generating and
Transforming Decoction (shenghua
tang).
Duden, Barbara, 126–27, 129

Easy Childbirth. See Treatise on Easy
Childbirth (Dasheng bian, Jizhai
jushi [Ye Feng])
eclampsia, 193
Edited Essentials of Medicine for Women
(Nüke jiyao, Zhou Jichang), 71, 73–
74
Efficacious Prescriptions from a Hereditary Medical Family (Shiyi dexiao
fang, Wei Yilin), 48, 136
Elman, Benjamin, 253n102
epidemics: cholera, 218–22, 307n97;
medicine for treating, 58, 120; path-
ogenic heat as cause of, 218–20;
state activism in medicine stimulated
by, 27
epistemology. See cosmological frameworks; religious beliefs, rituals, and
institutions; and specific religions
Essential Outline of Medicine for Women
(Nüke yaolue, Pan Wei), 71, 140
Essential Prescriptions Worth a Thousand
Golds (Beiji qianjin yaofang, Sun
Simiao), 27, 42–45
Essential Readings in Medical Learning
(Yizong bi du, Li Zhongzi), 104–5,
277n87
Essentials of Fecundity (Dasheng yaozhi,
Tang Qianqing), 67
Essentials of Medicine for Women (Nüke
yaozhi, Chen Nianzu), 121, 281–
82n1
Essentials of the Golden Cabinet (Jinkui
yaolue, Zhang Ji), 109–10, 194,
255–56n129, 300n18
Essential Teachings on Childbearing
(Taichan xinfa, Yan Chunxi): background on, 2–3, 239n1; on deficiency
of uterine vitalities, 114–15; on Generating and Transforming Decoction,
205–6; multiple editions of, 239n5;
terminology of, 280n130
Europe. See anatomy; Western medicine
"evidential scholarship" (kaozheng)
movement, 44–45

Fa family, 57
"famous doctor" (mingyi), 57
Fan Yuanpu, 54
Fan Zhongyan, 37, 76
female alchemy (nüdan), textual tradition
of, 53, 257n146
female practitioners: diversity and role
of, 18–19; few extant medical works
by, 19–22; on men's and women's
illness as different, 50–51; therapies
of, 247n41. See also midwives
female reproductive body: analytical approaches to, 3–5; changing views of
womb and, 99–105; de-exoticization
of, 43–45, 97; genital tract infections
and, 196, 301n25; key components
of, 86–97; medical and moral imperative of maintaining health of, 6–7;
narrowing scope of illness of, 47–
49; optimistic view of (women's
ailments essentially same as men's),
4, 18, 42, 43–45, 47–51, 86, 105,
228–35; regulating behavior of,
123, 135–36, 140–41, 145–46,
150; reproductive essences and,
141–42; vessels of, 90–92, 273n29,
273nn32–33. See also Blood; childbirth (labor and delivery); fertility
and conception; fuke (medicine for
women); infertility; menstruation;
miscarriage; pollution beliefs; postpartum period; pregnancy; qi;
womb; women
Feng, Ms., 34, 35
Feng Shaoqu, 227–28, 308n8
fertility and conception: Blood, vessels,
and womb interconnected in, 105–
7, 110–11, 116–17; case of blocked
womb impairing, 84–85; deities for,
263n44; earth equated with, 141–
42; as a focus of literate medicine,
17; life-gate (mingmen) and, 99–
105; religious rituals linked to, 65;
vessels of body central to, 90–92,
273n29, 273nn32–33; womb as
container in, 112–13; womb as crucible and field in, 113–16; womb as
passage and receptacle in, 107–12.

See also infertility; miscarriage; pregnancy

"fetal poison" *(taidu)*, 52–53, 99

fetus: arrested or delayed development of, 130–34, 138; avoiding miscarriage of, 135–37; classical understanding of development, 129–30; current understanding of, 126, 283n27; as dependent on fire of life-gate, 121; discourse on corrupted or weird, 114–15; displacement of *(taidong)*, 138–40, 287n82; formulas to slim and lubricate, 166, 168, 170, 293n64; ghost *(guitai)*, 128, 129, 134; leaking *(tailou)* of, 121, 123–24, 131, 139; malpresentation in labor, 155, 160–64, 186, 297n122; movement of, 137–38, 140; mutable state of, 96, 276n61; mummified following in utero death (withered fetus *[kutai]*), 132, 138, 285n54; nature metaphors for development of, 139; physical destruction of, to save woman, 180, 185, 186, 187, 297n125; "securing the fetus" *(antai)*, 137, 138–39, 140–41, 144–45, 175–76, 183–84; sex determination factors for, 94–97, 108, 113; weak qi of, 176–77; womb as abode of, 92–94. *See also* miscarriage; pregnancy

five phases *(wu xing)*, 5, 24, 28–29

folk practices. *See* daily life

forensic medicine manuals, 108, 189

Formulary of the Imperial Pharmacy Service for Benefiting the People in an Era of Great Peace (Taiping huimin hejiju fang), 211

Formulas for Universal Benefit (Puji fang, ed. Zhu Xiao), 110

Four Ingredients Decoction *(siwu tang)*, 217; changing assessments of, 212–15

fuke (medicine for women): approaches to, 12–14; Blood, vessels, and womb interconnected in, 105–7, 110–11, 116–17; Blood health and womb health central to, 86, 88–90; conceptual universe underlying, 3–4; continuing questions in, 122–23; as curriculum *(ke)*, 27–30; debate about traditional vs. scientific methods in, 226–28; de-exoticization of female bodies and, 43–45, 97; development of, 17–18; female knowledge not a source of authority in, 22; hereditary physicians of, 30–31, 250n72, 251n80; Hippocratic corpus compared with, 118–19, 281n139; his-

torical context of, 4–5; as male-authored tradition, 18–22; medical skills needed in, 74–75; nine categories of disease in, 49, 50; norms and dynamics underlying, 82–83; origins of, 26–27; patterns of, summarized, 228–35; ritual practices increasingly marginalized in, 158; scholarship on, 9–10; specialization in, 15–17, 25–30, 179–80; suspicions about monks and, 62–63, 261n30; and "thirty-six diseases of women," 48, 255–56n219. *See also* Blood; childbirth (labor and delivery); female reproductive body; fertility and conception; infertility; medical practitioners; miscarriage; postpartum period; pregnancy; qi; vessels; womb; yin and yang

fuke literature: accessibility of, 9; by amateurs, 57–59, 67–75; by Bamboo Grove monks, 54–55; disagreement and consensus underlying, 10–11; earliest manuscripts of, 7–8; female body in, 3–5; focus of, 6–7; format of, 88; overview of, 8–9. *See also specific authors and texts*

Fully Deploying the Formulary of the Imperial Pharmacy Service (Jufang fahui, Zhu Zhenheng), 201–2

Fu Qingzhu's Medicine for Women (Fu Qingzhu nüke), 206–7, 303–4n58

Furth, Charlotte: on androgyny and difference, 231; on Blood and female-ness, 87–88; on lack of male interest in childbirth, 179; on medical collections, 46, 281n137; on medicine and cosmology, 253–54n110; on medicine and gender, 233; on narrowing scope of female illness, 47; on rituals, 158; on Tan Yunxian, 19–20; on therapies of male and female practitioners, 247n41

Fu Shan (Qingzhu), 71, 205, 206–7, 303n57, 303–4n58

gall bladder, 275n47

Gaotan (monk), 59

Gao Yangsheng, 294–95n77

gender difference: in disease, limited to reproductive issues, 4, 18, 42, 43–45, 47–51, 86, 105, 228–35; in fetal movement, 137–38; life-gate *(mingmen)* function and, 99–105; origins of *fuke* and, 26–27; in patterns of childbirth practice, 179–86; in yin and yang/Earth and Heaven, 141–42

gender segregation: female healers in context of, 50–51; medical challenges of, 45–51, 255n122; Neo-Confucianism and, 6; in patterns of childbirth practice, 180
Generating and Transforming Decoction (shenghua tang): detractors of, 217–19, 220, 221, 222, 223; medical rationales for, 207–10; origins of, 204–5, 216, 302n42, 303n57; popularity and endurance of, 189–90, 205–7; for postpartum ailments, 190, 206, 207; proponents of, 213–16; social and intellectual substructures supporting use of, 223; various ailments treated by, 298n8
gestation. See fetus; pregnancy
ginseng, 2, 57, 176, 210, 239n3
Golden Mirror (Imperially Compiled Golden Mirror of Medical Learning [Yuzuan yizong jinjian], ed. Wu Qian): circulation of, 50; status of, 44–45, 254n116; title of, 254n112; specific topics: diagnosing pregnancy, 126; externally provoked illness, 107–8; female illness, 43–45; fertility and Blood, 113; fetal leaking vs. displacement, 139; Generating and Transforming Decoction, 206, 207; girdle discharges, 110–11; internal swelling, 112; li jing (pulse), 171–72; maternal and fetal health, 140; men's and women's illness as essentially the same, 50–51, 105; menstrual irregularities, 88–89; postpartum treatments, 213; qi and li, 41; sex selection, 105; sexual maturation, 105–6; stony accumulation, 129; vulnerability to illness during pregnancy, 123–24; womb, 109–10, 113–14
Goldschmidt, Asaf, 37
Gong Chunpu, 70, 266n64
Gong Jianyang, 239n1
government civil service: examination degrees for, 38–39, 253n102; legal specialists, 71, 189–90; medicine likened to, 181–82; staff advisors and administrative secretaries, 69, 71; practicing medicine as an alternative to, 38–39. See also shengyuan
government medical school, 37
government medical service: background of doctors in, 40; elevated status of, 37–39; hereditary physicians' role in, 30; Song reform of, 27–28; spe-

cialization institutionalized in, 37. See also Golden Mirror
Gowing, Laura, 130
gu: character for, 279n116; patterns of swelling and, 112; symptoms of poisoning with, 134–35; understanding of, 286n65
Guanyin (deity), 65, 66fig., 79
Gu Dehua, 20, 22, 244n17
Guidelines for Treating Illness (Zhengzhi zhunsheng, Wang Kentang), 283n17
Guo family of Hangzhou: female practitioners of, 34, 35; history of, 33–34, 40, 251n80, 251n82; "peony formulas" of, 34
Guo Jizhong, 161, 291–92n44
Guo Shaoqu, 35
Guo Shiyi, 34
Guo Yuan, 34
Guo Zhaoqian, 34

Handan yigao (Zhao Xianke), 248n50
Han dynasty (206 B.C.E. to 220 C.E.), 6, 23
Hang Shijun, 242n2
Hanson, Marta, 44, 218, 254n112, 264n51, 309n17
healers. See medical practitioners
health: cosmological patterns in, 41; universal dynamics of, 46–51. See also cosmological frameworks; illness and disease; medicine
hereditary physicians (shiyi): complaints about, 57; examples of, 31–36; fuke and, 30–31, 250n72, 251n80; included in medical compilations, 71; as patriline, 18; scholar-physicians vs., 39–42; secret techniques and perpetuation of, 33–34, 35, 251n77, 251n79; uxorilocal sons-in-law as heirs of, 35–36, 252n91; woman founder of, 35–36; women's training in, 18, 19–20
hermaphrodites, 96
He Rong, 303n53
He Zhongling, 258–59n15
Hinrichs, TJ, 58
How Scholars Serve Their Relatives (Rumen shi qin, Zhang Congzheng), 200–201
Huang, Ms., 120–23, 141, 143, 144–45
huan pulse, 85, 270n3
huoluan. See cholera; Treatise on Huoluan
Hucker, Charles O., 287–88n92, 288–89n2
Huizong (emperor, 1101–25), 37, 95

Hu Jishi, 29
Hundred Days' Reform (1898), 225
Hundred Masters of National Medicine, The (Guoyi baijia, Qiu Qingyuan), 226
Huyang (princess of Eastern Han dynasty), 167, 293n64

illness and disease: applying general principles in flexible, 25, 199–204, 219, 222–23; "below the girdle" (daixia), 26, 28, 247–48n47; categories of, 107, 278n92; changing nature of, 5; classification and systematization of, 199; concerns about behavioral causes of, 51–52; diverse causes of, 18; fatal, of postpartum period, 192; men's and women's as essentially the same, 4, 18, 42, 43–45, 47–51, 86, 105, 228–35; shift in thinking about gender difference in, 42–45; system of correspondences in, 23–25; "thirty-six diseases" of women and, 48–49, 255–56n129. See also epidemics
illness and disease, specific: cholera, 218–22, 307n97; consumption (lao), 129; postpartum infections, 193–94, 196–97, 198fig., 199, 301n25; puerperal fever, 197, 199, 301n31; smallpox, 52–53, 99; tetanus, 194–96, 195fig., 300nn17,23–24
Illustrated Supplement to "The Inner Classic Explicated by Topic" (Leijing tuyi, Zhang Jiebin), 97, 101, 103fig.
Imperial Editorial Office (Song dynasty), 23
Imperial Encyclopedia (Gujin tushu jicheng, comp. Chen Menglei, et al.): on fetal malpresentation, 163; on first three months for fetus, 139; on infertility, 143; on menstruation, 88; on postpartum treatments, 212–13, 221; on types of failed pregnancies, 135; on womb's opening and closing, 108
Imperial Medical Office (taiyi shu, Tang), 28
Imperial Medical Service (taiyi ju, Song), 27–28, 29
infertility: Blood, vessels, and womb interconnected in explanations of, 105–7, 110–11, 116–17; causes of, 106–7, 113, 120–23, 141, 143, 144–45. See also fertility and conception

Inner Classic. See Yellow Emperor's Inner Classic (Huangdi neijing)
Inner Classic Explicated by Topic, The (Leijing, Zhang Jiebin), 97
Introduction to Medicine, An (Yixue rumen, Li Chan), 101, 102fig., 103, 163, 168

Jiang Guan, 16, 114, 280n129
Jia Zhizhong, 266n59
Jikong (monk), 60
Jingxian (monk), 59–60
Jin Ying, 97, 276n66
Jivaka (Chinese name Qipo), 287n79
Jizhai jushi. See Ye Feng
Johnson, Timothy R., 299–300n14
Judeo-Christian tradition, childbirth as travail in, 151

Karlgren, Bernhard, 289n11
Katz, Paul, 263n43
ke ("curriculum"), 27–30, 249n57
kidneys: definition and function of, 99–100; infertility and deficiency of, 116; life-gate (mingmen) and, 100–101; water's importance for womb and, 142–43
King, Helen, 301n35
Ko, Dorothy, 19, 52
Kou Zongshi, 45–46, 49, 255n122
Kui Yutian, 78
Kuriyama, Shigehisa, 285–86n57

labor and delivery. See childbirth (labor and delivery)
laws on physicians killing or harming people, 2, 239n2
laypeople. See amateurs, medical; female practitioners; midwives
Lee, Jen-der, 248n51
legitimacy of medical practice: efficacy of treatments and, 64–66, 262n39; elite patronage as endorsing, 62–64; of scholarly amateurs and their publications, 72–75. See also authority of medical practitioners
Leung, Angela Ki Che, 41, 243n10
li and qi, 41. See also cosmological frameworks; qi
Liao Yuqun, 262n33
Li Chan: on birth-expediting medicines, 168–69, 294n71; on categories of doctors, 39; on fetal malpresentation, 163; organs depicted by, 101, 102fig., 103; on taidong, 287n82; on "teasing pains" (nongtong), 174

life-gate *(mingmen)*: androgynous, 86,
    100–101, 103–5, 234; debates over
    location of, 99–100; equated with
    womb, 100–105; fetus dependent
    on fire of, 121; illustration of, 101,
    103*fig.*
Li Gao, 46, 113
Li Heli, 79, 269n109
Li Jianmin, 33, 251n77, 274–75n45
Li Keqiong, 73–74
lineage medicine. *See* hereditary
    physicians *(shiyi)*
Lin Riwei, 254n118
Lin Rujin, 79
Li Shisheng, 291–92n44
Li Shizhen, 297n3
literature: depiction of medical activity
    in, 39; poetry production by women,
    20–21, 52, 244n17, 245n28; secret
    medical formulas in, 251n79. See
    also *fuke* literature; medical canon;
    medical texts; publishing
Liu Shijue, 303n52
Liu Wansu, 221
Liu Xiaogan, 152
liver, 115
Li Wenbin, 239n3
Li Zhongzi, 104–5, 277n87
Lo, Vivienne, 273n32
lochia (bloody postpartum discharges),
    15–17
Lodge of Ritual and Ceremony, 19
Lotus Sutra (Saddharmapundarikasutra),
    66*fig.*
Loudon, Irvine, 197, 301n31
Lou Ying: on fetal malpresentation, 161;
    on pushing too early, 172–73; on
    "securing the fetus," 175–76; on
    "teasing pains" *(nongtong),* 174
Luo Qilan, 21
Luo Shanqing, 74
Lu Yuan, 74

Ma, Ms., 133
male practitioners: categories of, 39–
    42; cautions about, 157; changes in
    backgrounds of, 38–39; competition
    among, 56–57, 229–30; diversity
    of, 11; expert judgment of, 98–99;
    female healers disdained by, 50–51;
    fuke integrated into sphere of, 17–18;
    key concerns of, 124, 191; master-
    disciple networks of, 20; medical
    ideals of, 37–39, 63, 74, 82; on mid-
    wife selection, 17, 184; midwives crit-
    icized by, 4–5, 150, 181–87, 226–29,
    297n122; and need to apply general

medical principles in flexible manner,
    25, 199–204, 219, 222–23; obstetrics
    disdained by, 179–80; professional
    and social aspirations of, 180–81;
    scholarly amateurs distinguished
    from, 55–56, 72–74; special subfields
    of, 15–17, 25–30, 37, 249n65. *See
    also* amateurs, medical; drug-based
    therapies; hereditary physicians;
    medical canon; scholar-physicians
Manchu conquest, 58–59
Mann, Susan, 19, 57
Mao, Ms., 35
Marshal Wen (deity), 263n43
massage, 9, 28, 285n56
*Master Chao's Treatise on the Origins
    and Manifestations of the Myriad
    Diseases (Chaoshi zhubing yuanhou
    lun,* Chao Yuanfang), 160
maternal mortality rates, 301n32
May Fourth Movement, 225
McCartney, James H., 187
McDermott, Joseph, 58
McKnight, Brian E., 278n95
*Medical Books of Chen Xiuyuan, The
    (Chen Xiuyuan yishu,* Chen Nianzu),
    68, 264–65n52
medical bureaucracy. *See* government
    medical service; *Golden Mirror*
medical corpus: bodily morphology
    described in, 117–19; few extant
    works by women, 19–22; key texts
    in, 23, 44–45; on men's and women's
    illnesses being essentially the same,
    4, 18, 42, 43–45, 47–51, 86, 105,
    228–35; multiplicity of coexisting
    opinions and strategies in, 8–9;
    plurality and synthesis in, 10–12,
    230; reinterpreted and systematized,
    6. *See also* Bamboo Grove Monas-
    tery texts; medical texts; *and specific
    texts*
medicalization, 4, 141. *See also* drug-
    based therapies; male practitioners;
    Western medicine
medical practitioners: complaints against,
    56–57, 73, 74; as experts in Yellow
    Emperor's art, 23–24; imperial
    posts for, 31–33; patron deity of,
    26; qualification of, 18; scholar-
    amateurs distinguished from, 55–
    56, 72–74. *See also* amateurs, med-
    ical; female practitioners; hereditary
    physicians; male practitioners; medi-
    cal specialization; midwives; scholar-
    physicians
medical specialization: in *fuke,* 15–17,

25–30, 179–80; in pediatrics, 30; in Qing, 29, 249n65; in Song, 27–28; in Tang, 28, 248n51; and term *zhuanke* ("expert in the discipline"), 15, 29, 30, 36; in Wang Shixiong's works, 250n69; in Western vs. Chinese medicine, 36–37

medical texts: by amateurs, 57–59, 67–75; amateurs' use of, 54–55, 60; availability of, 59; case collection (*yi'an*) genre of, 16–17, 19–22, 59, 74, 267n76; commercial success of, 58–59; concerns about propriety and, 45–51, 255n122; contents arranged according to body parts, 118, 281n137; continuing relevance and reevaluation of traditions in, 226–28; divine and mysterious sources of, 33–34, 58, 59, 63, 64, 65–66, 262–63n42; merit of publishing, 58, 75–81; motivation for creating primers, 41; nosological categories of postpartum ailments in, 193; on "nourishing life" (*yangsheng*), 52; practice of appending materials to, 67–68, 70–71, 264n49; produced as a public act, 21; proliferation and distribution of, 6, 9, 59; rhetorical devices in, 16–17; scholarly amateurs as compilers of, 70–75; sponsors of, 75–81, 258n8; tested prescriptions (*yanfang*) genre of, 71–72, 81–82, 267n69. See also *fuke* literature; medical corpus

medicine: ancient intellectual heritage of, 109–10; conceptual overview of, 5–6, 22–25; cosmology integrated with, 18, 98–105, 253–54n110; curriculum of *fuke* in, 15–17, 25–30; historical particularities of, 4–5, 36–37; Indian influence in, 287n79; multipolar nature of, 82–83; patterns in late imperial period, summarized, 228–35; perceptions of bodily structures and functions in, 117–19; plurality and synthesis in, 10–12, 230; post-Qing relevance and reevaluation of traditions, 225–28; scholarly medical ideal in, 37–39, 74; scholarly vs. hereditary, 39–42; state promotion of, 27; status of *Golden Mirror* in, 44–45; uniformity not imposed in, 22. See also cosmological frameworks; "currents of learning"; *fuke* (medicine for women); medical practitioners

Medicine Made Easy (*Yixue yitong*, Chen Nianzu), 261n27

men: Blood of, 87; civil service examinations and, 38–39; copulatory techniques of, for fetal sex selection, 96; deficiency of vitalities of, 115–16; exhortation to self-restraint for, 52, 288n102; as having body part analogous to womb, 86, 100–105; medical writing as public act of, 21; overindulgence of, 52; responsibilities of, 268n85; sexual maturation of, 91; as sponsors of texts, 77; as yang and associated with Heaven, 141–42. See also male practitioners; semen; sexual intercourse

Mencius, 6

Meng, Ms., 224, 226–27

menstrual ailments: blocked or interrupted menses, 48–49, 84–85, 109–10, 255–56n129; Blood stagnation and, 89–90, 107, 109–10, 128; externally provoked type of, 107–8; as false pregnancy, 128–30, 284n33; in pregnancy, 131. See also vaginal discharges, abnormal

menstruation: as female reproductive vitalities, 105–6; as foundation of women, 270n14; Greeks vs. Chinese on, 118–19, 281n139; at intervals other than monthly, 270n15; irregularities of, 88–89, 105; life-gate (*mingmen*) and, 100–101; male practitioners' focus on, 17; medical discourse on, 86–90; metaphors for, 113; and opening and closing of womb, 108–9; patterns of internal swelling associated with, 112; timing of conception in cycle of, 94–95; regulation of, 87, 88, 89, 142. See also menstrual ailments

meridians, pulse lore and, 125, 282n13

midwifery (Western obstetrics, *chanpoxue*), 226–28, 307–8n5

midwives: and gendered patterns of childbirth practice, 179–86; genitalia of female corpses examined by, 275n56; male practitioners on selecting, 17, 184; medical men's assertion of superiority over and criticism of, 4–5, 150, 181–87, 226–29, 297n122; older, female midwives preferred, 229, 308–9n10; reform movements and, 308–9n10; stereotypes of, 185–86; "teasing pains" (*nongtong*) and, 174; warnings about interventions of, 151, 160–61, 164, 165, 186, 297n122. See also female practitioners

Ming dynasty (1368–1644): context of, 4–5; expanding and revising medical doctrines in, 97–99; female practitioners in, 19, 247n41; "fetal poison" *(taidu)* concept in, 52–53, 99; ghost fetus in, 129; hereditary physicians in, 30, 31, 250n72; medical publishing expanded in, 57–58; misdiagnosis of pregnancy in, 129–30; pregnancy test in, 125–26; scholar-physicians in, 38, 40

Ming Taizu, 39

miscarriage: attempts to provoke, 293n65; causes of, 135–37; consultations about multiple, 54–55; contradictory approaches to preventing, 120–23, 141, 143; current understanding of, 122, 282n6; doctors' concerns about, 135–37, 145–46; fetal displacement *(taidong)* and, 138–40; influence of bodily water on, 142–43; terms for, 135; treatments to forestall impending cases of, 140–41

Monastery of Benevolent Aid (Huijisi). *See* Bamboo Grove Monastery (Zhulinsi)

monks, stereotypes of, 62–63, 261n30. *See also* Bamboo Grove Monastery (Zhulinsi)

muscles, disorders of, 194–96, 300nn17,23–24

Nationalists. *See* Republic of China

Neo-Confucianism: empirical investigations *(gewu zhizhi)*in, 98–99; five phases *(wu xing)* and, 5, 24, 28–29; *fuke* and gender difference in context of, 232–35; gender segregation and female chastity in, 6, 52; *li* and *qi* in, 41; medicine integrated with, 18, 98–105, 253–54n110. *See also* Confucianism; cosmological frameworks; yin and yang

New Book on Childbearing, A (Taichan xinshu, Bamboo Grove Monastery monks): on birth-expediting drugs, 294n69; copies and editions of, 257nn1–2; on Generating and Transforming Decoction, 206; on menstrual irregularities, 89

New Compilation of Tested Prescriptions (Yanfang xinbian, Bao Xiang'ao), 71–72, 267n69

Ni Zhiwei (Peiyu), 189, 216, 297n1, 297n4

Northern Song dynasty (960–1127):

cosmological frameworks in, 28; materia medica of, 25

nüke, use of term, 28. See also *fuke* (medicine for women)

Obringer, Frédéric, 279n116, 286n65

obstetrics *(chanpoxue,* Western midwifery), 226–28, 307–8n5

Opium War (1839–42), 224

organs: Blood linked to kidney, liver, and heart, 87; categorizations of, 275n47; circulation and, 274–75n45; color of vaginal discharge indicates afflicted organ, 111; diagrams of, 101–5, 102*fig.,* 103*fig.*; in explanations of bodily structures and functions, 117–19; as "five depots and six palaces" *(wu zang liu fu),* 24, 93–94; life-gate *(mingmen)* and, 99–105; potential damage to, in childbearing, 191–92; pulse pattern of pregnancy and, 125; unusual types of, 93–94; womb as female, 92–97. *See also* bladder; kidneys; spleen; womb

Overmyer, Daniel, 203

pain: false, in childbirth, 172–78; fetal displacement and, 139; menstrual, 89–90; as necessary part of childbirth, 148, 149*fig.,* 152, 156, 158, 172; postpartum, 188, 192, 193, 197, 208, 210

Pan Jingru, 62

Pan Wei: background of, 260–61n27; medical compilations of, 62, 71, 205; on "securing the fetus" *(antai)* and pregnancy, 140; on women's and men's illness as essentially same, 51; on women's medicine, 75, 268n85

Pan Yantong (Yiqin), 61*fig.,* 62, 261n29

"pathway of essence" *(jingdao),* 102–3

peony, white *(baishao),* 213–15

Peony Pavilion, The (play), 39, 52

Phoenix Grove Monastery, 65, 263n45

placebo effect, 64, 262n39

placenta: burial of, 27, 240n12; double, with twins, 15–17; early discourse on, 92–93; as obstruction, 163; retention of, 15–17, 151, 191, 298n8, 305n79; terms for and medicinal uses of, 274n37

plurality and synthesis (in healing practices), 10–12, 230

political metaphors: in descriptions of

drugs, 142–43, 287–88n92; in descriptions of organs, 93–94. *See also* agricultural and nature metaphors
pollution beliefs, 27, 28, 53, 63, 155, 157, 191, 203, 233
popular practitioners. *See* amateurs, medical; midwives
population, rapid growth of (1500–1800), 39, 253n101
Porkert, Manfred, 117
postpartum depression, 191, 298–99n10
postpartum mania, 193
postpartum period: abscesses in, 198*fig.*, 302n50; ailments and dangers in, 109, 190–93, 199; cholera epidemics and, 218–22, 307n97; deadly convulsions in, 193–97, 199; "doing the month" *(zuoyue)* in, 191, 203–4, 211; factors in differential diagnosis of illnesses in, summarized, 199–200; heat as injurious in, 111–12, 217–19, 220–21; infection in, 193–94, 196–97, 198*fig.*, 199, 301n25; internal swelling in, 112; as key concern of male practitioners, 17, 191; lochia in, 15–17; maternal tetanus in, 194–96, 300nn17,23–24; as mundane stage in reproductive cycle, 217; stagnation and, 188–90, 192, 197, 198*fig.*, 200–202, 204, 208–13, 215–16, 221, 297nn2–3; warming vs. cooling medicines in, 211–18
Precious and Felicitous Collection of Teachings on Childbirth (Chanyu baoqing ji, Guo Jizhong), 291–92n44
preeclampsia, 124
pregnancy: cautions about number of, 157; current knowledge of, 126; diagnosis of, 123, 127–28; difficult labor caused by mistakes during, 156–57; doctors' concerns about, 17, 136–37, 145–46; false, 128–29, 134, 284n33; fetal displacement in, 138–40; fetal movement in, 137–38; first three months critical in, 139; length of, 130–35, 159, 170–71; medicalization of, 141; medicines used during, 121, 165–66; misdiagnosis and disruptions of, 129–30; morning sickness in, 124, 126; mutability and unpredictability of, 122–23, 135; recognizing variations in individual cases of, 175–76; "securing the fetus" *(antai)* in, 137, 138–

39, 140–41, 144–45, 175–76, 183–84; "teasing pains" *(nongtong)* in, 173–74; tests for, 124–28, 130, 133, 283n26; unusually long, 130–35; vulnerability to illness during, 123–24. *See also* childbirth (labor and delivery); fetus; miscarriage; postpartum period
professionalization, in Chinese vs. European medicine, 257–58n4
publishing: of amateur compilations, 57–58; expansion of, 58–59, 258–59n15; religious and moral motivations for, 58, 75–81, 258n8; state-sponsored projects of, 6, 27, 37–38; of texts for free distribution *(yinsong)*, 77, 268–69n92; woodblocks for, 70. *See also* Bamboo Grove Monastery texts; *fuke* literature; medical canon; medical texts; *and specific texts*
pulse lore: to ascertain pregnancy, 124–25, 126, 127, 133; in childbirth, 171–73, 183–84, 294–95n77; *huan* type and, 85, 270n3

qi: channels and vessels of, 90–92; concept of, 23–24, 87; in explanations emphasizing bodily function over structure, 117–18; fetal, nourishing of, 138; heat and cold as influences on, 111–12, 128; interplay between maternal and fetal, 122–23, 129–30; life-gate *(mingmen)* as seat of, 99; men as ruled by, 28–29; production and manifestation of, 24–25; spleen's role in producing, 84–85; understanding of *li* and, 41; *zhen qi*, meanings of, 114, 280n130. *See also* Blood: depletion; qi and Blood; repletion; stagnation; vacuity; yin and yang
Qian family of Shaoxing: Generating and Transforming Decoction attributed to, 204–5, 206, 207, 302n43; lineage of, 71. *See also Secret Book of Childbearing, A (Taichan mishu*, Qian family)
Qian Biyi, 29–30
qi and Blood *(qi xue)*: birth-expediting medicines and, 164–65, 169–70; in childbirth, 155, 178, 192, 193; concept of, 24, 87; fetal malpresentation due to imbalance in, 161–64; long pregnancies and deficiency of, 130–35; medicines to nourish and replenish, 139–40, 165, 167–70,

qi and Blood *(qi xue) (continued)*
178; patterns of, 116–17; postpartum ailments of, 192, 299n13,
299–300n14; pulse pattern of
pregnancy and, 125; regulation of,
156–57, 189–90. *See also* depletion;
repletion; stagnation; vacuity
Qian E, 36
Qian Guobin, 133, 134
Qian Qingshi, 29–30
Qiao Guanglie, 78
Qi Bo, 23, 275n47
qing ("emotions"), 49, 51–52
Qing dynasty (1644–1911): Bamboo
Grove Monastery's reputation in,
60, 63, 65–66; civil service examination degrees in, 38–39; cultural
and social developments in, overview, 5–6; *Easy Childbirth* text
in, 67–68; feminist and reformist
thought in, 22; foreign imperialism
and overthrow of, 224–26; Generating and Transforming Decoction
used in, 190; hereditary status groups
eliminated in, 30–31; influential
people in, 120; intestinal spreading
and stony accumulation in, 129;
limited male interest in childbirth
during, 179–80; medical publishing
expanded in, 58–59, 258–59n15;
medical specialization in, 29, 249n65;
merit accumulation in, 75–81; misdiagnosis of pregnancy in, 129–
30; Neo-Confucian revival in, 52;
pregnancy test in, 125; scholar-
physicians esteemed in, 40; self-
diagnosing and self-dosing in, 55–57
Qiu Qingyuan, 224, 225–27, 297n4
Qi Zhongfu, 26, 28

rehmannia *(shudi)*, 211, 213–15, 242n3
religious beliefs, rituals, and institutions:
for childbirth, 157–58; medicine and
healing linked to, 64–66, 265n43;
merit medical publishing and, 58,
75–81. *See also* Buddhism; Confucianism; cosmological frameworks;
Daoism; Neo-Confucianism
repletion: factors in, 42–43, 202, 204;
postpartum, 202, 204, 209; Princess
Huyang's case of, 167; pulse lore
and, 172
Republic of China: feminist and reformist
thought in, 22; midwifery schools in,
265n56, 308–9n10; national medicine *(guoyi)* proponents in, 225–26;
traditional vs. scientific medicine

debates in, 226–28, 308n7; women's
health linked to China's future in,
228

Scheid, Volker: on characteristics of
scholar-physician, 39–40; on
medical "currents of learning"
(xuepai), 243n8; on modernizing
Chinese medicine, 308n7; on
plurality and synthesis, 10; on
uxorilocal sons-in-law as heirs
in medical lineages, 252n91
scholar-physicians *(ruyi)*: attributes
associated with, 39–42; criticism
of, 56; medical ideal of, 37–39, 82;
mental perspicacity of, 37; use of
term, 38, 252n95. *See also* amateurs,
medical
*Scientific Treatise on Easy Childbirth,
A (Kexue de Dasheng bian,* Yu
Songyun), 68
*Secret Book of Childbearing, A (Taichan
mishu,* Qian family): on fetal movement, 138; on Generating and Transforming Decoction, 206; on maternal
and fetal health, 140; publishing history of, 302–3n52, 303n53
*Secret Essentials from the Imperial Palace
(Waitai biyao,* Wang Tao), 291n31
*Secret Formulas of Women's Medicine
from the Bamboo Grove Monastery
(Zhulinsi nüke mifang)*, 60, 62
"securing the fetus" *(antai)*, 137, 138–39,
140–41, 144–45, 175–76, 183–84
"self-so principle" *(ziran zhi li)*, 152
semen: Blood as female analogue to, 53;
infertility caused by problems with,
115–16, 132; sex determination and,
113; womb as receiver of, 92, 108–9
sex determination factors, 94–97, 108,
113
sexual intercourse: components of
successful, 115–16; orgasms and
fetal sex determination, 94; in
postpartum period, 196, 299n11;
during pregnancy, 141, 156–57,
163; womb's opening and closing
and, 108–9
sexual maturation, 91, 105–6, 273n26
Shang dynasty (1600–1046 B.C.),
248n51
Shanghai: medical institutions in, 308n8;
midwifery training in, 308–9n10
Shan Yangxian (Shan Nanshan):
background of, 302n47; Generating
and Transforming Decoction and,
205; on postpartum treatments,

213–14, 305n82; post-Qing evaluation of, 226–27

Shaoxing Medical Journal Society, 226

Sharia law, 130, 285n45

shengyuan (degree): and book culture, 58; and social status, 70

Shen Shiyu (Shen Mingsheng), 210, 304n67

Shen Qiwan, 79

Shen Youpeng (Shen Yaofeng), 89, 90, 138

Shi Jiefan, 15–17

Shi Pusheng, 186

Shi Qiutao, 185

Shu Gui, 35

Sima Qian, 26

Sino-German Advanced Professional School of Midwifery, 308–9n10

Sino-Japanese War (1894–95), 225

Sivin, Nathan, 246–47n36

Six Classics: *Classic of Music* dropped from, 240n11; interpretations of, 253–54n110; on marriage and procreation, 7. See also *Classic of Changes; Classic of Odes*

"sleeping embryo" theory, 130, 285n45

smallpox, 52–53, 99

social system: assumptions about misogyny in, 11; behavioral regulation in, 145–46; female reproductive health and childbirth in context of, 6–9; marriage central to, 7; medical challenges linked to, 45–51, 255n122; pleasure and overindulgence in, 51–52. See also daily life; gender segregation; men; women

Sommer, Matthew, 134

Song dynasty (960–1279): Bamboo Grove Monastery's reputation in, 59–60; "below the girdle" *(daixia)* ailments in, 28, 247–48n47; birth-expediting medicines in, 165–66, 168, 170, 208; Blood and femaleness linked in, 87–88; hereditary physicians in, 31–33; Imperial Medical Service in, 27–28, 29; medical classics of, 6, 23, 247n46; medical publishing expanded in, 57–58; medical reform in, 27–28; medical specialization in, 27–28; origins of *fuke* in, 26–27, 28–30, 231, 233–34; pregnancy test in, 125; scholar-physician ideal emerging in, 37–39; views of maternal behavior and childbirth in, 156–58

Song family of Ningbo: childbearing text of, 227, 308n8; history of, 35–36

Song Chun, 63–64

Song Ci, 108, 189

Song Er'rui, 79

Song Guoying, 252n90

Song Hong, 293n64

Song Jing, 35, 252n88

Song Lili, 252n90

Song Lin'gao, 35, 36

sons: filial piety of, 21–22; social importance of, 6; uxorilocal sons-in-law as medical heirs in absence of, 35–36, 252n91. See also sex determination factors

spirit-writing sessions, 65, 78, 262–63n42

spleen: arrested fetal development and qi of, 132; dampness and impairment of, 84–85; deficiency and coldness of, 116; as earth in female body, 142–43

stagnation: childbirth and, 156–57, 165–66, 167, 169–70, 179; fertility and, 84, 113, 116, 125, 128–29; formula for cooling and breaking up, 242n3; illness from, 15, 25, 42–43; menstruation and, 89–90, 107, 109–10, 128; miscarriage and, 1–3, 132, 143; postpartum, 188–90, 192, 197, 198*fig.*, 200–202, 204, 208–13, 215–16, 221, 297nn2–3; vaginal discharge and, 111–12; women as prone to, 50

Sui dynasty (581–617), 6, 27

Sun Simiao: on female illness, 27, 42–44; on health of womb, 273–74n34; influences on, 255–56n129; other writers on, 45, 46–47; on postpartum behavior, 196–97, 299n11; on womb as gateway for illness, 108

Sun Yikui: background of, 270n2; case records of, 84–85, 270n4; cosmological frameworks of fertility in, 141–42; on impaired fertility, 84–85; on miscarriage, 210; on postpartum, 197; on sex determination, 113

"supplementing through warmth" *(wenbu)*. See currents of learning

Su Shi (Dongpo), 58

Suwen. See *Basic Questions*

Taichan shu (Book on childbearing, Mawangdui), 240n12

Taiping Rebellion (1851–64), 225

Tamba no Mototane, 302n47

Tang dynasty (618–907): aristocratic dominance in, 37; hereditary status groups in, 31; Imperial Medical

Tang dynasty (618–907) *(continued)*
  Office in, 28; medical classics of,
  6, 23; medical specialization in, 28,
  248n51; women's diseases as area
  of study in, 27
Tang Qianqing, 67, 264n49
Tang Yaoqing, 19
Tan Jinzhang, 30
Tan Yunxian, 19–20, 21
Taylor, Kim, 22, 246n33, 306n93,
  307n94
TCM. *See* traditional Chinese medicine
"terrestrial branches" *(dizhi)*, 117–18
tetanus: depiction of, 195*fig.*; maternal,
  194–96, 300nn17,23–24; neonatal,
  300n17
therapies: general principles in specific
  cases, 25, 199–204, 219, 222–23;
  ritual and manual, 28; secret techniques of, 33–34, 35, 251n77, 251n79.
  See also drug-based therapies
Tian Hou (deity), 263n44
Tongzhi reign (1862–74), 20, 245n20
*Tract on Action and Response (Ganying
  pian)*, 78
traditional Chinese medicine (TCM):
  assumed indifference to bodily
  structure in, 117; on circulation
  channels, 272n24; classical medicine
  distinguished from, 22; earliest use
  of term, 246n33; *Easy Childbirth*
  text referenced in, 68; female hereditary physicians of, 252n90; Generating and Transforming Decoction
  in, 190, 206; plurality and synthesis
  in, 10
*Transmitted Family Knowledge about
  Childbirth (Chanbao jiachuan)*,
  264n50
*Transmitted Secrets of Women's Medicine
  from the Bamboo Grove (Nüke
  michuan)*, 61*fig.*, 70, 262–63n42
*Treatise on Cold Damage Disorders
  (Shanghan lun*, Zhang Ji), 294–
  95n77
*Treatise on Easy Childbirth (Dasheng
  bian*, Jizhai jushi [Ye Feng]): authorship of, 68–70, 266n59; on childbirth as essentially easy process,
  148, 150, 151–54, 155–56, 158,
  168, 227; circulation and editions
  of, 12, 67–68, 265–66n58; citations
  of, 181; context of, 55; on fetal malpresentation, 160–61; on Generating
  and Transforming Decoction, 206;
  historical precedents for views in,
  154–58; included in other texts, 67–

68, 71, 264n49; legitimacy of
  scholarly amateur and, 72–75;
  meaning of title, 153; merit of
  publishing, 76, 77, 78–79, 81;
  popularity of, 68, 149–50, 179;
  print shop advertisements in, 78;
  on pushing too early in labor, 159–
  60; reprinted with added material,
  70–72, 78; rhetorical stance of, 72–
  73; signature line in, 269n109; as
  tested by experience, 82; title page
  of, 78, 80*fig.*; translations of, 67–
  68, 264n51; on women's illness, 13
Treatise on Huoluan (Huoluan lun, Wang
  Shixiong), 219–20, 221–23, 306n93
*Treatise on the Manifestations and Treat-
  ment of Diseases Caused by the
  Three Factors (Sanyin jiyi bingzheng
  fang lun*, Chen Yan), 278n92
*Treatise on the Origins of Medical Learn-
  ing (Yixue yuanliu lun*, Xu Dachun),
  50
*Treatments for Women's Illnesses from
  the Bamboo Grove Monastery (Zhulinsi nüke zhengzhi)*, 62

*Union Catalog of Chinese Medicine
  Works in Chinese Libraries (Quanguo zhongyi tushu lianhe mulu)*, 8,
  67
United States. *See* traditional Chinese
  medicine (TCM); Western medicine
Unschuld, Paul: on categorizations of
  organs, 275n47; on circulation
  channels, 272n24; on *Classic of
  Difficult Issues*, 26, 247n46; on
  Classic of the Divine Pivot, 246–
  47n36; on dynamics of illness and
  cure, 23–24; on political metaphors
  in drug classifications, 287–88n92
urbanization and commercialization,
  concerns about, 51–52
uterus: bicornuate, 95, 276n58; life-gate
  (mingmen) and, 100–103; prolapsed
  and inversion, 95, 275n57; use of
  term, 92. *See also* womb

vacuity: conception and, 113; difficult
  birth due to, 162; factors in, 42–43;
  illness from, 25, 131; miscarriage
  and, 116, 133, 135, 142; postpartum, 190, 201–4, 208–12, 216–17,
  221–23
vaginal discharges, abnormal: color of,
  111; "girdle discharges" *(daixia)*,
  26, 28, 105, 107, 110–11, 233, 247–
  48n47; postpartum, genital pus,

197; as potentially dangerous, 88–89; unique illnesses of, 110. *See also* menstrual ailments

Valussi, Elena, 53, 257n146

vessels: belt *(daimai)*, as source of uterine energy, 116, 280n132; Blood and womb interconnected with, 105–7, 110–11, 116–17; climatic influences on, 107; controller and thoroughfare, 90–92, 273n29, 273nn32–33; English translations of terms for, 272n24; life-gate *(mingmen)* and, 100–101; three causes of injury to, 107

Waguan Monastery, 261n30

Wang, Ms., 69, 266n61

Wang Bing, 91, 94

Wang Dejun, 56, 258n8

Wang Hengqi, 20

Wang Honglie, 65–66, 263n46

Wang Ji, 52

Wang Kentang: on drugs for difficult birth, 170; on *li jing* (pulse), 172; on postpartum behavior, 197; on pregnancy tests, 125–26, 283n17; quote attributed to, 279n122

Wang Lun, 135, 139–40

Wang Maocun, 70

Wang Qingren, 275n55

Wang Shixiong: on cholera-like diseases, 219–20, 221–23, 306n93; criticism of "doing the month," 220–21; criticism of Generating and Transforming Decoction, 217–19, 223; criticism of midwives, 185–86; on doctors and specialization, 250n69; on fetal movement, 138; on protracted labors, 185–86; on long pregnancies, 132; medical case collection of, 306n89; on men's and women's illness as essentially the same, 50; and "warm factors" *(wenbing)* current, 218–19; on Wei Zhixiu's *Continuation of the* Cases, 50, 241–42n1

Wang Sixun, 266n61

Wang Tao, 291n31

Wang Xi (Wang Shuhe), 171, 294–95n77

Wang Xueli, 79

Wang Yuwen, 78–79

Wang Zhu, 20, 245n22

Wan Mianqian, 264n50

Wan Quan, 108, 142, 278n98

"warm factor illness"*(wenbing)*. *See* currents of learning

Warring States period (403–221 B.C.E.), 25–26

Washing Away of Wrongs, The (Xiyuan jilu, Song Ci), 189

Water Margin (Shuihu zhuan, attrib. She Nai'an and Luo Guanzhong), 261n30

Wei, Ms., 188–89, 297n2

Wei Yilin, 48, 136, 138

Wei Zhixiu: background of, 242n2; on blocked menses, 85; on "experts in the discipline," 15, 29, 30, 36; flexible medical approach touted by, 37; formulas of, 242n3; on long pregnancy cases, 133, 134–35, 178–79; medical practice of, 22–25; on postpartum ailments, 15–17, 197, 210. See also *Continuation of the* Cases from Famous Doctors, A *(Xu mingyi lei'un,* Wei Zhixiu)

Weng Linzhong, 79, 81

Western medicine: Braxton-Hicks contractions in, 173; causes of false pregnancies in, 128, 129; correspondences for postpartum ailments in, 193, 299–300n14, 300n23; evaluation of Chinese medicine in comparison to, 226–28; fetus in, 126, 283n27; gendered discourse in, 85; male medical authority over childbirth in, 180; maternal tetanus in, 194–95, 300nn17,23–24; "natural childbirth" in, 148; obstetrical surgeries in, 295n104, 297n125; obstetrics in, 226–28, 307–8n5; physical destruction of fetus, to save woman, 187; pregnancy tests in, 126–27, 283n26; professionalization in, 257–58n4; puerperal fever in, 197, 199, 301n31; specialization as understood in, 36–37; understanding of ovulation in, 284n29

Will, Pierre-Étienne, 189, 298n7

Wilms, Sabine, 277n89

Wilson, Lindsay, 130

wind, as disease term, 111, 193, 194, 195–97, 208, 300n24

womb: as androgynous life-gate *(mingmen)*, 86, 100–105, 234; Blood and vessels interconnected with, 105–7, 110–11, 116–17; as container, 112–13; as crucible and field, 113–16; flexibility and variability of terms for, 92–93, 274n36; function, shape, and structure of, 93–97; medical discourse on, 85–86; as passageway and gate, 107–12; vessels and channels of, 90–92, 105,

womb (continued)
273n29, 273nn32–33; water's importance for, 142–43. See also Blood;
fertility and conception; infertility;
menstruation; uterus; vessels
women: China's future linked to health
of, 228–35; effects of miscarriage on
health of, 136; as founder of medical
lineage, 35–36; literacy of, 20; medicoreligious healing important for,
65; as more sickly than men, 42–43,
45–46, 48, 74; naming conventions
for, 238–39n1; number of diseases
of, 48–49, 255–56n129; as oven,
301n35; poetry production of, 20–
21, 52, 244n17, 245n28; sexual
maturation of, 91; social, contextual
causes of illness of, 45–53, 255n122;
as sponsors of texts, 77; as yin and
associated with Earth, 141–42. See
also female practitioners; female
reproductive body; fuke (medicine
for women); menstruation; midwives; sexual intercourse; women's
behavior
women's behavior: carelessness in, 168–
69, 293n63; difficult childbirth
caused by, 181–82; easy childbirth
due to, 156–57, 163, 293n63; in
postpartum period, 190–93, 196,
299n11; pregnancy successful due
to, 123, 135–36, 140–41, 145–46;
to provoke miscarriage, 293n65
wound wind (po shang feng), 196,
300n24
Wu, Ms., 35
Wu Bai, 19
Wu Qian, 198fig., 213
Wu Youyun, 257n2
Wu Yu, 54–55, 63, 257n1
Wu Zhiwang, 47–48, 125–26, 305n77
Wu Ziqing, 74

Xiao Xun: on birthing environment,
290n25; on dangers of miscarriage,
136; on doctor's limited role in
childbirth, 179; on false pregnancy,
284n33; on female reproductive
health, 6–7; on Generating and
Transforming Decoction, 205; on
long pregnancies, 131; on menses
and fertility, 278n99, 279n122; on
womb's function and structure, 96,
105
Xie Guan, 300n19
Xuanzong (emperor, r. 712–756),
252n88

Xu Bin, 110, 111–12
Xu Dachun: on competition among
doctors, 57; on drugs during pregnancy, 144; on medical amateurs,
56, 81; on men's and women's
illness as essentially the same, 50;
pregnancy case attributed to, 127,
284n31; on protracted labor, 183–
84; reputation of, 205; on secret
techniques, 33, 251n79; on vessels
of the body, 91; work of, in other
compilations, 71
Xue Ji: Chen Ziming's text revised by,
46–47, 305n77; on examining
women, 49, 255n122; on social
causes of women's illness, 52
Xu Lian: background of, 189, 297–98n5;
on Generating and Transforming
Decoction, 190, 216; postpartum
death of wife, 188–89, 297n2; on
regulation of qi and Blood, 189–90;
works attributed to, 298n7
Xu Ning (Guqing), 285n56
Xu Shuwei, 290n25

Yan Chunxi: agricultural metaphors used
by, 133; on arrested development of
fetus, 132; background of, 1, 239n2;
on Generating and Transforming
Decoction, 205–6, 207; medical, historical context of, 4, 10; on morning
sickness in pregnancy, 126; on postpartum ailments, 192, 193, 209–10,
299n13, 299–300n14; on postpartum treatments, 211, 213, 214–15,
305n79; on stagnation, 209–10; on
wife's death, 1–3. See also Essential
Teachings on Childbearing (Taichan
xinfa, Yan Chunxi)
Yang, Marion (Yang Chongrui), 68,
265n56
Yang Yanfei, 266n59
Yang Zijian: on birthing environment,
157, 220–21; on difficult vs. "correct" childbirth, 155–56, 172,
290nn21–22; on "expedited birth,"
175; on false labor pains, 173; on
fetal malpresentation, 160–61, 162,
163, 164; on length of pregnancy,
130; "Ten Forms of Childbirth"
written by, 155; Qing reference to,
179
Yan Yonghe, 167
Ye Feng (Weifeng): background of, 69,
71, 266nn60–61; on birthing medicines, 164–65, 167, 170; on childbirth as cosmologically resonant

process, 151–53; *Easy Childbirth* written by, 68, 69–70; on fetal malpresentation, 160–61, 163–64, 186; on Generating and Transforming Decoction, 206, 207; on historical precedents, 154; on lengthy labor, 147–48, 288n1; on midwives, 184, 185, 186, 297n122; on moral imperative to publish medical works, 76; noninterventionist approach of, 148–50, 149*fig.*, 164, 165, 168–69, 171–72, 173, 177–78; on pain, 172–73; on pushing too early in labor, 159–60; rhetorical stance of, 72–73; on tested methods, 82; wordplay in title of text by, 153. See also *Treatise on Easy Childbirth* (*Dasheng bian*, Jizhai jushi [Ye Feng])

Yellow Emperor's Inner Classic (*Huangdi neijing*): body as microcosmos in, 23–24; Buddhist sutras compared with, 66; essential study of, 99; interpretations of, 253–54n110; on muscular disorders, 194–95; on pregnancy tests, 124–25; on qi and Blood, 28–29; texts included in, 246–47n36; therapies in, 25; on vessels and channels, 91–92, 273n29, 273n33; on womb, 92–94; Zhang Jiebin's commentary on, 97–100. See also *Basic Questions* (*Suwen*); *Classic of the Divine Pivot* (*Lingshu jing*)

Ye Mengyu, 69
Ye Sheng, 69
Ye Wanpu, 69
Ye Wenshu, 101

yi ("medicine"), definition of, 22. See also drug-based therapies; medicine

yin and yang: agricultural metaphors in tension with, 143–45; as attributes of male and female fetuses, 137–38; as attributes of muscular disorders, 194–95; and childbirth, 202; conceptual system of, 5, 23–25, 46; corrupted or unusual pregnancies and, 133; in human gestation, 114–16, 122–23; as influence in medicine, summarized, 230–35; medical judgment rooted in knowledge of, 98–99; postpartum treatments and, 215–16, 218; pulse pattern of pregnancy and, 125; qi and Blood in context of, 87; root cause of illness in, 199; in schema of body, 103–5; sexual maturation and, 91; at time of conception, 95–97; women's

ailments in terms of, 28–29, 85. See also *Classic of Changes*; depletion; repletion; stagnation; vacuity

Yu, Ms., 35–36
Yuan dynasty (1279–1368): cults of medical gods in, 263n43; hereditary status groups in, 30; medicine esteemed in, 38; pregnancy test in, 125
Yuan Huang, 76–77
Yuan Lingmo, 210
Yuan Xiang, 35–36
Yu Songyun, 68
Yu Tuan, 131, 162–63, 175, 176
Yu Zan, 63–64

Zan Yin, 155, 290n18
Zeitlin, Judith, 270n4
Zeng Jifen, 19, 26/n69
Zeng Yi, 20, 21–22, 244n18, 245n21
Zhang family of Changzhou: complaints about doctor, 57. See also Zhang Yuesun
Zhang Baohua, 147–49, 171, 179
Zhang Congzheng, 129, 182, 200–201, 212
Zhang Hongmao Engraving Shop, 78
Zhang Ji: on cold damage disorders, 218, 294–95n77; on muscular disorders, 194, 300n18; on postpartum ailments, 208–9; reputation of, 66; on "thirty-six diseases" of women, 255–56n129; on womb-gate, 109–10
Zhang Jiebin: background of, 97, 276nn65–66; on belief that "medicine means judgment," 98–99; on birth-expediting medicines, 168, 169–70; on fetal movement, 137; on *fuke*, 45, 254n118; on Generating and Transforming Decoction, 204–5, 207, 216, 304n58; historical significance of, 97–98; on inherent sameness of men's and women's illness, 47–49, 255n128, 255–56n129; on life-gate *(mingmen)*, 99–105; on long pregnancies, 131; on menses, 270n14; on postpartum treatments, 200, 202–4, 210, 305n79; on right time for childbirth, 168; on "generation and transformation" *(shenghua)*, 216–17; on signs of true labor pains, 174, 176; on social causes of women's illness, 52; sources cited by, 277n77; on womb, 94, 96, 98, 108, 234; on Zhu Zhenheng's "*dasheng* powder," 153
Zhang Lu, 299n13

Zhang Sunzhen, 288–89n2
Zhang Yuesun, 181–82, 296n107
Zhang Zhao, 266n59
Zhang Zhuo, 299n13
Zhao Cunyi, 303n57, 304n58
Zhao Xianke, 248n50
Zhao Yizhen (aka Yuanyangzi), 277n77
zheng, use of term, 279n115
zhengjia (internal accumulations), con-
    cept of, 44, 49, 50, 256n135. *See
    also* female reproductive body; *fuke*
    (medicine for women); illness and
    disease
Zhou Dunyi, 253–54n110
Zhou dynasty (1045–256 B.C.E.), 153
Zhou Hanqing, 135
Zhou Heng, 306n89
Zhou Jichang, 51, 71, 73–74, 75
Zhou Lianggong, 134
Zhou Ting, 155, 157
zhuanke ("expert in the discipline").
    See medical specialization
Zhu Peng, 134, 135
Zhu Qixian, 78
Zhu Xi, 41
Zhu Xiao, 110

Zhu Xuzeng, 33, 250–51n76
Zhu Yungu, 70
Zhu Zhenheng (Danxi): on birth-
    expediting medicines, 167–68;
    "*dasheng* powder" invented by,
    153; on deficiency of Blood, 114;
    on difficult labor, 162; doctors'
    criticisms of, 121, 210; on fetal-
    slimming medicines, 293n64; on
    infertility in plump women, 113;
    infinitive body model and, 234;
    on maternal carelessness, 293n63;
    medicine and Neo-Confucianism
    linked by, 41; on postpartum ail-
    ments, 200, 201–2, 203–4, 209,
    210; on postpartum treatments,
    212, 215, 216, 218; on preventing
    miscarriage, 120–21, 230, 282n3;
    on Princely and Ministerial Fire,
    253–54n110; on provoking mis-
    carriage, 293n65; on womb's shape
    and sex of fetus, 95–96; work mis-
    takenly attributed to, 303n52; on
    yin and yang, 46, 97, 143–44
zigong ("child palace"), 93, 100–105.
    See also life-gate *(mingmen)*; womb

Text:	10/13 Sabon
Display:	Sabon
Compositor:	Integrated Composition Systems
Indexer:	Margie Towery
Printer and binder:	IBT Global